ORGANIZATION RENEWAL

Second Edition

ORGANIZATION RENEWAL

A Holistic Approach to Organization Development

Gordon L. Lippitt
The George Washington University

Prentice-Hall, Inc., Englewood Cliffs, New Jersey 07632

Library of Congress Cataloging in Publication Data

Lippitt, Gordon L.
Organization renewal.

Includes bibliographical references and index.
1. Organization. 2. Organizational change.
I. Title.
HD31.L48 1982 658.4'06 81-13876
ISBN 0-13-641845-7 AACR2

Editorial/production supervision and interior design: *Natalie Krivanek*
Cover design: *Carol Zawislak*
Manufacturing buyer: *Ed O'Dougherty*

Previously published under the title *Organization Renewal: Achieving Viability in a Changing World*

Printed in the United States of America

10 9 8 7 6 5 4 3 2 1

ISBN 0-13-641845-7

Prentice-Hall International, Inc., *London*
Prentice-Hall of Australia Pty. Limited, *Sydney*
Prentice-Hall of Canada, Ltd., *Toronto*
Prentice-Hall of India Private Limited, *New Delhi*
Prentice-Hall of Japan, Inc., *Tokyo*
Prentice-Hall of Southeast Asia Pte. Ltd., *Singapore*
Whitehall Books Limited, *Wellington, New Zealand*

This book is dedicated to the women in my life–

my mother, **Lois G. Lippitt**

my wife, **Phyllis**

daughters **Anne**, **Mary**, and **Connie**

and five granddaughters.

contents

preface

This revised edition is written and published at a time when most of our organizations are faced with dissensions, dilemmas, stress, turnover, strikes, conflict, and the complexities of survival. The evidence is seen in newspapers and newscasts that schools, voluntary agencies, businesses, government agencies, trade associations, unions, churches, communities, and industries are trying to cope with some of the most difficult issues that either old or new organizations have faced since their beginning.

The challenge to most of these organizations is not only their survival but also their relevancy to the age in which they live. Powerful changes in social responsibility, moral standards, economic pressures, educational requirements, and people's search for quality of life are but a few of the forces causing disequilibrium in today's organizations.

At no other time in my life has there been more need for organization renewal. The need for organizations to reexamine their objectives, review their structures, improve their relationships, and rediscover their responsibilities to their members, clients, and employees is evident. The organization that will remain viable, creative, and relevant must engage in the process of search that the renewal process involves. Such renewal will not take place by chance. It must be a purposive effort that embodies more than good intentions. An organization renewal process takes time, commitment, energy, money, and skill.

In these pages I have attempted to share some research, experiences, and challenges with both the practitioner and the student of organizational life. There are many persons in organizations who can be the creative renewal facilitators so needed in today's organization world. The facilitator might be an executive, a board member, a professional employee, a staff specialist, the organization development office, the training officer, an important supervisor, or a group of concerned persons. This is not, therefore, intended to be just a textbook or an oversimplified "how to" book. Implementation of organization renewal will require all we know about management and human systems to be mixed with the best of experimentation in practical application.

In preparing this revision I have wanted to present a new frame of reference for initiating and maintaining renewal processes. The reader will sense that I have blended the utilization of behavioral and management science with my own experiences in government, education, voluntary agencies, and industry.

In the twelve years since publication of the first edition of *Organization Renewal,* I have found it important to take a "systems" look at renewal. Modern complexities require a systematic way of linking financial, technological, structural, and social factors of organizations. This revised edition, therefore, is based on more of a holistic concept—and presents a human systems model that interrelates individual, group, and organization development processes. Although this integration is necessary, it is not proposed that renewal is a basic science. In many ways renewal is a performing art that requires commitment, competence, feedback, practice, and professionalism.

My experience as an administrator in various types of organizations hopefully lends a note of reality. My practical failures, successes, and frustrations have been helpful ways to test and clarify my own research and that of many colleagues.

Although every author must assume responsibility for his or her own words, I want it known that I am indebted to not a few others for bringing me to that point in life where I feel I have some thoughts, ideas, and experiences worth sharing. Ten years of my early career were spent in helping develop and build the National Training Laboratories Institute for Applied Behavioral Sciences. In such a position I was privileged to work closely with Leland P. Bradford, the director of NTL, who contributed more than anyone else to my professional growth. Association with the NTL network at numerous laboratories, consultations, and programs during the past thirty years has provided a continuing stimulus for which I am indeed grateful, if for no other reason than that I was able to experience the birth and survival realities of a new organization. The twenty-one years I have spent at the George Washington University have been an opportunity to pursue teaching and research with faculty and student associates, who have made it possible for me to test and refine the ideas expressed in this book. Jerry Harvey, professor, School of Government and Business Administration, has been particularly helpful.

My experiences as a founder and first president of Leadership Resources, Inc., of Project Associates, Inc., and of Organization Renewal, Inc., gave me a chance to practice leadership skills in the practical world of business that are not inherent in the roles of teacher, researcher, and consultant. I also learned something about the realities of cash flow, overhead, and marketing.

My pre-NTL experiences as an administrator with both a government and a community agency developed my interest in organizational dynamics. In addition to my associates at NTL, the George Washington University, and three consulting firms, I learned much by serving for five years on the board of directors and as president (1969) of the American Society for Training and Development. My association with professional training and educational practitioners in the United States and overseas has helped focus on the problems of communications, coordination, and personal relations. As cofounder of the International Consultants Foundation, I found that trying to cope with the need for renewal in other cultures provided valuable learnings.

These relationships, and my own interests and skills, have made it possible for me to consult and work with numerous clients who have tolerated both my successes and failures, affording another testing ground for the ideas and actions that are important in the area of organization renewal—particularly, the realities of productivity, accountability, and responsibility.

All this has heightened my appreciation for people who manage and lead. It is the supervisors, managers, public administrators, city managers, entrepreneurs, elected officials, and other responsible persons of such caliber who must face the hard realities of this changing world. As stated by poet Robert Graves:

Bullfight critics ranked in rows
Crowd the enormous plaza full,
But only one is there who knows,
And he's the one who fights the bull.

Thus, renewal depends upon the interest, skill, and commitment of the doer, not of the theorist.

In the process of developing this revised version, I initially prepared a draft text twice as long as the publisher felt to be economically feasible. In reducing this first draft, it was regretably necessary to abandon discussion of some material that now appears only in concise lists; and much had to be left out entirely. The reader's understanding of the resultant truncation will be appreciated.

Although the foregoing personal history might appear to be somewhat self-serving, and perhaps not even necessary, it provides my reasons for presuming to devise a single representation of organization renewal processes—the human systems renewal model in Chapter 2.

My thanks need again to be expressed to selected students in my classes on organizational development at the George Washington University. Some of their research appears in Chapters 7 to 9.

I also want to express my appreciation to the professional journals, books, and magazines from which I have been allowed to use revised portions of my own writings that first appeared in their pages.

I am especially indebted to Warren Schmidt, professor, Graduate School of Public Administration at the University of California at Los Angeles, and to Leslie This, past president of Project Associates, Inc., for their friendship, encouragement, coauthorship of earlier writing ventures, and detailed critiques of early drafts of this manuscript.

I would be remiss in not mentioning Betty June Chakaris, president of Organization Renewal, Inc.; Oscar Mink, research associate, University of Texas; Ronald Lippitt, professor emeritus, University of Michigan; and Mary Burner, manager, management development, Racal-Milgo, Inc., for their invaluable assistance in reviewing the final draft of this manuscript prior to publication.

A sincere expression of gratitude goes to Reuben Elmore Stivers of Major Manuscripts, not only for copyediting the complete manuscript but also for considerably improving its readability; and to Edith Giddings Stivers, also of Major Manuscripts, whose capability and careful attention to detail in typing the manuscript through several stages were essential.

Last but not least, as they say, a word of thanks and much love to my wife for her patience and encouragement during the many occasions when this effort created fatigue, impatience, and moodiness.

glossary

The field of organizational systems theory, research, and practice is a relatively new area for the researcher, practitioner, and student. Although much has been written in the behavioral and management sciences about individual and group functioning, it has only been in the last two decades that major attempts have been made to study the complexity of the total system as well as those things that benefit the individual and group. As a consequence of these developments, many new concepts and words have been used in different ways by different writers and advocates of one approach or another. I feel it will be helpful to the reader to have a glossary of some of the words and concepts as I have used them in discussing this relatively new field:

Behavioral Science: the study of the problem-solving behavior of human beings; such study uses primarily findings and insights from the disciplines of psychology, sociology, and anthropology, but it may also include the behavioral aspects of economics, political science, and biology.

Change: any planned or unplanned alteration of the status quo in an organism, situation, or process.

Closed System: an isolated system having minimal or no interaction with an environment in light of fixed boundaries.

Community and Societal Development: the process by which human beings can become more competent to live with and gain some control over the multiple local subsystems that constitute their community; it provides means to cope with a frustrating and changing world.

General Systems: a new outlook, not a theory, that grew out of a need to overcome the fragmentation of the sciences; a holistic, transdisciplinary movement of researchers to apply to unified methodology of conceptualization to examining all kinds of human and nonhuman systems.

Group Development: the process of understanding the ways in which groups behave, and of helping the group mature through purposeful group self-analysis, education, and training processes, so as to perform more effectively in terms of teamwork and problem solving.

Holistic: (in the subtitle of this book refers to) an overall and integrative look at Organization Development so as to examine both the micro and macro aspects of human systems. It means whole or entire and is derived from the Greek word holos or whole.

Human Resource Development: a series of plans, processes, activities, or programs that are initiated or planned so as to provide for the optimization of people at a given time or place for improved problem solving, enrichment, and coping by individuals, groups, organizations, and communities; it is dependent upon the values, norms, and beliefs of a given culture. If effective, human resource development builds in problem-solving and coping skills for one situation that can be carried over and applied to other times and places.

Human Systems Renewal: a holistic way of examining micro (individual) and macro (society) human organisms so as to understand their energy input and output leading toward their potential for directing or redirecting their energies toward increased effectiveness and great maturation.

Individual Development: the ways by which a person learns, matures, and grows as a consequence of analyzed life experiences, with positive interaction with internal and external environments, and of participation in planned education, training, and development activities of either a formal or informal nature.

Interfacing: a process by which human beings confront common areas of concern, engage in meaningfully related dialogue,- actively search for solutions to mutual problems, and cope with these solutions purposefully; interfacing may also involve the confrontation between human beings and machine processes or technological systems.

Model: a representation of structures and processes describing in simplified form some aspect of the world; every model is based upon a theory, but the theory may not be stated in concise form.

Open System: a system that interacts with an environment so that it receives inputs and produces outputs, and adapts internal structures and processes to the environment.

Organizational Change: any planned or unplanned alteration of the status quo that affects the structure, technology, or personnel of the total organization.

Organizational Growth: the concept that organizations are complex organisms having a life cycle with stages of development commencing with birth and progressing through survival to later stages of maturity.

Organization Development: any planned, organization-wide effort to increase the effectiveness and health of an organization through various "interventions" in the organizational processes using behavioral and management sciences technologies.

Organization Renewal: the process of initiating, creating, and confronting needed changes so as to make it possible for organizations to become or to remain viable, to adapt to new conditions, to solve problems, to learn from experiences, and to move toward greater organizational maturity; it is the application of the planning, development, and problem-solving process to the overall functioning of the organization in such a way that it strengthens the physical, financial, technical, and human resources; it improves the process of interface; it helps the organization mature and is responsive to the environment of which the organization is a part.

Planned Change: an intended, designed, or purposive attempt by an individual, group, organization, or larger social system to influence directly the status quo of itself, another organism, or a situation.

Quality of Work Life: defines the nature of human work in a particular environment; and it defines a way of working or an approach to work incorporating the precepts that work is cooperative, change-oriented, problem-solving-oriented, and based on mutual respect.

Renewal Facilitator: a person or group that initiates an action, process, or activity intended to bring about planned change contributing to organizational renewal. If a person, he or she may be internal or external to the system.

Social System: to the system of subsystems within an organization made up of individuals, dyads, and groups having common social elements.

Sociotechnical System: the organizational concept emphasizing that both human and nonhuman factors—including technology, structure, and process—interact to determine individual and organizational functioning.

I

Human Systems in Transition

Organizations today face multiple environmental forces affecting their survival, growth, and success. In such a complex reality it is desirable to see an organization as a social, technological, economic, and human system. In this context it is important to see the interrelationship of individual, group, and organization development processes as needed for organization renewal. Renewal, in this context, implies purposeful and planned change.

Chapter 1 presents the trends in the environment affecting organizations and the resultant need for systems renewal. Chapter 2 presents the systems way of looking at organizations and a conceptual model for perceiving organization renewal. This model forms the sequential basis for all the chapters. Chapter 3 discusses the change process and the management of change with optimal attention to effective planning.

The shaded area of Figure P-1 indicates the portion of the systems renewal model that is discussed in Part 1.

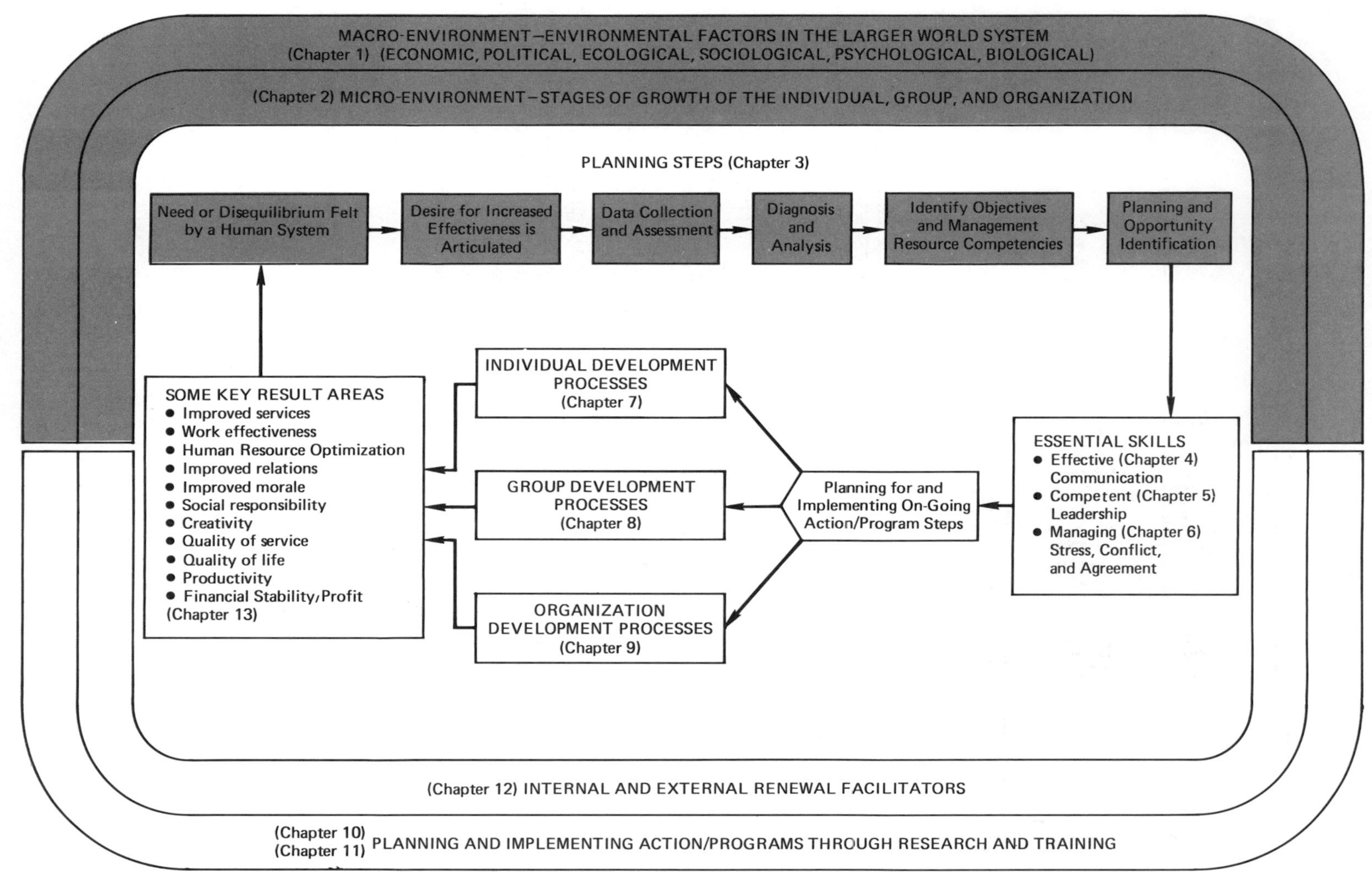
SYSTEMS RENEWAL MODEL
MACRO-ENVIRONMENT–ENVIRONMENTAL FACTORS IN THE LARGER WORLD SYSTEM
(Chapter 1) (ECONOMIC, POLITICAL, ECOLOGICAL, SOCIOLOGICAL, PSYCHOLOGICAL, BIOLOGICAL)
(Chapter 2) MICRO-ENVIRONMENT–STAGES OF GROWTH OF THE INDIVIDUAL, GROUP, AND ORGANIZATION
PLANNING STEPS (Chapter 3)
Need or Disequilibrium Felt by a Human System
Desire for Increased Effectiveness is Articulated
Data Collection and Assessment
Diagnosis and Analysis
Identify Objectives and Management Resource Competencies
Planning and Opportunity Identification
ESSENTIAL SKILLS
● Effective (Chapter 4) Communication
● Competent (Chapter 5) Leadership
● Managing (Chapter 6) Stress, Conflict, and Agreement
Planning for and Implementing On-Going Action/Program Steps
INDIVIDUAL DEVELOPMENT PROCESSES (Chapter 7)
GROUP DEVELOPMENT PROCESSES (Chapter 8)
ORGANIZATION DEVELOPMENT PROCESSES (Chapter 9)
SOME KEY RESULT AREAS
● Improved services
● Work effectiveness
● Human Resource Optimization
● Improved relations
● Improved morale
● Social responsibility
● Creativity
● Quality of service
● Quality of life
● Productivity
● Financial Stability/Profit
(Chapter 13)
(Chapter 12) INTERNAL AND EXTERNAL RENEWAL FACILITATORS
(Chapter 10)
(Chapter 11) PLANNING AND IMPLEMENTING ACTION/PROGRAMS THROUGH RESEARCH AND TRAINING

Figure P-1 Systems Renewal Model

1

the changing nature of organizational life

It is horrible to think that the world could one day be filled with nothing but those little cogs, little men clinging to little jobs and striving toward bigger ones—a state of affairs which is to be seen once more, as in the Egyptian records, playing an ever increasing part in the spirit of our present administrative system, and especially of its offspring, the students. This passion for bureaucracy . . . is enough to drive one to despair.

Max Weber, 1864–1920[1]

Many people today wonder if they and their institutions can meet the demands of increased and improved delivery of products and services in a changing society. The present turbulence faced by government, business, and other organizations is caused both by the increased complexity of their sociotechnological functions and by multiple revolutions in contemporary society. In addition, predictable strains are being exerted by similar and more dynamic interrelationships and increased interdependence among government agencies (at all levels), industry, communities, and educational institutions. These multiple forces must be met with a process of renewal adaptation, and planning for change at the individual, group, and organizational level. I refer to this as *human systems renewal.* Max Weber himself expressed real misgivings about the whole rationale of the system he had so highly praised.

MAJOR TRENDS INFLUENCING HUMAN SYSTEMS[2]

The need for renewal is reflected in the multiplicity of crises in the world today. The trends at work in the current world situation vary in their impact on organizations. Nevertheless, we can analyze the transformations in our society and perhaps plan so as to more effectively cope with these tumultuous times.

World Population Growth

A list of key problems in the world today might well begin with the population explosion. There has been so much talk about the explosion in numbers of human beings that those of us in countries where the rate of growth is relatively slow are inclined to say: "When are those people in China and India going to learn?" We turn our eyes away from what we consider to be *their* problem alone. Obviously, it is not solely their problem, as front-page stories in our newspapers daily make clear. Is the population explosion a problem that we can safely ignore? Can we afford not to think about sources of manpower as we see the desire of people to immigrate to countries where jobs are more available as well as the creation of new work opportunities through economic and social development in their own country? Population growth is putting heavy pressure upon food supplies that are already short of meeting world needs; upon all our public services; upon economic growth trends that, in some cases, are being limited; and upon our professional skills and organizational capacities.

Economic and Social Imbalance Between Nations

Countries of the world are unequal in their resources and utilization of resources. The developing countries represent major geographical and population areas. The United Nations estimates that there are over 4 billion people living in 126 underdeveloped areas throughout the world.

Among the characteristics of an underdeveloped country are widespread poverty, a lack of power and light, inadequate communications systems (roads, railroads, telephones, etc.), and insufficient government services. There are too few hospitals, schools, and institutions of higher learning. The majority of the people can neither read nor write. The banking system is rudimentary and interest rates are unreasonably high. Major exports, frequently controlled by foreign companies, are raw materials of either extraction type (tin, copper, oil) or cultivation type (rubber, coffee, copra). In spite of these adverse conditions, there is always a small group of people in these areas who live in luxury. Such trends can also be seen in the developed countries.

What are the major needs for improved development in many areas? They are too numerous to list in detail, but three are: (1) to increase production, (2) to improve distribution of production, and (3) to stimulate in the people a favorable attitude toward change. Such needs form the essence of renewal.

World Food Crisis

One of the great crises of the world is that of hunger and famine in Africa, Latin America, and Asia. This crisis is imposing great burdens in countries that do not have the agricultural or economic experience to feed growing numbers of their own people. Further increases in population, combined with the need for more food, could convert what is now a crisis into a global catastrophe in our lifetime—unless the producing nations quickly assist the limited production countries to meet their basic need for food. The experience of agricultural producers in Canada, Europe, the United States, and other areas is needed to help confront the issue.

Energy Crisis

In the 1970s, an energy shortage emerged as a key factor affecting all societies, economies, organizations, and individuals. The lessening of fossil fuels in the world and growing dependence on Middle-East oil while other forms of energy are sought has created economic stress and inflation in the energy-hungry nations of the world.

Interdependency Needs Between Nations

It is a well-recognized fact that the world is now economically, geographically, and sociologically interdependent. The recognition that one country can learn much from another is a modern phenomenon. This provides the underlying foundation for the values of cross-cultural interchange. Every culture can contribute something to the knowledge and practices of another. In addition, they affect each other economically and politically.

National Pride and Cultural Uniqueness

There is increasing self-recognition in developing countries of their heritages, and a mounting pride of these peoples in their history. In struggling to improve their condition, it will be important—as they learn from others—that they also preserve their identity, their unique character. It will be necessary not only to help channel such pride, but to protect it, a key factor in cross-cultural relations.

Industrial Revolution: A Tempo and an Evaluation

Economic imbalances are hastening industrial revolution in the developing countries. In most of the world the average annual per capita income is somewhat or considerably less than the weekly earnings of an American, Swedish, or West German factory worker. The need is imperative to raise the standards of living of citizens of the developing countries. Such change is required not just for them to achieve luxury—but simply to stay alive. What greater challenge could there be to human systems worldwide?

Authority and Power Shifts

As the nations of the world develop and mature, we will see change in power spectrums—continuing evolution and revolution. New groups will develop authority, new leaders will come to the fore, and a new middle class will emerge to play its role in economic and social development. In many cases, these permutations of control and power may resemble anarchy. The United Nations General Assembly well demonstrates the changing nature of such power shifts, and people concerned with human systems need to be deeply concerned.

International Tensions

Based on what is presently happening, we can predict an era of international tension as we move into the twenty-first century. What does this mean to organizations? Certainly, we will be relating to people who are fearful of nuclear warfare, which will be a threat for a long time to come. We must help people become more aware of what to expect from themselves and others. Never has there been so great a need for knowledge of human behavior, economics, and religion, in order that men and women may better understand and cope with problems that affect their physical, mental, and spiritual balance.

Inflationary Factors

The energy situation, demands for a higher standard of living, and large governmental and trade-union influences will continue to increase inflationary trends. In recent times, Brazil, a typical rapidly developing nation, underwent 60% to 80% average inflation, and in the United States a trend developed toward an annual inflation rate of 13% or higher. The inflationary effect on capital investment, wage/price spiraling, purchasing power, and persons with relatively fixed incomes has become obvious.

Multinational Corporations and Organizations

In the 1960s and 1970s, more and more multinational corporations came into existence as the complex economic realities of the world market evolved. In addition, the number of international associations, both governmental and nongovernmental, have multiplied. Such growth means more interdependency, linkage, and collaboration across national boundaries and cultures.

Knowledge and Technological Expansion

The continuing rapid increase in our knowledge from scientific research, innovation, and development is a key factor in our society. Some examples: knowledge of DNA; atomic nuclei; the moon, Mars, and Jupiter; black holes; what we are and where we are; and how we have constructed or destroyed our human-made world. The medical discoveries that led to the eradication of malaria, tuberculosis, and yellow fever, as well as to heart transplants, are evidence of greater medical knowledge. In the fields of nutrition, public health, productivity, behavioral science, and other areas, the knowledge explosion is easily perceived.

The continuing development of the computer, which in its fourth generation of complexity has given us the mini- and microcomputer, is continually improving data processing's capability to cope with expanded knowledge. Also, television and videotape have contributed to instant communication, rising expectations, cross-cultural awareness, and the expansion of leisure.

Our sense of understanding—our faith that what is not understood today will be learned tomorrow—differs vastly from the ignorance that once engendered mysticism, superstition, and terror.

Activism by Consumers and Special-Interest Groups

There is both a strong trend toward and the means of communication for people to protest against the faulty or dangerous or senseless. Deep concerns about industrial products, the ineptitude of government, impersonal institutions, energy policies, pointless wars based on a "no-win" philosophy, and similar issues are abroad in the world today. People of all walks of life no longer fear to "speak up and out" on such issues. They are no longer subservient to either leaders or institutions. It may be that we will be grateful to those who care enough about our institutions to want them changed. It is obvious that "established institutions (government, industry, education, the church, the courts) have come to be perceived as decreasingly competent in managing their responsibilities."[3]

In a poll taken in the United States in 1979 there was revealed a lack of trust and confidence on the part of the American people in almost all of our institutions—including Congress, labor unions, banks, oil companies, government, and even universities and churches.

Larger Complex Organizations

Concern about and lack of trust in many modern organizations may be related to the trend toward bigness. It may well be that we are reaching the limits of our ability to manage such gargantuan and complex human systems. Many of our human systems have grown to colossal size: government, business, hospitals, churches, unions, institutions of learning, and so on. In a recent study[4] completed for the National Science Foundation by the Center for the Study of Social Policy, propositions associated with the unrestricted growth of human systems were identified:

> It is hypothesized that if a social system grows to extreme levels of scale, complexity, and interdependence, the following characteristics will *tend* to become manifest:
>
> 1. Diminishing relative capacity of a given individual to comprehend the overall system
> 2. Diminishing level of public participation in decision making
> 3. Declining public access to decision makers

4. Growing participation of experts in decision making
5. Disproportionate growth in costs of coordination and control
6. Increasingly dehumanized interactions between people and the system
7. Increasing levels of alienation
8. Increasing challenges to basic value premises
9. Increasing levels of unexpected and counterintuitive consequences of policy action
10. Increasing system rigidity
11. Increasing number and uncertainty of disturbing events
12. Narrowing span of diversity of innovation
13. Declining legitimacy of leadership
14. Increasing system vulnerability
15. Declining overall performance of the system
16. Growing deterioration of the overall system unlikely to be perceived by most participants in that system[5]

PROBLEMS OF LARGE, COMPLEX SYSTEMS

If we are to bring about human systems renewal, it must take place first within large organizations. In reality, however, the most difficult organizations to change are those that are *large, old,* and *successful.* Richard Goodwin, writing in the *The New Yorker* magazine, describes the resistance of large social systems to fundamental structural changes:

> The passion for size, reach, and growth is the soul of all bureaucracy. Within government, the fiercest battles are waged not over principles and ideas but over jurisdiction—control of old and new programs. Radically new pronouncements and policies are often digested with equanimity but at the slightest hint of a threat to the existing structure . . . the entire bureaucratic mechanism mobilizes for defense. Almost invariably, the threat is defeated or simply dissolves in fatigue, confusion, and the inevitable diversion of executive energies.[6]

In a study conducted by David S. Brown,[7] 520 persons were asked to indicate what, in their opinion, were the five most serious deficiencies found in large organizations. The chief criticism was that large organizations are "incapable of taking immediate action save in crises; slow, ponderous, wedded to old habits and processes." Nearly 46% of those questioned included this in their list of five faults. The second most frequently noted criticism was that "they are efficient only to a point, declining in efficiency as their size increases beyond it." This was mentioned by 36%. Over 53% agreed that "individual responsibility for what is done is difficult to establish or determine." Similarly, 31% agreed that "they are more concerned with rules, regulations, and procedures than with achievement of objectives." Only slightly fewer assigned to fifth place their belief that "individuals and units are not well coordinated" and "are poorly integrated."

The fourteen trends affecting human systems that are listed above are not all-inclusive. They do, however, form the necessary minimum background for an examination of the transitional nature of today's large organization as faced by the individuals who work within it as employees or managers.

HUMAN SYSTEMS IN TRANSITION

Observers of the world scene now view our human systems as being in a period of transition. These changing trends are accelerating at an uneven rate, but at a rate that is challenging all our institutions as well as the individuals who work within them. This total picture can be described as a transition from the industrial to the postindustrial society, and it involves massive changes that are not yet under control. Organizational renewal can create out of this transition a type of organizational functioning that is different from what has been known in the past.

Jonas Salk, in his book *The Survival of the Wisest,* describes our world as being in a transition area between the A and B stages of the sigmoid curve, common in biological growth (see Figure 1-1). Stage A represents industrial society and stage B, postindustrial society.

In the industrial stage, all feedback says, "grow, expand, increase." At the transitional point, feedback becomes confused and says, "grow, don't grow, change." In the postindustrial stage, a transition is completed and stabilization achieved. Applied to organizations, if we are emotionally able to confront the data and professionally competent to respond to this changing feedback we will, in years hence, have made the transition from a stage A "quantity" to a stage B "quality" set of values, methods, policies, and practices.

Alvin Toffler refers to the agricultural revolution, the industrial revolution, and in the 1980s, the "third wave," a time when multiple trends will create a society of complexity.[9]

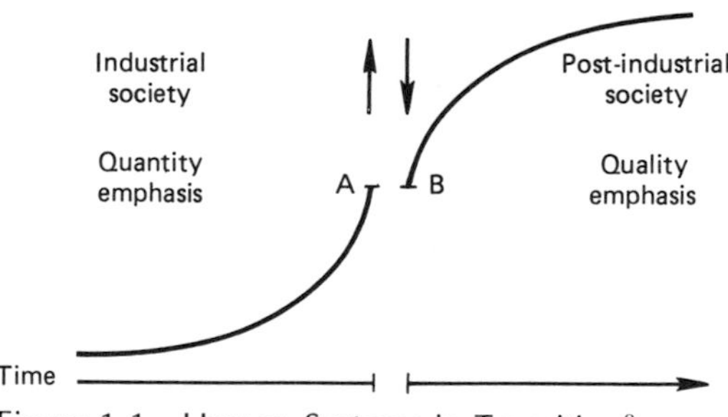

Figure 1-1 Human Systems in Transition[8]

The dilemma created by such change is well stated by Eric Trist:

> The contemporary environment . . . is taking on the quality of a turbulent field. . . . This turbulence grossly increases the area of relative uncertainty for individuals and organizations alike. It raises far-reaching problems concerning the limits of human adaptation. Forms of adaptation, both personal and organizational, developed to meet a simpler type of environment, no longer suffice to meet the higher levels of complexity now coming into existence. . . . The planner's dilemma . . . may be summarized as follows: the greater the degree of change, the greater the need for planning—otherwise precedents of the past could guide the future; but the greater the degree of uncertainty, the greater the likelihood that plans right today will be wrong tomorrow.[10]

Leaders of all institutions are coping with this transition more slowly than it is occurring. They are still managing with the values, organizational structures, and leadership styles that characterized the industrial era. That era adhered strongly to the values and beliefs of the Christian work ethic, economic efficiency, and an unresponsiveness to the external environment. The contrasts cited in Table 1-1 reveal some of the differences between industrial and postindustrial society.

These transitions are now taking place in advanced industrial and urbanized societies. Change is always difficult, but these shifts are particularly painful, complex, and frustrating. Margaret Mead has described this generation as "immigrants in time," as members of the first generation to live in an era when it is not obvious or even plausible that "experience is the best teacher," since the circumstances of today are unlike anything faced by those who are now

Table 1-1
Changes in Emphasis in the Transition to Postindustrialism[11]

Type of Change	From:	Toward:
Cultural values	Achievement	Self-actualization
	Self-control	Self-expression
	Independence	Interdependence
	Endurance of distress	Capacity for joy
Organizational philosophies	Mechanistic forms	Organic forms
	Competitive relations	Collaborative relations
	Separate objectives	Linked objectives
	Own resources regarded as own absolutely	Own resources regarded also as society's
Organizational practices	Responsive to crisis	Anticipative of crisis
	Specific measures	Comprehensive measures
	Requiring consent	Requiring participation
	Short planning horizon	Long planning horizon
	Damping conflict	Confronting conflict
	Detailed central control	Generalized central control
	Small local units	Enlarged local units
	Standardized administration	Innovative administration
	Separate services	Coordinated services

of middle age.[12] Organizations and their leaders, as well as employees, will be living in this transitional period throughout the 1980s and 1990s.

The task, then, amounts to reorienting institutions so that, amoeba-like, they are capable of continuously and consciously undergoing change and renewal. It is no longer sufficient to depend upon remedial splinting of institutional fractures caused by excessive rigidity. Such a transformation in our human systems would be of a major magnitude and pervasiveness. But recognizing a requirement for human systems renewal is not equivalent to being able to initiate and cope with change. The problem for managers today is whether or not they have the resources and skills to bring about sufficient, timely renewal in their organizations to meet the challenges of the only partially known future.

Organizations have grown in size, but have they matured? Maturation requires adaptability, flexibility, health, and identity, particularly in this era of technological and sociological innovations. Toward what end are institutions growing? This question is brought into focus by changes wrought not just in human and managerial technology but in philosophy:

> A new concept of *persons,* based on increased knowledge of their complex and shifting needs, which replaces an oversimplified, innocent, pushbutton idea of human beings
>
> A new concept of *power,* based on collaboration and reason, which replaces a model of power based on coercion and threat
>
> A new concept of *organization values,* that is based on humanistic/democratic ideals, which replaces the depersonalized, mechanistic value system of bureaucracy[13]

As Willis W. Harman puts it:

> Our research leads me to the conclusion that the industrialized world is

> simultaneously undergoing a conceptual revolution as thoroughgoing in its effects as the Copernican Revolution, and an institutional revolution as profound as the Industrial Revolution.[14]

He notes that there probably have not been more than half a dozen profound transformations in Western society since primitive man. The reasons for such a transformation now being plausible are the complexity of present-day racial problems, social indicators in human behavior, and a shift in values. In discussing the possibility of such a transformation, Harman points out that, in other periods of historic cultural change, certain typical occurrences tended to become evident one to three decades ahead of the basic change. These changes are:

Decreased sense of community
Increased sense of alientation and purposelessness
Increased frequency of personal disorders and mental illness
Increased rate of violent crime
Increased frequency and severity of social disruptions
Increased use of police to control behavior
Increased public acceptance of hedonistic behavior (particularly sexual), of symbols of degradation, and of lax public morality
Increased interest in noninstitutionalized religious activities (e.g., cults, rituals, secret practices)
Signs of specific and conscious anxiety about the future
In some cases, economic inflation

If such transformation is occurring now, it is obvious that individuals, groups, and organizations will need to react, adapt, and effectively respond to the forces in the macroenvironment. It is therefore necessary to begin any examination of human systems renewal by giving credence to the environmental forces that place stress on human systems, as shown in Figure 1-2.

TRANSITION MANAGEMENT

"The implication to management in transition is to manage in a different manner."[16] Transition management is in contrast to more conventional methods of *steady-state management.* Steady-state management in

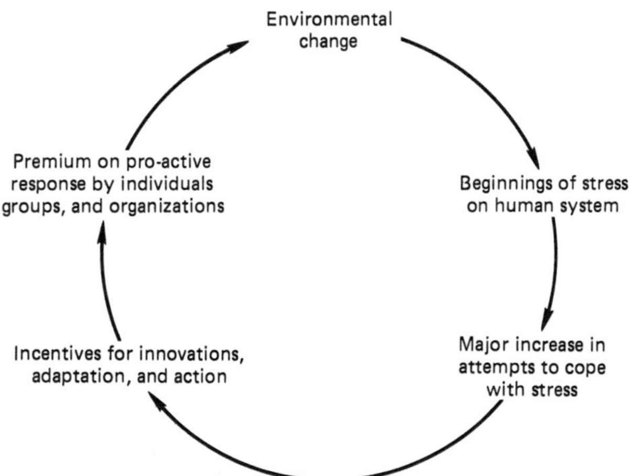

Figure 1-2 Environmental change forces change in human systems[15]

times of rapid change is doomed to failure because it is precedent-oriented, whereas the problems of transition are almost always unique. In such precedent-oriented steady-state management the tendency is to fit current difficulties into a conceptual framework provided by a similar situation from past experience. When conditions are relatively stable, this is an appropriate and expeditious approach. It not only provides a structure for thinking about the problem but suggests a potential solution. However, when conditions are changing extensively and rapidly, it is probable that there are unique elements in the situation which find no place in the conceptual framework provided by a similar situation is then a tendency to underrate the importance of such unique elements or, more often, to simply ignore them. This leads to a distorted perception of the problem and greatly lowers the probability of an effective solution. It often leads to the right answer to the wrong question.

In contrast, change-oriented transition management focuses on identifying the unique elements of a situation and developing new approaches accordingly. In so doing, it does not ignore precedent but uses it as a benchmark for identifying the need for change.[17] Transition management directs its attention to the irrational (or nonrational) human behavior that occurs when people are bombarded with too much new and unfamiliar change. It consists primarily of an interrelated set of skills and concepts centered around the management of human systems under conditions of stress and the recognition of patterns under conditions of novelty and ambiguity. Intellectually, transition management is relatively simple to understand. However, there are habits, attitudes, and beliefs held by most individuals as a result of intensive cultural conditioning which constitute effective barriers to the implementation of transition management. Effective application of the principles to managing the problem of rapid, comprehensive change requires some intellectual learning, but primarily it requires behavioral deconditioning and reconditioning, which can only occur through development of individuals in the actual process of dealing with real and complex problems.

History has shown that homeostatic forces operating to maintain the status quo have acted to make institutional change lag far behind changes in environmental factors. This eventually results in a large gap between institutional behavior and environmental conditions.

The times when there is a wide divergence between environmental conditions and institutional behavior are just those times when past precedents no longer provide adequate guidance for current behavior. Leaders then tend to polarize around the conservative forces who want to keep things as they "were," and the new liberal leaders who want to change everything. Such polarity tends to highlight value differences and, in the process, to accentuate them. All agree that something must be done but, because of the difference in values, there is no consensus as to what that "something" should be. There are compromises that lead to programs which, because of lack of consensus, are fragmented and, in the main, tend to cancel each other out. The result is much action with little progress, which eventually leads to unbearable frustration. Frustration then generally leads to the destructive results of either repression (i.e., we don't really have any major problems) or projection (i.e., either "he" or "they" are the source of our problems; therefore, if we can get "him" or "them" to change or, alternatively, if we can "neutralize" or "eliminate" "him" or "them," our problems will be solved). In other words, given unbearable frustration, the two most often selected alternatives are either "flight" from the problem or "fight" with those who are seen as the cause of the problem.

The early phases of transitional change and the two most common responses are illustrated in Figure 1-3.[18]

A state of frustration for individuals, groups, or organizations is a nonfunctional and unsatisfactory response to environmental forces. It is hoped in this book to indicate concepts, methods, procedures, and criteria that people can use to lessen the gap between the pressures of change and creative response. It is essentially a human response that we will call *renewal.*

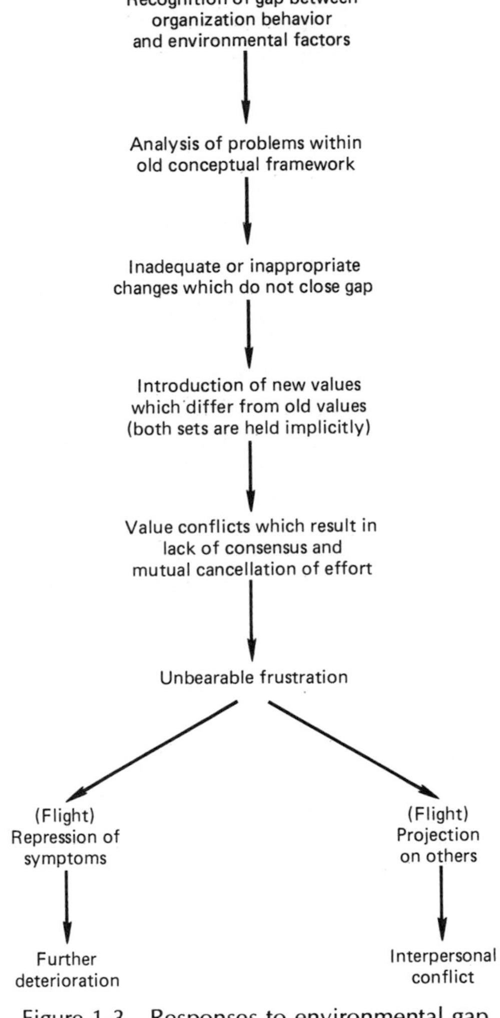

Figure 1-3 Responses to environmental gap

The buildings, real estate, typewriters, computers, and financial resources of modern organizations are no more than useful tools, the material side of enterprise. These tangibles could be dispensed with and there could still be an organization. This is because basically an organization is made up of human resources—people. In a way this is paradoxically both fortunate and unfortunate. On one hand, the prospect of an enterprise that could function endlessly and efficiently without human guidance is the substance of nightmares; on the other hand, the greatest obstacles to the successful functioning of human organizations are people.

No one denies that few tangible evidences of organization last forever—that, for example, there usually must be a purchasing schedule for new machinery. Every personnel director is plagued with the realities of employee turnover. In the language of ancient adage, philosophers and physicians warn that all work and no play make Jack a dull boy. Peculiar to themselves, of course, the necessary processes of replacement and restoration contribute to organizational needs for revitalization. However, these processes are not ordinarily applicable to another essential form of renewal, which has to do with the manner in which an organization undertakes decision making or the way it deals with the world around it. The renewal of people and tools is, at best, incremental; renewal of attitudes, aspirations, and purposes, because they rest basically on the will and ideas of human beings, involves the interrelationships of people with people, and of people with situations. In other words, the human systems in all our institutions. As one author states:

Actually, of course, it is through their people that the adaptive organizations must respond to these many inescapable change demands, and it is bound to be a stressful experience. Stress is neither good nor bad in itself; it is the outcomes that matter. Good outcomes result in growth and mastery; bad outcomes result in failure to meet change demands and consequently diminished self-esteem and emotional disturbances. In periods of transition, the organization can provide supports that ease the strain, reduce the likelihood of poor adaptation, and increase the likelihood of successful response to change. Thus, the risks and uncertainties of change can be converted to opportunities for growth—if, scrambling to maintain immediate profits, the organization does not neglect its people's needs in the face of change.[19]

R. G. Hirschowitz states his belief that the mismanagement of change has been caused by six factors:[20]

1. Failure to appreciate complexity
2. Failure to make investments in human assets
3. Failure to engage in psychological cost accounting
4. Violation of cherished values
5. Outmoded theories of individual motivation
6. Failure to budget adequate "test and lag" time

We cannot cope with change without taking into account its effects on people. We must help the human system to be human.

In examining the response of organizations to their environment in a systemic way, there is a need for action, change, and development at the individual, group, and total organization levels. These three levels of human systems are essential for organization renewal.

Organization renewal, with which we are dealing here, involves planned change. In examining approaches to organization renewal, there have been three models identified by Warren Bennis[21] that provide a frame of reference by which to understand new approaches to organizational change:

The equilibrium model of organizational change. This approach places value on developing a "conflict-free" social structure. It is seen as desirable to release tensions in the organization and try to make subsystems less defensive. The planned change efforts focus on identifying problem areas and try to alleviate tensions through whatever means of catharsis, group discussion, or problem clarification seems to be appropriate to the situation.

The development model of organizational change. In this approach an attempt is made to develop authentic and open relationships among the persons in the organization so that human and interpersonal values are furthered to help the organization maintain itself and grow. The goal here is to develop interpersonal competence among the individual members of the organization so that they can carry out valid communication in the formal and informal aspects of organizational life. The use of T-group and laboratory training to improve the interpersonal skills, attitudes, and values of persons in the organization is one of the major means in achieving such a goal.

The organic model of organizational change. A third model of organizational change identified by Bennis rests on the desirability of achieving productivity and results through team management in the organic functioning of the various units of the organization. The work of Blake and Mouton[22] in applying the managerial grid concept to organizational change is a foremost example. The desirability of management acquiring new concepts for teamwork leadership, so that they can solve organizational problems, is a basic premise; and the need for management to be adaptive and collaborative is stressed. The ability to integrate the technological, structural, financial, and human systems in a holistic way is needed (i.e., the interdependence of multiple systems).

The human system renewal concept developed with Warren Schmidt[23] is based on the idea that organizations have stages of potential growth in their life cycles, and that each experiences crises and situations demanding certain management and/or organizational responses that are indispensable if the organization is to achieve its next stage of growth.

Such a model, closely related to the organic change concept, stresses the need for reality assessment within the organization with respect to its present state of affairs, for identification of the key issues or concerns the organization is now facing, and for planned efforts to confront that situation with those activities, processes, or actions that will help cope with the present situation so as to achieve growth for the individual, group, and organization. The emphasis on situational confrontation reemphasizes the relevance of planning and action through existential leadership.

Such renewal sees the organization as a sociotechnical system, a term first developed by Eric Trist and his associates at the Travistock Institute, London, England. The organization is thought of in terms of a multifaceted "personality" or organism. For a long time the law has dealt with organizations as if they were persons, and the same viewpoint can be applied to the birth and potential maturity of an organizational enterprise.

We know that many organizations die aborning, or nearly so, while a few, such as Lloyd's of London and DuPont, seem to live forever. Perhaps this indicates that the bedrock of any discussion of organization renewal—whatever the limitations or disadvantages of such an analogy—lies in an examination of what happens when we apply theories of biological and human development to the creation, growth, maturization, and decline of an organization. This may be an initial step toward helping us understand and predict organizational growth and give useful answers to some typical introspective questions:

Why don't we have the spirit of excitement we used to have?
Why can't the various departments pull together instead of competing and undermining one another's efforts?
Why do we seem to have so many conflicting pressures and so much confusion?
Why can't our people understand that we have to economize if we are going to survive?

Most managers learn the dimensions and characteristics of *financial* problems within an organization because these kinds of problems are reducible to familiar, inflexible, finite terms. But the problems that are common to organizational growth, being largely derived from *nonfinancial situations,* are more difficult because they are seldom finite, and because they are often a matter of subjective judgment.

Managers, external change specialists and consultants, employees, and others need to perceive their organization as a complex system. As they examine and assess the human systems at the individual, group, and complete organization level, the interdependency of the forces becomes evident. The premise of this book is that each level of a human system is encompassed by the macroenvironment of the larger world in which the organization exists. Another all-encompassing aspect is the reality that systems have an organic life of potential maturation at the microlevel of the human system that makes up the complex organization. To understand human systems, one needs to comprehend the developmental potential at each level. Such understanding provides a target for change for the individual, group, and organization.

In the first edition of this book (1969) the term "organization renewal" was used, for three reasons:

1. It avoids the trap of a narrow definition of organization development.
2. It seems a more dynamic expression of action-taking.
3. It avoided the connotation that all organization change is implemented by behavioral change.

Since that time the author has only increased his feeling that organization renewal is a planned change effort utilizing both behavioral and management science methods.

Organization renewal is the process of initiating, creating, and confronting those changes needed—so as to make it possible for organizations to become or remain viable, to adapt to new conditions, to solve problems, to learn from experiences, and to move toward greater individual, group, and organization maturity.

This process includes multiple methods, processes, and actions directly derived from the behavioral sciences (organization development) and, as well, management sciences. Some of the different functions in the process are shown in Table 1-2 and discussed in detail in subsequent chapters.

The field of organizational systems, theory, research, and practice is a relatively new area for the researcher, practitioner, and student. Although much has been written in the behavioral and management sciences about individual, group, and organizational functioning, it has only been in the last two decades that major attempts have been made to study the complexity of the total system, as well as those that benefit the individual and group in an organization. As a consequence of these developments, many new concepts and words have been used in different ways by different writers and by advocates of one approach or another.

THE NEED FOR HUMAN SYSTEMS RENEWAL

An attempt has been made in this introductory chapter to highlight the need for renewal by individuals, groups, and organizations. One criterion by which we can measure the appropriateness of renewal efforts is to assess the way we relate to the external environment within which a human system exists. Heretofore, attempts thus to examine organizational dynamics tended to ignore the relationship between environmental forces and organizational response. Every organization is embedded in a total environment that conditions its form, decision-making process, and the way it utilizes the resources of the organization. The technological, civil rights, political, economic, and knowledge revolutions cited earlier as trends are all examples of this modern environment. In appropriately responding to situations, an organization should manifest an awareness of its responsibility to the larger external environment.

An example of the relationship between environment and organizational response is the work of Lawrence and Lorsch, who examine the effects on organizations of an environment that is characterized by rapid rates of technological and market change, and a high degree of uncertainty and unpredictability.[25] The way the managers in a quickly changing environment (such as an electronics industry) respond is quite different from the response of those in the more stable environment of a public utility.

An industry may be in a quasi-governmental partnership where controls on wages, profits, and processes are important factors in the environment. On the other hand, a new and highly competitive field (such as the plastics industry) is con-

Table 1–2
Functions of Organization Development and Management Science[24]

Functions	Applied Behavioral Science and Organization Development	Management Science
Action research methods	×	
Salary administration		×
Auditing		×
Conflict management	×	
Change analysis	×	
Community analysis	×	×
Community development	×	
Creative risk taking	×	
Change agent training	×	
Case studies	×	×
Cost–benefit analysis		×
Computer modeling		×
Cost accounting		×
Delphi techniques	×	×
Environment assessment	×	×
Force-field analysis	×	
Facility development		×
Fund raising		×
Group or team development	×	
Human factors	×	×
Intergroup negotiation	×	
Individual career planning	×	
Innovation	×	×
Instructional unit analysis		×
Job enlargement		×
Management by objectives	×	×
Management training		×
Market analysis		×
Media research		×
Mutual goal setting	×	
Organizational mirroring	×	
Organizational sensing	×	
Participative governance	×	×
Performance testing		×
PERT		×
PPBS		×
Personnel evaluation		×
Quantitative analysis		×
Role playing	×	
Scheduling systems		×
Sensitivity training	×	
Simulation	×	
Social research	×	
Survey feedback	×	
Task group therapy	×	
Time and motion studies		×
Zero-based budgeting		×

fronted with the need to keep costs at a minimum, react quickly to changing markets, and be constantly alert to the cash flow balance in the corporate budget. This is equally applicable to a volunteer agency that finds its services to a middle-class suburban area not completely relevant to an economically stunted and culturally deprived urban area. If it wants to remain relevant to its constituency and viable as a system, sensitivity and adaption to its wider environment should be a prime consideration for any organization.

Man's continual search for compatibility between organized relationships and personal growth is being constantly explored by social scientists. That kind of organizational system that manifested itself early in history frequently exhibited a high degree of control by managerial coercion that no longer meets the needs of today's organized society or of the individuals in it. Rapid changes in society have brought with them changes in organizational systems and the need for even greater change. One of the most apparent changes has been control through benevolence and persuasion. Whether viewed from the paternalism of large organizations in the 1930s in the United States, or the more recent "sell-the-other-fellow" approach used by some sales and pseudo-human relations advocates, such control has been very much in evidence in the leadership of industrial, governmental, social, and welfare organizations. In fact, some writers give a great deal of credence to this kind of organizational leadership.

There is, however, a third way by which influence and power can be manifested in organizational life. As the situation stands, *existential pragmatism,* taking into account the interdependent nature of renewal for individuals, groups, organizations, and environment for attaining objectives, is the appropriate managerial response for the viable organization of tomorrow. This is truly the organic approach.

Complex organizations are a way of life. We cannot, and should not, hanker after Thoreau's Walden Pond. As Harvey Cox states:

> We must first realize that the organization is here to stay. There is simply no other way to run a world brimming with four billion people in the midst of an industrial epoch. Unless a nuclear war returns us to a culture of hunting and gathering tribes, our world will be increasingly organized as the decades go by. If we choose to live responsibly in the world, then we must face the issue of how we can harness organizational power for authentic human purposes.[26]

Many people today have become antiorganization thinkers and want to develop a society wherein only individuals or small groups mature and grow. This is not an acceptable alternative to our present degree of inability to utilize human resources collectively and creatively in organizations. The very nature of modern organizations places a requirement on the nature of those who manage them, and the evolving and relevant social system in today's world certainly offers a number of choices for maximizing human effort.

Cox indicates that although today's organizations are characterized by *anonymity* and *mobility,* these may not be completely negative forces. He elaborates the thesis that present-day organizations are marked by these four attributes:[27]

1. The organization is *flexible.*
2. The organization is *future-oriented.*
3. The organization is *secularized.*
4. The organization makes only a *limited claim on its members.*

If circumstances demand it, every organization could be reorganized, merged, or disbanded. Tradition is to be valued, but it is secondary. Organizations are formed to achieve certain future goals, managers are selected on the basis of their ability to solve the resultant problems, and nepotism belongs to a past generation. A modern organization should not be bound by rituals or taboos; it makes use of professional and technical capabilities as each situation demands, and this invites the moving of individuals from one organization to another. Finally, organizations are interested only in a limited claim on the life of an individual. Its power over the lives of its personnel is relative. People have additional loyalties and responsibilities; all their activities cannot be wrapped up in the organization by which they are employed.

This brings into focus the suitability of existential or pragmatic leaders. Such managers concern themselves with actually working out a problem or idea. They are interested in tackling situations confronted by the organization and in what will change them; they see organizational life as a set of problems or opportunities, not as a mystery, or as a set of absolutes, or as a systematic ideology. They see the organization as a resource that should be equipped to respond appropriately to the task or opportunities it faces. Effective leaders among them encourage and live with provisional solutions. Such a leader's existential approach sees the potency and capability of the system to solve problems, even though he recognizes no simple, all-encompassing approach. There is a certain confidence inherent in such pragmatism and existentialism:

> The fact that we approach life today without feeling the need for a big key that fits everything together as one great whole, and are able to concentrate instead of isolating particular issues and dealing with them as they come up, shows that we have a basic confidence that the world is held together, is strong, is self-consistent, has regularity in it, and can be put to the test without everything in life going to pieces.[28]

No attempt to be simplistic is intended, however. We must face the complexities of human systems renewal with multiple processes. In the past 30 years the behavioral and management sciences have made an ever-growing contribution to the field of human systems functioning.[29] In the textbooks of schools of business and public administration and in the executive development programs of government and industry, we find constant reference to the mounting importance of these sciences in our understanding of management. One reason has been the increased quality and quantity of research in organizational problems; another, related reason is the increased demand by management for answers to organizational situations that become more and more complex.

Behavioral and management science together cover a vast intellectual area. The behavioral sciences are usually thought of as being psychology, sociology, and cultural anthropology. Although these may be the three major behavioral sciences, it is also well to include the behavioral aspects of political science, economics, educational psychology, and biology.

In a real sense, the behavioral and management sciences are a study of the problem-solving behavior of the human being. Using this definition, one can envision readily their importance to the processes, concepts, and practices of management. New findings in the behavioral and management sciences are relevant to organizations as well as to systems of the culture, but the word "science" must be placed in perspective:

> Pure science is not technology, not gadgetry, not some mysterious cult, not a great mechanical monster. Science is an adventure of the human spirit; it is an essentially artistic enterprise, stimu-

> lated largely by curiosity, served largely by disciplined imagination, and based largely on faith in the reasonableness, order and beauty of the universe of which man is a part.[30]

It is obvious that behavioral science research is causing us to reexamine our assumptions about people and their motivation. The research conducted in the field of management science is helping us understand the structural, quantitative, information technology, and systems impact on organizations. This research is also giving us an improved understanding of the behavior patterns of managers and the effects of their leadership or nonleadership within an organization. In this sense the following implications seem to be highly important:

The increased interdependence between the creators and appliers of knowledge. Research coming from behavioral science indicates a need for a closer link between those who do research and create new knowledge, and those who apply such knowledge. Managers who graduated from a school of business administration or public administration 10 years ago may now be out of date with respect to their usefulness. Rapid managerial obsolescence emphasizes the need for creative interrelationships between organizational researchers and managers. Their common concerns must be more closely interwoven to stimulate further study and produce mutual benefits.

Closer focus on the education of managers. The rate at which managerial knowledge becomes outmoded today makes it almost essential to develop management through both internal and external (to the organization) training and educational programs. Opportunities for managers to acquire new knowledge and skills should have high priority.

Situational focus on the role, skills, and practice of managerial leaders. Research on leadership indicates that there is no one concept or simple set of rules for effectiveness. It is increasingly obvious that the manager must examine each situation, and the persons in that situation, to determine the appropriate action. More and more managers are coming to realize the relative importance of focusing on the situation, as opposed to proceeding on the assumption that there exists a ready-made set of all-weather techniques that guarantee effective leadership.

Need for developing adaptive organizational systems. Research indicates that the organization of the future must remain adaptive if it is to remain viable. It will need to remain flexible to cope with ever-changing consumers, services, production techniques, technical skills, changing market conditions, social demands, economic forces, and all the other many factors that affect an organization. A particular theory of management suggesting that an extreme of either scientific management or human relations is the right approach will not be adequate. Management needs to recognize that its organization has to meet the multiple requirements of the various social systems to which it is related.

Greater focus on the transactional nature of management. Research in the behavioral and management sciences indicates that the quality of personal interrelationships is far more important than their quantity. In searching for quality, the manager of tomorrow needs to recognize the value of confrontation, of search, and of coping in the process of interfacing.

Need for integrating management and behavioral sciences. Research in the behavioral sciences indicates that separation of productive work requirements, finances, and human relations tends to result in ineffective management. Relatively heavy emphasis on one or the other will be inadequate. A manager needs to see the importance of all relevant factors. People need a sense of accomplishment and achievement. This is best done through effective work achievement, job enhancement, and production. The systems concept needs to be seen in the perspective of both the social and technical natures of an organization.

The need for a manager to be a diagnostician and planner rather than only a treater of symptoms. Research indicates the importance of the manager's ability to diagnose the causes, and to improve the appropriate treatment of symptoms is not adequate. Absenteeism, turnover, apathy at staff meetings, and similar phenomena are symptoms, not causes. The manager of tomorrow will be required to understand the dynamics of systems, to diagnose causes, and to improve the appropriate problem-solving skills needed in particular situations.

Although behavioral and management sciences are making many contributions to our understanding of organizational complexities, they have a long way to go in giv-

Table 1-3
Characteristics of Management[31]

Past	Future
	Values and attitudes
Surrogate owner	Professional
Committed to laissez-faire	Committed to social value of free enterprise
Profit optimizer	Social-value optimizer
Seeks economic rewards and power	Seeks job satisfaction
Seeks stability	Seeks change
Prefers incremental change	Prefers entrepreneurial change
	Basis of managerial authority
Surrogate asset ownership	Knowledge ownership
Power to hire and fire	Expertise
Power to reward and punish	Ability to challenge
	Ability to persuade
	Management decision-making
Change absorbing	Change generating
Risk minimizing	Risk propensive
Triggered by problems	Triggered by opportunities
Serial diagnosis	Parallel diagnosis
Convergent	Divergent
Consistent with experience	Novel
Incremental	Global
Sequential attention to goals	Simultaneous attention to goals
Satisfying	Optimizing
	Systems
Financial	Human resource accounting
Capital budgeting	Capability accounting
Expense budgeting	Capability budgeting
Historical control	Action budgeting
Long-range (extrapolative) planning	Strategic entrepreneurial planning
	Forward control

ing definitive answers in many areas. The organization is at the same time an open and closed system that has multiple subsystems and functions. These subsystems have mutual dependence and interdependence.

This new kind of management has been clearly perceived and described by Igor Ansoff (see Table 1-3).

Every organization exists in a dynamic environment consisting of other systems that affect it, and behavioral scientists and management scientists have learned to look at managerial effectiveness in terms of all the various organizational complexities.

Earlier theorists of organization were content to talk of measuring effectiveness in terms of adequate profits, efficient service, good productivity, or effective employee morale. These things are not adequate in and of themselves. Managers of human systems need to define effectiveness in terms of the capacity to survive, maintain oneself, adapt, and develop toward our own goals, and in terms of the performance of multiple functions that also relate to the larger environment.

In one sense, this book deals with individuals, groups, and organizations as human systems, with a major focus on the organization. The great theologian, Reinhold Niebuhr, pointed out that we say "moral man" because we still do care for each other.[32] But we say "immoral society" because we do not care about our institutions. We must do both if we are to optimize the potential of human systems.

In the 1980s there will be an increasing emphasis placed on organizations to be both *viable* and *relevant* to the society of which they are a part. This will demand that more and more organizations examine the multiple systems affecting them. Following such examination then requires action to innovate solutions appropriate to our age and times. This book is based on a belief that there is time for our planet to progress and change.

SUMMARY

Dramatic trends in the world are affecting organizational survival and functioning. In the transition from one stage or revolution to another stress is created for individuals, groups, and organizations. Coping with the transition requires effective management response to both the internal and external environment of the organization. Such response will require organizational change and renewal. Therefore in examining organization renewal we need to look at individual, group, and organization development/human systems renewal. Such renewal will utilize management and behavioral science.

QUESTIONS

1. What additional trends would you add to the fourteen cited in this chapter?
2. What additional kinds of stress have you experienced or observed as organizations experience transition to the postindustrial society?
3. How would you define behavioral science?
4. How would you define management science?
5. What will be required for managers to be able to provide the leadership for renewal?

NOTES

[1]Max Weber, as quoted by Reinhard Bendix in *Max Weber: An Intellectual Portrait* (New York: Doubleday & Company, Inc., 1960), pp. 455–456. Copyright © 1960 by Reinhard Bendix; reprinted with permission of Doubleday & Company, Inc.

[2]Adapted from Gordon Lippitt and D. Hoopes (eds.), *Helping across Cultures* (Washington, D.C.: International Consultants Foundation, 1978), p. 12.

[3]Philip Handler, "Science, Technology, and the Human Condition," *IEEE Spectrum,* August 1979, pp. 49–50.

[4]Duane S. Elgin, "Limits to the Management of Large, Complex Systems," part of a project on *Assessment of Future National and International Problem Areas* (Project 4676; Menlo Park, Calif.: SRI, Inc., 1977).

[5]Duane S. Elgin and Robert A. Bushnell, "The Limits to Complexity: Are Bureaucracies Becoming Unmanageable?" *The Futurist,* December 1977, p. 337. Published by The World Future Society, 4916 St. Elmo Avenue, Washington, D.C. 20014

[6]Richard Goodwin, "Bureaucracy and Complexity: A World in Transition," The *New Yorker,* November, 1978, New York, N.Y.

[7]David S. Brown, *Bureaucratic Management in the Public Sector: Is Bureaucracy the Only Way?* (unpublished paper; Washington, D.C.: The George Washington University, August 1979).

[8]Jonas Salk, *The Survival of the Wisest* (New York: Harper & Row, Publishers, Inc., 1973), p. 18. Copyright © 1973 by Jonas Salk; reprinted with permission of Harper & Row, Inc.

[9]Alvin Toffler, *The Third Wave* (New York: William Morrow & Company, Inc., 1980), p. 25.

[10]Eric Trist, "Between Cultures: The Current Crisis in Transition," in Warren Schmidt (ed.), *Organizational Frontiers and Human Values* (Belmont, Calif.: Wadsworth Publishing Company, Inc., 1970), p. 29.

[11]Ibid., p. 32 (with minor adaptations).

[12]From a speech by Margaret Mead, given at the Young Presidents Organization Conference, San Juan, Puerto Rico, November, 1971.

[13]Warren Bennis, "Organizations of the Future," *Management of Organization Development* (University of Bradford, England, 1971), p. 16.

[14]Willis W. Harman, "The Coming Transformation," *The Futurist,* April 1977, pp. 105-112. Published by The World Future Society, 4916 St. Elmo Avenue, Washington, D.C. 20014.

[15]Ibid., p. 107.

[16]Gordon L. Lippitt, "Transition Management: Coping," *Management World,* January 1975, pp. 128-132.

[17]Michael J. Marquartdt, "Introduction to Transition Management," *Systems Management Corporation,* January 1973, p. 3.

[18]Ibid., p. 11.

[19]Ralph G. Hirschowitz, "The Human Aspects of Managing Transition," *Organizational Dynamics,* Vol. 5, No. 1, 46.

[20]Ibid., p. 48.

[21]Warren Bennis, *Changing Organizations* (New York: McGraw-Hill Book Company, 1966), Chap. 7.

[22]Robert Blake and Jane Mouton, *Corporate Excellence through Grid Organization Development* (Houston, Tex.: Gulf Publishing Company, 1968).

[23]Gordon Lippitt and Warren Schmidt, "Crises in a Developing Organization," *Harvard Business Review,* November-December 1967, pp. 102-112.

[24]Oscar Mink, Janis Schultz, and Barbara Mink, *Developing and Managing Open Organizations* (Austin, Tex.: Learning Concepts, Inc., 1979), p. 80.

[25]Paul Lawrence and Jay Lorsch, *Organization and Environment: Managing Differentation and Integration* (Boston: Harvard Business School, 1967).

[26]Harvey Cox, *The Secular City* (New York; The Macmillan Company, 1966), p. 173.

[27]Ibid., p. 176.

[28]Harry Morton, "The Mastery of Technological Civilization," *The Student World,* first quarter 1963, p. 48.

[29]This portion of Chapter 1 is based on Gordon Lippitt, "Implications of the Behavioral Sciences for Management," *Public Personnel Review,* Vol. 27, No. 3, 1966.

[30]Warren Weaver, "A Great Age for Science," *Goals for Americans* (The American Assembly, Columbia University; Englewood Cliffs, N.J.: Prentice-Hall, Inc., 1960), p. 105. Copyright © 1960 by The American Assembly, Columbia University; reprinted with permission of Prentice-Hall, Inc.

[31]Igor Ansoff, "Challenge to Leadership: Management in a Changing World," *Management in Transition* (New York: The Free Press, 1973), pp. 40–42.

[32]Reinhold Niebuhr, *Moral Man and Immoral Society* (New York: Charles Scribner's Sons, 1932).

2

a systems approach to organizational renewal

Life cycle patterns are found in human artifacts, such as automobiles, buildings, and so on. The concept is less applicable to social organizations which often have the capacity for self-renewal. Neither organizations nor civilizations are under the necessity of aging, although this does sometimes happen. The fact that people die, however, means that organizations can renew their youth as the old occupants of powerful positions die off and younger occupants take their place. We do not seem to be able to do this with neurons.

Kenneth E. Boulding, 1910–[1]

We have examined some of the multiple environmental changes that are influencing modern organizations, and the need for organization renewal was cited; but what are the goals of such renewal? Perhaps the latter can best be illustrated by mentioning some of the sought-for results:

1. Continuous examination of the growth of organization, together with diagnosis of the multiple internal and external influences affecting its state of being
2. Improvement in the manner in which problems are solved at all levels of the organization
3. Development within the organization of formal and informal groups that are effective and communicative
4. Development of leadership that is appropriate to the situation facing the organization at any given time
5. A way for people within the organization to learn from their experiences of success or failure
6. Maturity of individuals and groups within the organization as well as maturity of the organization itself
7. Development of a climate that encourages and channels creativity by people throughout the organization
8. Development of a system to which all employees of the organization feel committed, thereby securing their motivation

All of the above involve *change,* which is a word much used in organizational development and renewal, but often misunderstood in context. Organizations are goal-seeking complex systems of human and nonhuman resources. Stability within such a complex is not synonymous with growth. Growth of such a complex, in terms of mere numbers, is not synonymous with maturity. Change occurs within an organization—or it should so occur if survival is to be achieved—as from time to time its goals and circumstances vary. These variances cause the human resources of the organization to engage in problem solving as they seek reorientation and try to adapt to new environmental influences.

Organization renewal, therefore, affects the organic functioning of the system, confronts a real situation, and helps the organization mature while being responsive to the environment. The many programs of management and organization development may contribute to and be a crucial part of organization renewal, but successful renewal is a *total* response by the human, financial, and technical resources of the organization. Organization renewal enables human resources to become increasingly viable, to cope with the future, and to contribute to it in a relevant manner.

It can be understood, therefore, that organization renewal is concerned with the manner in which individuals, groups, and organizations, first, confront situations and search for solutions to them, and second, cope with facts and circumstances in implementing solutions. Solutions can be, and not infrequently are, found without appropriate processes, being achieved by vaguely intuitive or haphazardly venturesome actions, and with little understanding of what really has happened once the dust has settled. Or they can be accomplished by one of the more formally structured methodologies based on directive or participative management currently espoused by different organizational theorists. Intuitive solutions, while occasionally unavoidable, are sometimes as harmful as wishful bookkeeping, haphazard marketing, or lack of long-range planning, and seldom add to the understanding of cause and effect. Solely directive or participative management are sometimes patently unsuitable in the face of certain circumstances and, therefore, simplistic and discouraging.

Between the two extremes of guesswork and formula there is a middle ground on which most leaders operate. Here they recognize occasions that demand situational leadership—appropriately autocratic, participative, or laissez-faire—and other occasions that permit the integration of human systems with conscious renewal processes. Organization renewal can live quite comfortably and effectively in this middle ground, integrating the structure and processes part of an organizational system as the need for change is diagnosed.

Most organizations are not initiating such action. Why? In most instances, because they are working from an inadequate model or concept of an organization.[2] Many organizations still indirectly value and practice the *power view* of organization that traces back to Machiavelli's (1515) hard view of persons: "Because of Man's rebelliousness and uncooperative behavior, he must be strictly and ruthlessly controlled."[3]

In this context, organizations are controlling and inhibiting systems. It is interesting to see that many modern organizations, both profit and nonprofit, base their models on an *economic view* of human beings, as advocated by Adam Smith (1760): "Under the laws of supply and demand and by pursuing his self interests, each individual can further not only his own fortune, but that of society as a whole."[4]

Although power and economics are realistic and understandable organizational frames of reference, the most predominant contribution to managing our institutions has been the *mechanistic view* advocated by Frederick Lewis Taylor (1910):

> The employee is (1) a constant in the production equation, (2) an inert adjust of the machine, prone to inefficiency and waste unless properly programmed, (3) by nature lazy, and (4) his main concern is self-interest. He must therefore be tightly controlled and externally motivated in order to overcome

his natural desire to avoid work unless the material gains available to him are worth his effort.[5]

to achieve organization requirements, tends to produce the greatest productivity and the highest quality of work.

This view has led to all the advantages and traps of bureaucracy. The principles of planning, organizing, controlling, and specializing have provided a model of supposed efficiency that all too often blocks effectiveness by stumbling over its multiple mechanisms and controls.

In midcentury, the *human relations* view of organizations came into vogue. One of its advocates, Douglas MacGregor (1960), challenged the old models when he said: "If employees are lazy, indifferent, unwilling to take responsibility, intransigent, uncreative, uncooperative, this is due to the traditional assumptions and methods of organization and control."[6]

The human relations view, however, was often seen as paternalistic, non-goal-oriented, and "soft" management. Where does this leave us as we approach the end of a century of study and application of methods of organizational functioning? The need to make the most of human potential is primary in our modern society. Three interrelated conditions have now aroused interest in how best to better the quality of life of those working:

1. In the advanced society in which we live, with almost full employment, minimum wage, unemployment insurance, and rapid technological changes and challenges, it is ever more possible for people to make a choice of where they will work, and this choice can be based upon their own needs and goals.
2. Increasing importance is attached to human dignity in our society, with greater recognition that work must be so organized and managed as to take human dignity fully into account.
3. Findings from the behavioral and management sciences show that work organized to meet people's needs, as well as to achieve organization requirements, tends to produce the greatest productivity and the highest quality of work.

When Sigmund Freud was asked to state the two most important aspects of life, he replied, "Lieben und arbeiten" (To love and to work). Probably in these simple words lies the key to why people in organizations are restless today. Work without love produces a fractured life. Love without work may irresponsibly deny a love of humanity. Perhaps love and work are essential in combination. And perhaps the most advantageous ratio of one to the other is as individualistic and unduplicatible as a fingerprint. The promise of open organizations, as human systems, is to provide for the accommodation of both.

Given the complexities of our society, we may well need another way of looking at organizations. This brings us to the contributions and values of the *systems view* of organization. Recent contributors to this concept include Stafford Beer, Jay Forrester, James Miller, and Eric Trist. Whereas some interpreters of this field focus on complex mathematical models, the systems view is a broader, more comprehensive, and potentially divergent or creative concept than those embodied in operations research.

The concept of sociotechnical systems is based on the fact that any production or service system requires both a technology and a work-relationship structure that relates human resources to technological resources. An organization's total system provides a total set of human activities, together with interrelationships to the technical-physical-financial resources and the process to make and deliver products or services. To think about an organization as a sociotechnical system helps make viable the human-machine relationships of today's society.

We have continually searched for compatibility between organized relationships and human potential. For centuries, the control of organizations has been characterized by managerial patterns which are now considered by many management and behavioral scientists to be no longer adequate for the needs of most organizations or of the individuals in them. In other words, until comparatively recently the organization has not been viewed as a system with growth characteristics, much less a system of systems; nor has it been recognized that the subsystems making up an organization have certain things in common. Today, our conceptual grasp enables us better to understand that:

> Organizations are extremely complex systems. As one observes them they seem to be composed of human activities on many different levels of analysis. Thus, personalities, small groups, intergroups, norms, values, attitudes all seem to exist in extremely complex multidimensional patterns. The complexity seems at times almost beyond comprehension. Yet it is this very complexity that is, on one hand, the sole basis for understanding organizational phenomena, and on the other, that makes life difficult for an administrator.[7]

Modern organizations are becoming ever larger. We live and work in an environment of big organizations: business, government, labor, agriculture, religion, voluntary agencies. Such large-scale, usually rationalized, frequently formalized, and hopefully efficient types of organizations are a major reality of the twentieth century.

Some of the significant effects of "bigness" are *specialization, fragmentation of knowledge, coordination*—the bringing together of human and other resources to achieve certain conditions in organizations, to produce a product, to solve a problem, to do a job—and, finally, *integration.*

There are some significant effects of living in and through big organizations. Some of these are the feelings of remoteness, powerlessness, and impersonalness. There are the feelings of isolation and of conformity—emphasized by incompatible and antimaturing demands.

We need to understand organizations better. In them we find many of our satisfactions and frustrations; in them we achieve or fail, individually and as a society. Through organizations we realize our aspirations or are manipulated into the realization of alien goals.

Basically, organization means regularity and predictability in people's relationship with each other. A collection of people may have all the trappings of organization but have no real organization in the sense of regularity and predictability. Thus regularity can be achieved formally by making such explicit rules, regulations, and procedures—and informally by then developing a regularity that comes from living and working together. An organization is not a thing, therefore, but a way of relating human beings so as to work toward shared objectives and interdependence.

In observing organizations, we are frequently in the predicament of the blind men and the elephant. The phenomena of organization, and particularly of individuals in organizations, are too many and too complex to be observed in total and all at once. When one or two people have a job to do, there are no serious problems in knowing what the job is and being able to communicate about it. When many people try to work on a larger job, there will be less understanding about the job and difficulties in communicating accurately about it.

Our solution to this problem has been to ask one person to stop working directly on the job, and to *coordinate* the work of other people so as to reduce the duplication of effort and make sure all parts of the job are being accomplished correctly. This arrangement produces more effective use of the total energy of the people, even though one person, the coordinating person, is no longer directly productive.

When a group asks a person to plan and coordinate their efforts, they give him or her *the right to make decisions* about their activities. They say, in effect, that it will be easier and more efficient for that person to make certain decisions for them while they concentrate their efforts on the task itself. Coordination of work, when many people are involved, requires delegating to certain people a power of decision and giving them *authority* over others.

Organization is the arrangement of people in patterns of working relationships so that their energies may be related more effectively to the large job. The need for organization arises from the problem of dividing labor and decision making in relation to large tasks, and the need for coordinating both with respect to available energies and resources.

Some attempts have been made to examine organizations as populations of individuals in their proper place and function. This approach emphasizes how organization affects the individual, how the individual achieves his or her goal in organization, and how the personality of a leader does influence the organization. Another way of looking at the organization has been to see it as a population of overlapping groups. Here the emphasis is on characteristics of group cohesiveness and the allocation of group effort (e.g., building the group and getting a job done).

Thinking about an organization as a system helps us accept the human-machine relationships of today's society. All organization systems include in their makeup many elements and processes. This is true for all, including subsystems, the smallest groups (or dyads), and the most complex multigroup structures of the international organization. When no attention is paid to the elements and processes of the system, it cannot function effectively. A systems view may suggest that other models of organization operating as parts of that organization serve only to contribute to its complexity. The relevance test for systems models is how appropriate is the response to them, in terms of the interaction and interdependence between the individual, group, organization, and environment for effective functioning.

GENERAL SYSTEMS CONCEPTS

To understand the systems approach, one should first have an understanding of a system. According to *Webster's Collegiate Dictionary,* a system is "a regularly interacting or independent group of items forming a unified whole."[8] Its parts are known as subsystems. A system is a means for accomplishing some purpose or set of purposes. It connotes plan, method, order, and arrangement. For example, in the weapons-system concept of the modern day missile, the nose cone is conceived as a subsystem; propulsion and guidance are subsystems; and the missile, its ground support equipment, material, and personnel are the system.

System, therefore, means both the structure and the process of the associations of people with which we work—not only the components of an organization, but also the interrelationships among those components. Indeed, it is the very *complexity* of these interrelationships that makes today's world of multinational problems increasingly difficult.

It is more and more apparent that systems concepts are not only helpful but also necessary for understanding and renewing complex organizations. Systems can be as varied as, for example:

Social systems
Information systems
Marketing systems
Decision-making systems
Financial systems
Computer systems

General systems theory is a perspective of organization that sees human systems as a collection of interdependent, living parts (subsystems), much like the human biological makeup. The system is a whole that functions as a whole by virtue of its interdependent parts. Unlike the physical sciences, which tend to isolate phenomena and classify variables, general systems theory, which applies to biological and social sciences, observes phenomena within the context of whole systems and seeks to identify and predict patterns of behavior that operate throughout the various levels of complexity. It teaches that information about one group or subsystem says something important about the whole system (process); and that the activity and behavior of a subsystem is reflective of its functioning *position* in a total system (structure).

A healthy state refers to a synergistic relationality among and between interdependent parts and between the whole system and its environment.

The possible contribution of so-called "systems approaches" to the solution of multivariable, socioeconomic problems confronting organizations is attracting a great deal of public attention.[9] Shrode and Voich[10] suggest that the reason revolves around four general limitations of traditional management thinking that originate in two major developments: changes in organizational environment and changes in organizational attitudes. This concept is illustrated in Figure 2-1."

Both management science and behavioral science have provided important insights to managers that are useful in attacking problems related to uncertainty and change, the expanding knowledge base, worker specialization, and the integration of ever-changing and developing management styles. But none of these in-

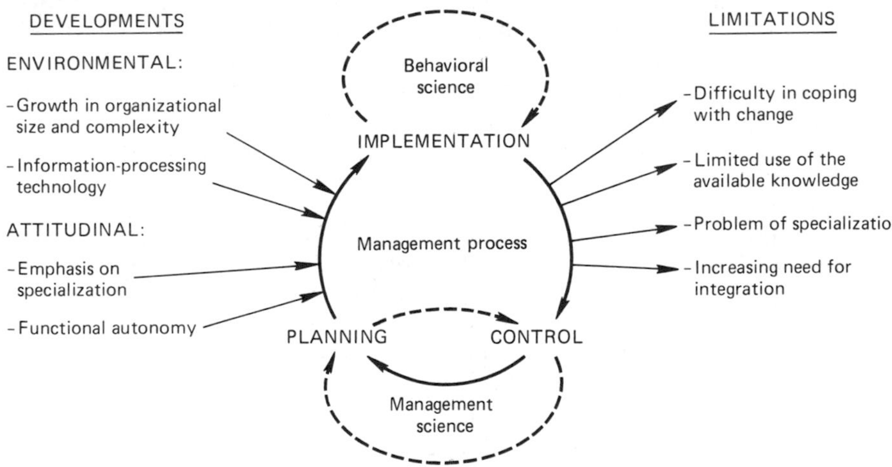

Figure 2-1 Limitations of traditional management theory[11]

sights attempt to deal with the *entire* management process as a unified whole. This concept of "holism" is the challenge to effective management accepted by *general systems theory*. To meet this challenge, general systems theory attempts conceptually to model a set of theoretical constructs that describe general relationships within the real world.

These models are interdisciplinary in nature, identifying developments in an individual discipline, and showing how these developments can be useful in other disciplines. For example, cybernetic models utilize concepts from such disciplines as electrical engineering, neurophysiology, physics, and biology. Organization theory models utilize, among others, concepts from sociology, psychology, economics, and political science. Management science models utilize concepts from mathematics, statistics, engineering, and information theory. General systems theory does not prescribe concrete techniques for resolving problems, but rather furnishes conceptual implications or suggestions that the multidisciplinary approach might be useful for solving problems in the real world.

The systems concept builds on the traditional view of the management process and on the management science and behavioral science areas to provide an integrated approach to managing the basic elements of people, techniques, information, structure, and purpose, as shown in Figure 2-2.[12]

Systems philosophy is not a distinct body of knowledge separate from that of management science, behavioral science, or the management process. It utilizes the techniques and principles in these areas, but with a more integrated scope and frame of reference so as to maximize both productivity and satisfaction.

One of the leading contributors to this field was Ludwig von Bertalanffy, who pointed out the goal-seeking behavior of both living and nonliving systems, more especially the search for a steady state.[13] He envisioned systems as being recurrent in nature. Open systems, especially, exhibit this characteristic and seem to defy the second law of thermodynamics that dictates entropy and equiprobability. Bertalanffy identified living systems as open systems with fundamental features, such as homeostasis, equilibrium, and adaptation.

This concept, when applied to organizations (as open systems), can serve as a useful tool for organization renewal, both for prescriptive and diagnostic procedures. Systems are usually considered to be recursive (i.e., recurrent). Organically stated, larger organisms are composed of smaller organs or units that mimic the functions of the larger organism. To illustrate this concept, Stafford Beer's "brain model"[14] of the decision-making process is a well-known contribution.

Another leader in the general systems area is James G. Miller.[15] He presents a conceptual system concerned with seven levels of living systems—cell, organ, organism, group, organization, society, and supernational system. His theory is then applied, in separate and extensive published articles, to each of the seven levels. Miller feels that "though every living system and every level is obviously unique . . . there are important formal identities of large generality across levels."[16] He stresses the concepts of *matter* (that which has mass and occupies space), *energy* (ability to do work), and *information* (the degree of freedom in a given situation to choose among signals, symbols, messages, or patterns to be transmitted; the contents of such symbols; the expression of the organization of a system). Matter and energy are equivalent (can be converted into each other) and, when conveying informational symbols, often are known as *markers*. Living systems need forms of matter-energy and patterns of information, the latter requiring less energy but also a marker to be moved over space.

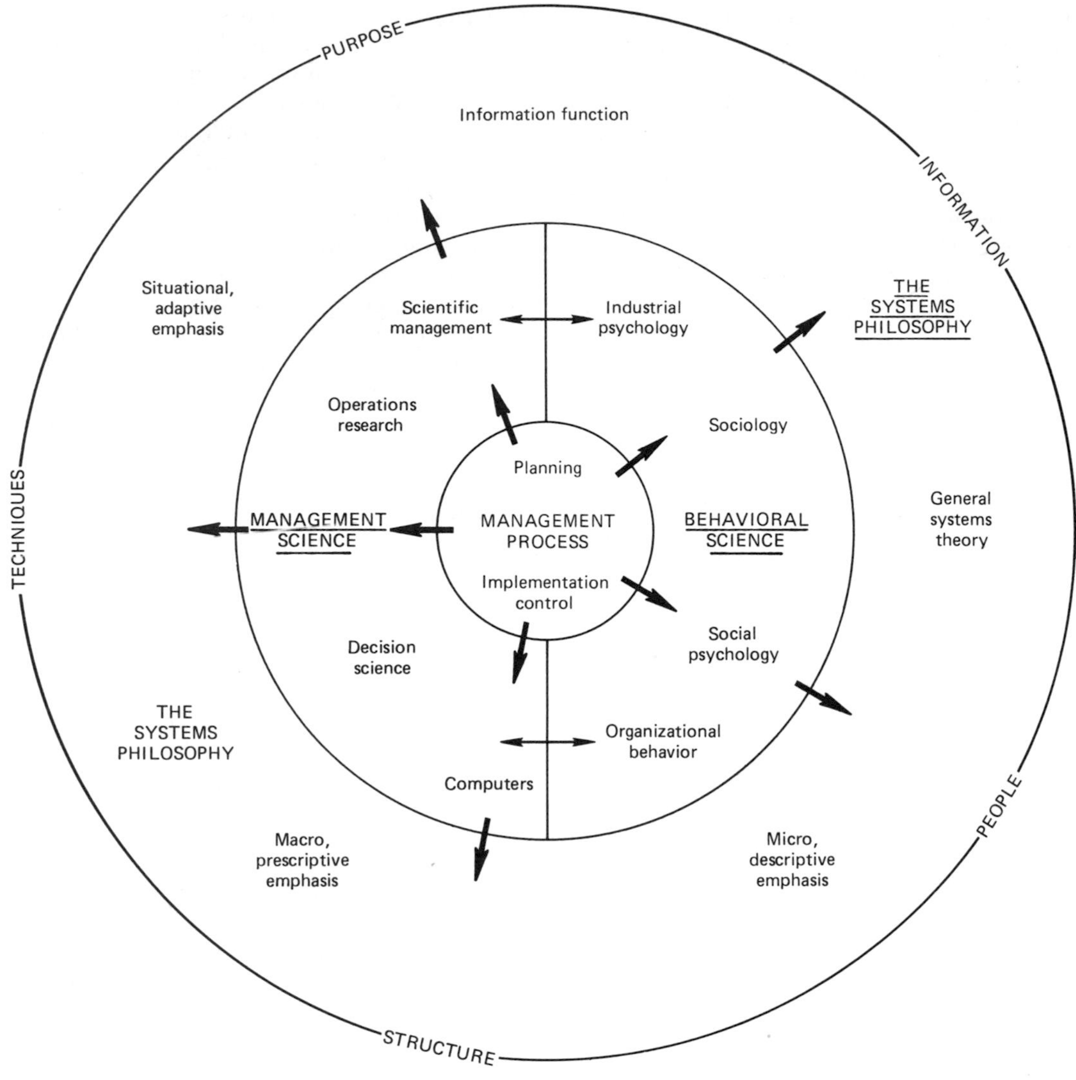

Figure 2-2 Emergence of the systems philosophy

A *system* may be considered as a set of *units* having *relationships* among them. Of the systems known to us—conceptual, concrete, and abstracted—the concrete system contains units and relationships which are empirically determinable and can be described (units by nouns and pronouns, relationships by verbs). Living systems are a subset of the concrete system and, for survival, differ from nonliving systems in that they require critical subsystems.

In the history of thinking about categories, we have seen the need for bringing together body-mind, right-left brain, group task-process functioning, morale and productivity, and individual goal-organizational goals. Such an integration is part of the potential contribution of general systems thinking. This linkage, as related to organizations, should be viewed as follows:[17]

1. *Organizational structure.* Here we are dealing with divisions of *labor* and *authority.* If not clear, confusion results; also low productivity, some work repeated, other work never done. Issues of *responsibility* and *accountability* get resolved here.
2. *Organizational processes.* Here we are dealing with the internal dynamics that interact with the structure. The organizational structure will determine the process to be positive or negative (i.e., if the heart were located in the feet, there would be poor circulation to the head, and vice versa).
3. *Levels of organizational processes*

   Intrapersonal—an individual's relatedness to self; ego-gratification wishes, fantasy life, management of anxiety, and impulse.

   Interpersonal—member-to-member interaction and relations.

   Group—organizational role patterns and member identity patterns.

   Intergroup—group-to-group relations; the interdependence of subsystems in an organization.

In summary, the systems concept is the recognition that any organization is a system made up of subsystems, each of which has its own goals. Managers should realize that they can achieve the overall goals of the organization only by viewing the entire system, seeking to understand and measure the interrelationships, and to integrate them in a fashion that enables the organization effectively to pursue its goals.

There appear to be five system properties, or elements: input, output, processor, control, and feedback. These are the attributes of any ongoing process, structured or unstructured. Figure 2-3,[18] conceptualized by Irving Stubbs and Richard Hill, provides a way of looking at the functional relationships that exist in any ongoing process.

Attempts to define a general systems approach have not always been easy or useful. It is often confused with systems analysis, systems engineering, or systems management. Our principal focus here, however, is not upon systems engineering but rather the phases of systems analysis. It will be helpful if general systems ideas can assist us identify, define, and better understand individuals, groups, and organizations.

Systems analysis, according to Ernest Jones, is "analysis undertaken with a view to supporting decisions as to the design, selection, or operation of a system," the

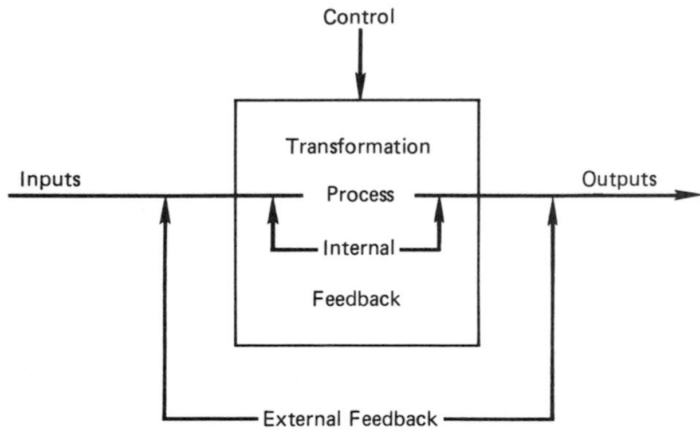

Figure 2-3 A systems model of an organization

"ideal result" of which is "clear identification of one best system and its manner of operation."[19] Systems analysis attempts to formulate a model of representation of a system to be created, engineered, or managed. A definition of systems analysis is that it makes "a problem understandable, offering possible avenues for its solution, and establishing criteria for the selection of the best alternative."[20]

Systems management is defined by Jones as "a special method for managing the production or operation of a system," and as "a lower echelon general management . . . organized around a task within the scope of the system" that "can be considered as an extension of the concept of decentralized management."[21]

Since our principal focus is upon systems analysis for organization renewal, the following rationale may be helpful:[22]

1. Understanding the objectives in the context of the environment in which the system is to operate
2. Stating in an analytically manageable way the interrelations between variables chosen for the analysis and the objectives; this amounts to the construction of a model
3. Quantifying functional relationships between elements of the model and "output," which is often described as the "benefits"
4. Quantifying functional relationships between elements of the model and "inputs" or resources needed
5. Combining (3) and (4) into an overall model characterized by an input–output relationship that flows through the model
6. Determining from the input–output relationship that choice of all possibilities of systems characteristics and manner of operation that produces the most desired results, and operating rates that correspond to that optimum

Systems analysis often borrows methods and techniques of analysis from other disciplines. Moreover, its "procedures vary widely, reflecting the uncertainties and confusion . . . found in intellectual endeavors in ill-defined areas" and indicating "differences among organizations."[23] These procedures include measurement, quantification, mathematical models, simulation, gaming, and game theory;* statistical theory, a variety of devices for coping with uncertainty (such as sensitivity analysis); contingency analysis; a fortiorari analysis; break-even analysis; adversary procedures; and the Delphi method.

ORGANIZATIONS AS SOCIAL/HUMAN SYSTEMS

Now let us move to the way the behavioral sciences look at organizations as social systems.

A *social or human system* may be defined as a "stable pattern of interaction between interdependent social units." It is a set of parts that stand in definite relationship to one another. This concept can be applied to *individuals,* in which case there is an interaction between the different roles that the individual person performs. It can be applied to *organizations,* in which case there is an interaction between social institutions (e.g., economic system, political system). An organization, in common with individuals, groups, and communities, may be regarded as an open, organismic system. We see the organization as a set of dynamic elements that are in some way interconnected and interrelated and that continue to operate together according to certain laws and in such a way as to produce some characteristic total effect. This serves equally well in referring to individuals, groups, organizations, or communities. All four levels of systems have their bound-

*Operations research is now identified with specific techniques, such as linear programming, Monte Carlo (randomizing) methods, and gaming and game theory.

aries which separate them from their environment; each is constantly exchanging material and energy with this environment; each has a number of subsystems within it which have to be functioning together to form a dynamic unity.

Such a human system performs certain necessary functions:

1. To keep the random actions of its members within limits so that they behave in accordance with *role* definitions. Supervisors are expected to supervise, workers to work, managers to administer, custodians to maintain the building, and so forth.
2. To reduce randomness and uncertainty in the relationships among the individuals or groups that make up the system (i.e., to meet the human need for structure and predictability).
3. To satisfy the shared needs and fulfill the shared goals of its members, both the implicit (usually not talked about) and the explicit (talked about), as defined by the system.
4. To survive as a system by meeting new concerns of its members and new demands directed toward it from the outside.

The nature of such a human system, however, is not that obscure; it can be simplified for the purpose of examination. Figure 2-4 illustrates the progression from the individual human being to a complex organization of many human beings.[24] The basic, microorganismic unit—the subsystem we know as the *individual*—is indisputably as complex as other parts of the system, a fact that explains one of the reasons why organizations have problems.

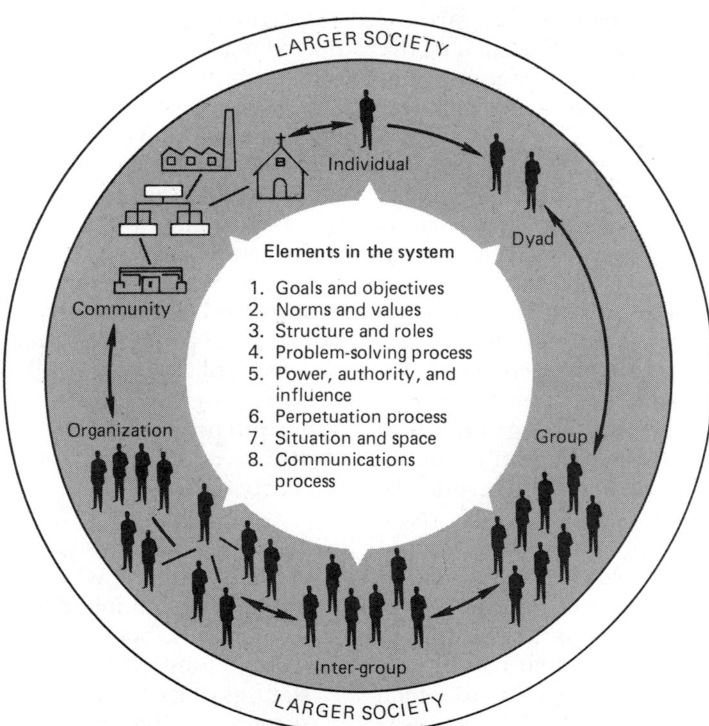

Figure 2-4 Behavioral factors in social systems

Two individuals constitute a *dyad,* more than two individuals form a *group,* and both the dyad and the group are subsystems. The *intergroup* is created when two or more groups establish a relationship. An *organization* usually is comprised of two or more groups having a more or less common reason for working together, although an organization can at any time consist of only a single group. A *community,* which in this scale is macroorganistic, is made up of individuals, groups, and organizations in various intermixtures and associations. Schematically, as well as practically, all this forms a never-ended circle, and the whole of a society is made up of countless such circles interlocked like chainmail.

If we consider an organization to be a sociotechnical system comprised of subsystems (i.e., individuals, dyads, and groups), we find that the subsystems are influenced by certain behavioral elements regardless of their size or complexity. For each of the elements, therefore, we can see it as applicable to the individual, group, or organization.

Goals and objectives. Each subsystem has certain goals toward which its behavior is directed. The conscious or unconscious perception of these goals may range from clear to vague. They may be short range or long range, fixed or flexible, explicit or implicit. Although not necessarily with absolute certainty or unanimously, goals reflect what the subsystem "wants to do." In small, informal, face-to-face groups, the relevant goals are those that involve the interaction of the members of the group. In formal organizations, goals are the rationally contrived purposes of the organizational entity.[25] The goals set up by organizational subsystems may be sought in different degrees as a result of the clarity with which they are conceived, their consistency with other goals, and the extent to which such goals are integrated with the next larger unit in the social system.

The functioning of an organization is often strongly affected by the nature of both its formal and informal goals, and by the extent to which those goals are understood and accepted by all members of the system. Vague or mixed goals tend to produce apathy and internal competitiveness; clear, accepted goals do tend to produce greater commitment and interdependence.

Norms and values. As it interacts with the environment, a social system will develop expected and prescribed ways of acting in relationship to its goals and objectives. These standards of behavior will be influenced by what has happened in the past as well as new experiences and requirements. These norms will include how people dress, whether personal relations are stiff or relaxed, how much "enthusiasm" about one's occupation is appropriate—and dozens of similar, unspoken but powerful dictums. To act contrary to the norms may bring severe censorship or even total rejection by the group. Some norms are functional in getting the organization's task done; others may be incidental and nonproductive. Standards may rest on tradition as well as on changes produced by new experiences and requirements. Because norms and values sometimes persist beyond the point where they are functional, some groups and organizatons find it useful in the renewal process to make their operative norms explicit periodically. They ask: "Is this the way we really want to behave? What purpose is served by this norm?"

Norms and values form the culture in which people work.

> A social system is a function of the common culture, which not only forms the basis of the intercommunication of its members, but which defines, and so in one sense determines, the relative statuses of its members. There is, within surprisingly broad limits, no intrinsic significance of persons to each other

> independent of their actual interaction. Insofar as these relative statuses are defined and regulated in terms of a common culture, the following apparently paradoxical statement holds true: what persons *are* can only be understood in terms of a set of beliefs and sentiments which define what they *ought to be*. This proposition is true only in a very broad way, but is none the less crucial to the understanding of social systems.[26]

Structure and roles. A human system develops a pattern of expected behavior that determines the interrelationships of individuals and groups and, thereby, the structure of the organization. In the small group, organization for work is flexible, and can meet both group goals and member needs. The positions in the group are interchangeable, and usually there is no stable, sharp role differentiation. Occupants of a position (e.g., group member, chairman) can move in and out of a small group, and in and out of a particular position, with relative ease. The behavior of the members of a small group is highly visible to all members of the group. Finally, the sequence of work operations can be relatively casual and circuitous without serious difficulty.

In the formal organization, on the other hand, we have closely defined positions in a network. These organic positions have *continuity*—they are maintained by the expectations of occupants of other positions. All this makes for more stability, but less flexibility. The positions usually are *not* easily interchangeable (e.g., the sales manager may not understand and therefore could not perform the chief engineer's job). Positions are clearly differentiated for an effective division of labor. Position occupants accordingly cannot move easily in and out of positions other than their own. Job behavior is not highly visible (e.g., most members do not know very much about what other members *do*) and sequence becomes very important (e.g., order slips have to be routed *this* way or we'll have confusion).

These organizational features both raise and answer many questions. How much social distance should exist between a boss and his subordinates? What sphere of influence does the controller have—and what data can he ask for without being accused of invading the privacy of some individual or department? These role expectations, like norms, become powerful determinants of behavior within the organization.

Problem-solving process. Each subsystem adopts a way to resolve its internal and external conflicts, and to eliminate threat or ambiguity. These processes may result in such behavior as flight, fight, or dependency; or they may involve behavior that copes with the situation *as it is* through proper analysis, progression, and evaluation. Members of the organization develop a general feeling that "We're pretty realistic here" or "We really don't know how to come to grips with problems." In some systems, problem solving is viewed as primarily an individual responsibility; in others, it is viewed as group effort.

Again, basically, organization renewal is the process of realistically confronting situations so that problems are resolved in such a manner as to produce growth of individuals, groups, and the organization, as well as mature the process of problem solving itself.

Power, authority, and influence. This element reflects the ability of a subsystem to exert change on other subsystems within the same organization, and the ability of that organization to effect change within its subsystems or to influence change in other organizations. Some of the factors affecting the results of power and authority are the subsystem's place in the hierarchy of the organization, the sanctions imposed upon it, the expertise it possesses, the capacity of one subsystem to reward or punish another, and the interpersonal skills that are brought into play. Power, in the sense of capacity to influence behavior, becomes more and more central as positions become more differentiated. Authority is here used to mean "legitimized" power (who has the right to make this particular decision?), but it is clear that much "illegitimate" power is exerted in keeping any organization going.

The influence by participation in small, work group decision making can be full and complete. Non-face-to-faceness, however, unavoidable as it is in the large, formal organization, means that participation in *all* decisions by *all* persons within the organization is an impossibility, and that such participation would be highly disruptive and ineffective. Trust or mistrust of those with greater power and efficiency becomes a pattern in organizations. As members of an organization gain in sophistication, skill, and self-confidence, they increasingly resist direct commands and respond to the more sophisticated and sometimes informal influence of involvement and recognition.

Perpetuation process. Every subsystem in an organization wishes to maintain its existence. The need felt by each subsystem to continue functioning is a dynamic factor in the development and growth of an organization, either positively or negatively. This need is a dynamic factor behind attempts to reorganize a personality or an organization. To demonstrate the power of this behavioral element, one need only note the number of committees, agencies, and organizations that continue to exist long after their stated mission has been accomplished.

Situation and space. Every system and subsystem exists within the sphere of influence of an even larger system, and the limits constraining each system or subsystem are determined by its particular circumstances with respect to situation and space. Studies in the field of sociotechnical systems underscore the impact of physical arrangements on the operation of an organization. The location of an office inevitably determines the persons talked to most frequently and influenced. Recognition of this fact—that physical arrangements can strongly influence interpersonal relations—has led some to complain that too often architects and engineers determine the climate of an organization without fully realizing the ultimate results of their decisions.

Communication. A social system must communicate to survive and grow. Communication is the means for providing information that permits the system or subsystem to change, grow, achieve its goals. In the smaller group, the communication net is usually fully interconnected—all persons can talk to all other persons, either singly or as a group. Under these circumstances, few rules are necessary to channel communications, and members tend to follow these rules because they are clearly functional (e.g., one person should talk at a time). Since people are face to face, information is transmitted with less distortion. Small group information handling is as good as possible because errors can be checked and corrected immediately ("Joe, do I hear you saying that . . . ?").

In a formal organization, on the other hand, the communication networks limit and channel the exchange of information. Much information must travel through a number of persons in sequence; distortion increases sharply as data are abstracted and simplified, as some information is blocked, or some is added deliberately or via projection. Rules for communication become important (X reports to Y and sends carbons to Z, *only*). As work and authority problems mount, occupants of positions almost inevitably find that the formal communications channels are providing data of poor quality or insufficient quantity. Therefore, the rules are circumvented, persons are "gone around," coffee-break chats become essential, and an informal communication network appears. Finally, correcting information in an organization is a difficult and lengthy process (phone calls, memos, special meetings). Many problems can be attributed to "breakdowns in communication." This process has been studied extensively and much is now known about the conditions that facilitate effective communications.[27]

Understanding and examining these behavioral elements is essential to the change process and organization renewal. The subsystems of the organization are complicated. One feature that makes organizations of particular interest as larger social systems is that they are composed of parts which are themselves more or less complete social systems. These subsystems develop their own structures in each of the areas noted above and, especially, their own norms.

The degree to which the organization is integrated as a social system depends on the degree to which the subsystems, with their own norms and procedures, work congruently with each other toward organizational goals. One of the major problems of organizations arises when subsystems work at cross purposes with each other. The following typical kinds of special problems result:

- Intergroup competition, possibly leading to collusion
- Restriction of output
- Bureaucratization, formalization, and professionalization
- Split loyalty for the individual
- Communication difficulties, especially for smaller subsystems
- Decision-making difficulties, such as integrating the separate goals of different individuals or groups

These problems put a special demand on the need for teamwork and openness throughout the modern organization. Such team development will be particularly relevant for the temporary and permanent face-to-face groups that function in the organization, and the elements of a social system will be evident in all such team situations.

The "behavioral elements" of social systems, and their formal and informal manifestations, can be related to mathematical and engineering models so as to show us the forces in a social system that are constantly changing:

1. *Inputs and outputs.* One of the characteristics of individuals, groups, organizations, and communities is that there is a continual input into the system and output from it. Things go into the system, something happens to them inside, and they come out in an altered form.
2. *Fluctuation of being open and closed.* Systems such as individuals, groups, organizations, or communities are neither completely open nor completely closed. They are some of both. Sometimes they tend to be more open; sometimes they tend to be more closed. Systems seem to go through a continuous cycle of alternate opening and closing. Sometimes one part of the system may be open while another is closed.
3. *Maintenance of a steady state.* They strive to maintain a particular kind of equilibrium which may be called a *steady state.* The maintenance by a human being of a fairly constant body temperature during changing hot and cold environmental conditions is a good example. The financial resources available to an organization, such as a voluntary agency, will fluctuate, but through a complicated process of self-regulation the organization is able to maintain itself in a more or less steady financial state, unless, of course, resources decrease beyond some critical point.
4. *Defense against injury and repair of damage.* It is a characteristic of organizational subsystems that they will repair any damage they incur. This feature indicates that most organizations have a built-in potential for organization renewal.

5. *Maintenance of boundaries.* All social systems and their subsystems appear to have a need for a clear sense of identity. There is, for example, a need for an organized subsystem to know where its jurisdiction begins and ends; thus, it strives for a clear definition of its boundaries and tends to resist any external effort to change it. This boundary maintenance phenomenon might account for the contention that often exists between organizations or organizational subsystems that operate close to one another. It is also one of the complications that emerges in this age of acquisitions and mergers.

   Another complication is the effect that *external* factors have on the system's existence and *internal* processes. External factors will tend to affect primarily the input part of the system, but the data and output can also be affected.

To fully understand a sociotechnical system, it is necessary to appreciate both the external and internal forces at work, the formal and informal nature of the behavioral elements affecting the subsystems, and the input–output process of the system itself.

In examining the response of organizations to their environment in a systemic way, there is a need for action, change, and development at the individual, group, and total organization levels. These three levels of human systems are essential for organization renewal.

LOOKING AT ORGANIZATION RENEWAL AND ORGANIZATION DEVELOPMENT

Organization development is described in multiple ways. This is referenced by Schien and Bennis when they comment that many programs indicate they are "doing OD." They observe:

> Four examples would be: (1) the Organization Development Program, an alumni program, developed by an NTL committee, for directors of management development activities who were presumed to be already in influential change agent roles in their organizations. . . . Here the OD program was seen as designed for directors of management development activities; (2) the development of advanced programs for experienced persons by the American Management Association and the American Society for Training and Development; (3) a third school has a definition similar to those described above, but interestingly, and understandably, equate OD with laboratory training. The two terms are identical with this group. We have observed that England seems to subscribe to this limited definition—but many U.S. organizations also hold to this definition; (4) the fourth school would equate the term OD with systems development, systems research, and/or training/developing/improving a sub-system.
>
> Sometimes this appears to be in the sense of laboratory training—others equate it with any sub-system improvement; including procedures, hardware, technological, time-motion studies, etc.[28]

A fifth school, and this seems to be growing, equates organization development with being concerned not only with the organization's human resources—but the nonhuman resources and factors as well. Many in this school, despairing of getting the term "organization development" to be understood in this sense, have developed another phrase to encompass their concept—*organizational renewal.*

Increasingly in recent years, there has been a heightened awareness that organization development should connote more than improving the human resources of the organization—that nonhuman aspects must also be considered. This is increasingly seen in comments by persons who have predominantly, in the past, seen organization development as primarily concerned with the human side of organizations.

Warren Bennis, discussing the managerial revolution, comments:

> The challenge for organization development and the challenge for education, it seems to me, are these:
>
> How do we produce in our organization development efforts "learning persons," persons who have poise, persons who can adapt, persons who have the right balance between commitment and inquiry, and persons who will be able to tolerate future shock?
>
> How do we develop problem-centered organizations, organizations that react to problems as they emerge and don't get over committed to techniques that worked yesterday but can't work tomorrow?
>
> How can we develop within our organizations "centers for revitalization," centers for development, if you will, that have as their main mission organizational adaptation and helping to shape the future of society?
>
> Finally, how do we develop a system of organization which is oriented to the future to possibilities and potentials, rather than basing most of its learning on a past that will no longer be adequate to handle very new kinds of problems, problems which we can't even contemplate today?[29]

In the past, organization development has been equated with such unlike things as an enlightened wage and salary program, ongoing training programs, role plays, case studies, T-groups, laboratory training, operations research, and systems research.

As organizations use the term, a lot depends on their philosophy. If the criteria of success are growth and better-than-industry return to shareholders, you get one view of what organization development is. If the organization has a philosophy that also to be considered are the employees their goals and aspirations, and the meaning of work to people, you get still another view. If the organization has a philosophy that both of the above are important, and add concerns of the nation, our way of life, our partnership with government, an awareness of community and social "good," then still another meaning of organization development evolves.

With these broad and sharp variations, it is quite understandable why organization development is defined so differently and programs constructed that look so different. It is also the reason for the new term "quality of work life" (see Chapter 8).

John W. Gardner, if he did not coin the term "organization renewal," brought it into the vocabulary of organization development practitioners. As initially used by Gardner, the term had a fairly restricted meaning:

> . . . a "self-renewing agency" [is] one in which the total organization (and the consumer of the service) participates in defining its own problems. Successful self-renewal depends upon employing the model of complex causality and remaining alert to ever changing goals.[30]

A number of persons concerned with organization development began uncomfortably to suspect that the "development" of an organization had something to do with more than human relations training and teamwork.

Because of the difficulty in so gaining common acceptance of an expansive definition of "organization development," I began to use the term *organizational renewal.* Robert Blake and Jane Mouton also saw the problem of definition when they wrote:

> It seems to us that the "O" in Organization Development deserves to be respected for what it is: the total system existing within a larger external environment which consists of interacting parts, including traditions, precedents, and past practices, all of which are geared, or should be, toward achieving an overriding purpose.[31]

This definition is helpful, but individual and group development can contribute to renewal even while organization development is seen as a system-wide effort. One of my reasons for using the term "organization renewal" is that "organization development" is so variously defined. "Organization renewal" is intended to convey a concept that includes but goes beyond what "organization development" originally was meant to convey. Other practitioners and behavioral scientists—among them Matthew B. Miles, Paul C. Buchanan, and Dale G. Lake—are also using "organization renewal." Some others reject the term on the grounds that "renewal" connotes something that has gotten old and is being renewed (e.g., urban renewal), whereas "development" connotes an attempt to keep an organization in step with internal and external factors.

One confusing aspect in discussing organization development is the way the term is frequently associated with "planned change." Many use the two terms synonymously. Planned change generally seems to assume resistance to change, whereas organization development does not necessarily imply inevitable resistance. Planned change generally implies the use of an outside change agent; organization renewal most often is considered an internal operation, but uses both. The focus in planned change seems to be on human relationships; organization renewal is not so limited. The change efforts in planned change usually involve a limited goal; stop smoking, introduction of a new billing system; installation of a new machine; organization renewal implies broader, more significant change goals achieved over a longer period of time. Organization renewal must, of course, concern itself with planned change, and limited change goals introduced sequentially to reach a broader change goal. It would be helpful if this differentiation was clearly understood; it is the same as confusing a skirmish with a war.

Paul C. Buchanan illustrates this principal when he uses a title such as "The Concept of Organization Development, or Self-renewal, as a Form of Planned Change," and says:

> Organization development is directed toward developing the capabilities of an organization in such a manner that the organization can attain and sustain an optimum level of performance; it is a problem-solving process; it is undertaken on a collaborative basis by the members of an organization and behavioral science practitioners; and it reflects the belief that even in organizations which are operating satisfactorily or adequately there is room for further improvement.[32]

The parameters of organization development, in this broad perspective, and the reasons for concern, were sketched by Norman J. Ream in a panel discussion entitled "The State of Information Retrieval and Data Processing in the Year 2000 and Its Implications for Management." He was not discussing organization development per se, but the pronounced change and complexity to be expected in the world in the years ahead:

> No product or service will be safe in an innovative world.

> No enterprise, however big, is safe in an era of radical change; all organizations must live dangerously and try to hear the potentialities in the marketplace.
>
> No management technique can survive as a conditioned response to a given situation, for the situations will not remain static.
>
> No business or marketing plan can avoid becoming obsolete when there are vast swings into mass habits, when there is intense and imaginative competition.
>
> No member of management is secure in his position unless he can cope with extreme changes. Past successes will not secure his future.[33]

The field of organization development is in a state of flux. Warner Burke points out that organization development is experiencing eight key transformations:

1. From a field limited almost exclusively to business/industrial organizations to a field affecting many different types of organizations
2. From advocating a specific managerial style to emphasizing a situational or contingency approach
3. From democracy as the primary value advocated to authenticity
4. From a field based largely on the social technology of laboratory training and survey feedback to a field based on a broader range of social technology
5. From the consultant as a nondirective, purely process-oriented practitioner to the consultant as an authoritative specialist
6. From considering the organization development practitioner as the change agent to thinking of the line manager/administrator as the ultimate change agent
7. From the role of the practitioner as working almost exclusively with management to the role of the practitioner as working with both managers and other persons at all organizational levels
8. From the organization development function being merely a more glamorous name for training to a function that has organizational legitimacy in and of itself, with attendant power and official status[34]

There is an accelerating awareness that while an organization does nothing without people, conversely, people do little without organization and tools and nonhuman resources. Somehow the two interface and are interrelated—and the discussion about theory X or theory Y is not materially helpful.

One other issue needs to be surfaced and confronted—an issue that is not dealt with much in the current literature. Organizations are said to be either reactive or proactive. Few organizations would readily admit to being reactive—responding to emergencies and forces only when they present themselves and demand a response. The critical issue for organization development or organization renewal with respect to a proactive course would seem to be this: Is it possible for an individual, group, or organization to sustain high interest, awareness, and constantly make the changes, decisions, and planning that are called for in such a viable concept?

Both organization development and organization renewal need to be concerned with the *ying* of change and the *yang* of stability. Organization renewal calls for a process of diagnosis and planning that holds on to those valuable beliefs, norms, and practices that should not change, and identifies those that should be changed. This is the essence of professional management and an integral part of a leader's responsibility.

In light of this historical background, it is possible to present an organic model of systems renewal that can lead to change and renewal in organizations. This model attempts to integrate all five schools of thought—cultural, developmental, training, laboratory education, and systems; and, as well, human and nonhuman approaches—into a comprehensive presentation. This model forms the organizational basis of this book (see Figure 2-5).

A SYSTEMS RENEWAL MODEL

The environmental forces interacting with the stages of growth of the organization give the larger frame of reference for what Bakke refers to as an *organizational charter*. The subsystems are the basic human resources which, when combined with the material and capital resources of the organization, form the "critical mass" of the organization. His *activity process* is illustrated in the discussion of the process of communication that involves the confrontation, search, and coping phases. Planned or unplanned situational responses, with continuing renewal stimulus, provide his *bonds of organization*. These ways of conceptualizing the organization place emphasis on the problem-solving nature of organizational functioning. They also point out the many factors that affect and contribute to this problem solving.

It is important to take into account the fact that individuals and groups within organizations really are "systems" in a biological, psychological, sociological, and anthropological sense; and that organizations themselves are human as much as technological systems. The concept of the organization as a sociotechnical system is entirely valid and, rather than urge the democratic overtones of participative management upon every situation, leaders would do better to take advantage of *all* the contributions that management and behavioral sciences have made to understanding how and why a sociotechnical system functions best. We know, for example, that the human organism is a lot tougher than we give it credit for being, that the individual can absorb more punishment than we ordinarily suspect, and that one is not always injured by not being involved. We know, also, that groups and organizations find it hard to go out of existence, even though the survival stage is difficult.

In the renewal model (see Figure 2-5), the need for individual, group, and organization development is treated in essential relationship to the planning process derived from a requirement or disequilibrium in the system. Such planning demands research, training, and action. In such processes, therefore, an internal leader/consultant/facilitator and/or external consultant/facilitator will be helpful and useful, no matter what kind of action is anticipated and implemented. It is also obvious that some key competences will require skills in managing change, effective communications, competent leadership, and handling conflict and agreement.

In any discussion of systems thinking, we find frequent reference to *closed* and *open* systems. Systems renewal that includes individual, group, and organization development will require open-system characteristics at all levels.

OPEN SYSTEMS

Subsystems and the total organization manifest both open and closed aspects of their nature. One of the social scientists who has contributed a great deal to our understanding of this field is Milton Rokeach. He proposes that every person, group, or organization has a belief system that represents the total beliefs, opinions, mind sets, and expectancies—conscious or unconscious—that are accepted as being true; at the same time, it has a system of

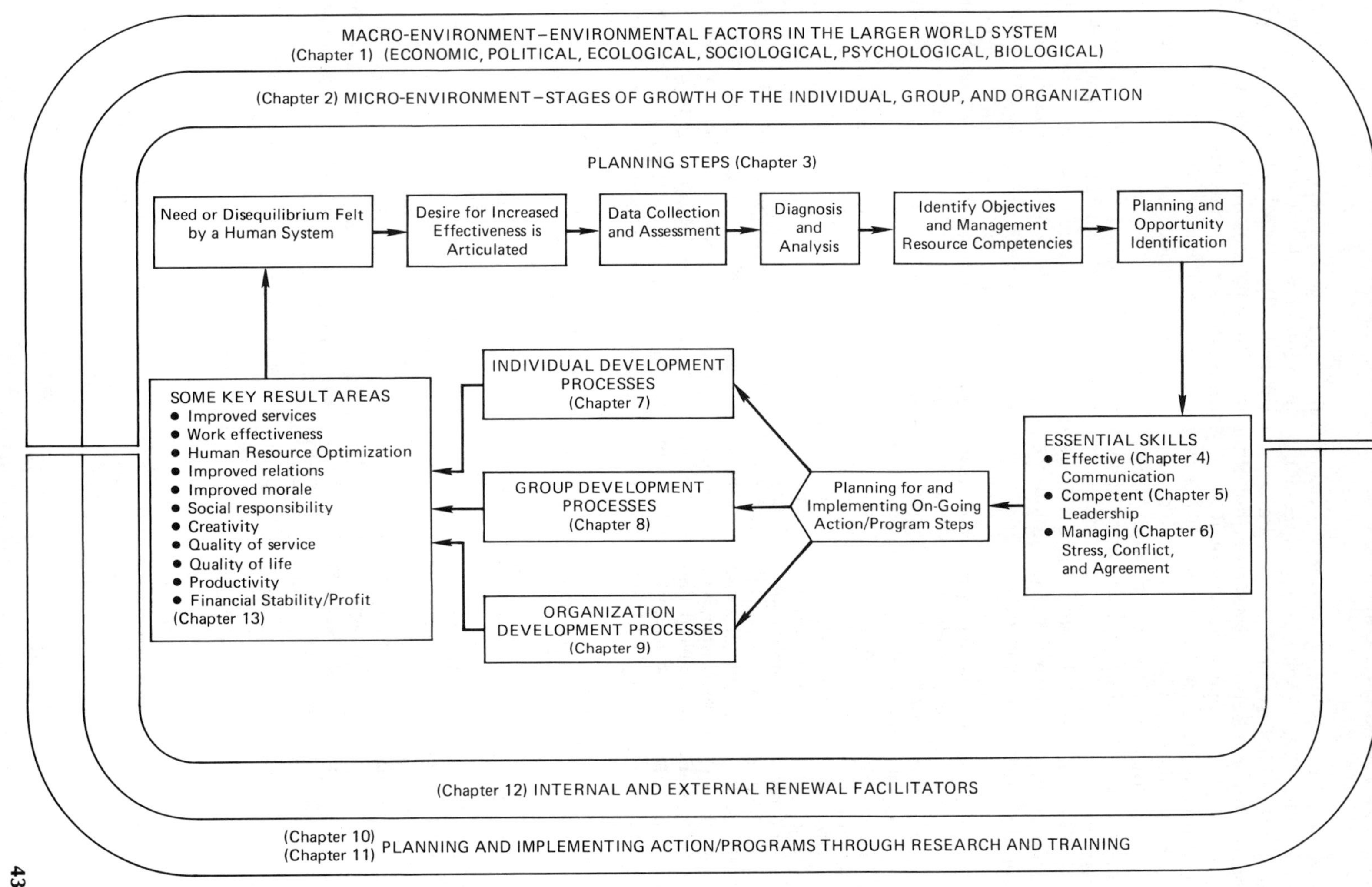
SYSTEMS RENEWAL MODEL
MACRO-ENVIRONMENT–ENVIRONMENTAL FACTORS IN THE LARGER WORLD SYSTEM
(Chapter 1) (ECONOMIC, POLITICAL, ECOLOGICAL, SOCIOLOGICAL, PSYCHOLOGICAL, BIOLOGICAL)
(Chapter 2) MICRO-ENVIRONMENT–STAGES OF GROWTH OF THE INDIVIDUAL, GROUP, AND ORGANIZATION
PLANNING STEPS (Chapter 3)
Need or Disequilibrium Felt by a Human System
Desire for Increased Effectiveness is Articulated
Data Collection and Assessment
Diagnosis and Analysis
Identify Objectives and Management Resource Competencies
Planning and Opportunity Identification
ESSENTIAL SKILLS
● Effective (Chapter 4) Communication
● Competent (Chapter 5) Leadership
● Managing (Chapter 6) Stress, Conflict, and Agreement
Planning for and Implementing On-Going Action/Program Steps
INDIVIDUAL DEVELOPMENT PROCESSES (Chapter 7)
GROUP DEVELOPMENT PROCESSES (Chapter 8)
ORGANIZATION DEVELOPMENT PROCESSES (Chapter 9)
SOME KEY RESULT AREAS
● Improved services
● Work effectiveness
● Human Resource Optimization
● Improved relations
● Improved morale
● Social responsibility
● Creativity
● Quality of service
● Quality of life
● Productivity
● Financial Stability/Profit
(Chapter 13)
(Chapter 12) INTERNAL AND EXTERNAL RENEWAL FACILITATORS
(Chapter 10)
(Chapter 11) PLANNING AND IMPLEMENTING ACTION/PROGRAMS THROUGH RESEARCH AND TRAINING

disbeliefs, which are defined as a *series of subsystems* related to and not in agreement with the belief system.[35] For example, a person may accept a system of thought concerning a social organizational structure as being true for a particular situation. If this is taken as a belief system, he or she simultaneously rejects, to a greater or lesser degree, all other organizational value systems.

If we applied Rokeach's characteristics of open–closed systems to organizations we could observe the following:

> An organization system is open to the extent that the *specific content* of beliefs by people in the organization is to the effect that the organization offers a work-life environment that is *primarily friendly;* it is closed when the work world is seen as a threat.
>
> Open organization systems hold to a scheme of values founded on the belief that *authority is rational and tentative,* and that persons are not to be judged according to their agreement or disagreement with authority. In closed systems the value is that authority is considered absolute, and that persons are to be accepted or rejected in accordance with their relation to such authority.
>
> Open organization systems will value and practice a relatively *open communication* pattern among persons, and in a closed system the converse will apply.
>
> The closed organization tends toward formal and inflexible structure, communications, and relations. An open organization is more flexible in its structure, informal in its human relationships, and leveling in communication. The formal aspect puts the individual at the summons of external demands—forces that originate outside his personality and are only indirectly fashioned out of his needs. The necessary submission brings its cost to the human personality; it causes fatigue, drains nervous energy, and produces anxiety.

Three types of systems are sometimes distinguished according to the kind of interaction between system and environment: (1) *absolutely closed systems,* where no interaction with the environment is considered; (2) *relatively closed systems,* where little interaction with the environment acts upon the system (inputs), and the paths over which the system acts on the environment (outputs) are narrowly defined; (3) *open systems,* where all possible effects of the environment on the system and the system on the environment are considered.

All organization systems and subsystems, from the smallest group (a dyad) to the most complex multigroup structure of an international organization, include many elements and processes. Without attention to these interdependent elements and processes the system cannot function effectively.

In the open-systems context the organization is seen as an energy-exchange system:

> A more recent way of looking at organizations is to consider them as energy exchange systems in which there is an input of energy from the environment, and a patterned internal activity that transforms the energy into output, which in turn provokes a new energy input. The organization is thus seen as an open system engaged in constant transactions with its environment, which can be visualized as a system of systems. These systems include the sub-systems within the corporations (divisions, departments) which are constantly engaged in energy exchanges, and the systems operating outside the organization, but affecting it—other members of the same industry, members of the same industries, suppliers, government institutions, etc. The energy exchanges—transactions—that take place both internally and externally occur in a field of force operating in space/time and made up of all the patterned but individual desires and aspirations of all the people who make

up both internal and external environmental systems. This way of looking at an organization offers a picture that is fairly close to modern physical theory and one which should be capable of expression and measurement in scientific, quantitative terms.[36]

Although such a definition may seem rather general, it has specific implications for organization functioning. In Table 2-1, a long-time colleague and friend, Malcolm Knowles, has put static organization versus open-systems organization in chart form for comparison purposes.

The open organization concept presented here correctly assumes that people have a great capacity for being creative, inventive, and ingenious. It recognizes that an inner energy exists within the individual, ready to be turned on and in turn to release that creativity, inventiveness, and ingenuity. It

Table 2-1
Characteristics of Static Versus Open-Systems-Oriented Organizations[37]

	Characteristics	
Dimensions	***Static organizations***	***Open-systems organizations***
Structure	Rigid: permanent committees; reverence for constitution and bylaws, tradition Hierarchical: chain of command Role definitions: narrow Property: bound and restricted	Flexible: temporary task force; readiness to change constitution and bylaws, depart from tradition Linking: functional collaboration Role definitions: broad Property: mobile and regional
Atmosphere	Internally competitive Task-centered: reserved Cold, formal: aloof	Goal-oriented People-centered: caring Warm, informal: intimate
Management and philosophy	Controlling: coercive power Cautious: low risk Errors: to be prevented Emphasis on personnel selection Self-sufficient: closed system re: resources Emphasis on conserving resources Low tolerance for ambiguity	Releasing: supportive power Experimental: high risk Errors: to be learned from Emphasis on personnel development Interdependent: open system re: resources Emphasis on developing and using resources High tolerance for ambiguity
Decision making and policy making	High participation at top, low at bottom Clear distinction between policy-making and execution Decision making by legal mechanisms Decisions treated as final	Relevant participation by all those affected Collaborative policymaking and execution Decision making by problem solving Decisions treated as hypotheses to be tested
Communication	Restricted flow: constipated One-way: downward Feelings: repressed or hidden	Open flow: easy access Two-way: upward and downward Feelings: expressed

also recognizes individual needs for survival and security and that we tend to rush past the line that divides us from the lower order of animals, seeking satisfaction of our higher needs. Organization openness calls for restructuring work to provide opportunities for the worker to express initiative, responsibility, and competence—elements that contribute to the higher need for self-fulfillment. If the desire for self-fulfillment triggers creativity, inventiveness, and ingenuity, the worker's self-fulfillment results in both high personal satisfaction and greater output.

In an open-systems context, the manager may be viewed as a systems integrator with a major responsibility to maintain some degree of consistency and interdependence between the demands imposed by the many subsystems that are a part of the organization. And if we examine the underlying theory base for open systems, we find that it:

1. Views the organization as an energy-exchange system
2. Emphasizes the close relationship between organization structure and its supporting environment
3. Recognizes that energy enters the organization from its environment
4. Sees this energy processed and transformed within the organization
5. Results in outputs that generate more inputs, to continue the process

Table 2-2, a model developed by Oscar Mink, James Schultz, and Barbara Mink, indicates that open behavior requires unity and internal and external responsiveness.

Reality behavior which demonstrates that an organization is moving toward an open system can be outlined in this manner:[39]

1. Is in functional touch with its external environment.
2. Has all its parts integrated toward common goals.
3. Has leadership that draws employee commitment to a common organization purpose.
4. Has no isolated units; all subunits are open to each other.
5. Is willing to engage in "high-risk" experiments.
6. Centralizes broad policy; develops its strategies and tactics inputs up and down within the organizational structure; and decentralizes implementation, innovation, and governance.
7. Is able to adapt quickly and constructively to rapid change on a proactive basis.
8. Wants problems to be solved at the lowest possible level.
9. Supports needed creative and rational problem-solving processes.
10. Reduces levels of supervision by decentralizing performance control.
11. Is managed by persons who demonstrate high expectations of other persons; who attempt to respond to employee needs in a way that will develop their potentialities; and who generate synergy through motivating management practices—thus:
    a. Broad rather than narrow job descriptions.
    b. Encouragement of employee communication directly to those whose cooperation is required to achieve the organization's objectives.
    c. Effective use of matrix task forces.
    d. Confront and minimize organizational games.
    e. Decrease negative stroking and increase positive stroking.

The basis for general, social/human, and open systems ideas is that any production or service system calls for both a technology and a work relationship structure relating human resources to technological resources. That is, an organization's total system has a complete set of human activities plus interrelationships to the technical, physical, and financial resources; and to the processes for turning out products and services.

Table 2–2
Open-Organization Behaviors[38]

Level	Unity	Internal Responsiveness	External Responsiveness
Individual	Identification of my basic beliefs; who I am; my uniqueness; self-concept, perceived self. Values: Am I open and other-oriented or closed and self-oriented?	Awareness of myself, my feelings, my needs, my defenses; freedom to fulfill my wants and needs	Hearing and responding to others; active listening; openness to ideas, experiences, persons; love—ability to enter into and establish enduring relationships; interpersonal attraction and involvement
Group	Identification of team goals and objectives; building the team; group achieves syntality (personality) and synergy (group output is greater than the sum of individual outputs)	Interpersonal skills; facilitation of interaction among team members; process observation; sensitivity and coherence; interpersonal attraction *or* cohesiveness develops	Gathering and relating external information relevant to task of team; linkage with other individuals and groups; cooperation for achievement of common purpose with other systems
Organization	Development of common goals of organization; management according to purpose and mission	Ways components within an organization react to and affect each other; data sharing; organization development and human relations; linkages between individuals and groups	Organization responsiveness to larger community; social relevance, profitability

The need to initiate moves toward organization renewal, then, arises partly from changes in our technological environment—from the insensate hardware through which we wander every day. It also arises, and more significantly, from the changes in philosophy that have moved the worker from a victim of serfdom to a victim of scientific management, an evolution in the software of work that has progressed from complete coercion and threat to nearly complete collaboration and reason. The potential of organization flexibility and openness is within ourselves, and in those internal and external others operating in a state of interdependence. Yet making the most of that potential is as much an opportunity for the top executive as for the least-paid employee. Realizing the potential for organization renewal that requires an open system is measured not only by how much money we have, how much floor space, how much production, or how much profit. It lies in how much meaning we realize in our work, how much personal satisfaction, and how much peace of mind. It is demonstrated in our belief in the desire of people to live in the full measure of their capabilities and still reach beyond them. Only then can we say that we have an open organization and that organization renewal is taking place.

SUMMARY

Organizations have been viewed in various ways by society, leaders, managers, and scholars. The reality may be that there is some of all five approaches in most organizations. In the light of the complexity of modern organizations, however, the systems point of view seems to be helpful. General systems thinking provides a frame of reference that can include multidisciplines and technologies. In the organization development field the social systems' frame of reference is most relevant for diagnosis. Organization development is a rapidly changing field moving from a purely interpersonal focus to a more results-oriented approach. The use of the term *organization renewal* is proposed to extend to the human and nonhuman aspects of organizational viability.

In the systems renewal model the reader will find a holistic way of combining individual, group, and organization development into the totality of internal and external forces impacting the organization. Renewal at each level of complexity will depend upon achieving an open-systems orientation and practice.

QUESTIONS

1. As a person examines the five different ways of looking at organizations, which approach seems most prevalent in the organizations with which you are familiar?
2. What is an operational way of defining general systems? How does cybernetics relate to general systems?
3. What are the key elements of individuals, groups, and organizations as social systems?
4. What major trends are identified in the organization development field? Can you give examples in which you support of differ with these trends?
5. How does organization renewal differ from organization development?
6. In reviewing the systems renewal model, what examples of macro and micro environmental forces can you cite?
7. What examples can you cite of an open system? a closed system?

NOTES

[1]Kenneth E. Boulding, *Economic Analysis,* 2nd ed., (New York: Harper & Row, 1948), p. 508.

[2]Adapted from foreword by Gordon Lippitt in Oscar Mink, James Shultz, and Barbara Mink, *Developing and Managing Open Organizations* (Austin, Tex.: Learning Concepts, Inc., 1979). Hereafter cited as Mink et al.

[3]Henry P. Knowles and Borje O. Saxberg, *Personality and Leadership Behavior* (Reading, Mass.: Addison-Wesley Publishing Company, Inc., 1971), p. 103.

[4]Ibid., p. 105.

[5]Ibid., pp. 107–108.

[6]Ibid., p. 116.

[7]Chris Argyris, *Integrating the Individual and the Organization* (New York: John Wiley & Sons, Inc., 1964), p. 11.

[8]*Webster's Seventh New Collegiate Dictionary* (Springfield, Mass.: G. and C. Merriam Company, 1967).

[9]Earnest M. Jones, *Systems Approaches to Multivariable, Socio-economic Problems: An Appraisal* (Staff Paper 103, Policy Studies in Science and Technology; Washington, D.C.: The George Washington University, August 1968). Hereafter cited as Jones.

[10]William Shrode and Dan Voich, Jr., *Organization and Management: Basic Systems Concepts* (Homewood, Ill.: Richard D. Irwin, Inc., 1974).

[11]Ibid., p. 89; copyright © 1974 by Richard D. Irwin, Inc.

[12]Ibid., p. 102; copyright © 1974 by Richard D. Irwin, Inc.

[13]Ludwig von Bertalanffy, *General Systems Theory* (New York: George Braziller, Inc., 1968).

[14]Stafford Beer, *Brain of the Firm* (New York: Herder and Herder, 1972).

[15]James G. Miller, "Living Systems: The Organization," *Behavioral Science,* Vol. 17, No. 1, 1972.

[16]Ibid., p. 2.

[17]Salathiel E. Smith, *Report on General Systems Theory* (unpublished paper; Washington, D.C.: The George Washington University, December 1977).

[18]Adapted from Donald Ralph Kingdon, *Matrix Organization* (London: Tavistock Publications Ltd., 1973), p. 46.

[19]Jones, p. 3.

[20]Ibid., p. 3

[21]Ibid., p. 4.

[22]Ibid., p. 5.

[23]Senate Executive Document, 90th Congress, 1st Session: statement of Thomas E. Rowen, Hearings on S. 2662, Note 1; similar descriptions of the "phases" or "sequences" of a systems approach are contained in the statement of Michael Michalis, Hearings on S. 430 and S. 467.

[24]Adapted from Gordon Lippitt and Warren Schmidt, *Managing the Changing Organization* (Washington, D.C.: Leadership Resources, Inc., 1968), pp. 14–17.

[25]Robert Tannenbaum, Irving R. Weschler, and Fred Massarik, *Leadership and Organization* (New York: McGraw-Hill Book Company, 1961), pp. 28–29.

[26]Talcott Parsons, *Social Structure and Personality* (New York: The Free Press, 1964), p. 32.

[27]William V. Haney, *Communication and Organizational Behavior* (Homewood, Ill.: Richard D. Irwin, Inc., 1978).

[28]Edgar H. Schein and Warren B. Bennis, *Personal and Organizational Change through Group Methods* (New York: John Wiley & Sons, Inc., 1966).

[29]Warren B. Bennis, *Changing Organizations* (New York: McGraw-Hill Book Company, 1966), p. 43.

[30]John W. Gardner, as quoted in Leonard J. Duhl, "Planning and Predicting: Or What to Do When You Don't Know the Names of the Variables," *Daedalus,* Vol. 96, No. 3, 1967, 786.

[31]Robert Blake and Jane Mouton, "Why the O.D. Movement Is Stuck and How to Break It Loose," *ASTD Journal,* September 1979, p. 18.

[32]Paul C. Buchanan, "The Concept of Organization Development, or Self-renewal, as a Form of Planned Change," in Goodwin Watson (ed.), *Concepts for Social Change* (Arlington, Va.: NTL Institute for Applied Behavioral Science, 1967), p. 2.

[33]Excerpted from *Management 2000* (New York: The American Foundation for Management Research, Inc., 1968), pp. 80–81.

[34]Warner Burke (ed.), *The Cutting Edge: Current Theory and Practice in Organization Development* (San Diego, Calif.: University Associates, Inc., 1978), pp. 2–3.

[35]Milton Rokeach, *The Open and Closed Mind* (New York: Basic Books, Inc., 1960), p. 33.

[36]Don Fabrun, "The Corporation as a Creative Environment," *Kaiser Aluminum News,* No. 2, 1967, p. 12. Copyright © 1967.

[37]Malcolm Knowles, *Adult Learner: A Neglected Species* (Houston, Tex.: Gulf Publishing Company, 1978), p. 93.

[38]Mink et al., p. 80.

[39]Irving Stubbs and Richard Hill, *The Open Systems Organization* (unpublished proposal to Diamond Shamrock Corp., 1976), p. 8.

3

planning and managing change[1]

No great improvements in the lot of mankind are possible, until a great change takes place in the fundamental constitution of their modes of thought.

John Stuart Mill, 1806–1873

More hours and dollars are spent on managing organizational affairs than on any other peacetime activity. For the most part, this managerial leadership is undertaken in small and large organizations alike without special training in the skills required to cope with planning, problem-solving, and change. The very behavior of those trying to achieve change often erects an impenetrable barrier between the led and the leaders.

Such a condition exists even though we have numerous management development programs and increasing numbers of persons in managerial positions who have college degrees in such areas as business administration, public administration, or engineering. A major reason for the dearth of more effective managerial leadership is a lack of ability to cope with the processes of change that are rapidly taking place in today's organizations.

Today, we do indeed live in a world of rapid change. In less than two decades, modern technology has leaped from conventional to nuclear power, from the piston age to the jet age, from earth men to space men.

Change brings with it challenges for those of us who help and lead people. Coping with change mainly involves the proper understanding and proper utilization of the human resources of the organization. Clarence B. Randall, former board chairman of the Inland Steel Company, has laid much of the failure to cope with change squarely on management's own doorstep:

> The timorous and hard-pressed executive, who deep down inside resents and resists change . . . seeks refuge in meaningless statistics. Not sure of his own thinking and hesitant to plunge boldly ahead on a plan that would put his personal status in hazard he takes protective covering in conformity with whatever general level of conduct seems to be emerging.[2]

An organization can be described as the way in which people arrange themselves and their relationships in order to get something important accomplished, and to solve problems either for themselves or for society. An industrial organization is such an arrangement, usually with the goal of manufacturing and distributing a consumable product. A voluntary organization brings together persons interested in some social need and in providing a service or promoting a best common interest. A neighborhood civic group may be a small organization, in that people work closely together in their common action, but it is still an arrangement of persons for a useful and productive activity.

Success in accomplishing improved productivity, greater efficiency, or better service—all examples of indirect results of organization renewal—depends on management's mastery of human resources in order to cope with changing demands. The human system upon which so much depends is the potential response of a person as an individual or in consort with other individuals. Thus, the basic human resource is the individual: a single, complex organism working in a variety of ways to supply his or her own needs. One can do this alone, or in informal or formal face-to-face groups made up of other individuals working in a variety of ways to supply their common needs.

Frustration is experienced by those who think success in changing self, in mobilizing human resources, or in initiating organization renewal is simply a matter of education and, perhaps, of using persuasive stimuli reinforced by annual picnics, newsletters, and adequate coffee breaks. A newly identified but actually old-fashioned key to obtaining commitment for a new idea method, or procedure, is to involve the human resources in face-to-face situations for the explicit purpose of self-determination. This general principle, however, requires specific explanation of the process of change. We know a great deal about change. Some think that like the weather, it is a subject everybody talks about but nobody does anything about. This is not true. Many useful beginnings have been made and various approaches to problems of social change have been suggested.

Change may be studied in a variety of approaches and dimensions. This chapter considers the problem-solving planning of change, especially as it relates to complex organizations. Economically, politically, religiously, recreationally, and throughout other aspects of American life, the individual is increasingly involved with a multiplicity of such complex organizations.

Wilbert Moore has summarized some of the major characteristics of contemporary change. Their meaning for organizations can be stated thus: "Organizational changes are isolated neither in time nor space. They interact, and their consequent impact both on the organization and on systems is increasingly distant."[3] The proportion of contemporary organizational and other change that is either planned or results from the consequence of deliberate innovation continues to increase. The range of technology and social strategies is expanding rapidly, and the net impact on organizations and their functioning is cumulative despite the rapid obsolescence of some procedures.

The late Margaret Mead said, not long before she died, that one of the things that is different about change in these times is its complexity and rapidity. She went on to say that the challenges are that there are no precedents for dealing with some of the changes. This means that the decision-makers need to be creative persons. They cannot rely upon what worked five/ten/twenty years ago. Some people find this challenging, others frightening.

If we are planning to change human systems, we need to have, as a prerequisite to effective planning, a thorough understanding of the phenomenon of change itself. Max Ways has stated:

> Change has always been a part of the human condition. What is different now is the pace of change, and the prospect that it will come faster and faster, affecting every part of life, including personal values, morality, and religion, which seem almost remote from technology. . . . So swift is the ac-

> celeration, that trying to "make sense" of change will become our basic industry.[4]

As we examine the needs of human systems to cope with change, it is evident that there are two basic categories of change. One type is *unplanned change,* which will happen to and in all human systems. A tornado that blows down a warehouse, a new interest rate on bank loans, a power failure—these are situations to which the human organism *must react.* In its reaction it will try to maintain homeostasis, which, by definition, is the tendency shown by an organism or a social system to seek a new balance when its elements have been disturbed. Homeostatic change, then, is reactive response to outside stimuli when they occur, and it may be competitive or cooperative, but it is not anticipatory. The goals of homeostatic change are the *goals of adjustment,* holding on to a balance of material and psychological expenditures and rewards. Examples might be: management introduces a new computer system solely because a competitor has taken this step; an educational system relooks at itself because the Soviet Union puts a Sputnik into space; a training director buys and uses video tapes in training programs because a well-known figure in the field has made advantageous use of them.

A second category of change is *planned change,* the type of change involved in the process of human systems renewal. It can be defined as a conscious, deliberate, and usually collaborative effort to improve the operations of a system—whether it be self-system, social system, or cultural system—through the utilization of knowledge and skills. It usually involves both a renewal facilitator and some kind of organized effort. Persons are brought together to solve a problem or to plan and attain an improved state of functioning in the human system by utilizing and applying valid knowledge. A person, a group, or an organization can be the renewal target in the process.

The managers, consultants, behavioral scientists, or management scientists engaged in planned or inventive change have some social "goals" (objectives) and they have a well-structured "design" (scheme) for achieving this end. Planned change, therefore, involves inventing a future, and creating conditions and resources for realizing that future.

Changes, planned and unplanned, are ubiquitous aspects of modern organizations. Unplanned changes occur because of maturation, depressions, accidents, death, or loss of resources. Planned changes occur because of the need for improved technology, new organizational structure, or new procedures. Suppose that you are a responsible member in an organization where organization renewal involving change occurs or is contemplated. What might you expect? What might you do? How could you start? Will we be overactive or merely react to change? In the future it will be the individuals, groups, and organizations which, by manipulating their physical and social environments, by contributing to planned change, by coping with obstacles and persisting toward their goals, tip the scales toward the betterment of humankind. Those that are less venturesome will be easily sidetracked or defeated by obstacles and become victims of change.[5]

Dealing with change that involves human beings, who have nearly 10,000 thoughts pass in and out of their minds each day, is most complex. To be able to initiate and maintain planned or unplanned change, particularly as it involves people, is no easy task. It is helpful first, of course, to have a schematic model of the different types of change (see Figure 3-1).

The very nature of change implies there is some perceptible difference—in a situation, a circumstance, a person, a group, or an organization—between some original

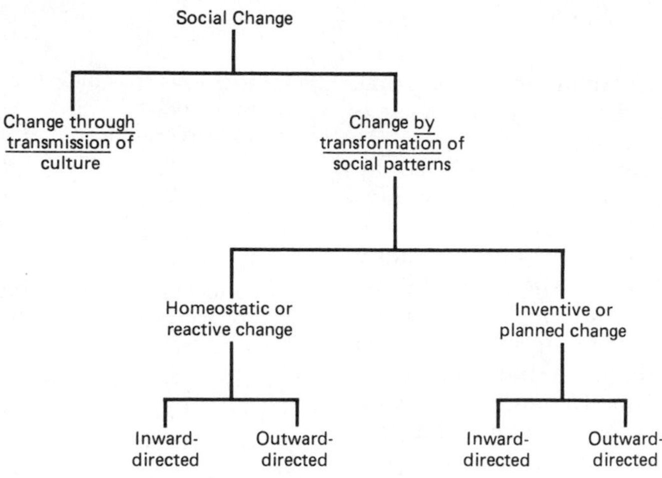

Figure 3-1 Taxonomy of social change[6]

time and some later time. Hardly anything is measured that will not display some difference between two successive points in time, if the time interval is long enough. The general category of social change is subdivided into change through *transmission* and change *transformation.* In transmission we are usually talking about evolutionary change, normally not measured by methods typical to the behavioral sciences but rather the methodologies of history and anthropology. When these two disciplines study changes in family life, classroom education, or the social values of youth, they are looking at changes that have been, for the most part, evolutionary in nature. That is, they occur without conscious direction and without reference to design or some intentional force. These changes, like the growth changes of a child, "just happen." This does not mean that in a culture changes by transmission are random, but neither are they planned or intended.

The opposite is true of change by *transformation,* which occurs when individuals, groups, or organizations change themselves or others through conscious action or decisions. As indicated in the model, change by transformation is further divided into *homeostatic* change or *planned* change.

Homeostatic change is a conscious effort that might result in an immediately noticeable and measurable effect. This kind of change occurs as a response to some specific "triggering" and is referred to as reactive, implying that it is essentially automatic and instinctive. Homeostatis is the tendency shown by an organism or social system to seek a new balance whenever an existing state of balance has been disturbed. Homeostatic change is a reaction to any external stimuli that affects the existing balance of equilibrium. The term "homeostasis" is borrowed from the biological sciences, where it is used in a sense of automatic regulation and adjustment. In the biological context it is good to have homeostasis in such things as body temperature, blood pressure, heart rate, and similar bodily functionings. Thus, homeostatic change has built into it the *goal of adjustment.*

A third type of change by transformation has been identified as *neomobilistic* change.[7] Such change also results from conscious, planned effort, but its essential feature is that it moves the system, the organization, or the individual in a new direction. This kind of change implies that an organism must be so out of balance (disequilibrium) that an entirely new organization, structure, or mechanism may be required. A good analogy for homeostatic change mechanisms may be found in industry in the process control system, while a good analogy for the neomobilistic change mechanism may be found in the research and development system. I feel that this third category is but one of the ways by which planned change is enacted through a systems approach and that it is not necessarily a category equal in importance to planned change.

Whether we are discussing planned or homeostatic change, there is the reality that the change may be outwardly directed toward some other group or organization or internally directed toward self-change. Any complicated planned change effort, perhaps, will involve both inner-directed and outer-directed aspects of the planning and implementation. In both homeostatic and planned change, there is a definite achievement *goal.* Thus, the homeostatic goal may be simply to reestablish an equilibrium or come back to the proper state of affairs; in planned change the goal must be known in advance and designated as such. One of the characteristics of a planned change effort will be recognition that the use of a plan is "to help us get somewhere" (i.e., that the change has some direction). Such a goal may be an end state that the human system has in mind, it may be the process of becoming more mature, or it may be achievement of a particular skill or attitude. Goal-seeking behavior is a process that takes place in an organism in direct relationship to its environment. A change effort, therefore, will be goal-oriented and will have one or more of the following characteristics:

- A system that features or desires goal-seeking behavior
- A goal toward which the system is directed by its behavior
- Some forces, external or internal, which will direct the system toward its goal
- A representation of the goal in the internal and external forces
- Some disturbing forces that are hindering this system from attaining its goal
- A connection between the goal and the resource forces of the system

In the systems model, a change effort is initiated when the human system is "hurting" or in disequilibrium. An individual, group, or organization will want to achieve a state of improvement when it feels and sees a need. Whether it is need for more varied products, the loss of an important client, a failure in providing a service, or some other work-life crisis, these provide the motive and drive to initiate change.

There is a need to recognize that change always involves a process of confronting needs. Such confrontation will involve the areas of knowledge, skill, and values. That is, we must recognize that planned change can take place in four different areas; and that all four undoubtedly are required in almost any planned change effort that is meaningful and maintained:

- *Knowledge change area:* generalization about the change experience, cognitive or conceptual understanding about the change
- *Skill change area:* the incorporation of new ways of performing through practice of the changed behavior
- *Attitude change area:* the adoption of new feelings through experiencing success with them
- *Values change area:* the adoption and rearrangement of one's beliefs

The need for planned change to be a process of confronting reality is the first aspect of a model of planned change. This need must also be combined with *search* and *coping,* and these two things tend to eliminate the extremes of pleasantry or recrimination.

Confrontation implies a facing up to the tangled web of relationships, issues, problems, challenges, values, and potentialities that invariably hang like a curtain between the entities into which human systems are divided or into which we divide ourselves. Unless each entity involved—conceived here for the sake of clarity and brevity as being, singularly or collectively, an individual, a group, an organization, or a political or natural subdivision of human society—sincerely tries to penetrate this curtain, communication rebounds in sterility. If confrontation is only tolerated and neither processed nor acted upon, change ends in a cul-de-sac. If a change idea is received and processed in a rational mind but not acted upon, neither the human being nor the society benefits. But if the elements of receiving, processing, understanding, and acting are present in an exchange of ideas, the first elementary step has been taken in the search for interfacing.

This is the aspect of the search for the self and the other in the process of interfacing. Martin Buber's concept of the I-Thou relationship exemplifies the essentials of the search for comprehension and understanding between persons. As he stated, "Existence cannot be possessed but only shared in."[8] The energizing effort to reach out to the other releases one's self in the process. Such a search is the essential linkage between confrontation and coping. Once this search is under way, the act of coping becomes a mutual attempt to solve, to know, to empathize, to understand by means of equitable change whatever relationship is confronted. This is the third essential step in interfacing, and together with confrontation and search, it produces a dynamic interaction in which the reality of change is faced, resolution produced, and action effected. Suffice it to say, therefore, that whatever concept of change is contemplated, a variety of planned change efforts is taking place all the time between, for example, parents and their children, teachers and students, administrators and subordinates, and federal government and state government.

RESPONSES TO CHANGE

Research indicates that individuals respond to unplanned and poorly planned change in certain stages:

Shock. An intense feeling of disequilibrium.
Disbelief. A feeling of unreality about "why" the change is occurring.
Guilt. A feeling by the receiver of change that he or she has done something wrong and that that error has brought about the change.
Projection. The act of blaming someone else for the change.
Rationalization. The organism tries to "make sense" of the change.
Integration. The receiving system tries to turn the change into an advantage.
Acceptance. Either in resignation or enthusiasm, the organism accepts the new state of affairs.

The stages that have been observed in planned change efforts by such people as parents, civic leaders, managers, and change facilitators are similar to the stages of dying identified by Elizabeth Kübler-Ross in her book *On Death and Dying.*[9] She talks about the initial stage as denial and isolation, the second stage as anger, the third stage as bargaining, the fourth stage as depression, and the fifth stage as acceptance—with a sense of hope running throughout. In the article "Human Aspects of Managing Transition," Ralph Hirschowitz describes "a period of impact in which the newness is assimilated . . . followed by phases of recoil-turmoil, adjustment and reconstruction."[10]

Although these phases are derived from research and observation with individuals, it is interesting to note that similarity is encountered when one examines stages of systems-wide, organizational response to change (see Table 3-1). In this model we see the four levels of organizational response to change and the corresponding effects on various aspects of the processes of an organization. The changes that can be observed and studied in human systems are of endless variety. Examples are changes in tools, in procedures, in the structure of the organization, or in its policies.

In general terms such changes imply, for each of us, uncertainty about our future role and our behavior in that role. These changes also imply, in our relations with others, uncertainty about who will be doing what, what we can expect of others, and what relations other persons will have with one another. Such ambiguity is unsettling; it generates a need to give meaning to the situation, to try to understand it; it also generates a tendency to react in terms of the meaning we discover, whether or not it is correct.

Two decades of research and experience by social scientists have provided some guidelines as to why people reject ambiguity and resist change.

We can no longer shrug our shoulders and say, "You can't change people." Research shows that we can change people. In fact, people *like* change. What they resist are the *methods* that are used to put changes into effect. Much of this concern was started early in life when most of us resented the dominance and manipulation of parents, teachers, and other authority figures. The word and concept of *change* is feared because it upsets a way of doing things and threatens security. This feeling is balanced by a desire for new experiences and for the benefits that may come as a result of change.

The practical reality of life is that people resist change in light of prosperity, growth, new situations, and the inadequate skills of leaders. As Albert Schweitzer said:

> Anyone who proposes to do good must not expect people to roll stones out of his way, but must accept his lot calmly even if they roll a few more on it. A strength which becomes clearer and stronger through experiences of such obstacles is the only strength that can conquer them. Resistance is only a waste of strength.[12]

Although Schweitzer implies that resistance is foolish, anyone initiating change and human systems renewal must identify existing resistances, diagnose them, and confront them with planned change. Some of the more typical reasons for resistance to change have been identified in research:[13]

- When the purpose of the change is not made clear
- When persons affected by the change are not involved in the planning
- When an appeal for change is based on personal reasons
- When the habit patterns of the work group are ignored
- When there is poor communication regarding the change
- When there is fear of failure
- When excessive work pressure is involved
- When the "cost" is too high or the reward inadequate
- When anxiety over job security is not relieved
- When "vested interest" of the individual or a subunit of the organization is involved
- When there is a lack of respect and trust in the initiator
- When there is satisfaction with the status quo
- When change is too rapid
- When past experience with change is negating
- When there is an honest difference of opinion

Table 3-1
Phases of Organizational Crisis[11]

Phase	Interpersonal Relations	Intergroup Relations	Communication	Leadership and Decision Making	Problem Handling	Planning and Goal Setting	Structure
Shock	Fragmented	Disconnected	Random	Paralyzed	None	Dormant	Chaotic
Defensive retreat	Protective cohesion	Alienated	Ritualized	Autocratic	Mechanistic	Expedient	Traditional
Acknowledgment	Confrontation (supportive)	Mutuality	Searching	Participative	Explorative	Synthesizing	Experimenting
Adaptation and change	Interdependent	Coordinated	Authentic congruent	Task-centered	Flexible	Exhaustive and integrative	Organic

Time →

This is not a complete list of the causes of resistance to change, but it does suggest some of the forces at work when change is attempted. In recent years an attempt has been made to develop a typology of resistance to change as it relates to an organization's need for new methods and processes. Robert Drazin and William Joyce have prepared such a typology that is applicable to innovative decision making (see Table 3-2). In all the typologies examined here, it seems clear that any person introducing systems change should not only understand resistance to change, but also the phases in which such resistance occurs.

Table 3-2
Resistance and Stages of Organization Innovation Decision Making[14]

Decision-Making Stage	Nature of Resistance
Knowledge awareness	Need for stability Coding scheme barrier Impact on existing social relationships Personal threat Local pride Felt need
Attitude formation and decision	Division of labor Hierarchical and status differences Physical separation Resistant parties
Initial implementation	Forces altering the innovation Feigned acceptance and utilization Conflict Passivity Perceived manipulation Felt mistrust of subordinates by superiors
Continued-sustained implementation	Continued conflict Occurrence of unintended dysfunctional effects Functional effects Disillusionment because of false expectations

APPROACHES TO CHANGE

The most obvious way for people to understand and favorably anticipate a change is to obtain information, to ask questions. Even full information, however, is seldom wholly satisfactory since parts of it are likely to contradict prior preferences or decisions. This contradiction between existing beliefs and new ideas creates a state of dissonance which can hardly be tolerated easily. Such dissonance is most easily reduced by attributing favorable qualities to the change that are not obvious and attributing less favorable qualities to previously held ideas. Adverse meanings in change may be found in the hidden purposes of those who advocate it, or in the implications concerning others' evaluations of the work that has been done, which is often feared to be negative.

Depending upon the meaning we give to a change, a variety of reactions follow. We may fully accept the change, but even when we do, remaining uncertainties may soon generate flight, withdrawal, rigidity, apathy, or a counterplan. Clearly, the frequency and vigor of these reactions is a function of the security an individual feels in the part to be taken in the proposed change. Many of these reactions are efforts to protect ourselves from the consequences of the contemplated change. Energy put into such reactions is drained from the efforts to implement the change.

It is apparent from the foregoing that changes in persons must occur at several levels if the change in the organization is to occur effectively. Changees must understand both the problem that generated the need for change, and the nature of it; and, somehow, reduce their negative attitudes. Changees must have an opportunity to learn their new functions; that is, they need to practice the needed new skills where new skills will be required.

Persons who are responsible for stimulating change have a variety of methods available to them. The choice of method depends upon a diagnosis of the possible sources of resistance the relative importance of resistant acts to successful introduction of change and, when necessary, ways in which resistance can be reduced. Consider the approaches a manager, leader, or supervisor may use:[15]

Issue instruction. This will work where the change is relatively minor, the attitudes of individual groups are likely to be favorable, and the right to give such instruction is seen as within the renewal stimulator's legitimate domain of authority.

Force compliance (decree). This will work if the change is a public one, if negative attitudes are unimportant, and if new skills are not needed by those who must make the change.

By technology. The assembly line or the initiation of a management information system can bring about change.

By reorganization. Changing or replacing key people can be a strong force for change.

Provide opportunity for others to share in the decision. This will work if the problem is not too complicated, if those affected believe that their own ideas are being used, and when those affected are comfortable in the position of decision making.

Studies of change regarding the transfer of acceptance from one system to another—with significant meaning for organization renewal—suggest that this transfer is enhanced by (1) its simplicity; (2) its consistency with existing values; (3) the prestige of the bearers of novelty; (4) an already changing situation in the receiving system; (5) lack of close integration of the receiving system, such as actual or incipient conflict among existing groups or ideologies; and (6) long and continued contact.[16]

Studies on overcoming resistance to change reported by Goodwin Watson seem to indicate the following steps as being helpful: (1) encourage participation; (2) start with top officials; (3) show that change will reduce rather than increase burdens; (4) connect proposal with traditional values; (5) bring out novel and exciting aspects; (6) give assurance that autonomy will not be threatened; (7) include participants in diagnostic efforts; (8) try for consensual decisions; (9) empathize with resistors and reduce their apprehensions; (10) build in feedback mechanisms so that officials are aware of difficulties before they become serious; (11) build mutual trust among participants; and (12) keep a pathway open for reappraisal and revision.[17]

Although different strategies for planned change have advantages and disadvantages, there are certain common elements to any planned change effort:

Advocacy is the first step toward change. There needs to be some individual, group, or collection of groups that are advocating a change and that will persevere in securing such a change.

Time is always a factor in any planned change effort. One of the naive assumptions that some of us have made about individual, group, or organizational change is that it can be effected quickly. We now know differently from some of our failures and successes. Whether you look at the psychotherapist's work for two years with an individual, a group change that might take place over several months, or an organizational change that might take seven years, the reality that change does not come quickly is an essential of any understanding of planned change.

Collaboration and *cooperation* between certain power forces in the system are essential to make the change permanent. The support of the power persons early in the advocacy of a change may not be necessary, but if it is to be sustained, they will need to be affected and involved, and their cooperation must be secured.

System approach is a key element in looking at the true complexity of any planned change effort. The interrelationships between subparts of any change situation must be understood or the change effort will end in futility.

Interrelationship of change programs to the other aspects of system behavior is necessary. A single change effort cannot stand alone; it must be phased into and related to other interdependent activities of the system.

Change involves both emotionality and rationality in getting to the change goal. People need to be involved with their total being, which includes their feelings, emotions, and values, or the change will be neither accepted, tolerated, nor supported. In this era when many planned change efforts are brought about by temporary systems—a housing development, resisting a new interstate highway, protecting trees, influencing the battle against pollution, making organizations more participative, or getting government to involve their citizens in depth and listen to their complaints—many efforts fail because there is not sufficiently effective implementation and "follow through." This is usually the weakest part of planned change.

Not a little of the change within organizations is planned and largely effected by professional change facilitators in collaboration with line managers. In such instances, the group or the organization becomes a *client* and the organization's system is viewed as a *client system.*

The significance of the role of the change facilitator is an essential part of any planned change effort. Confrontation, search, and coping are most productive when based on a strong advocacy position. Generally speaking, behavioral scientists have been too "nondirective" when in the role of change agent. There is a need for taking a stand on certain goals and expressing one's human values as an advocate. There is another premise basic to this role, although of a different order, and that is that the advocate can achieve results best by doing things to, or planning for, people rather than with them.[18]

Suffice it to say, however, that there are numerous kinds of advocates attempting the role of change agent. The names of those who would change others are legion. Perhaps one of the greatest attractions of life seems to be to influence and change the behavior of someone else, if not oneself. These would-be change agents have been classified as militants, apocalyptics, regressors, retreaters, historians, technocrats, and reformers.[19]

As one hears about these seven types, it would seem obvious that they tend not to represent either a focus on responsibility or a development process. This is why confrontation is not enough in the process of change. It must be accompanied by the search for methods, procedures, communications, processes, and other innovations that aid in the search for new ways of coping with changes that one has not experienced before. As Margaret Mead said: "As we move through the industrial to the post-industrial society, we may well be finding ourselves as 'passengers in time' where it is evident that experience is not the best teacher, because we have never experienced times like these."[20]

Because of this complexity and ambiguity we need persons—line managers and professional facilitators—who are experienced in coping with change, who can effectively carry out the data collection and assessment needed to diagnose and analyze the needed areas of change. The application of scientific process to the planning of change is valuable, but it is also important to recognize that planned change is not yet wholly a science. It is both an art and a science. Someone has suggested that art can "describe" while science "predicts."

In most change processes we usually think of four distinct phases: diagnostic, planning, implementing, and evaluating; and the most neglected of these phases is that of diagnosis.

In collecting data about systems we must envision the planned change process within a total frame of reference, including the human and nonhuman resources and the relationships among the people, the situation, and the environment. Both the theory and practice of change are assisted when conception-minded practitioners develop models that demonstrate this total frame of reference and that are appropriate to their intended change purpose. In this early stage of the science and art of change, the systems concept is useful in that it helps in grasping all the key understandings of the dynamics of the change process itself.

Robert Chin gives us three models of change: *systems, developmental,* and *intersystem* (see Table 3-3). He favors the intersystems approach—with systems that are connected to each other. This connection might be lines of communication, leadership, branch units of a large organization, or the various ties that might exist between members of different subgroups. He extends the system model so that each subsystem can be treated as an autonomous unit. You will notice that Chin's preference for

Table 3-3
Assumptions and Approaches of Three Analytic Models[21]

Assumptions and Approaches to:	System Model	Developmental Model	Model for Changing: Intersystem
Content			
Stability	Structural integration	Phases, stages	Unfreezing parts
Change	Derived from structure	Constant and unique	Induced, controlled
Causation			
Source of change	Structural stress	Nature of organisms	Self and change agent
Causal force	Tension reduction		Rational choice
Goals			
Direction	Emergent	Ontological	Deliberate selection
Set by	"Vested interests"		Collaborative process
Intervention			
Confronting symptoms	Stresses, strains, and tensions	Discrepancy between actuality and potentiality	Perceived need
Goal of intervening	Adjustment, adaptation	Removal of blockages	Improvement
Change Agent			
Place	Outside the "target" system	Outside	Part of situation
Role	External diagnoser and actor	External diagnoser and actor	Participant in here and now

the intersystem model is clear. Although this model appropriates some of the ideas from systems models and development models, it looks to the stability process to unfreeze the present situation and to move some part of the system so that change can take place. He feels that the intersystem model provides a more effective way of examining the role of the change agent than either the developmental model or the systems model.

Such a choice is not required. The systems model utilizes all three of Chin's approaches, with the acknowledgment that all three require a research, training, and action mode.

A highly valued resource in most change situations is time. The time required to meet individual, group, and organizational change needs and the total time available are not always the same. The former may hinge on the aspiration level of the human resources involved. The environment in which social systems exist requires that time be allocated to multiple goals.

One viewpoint presents five factors as characteristics of the time and needs of any large, planned change:[22]

1. The state of the organization before change and the condition of the organization when operations are relatively normal.
2. Recognizing the need for a change, usually triggered by some economic, technological, or other event that impels the organization to seek more satisfactory procedures, machines, or structure.
3. Planning the change, including selecting objectives and means of attaining them and conducting necessary training.
4. Executing change actions, which embrace execution of the plan, assessment of the results, and modification of the plan as required.
5. Stabilizing the change; that is, consolidating and reinforcing required behavior patterns.

While these stages in planned change efforts are indicative of steps in the time sequence of any change project, they indicate both a particular bias toward the collaborative and democratic problem-solving orientation to planned change. As indicated earlier, although most managers and behavioral scientists may tend toward this kind of commitment and process, it is important to recognize a variety of ways in which change programs have been initiated and carried out.

Most change efforts tend to focus on the use of knowledge to gain some desirable change.[23]

The assumption that knowledge *about* something means that there will be some intelligent action or change *is not true*. In change we usually find a situation that involves experimentation, risk, insecurity, challenge, fear, and courage. Data alone are not the answer. How many times have we seen individuals secure data about their behavior and neglect the information; groups analyze their performance and fail to face up to the need for change; or an organization conduct an employee climate survey and ignore the signs of deteriorating morale because of inadequate leadership and planning.

PLANNING AND CHANGE[24]

"Plans" and "planning" are in such common use that we may give them too little attention as they relate to individual, group, and organizational change. We may also overlook the fact that planning is not a panacea, a mystique, or something new.

Unfortunately, present-day experts on planning are prone to ascribe the glamor of originality to what is in reality merely a revival of a recurrent movement that has manifested itself at one point or another in almost every civilization and culture of which we have anything approaching a complete historical record. Certain fragmentary Mayan documents, for example, testify to the existence of a strong agricultural planning movement in A.D. 1350,[25] and the scholar Alcibiades mentions a controversy between several Athenian citizens and the Piraeus Port Authority over the quartering of slaves in the sections zoned for freemen's residences. During the Greco-Trojan war, the hastily established all-Hellenic planning board was constantly attempting to coordinate military, naval, and economic activities, but it fell from power shortly after the incident of the wooden horse, which the planning board had damned as doomed to failure because the plan has not been preceded by the collection of sufficient base data.

Planning on the North American continent became evident as early as the discussion in the constitutional convention in Philadelphia in 1788–1789, when a small group of planning-minded thinkers drew up a rough draft of a proposed union on a regional basis, with provisions prohibiting pressure politics and limiting graft. The scheme was regarded as impractical, however, and was never introduced into the convention. The only way we have any knowledge of these proposals, in fact, is that Benjamin Franklin used the back of several pages of the draft to make some rough sketches of a self-emptying privy.[26]

Some of these historical experiences have caused leaders, administrators, bureaucrats, and citizens to become sarcastic and even humorous about the attempt to plan. Someone said: "Long-range planning is when you lose sight of both the forest and the trees." And there is a sign at the Pentagon which reads: "Don't plan vast projects with half vast ideas."

Slightly over a decade or so ago, the term "planning" was still highly suspect in a large portion of the U.S. management community because of its long-held and unpleasant associations with the New Deal, impractical intellectuals, and creeping socialism. Within recent years, all that has been changed and managers have come to realize the importance of a quality-oriented planning process and function. Of course, some leaders still feel uncomfortable with planning, but its respectability in management circles is no longer in question.[27] Much of the reason for this ridicule and humor stems from the fact that more often than not, the planning process left out *good data collection, appropriate involvement, consequence assessment, action taking, evaluation,* and *provision of flexibility for change and replanning.*

Perhaps a useful definition of planning for our purposes is as follows: *Planning is a description of what we want to accomplish in the future and the means for achieving these objectives.*

Planning may take many different forms. Planning may be informal, completely within the mind of human system leaders; or it may be formal, with plans that are fully written, including specifications for carrying them out *in toto,* and schedules and deadlines for their execution. The nature of the situation determines the formality, the detail, the responsibility, and the methods of planning. Whatever the nature of the planning process, it is generally agreed that planning is a most important management function.

Planning is not a virtue in itself, but it brings many virtues in its train. It is one way to avoid entropy, which is the tendency of all created things to seek rest, to "run down." Planning—which involves looking ahead—takes us out of the complacency that accompanies seeing things only as they are, not as they might be. It protects us from thinking that this is the final chapter in our career, our personal relationships, let alone that it is obvious that there may be a next chapter. People who set themselves to succeed in a project by planning its course are greatly helped because so many have no aim or plan. Effective planners take the measures necessary to influence and make sure of the fulfillment of their aims. The only link between a desire and its realization is the blueprint showing the parts needed, how they are put together, and the order in which to handle them.

Planning is the essence of the human systems renewal concept and application. The process of leadership for change is a performing art, and planning is one of the necessary skills to be practiced. Management is not a deductive science. Despite the theory and research that exists in our modern literature and schools of administration, management is not a complete science. This truth has been well stated by Peter Vaill:

> At this point, perhaps I should try to give you a personal, amateur, and unofficial definition of what I think an "art" is. I want to be clear that I am not talking about results which are merely handsome or pleasing or esoteric, nor am I talking about results which are always correct and beneficial.
>
> An "art" for me is the process of struggle that wrests coherence and meaning out of more reality than we ordinarily try to deal with. The reality is "out there" in the complexity of the self. For the practitioner of the art, whatever it is, there is no choice about whether to try for coherence and meaning: they are experienced as imperatives.[28]

So it is with all of us living in a web of imperatives, of things that need to be done, struggling to wrest coherence and meaning not just out of planning, but also out of a host of ill-structured and flowing realities where the imperatives reside within, in the desire to do the right thing, and without, in the need the individual and organization have to survive and prosper. Planning must take place within the context of the goals of the individual, the group, and the organization: first, by setting goals and developing strategies to achieve them; and second, by translating that strategy into detailed operational programs and ensuring that the integral plans are carried out.

Thus, long-range goals are concerned with planning for the utilization of the total resources of human systems in order to achieve quantified objectives within a specific period of time. Short-range plans are much the same as long-range plans, but they are limited in the budgetary cycle (e.g., 30 days, 60 days, 90 days). Strategic planning is concerned with anticipating events, making a diagnosis, and shaping appropriate courses of action, so that an organization can be in the best possible position, ready and capable of responding effectively to contingencies.

If we agree that planning is a process that requires continuous activity, input, and monitoring, one is able to understand why the basic assumption for interchanging the terms "plan," "objective," and "goal" is related to the commonality of directing one's efforts toward an end product. However, there is a distinct difference in the terms. Each term is defined at different levels in an organization. All concerned—the manager, the leader, the renewal facilitator—need to be aware of the different definitions.

Objectives are general statements describing the size, scope, and style of an organism.[29] Some elements in an objective are: (1) a sense of agreement, (2) intent, (3) focus, (4) guidance in terms of planning, and (5) reduction in competition among many groups with common interest.

Objective embodies the values and aspirations of those concerned, based on their assessment of the environment and of the capabilities and conditions of the associations. For example, a large diversified multinational corporation's financial objective might be to rank in the top 10% worldwide in compound rate of growth in earnings per share.[30] Objectives are usually stated at the top level of an organization, whereas goals are more commonly set at the middle level.

A goal is much like an objective, but it is more of a specific statement as to what is to be achieved within a certain time span. It contains such elements as (1) a time dimension and (2) systems for evaluation and control. "Goals facilitate two functions or organizations or systems: evaluation of program effectiveness relative to receiving systems and control over system behavior."[31] Using a system approach to human systems renewal, a goal is defined as the evaluation and control of system effectiveness. A planner for human systems renewal can find a number of sources for setting and prioritizing goals:[32]

1. *Input from those being served.* The needs, expectations, and confrontations of those we are trying to serve through our educational efforts (i.e., students, clients, and consumers) are a very important source of input. What are the signs of their discontent and boredom? How are they feeling about learning? What growth are they showing or not showing? What needs and expectations are they expressing?
2. *Interdependence with significant others.* Each system is surrounded by and interdependent with other systems and persons that make up its environment: for example, the economic system of business and taxpayers; the political system of voters, liberals and conservatives; the citizens with their expectations, hopes, concerns; and other human service agencies, which can offer or withhold collaboration and have their own goals.
3. *Observing successful goal achievements of others.* Other systems are also continuously projecting goals and trying to achieve them. Some have had very exciting success experiences that have relevance for us. What are they?
4. *Identifying policy-practice discrepancies.* We have set previous goals and policies. What are the discrepancies between these intentions and what we are actually doing? Closing some of these gaps could be important goals. What is still unfinished on our agenda?
5. *Present problem pain.* Often the most salient data for goal setters and planners are those comprising the inventory of present problems or the sense of pain to be coped with. To what degree are these symptoms rather than underlying causal problems? Does the pain-stimulated urgency distract from good diagnosis and futuring?
6. *The goals of our own system leadership.* What ideas for goals and plans are in the minds of the leadership of our systems? Have they been set down in writing? How much commitment is there for us?
7. *Extrapolations of current trends.* Sometimes an assumption is made that the rate of change is relatively stable and predictable, so that extrapolations of current rates or shapes of curves provide a basis for projecting the future.
8. *Predictions about the future.* Many predictions and projections of the future are being made by futurists and long-range planners. What implications do these predictions have for our goal setting?
9. *Projecting our desired or preferred images of potential.* What would the best outcomes we can imagine look like in action one or two or five years from now? Do we agree? Would others agree? What criteria would we use in "choosing our future?"

The clearer our goals, the stronger our motivation to accomplish these goals. When our goals are clear, we are able to focus more energy toward their accomplishment, and not as much energy gets dissipated in less important activities. All of us can think of examples (perhaps oversimplified) when we firmly made up our minds to fix the car, sew the button, finish the homework, or cut the grass, and we went at it and stuck with it until it was done. Accomplishment took very little time when energy was focused on specific action.

Planning—with clear goals—is a useful methodology in organization development. Wendell French and Cecil Bell give the *purposes* for planning interventions:

> Both organizations and individuals need to manage their affairs against

goals—explicit, measurable, obtainable goals. To help achieve this for the organization, OD interventions may be directed toward examination of the planning function, strategy-making processes, and goal-setting processes at the individual, group, and organizational levels.[33]

Those organizations that indicate involvement in organization development efforts consistently use goal setting and planning at more levels of the heirarchy than do organizations not so involved (see Table 3-4). It is also interesting to observe in the Industrial Conference Board Study that more use of management by objectives and group planning took place in the organizations practicing organization development.

This study implies the pervasiveness of planning. As shown in the systems model, the steps involving data collection, need assessment, and developing plans are prerequisites to any good development process. Some of the essential factors are:

Conformance with overall goals and objectives. The objectives of a plan of action should be consistent with the overall goals and objectives of the system. In this capacity, it may be related in a specific sense to one or more goals. Conflict between action planning and overall goals place the entire planning process in jeopardy.

Assumptions of the plan must be valid. This aspect is a very critical component of an ac-

Table 3–4
Goal Setting in Companies[34]

	102 Non-OD Companies	45 OD Companies
Companies reporting special goal-setting methods ...	83 (81%)	44 (98%)
Organization levels involved in goal setting		
Long-range goals		
Top-management level only	72	18
Top and middle management only	11	8
All management levels	0	18
Short-range goals		
Top-management level only	38	5
All management levels only	45	25
Rank and file participate with management	0	14
Work groups set own goals	4	27
Kinds of goals		
Individual goals	43	30
Group goals	56	35
Intergroup/total organization goals	59	37
Economic/business goals	69	39
Personal/interpersonal goals	11	17
Other (company-public relations goals)	1	0
Have objective measurement	11	25
MBO or variation for individuals	10	16
Group objectives within larger organization's goals .	1	14
Pre-post group productivity measures	0	3
Managerial Grid Phase 4 evaluation	0	2

tion plan because a good action plan based on invalid assumptions is practically worthless.

Plan must contain measurable goals. An action plan should contain objectives or end points which could be subjected to some form of measurement that can be used to determine whether the plan is accomplishing what it is supposed to do. Proper evaluation cannot be done in the absence of measurable goals.

Plan must contain implementation. An action schedule, with a time sequence of activities that should be accomplished by certain dates, should be developed. Devices such as the Program Evaluation and Review Technique (PERT) or the Critical Path Method (CPM) enable planners to see how well individual pieces can be fitted into a parcel that will move the plan along from objective to objective until a goal is achieved.

Plan must have support of key decision makers. Some researchers have found that action planning is not effective without the personal involvement and leadership of key persons. If leaders give only lip service to the planning process, action plans resulting from such a process stand little chance of being implemented. In other words, without the involvement of key managers, action planning becomes only an academic exercise. On the other hand, with the involvement of key leadership, action planning can be workable and successful.

Evaluation of a long-range planning effort is a very critical component of the total process for it determines action—both on the part of the evaluator and the process evaluated—and thereby directs, limits, and motivates behavior and performance of the business enterprise. In other words, since what we evaluate and how we evaluate determines what is considered relevant and what is not, we must be careful to design the appropriate evaluating mechanism so that we have proper feedback which in turn leads to better control. In a sense, evaluation is the mirror image of planning in that it is the process of looking back upon action and making a judgment about it in order to provide the necessary and relevant information for future planning.[35] Evaluation is needed to tell us whether we are doing that which brings us what is wanted, whether we are doing it effectively and in an efficient way, whether our planning methods are any good, and what we should do the next time around.

Also, it must be remembered that planning does not deal with observable events: it deals with future expectations. Thus, unless expectations are developed within the planning process in such a way that it can be early determined whether they are actually being fulfilled or not—including a fair understanding of what are significant deviations both in time and scale—good long-range planning cannot be accomplished. In addition, evaluation should not only be concerned with achievement in terms of measurable expectations or goals, but it should also examine the validity of assumptions made in the plan and search for evidence of their continued desirability. Thus, evaluation can be seen as a continual forward-moving process along a time continuum in which there is a cycle of evaluation-planning-action planning/implementation-evaluation. Although these factors provide essential guidelines, it is necessary to see planning as a process.

In summary, we can highlight some key elements about effective planning:

Planning is based upon *clear goals.*
Planning is based upon an *image of the future.*
Planning requires continuous *input of reliable information.*
Planning needs *intelligent, appropriate, and enthusiastic participation.*
Keep it *simple.*
Keep it *practical.*
Keep it *flexible.*
Keep it *measurable.*
Keep it *comprehensive.*
Minimize paperwork.
Use professional help.
Assess consequences.
Take appropriate action.

Evaluate results.
Preplan based on evaluation.

Without planning we indeed have chaos. Whether it is political planning for an election or a coup d'etat for the overthrow of a political system, or a farmer planning his crop allocations, or military planning for a battle, or planning for human systems development, the fundamentals of planning are the same.

The performing art of professional planning is to help our human systems fulfill human values and goals. Many people, however, say that we cannot change, or that now is not the time. They maintain that planning is too complicated.

It may be like what the little boy said to the minister. The minister had finished his sermon, shaken hands, and was going to his car when he saw three little boys out in front of the church. He went up to the first little boy and said, "Do you want to go to Heaven?" "Yes, Reverend." Second little boy—"Do you want to go to Heaven?" "Yes, Reverend." Third little boy—"Do you want to go to Heaven?" "No!" "You don't want to go to Heaven?" "No!" "You mean to say that when you die, you don't want to go to Heaven?" "Oh, yes, when I die, but I thought you were getting up a group to go *now*."

Many people—as they look at the need for organizational change, at revitalization and renewal, are inclined to say: "Not now, I'm waiting for ideal circumstances. Maybe when we get a new leader, maybe when we get more funding." These responses usually are window dressing for unfounded apprehensions. Our human systems need help from enlightened professional managers who are able to plan change.

MANAGING THE CHANGE PROCESS

As an individual, group leader, or organizational manager it is necessary not only to understand change and plan for change, but also to *manage* the process of change. A review of the manner in which human systems respond to change provides a number of guidelines for managing change and for lessening the resistance to change:

Involve individuals in planning for change. Resistance to change will be less intense when those to be affected, or those who believe they might be affected, know why a change is being made and what the advantages are. This can be done most effectively by letting them participate in the actual planning. Besides helping them to understand the when, what, where, and why of a change, participation eases any fears that management is hiding something from them. In addition, participation can stimulate many good ideas from those who probably are best acquainted with the problem that necessitates the change. It also alerts a leader to potential problems that might arise when the change is implemented. Such an approach, because people tend to better understand what they create, also advantageously involves people in the diagnostic and creative processes. Thus, if they help make the diagnosis, they more readily accept the prognosis—which is to say that employees can seldom be successfully treated like a doctor treats a patient, by mysterious prescription.

Provide accurate and complete information. When workers are kept in the dark or get incomplete information, alarms and rumors start to circulate. This creates an atmosphere of mistrust. Even when the news is bad, employees would rather get it straight and fast than receive no news at all. Lack of information makes them feel helpless, whereas the whole story—even if it's unpleasant—lets them know where they stand.

Give employees a chance to air their objections. Change is more easily assimilated when a supervisor provides an opportunity for employees to blow off steam. A gripe session also gives leaders useful feedback which may reveal unsuspected reasons for opposition. For example, a worker may balk at using another machine only because he will be moved away from a window.

Always take group norms and habits into account. For example, leaders should ask themselves if a contemplated change will:

- Break up congenial work groups
- Disrupt commuting schedules or carpools
- Split up long-standing luncheon partners
- Unfavorably affect anticipated vacations, priorities, preferences
- Require temperamentally incompatible employees to work together
- Violate a value norm of the group

Make only essential changes. Most employees can tolerate only so much change. When they are confronted with many trivial or unnecessary changes, their reaction will be irritation and resentment. Even more important, they will be less receptive to major changes.

Provide adequate motivation. Motivation affects persons' willingness as an effective *human resource* to give or not to give themselves to their organization. Resistance may be reduced if these factors are taken into account seriously:

Meaningful reward. It varies with individuals. They may be concerned with self-expression, recognition, the need to feel useful and important, the desire for new knowledge, the need to meet new people, or a genuine desire to meet unmet needs.

Relationship. However small it may be, the individual must be able to relate his or her contribution to a total effort.

Importance. Has the contribution had any real meaning to the organization, or was it a wasted effort? The human resource may not particularly care whether the answer to this question is happily "yes" or miserably "no," but one does want to feel important enough to be told which it turned out to be, and does not want to repeat a wasted effort. A person works best in a warm but work-oriented atmosphere where real effort is obviously needed and appreciated.

Initial success. A little succeeding goes a long way toward maintaining interest in new ways of doing things. The jobs people are given to do must be within their skills and experience, because frustration at the outset is sure death to efforts to stabilize or initiate change.

Opportunity to grow. Interest stops when stagnation is produced by doing the same thing over and over again; and continued involvement demands new challenge to learn and grow on.

Appropriate involvement in key decision making. People should be allowed to take part in this process. One of the hardest jobs a leader has in organizational management is to refrain from making most of the decisions alone.

Develop a trusting work climate. Mistrust arises when people have inadequate or incomplete information, when they are kept in the dark, when rumors disseminate false alarms. One major reason for this is that they feel helpless—they cannot influence the situation. To build a trusting climate, tell the truth. It has been proven time and again that people would rather have bad news than no news. Given the facts, they feel they may be able to *do* something about a problem. In one case, a company was threatened with going out of business because its high costs made it impossible to compete with a similar product made in Japan. Top management decided to give its employees the facts. The employees increased their productivity—and reduced costs—to the point where the organization got back on its feet and is flourishing today.

Learn to use the problem-solving approach. Research in behavioral science furnishes some useful guidelines in solving problems that arise from implemented change. First, identify the real problems. A leader may think, "If I could only get Mary to retire, the morale of the group would improve." But deep-seated attitudes rarely are caused only by a single individual in a group. Second, be aware of timing. It is much easier to influence people favorably toward new data-processing equipment before it is installed than afterward. Third, help people solve problems to their own satisfaction. They will react negatively to such advice as, "You shouldn't take that attitude" or to such persuasion as, "I'm sure when you have all the facts, you'll see it my way." Adjusting to change is sometimes difficult under the best of conditions, but it can best be confronted when the initiator of change is committed to the problem-solving approach and process.

Effective organization renewal must be related to the *process of solving the real problems* that face an organization. Usually, problem solving proceeds in this direction, by fits and starts, rationally and irrationally, but the phases of the process can be seen to proceed through several steps, as indicated earlier.

The question is frequently asked about the decision-making phase of problem solving. Who really makes the decision? Who should be involved? One way is for the decision to be made on the basis of authority; the chairman, the superior, the person with most status or power makes it. This method is frequently used even when it is not the one intended; unless a group has reached a certain stage of maturity, work group members are likely to look to the boss without being fully aware that this is what they are doing.

A second way is by some form of vote. The usefulness of this method, as well as its limitations, is quite well known.

A third way is by consensus. This way of reaching a decision requires some explanation since it is easily misunderstood and misapplied—as well as frequently difficult to obtain. This word is derived from *sensus,* meaning a mental process, not from *census,* meaning counting. Thus, it refers to a "meeting of minds." Consensus has been reached when the group, as a group, agrees to take a given action. Some may have doubts about the wisdom of the action, but are willing to commit themselves to implement the action because (1) the consequences of failure seem to be not too great, (2) the group can learn from failure and improve its next attempt, and (3) a next attempt will be possible.

Thus, to be "for" the action means that one is willing to implement for any reason—especially when (1) the consequences are severe, (2) it will not be possible to learn from failure, or (3) there can be no second chance—even when there is no opportunity to use any learning. To be "undecided" means that one is not yet sure about whether he or she is willing to implement the plan.

Another way in which decisions are made is by avoidance, not confronting the problem. The situation may end inconclusively with no one knowing what was decided, members may propose getting more information, or they may schedule another meeting. Unfortunately, this often happens without the members realizing that their action constitutes avoidance. Sometimes both individuals and groups avoid coming to grips with a situation or problem. The perplexing reality to problem solvers in groups lies not only in the great number of difficulties that confront them, but also in the need to diagnose the specific blocks and to take facilitating action. Several problems may operate concurrently, and at both the *task* and the *maintenance* level.

In improving group problem solving, a number of challenges confront the manager-leader: the orientation challenge, arriving at a common perception of the problem situation; the evaluation challenge, achieving an accepted value system by which the various alternative solutions can be judged; the control challenge, efforts by the group to influence each other; the decision challenge, achieving the final decision out of the choice of alternative solutions to the problem at hand; the challenge of managing tensions, handling the tensions that arise in the group as a result of its task activities; the integration challenge, preserving the social cohesion of the group as it relates to the total organization.

FORCE-FIELD ANALYSIS

A useful concept, theory, and method for thinking about change has been developed by the social scientist Kurt Lewin.[36] He looks upon a level or phase of behavior within an institutional setting not as a static habit or custom, but as a dynamic balance of forces working in opposite directions within the social-psychological space of the institution. He believes that we should think diagnostically about any change situation, in terms of the factors encouraging and facilitating change (driving forces) and the factors against change (restraining forces). These forces may originate inside the organization, or in the environment, or in the behavior of the renewal facilitator.

We can think of the present state of affairs in an organization as an equilibrium which is being maintained by a variety of factors that "keep things the way they are" or "allow me to behave in my customary ways." The renewal facilitator must assess the change potential and resistance and try to change the balance of forces so that there will be movement toward an improved state of affairs.

Looking at patterned behavior, as illustrated in Figure 3-2, it can be seen that change occurs when an imbalance occurs between the sum of restraining forces and the sum of driving forces. Such an imbalance unfreezes the pattern and the level changes until the opposing forces are again brought into equilibrium. An imbalance may occur through a change in the magnitude of any force, a change in the direction of a force, or the addition of a new force.

Lewin pointed out that the effect of change will be maintained if the initial set of forces is unfrozen, initiates the change, and then refreezes at the new level. In many situations, however, the evidence of change is only temporary. Everyone knows that change in an organization is often followed by a regression toward the old pattern after the pressures effecting change are relaxed. A company or school system may implement the recommendations of a study under pressure from the board or

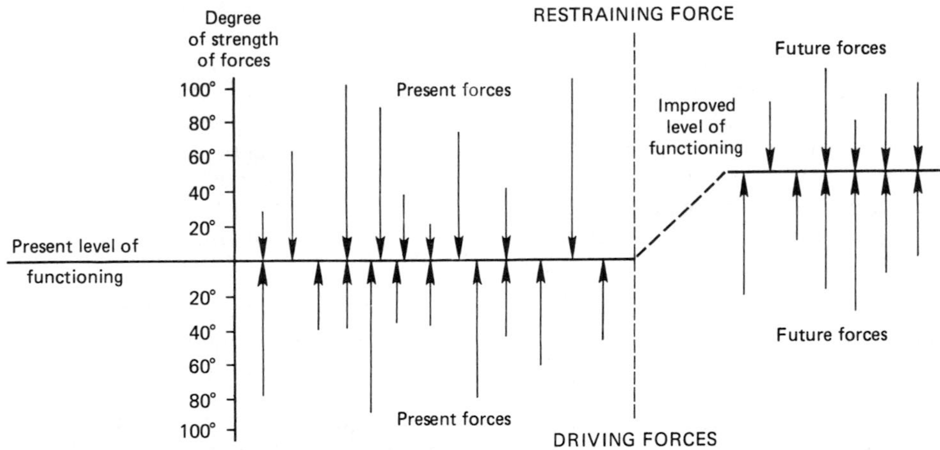

Figure 3-2 Force-field analysis

manager, but as soon as vigilance is relaxed, the old patterns usually creep back in. This raises the problem of how to maintain a desirable change once it has been accomplished, how to refreeze the institutionalized pattern at a new level. Two examples of ways backsliding may occur are appropriate here. Those affected by the change may not have participated enough to have fully internalized the change that those in authority are seeking to induce; thus, when the pressure of authority is relaxed, there is no pressure from those lower down to maintain the change. Or the change of a part of the institution may not have been accompanied by enough cooperative changes in other subsystems to maintain the temporary change in only one part.

Keeping this frame of reference in mind, it might be helpful to interrelate the process of change, Lewin's three-stage concept, and the problem-solving process into some helpful guidelines for renewal facilitators. Ronald Lippitt and others,[37] after studying the actual behavior of many renewal facilitators, have expanded these phases into seven. Here, in some respects, the term "aspect" may be preferable to "phase," for the latter has too much the sense of an unalterable sequence. There is a good deal of evidence that a renewal facilitator and an organization work on problems in a rough order of priority, but it is important to keep in mind that they may subsequently return again and again to the same concerns and processes that were in evidence at the onset of the relationship. Confrontation, search, and coping must take place at each of these "aspects."

Diagnosis of the Organization's Problem

It is not easy to overstate the importance of diagnosis in the renewal process, although in the same breath we must note that diagnosis generally does not stand as an end in itself and that in most cases it must be translated into a course of action for change. The history of planned change shows that most renewal facilitators approach each problem with predetermined diagnostic orientation. Some of them always believe that the basic problem is either a maldistribution of power, caused by faulty interchange of ideas, or the result of poor utilization of energy by the organization. It seems almost axiomatic among industrial consultants that poor intraorganizational communication lies at the root of low productivity. A renewal facilitator with a particular diagnostic orientation undoubtedly will find data to fit such a preconception; this does not limit the usefulness of a diagnosis provided that the facilitator is willing to change it in the face of contrary data.

Ronald Lippitt has pointed out that renewal facilitators vary greatly in the extent to which they feel it is necessary to share their diagnostic insights with the organizational system. Some contend that disclosure of data might stimulate so much resistance within the organization as to endanger the solidifying of change. On the other hand, the more psychologically oriented renewal facilitators hold that all data gathered represent a part of the reality with which an organization must deal if it is to introduce necessary innovations. The methods used by renewal facilitators to collect data represent a wide range of skills and approaches. Direct questioning is probably the best way, but it often turns out that the best diagnostic data result from the relationship itself.

Assessment of Motivation and Capacity of the Organizational System to Change

If change is to occur, it will come about largely through hard work within the organization itself. It is not enough that an organization experiences some discomfort. Problem awareness must be translated into a desire to change, and this in turn requires a readiness and capacity to change. In a community, for example, people will have conflicting desires; on the one hand, they want the advantages that change may bring, but on the other, they do not wish to give up the known security and satisfaction which they currently enjoy. The ability to recognize readiness for change, and to handle resistance to it, requires considerable sophistication on the part of the renewal stimulator.

Assessment of the Renewal Facilitator, Motivation, and Resources

From a practical point of view, it is important that the initiator of change clearly assess his or her ability to help the organization in a particular situation. If it is decided that special skills and knowledge may be helpful, there is a further responsibility for defining what may be reasonably expected from the change project. Perhaps most persons and organizations who seek help tend to feel that once they have contacted the right expert or authority, half the battle is won. Most renewal facilitators know that if no attempt is made to clarify mutual expectations, then the organization's leaders may find that their own expectations are going unmet, become disenchanted with the whole process, and withdraw.

Beyond the question of professional responsibility and personal motivation is the problem of professional ethics. People may ask what right has one person to remake another. It is enough here to say that the renewal facilitator or manager may provide the tools and support, but alone they do not and cannot create change. To emphasize this, some stress the means by which change objectives can be reached and organizational leaders can make decisions about goals. It is a commonly held view of almost all consultants that policy decisions can be made only by these leaders.

Selecting Appropriate Change Objectives

The first three aspects of the planned change process have to do with diagnosis: What is wrong and what resources do we have to change what is wrong? A difficult part of the task of the renewal facilitator is the conversion of diagnosis into action. In the medical field, diagnosis has become a separate specialization. Similarly, some renewal facilitators, emphasizing a methodological approach, feel that little more than diagnosis is enough to stimulate an impetus for change. Most of them, however, are not in a position to stop at this point in the change process and must go on to handle the question: Knowing this, what should we do first?

Many leaders and other renewal facilitators state that after diagnosis, the movement toward the final goal is a sequential process that requires a number of subgoals and, therefore, that the place to begin must be chosen in terms of an overall strategy. This starting point is frequently referred to as the leverage point. This may be a person, persons, or a group especially salient or accessible to change, and therefore receptive to communication. On the other hand, we may think of the leverage point in terms of patterns of behavior, or in terms of organizational facts of life. Renewal facilitators and organizations work from one problem area to another or from one leverage point to another.

Choosing the Appropriate Type of Role for Renewal Facilitator

Tied up with the selection of leverage points is the selection of the appropriate help role. In what way will the renewal facilitator relate to the problem? There are a number of possibilities. One way is to make possible new connections and to reorganize old ones. Another role is that of an expert on procedure or method. This may include, for example, providing the organization with techniques that will enable it to find out more about itself through the use of community self-surveys or self-education devices for small groups. Or consultants in human resources development may advise skill training or a program of supervisor training. There is the danger, however, that in a culture such as ours, where self-improvement is so valued, follow-through procedures may become ritualized and sterile unless they are accompanied by the means of obtaining fuller understanding of motivation.

We should note the advantage of creating a special environment for change. Sometimes environment is a direct impetus toward change; in other cases it may be merely a necessary background that must be present to promote the effectiveness of other change forces.

Establishment and Maintenance of the Relationship with the Organization

A further important problem the renewal facilitator faces is the maintenance of change once it has been started. Some use the relationship with the organizational system to this end, and continue to offer them support and reinforcement. Even though the renewal facilitator should not stand at the elbow of an organization leader while that person is trying something new, periodic opportunities to review the change attempts should be provided.

Another way of reinforcing change is to build into the organization means by which change may be maintained. This may involve the inception of an ongoing training program in an industry or the freeing of communication so that feedback may be made available to policymakers. It is also more conducive to establishing lasting changes in one part of a system if other, related parts are prepared for change. At the community level it is always more effective to attempt change among members of a large group rather than to effect change in a few isolated individuals. Persons who have a similar change experience can reinforce each other's efforts. The renewal stimulator can also help to maintain change by helping the organization to accept the legitimacy of seeking help when needed. Everyone needs support while working for change, and this usually can be provided if the person desiring change is assured that experimentation in new directions is useful and desirable.

Termination of a Supportive Relationship

The problems surrounding the termination of the helping relationship are more profound in those cases where it is used directly to effect change, as is the case in psychotherapy. Even with larger organizational systems, the resolution of dependency needs on the part of both may be a matter of concern. Generally, there is likely to be considerable dependency in the early stages of the relationship and if thereafter the organizational leaders come to rely heavily on the renewal facilitator for support and guidance, the termination is likely to be a painful affair.[38]

A special effort is sometimes made to build into the permanent structure of the organizational system a substitute for the renewal facilitator. This may take the form of procedures, or training programs, or the possibility of continued consultation on new problems and new personnel.

The system model for renewal suggests these steps:

Define objectives and needs.
Decide who should be involved in the planning process.
Review the data base and decide if additional facts and need assessment are required.
Outline specific planning steps and create a timetable.
Look at the planning steps and determine where skills training is needed.
Plan individual, group, and organizational development processes.

This analysis of the problem-solving process hopefully offers a workable frame of reference for those initiating and implementing planned organization renewal and change. These guidelines, which are primarily from behavioral science research, may also help the professional renewal stimulator.

The change facing our systems and their leaders demand maximum knowledge, skills, and courageous attitudes by those who bear the responsibility for managing complex problems with the multiple resources available to us today. Planning change is an act of leadership.

SUMMARY

The changes in today's systems are both planned and unplanned. In addition, changes take place at the knowledge, skill, attitude, and value levels. While change usually shocks the system, this trauma can be lessened by attention and effective planning. Persons in authority can manipulate variables to "form" change, but a diagnostic and problem-solving mode will be more helpful and, in the long run, more effective. It is obvious in theory, but not necessarily in practice, for planned change to have clear goals and commitment to these goals. The process of diagnosis can be facilitated by use of force-field analysis. The steps for implementation following diagnosis are the important factor in achieving results.

QUESTIONS

1. Can you cite a recent example of an *unplanned* change at the individual, group, or organization level?
2. Can you cite a recent example of a *planned* change at the individual, group, or organization level?
3. What were some of the reasons for any resistance to the planned change effort you cited above?
4. How could the management, manager, or leader (in the example of planned change you cited above) have been more effective in planning so as to lessen the resistances?
5. What has been your experience with *successful* and *unsuccessful* planning? What were the principal factors in the differences between the two experiences?
6. Take a change situation in which you are involved and try using the force-field analysis method. Was it helpful? What did you learn in doing diagnosis in this manner?

NOTES

[1]Chapter 3 utilizes two articles on change by Gordon Lippitt: "Managing Change: Six Ways to Turn Resistance into Acceptance," *Supervisory Management,* August 1966; and "Overcoming People's Suspicion of Change," *Nation's Cities,* Vol. 3, No. 12, 1965.

[2]Clarence B. Randall, "The Myth of the Magic Numbers," *Dun's Review of Modern Industry,* March 1961, p. 34.

[3]Wilbert E. Moore, *Social Change* (Englewood Cliffs, N.J.: Prentice-Hall, Inc., 1963).

[4]Max Ways, "The Era of Radical Change," *Fortune,* May 1964, p. 113.

[5]This portion of Chapter 3 is adapted from Gordon Lippitt, *Visualizing Change* (La Jolla, Calif.: University Associates, Inc., 1973).

[6]Harbans Singh Bhola, *Categories of Social*

Change (unpublished paper; Columbus, Ohio: Ohio State University, December 1965).

[7]Egon G. Guba, *A Model for Instructional Development* (Bloomington, Ind.: National Institute for the Study of Educational Change, June 25, 1968), pp. 14–16.

[8]Martin Buber, *Daniel—Dialogues on Realization,* translated by Maurice Friedman (New York: McGraw-Hill Book Company, 1964).

[9]Elizabeth Kübler-Ross, *On Death and Dying* (New York: The Macmillan Company, 1969).

[10]Ralph C. Hirschowitz, "Human Aspects of Merging Tradition," *Personnel,* May–June 1974, p. 46.

[11]Stephen L. Fink, Joel Beak, and Kenneth Taddeo, "Organizational Crisis and Change," *Journal of Applied Behavioral Science,* Vol. 7, No. 1, 1971, 21. Reprinted with special permission of NTL Institute for Applied Behavioral Science.

[12]Albert Schweitzer, quoted in *This Week,* September 26, 1966.

[13]Alvin Zander, "Resistance to Change: Its Analysis and Prevention," *Advanced Management,* Vol. 15, January 1950, 9–11.

[14]Robert Drazin and William F. Joyce, "Toward a Typology of Resistance to Change Behavior," *Academy of Management Proceedings,* 1979, p. 305.

[15]Michael Beer, *Organization Change and Development* (Santa Monica, Calif.: Goodyear Publishing Company, 1980), p. 53.

[16]Wilbert E. Moore, *The Conduct of the Corporation* (New York: Random House, Inc., 1962), pp. 199–201.

[17]Goodwin Watson, "Resistance to Change," *SEC Newsletter* (Ohio State University), Vol. 1, No. 7, 1966, 5.

[18]Art Gallaher, Jr., "The Role of the Advocate and Directed Change," in Wesley C. Meierhendy (ed.), *Media And Educational Innovation* (Lincoln, Nebr.: University of Nebraska Press, 1964), pp. 33–34.

[19]Warren Bennis, "A Funny Thing Happened on the Way to the Future," *American Psychologist,* 1970, pp. 596–597.

[20]Statement by Margaret Mead on panel at Young Presidents Association conference, San Juan, Puerto Rico, 1968.

[21]Robert Chin, "The Utility of System Models and Developmental Models for Practitioners," in Warren Bennis, Kenneth Benne, Robert Chin, and Kenneth Corey (eds.), *The Planning of Change,* 3rd ed. (New York: Holt, Rinehart and Winston, rev. 1976), p. 102. Copyright © 1961, 1969 by Holt, Rinehart and Winston, Inc. Copyright 1976 by Holt, Rinehart and Winston. Reprinted with permission of Holt, Rinehart and Winston.

[22]George C. Homans, "Social Systems," in Joseph Literer (ed.), *Organizations: Structure and Behavior* (New York: John Wiley & Sons, Inc., 1963), pp. 4, 187.

[23]Floyd Mann and Franklin Noff, *Managing Major Change in Organizations* (Ann Arbor, MI: The Foundation of Research on Human Behavior, 1961).

[24]Adapted from Gordon Lippitt, *Is Planning Necessary?,* presented at the annual meeting of the National Assembly of State Arts in 1979.

[25]George Meyer, *World History Encyclopedia,* Vol. 11 (New York: Reinhold Publishing Corporation), pp. 47ff.

[26]Charles Beard, *The Story of Civilization* (New York: Heritage Press, 1937), p. 455.

[27]David W. Ewing, "Corporate Planning at the Crossroads," *Harvard Business Review,* July–August 1976, p. 77.

[28]Peter Vaill, *Management in Perspective* (commencement presentation at The George Washington University, May 9, 1975).

[29]Richard Vancil and Peter Lorange, "How to Design a Strategic Planning System," *Harvard Business Review,* November 5, 1976, p. 89.

[30]Ibid., p. 74.

[31]Robert Morosky, "Defining Goals: A Systems Approach," *Long Range Planning* (London), Vol. 10, April 1977, 87.

[32]Contained in a paper presented by Gordon Lippitt and Ronald Lippitt as part of a seminar on human resources and productivity at the University of Eastern Michigan on February 28, 1978.

[33]Wendell French and Cecil Bell, Jr., *Organization Development: Behavioral Science Interventions for Organization Improvement* (Englewood Cliffs, N.J.: Prentice-Hall, Inc., 1973), p. 59.

[34]Harold M. F. Rush, *Organization Development: A Reconnaissance* (New York: The Conference Board, Inc., 1973), p. 42.

[35]Mary Arnold, "Evaluation: A Parallel Process to Planning," *Administering Health Systems: Issues and Perspectives* (Chicago: Atherton Press, Inc., 1971), Chap. 16.

[36]Kurt Lewin, *Field Theory in Social Science* (New York: Harper & Row, 1951).

[37]Adapted from Ronald Lippitt, Jeanne Watson, and Bruce Westley, *Dynamics of Planned Change* (New York: Harcourt, Brace & World, Inc., 1958), Chap. 2.

[38]Ibid., Chap. 6.

II

Elements in Organization Renewal

Some critical skills are needed to maintain and increase organization effectiveness. These include the ability to develop open communications; to provide competent leadership; and to manage the stress, conflict, and agreement that emerges in any renewal process.

In Chapter 4 the dynamics of the communication process is discussed, with particular emphasis on the need for open communication, and the process of dialogue is explained. Chapter 5 deals with styles of leadership and the characteristics of an effective leader. Here, too, the use of power is examined as a reality in any organization. In Chapter 6 the reality of stress is discussed, with emphasis on how to manage it as a reality; and a thorough examination is made of the opposing forces of conflict and agreement and the skills required to control them in the modern organization.

The shaded areas in Figure P-2 indicate the portion of the systems renewal model that is discussed in Part 2.

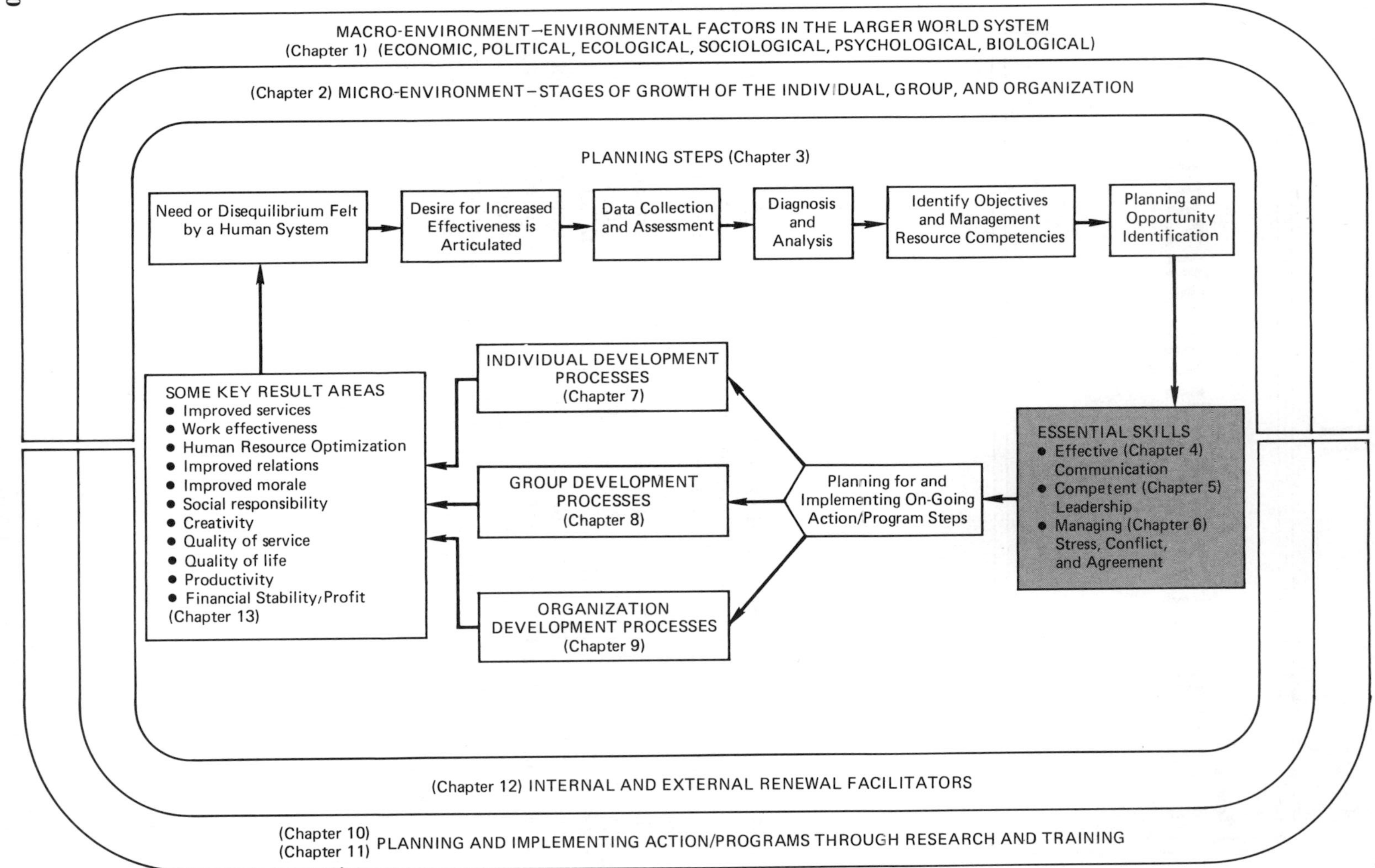

Figure P-2 Systems renewal model

4

the interface process—information and communication at work

The biggest block to personal communication is man's inability to listen intelligently, understandingly, and skillfully to another person. This deficiency in the modern world is widespread and appalling.
Carl Rogers, 1952[1]

In an age when computers, electronic data processing, microwave capabilities, satellite connections, teleconferencing, desktop terminals, computer conferencing, and other complex means of collection are utilized in the storage, retrieval, and sharing of information, the decision as to what information is useful is a strategic determination.

The renewal process will require open and effective communications. Many leaders and managers today have become concerned with developing intricate management information systems. Few such systems have matched the expectations of their creators and users. Some have been outright failures, whose causes may be found among the following:

Overabundance of irrelevant information
Lack of real clarity as to who needs what information
Lack of distinction between information and communication
Inability to synthesize relevant information
Poor identification of information requirement
Inability to build two-way communication processes

The use of the term "interface process" is quite intentional. The much-abused words "communication" and "information" should not be thought adequate to describe the *process* by which an organization can use and apply information so as to realize its potential for renewal and growth. Every organizational system has within it the potentiality for bringing about its own death, maintaining the status quo, or growing into maturity. To cope adequately with these alternatives, and hopefully to choose the latter, the people in an organization must confront each other realistically, search for ways to discover the basis for the confrontation, and then deal with the problem or situation being considered.

Such a process will achieve authenticity when individuals can trust the reality of what they feel, read, and hear in the organization. The process of search will lead to congruence and credibility for those involved in the interfacing, but more important, it will seek the common attitudes, skills, and means by which the coping process may take place.

Interface implies a relationship between people as well as between person(s) and machines. In this technological era, both are utilized to enable individuals, groups, and organizations to handle large amounts of data for appropriate action-taking. Appropriate response is therefore defined as those actions that will contribute to improved interfacing in the organization and effective utilization of human resources, and result in growth of the organization and positive adaptation to the environment.

It may be helpful to discuss in some detail the differences between "information" and "communication."

Information

James Miller's concept is helpful: that information is the patterned movement of energy in a system, and that this occurs from the smallest system to the largest. Energy transfer of information can be made by sound, light, printed message, and so forth. When people perceive and understand the patterning, information is possible. In this definition the key factor is the perpetual process of the human observer. Morse code is "noise" to the uninitiated because it is not perceived as being patterned.[2]

A similar belief is expressed by Walter Buckley:

> Though "information" is dependent on some physical base or energy flow, the energy component is entirely subordinate to the particular form or structure of variations that the physical base or flow may manifest. In the process of transmitting information, the base or carrier may change in many ways—as in the production or reproduction of sound via phonograph records—but the structure of variations in the various media remains invariant over the carrier transformations.[3]

In its most primitive form, then, the concept of information refers to the movement of matter-energy, which on occasion exhibits patterning that is perceived by some members of the system. An individual, group, or organization has much more patterned energy—information—than it can use or absorb. There needs to be a distinction between information that is *available* to its human system and that which is ultimately *utilized.* This distinction is illustrated in Figure 4-1.

Among dozens of other things, we see computer printouts, memoranda, newsletters, correspondence, quarterly reports, and guidelines that give us patterned information; but unless such information is perceived, understood, and used, it is not communication.

Communication

"Communicate" is a battered, abused word meaning practically anything from sending up smoke signals to extrasensory perception. Let us try to put a limit on its meaning. First, it is more than telling, influencing, propagandizing, or making information available. We are communicating when the messages flowing between two parties have arrived at a stage where the images and ideas—which each is trying to pass to the other—have the same meaning to the receiver as to the sender. Messages can be transmitted in a variety of ways: orally, mechanically, in writing, in word symbols, or by facial expression, body language, attitude, behavior, action, or inaction. Any signal or message that a

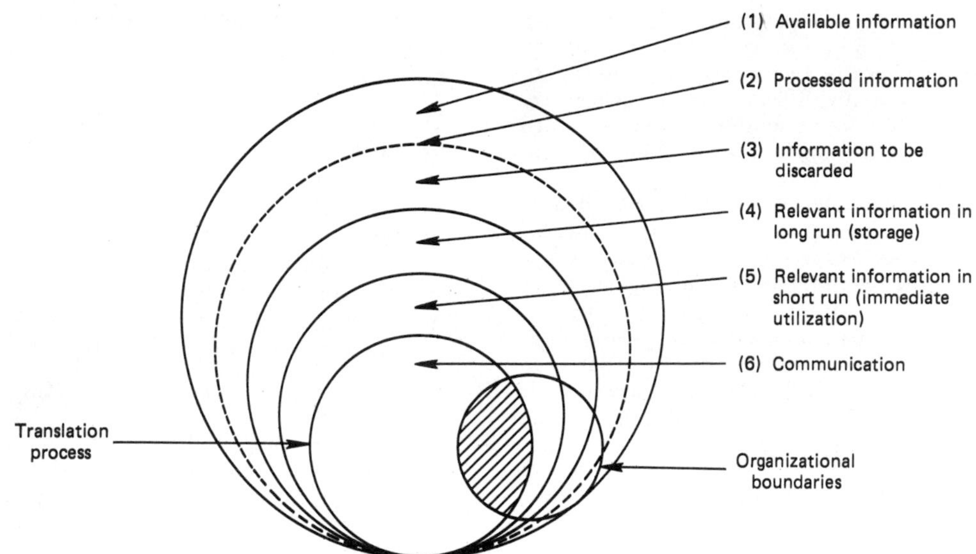

Figure 4-1 Information for decision making in organizations[4]

receiver interprets, through a background of experience, as having a specific meaning is communication.

We have had the mistaken concept that if we informed others of what we thought they should know, we were doing a good job of communicating. Not true. How the "others" you inform receive and interpret your "communications" is the sum total of their experience with you, your facilities, your methods and procedures, your policies, and your perceived attitude and purpose. Such experience is then filtered by the "others" through all the feelings and attitudes they have developed thus far in their lives. In other words, to bring this down to an example, if an organization such as a corporation wishes to have a good image with its consumers, it must provide good, reliable, convenient, consumer-oriented services; its employees must be courteous and helpful; its suppliers need to be informed; policies must be formed and articulated; and a process of effective communications must be implemented.

Communication means the process of "communing": the process of exchanging and sharing thoughts and feelings. Underlying all we know about ourselves, about other people, and about our world is the act of communication. Also, underlying all our attempts to work together is the act of communication. In the final analysis all communication is a process that takes place at the level of the individual, even though the individual may be interacting with a machine, a group, or an organization. We are concerned, therefore, with *what the machine, individual, group, or organization is saying.* What, indeed, is one of these entities *trying to say?* What does the receiver hear and see? How is the interpretation made? How do the policies and standards of the group or organization, as well as cultural norms, affect the receiver's interpretation? Actually, too many managers trying to communicate within an organization frequently use three approaches:

1. *The "decibel" approach.* The basic assumption of this method is that to "communicate" you must talk loud enough and long

enough and repeat yourself often enough. The receiver will hear what you mean because of sheer volume and repetition. Usually, however, the receiver is responding to the sender's power to reward and punish and not to the loudness and repetition.
2. *The "sell" approach.* Package the idea so attractively that the receiver is "seduced." Witness how common it is to advertise a product with pictures of attractive men or women using or holding the product.
3. *The "minimal-information" approach.* Give the receiver a minimum of information, so that there will be little to object to, little to ask questions about, and little that can be used to form any negative judgments. This theory is particularly appealing to managers who feel they do not have the time to communicate.

We might call these the "unilateral" or "one-way" approaches to communication. They imply that the communication is not a process of mutual exchange, but rather a process of one-way influence. They imply that the sender does something to the receiver. The sender is assumed to be completely active. The receiver is assumed to be completely passive. These approaches assume that the sender knows what the receiver hears and how the receiver reacts.

Two-way communication is called dialogue. If communication is not achieved, we can observe the distortions and misunderstandings that occur—as in this humorous but all too realistic example:

Operation Halley's Comet

A Colonel issued the following directive to his Executive Officer:

Tomorrow evening at approximately 2000 Halley's Comet will be visible in this area, an event which occurs only once every 75 years. Have the men fall out in the battalion area in fatigues, and I will explain this rare phenomenon to them. In case of rain, we will not be able to see anything, so assemble the men in the theater and I will show them films of it.

Executive Officer to Company Commanders:

By order of the Colonel, tomorrow at 2000, Halley's Comet will appear above the battalion area. It it rains, fall the men out in fatigues, then march to the theater where this rare phenomenon will take place, something which occurs only once every 75 years.

Company Commander to Lieutenant:

By order of the Colonel in fatigues at 2000 tomorrow evening, the phenomenal Halley's Comet will appear in the theater. In case of rain, in the battalion area, the Colonel will give another order, something which occurs once every 75 years.

Lieutenant to Sergeant:

Tomorrow at 2000, the Colonel will appear in the theater with Halley's Comet, something which happens every 75 years. If it rains, the Colonel will order the comet into the battalion area.

Sergeant to Squad:

When it rains tomorrow at 2000, the phenomenal 75-year-old General Halley, accompanied by the Colonel, will drive his Comet through the battalion area theater in fatigues.[5]

Some research in downward communications indicates that each time a message goes one level lower, a 25 percent distortion occurs. How, then, can we begin to build two-way uses of information through communication processes?

In this second half of the twentieth century, we have had the opportunity to develop instruments of communication, and the assimilation of information necessary to communication, beyond any stage yet achieved. This process unavoidably requires more than merely the efficient expansion of our internal and external technological capabilities. Our critical concern is the need for a process involving internalizing of communication so that something other than information is transmitted. The latter process can be called interfacing, which is a combination of dialogue, confrontation, search, and coping.

In its simple sense, dialogue is "a talking together."[6] That in itself may be a mild exchange of pleasantries or violent recriminations. In its larger, more resultful sense, it is not only a need of humankind, but also much more than ordinary conversation. Reuel Howe defines it as "the serious address and response between two or more persons in which the being and truth of each is confronted with the being and truth of the other."[7] The need for *confrontation* must also be combined with *search* and *coping,* and these things tend to eliminate the extremes of pleasantry and recrimination.

Confrontation implies a facing up to the tangled web of relationships, issues, problems, challenges, values, and potentialities that invariably hang like a curtain between the entities into which people are divided or into which they divide themselves. Unless each entity involved* sincerely tries to penetrate this curtain, communication rebounds into sterility. Human beings, exclusively among the animals, are capable of receiving, processing, understanding, and acting upon complex ideas. Because of this unique capability, then, a human being is superior to all other animals. Paradoxically and perhaps also inexplicably, however, our attempts at communication in matters of emotion and feelings are often devious and confused, whereas those of all other animals are positive and direct. Human beings do not always use their exceptional capability of communication to its full extent. If an idea is received only, and neither processed nor acted upon, communication ends in a cul-de-sac. If an idea is received and processed in a rational mind but not acted upon, neither the person nor society benefits. But if the elements of receiving, processing, understanding, and acting are present in an exchange of ideas, the first step has been taken in the quest for interfacing. These four processes constitute an overt attempt to reduce to manageable scope the often enormous problem of unlikeness between entities.

Once this search is under way, the act of coping becomes a mutual attempt to solve, to know, to empathize, to understand, by means of equitable interchange, whatever new relationship is confronted. This is the fourth essential step in interfacing, and together with dialogue, confrontation, and search, it produces a dynamic interaction in which reality is faced, resolution produced, and action effected.

On the other hand, these things have always been so. They are not new, but their implementation has been made vastly more difficult by the increasing complexity of the world in which we live. Educated humankind shares a common worry about the growing impersonality of human relationships, the hugeness of institutions, and what John Locke called "an age at enmity with all restraint." These things generate a feeling of powerlessness to act, to influence either the parade of montonous events or the constant trickle of small annoyances that mark our all too brief time on earth. Yet it is because people as individuals and humankind as a society have tried to influence events and circumstances that all human progress has materialized.

Those who are somehow compelled by

*For the sake of clarity and brevity, conceived here as being, singularly or collectively, an individual, a group, an organization, or a political or natural subdivision of human-made society.

motivations larger than themselves to react, to respond to situations even of apparent hopelessness, to overcome the restlessness and rootlessness that people inflict upon themselves, have turned to interfacing. The mold from which they were cast has not been broken, people are shaped in it still, and there is a constant search for ways in which to improve interfacing. Those who would place their feet in these footsteps are numerous, and far more resilient than their acts portray. Desire is strong, but it is essential to the purpose that we first comprehend the elements of interfacing, for it is a skill that few inherit or acquire.

The quest for interfacing is evidenced on all sides of us, by all kinds of entities (see Figure 4-2). It is present in the attempt to express love for one's spouse. It exists when an individual expresses creative disagreement rather than conformity, or when one seeks to influence the direction of an organization by persuasion alone. It is evidenced in the voicing of responsible community action by an individual in a group, and by those who individually contribute to their country through constructive criticism. It is obvious in speeches at the United Nations that urge peace, and in hundreds of diplomatic conversations throughout the world between individuals representing opposing ideologies.

Each of these is in itself but a microcosmic example of interfacing related to change in the various subsystems of world society. In each such contact between individuals as entities, people are influenced by their grasp of the universe, the economics of survival, and the ecological factors that affect the thinking organism.

Any attempt to categorize communication is complex and open to controversy. One approach has been suggested by Rus-

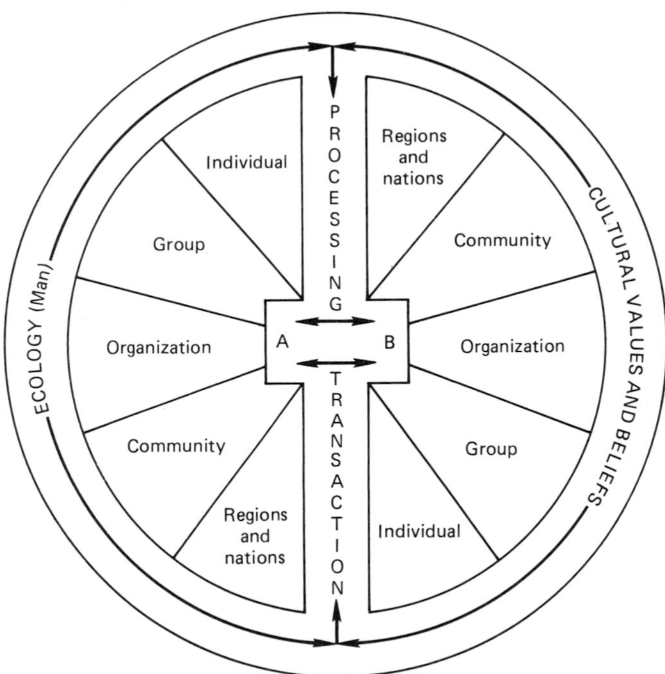

Figure 4-2 Various levels of interfacing

sell Ackoff—that messages can be indexed according to the degree of information, instruction, or motivation:

> We shall say that a communication which changes the probabilities of choice, informs; one that changes the efficiencies of courses of action, instructs; and one that changes the value of outcomes, motivates.[8]

Two serious problems are encountered in this approach. The first is that where studies have been conducted, the amount of variance explained by these measures of category have been relatively small. Second, the techniques for categorizing messages have not been worked out effectively.

Another communication expert, David Berlo, suggests three functional categories of messages: production (getting a job done), innovation (exploring new behavioral alternatives), and maintenance (keeping the system and its components operating).[9] The production function deals with messages whose effects are to ensure that the members of the organization carry out the tasks that must be done

Table 4–1
Communication Variables at Levels of Analysis[10]

Level of Analysis	Variable Label	Comment
Individual	Frequency of communication	"Direction"—up, down, peer
	Duration of communication	(As above)
	Message consumption	Mediated Interpersonal
	Participation in the information system	Suggestions Grapevine Control of message channel, timing content
	Mode of communication	All, including the nonverbal
	Content function	Production, innovation, maintenance
	Load	Overload, underload processing behavior
	Contact diversity	Location, status, relation to system boundaries
Dyad	Reciprocation	All combinations of ego-alter; agreement, accuracy
	Sequence	Initiation, response, escalation
	Punctuation	With sequence, indicates pattern
	Relational aspects	Complementary, symmetrical
Work group	Structure	Duration, integration (centrality)
	Flow	Time, route, modes, transmission vs. feedback loops, saturation, distortion
	Roles	Liaison, bridge, group member, isolate
	Openness	Several measures of "climate"
	Code	Intergroup translation
Organization	(All of the above, with previous levels taken as units)	

in order to generate the organization's output. Most of the flow of such messages is along the lines of authority and hierarchy. Information systems developed in many organizations are basically for this purpose. The innovation and maintenance functions are more complex. The importance of innovation is measured by the extent to which managers or leaders view their environment as changing. The innovation function, essentially, has two basic components—eliciting or generation of proposals, suggestions, new ideas (which can be called creativity), and the implementation of the new ideas that are chosen to improve efficiency. Maintenance communication serves a different purpose. Berlo discusses the maintenance function in terms of three subcategories: the maintenance of self-concept, the maintenance of interpersonal relationships with others in the organization, and the maintenance of the production and innovation functions within the system.

Richard Farace and Donald MacDonald have presented a useful taxonomy, shown in Table 4-1. We should study these levels of communication in order to understand communication in and between human systems.

INTERPERSONAL COMMUNICATIONS

The interpersonal aspect of communication involves the search for the self and the other in the process of interfacing. Martin Buber's concept of the I–Thou relationship exemplifies the essentials of the search for comprehension and understanding between persons.[11] In the energizing effort to reach out to the other, the self is released in the process. Such a search is the link between confrontation and coping.

Because interfacing is a dynamic process not always uncomplicated by confusions and doubts, its implementation involves a complex transaction (see Figure 4-3).

Self-Image. Each entity wears a mantle of self-perception. What a human being or a group or a nation thinks of itself—and this is a combination of such things as its ego, pride, traditions, ambitions—is inescapably reflected in behavior with and toward other entities.

Needs. Each entity will believe itself to possess unique needs—the need to love, to belong, to give, to be recognized, to be creative, to be secure, to acquire, to work, to be successful, and to solve problems—all yearning to be satisfied.

Values. Each entity will subjectively hold dear those things that heritage or education or environment has made valuable to it.

Expectations. No matter how disproportionate they may be, great expectations are consultants sitting at the elbow of each participant in a dialogue. They tend to implant a "mental set" that affects flexibility, they counsel against faith and goodwill, and they rationalize failure.

Goals. Unilaterally worthy though they are, the fixed objectives of an entity can become barriers to vision if no effort is made to take a look from a higher elevation.

Standards. Each entity will cling to fixed norms that reflect its cultural background and experience, and probably nothing is so difficult to lay down even for the purpose of temporarily trying on another viewpoint.

Perceptions. These are eyeglasses worn by each entity that tend to distort rather than to increase conceptual clarity. It is quite traumatic for either entity to take them off, even for a moment; a still more painful experience is to have the lens reground.

These factors, and sometimes others less pronounced, must be thrown into the scale of balance. In addition, it is necessary to compensate for the effects of outdated or erroneous information and incongruous gaps in understanding that are the by-

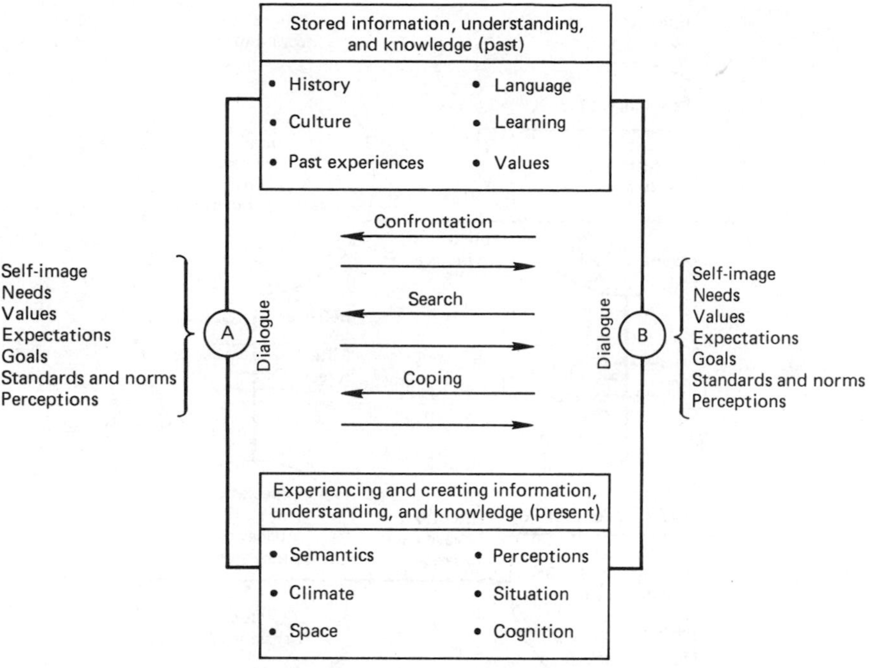

Figure 4-3 Process of interfacing

products of faulty education, limiting environment, and differences in languages, cultural levels, and noncomparable value systems.

Leo Rosten has pointed out that:

> This problem of getting an idea from one head to another is . . . apparently more complicated than any the physical sciences have had to deal with. . . . We go on the assumption that there is something called "the truth" and forget that there are truths. We think we can talk about facts and forget there is something called context.[12]

It is the context in which interfacing must take place that makes reality in its execution elusive. Both the entity sending and the entity receiving an idea in the process of interfacing bring to the transaction personal attributes that limit and color their effectiveness.

Another helpful way to analyze interpersonal communication is to see it as an inevitably circular process, as shown in Figure 4-4.

Let us look at this concept step by step:

1. You have a picture of yourself, and an understanding of what kind of person you are (this is self-image).
2. You also have a set of attitudes toward the person or persons with whom you are communicating (you like them; you are afraid of them).
3. As a result of this self-image and set of attitudes, you have intentions to behave in a certain way. If your self-image is that you can make a contribution and have something important to offer—and if your attitudes are that your ideas are wanted and appreciated by others—we can predict that your behavior will be confident, warm, and supportive.
4. Under these circumstances, you will behave in a certain way in accordance with

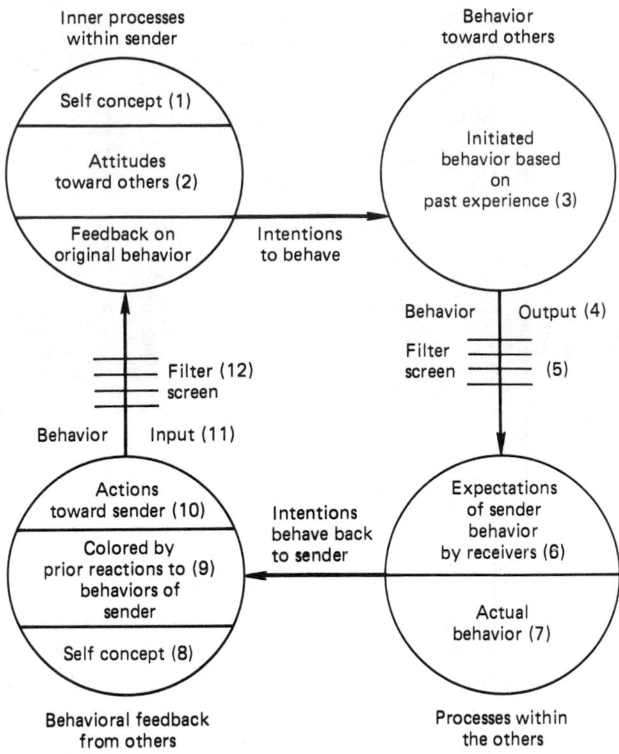

Figure 4-4 The circular process of interaction

your past experiences in similar situations. We call this *behavior output.*

5. We come now to the listener or receiver. The behavior is received but only after being screened through a picture of the sender. This means that if the receiver dislikes the sender, what is received will have passed through a filter of dislike and what is actually received is thereby colored.
6. The receiver will have had some prior expectations about how the sender should behave. The sender's behavior, as received, will either meet these expectations or differ from them. The receiver will evaluate incoming behavior in the light of these expectations.
7. As a result of this evaluation, the receiver will behave back (respond) to the sender. From the sender's point of view, this is called *behavior input.*
8. The original sender also has a screen of filters, which include prejudices, attitudes, and so forth. What comes back to the sender from the receiver must go through this filtering screen.

This apparently abstract and complex process can perhaps be simplified through three illustrations. Let us suppose that we are talking about a member of a group. She is a secure person, sees herself as effective in her relations with others, and feels warmly toward others. Her intentions, based on this combination of feelings and attitudes, are to express her ideas, to cooperate, and to be quite active in a group. Her behavior output is thus active and friendly. This behavior output is perceived by others as being warm, friendly, competent, cooperative, and demonstrating a willingness to listen to others. Given these perceptions of this member, the intentions of other members toward her are friendly, respectful of her opinions, inquiring regarding her ideas, and being generally willing to accept her influence attempts.

These intentions again show themselves in the behavior of other members toward her. She perceives the behavior of others as telling her that she is liked and accepted and that she is satisfying her needs to be respected and influential. In other words, the feedback confirms her initial image and she therefore continues to produce similar types of intentions and behavior. This person is likely to maintain high status in the group and to be in a position of leadership.

Perhaps of more interest to us is what happens to people who do not have this initial image. For example, if the same person sees herself as quite inadequate and her attitudes toward others are that they see her this way also, her intentions are likely to be cautious, which will produce very low behavior output in a group. This low behavior output may well be perceived by others as somewhat neutral, neither friendly nor unfriendly, and it thus tends to produce very few intentions to behavior toward her. Operationally, this means that very little behavior is addressed to her. Such a member is likely to interpret this lack of attention as a confirmation of her own low evaluation of herself. This tends to reinforce her behavior pattern of withdrawal.

A third illustration would be that of a person who feels that she is quite adequate but that others tend to be unfriendly and competitive toward her. This produces intentions to keep them from blocking her, or to compete or get her way in spite of their attitudes. Such a person is likely to be very active. She probably initiates many ideas and probably reacts critically to others. If this behavior is received, it probably makes others feel irritated and makes them tend to reject her ideas even when they are good. This produces intentions to either reject or resist her. Their behavior toward her is then either to ignore her or to fight her. She perceives this behavior as a confirmation of her initial attitudes, and so the circle begins again.

This model or way of thinking about communication is called the *self-fulfilling-prophecy concept.* It predicts that you frequently get back in behavioral feedback what you send out. Inasmuch as perception and attitude form such an important part of the process of interpersonal communication, it is helpful to examine these phenomena more closely.

Perception is how individuals and groups "see" or perceive the situation. *Attitude* is the enduring organization of individuals' and groups' perception as it centers upon the situation. Together these create the social-psychological basis for how people develop their feelings—likes, dislikes, or neutrality—about the context in which communication takes place. How, then, do people form their perceptions? A number of studies indicate that they are primarily determined and influenced by the following factors.

First impression. The first experience a person has with an individual, group, or organization is very important. First impressions frequently tend to be lasting ones—particularly if later experiences are infrequent or casual.

Past experience. The background of a group or individual's relationship with another human system will affect the interface process. Some refer to this as the "halo" effect. Despite a system's effort to change, or the reality of a change in a more favorable direction, our past experiences with the system will continue to affect our perception image for varying periods of time.

Particular situation and setting. If the relationship with another human system is associated with either a happy or an unhappy event, it "colors" the individual's feelings. This event, unfortunately, may be with the organization—or entirely separated from the control of the organization. It can create a negative or a positive attitude.

Nature of the communication. If the sender is seen as "telling" and not "listening," it makes a real differnce to the receiver. People want to be able to influence the "inputs" and "outputs."

Stereotyping the sending system. The receiver formulates stereotypes about individuals, groups, and organizations. He or she refers to "those folks at X organization." Or the receiver tends to stereotype individuals in a particular profession. All of us are familiar with stereotypes of social workers, teachers, and those engaged in social action.

Persistence of people's perception. Research on people's opinion shows that it tends to remain fixed once the perception is established. This is another evidence of the halo effect. Apparently, we human beings need to have our perceptions or values remain fairly fixed. Most of us tend not to modify them in accord with current knowledge or facts. Normally, it takes a rather significant experience or really meaningful feedback, or long hammering at obvious data before we are willing to examine and modify our perceptions.

One helpful way to understand how individuals can look at themselves, and secure feedback, is the concept contained in the Johari window, illustrated in Figure 4-5. The Johari window graphically visualizes the relationship between individuals. It is simply a window with four quadrants, each quadrant representing the whole person in relation to others.[14]

Quadrant 1 encompasses behavior and motivation that is known to self and others. It shows the extent to which two or more persons can freely give and take, work together, and share experiences. The larger this area, the greater is a person's contact with reality and the more available are his

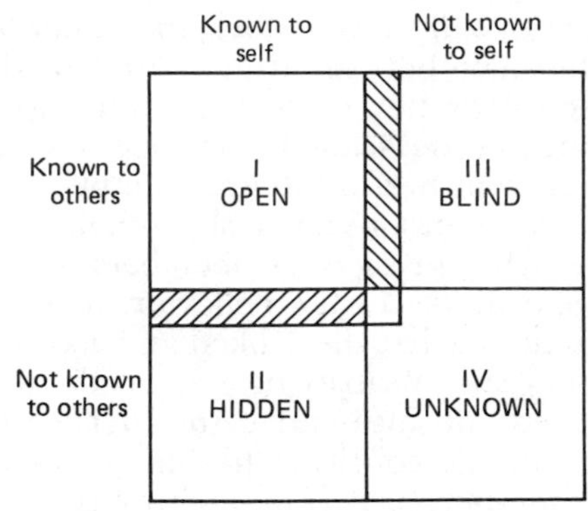

Figure 4-5 The Johari Window[13]

abilities and needs, to himself and to his associates. This can also be labeled the quadrant of openness, honesty, and frankness (but not naiveté).

Quadrant 2 comprises behavior and motivation that is open to the self but kept from other people. This quadrant is sometimes referred to as the *hidden agenda.* For example, a person may want to get a particular assignment in order to look good as a result of carrying out the assignment, but neither says why the assignment is desired nor goes about trying to get the assignment in an obvious way. Another illustration is the person who carefully conceals resentment of a remark made by another individual. Or in a meeting a member may focus attention on a particular project that is embarrassing to one of the other members.

Quadrant 3, the blind area, represents behavior and motivation that is not known to the self but is readily apparent to others. The simplest illustration of this quadrant is a mannerism in speech or gesture of which an individual is unaware but which is clear to others. This could be a certain habit or tic, for example. Or an individual may have an excessive tendency to dominate when in a committee meeting. This tendency may be perfectly obvious to everyone else but not in the least obvious to the person doing the dominating. Most people's quadrant 2 is larger than they think. This is evident particularly in a group situation in which an individual's behavior is under the scrutiny of others.

A convenient way of differentiating quadrant 1 and quadrant 3 is to think of quadrant 1 as including those things that are *on top of the table* and quadrant 3 as behaviors that are motivated by an issue that is *under the table.*

Quadrant 4 incorporates the area of unknown activity, in which behavior and motivation are known neither to the individual nor to others. We know that this quadrant exists because both the individual and persons with whom he or she is associating discover from time to time new behavior or new motives which were really there all along. People surprise themselves with others, for example, by taking over the group's direction during a critical period. Or someone may discover that another person has great ability in bringing warring factions together, and that the potential for this activity and the actual behavior were there all along.

In Figure 4-5, the shaded area added to quadrant 1 indicates the well-known reality that if one opens up a bit to other persons, they will tend to provide constructive feedback so as to make quadrant 3 somewhat smaller. Organization renewal advocates open systems—individual, group, and organization. Why should not an individual be open? First, it is important to physical health. As we study stress, we find that uptight people, those who do not understand themselves or let others know them, tend to be susceptible to high blood pressure, heart disease, ulcers, asthma, and other chronic illnesses. Second, being open is valuable for mental health. If one's personal ego strength can permit appropriate leveling and disclosure, it will lessen the personality rigidities that may lead to mental illness. Third, if an organization is not going to face up to its data about such things as tension, poor morale, and high incidence of accidents, it lessens its chance for survival. The value of leveling and being open, therefore, seems obvious—but this is not to suggest that individuals should reveal all they know about themselves. We must be granted our right to privacy. It is, rather, to insist that it is healthy to level about your job, about problems to be solved, or about what "bugs" you. John Keltner has put it rather succinctly:

> We probably do not reveal enough of ourselves in speech-communication to enable our co-communicators to understand us better. The complexities of the world we live in demand better communication than we have known. *To communicate better, we must understand each other better. To understand each other better, we must reveal more of ourselves through speech and speech-communication events.*[15]

It is not easy to level with another person in such a way as to provide constructive data and useful feedback. One of the frequent misconceptions about leveling is that of laying another person out cold. Such leveling, if that is what it is, seldom leads to learning or problem solving. The goal of the aggressor here is often not to help the other person, but to give vent to own feelings. Such behavior is not in keeping with the rationale and principles of effective communication.

Leveling also does not mean just saying what one prefers to say. If a person feels that there are significant things to be said to another person, but instead spends time talking about the weather, or fishing, or problems with someone else, that is not leveling. To the degree that other than the current and most pressing problems of the work or interpersonal relationship between the people present are discussed, leveling is diminished. One might be talking about other things because of a fear of the consequences of talking about more significant happenings. In contrast to the openness of leveling, this kind of relationship is one that is closed. Here stress is high, and the felt need for self-protection reduces the willingness to level. When things are undercover and there is not enough trust in the relationship to warrant talking about things that are important, a very significant avenue for increasing the effectiveness in the relationship is closed. Leveling is saying the things that one thinks are most significant to say in any relationship, with the intention of helping the other person to learn from the experience and to solve problems.

There are at least three aspects of leveling behavior, which to the degree that they are skillfully integrated, will produce more effective results: the general conditions under which leveling occurs, the giver's behavior, and the receiver's behavior.

By *content,* we mean what is being talked about. If one attempts to level, using terms that are vague or abstract, it is hard for the receiver to understand. To communicate vague ideas leaves wide latitude for personal misinterpretation of the meaning the sender is attempting to convey and enhances the chance of defensive behavior on the part of the receiver. When a receiver of leveling has concrete information, it is possible to perceive what has occurred and how this affects another person.

Timing, as well as stating information in terms of observable behavior, is also important. That is, the information should be current in time and space. The receiver can thereby more readily understand how it relates to his or her intentions, and thus is in a position more readily to accept alternative patterns of behavior for trying to solve problems. To the degree that there is a delay in the communication of significant information, there is forgetting, and often what is forgotten is a particular factor that would facilitate a change in behavior that may be desired or the problem solving that may be needed.

The general climate in which one levels is an extremely important condition, and one that is generally overlooked. In climates where distrust is high and the need for politeness is uppermost, it is extremely difficult to level. It is also this kind of interpersonal situation in which leveling is most needed. In a situation where support is present, leveling becomes appreciably easier. Leveling should not be rushed or done under pressure.

Here are some general principles to observe when leveling and giving feedback:

Focus on behavior rather than personality.
Focus on real observation, not inferences.
Focus on description, not judgment.
Focus on present situation, not the past.
Focus on sharing of ideas and information, not giving advice.
Focus on developing alternatives, not merely a solution.
Focus on help to each other, not just release of feelings.
Focus on the amount of information the other person can assimilate and use.
Focus on what is said, rather than why it is said.

Openness in communication is an extremely powerful element of interface. It can be used to destroy a person or it can be used to help. The consequences of leveling are a function of the intention of the giver, the skill with which it is given, and the willingness to enter into an interdependent relationship with the receiver. The receiver can facilitate and enhance the leveling situation by developing a readiness for acceptance, being a good listener, giving support to the giver's efforts, and asking for examples of behavior that are related to the information being received. The greater the trust between people, the easier it is to level. The greater the distrust, the more difficult it is to level, but the need for leveling is that much greater. One begins to break down the distrust by selecting areas in which the data are clearly objective and the intentions of the leveler are clear and open. Once leveling has begun to develop, even with relatively insignificant kinds of material, trust begins to be enhanced between the parties. As trust develops, leveling becomes more significant and more effective. In short, the giving (and receiving) of information requires courage, understanding, and respect for self and others.

Organizations can improve interpersonal dialogues in these ways:

- Help individuals better understand the communications process.
- Give correct information (feedback) to an individual about how others perceive his or her behavior.
- Help a person get better information as to the effects of his or her own behavior, so that, if desired, it can be modified.
- Help people to see how they might be preevaluating or coloring their listening.

On a personal level, individuals can ititate some key steps with respect to their own behavior:

- Develop an awareness that you are a person with feelings and that you can live with the fact that your feelings influence you and your communications.
- Develop tolerance of other people's feelings and an awareness that their feelings, which may be different from yours, affect their sending and receiving communications.
- Develop the intention as a sender to build feelings of security in the receiver.
- Develop the intention as a receiver to listen from the sender's point of view, rather than evaluating the communication from your own point of view.
- Further your willingness to take more than half the responsibility for the effectiveness of communication, whether as sender or receiver.
- Further your conscious effort to build feedback into all communications.
- Develop the ability to resist acting on and reacting to your own assumptions about another person's reasons behind a particular communication.
- Develop a recognition that communications are at best imperfect, and avoid being unduly cynical regarding difficulties or failures to communicate.

Interpersonal sending and receiving is complicated, necessary, and challenging; but it is the essential base of all effective communication.

COMMUNICATION IN GROUPS

The next level of human system complexity, in our understanding of the communication process, is the group. In some early research on communication channels in groups, Harold Leavitt studied the characteristics of five different networks (see Figure 4-6). He found that the central person in a network (e.g., the wheel) usually becomes the leader and enjoys the position more than those on the periphery whose communication is much more restricted. That is, the central person can communicate with any other person, but they must direct all their comments through the center. Both the chain and the Y networks have similar characteristics to the wheel. On the other hand, the circle and the all-channel patterns are much less centralized and are sometimes leaderless.

A person who dominates the communication will sometimes create a network similar to the wheel. Although this may be more centralized and speedy, it results in a dependency on the leader and lowered group satisfaction for everyone but the leader. The chain or the Y network allows members to communicate with one or two other persons, but not with all others in the

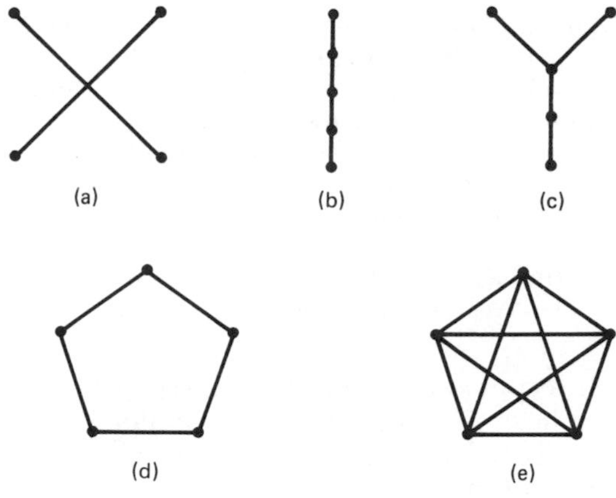

Figure 4-6 Communication Networks[16]

group. This produces subgroups, decreased satisfaction, and a relatively poor amount of idea sharing.

The all-channel network may be relatively slow, but it is superior in terms of idea sharing and membership satisfaction. Feedback is more immediate and furthers accuracy of communication.

A more functional way of looking at group communications has been developed by Kenneth Benne and Paul Sheats.[17] They suggest a classification of functional roles in three broad categories: (1) task roles, (2) group building and maintenance roles, and (3) individual roles. This approach is one of the most useful for learning to identify group roles and to measure the contribution of each role in communicating.

Group task roles are directed toward accomplishing the group's objective through the facilitation of problem solving:[18]

Initiating-contributing: proposing new ideas or a changed way of regarding the group goal. This may include a new goal or a new definition of the problem. It may involve a suggested solution or some way of handling a difficulty the group has encountered. It may also include a new procedure for the group to better organize its efforts.

Information seeking; asking for clarification, authoritative information, and facts relevant to the problem under discussion.

Opinion seeking: seeking information that is related not so much to factual data as to the values underlying the suggestions being considered.

Information giving: offering facts or generalizations based on experience or authoritative sources.

Opinion giving: stating beliefs or opinions relevant to a suggestion made. The emphasis is on the proposal of what ought to become the group's values rather than on factors or information.

Elaborating: expanding on suggestions with examples or restatements, offering a rationale for previously made suggestions, and trying to determine the results if a suggestion were adopted by the group.

Coordinating: indicating the relationships among various ideas and suggestions, attempting to combine ideas and suggestions, or trying to coordinate the activities of group members.

Orienting: indicating the position of the group by summarizing progress made, deviations from agreed-upon directions or goals, or raising questions about the direction the group is taking.

Evaluating: comparing the group's accomplishments to some criterion or standard of group functioning. This may include questioning the practicality, the logic, or the procedure of a suggestion.

Assisting on procedure: helping or facilitating group movement by doing things for the group, such as performing routine tasks such as distributing materials, rearranging the seating, or running a tape recorder.

Group building and maintenance roles help the interpersonal functioning of the group; they help alter the way of working, to strengthen, regulate, and perpetuate the group:

Encouraging: praising, showing interest in, agreeing with, and accepting the contributions of others; showing warmth toward other group members, listening attentively and seriously to the ideas of others, showing tolerance for ideas different from your own, conveying the feeling that you believe the contributions of others to be important.

Harmonizing: mediating the differences between the other members, attempting to reconcile disagreements, relieving tension in moments of conflict through the use of humor.

Compromising: operating from within a conflict situation, one may offer a compromise by yielding status, admitting a mistake, by disciplining oneself for the sake of group harmony, or by coming halfway toward another position.

Gatekeeping and expediting: attempting to keep communication channels open by encouraging the participation of some or by curbing the participation of others.

Setting standards or ideals: expressing standards for the group and/or evaluating the quality of group processes (as opposed to evaluating the content of discussion).

Following: going along with the group, passively accepting the ideas of others, serving as an audience in group communications.

Individual roles are designed to satisfy an individual's needs to contribute to the requirements of the group; these are sometimes called "self-centered" roles:

Aggressing: may be accomplished by deflating the status of others, disapproving of the ideas or values of others, attacking the group or the problem it is attempting to solve, joking maliciously, resenting the contributions of others, and/or trying to take credit for them.

Blocking: resisting, disagreeing, and opposing beyond reason, bringing up dead issues after they have been rejected or bypassed by the group.

Recognition seeking: calling attention to one's self through boasting, reporting on personal achievements, acting in inappropriate ways, fighting to keep from being placed in an inferior position.

Self-confessing: using the group as an opportunity to express personal, non-group-related feelings, insights, and ideologies.

Acting self-indulgent: showing a lack of involvement in the group's task. Displaying nonchalance, cynicism, horseplay, and other kinds of "goofing-off" behaviors.

Dominating: trying to assert authority or superiority by manipulating others in the group. This may take the form of flattery, asserting a superior status or right to attention, giving directions authoritatively, and/or interrupting others.

Help seeking: attempting to get sympathy from other group members through expressions of insecurity, personal inadequacy, or self-criticism beyond reason.

Special-interest pleading: speaking on behalf of an interest group, such as "the oppressed," "labor," or "business," usually cloaking one's own prejudices or biases in the language that best fits only one's momentary need.

It is valuable for persons to learn to fulfill these roles as appropriate to the requirements and life of a group. While the individual roles may not be constructive, a group can and should learn to tolerate and assimilate them if the task and group-building functions are also present and operating.

A third way of examining group communications is to focus on the climate for effective or ineffective interface within the group. Jack Gibb conducted research over a period of eight years in order to explore the effects of defensive communication:

> Defensive behavior is defined as that behavior which occurs when an individual perceives threat or anticipates threat in the group. The person who behaves defensively, even though he also gives some attention to the common task, devotes an appreciable portion of his energy to defending himself. Besides talking about the topic, he

> thinks about he appears to others, how he may be seen more favorably, how he may win, dominate, impress, or escape punishment, and/or how he may avoid or mitigate a perceived or an anticipated attack.[19]

It is valuable to learn how to communicate so that we can avoid arousing the defenses of others. Gibb describes six differences between what he calls defensive and supportive communication climates:

Supportive climates	*Defensive climates*
Description	Evaluation
Problem orientation	Control
Spontaneity	Strategy
Empathy	Neutrality
Equality	Superiority
Provisionalism	Certainty

When we feel that we are being evaluated, especially when someone is criticizing us, we are likely to rise to our own defense. However, when we feel that a person is objectively describing us without adding an evaluation, we are not as likely to become defensive. When someone tries to control or coerce us, it usually is less pleasant than when a person seeks to solve a problem without forcing us to go along with his or her solution. Then, too, a person who has a predetermined plan usually turns us off, as opposed to one who spontaneously reacts to situations. Strategy often implies a gimmick or some deception. Similarly, when a person is neutral toward us, as opposed to empathetic or sympathetic, it usually makes us more defensive. When a person acts in a superior manner instead of as an equal, we say that he or she is on an ego trip. Such superior behavior is deflating to our self-esteem and arouses our defenses. Finally, when someone acts as a "know-it-all," this attitude of certainty or dogmatism is less pleasant than when the person is willing to have an open mind and act with a degree of provisionalism. Gibb found that groups with more defensive climates got more bogged down in worthless ego-protecting discussion and accomplished less than those groups with a more supportive climate.[20]

It is important to the process of communication, whether at the individual, group, or organizational level, to develop a supportive climate. Managers, as well as other individuals, should recognize this essential reality. As persons in groups relate as members, they are always coping with four distinct problems; and these problems produce many different kinds of emotional behavior:[21]

The problem of identity
The problem of power and influence
The problem of goals and needs
The problem of acceptance and intimacy

As a group works together, a number of characteristics will indicate its growth toward maturity:*

Ability to integrate group and individual goals.
Different members perform appropriate leadership functions, as needed.
Balance of communication between content and feeling—and freedom to communicate both.
Tolerance for a wide range of individual behavior.
Adequate cohesion for efficient functioning.
Appropriate decision-making procedures—with minority viewpoints being considered—and a growing awareness of consensus.
Flexible group procedures adapted to accomplish the task.
Ways of examining group operation, with members giving and receiving frank reactions to individual behavior.
Appropriate use of the resources available to the group.

*See Chapter 8 for criteria for developing effective group team work.

COMMUNICATION IN ORGANIZATIONS

The next level of communications is the total organization as a system. In looking at the various types of organizational communications, we know that four sublevels exist: *formal, work related, informal,* and *external.* Informal communication, including the grapevine, usually has a two-way component. The other three sublevels of communication, whether written or oral, usually take place in a downward manner and experience specific filters as they progress down through the organization:

Sheer mass of communication.
Boss is not available.
Overresponse to secrecy/sensitivity of information.
Lack of confidence and/or trust in subordinates.
Originator overresponds to trivia by those above him or her.
Deliberate generalizations when management is unsure what is wanted by those above.
Boss adds his or her embellishments.
Boss wants only an assured, predictable response—selects carefully what is communicated.
Background differences: format, semantics, idiosyncrasies.
Oversimplification of the problem expressed in the message.
Communication does not make clear the action desired or who is responsible for such action.
Multichannel distortions (i.e., several top people disseminate different versions of the message).

Similarly, when subordinates send messages upward in an organization, there are specific filters that impede effective communication:

Lack of two-way communication.
Inappropriate timing of message.
Overformalization (e.g., everybody in the act; everyone must sign off on the message).
Supervisors' insensitivity to problems and issues (e.g., trivia reported).
Conscious, deliberate distortion, omission, or expurgation.
Overassessment by originator of his or her ability and of what he or she has a right to communicate.
Personal relationships get in the way.
Poor "packaging" of information (e.g., need to follow required organizational format).
Complexity of data, especially that presented by professionals.
"All is well" is only thing reported.
Defensive of top echelon.
Unstable upper management (e.g., many and frequent changes of personnel).

My colleague of many years, Leslie This, has identified some of the major barriers in all types of organizational communication.[22]

Distance. In some complex organizations, supervisors are physically at a distance from those supervised. Infrequent face-to-face supervision creates difficulties. Often, managers spend much time seeking gadgets, gimmicks, techniques, and systems to overcome this communication problem. There is no easy solution—improvement is bought at a heavy price.

Distortion. When communication problems come to the attention of the manager, they are frequently quite complex and diffused. Too often they are not perceived while still simple, readily identifiable, and remediable. When finally grasped, so many persons have said so many things over so long a period of time that it becomes extremely difficult to separate factual data from feelings, emotions, and psychological distortions. It is helpful for the manager to recognize that sometimes, in communication, management is not of people, processes, materials, or functions but rather of the perceptions, needs, and prejudices of people.

Lack of Leveling. Subordinates usually find that it is hard to "level with" their manager. If the actions of the manager have resulted in faulty operations, it is difficult to communicate this information without fearing how the manager will react.

Lack of Trust. What will consistently be communicated is in large part dependent upon what the subordinate believes the manager has done with previously reported information. If, for example, bad news previously reported resulted in a "dressing down," little future bad news will be reported. Or if the subordinate senses that submitted reports are not acted upon few, if any, reports are likely to be made voluntarily.

Inaccessibility. If the manager is inaccessible, physically or psychologically, communication attempts will fall off.

Type of Organization. The nature of the organization will affect communication. For example, the distance between the policy formulators and the action implementers may be too great. Or those who implement a policy or decision may have no role in establishing the policy or making the decision, and thus feel little responsibility for it.

Communication Gap. There may be a defect in the formal network of communication. The organization and its system of communication may be large and complex. Sometimes there is a gap in the communication chain that has gone undetected. One element in the "chain" that has fallen down on its communication job creates a gap. This gap will need to be bridged to make communication function properly.

Lack of Clear Responsibilities. There may be status and role ambiguities. When we feel that we have low status, we may become overly critical of our ideas and tend to inhibit them. Conversely, if we have high status, we may fail to listen to and weigh carefully the ideas of others. If we are inconsistent in our leadership roles, we are apt to find that this lack of predictability creates confusion and errors of response. The manager can check distribution of responsibilities and job description. Many role problems can be traced to lack of clarity, either written or verbal.

Paper Channels. A study of the organizational chart may be in order to determine which formal channels are being used and which exist only "on paper." As a general guide, the informal and work-relationships communication networks can often give ideas for analyzing and modifying the formal network. In some instances, these networks can form the basis for new channels or groupings in the formal network.

Semantic Differences. There may be language or semantic differences. Sometimes we are blocked by our failure to understand clearly the words or terms used. There are the different connotations and meanings accorded words in various sections of the country, and by different racial, occupational, and other groups. Even within a single organization, these factors often blur understanding between occupational and professional groups. The manager can alert staff to these differences and review terminology used in communications to the different occupational groups—such as written forms, meeting formats, and the type and extent of verbal orders.

Personal Incompatibility. Sometimes subtle personality clashes create communication blocks; sometimes issues are personalized, rather than being treated in terms of organizational or task needs. Sometimes there are power struggles to gain control of a group or a situation, with the result that true communication becomes almost nonexistent. The manager can identify and analyze stress points (noticeable tension or open conflict) to determine causes. It is important to remember that although some conflicts are conscious, many are not consciously recognized by the participants.

These factors should be diagnosed, areas requiring improvement identified, training initiated, and action taken by organizational leaders and managers. Each manager, for example, should be a fact-finder and information linker.[23] The manager should undertake data collection by which to assess the present functioning of the organization; in this role the manager will also need to serve as a *seeker, clarifier, synthesizer, reality tester,* and a *provider* of information—as well as a *communications link* in the system.

As a *seeker of information,* the manager must know the goals and expectations of the human system. A manager must know what objectives and results are desired. A leader will want to request certain information from those who will guide action and change. The manager will need to seek out information from those who know about the goals to be achieved, and whether other input/output information is necessary so that training or greater involvement should take place.

As a *clarifier of information,* the manager will impart to the involved people the multiplicity of ideas and concepts collected. Implementation is doomed to failure if there is no common understanding of intentions, plans, and objectives.

As a *synthesizer of information,* the manager will put into a proper frame of reference the different ideas and concepts, bringing it all into focus so that the action is not a hodgepodge of conflicting parts, but becomes an integrating experience with a proper sequence of events centered on a specific goal.

As a *reality tester of information,* the manager should always help others see that the plans they approve are feasible, workable, and realistic.

As a *provider of information,* the leader will give proper information to those in the system, presenting ideas, opinions, and concepts from his or her own experience that will be helpful in successful planning.

As a *communications link,* the manager has access to the various subsystems in the organization; to be an effective multiline communicator, he must:

Be accessible to those who are working on a given situation or who will participate in it.
Develop trust between and among all concerned.
Level with participators on plans and problems.
Keep the goals clearly in mind and help others to do the same.
Define the responsibilities of others.
Develop listening skills.

In many ways, a leader or manager will find that these roles are not only essential but also contribute to greater assurance of successful interfacing throughout the organization.

No discussion of organizational communications would be complete without a look at *transactional analysis* and the *management information system:* Transactional analysis is a method for communicating and explaining our individual and social behavior.[24] It provides a frame of reference that most people can understand and put to use in their own lives.* Transactional analysis is concerned with four kinds of analysis:

1. *Structural analysis:* the analysis of individual personality

*Eric Berne, the leading exponent of transactional analysis, was trained in Freudian psychoanalysis, but developed his own therapy techniques during World War II while working in a military hospital with soldiers. His goal for the development of the technique was to find a method of providing patients with insight into their own behavior without the time-consuming process required by years of therapy and psychoanalysis.

Berne's original work has been popularized and expanded by several persons, especially Tom Harris (*I'm OK, You're OK*), Claude Stiner (*Games Alcoholics Play, Scripts People Live*), and Muriel James and Dorothy Jongeward (*Born to Win*).[25]

2. *Transactional analysis:* the analysis of what people do and say to one another
3. *Game analysis:* the analysis of ulterior transactions leading to a payoff
4. *Script analysis:* the analysis of specific life dramas that persons compulsively play out

Structural Analysis

Structural analysis provides one way of understanding ourselves and the reasons for our own behavior. It is based on an understanding of ego states or "consistent patterns of feeling and experience which is directly related to a corresponding consistent pattern of behavior."[26]

Each person has three ego states which are separate and distinct sources of behavior:

1. *Parent ego state:* This state contains the attitudes and behavior incorporated from external sources, primarily parents. Outwardly, it often is expressed toward others in prejudicial, critical, and nurturing behavior. Inwardly, it is experienced as old parental messages which continue to influence the inner child.
2. *Adult ego state.* This state is not related to a person's age. It is oriented to current reality and the objective gathering of information. It is organized, adaptable, intelligent, and functions by testing reality, estimating probabilities, and computing without emotion.
3. *Child ego state.* This state contains all the impulses that come naturally to an infant. It also contains the recording of your early experiences, how you responded to them, and the "positions" you took about yourself and others.

When you are acting, thinking, feeling, as you observed your parents to be doing, you are in your parent ego state. When you are dealing with current reality, gathering facts, and computing objectively, you are in your adult ego state. When you are feeling and acting as you did when you were a child, you are in your child ego state.

Transactional Analysis

Our transactions or communications with others can be analyzed in terms of the ego state that is being expressed—parent, adult, or child. When we communicate with others, we expect a response. These responses can also be analyzed in terms of the origin of the ego state. Thus, our communications or transactions with others can be understood as complementary, crossed, or ulterior.

1. *Complementary transactions.* These occur when a message sent from a specific ego state gets the predicted response from the specified ego state of the other person.
2. *Crossed transactions.* These occur when a stimulus elicits an unexpected response from the other person.
3. *Ulterior transactions.* These involve more than one ego state and are designed to achieve purpose.

Game Analysis

The basic function of transactions is found in our biological and psychological needs, which Eric Berne has called "hungers." One of the most basic hungers is the hunger for touch and recognition. This hunger for touch and recognition is fed by what Berne calls "strokes," which are acts that imply recognition of another's presence. Strokes can be given in the form of actual physical touch or by some symbolic form of recognition, such as a look, a word, a gesture, or any act that says, "I know you're there."

Receiving positive strokes as a child is basic to the development of good emotional health or a sense of "OKness." The need for positive strokes continues throughout our life, and these can range from maintenance strokes of a simple smile to a depth encounter of intimacy.

If we do not get enough positive strokes, we may provoke negative ones which can also feed the recognition hunger. Negative strokes or discounting is either the lack of attention or negative attention that hurts emotionally or physically. A discount occurs if a problem is not taken seriously; the significance of the problem is denied; the solution is denied; or when a person denies his or her own ability to solve a problem.

Script Analysis

In the life of every individual, the dramatic events, the roles that are learned, rehearsed, and acted out, are originally determined by a script. A psychological script is a person's ongoing program for their life drama which dictates where they are going with their life and how they are to get there.* Life dramas begin at birth. Our script instructions are programmed into the child ego state through transactions between parent figures and their children. As we grow, we learn to play parts—heroes, heroines, villains, victims, and rescuers—and unknowingly, seek others to play complementary roles. Scripts can serve the function of giving a person fairly realistic ideas about what he or she can do with his or her talents. Others misdirect the person to follow a path that is unrealistically or perhaps resentfully selected.

The goals of transactional analysis (TA) are not to eliminate any of our ego states but to place them in a proper balance. TA is designed to encourage more adult interaction and to achieve awareness, spontaneity, and intimacy. The primary applications to management have been organized around the personal growth and development of the individual. It has been used with employees as a means of:

- Teaching them communications that respond to the ego states that are being expressed, to avoid crossed transactions (e.g., flight attendants, betting tellers, teachers, and counselors)
- Diagnosing the interactions of work groups and assisting them to move toward a level of intimacy that can facilitate creativity and production
- Counseling employees with personal problems (e.g., alcoholism, marital difficulties, and child-rearing problems)
- Career and life planning—analyzing and rewriting scripts for development

In the last analysis, the goals of individual, group, and organizational communication are to achieve adult-to-adult types of interface.

*See the discussion of career and life planning in Chapter 7.

DEVELOPING A MANAGEMENT INFORMATION SYSTEM

The designers of management information systems (MIS) ask the manager what information is wanted. This assumes that the manager knows what information is needed, which is not necessarily the case. What is needed, first, is a plan for developing an information system for effective managing. Initially, the organization must analyze its own particular decision system. It is possible to devise a taxonomy of the kinds of decisions required and the human relationships thereby determined; and these relationships can then be flowcharted. Second, there is a need for an analysis of information requirements, and for this to be presented in terms of regular heuristic, problem/crisis types of situations. Provision should be made in the information system for measurement of actuality feedback. Third, decisions that are related should be grouped together and assigned to the manager responsible for that area.

Fourth, the procedures within a management information system should be designed to expedite collecting, storing, retrieving, and treating information—predicated on the regularity of reporting as well as the exceptional revelation. Volumes have been written about the design of information processing; as we look at the office of the future, however, the use of the desktop terminal, teleconferencing, and computer conferencing should be an established part of any management information system. Fifth, a management information system will require a control system that provides evaluation of the deficiencies of the information and distribution system. Sixth, the management information system should be flexible and adaptive.

Seventh, in developing such a system there should be adequate interface and joint planning between information specialists, general systems personnel, human systems specialists, and *operating managers.* If the latter's ideas, requirements, and concepts are not included in the planning for and design of the system, its utility will be sharply curtailed. Furthermore, such inclusion will assist the manager to make use of the management information system; and such interdisciplinary interface is a key to processing information so as to make it communication useful to action taking.

Recently, in the onrush of technological advance, humankind has devised new ways to store and retrieve information that do not rely solely upon our brains. As this physical process is developed, and as it is controlled and used wisely, there is an increasingly greater chance that each entity participating in interface will come more and more to see the world as it really is, and to evaluate the other's words as more than unintelligible noise.

When this begins to happen, however, interfacing itself will create new information and experience, for its very essence is new understanding. The fundamental action resulting from search and coping is the removal of the curtain that hangs between the protagonists, the transfer of reality from the shadow of suspicion to the sunlight of reason. In a new light, there will be coined semantics and a strange climate, unfamiliar physical and psychological distances, frightening perspectives seen for the first time, and uncertain recognition. These are the challenges, but they are also indicative of the rewards.

Much of the civilized world is already thirty years into an information revolution, and this phenomenon is touching the souls of men and women everywhere in countless and multiplying ways. It is realigning perspectives for both large and small organizations, and for those which are in the birth stage as well as those which have gained maturity. It can serve to protect and enhance human dignity and vastly enlarge the mobilization of human energy. Unfortunately, as has been mentioned, information in and of itself, even when communicated, is not enough to establish effective interfacing. Those who attempt to engage in interfacing must fully appreciate beforehand all the conditions that must be obtained, the many hazards that must be encountered, and the roadblocks that must be faced in the process of using information in a meaningful manner.

AN APPLIED LOOK AT INTERFACE

Interfacing is an exercise in confidence in understanding, and a key element, therefore, is a readiness to listen while the other entity expresses itself without artificiality, in its own way, out of its own culture, in its own manner and language. At its best, it creates new words and meaning from the shared experience. Since communication is inevitably evaluative, an element most troublesome to achieve is an absence of judgmental attitude. Because each participating entity has a right—in self-defense—initially to expect the other to seek an advantage, it is incumbent upon both to contribute a modicum of trust, not as a gamble but in demonstration of caring, and to suspend judgment until the understanding is as complete as possible.

Interfacing itself is experimental, by its very nature a treading on quicksand, for with failure it can and usually does result in disaster qualified only by the practical limits of consequent irrationality.

Interfacing is worthwhile in human affairs if only to ensure that all terms of reconciliation, understanding, and solution may reflect all circumstances of disagreement. Stress, tension, and suffering are all part of the painful and joyful nature of obtaining such a reflection. Confrontation by entities without a balance of flexibility is bound to be fruitless, and it should be recognized that acceptance of alternatives is basic to any context of resolution in which the Lewinian concept of "unfreezing, change, and refreezing" is to be involved, as it almost always is.

Strangely enough, it is not the absolute truths with which we abide that cause our travail, so much as it is interpretations of these truths. As someone has pointed out:

> There are subjects—mathematics, physics, and the descriptive sciences supply some of them—which can be discussed in terms of verifiable facts and precise hypothesis. There are other subjects—the concrete affairs of commerce, law, organization, and policework—which can be handled by rule of thumb and generally accepted convention. But in between is the vast corpus of problems, assumptions, adumbrations, fictions, prejudices, tenets; the sphere of random belief and hopeful guesses; the whole world, in brief, of abstract opinion and disputation about matters of feeling. To this world belongs everything about which civilized men care most.[27]

The quest for interfacing is not a choice—it is a necessity at all levels of organization renewal and, as well, for the individual and group. And whether one is examining the communication between one person and another or between one nation in the West and another in the East, some common elements are essential, as illustrated in Figure 4-7.

Understanding. Interfacing depends on confidence in the parties of both parts that

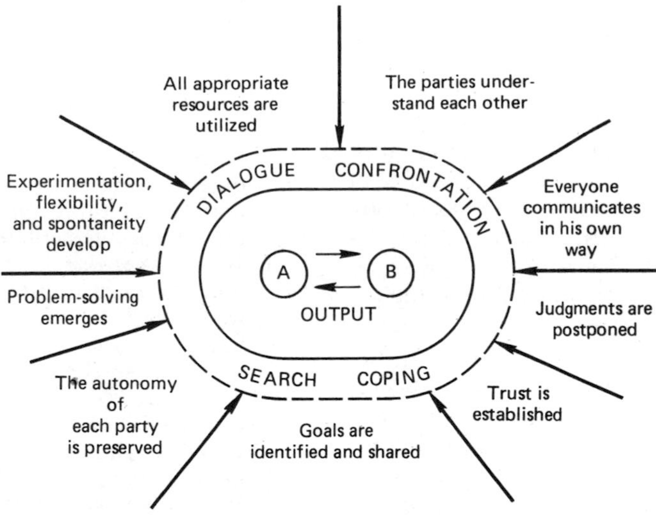

Figure 4-7 Elements in the process of interfacing

one is being understood. A real expression of interest and a readiness to listen are key elements in this understanding.

Communicating in one's own way. Interfacing permits each person to express himself in his own manner, language, and culture. We may seem to others to be different and incoherent, but the necessity of being allowed to tell one's story in one's own way is paramount.

Lack of judgmental behavior. It is difficult in communications not to be evaluative. If, however, we are to establish interfacing, we must not judge the other person, group, or organization. This is one of the most difficult elements for any person to put into practice.

Establishing trust. To be able to establish a modicum of trust is essential. As each party feels that he or she is influencing the other, the trust begins to emerge. It is only when mutual influence is seen, given, received, and acted upon that trust becomes evident.

Minimum attempt to control. Interfacing is a process of jointly coping with a solution to understood problems and not a process of control of one participant over another.

Automony is presevd. The need for a person to feel his or her own independence is an essential thing to protect in the process of interfacing. One remembers the statement of Henry David Thoreau, who commented: "If a man does not keep pace with his companions, perhaps it is because he hears a different drummer." We all have the right to hear on the basis of our own idiosyncratic nature; and to have respected by others what we say we hear.

Problem-solving approach. The interfacing process utilizes the best commitment to problem solving as a procedure for coping. Such a problem orientation communicates a desire to collaborate in the solution of a mutual problem between the parties involved.

Experimentation, Flexibility, and Spontaneity. An essential element of interfacing is that there is no definite answer or absolute in the process. Both parties need to be willing to experiment in a number of ways to cope with the problem they are confronting. In such experimentation, the value of spontaneous approach to the problem-solving process lessens any fear of deception on the part of the other person.

The ability to be open to new alternatives and to be open to change is an essential aspect of the process of interfacing. In coping with change, we find the need for maintaining flexibility of position, attitudes, and behavior in order to be able to respond—by way of creative growth—to the new potentials in the confrontations of life.

Thus far I have endeavored to explore the multiple factors involved in the quest for effective interfacing. Let us also examine what each of us might do to prepare ourselves to achieve the interfacings of life with a greater consistency and frequency than in the past.

1. *We must start with ourselves.* To understand oneself is the essential element in mental health, communication, and interfacing. It requires, however, more than merely knowing oneself. It also involves the giving of oneself.
2. *We must develop our ability to diagnose situations.* The increased knowledge from the behavioral and management sciences makes it possible for each of us to be more knowledgeable in our ability to diagnose our problems in communication. Such knowledge is a prerequisite for effective implementation of our intent.
3. *We must examine our philosphy and our beliefs.* We need to ask ourselves what it is we really believe. It is an easy thing in today's world for people to scorn idealism. We should not be afraid of looking at our ideals, goals, and objectives. It is when we understand these things that we know where we stand in the quest for interfacing.
4. *We need to be genuine.* Interfacing requires us to be genuine in our relationships with

each other. A person needs to avoid being a facade, a role, or a pretense. It is only by providing a genuine reality in dialogue that interfacing becomes at all possible. Another person, sensing falseness, will become cautious and wary, and interfacing will not develop.

5. *We must develop our creative leadership.* As never before, the world needs creative leadership that is looking for new paths, new methods, new approaches, and the search for innovations yet to come. We must accept modern technology and use it rather than be afraid of it. To see such technologies as tools to improve rather than to control people is the best attitude.

The quest for interfacing is almost always worthwhile, but not always successful. It is an essential ingredient for systems renewal.

SUMMARY

Interface for effective communications is essential to the renewal process. Communication goes beyond information interchange. It involves the dynamics of dialogue that embodies confrontation, search, and coping. Here again the concept of openness is a valuable element. Open communications is confronting the "self-fulfilling prophecy" nature of interface and that we communicate from the parent, adult, and child states of being. The manager is a principal factor in systems communication, being the link between subsystems. An effective information system is essential, but can only be as good as the data, the trust, and the problem-solving skills of those who utilize such a system.

QUESTIONS

1. How would you differentiate between communication and information?
2. How is dialogue defined in this chapter?
3. When you apply the Johari window concept, in what areas of your life do you have the largest open window? Why?
4. In transactional analysis, the idea presented is that we communicate as parent, adult, or child in different situations: Can you think of a situation where you communicated as a parent? As an adult? As a child?
5. As you think of communications in your organization, what are some of the most damaging *blocks* to effective communication?
6. What are some of the major *supports* to effective communication in your organization?

NOTES

[1]Carl Rogers and Fritz Roethlisberger, "Barriers and Gateways to Communication," *Harvard Business Review,* July-August 1952, p. 36.

[2]Richard V. Farace and Donald MacDonald, "New Directions in the Study of Organizational Communication," *Personnel Psychology,* Spring 1974, pp. 1-19. Hereafter cited as Farace and MacDonald.

[3]Walter F. Buckley, *Sociology and Modern Systems Theory* (Englewood Cliffs, N.J.: Prentice-Hall, Inc., 1967), p. 47.

[4]Michael H. Reindl, *Propositions on Information Management of Innovation Processes in Organizations* (doctoral dissertation; East Lansing, Mich.: Michigan State University, 1970), p. 37.

[5]From a speech by Dan Bellus of Dan Bellus and Associates, Santa Monica, CA; published in *DS Letter,* Vol. 1, No. 3 (Westbury N.Y.: Didactic Systems, Inc., 1971).

[6]Adapted from Gordon Lippitt, *Quest for Dialogue* (Philadelphia: Religious Education Committee, Friends General Conference, 1966).

[7]Reuel Howe, *The Miracle of Dialogue* (New York: The Seabury Press, 1963).

[8]Russell L. Ackoff, "Towards a Behavioral Theory of Communication," *Management Science,* Vol. 4, 1957, 32.

[9]David K. Berlo, *Human Communication: The Basic Proposition* (mimeographed paper; East Lansing, Mich.: Department of Communication, Michigan State University, 1970), p. 18.

[10]Farace and MacDonald, p. 15.

[11]Martin Buber, *Daniel—Dialogues on Realization,* translated by Maurice Friedman (New York: McGraw-Hill Book Company, 1964), p. 101.
[12]Leo Rosten, in *Newsletter* (Ohio State University), Vol. 32, No. 4, 1967.
[13]Joseph Luft, *Of Human Interaction* (Palo Alto, Calif.: Mayfield Publishing Company, 1967), p. 13.
[14]Adapted from "take home packet" of National Training Laboratory in Applied Behavioral Science, 1967.
[15]John Keltner, *Interpersonal Speech Communication* (Belmont, Calif.: Wadsworth Press, 1970), p. 54.
[16]Harold Leavitt, "Some Effects of Certain Communication Patterns in Group Performance," *Journal of Abnormal and Social Psychology,* Vol. 46, 1951, 38–50.
[17]Kenneth Benne and Paul Sheats, "Functional Rules of Group Members," *Journal of Social Issues,* Vol. 4, No. 2, 1948, 41–49.
[18]Stewart L. Tubbs, *A Systems Approach to Small Group Interaction* (Reading, Mass.: Addison-Wesley Publishing Company, Inc., 1978), pp. 209–211. Hereafter cited as Tubbs. Copyright © 1978 by Addison-Wesley Publishing Company. Reprinted with permission of Addison-Wesley Publishing Company, Inc.
[19]Jack R. Gibb, "Defensive Communication," *The Journal of Communication,* Vol. XI, No. 3, 1961, 141.
[20]Tubbs, p. 188.
[21]Gordon Lippitt and Edith Seashore, *The Leader Looks at Group Effectiveness* (Fairfax, Va.: Leadership Resources, Inc., 1971), pp. 10–11.
[22]Leslie E. This, unpublished list.
[23]Gordon Lippitt, *Visualizing Change* (La Jolla, Calif.: University Associates, Inc., 1973), pp. 60–61.
[24]Adapted from a paper by Shirley McCune (The George Washington University, 1978) based on Muriel James and Dorothy Joneswood, *Born to Win: Transactional Analysis with Gestalt Experiments* (Reading, Mass.: Addison-Wesley Publishing Company, Inc., 1971). Hereafter cited as McCune.
[25]Eric Berne, *Games People Play: The Psychology of Human Relationships* (New York: Grove Press, Inc., 1964).
[26]McCune, p. 4.
[27]Ivor A. Richards, *Practical Criticism* (New York: Harcourt Brace Jovanovich, 1929), p. 118.

5

power and the leadership function

There is nothing more difficult to take in hand, more perilous to conduct, or more uncertain in its success, than to take the lead in the introduction of a new order of things.

Niccolo Machiavelli, 1469–1527

Leadership and *power* are two terms that have been extensively researched, discussed, and argued about during the past several decades. They are interrelated human activities that have been studied with ever-increasing intensity. We have learned that it is easy to pontificate that viable and effective organizations and countries must have effective leadership, but that it is not so easy to prescribe a formula for such leadership, or to describe a leader in absolute terms or, for that matter, to develop a leader. The ingredients, prerequisites, and optimum styles of leadership have long eluded researchers, even though they have thrown the spotlight of specific inquiry on it.

A key part of that search has been to determine the degree of power, possibly compelling and insensitive, a leader should manifest in exercising leadership. The distinguished political historian, James MacGregor Burns, says that great leaders are sensitive to the fundamental needs and values of others:[1]

Leadership is an aspect of power, but leaders differ from powerholders. Powerholders are concerned with achieving only their own goals, whereas leaders address themselves to the wants and needs of followers as well as to their own.

Leadership may be transactional or transformational; simply an exchange of valued things with no enduring purpose, or an engagement in which leaders and followers raise one another to higher levels of motivation and morality.

Moral leadership goes beyond everyday wants and needs to higher levels of reasoned, conscious values.

Power and leadership are not concentrated in a few people but are widely distributed. "The vast preponderance of personal influence is exerted quietly and subtly in everyday relationships," so top leaders are more effective if they help their followers become leaders in their own right.

Leadership can be taught in the sense that great teachers are leaders (and great leaders teachers); they "treat students neither coercively nor instrumentally but are joint seekers of truth and mutual actualization."

The dilemma arising from a leader's use of power is complex and differentiated. All leaders hold power, but all powerholders are not leaders. Many of those who wield power treat people as things. Leaders bring their followers into the achievement of purposes. Some even see leaders as being servants to those with whom they work.[2]

The key factor is the purpose of a leader's use of power. Is power being used to achieve the goals of *both* the leader and the followers. Leaders perceive and act upon their own and their followers' values and motivations. In the United States, the concept of national consensus has been of value:

> To a fault, no doubt, but in reality, nonetheless, we are arranged around the principle of consensus as the engine of authority.
>
> The leader is the one who knows how to build it, activate it, maintain it, and use it. He needs to be "tough" in the sense of being serious and consistent and aggressive in the way he exercises this power, and that includes making it costly for those who oppose him and worthwhile for those who comply. But finally and always the blunt instrument will depend on some measure of public support.[3]

The use of leadership power is further complicated by the increasing size of today's organizations. The economist, E. F. Schumacher, raises the question from the economic viewpoint: Is it right or is it best that government be large, churches be huge, universities be multicampused with thousands of students?[4] Is this the best way for us to run organizations? We now are talking about the implications of the postindustrial society. We're moving into a society that's emphasizing quality—quality of service, quality of product, quality of work life, and quality of life in general. And this is raising dilemmas for leaders in many walks of life, but especially in business and government. When we start coping with these dilemmas, we are trying to search for the kind of leadership style and practices that make sense.

Here are some definitions of managerial leadership:

> Two Princeton researchers recently made a study of successful executives and they came up with some baffling results as a group. The top persons had only two distinguishing characteristics, neither of which would suggest itself to anyone selecting or using the common place approach to the selection of executives. These characteristics were: (a) a fear of illness, and (b) a tendency to depend on others when confronted with complex problems.[5]

Robespierre said during the French Revolution: "There go the people. I must catch up to them for I am their leader." If there's nobody following, you are not a leader. This quotation is from Emmet Hughes's book about former president Eisenhower, *The Ordeal of Power:*

> Now look. . . . I happen to know a little about leadership—I've had to work with a lot of nations, for that matter, at odds with each other. And I tell you this: you do not lead by hitting people over the head. Any damn fool can do that, it's usually called "assault"—not "leadership." . . . I'll tell you what leadership is. It's persuasion—and conciliation—and education—and patience.[6]

Antony Jay, in his interesting book, *Management and Machiavelli,* comments:

> It seems to be characteristic of the creative leaders that his personal loyalties are downward and not upward. His first loyalty is to his own ideas, his second to the people who he believes will help him realize them. Both these take a far higher priority than his superiors.[7]

Lenin is quoted as saying: "The true leader must submerge himself in the fountain of the people."[8] Napoleon is reported to have said: "The only way to lead people is to show them a future. A leader is a dealer in hope." Finally, to put in perspective this search for the relationship between power and leadership, there is a quotation from the Chinese philosopher Lao-Tzu, who lived in the 6th century B.C.:

> A leader is best when people barely know that he exists. Not so good when people obey and acclaim him. Worse when then they despise him. Fail to honor people, they fail to honor you. But of a good leader, who talks little, when his work is done, his aim fulfilled, they will all say—we did this ourselves.

One other introductory observation is to differentiate among the terms *administrator, manager,* and *leader.* These words frequently are used interchangeably, but there is a considerable difference:

Administrators have the responsibility of fulfilling certain functions relevant to their position.

A *manager* coordinates and utilizes the technical, financial, physical, and human resources presented by the system.

A *leader* releases and channels his own and followers' energies to achieve common goals.

Our leadership theories have been short-range and atomistic, focusing on leader-group relations and neglecting the leader-group-*system* relationship.[9] In Stogdill's massive review,[10] no section deals with the systems concept. Sergiovanni has joined the chorus of practitioners and scientists who are frustrated at the many ways of looking at leadership. Some caustic critics, such as Perrow[11] and Miner[12] have even suggested that the term *leadership* is no longer useful. We have expected too much of the leader. We teach leadership as an independent variable and ignore the reality of organizational life.[13] Many organizational variables are outside the leader's control, such as tax cuts, public expectations, inflation, political realities, and cultural changes.

Different *leaders* are needed at different stages of organizational life and maturity. The numerous attempts to classify leaders as one type or another is neither accurate or helpful. Whether one is a "wolf," "fox," "craftsman," "bureaucrat," or "gamesman" is a descriptive way to define leadership complexity, but too narrow.[14]

A new way of looking at a leader may be through the way he or she directs the activities of people:

1. *Force.* The leader uses control of means to *force* the choice of certain activities that are desired as goals.
2. *Paternalism.* The leader provides means, and hopes for acceptance of leadership out of loyalty and gratitude.
3. *Bargain.* The leader may arrive at a *bargain,* a more or less voluntary choice, made by each party to furnish certain means in return for certain means.
4. *Mutual means.* The leader creates the situation in which certain own activities and those of the group, if performed together, will serve as *mutual means,* means for each to satisfy own (perhaps different) needs.

The leader is *not,* however, always free to choose among these methods. To a greater or lesser extent, the method is prescribed by the nature and policy of the organization. The initial concept of leadership seems to have been that of force. Paternalism enjoyed popularity for many years among some managers. The rise of unions created the necessity for bargaining.

The fourth method listed above is not an impossible step, but it requires skill, understanding, and imagination of a high order. When leaders successfully create the necessary conditions, the organization and its objectives become a means not only to employees but also to the purposes of the organization; but the development of such leaders is difficult when organizations are complex systems.

Jack Gibb has summed up the need for an integrated systems view in a statement concerning group training that is echoed in other reviews of general management and human resource development.

> [They] are ineffective unless they are integrated into long-range efforts that include such elements as a total organizational focus, system-wide data collection, provision for feedback and information flow, organization-focused consultation over an extended time and data-supported theory.[15]

Leadership training is required in many areas of skill development—such as communication, conflict resolution, financial management, problem solving, and systems concepts—that are needed in effective managing. However, leadership is a *performing art,* not a science. Professional standards, skills, and values are required. To lead complex systems we need to broaden our ways of examining leadership beyond academic research and educational writings. Sources of data about leaders include *The New Yorker, Business Week, Wall Street Journal,* biographies, historical reports, and others that can broaden our concepts and practices of, and our values regarding leadership.

APPROACHES TO THE UNDERSTANDING OF LEADERSHIP

The early leadership studies, which focused largely on personality traits, were generally disappointing, and resulted in little agreement about the importance of any particular set of traits. Twenty years ago, an analysis of 106 studies of leadership revealed that only 5% of the total number of traits isolated appeared in four or more of the studies. In the late nineteen thirties, several pioneering studies were made of autocratic, democratic, and laissez-faire styles of leadership. A style called "benevolently autocratic" was uncovered somewhere along the line of search. More recently, researchers have concentrated on the functions of leadership that are necessary to get a particular job done. Some of this research has dealt with leadership actions affecting group action, but in spite of all the ground that has been covered, neither the behavioral sciences nor successful leaders can provide simple, definitive answers.[16]

There are indications that effective leaders are those who are flexible rather than rigid, aware of their own forces and understanding their own motivations, and trusting in relationships with those they lead. It seems that most leaders take into account both the short-range and the long-range nature of the situation they face, and that they more or less involve in making it those who are to implement a decision.

So much has been so well written about leadership, and about the larger function in organizations to which it contributes—management—that no good purpose will be served here by anything other than an overview discussion of those aspects of leadership and the principles involved, which seem to have a pertinence to organization renewal. We have come to realize that leadership is dispersed in many groups and fragmented among many people. No one person is powerful in all ways. A leader in one field often does not know leaders in other fields. Thus, important organizational issues and problems are settled, not by one leader or one power group, but by a balance of power.[17]

In trying to identify leaders in various ways, to determine what makes a person a leader and not a follower, the behavioral scientists have identified at least six different concepts:

1. *Great man theory.* We used to hold to the theory that a leader is a great man (or

woman), that leadership qualities are inborn, that people naturally follow the individuals who have these qualities. In this theory the great man is responsible for history, rather than history responsible for the great man.

2. *Trait approach.* In this theory we try to identify the traits of a great leader that make him or her different from the rest of us. There do not appear to be any characteristic physical attributes, nor is the leader necessarily endowed with superior intelligence. Chromosomes and genes have not been positively related to leadership in terms of inheritance, nor has a particular personality or behavior pattern been identified. The only conclusion so far reached is that there is nothing conclusive about leadership traits.
3. *Functions approach.* It has been learned that most leaders, to one extent or another, perform four major leadership roles or functions. One may be essentially decision making, with implementation to be carried out by others. Another may be that of providing information and advice. A third, and probably the most common, is that of planning. The fourth is largely symbolic, such as that which Queen Elizabeth serves in England.
4. *Situational approach.* Here it is assumed that there are certain traits and capacities that are crucial for effective leadership in one situation and not in another. Studies in this area indicate that there is a need for flexibility in the selection and training of leaders for different situations.
5. *Contingency approach.* Fred Fiedler's contingency theory of leadership[18] suggests that the key factor in determining style effectiveness is the extent to which the leader can or cannot influence followers. Fiedler's rather extensive and impressive research, spanning more than thirty years, strongly suggests that in situations where leaders are either exceptionally influential or not influential at all, task styles are more effective. In situations of moderate influence, his evidence suggests that relationship styles tend to be more effective.
6. *Organizational norms approach.* The norms of an organization will determine leadership response patterns. Abraham Zaleznik suggests that a bureaucratic society, which breeds bureaucratic managers, may stifle leaders who need mentors and emotional interchange to develop.[19] Leadership will always depend upon organizational norms and climate, the structure and use of communications patterns, and power.[20]
7. *Functional approach.* This deserves a bit more explanation. Here the leader seeks to discover what actions are required by groups, under various conditions, if they are to achieve their objectives, and how different members take part in these actions. Leadership is viewed as the performance by the leader of those acts that are required by the group.

This group-functions approach to leadership may incorporate the other approaches. Groups differ in a variety of ways, actions vary from one group to another, and the nature of the leader's acts will vary from group to group. Situational aspects (e.g., nature of the group's goals, structure of group, attitudes of members) will determine what functions are needed and who will perform them. There appear to be two main leadership needs in groups: the achievement of the group goal and the maintenance or the strengthening of the group itself. A specific function may be helpful to both or favor one at the expense of the other. For example, a group and its leader may be so intent upon maintaining good relations that they avoid interpersonal friction at all costs, thereby retarding the problem-solving process. On the other hand, a problem's wise solution forged in conflict may help the solidarity of the group.

The distribution of leadership functions in a group occurs in several ways. Usually, in a mature group, members will assume responsibility for group roles necessary for effective functioning. Studies and experiments indicate that groups which distribute leadership functions usually achieve greater productivity and morale.

Studies of the roles of group members show that there tend to be group-centered, task-centered, and self-centered member functions. Studies of the effects of these roles indicate that certain functions are required for a group to make a decision, to come to a conclusion, or to resolve a conflict.

Functional leadership means that group members have a shared responsibility to carry out the various tasks of leadership. The designated leader, however, has a responsibility for being sensitive to those functional needs and for seeing that they are accommodated.

One observation frequently made by leaders is: "Democratic or problem-solving leadership is all right, but it is too time-consuming, and I have a job to get done." It is true that when reaching a decision is the sole objective, problem-solving leadership usually takes longer than manipulative or autocratic leadership. However, studies show that problem-solving leadership can be more effective even from the point of view of time consumed if we consider the total time elapsed from the emergence of a problem to the implementation of a solution.

Figure 5-1 shows that although problem-solving leadership takes longer to reach a decision, implementation is much more rapid than in the case of manipulative leadership because the members of a group that participate in making the decision feel more responsible for carrying it out. In the autocratic style of leadership, the decision-making function resides in the leader; in the laissez-faire, it resides in the individual; in the democratic, it resides in the group. The benevolently autocratic style, although distinct, seems to be most like the democratic style, except that this kind of leader does not possess the basic skills in human relations that permit a really shared problem-solving approach in the leader's relationships with others.

Which of these styles is best? In some situations, autocratic leadership is best. In some, democratic leadership is more effective. In still other situations, the laissez-faire style does the best job. There can be no one set style of leadership that we can develop in ourselves or teach to others. Leadership must be flexible in style to meet the need of a particular situation which involves an individual, a group, an organization, or a nation.

In this context, the concept of a leadership continuum, introduced in works by Tannenbaum and Schmidt, who point out that forces in the leader, forces in the group members, and forces in the situation apparently combine to make it necessary for a leader to respond at any given moment with a style of leadership appropriate to that particular situation, can be further developed.[21]

This concept is in keeping with the position that a renewal facilitator in an organization should respond to situations as a professional *existential pragmatist.* It is not appropriate to classify leaders by the stereotypes of autocratic, benevolently autocratic, democratic, and laissez-faire. In similar fashion, classifying organizations as

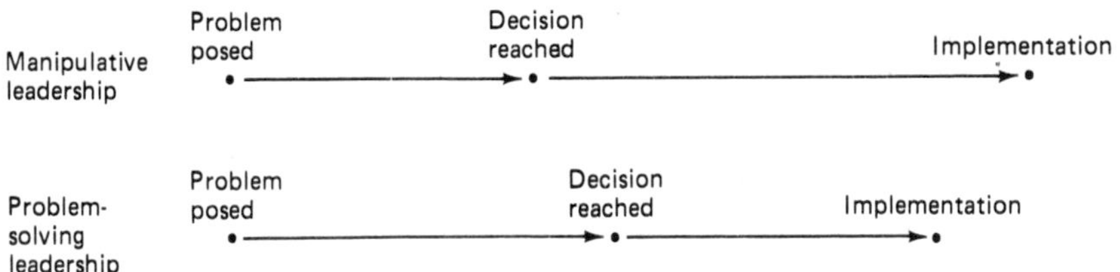

Figure 5-1 Leadership Style and Problem Solving

authoritative or participative may do a disservice to the reality of situational needs and demands.[22]

In whatever manner a leader or management responds, there will always be a *degree* of participation, as indicated in Figure 5-2. The amount of appropriate participation, involvement, and delegation is related not only to the skills of the leader and the ability of the group members, but also to the nature of the existential situation as it is influenced by organizational needs, response to the environment, and the interfacing process in the human subsystems of the organization. It may well be appropriate in the case of a company policy, safety regulation, or the announcement of a budget cut for a manager to permit only a "tell or persuade" degree of participation. The survival of the organization or the safety of employees may be the key element in the situation. In determining a new product or service, the manager may want to consult research scientists, product engineers, marketing people, an accountant, and a patent lawyer before making a decision. In another case, the manager may find that a group problem-solving process is the best way to decide how the company will solve a bottleneck on shipping orders.

A professional manager-leader will recognize, however, that leadership response will depend on a sophisticated diagnosis of the complex forces in the existential situation that will provide guidance in taking the appropriate leadership stance. Leadership is the effective meeting of the situation—whatever the situation is. And this effective meeting comes through confrontation, search, and coping.[23]

Confrontation. Effective leaders do not run away from involvement. They confront people and situations; they take the initiative, do not pussyfoot, do not play games, do not just react to a situation. They act, facing up to issues and problems. Effective leaders understand themselves, and the person who has such understanding is best able to confront situations and lead others. Further, in growing into leadership, a person needs to avoid trying to copy someone else. A leader does not put on the role or mantle of leadership. Effective leaders must confront the needs of people in each situation, with a solid understanding of their follower's needs, their own goals, and the goals of the organization. Without confrontation and the adequate communication confrontation involved, a person cannot be an effective leader.

Search. Here the leader seeks understanding of the people, the situation, and

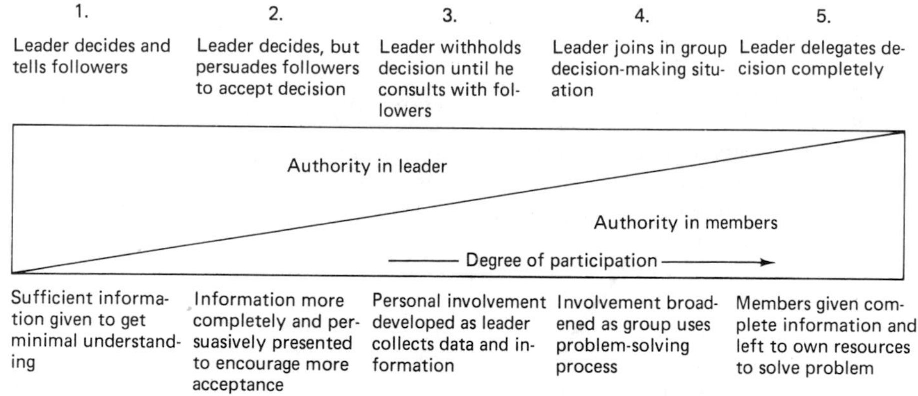

Figure 5-2 Degrees of Participation Related to Leadership Response

the causes involved—and examines the shadows cast by deep-seated causes. As a leader, using the delicate radar of our five senses, you tune in on your followers and develop mutual empathy by placing yourself in their situation. Similarly, one searches for facts, for data, that will help make sound decisions and obtain the confidence of those being led.

Coping. The best kind of coping with problems and situations involves a minimum attempt to control other people, a minimum pulling of strings, because whereas people like to be told honestly what to do, they do not like to be controlled, clobbered, or manipulated.

An effective leader uses a problem-solving approach to situations, knowing there are frictions and disagreements that often can be eliminated if they are brought out, looked at, and played out in an atmosphere of experimentation, flexibility, and adaptability to change. He or she is willing to take risks, is not afraid to rock the boat, does not fear failure. Attitudes and values condition personal leadership, contributing to a relationship between the leader's philosophy of life and his philosophy of leadership. If the latter is based on something akin to Douglas McGregor's theory Y—an assurance that people really want to do a good job, want to better themselves, and are willing to change as change becomes necessary to the organization—the results are favorable more often than not. Insofar as leadership is related to accomplishment, this philosophy expects much and obtains much, because the leader is trading on the followers' worth and potential.

Many a leader has learned that in certain situations an ability to confront, search, and cope depends on a trust *relationship* being established with the other members of the group or organization. All too often a cause of misunderstanding, and of damaged job performance and personal relations, is created when communications between the leader and the members of the group are merely superficial facades behind which those involved, on both sides, conceal their real feelings. A frequent reason for such a lack of real dialogue is a lack of trust.

What constitutes trust varies from person to person, largely depending upon the individual's situation. Trust can be unilateral, wherein one member of a dyad experiences certainty in his relations with the other, without reciprocity. Trust can be mutual, wherein the two members of a dyad reciprocally experience certainty. Each of these two kinds of trust, not dissimilar to the nature of the group interaction itself, can be either task or socially oriented, or a combination of both. Task-oriented, or working, trust is more or less impersonal and related solely to the trusted person's ability to perform his function as a member of a group. Social trust is limited to personal, informal relationships between people, as in friendships. Working trust seems to be largely subconscious.

A combination, a working-social trust, is the strongest form because it provides for the existence of an anticipated, positive, reality-based response from the trusted person. In this sense, positive response is perceived as helpful in achieving a goal (working trust) and helpful in strengthening the relationship bond (social trust). Reality-based response involves more than always looking on the bright side of things. Carl Rogers maintains that genuineness, acceptance, and empathetic understanding are the dynamic factors in a trusting relationship.[24]

Mutual working-social trust is important to organizational renewal. Change of performance and the solving of problems will occur most effectively when a climate of trust is developed (see Figure 5-3). In developing trust, Dale Zand indicates that the cycle starts with reality communication. The support given by leaders and accepted

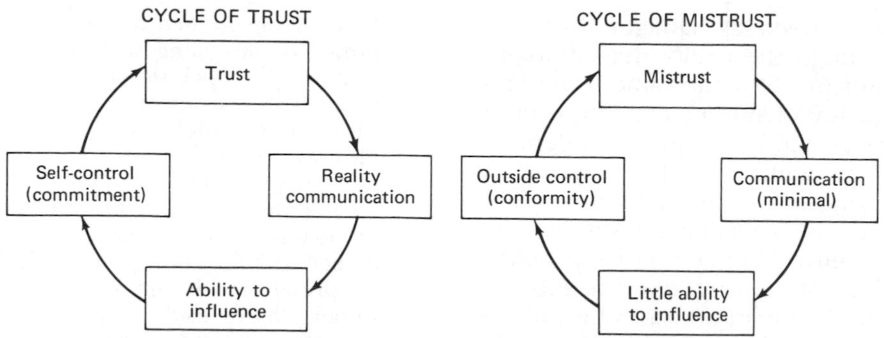

Figure 5-3 Cycles of Trust and Mistrust[25]

by followers is an outgrowth of open communication and related directly to the amount of caring that members of a group give in mutual influence circumstances. The latter, in turn, is related directly to the amount of cooperation and coordination exhibited between peers in the organizational hierarchy. Similarly, trust can be considered a factor in the forces affecting the attitude of each member of a group with respect to his wanting to remain in the group. It can be surmised, therefore, that trust can be a significant factor in each member's willingness to change and to communicate openly, both of which are essential to organization renewal.

A study of the "high-achieving manager" revealed a managerial response pattern that would probably be highly rewarding for subordinates:

> The results indicated that high-achieving managers are concerned with those aspects of the job that provide a sense of personal fulfillment. They talk about these things with their subordinates and attempt to structure the work situation so that subordinates can get personally involved and find the same kinds of fulfillment.... Low achievers are characterized by pessimistic outlooks and a basic distrust of both the intent and competence of their subordinates.[26]

The leader's ability to exercise influence is founded in trust—both the leader's trust in others and their trust in the leader. Research has indicated that the following basic characteristics promote trust:[27]

Integrity: Sound and honest in character and moral principles

Justice: Possessing a sense of right and equity

Ability: Capable of performing well in the task or relationship involved

Intention: Determined to achieve some desirable action or result

Reliability: Dependable in carrying out a commitment

Most people, in extending trust to peers having work-status equality, require only that they have the qualities of integrity and reliability. In a leader, however, most followers pay more attention to ability and intention, in such terms as "Does he know the job well?" and "Does she let me know why she takes certain actions when the actions seem to concern me?" Integrity places third in a list of personal qualifications desired in a leader, but this does not necessarily include his having a good, personal reputation. Too often, would-be leaders believe that a reputation as a "good fellow" is indispensable. Nothing could be further from the truth.

The multiple forces affecting a trust relationship between a manager and employee highlight the reality that although they are not precisely the same thing and do not call for identical capabilities, most organizations tend to equate leadership with management. With this in mind, it seems appropriate to determine their place concurrently in a scheme of systems renewal. Certainly, both emphasize problem solving, decision making, and the successful implementation of decisions by and for the organization. Far too often, the ordinary concept of leadership or management stops with this relatively simple outline of functions—which has led to the *inadequate* definition: "Management is getting things done through people."

Actually, there are in almost all organizations of significant size, at all levels, six distinct roles to be played by a manager:[28]

1. *Implementer.* A great premium on qualities of leadership; ability to communicate and to identify the best abilities in people; and to motivate people to exercise these abilities to the fullest; gregariousness; understanding of human motivation and behavior; and some degree of personal charisma.
2. *Administrator.* Basically, a matter of control, calling for a thorough understanding of how the organization gets things done and of the things critical to its success; and an ability to pinpoint existing or impending troubles and the imagination to develop corrective courses of action; an awareness of human elements, but not so conscious of them as to permit personal loyalties and influences to obscure recognition of the substantive causes of problems; and willingness to face up to the personal conflicts often precipitated by tough-minded decisions.
3. *Extrapolative planner.* Basically an organizer, inward-oriented toward internal problems; skilled in creating a structure of relationships between people and physical resources so as to assure the organization's greatest performance potential; ability to develop guidelines, programs, and budgets that assure smooth functioning of such a structure; an aptitude for designing such a structure as contrasted to operating it, which involves an ability to extrapolate the past into the future, to consolidate and schedule complex operations.
4. *Entrepreneurial planner.* Basically a risk-taker, outward-oriented toward changing or enlarging the organization; more concerned with the future than with the past or present, with opportunities outside rather than inside the organization; searches out and establishes new and challenging organizational goals.
5. *System architect.* Primarily concerned with management of the "information explosion," its volume, and substantive content relevant to the needs of management in decision-making; skilled in or knowledgeable about acquiring, disseminating, displaying, and interpreting information in proportion to the organizational investment in computers.
6. *Statesman.* Capable of seeing the organization in the broadest perspective, as a part of the total environment; cognizant of the growing importance of organizations as a social force, and society's concern with social welfare; able to compete or cooperate effectively with other organizations, including government agencies, universities, foundations, and non-profit institutes; able to cope with decision making in complex economical-social-political-cultural interaction in various widespread geographical locations all over the world.

All six roles are not necessarily in the forefront simultaneously, but sooner or later most organizations will be faced with a serious need for the particular skills each involves, although perhaps not to the same extent as an international industrial giant. One peculiarity is that these roles are seldom interchangeable in the same person.

A study conducted in 1977 and 1978 examined the roles and functions of career civilian executives in the Department of the Navy at the levels GS-16, GS-17, and GS-18.[29] A multimethod approach was used in this study. Data were collected through a sequence of interviews, observations, work-activity diaries, structures questionnaires, and an analysis of the CSC Executive Inventory Records of navy civilian executives. As illustrated in Table 5-1, eleven roles were found to be prevalent among key executives.

In Table 5-2, the rank order of those items receiving a mean of 4.0 or above, on the seven-point scale, are indicated.

The responses obtained in this study indicate that all 11 executive roles are relevant, but that leadership and resources allocation are the key functions. The five most frequently mentioned items with respect to time spent in the executive function relate to guidance to others, allocating resources, keeping others informed, learning what is going on, and taking immediate action. As a matter of fact, the time consumed by these five items represented 20% of the executives' time on the job. The same executives were then asked to fill out a questionnaire that probed their concept of the most important personal characteristics required in their position. The results are shown in Table 5-3.

It is interesting that the top three items relate to communication skills, and that ability in the areas of problem solving, technical skills, persuasiveness, flexibility, and planning capability also ranked high.

Another effort to clarify the competence of executive level managers was undertaken by the U.S. Office of Personnel Management (OPM). As a result of the Civil Service Reform Act of 1978, this office was created to provide appraisal, training, consultation, and development services. One objective was to develop the Senior Executive Service from top-ranked leaders in the federal civil service. An OPM task force was required to prepare a report dealing with an executive/managerial curriculum and a continuing research project on executive/managerial activities and competencies. This report, in its final form, focused on four categories of competencies:[30]

1. *Management and management processes.* This competency area deals with the general principles and concepts of management, and with utilizing those tools, aids, and other resources that have been developed in support of carrying out basic management functions, such as planning, budgeting, and staffing. It must be remembered that these have to be utilized within the context of an agency's processes, procedures, organization, and rules, and that of the individual's role as executive or manager.
2. *Personal/interpersonal.* The competencies in this category relate to individual intellectual, communication, and interpersonal relations capabilities.
3. *Environmental.* Competencies relating to the interaction between the organization and the broader context within which it operates (e.g., social, political, economic). Generally, these competencies involve being able to assess and understand both the current situation and the immediate and long-range prospects in terms of their implications for agency programs and program impacts.
4. *Professional/technical program.* Competencies relating to an understanding of the agency's undertakings, including the theoretical and/or legislative basis for agency programs and the immediate and long-range developments in the professional/technical fields.

The competencies selected for immediate attention were:

Dealing with executive role requirements and expectations. This obviously is a broad area and one that encompasses and reflects the various categories and subcategories of specific executive/managerial competencies. The role competency is intended to underscore the need for persons in public executive positions to have a wide perspective and understanding of the responsibilities associated with these positions. The role competency should be

Table 5–1
Summary of Executive Roles Investigated

Role	Definition[a]	Identifiable Activities from Study of Chief Executives
	Interpersonal	
Figurehead	Symbolic head; obligated to perform a number of routine duties of a legal or social nature	Ceremony, status requests, solicitations
Leader	Responsible for the motivation and activation of subordinates; responsible for staffing, training, and associated duties	Virtually all managerial activities involving subordinates
Liaison	Maintains self-developed network of outside contacts and informers who provide favors and information	Acknowledgment of mail; external board work; other activities involving outsiders
	Informational	
Monitor	Seeks and receives wide variety of special information (much of it current) to develop thorough understanding of organization and environment; emerges as nerve center of internal and external information of the organization	Handling all mail and contacts categorized as concerned primarily with receiving information (e.g., periodical news, observational tours)
Disseminator	Transmits information received from outsiders or from other subordinates to members of the organization; some information factual, some involving interpretation and integration of diverse value positions of organizational influencers	Forwarding mail into organization for informational purposes, verbal contact involving information flow to subordinates (e.g., review sessions, instant communication flows)
Spokesman	Transmits information to outsiders on organization's plans, policies, actions, results, etc.; serves as expert on organization's industry	Board meetings, handling mail, and contacts involving transmission of information to outsiders
	Decisional	
Entrepreneur	Searches organization and its environment for opportunities and initiates "improvement projects" to bring about change; supervises design of certain projects as well	Strategy and review sessions involving initiation or design of improvement projects
Disturbance handler	Responsible for corrective action when organization faces important, unexpected disturbances	Strategy and review sessions involving disturbances and crises
Resource allocator	Responsible for the allocation of organizational resources of all kinds—in effect, the making or approval of all significant organizational decisions	Scheduling; requests for authorization; any activity involving budgeting and the programming of subordinates' work
Negotiator	Responsible for representing the organization at major negotiations	Negotiation
Technical expert	Providing expertise to projects; serving as a consultant to internal or external projects	Directing a project or subproject; solving project-centered problems

[a] Definitions for all roles but "technical expert" based on *The Nature of Managerial Work* by Henry Mintzberg (New York: Harper & Row, 1973).

Table 5-2
Ranked Order of Job Activities Performed by Executives

Role	Item	Importance[a]
Resource allocator	Determining the long-range plans and priorities of your unit	5.8
Leader	Evaluating the quality of subordinate job performance and providing recognition, encouragement, or criticism	5.8
Leader	Providing guidance and direction to your subordinates	5.8[b]
Resource allocator	Allocating resources (manpower, money, material) among programs or units	5.7[b]
Resource allocator	Allocating your own time	5.7
Disseminator	Keeping members of your unit informed of relevant information through meetings, conversations, and dissemination of written information	5.6[b]
Monitor	Learning about fleet requirements and needs	5.6
Leader	Attending to staffing requirements in your unit such as hiring, firing, promoting, and recruiting	5.4
Resource allocator	Participating in defining command strategies and policies	5.4
Technical expert	Judging the accuracy of approach and utility of technical programs and proposals	5.3
Leader	Keeping abreast of who is doing what in your unit or command	5.2[b]
Disturbance handler	Taking immediate action in response to a crisis or "fire drill"	5.1[b]
Technical expert	Providing technical quality control through the review process	5.1
Spokesman	Keeping sponsors, consumers, or other important governmental groups informed about your unit's activities and capabilities	4.9
Monitor	Staying tuned to what is going on in outside organizations, including the professional and scientific communities	4.9
Disturbance handler	Resolving conflicts either within your unit or between your unit and other organizational components	4.9
Liaison	Developing personal relationships with people outside your unit who sponsor your work or services	4.8
Disturbance handler	Preventing the loss or threat of loss of resources valued by your unit	4.8
Leader	Attending to the training and development needs of your employees	4.7
Spokesman	Defending your unit's projects and activities to other groups	4.7
Resource allocator	Programming work for your unit (what is to be done, when, and how) and assigning people to work on it	4.7
Technical expert	Consulting with others on technical matters	4.6
Entrepreneur	Exploiting or initiating opportunities to improve or expand as a unit	4.4
Disseminator	Implementing the directives of higher authorities	4.4
Negotiator	Negotiating with groups internal to your command for necessary materials, support, commitments, etc.	4.4
Leader	Integrating subordinates' goals (e.g., individual development plans, career goals, work preferences) with the command's work requirements	4.4
Disseminator	Transmitting ideas and information from your outside contacts to appropriate people inside your command	4.4
Entrepreneur	Maintaining supervision over planned changes to improve your unit	4.3
Disturbance handler	Dealing with previously ignored problems (ones that people have known to exist but avoided) which have come to a head	4.3
Negotiator	Negotiating with groups outside your command for necessary materials, support, commitments, etc.	4.3

(*continued*)

Table 5–2 (*Continued*)

Role	Item	Importance[a]
Figurehead	Answering letters or signing documents as an official representative of your unit	4.2
Liaison	Attending outside conferences or meetings	4.2
Leader	Participating in EEO activities and responsibilities	4.1
Figurehead	Making yourself available to "outsiders" (such as consumers, sponsors, the public) who want to go to "the person in charge"	4.0

[a] Based on a scale where 0 = none and 7 = great deal.
[b] One of the five highest-ranked items as to time spent.

given particular emphasis in planning developmental experiences for those persons who have progressed up career ladders on the strength of professional or technical abilities and performance without extensive managerial experience or training (e.g., scientists, engineers, lawyers).

Dealing with the career executive/political executive interface. The nature of the interaction of career executives and political executives within and between organizations is a factor that is critical to the efficiency and effectiveness with which public programs are carried out. To the extent possible, career and political executives need an in-depth understanding of the factors that contribute to the difficulties that frequently arise around the career/political executive interface and how to deal more effectively with them.

Assessing one's strengths, limitations, and needs. Persons in managerial positions, by definition, have to rely upon and work with others to accomplish many of their objectives. Critical to such work activities as delegation is an understanding of one's capabilities and needs vis-à-vis others. This self-assessment competency is also important to deciding upon career goals and how to achieve them.

Understanding the broader context of agency operations. This includes, in particular, social and political forces, general economic conditions and issues, national priorities, and the governmental framework and relationships. These competencies fall within the environmental category and underscore the importance of having persons in executive-level managerial positions who can deal with the many interactions that occur (or should occur) between the agency and external groups and forces during the course of setting, implementing, and assessing agency programs.

In developing the more specific skills and knowledges required to achieve executive and managerial competence, a series of thirty-four areas were identified within the first three categories.[31]

The task force presented guidelines to the government agencies that spelled out a description of each of these thirty-four competencies and the typical indicators of when that skill or knowledge is being manifested. Such studies provide an operational way of looking at leadership, as well as the knowledge and skills that a part of the competency of executive leadership. It is interesting to observe that the matter of using influence and power, and the ability to take command of a situation, are ever-present dimensions of leadership behavior.

FURTHER EXAMINATION OF THE POWER ISSUE

While the political scientists have been examining the exercise of power by historical

Table 5-3
Civilian Executives' Perceptions of the Importance of Personal Characteristics Required in Their Jobs

Characteristics	Average Score[a]	Characteristics	Average Score[a]
Ability to communicate verbally (orally)	6.4	Good memory for facts	5.3
Ability to communicate in writing	6.3	Ability to reach conclusions with a minimum of information	5.2
Listening carefully to others	6.2	Keeping up to date in your technical specialty	5.2
Technical ability in your specialty (e.g., science engineering, personnel, financial management)	6.2	Administrative ability (ability to efficiently progress routine paperwork and other organizational demands)	5.2
Managerial ability (ability to plan, direct, and evaluate the work of your unit)	6.2	Time management ability	5.1
Ability to create an environment in which subordinates work effectively	6.1	Willingness to question directives or orders from above	5.1
Critical thinking; questioning methods and techniques that others take for granted	6.1	Crisis management ability	4.9
Ability to sell one's ideas; persuasiveness	6.1	Ability to recognize when you are licked on a given matter	4.8
Flexibility	6.0	Knowing budgeting and finance	4.6
Coolness under stress	6.0	Friendships and connections with superiors	4.1
Being achievement-oriented	5.8	Working long hours	3.9
Ability to undertake systematic planning	5.7	Mathematical skills	3.7
Patience	5.6	Survival skills, being able to protect one's self and one's position from others	3.4
Developing and maintaining sponsor and consumer satisfaction	5.6	Developing and maintaining social relationships with work associates	3.2
Willingness to take risks	5.5	Building a power base	2.9

[a]Based on a scale of 7 = very important and 1 = not at all important.

leaders, the social psychologists have been researching the form in which such power is manifested. Power is a key ingredient of almost all human relationships, person to person or system to system. To many, the word *power* has a negative connotation. It is frequently allied with negative acts. Power readily comes to mind when one discusses the role of a dictator, but it is rarely considered when one speaks of the relationship of a parent and child. Yet in both cases, real and considerable power exists; its value is determined in the light of the situation in which it is manifested. Thus, people have defined power in many ways; here we will define power as the capacity of an individual or group of individuals to modify the conduct of other individuals or groups in a desired manner, and to prevent one's own conduct from being modified in a way that is not desired.[32] In other words, power is A's ability to modify the behavior of B in A's desired direction without altering A's own behavior.

The use of power in organizational life

is always in evidence. In fact, for many it is the elixir of managerial life:

> Whatever else organizations may be (problem-solving instruments, socio-technical systems, reward systems, and so on), they are political structures. This means that organizations operate by distributing authority and setting a stage for the exercise of power. It is no wonder, therefore, that individuals who are highly motivated to secure and use power find a familiar and hospitable environment in business.[33]

How is such power manifested by leaders? The classic sources of power used by leaders are:

Position power or *legitimate power* derives from the position of a leader in the organizational hierarchy due to ownership and/or appointment or election. It includes the power accruing due to possession of information, veto powers, and power to set policy.

Coercive power is based upon the followers' fear of punishment and the leader's power to inflict it.

Reward power is based upon the follower's expectation of positive rewards and the leader's power to grant them.

Connection power is related to "who you know" in the system.

Expertise power is derived from followers' and others' deference due to leader's special knowledge or skills.

Referent or *charismatic power* is based upon followers' and others' identification with the leader due to personal traits or characteristics.[34]

It seems appropriate to divide power into two types: *authority power* and *influence power*. Although this differentiation is a bit difficult to clarify, we are aware that those who have been given certain positions—such as a president, commissioner, mayor, chief executive officer—do have the authority to initiate and enforce policy; sign bills, contracts, and legal documents; and issue directives. These privileges represent the use of authority. In the history of research into organizational leadership, many authors have cited the importance of authority:

> Legitimate authority is the basis of all organization.[35]

> Legitimate authority is relative, not absolute.[36]

Some writers have questioned the effectiveness of authority:

Glendower: I can call spirits from the vasty deep.

Hotspur: Why, so can I, or so can any man; But will they come when you do call for them?[37]

Even one of the pioneers in the science of management raised a question concerning the effectiveness of authority when that is the only power used:

> Now a most significant fact of general observation relative to authority is the extent to which it is ineffective in specific instances. It is so ineffective that the violation of authority is accepted as a matter of course and its implications are not considered.[38]

In the last few years it has become increasingly evident that leaders cannot expect to achieve goals without a much greater use of the power of *influence*. This has been reinforced by an increase in worker power.[39] References to the lessening of management authority power are evident in both professional studies and the daily newspaper. Some of the more obvious ways in which limits on a leader's power are manifested are:[40]

Collective power derives from subordinates' membership in a union or informal association of workers which can collectively alter leader behavior or prevent the leader or the organization from reaching objectives.

Legal powers emanate from laws governing the treatment of employees or their associations regarding selection, hours, pay, race, sex, national origin, religion, fringe benefits, and working conditions (safety and health).

Referent or *charismatic power* is based upon subordinates' influence on the leader, superiors, and co-workers, due to personal traits.

Affluence power derives from the reduction of subordinates' inclination to resist change or quit their jobs, and through absenteeism, tardiness, and threats to violate leaders' rules or company policy.

Expert power derives from leaders' and organizations' dependence upon subordinates' expertise, special skills, or knowledge. Included is power accruing to difficult-to-replace personnel.

In the light of such reality, the leader needs to develop competence in various influence processes. This is considered to be the highest skill developed by human beings. Robert Carcuff has devised a model (see Figure 5-4) that illustrates this principle.

In developing the use of influencing skills, these methods are relevant:

Legitimatization. Your role in the organization is clear, understood, and relevant.

Knowledge. Your behavior is such as to demonstrate appropriate knowledge, and you are up to date on the latest practices in your field.

Reference groups. Your influence is related to those people in the system with whom you can coordinate and collaborate in providing effective problem solving.

Competency. Your influence is closely related to competency to do your job, and to relate to peers and colleagues.

Openness in communication. Your influence is related to the degree to which you openly share and channel communications, as well as the manner in which you develop trust by your leveling behavior.

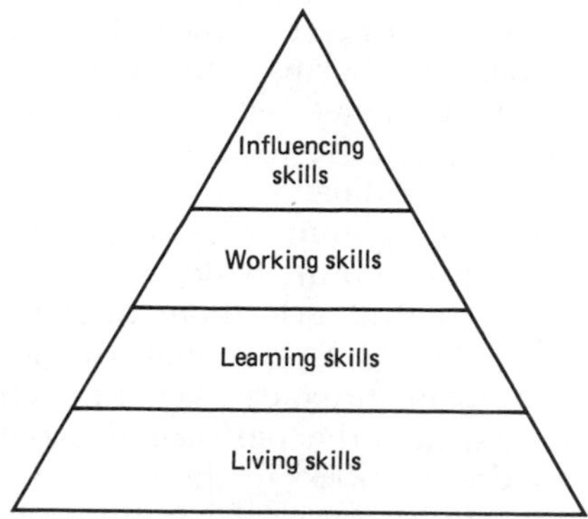

Figure 5-4 Hierarchy of Skills[41]

Those relationships a person has with others in an organization has an effect on influence power: "The real basis of a person's authority (or perhaps better, his influence) is his professional reputation among his peers and associations."[42]

We are always attempting to influence others. In human systems the concept of *influence* refers to the process through which the behavior of an individual or group is directed by others, usually within the context of superior/subordinate relationships. Influence is quite a general phenomenon in that it subsumes that a variety of particular types of influence are possible, such as the use of physical coercion, legal authority, social pressure, skill and expertise, and personal charisma. In this context, the concept of *leadership* refers to the use of influence by a leader for the purpose of effectively mobilizing followers; *power* is distinguished by being a latent potential, or capability for influence through reward or punishment, rather than through actual implementation.

One of the major issues in contemporary thinking about the relationship of people to an organization is the degree to which the organization infringes on their private lives.[43] Nevertheless, whether voluntary or coerced, acceptance of organizational goals and norms depends to a large degree on the perceived legitimacy of attempts by superiors to influence the behavior of subordinates. A key element of the culture of all human systems is the system of norms, and the basic values and assumptions that underlie them. Such values and norms deal with the goals of the system, the means to be employed in achieving these goals, the performance obligations of the members of the organization, and the "correct" way of handling the resources of the organization. These values and norms define how superiors will deal with subordinates, how closely they will supervise them, and in what areas they will attempt to influence them.

Although influence has been studied usefully from many viewpoints, an aspect of particular significance is the matter of legitimacy. Influence is legitimate when it is believed to be just and rightful, so much so that subordinates are prepared to comply because they believe they should do so. Legitimacy is the sine qua non for the successful use of power.[44] The effectiveness of influence ultimately rests upon maintaining the support of colleagues and subordinates. When legitimacy is lost, the influence of the leader easily may wane, as dramatically illustrated by recent events in corporations, political parties, and certain Third World nations.

In modern, complex societies, the methods of exerting influence are not as simple as they once were. In an earlier era, autocratic power generally was a clearly understood factor, because it was backed by force, physical or financial. Modern systems, however, usually must rely upon persuasion, reason, and self-interest to obtain compliance. Thus, available sources of influence seem to be growing increasingly subtle and intangible, causing the question of legitimacy to be of increasing interest: "The issue then is not whether influence occurs, and whether such influence is considered to be legitimate, but what the boundaries of the area of legitimacy are for different groups and organizations."[45]

Schein and Ott[46] have measured and analyzed attitudes concerning the legitimacy of supervisors influencing various types of subordinate behavior. Other studies have subsequently utilized this same conceptual framework to investigate different aspects of the topic. Schein and Lippitt[47] correlated supervisory attitudes toward the legitimacy of influence with key organizational variables; Davis[48] studied attitudes toward managerial efforts to influence employees; Heizer[49] surveyed the legitimacy of influence among minorities; Kemp[50] investigated the relationship between legitimacy and leadership; and Bedian[51] provided a cross-cultural comparison between the attitudes of managers in the United States and Germany. The original list of sixty-five questions was used in all these studies, and it dealt with:

Leisure time with subordinates
Faithful to spouse
Attitude toward savings
Drinks at home
Affiliation with clubs
Leisure time with superiors
Use of credit
Donation to charity
Leisure time with peers
Personal friends
Friendship in rival company
Life insurance
Location of residence
Attitude toward smoking
Ownership of home
Amount of entertaining
Type of home
Employment of spouse
Choice of spouse
Type of car
Political party
Number of children
Children's school
Choice of charge accounts

Vacation plans
Church attendance
Alcohol during work
Working hours
Temperament on job
Getting along with people
Tidiness of office
Criticism of company
Family calls
Job-related education
Use of profane language
Use of working time
Job-related reading
New job relocation
Alcohol during lunch
Supervision of secretary
Type of clothing
Form of addressing colleagues
Help in recruiting
Formality of clothing
Attitude toward unions
Competition with peers
Taking work home
Use of company products
Public activities
Company social functions
Sexual morality
Organizational politics
Organizational athletics
Attitude toward money
Wearing beard or moustache

The latest study[52] using these specific items of inquiry was completed 13 years after the original exploration by Schein and Ott, with results that are similar to those first determined; types of subordinate behavior more directly work-related tend to be considered legitimate to influence, personal areas generally were regarded as illegitimate to influence.

One of the more important findings, however, concerned changes in legitimacy that have occurred during the period since the first study was completed. The vast majority of the behavioral items in the list above showed a decrease in legitimacy, while only a few items increased in legitimacy. The magnitude of change was much greater for instances of decreasing legitimacy than for the few cases of increased legitimacy. On the basis of this evidence, the researchers conclude that significant decreases in legitimacy appear to have occurred during the period from 1962 through 1975 for large organizations in urban areas of the northeastern United States, where the study was conducted.

The greatest decreases were related to "attitudes toward unions," "company social functions," "public activities," and "sexual morality"—all of which decreased by more than 50 index points. It seems likely that the observed decreases in legitimacy reflect changes in attitudes that occurred over a dozen years. Increased economic security, changes in morality, higher educational level, lessening of the work ethic, stronger enforcement of rights for minorities, the more active role for women, affirmative action, privacy legislation, and decreasing trust of institutions and their leaders—all are key factors to be considered.

This trend toward decreasing legitimacy of various areas of influence does not necessarily imply that looser forms of influence are steering our organizations into chaos. Too great a loss of managerial control is so obviously dysfunctional that it could destroy an organizational system. A more reasonable expectation is that supervisors will hold subordinates accountable for work-related *outcomes* (that is, their job performance proper) rather than their non-work-related behavior. This could contribute to recently observed trends toward the development of more sophisticated leadership techniques for complex organizations, such as the use of *management by objectives, improved quality of work life, autonomous work teams,* and other alternative approaches to working relationships that attempt to engage subordinates in assuming more responsibility for the outcome of their working roles, in return for less supervision. The implication here is

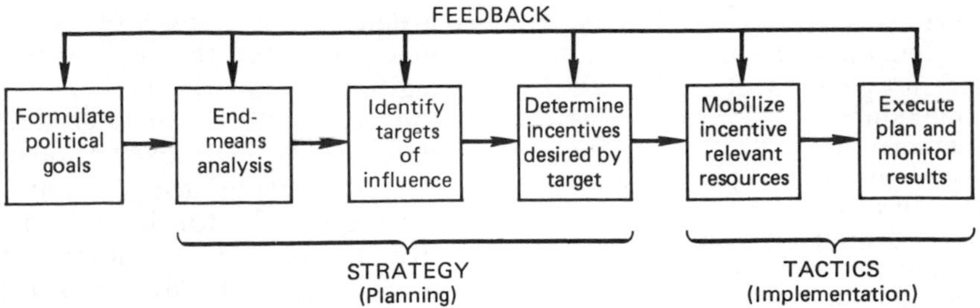

Figure 5-5 The Process of Management Influence[53]

the need for skills of influence in collaboration, rather than Machiavellian machinations. But using the power of influence can be anything but haphazard (see Figure 5-5).

While they were examining what they referred to as *political influence* in an organization, this manifestation of influence seems relevant to other leadership efforts. It might be well, in the light of new interest in using leadership to initiate change, to reflect that all of us use different strategies and tactics to bring about change. An instrument has been developed that helps us take a look at six different ways of exercising influence; the forty-eight items in this analysis form cover six distinct modes of wielding influence:[54]

1. Traditional, ethical, normal methods
2. Direct attempts to influence a superior
3. Manipulation of the formal system and structure
4. Aggressive actions
5. Use of external resources and persons
6. Waiting for the organizational milieu to change*

The use of such tactics will depend upon the individual's value system, skills, importance of the issue or problem, nature of the situation, kind of organization, and the style of the superior(s). In addition, we need to recognize that the use of power to effect change sooner or later involves the dynamics of conflict;† as well as collaboration, compromise, competition, withdrawal, accommodation, and other behavioral reactions when confronting the power politics of problem solving and change.

IDENTIFYING AND DEVELOPING LEADERS

Thus, although organizational management usually requires an extraordinary measure of leadership, in the connotation of guiding, influencing, and directing the behavior of others, such leadership in and of itself does not constitute all the needed skills, learning, and abilities organizations require. And successful leaders—those we call executives in the marketplace—although not born with executive leadership, or managerial talents, seem to have trod a somewhat similar upward path. Marvin D. Dunnette summarizes some major studies of executive predictability as follows:[55]

> Intelligence seems uniformly to be important wherever studied.
>
> Effective executives tend to show personalities characterized by dominance, self-confidence, and manip-

*These tactics are discussed in greater detail in Chapter 11.

†The dynamics of conflict is discussed in Chapter 6.

Table 5–4
Leadership Abilities at Stages of Organizational Development[56]

Critical Concern	Knowledge	Skills	Attitudes
To create a system	Clearly perceived short-range objective in mind of top man	Ability to transmit knowledge into action by self and into orders to others	Belief in own ability, product, and market
To survive	The short-range objectives that need to be communicated	Communications know-how; ability to adjust to changing conditions	Faith in future
To stabilize	How top man can predict relevant factors and make long-range plans	Ability to transmit planning knowledge into communicable objectives	Trust in other members of organization
To earn good reputation	Planning know-how and understanding of goals on part of whole executive team	Facility of allowing others a voice in decision making, involving others in decision making and obtaining commitments from them, and communicating objectives to customers	Interest in customers
To achieve uniqueness	Understanding on part of policy team of how others should set own objectives, and of how to manage subunits of the organization	Ability to teach others to plan; proficiency in integrating plans of subunits into objectives and resources or organization	Self-confidence
To earn respect and appreciation	General management understanding of the larger objectives of organization and of society	Ability to apply own organization and resources to the problems of the larger community	Sense of responsibility to society and mankind

ulative sociability; they are interested in power, money, and political manipulation . . . a desire for independence emerges quite often.

It appears that effective executives are people who have shown a total life pattern of successful endeavor. They have been good in college, had high socio-economic aspirations; they have been forceful, dominant, assertive, confident kinds of people. Their habit patterns have been rather consistent day-to-day and year-to-year demonstrations of success.

This extends certainly into the school situation, and some of the biographical data suggest that it extends also into the earlier background of the home situation.

We have information that effective executives, their wives, and their families are better educated.

We have evidence of open, less restrictive upbringing in the family situation, greater conscientiousness in school, and a more purposeful and more successful approach to college.

It seems that higher-level executives are persons who seek achievement, autonomy, and recognition more than they seek strictly money or interesting work. This is not to say that they do not appreciate the fact that achievement usually leads to increased material advantage.

Leadership is under the greatest pressure, and most often fails, when certain recognizable, nonfinancial crises occur in the life cycle of the sociotechnical system. Management cannot control the emergence of critical issues; it can only control how they are resolved. Table 5-4 shows some of the knowledge, skills, and attitudes that organizational leaders must bring into play in coping with each critical need, and this may help explain why it is that a person who is an effective leader in the developmental stage may prove to be quite ineffective in another stage.

Although it will be unlikely that an organization will change its type of leadership as each new stage of growth and need arises, it can and will develop a top-level team that will combine the multiple skills and abilities needed at different times and in varied situations. Does this mean that there are no guidelines to help a person improve a potentiality for organizational leadership? No, some focus can be provided out of the many studies in leadership in organizations.

Many variables enter into producing leaders. There are, however, only two forces that influence how a leader arrives at a leadership position. These are illustrated in Figure 5-6. Sometimes people are motivated by personal drives to become leaders; sometimes they find themselves in leadership positions as the result of external forces, of which they may or may not be aware. Usually, both factors are at work.

A more integrated concept of leadership relates the appropriate function of a leader to the kind of organization and the types of situations in which leaders find themselves. It seems, however, that regardless of the type of organization or situation, there is a need for some basic individual goals toward which the person who is attempting to develop leadership attempts to move. Some of these goals have become apparent in recent leadership-training and executive-development conferences:[57]

Insight into self. Some research findings clearly indicate the factor of self-insight as paramount to the healthy personality and, therefore, to the effective leader. Inasmuch as leaders, in the light of their power and influence in many situations, must understand their effect on others, it is essential that they also understand their own feelings and motivations.

A modicum of personal security. Research in the field of mental health indicates the importance of personal security in interpersonal relationships. Certainly, leaders need to have a modicum of such security so as to be nonpunitive in relationships with subordinates and with the groups with which they relate. He or she needs to be able to listen and work effectively with other people without the constant necessity for self-justification. The ability of leaders to behave consistently with their

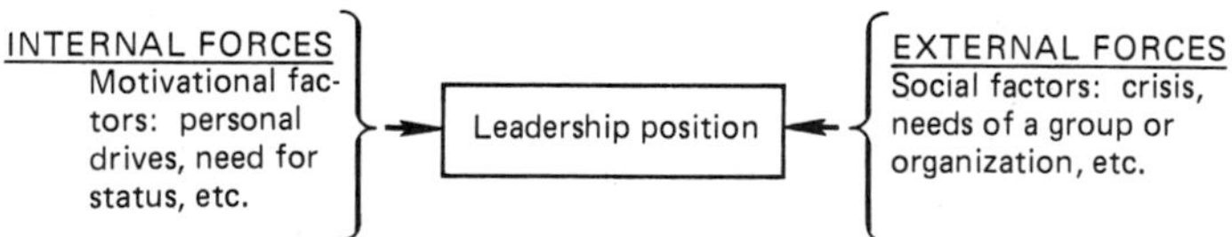

Figure 5-6 Leadership Development

intentions is an outgrowth of personal security and interpersonal skills.

Appropriate sensitivity to situations. Leaders must be sensitive, both emotionally and rationally, to the situations in which they find themselves, and sensitivity to interpersonal relationships—be it with an individual, a group, an organization, or a larger social system—is an important dimension in leadership action.

Diagnostic ability. Leadership is seldom adequate when performed on a "hunch" or "flying-by-the-seat-of-the-pants" basis. Too often, leaders treat symptoms of situations instead of making an adequate diagnosis of causes. The ability to diagnose a situation objectively is a prime "dimension" in any leader's self-development.

Flexibility in one's role relationships. The complexity of the situations in which a leader finds himself makes it necessary to be flexible to changing demands. Such flexibility is not to be confused with being unsure or ambivalent. The concept of role flexibility means the ability to function in the varied roles needed to resolve problems and secure action.

Rational relationships through application of scientific problem solving. To work effectively with others, the leader must practice the problem-solving approach used by scientists. To be sure, the web and fabric of life are emotional relations, but they are susceptible to the application of reason. The ability to understand and live through the application of the scientific process is an achievement toward which the leader must aspire.

Self-actualization and continuous learning. At the top of Abraham Maslow's hierarchy of needs, we find *self-actualization.* This is the same as Karl Menninger's concept of *personal fulfillment.* These terms denote both achievement and value. The way in which an individual discovers the surrounding, larger world and sees that world in perspective, is a basic element of self-actualization. This concept, as used in the field of mental health, is not to be confused with status or recognition. The internal–external dimension of this concept of self-actualization comes from the individual's ability to continue to learn from those associations, experiences, and awareness he encounters throughout his life span. One of the major achievements of any individual, particularly leaders, is learning how to learn. If leaders can learn from failures, frustrations, disappointments, achievements, and despair, they will have found major dimension of leadership.

These basic dimensions of leadership development are not mutually exclusive, nor are they a complete list. They do restore the dimension of personality role, and power to our understanding of leadership, and give some point of reference. In any development of leadership, the target will be the learning and growth of that individual in his or her ability to relate effectively to others in a variety of human situations. Working effectively with others requires many skills and insights; the search for these skills and insights is difficult, but the achievement is a discovery of self, a discovery of the mature person in action, and a discovery of the complexity of human systems.

ORGANIZATION RENEWAL AND LEADERSHIP

The success of organization renewal is dependent upon the behavior of leaders at all levels of the organization. In Figure 5-7, Marvin Weisbord illustrates the central role of leadership.

This tactical execution of "keeping the five boxes in balance" requires collaboration among line managers so that personal or vested interests do not block the attention of the total systems from these important, basic considerations. Can such leaders be developed?

Some aspects of leadership development were derived from a survey of top executives—who were asked to indicate the traits they believed to be essential to a suc-

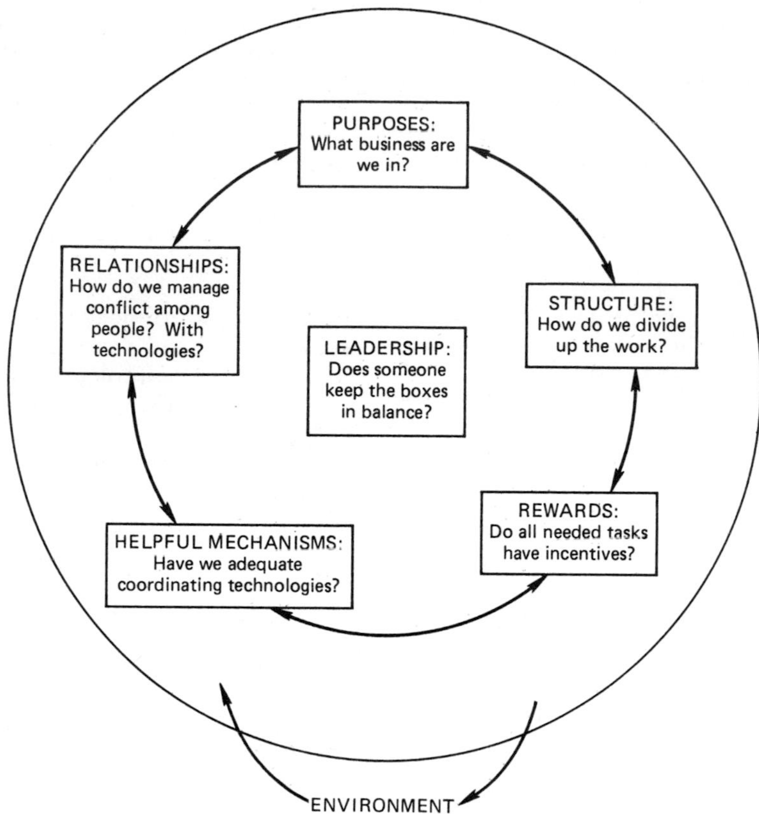

Figure 5-7 The Six-box Organizational Model[58]

cessful manager. Important factors were *people judgment, leadership, commitment, decisiveness,* and *personal drive.*[59] Although this survey covered only a few highly successful leaders in the United States, it has been found that these kinds of factors also show up in studies of leadership in other cultures; but they are expressed differently, behave differently, and emphasized differently in different cultures.[60] Nevertheless, core elements exist.[61]

The capacity to conceptualize. As you take a look at different cultures in terms of managerial leadership, most any culture finds that managers need to have a capacity to conceptualize their role and their function, to distinguish the overall from detail. Good managers can see the whole picture. An effective leader can separate the essential from the tangential, the factual from the inferential, and the hypothesis from the data. So many people get bogged down in excessive information that they do not know the key issue.

The ability to communicate. One of the core capacities for leadership in any culture is the ability to communicate; the ability to speak, write, listen, and read.

The capacity for self-confidence and security. It is difficult to be a leader and not have confidence. You don't see too many shrinking violets—with insecurity or inferiority complexes—being leaders. Leaders seek power for social, not personal purposes.

The capacity to command. Perhaps that is

a poor use of the word. Leaders do not really command anybody. Although leaders do a lot by influence and indirection, as in any leadership position, they also give directions. There are four elements involved in the capacity to command. The manager must direct work effectively, inspire cooperative effort, encourage high standards of performance, and build a productive relationship.

The capacity to initiate and sustain action. The ability to initiate action and get results is essential. This does not mean that you do all the work, but it does mean that you persevere despite discouragement. A manager must give leadership despite frustrations and disappointment.

The capacity for having and living by a sound value system. McGregor's theory X and theory Y were based on his thesis that people tend to manage from the point of view of their value system. It has nothing to do with bad or good. People lead according to their beliefs. Why is certain behavior right? Because we believe it. Why do we believe it? Because we value it.

Harry Levinson feels that no one person has all the qualities of an ideal leader. Real people are like diamonds—with facets of personality, and flaws. He feels that leadership competencies revolve about thinking, interpersonal relationships, and outward behavior characteristics.[62]

The needs, attributes, and competencies of leaders are complex, but identifiable. They may differ in degree but not in the essence of their manifestations. Leaders are indeed *made,* not *born.* The vital issue is how we can make better and more effective leaders to help individuals, groups, and organizations to mature and renew.

SUMMARY

Leadership and the relevant use of power is of concern when exploring the potential for renewal. Many philosophers, scholars, writers, and researchers have attempted to define the elusive concept of leadership. In today's world the leader will tend to use influence more than authority to accomplish goals. Different situations will require different approaches to the exercise of leadership. One of the skills needed is to assess the situation and the process so as to choose the appropriate leadership response. There is no one right way to lead or manage. A leader must be competent in a number of roles. It is important to know that leaders are made, not born. The search is for ways to develop leaders more effectively so that renewal is initiated, encouraged, and supported by competent and mature persons.

QUESTIONS

1. Identify four effective leaders you have known. What made them effective? What common behaviors did they possess? In what ways were they unlike?
2. In what areas do you find it appropriate for superiors to influence your performance and/or behavior? What areas are inappropriate?
3. Examine some operational situations:
   a. When is it appropriate to *tell* people what to do?
   b. When is it appropriate to *sell* someone on a course of action?
   c. When is it appropriate to *consult* with others before taking an action?
   d. When is it appropriate to *join* in a group decision-making approach?
   e. When is it appropriate to *delegate* the action to another person?
4. What do you feel are the best ways to identify effective leadership?
5. What do you feel are the best methods for selecting and/or promoting someone to a leadership position?

NOTES

[1]James MacGregor Burns, *Leadership* (New York: Harper & Row, Publishers, Inc., 1978);

summarized in book review by Ron Brandt in *Educational Leadership,* March 1979, p. 379.

[2]Robert Greenleaf, *Servant Leadership: A Journey into the Nature of Legitimate Power and Greatness* (New York: Paulist Press, 1977), p. 8.

[3]Meg Greenfield, "Leadership Chic," *The Washington Post,* October 17, 1979, p. 14.

[4]E. F. Schumacher, *Small Is Beautiful: Economics As If People Mattered* (New York: Harper & Row, Publishers, Inc., 1973), p. 12.

[5]Magazine section, *The New York Times,* April 13, 1972, p. 38.

[6]Emmet Hughes, *The Ordeal of Power: A Political Memoir of the Eisenhower Years* (New York: Atheneum Publishers, 1963), p. 124.

[7]Antony Jay, *Management and Machiavelli: An Inquiry into the Politics of Corporate Life* (New York: Holt, Rinehart and Winston, 1967), p. 171.

[8]John Gunther, *Inside Russia Today* (New York: Harper & Brothers, 1957), p. 125.

[9]Adapted from Gordon Lippitt, "Commentary on Leadership," *Educational Leadership,* March 1979, pp. 398–399.

[10]Ralph M. Stogdill, *Handbook of Leadership* (New York: The Free Press, 1974).

[11]Charles Perrow, *Complex Organizations: A Critical Essay* (Glenview, Ill.: Scott, Foresman and Company, 1972), p. 8.

[12]John B. Miner, *The Uncertain Future of the Leadership Concept: An Overview* (paper presented at the Third Leadership Symposium, Southern Illinois University at Carbondale, March 1975).

[13]Morgan W. McCall, Jr., and Michael M. Lombardo (eds.), *Leadership: Where Else Can We Go?* (Durham, N.C.: Duke University Press, 1978).

[14]Michael Maccoby, *The Gamesmen* (New York: Simon and Shuster, 1977), p. 12.

[15]Jack R. Gibb, "The Message from Research," in J. William Pfeiffer and John E. Jones (eds.), *The 1974 Annual Handbook for Group Facilitators* (La Jolla, Calif.: University Associates, Inc., 1974), p. 26.

[16]Ibid., p. 160.

[17]Adapted from Gordon Lippitt, "What Do We Know about Leadership?" *NEA Journal,* December 1965.

[18]See, for example, Fred Fiedler, *A Theory of Leadership Effectiveness* (New York: McGraw-Hill Book Company, 1967). For popular treatment, see Fred Fiedler and Martin Chemers, *Leadership and Effective Management* (Glenview, Ill.: Scott, Foresman and Company, 1974).

[19]Abraham Zaleznik, "Managers and Leaders: Are They Different?" *Harvard Business Review,* May–June 1977, p. 67.

[20]David G. Bowers, *Systems of Organizations* (Ann Arbor, Mich.: University of Michigan Press, 1967), p. 18.

[21]Warren H. Schmidt, *The Leader Looks at the Styles of Leadership* (Looking into Leadership Monographs; Washington, DC: Leadership Resources, Inc., 1961), p. 4.

[22]Rensis Likert, *The Human Organization* (New York: McGraw-Hill Book Company, 1967), p. 11.

[23]Adapted from Gordon Lippitt, "Leadership—A Mix of Many Ingredients," *Nations Cities* (publication of the National League of Cities), July 1967; and Gordon Lippitt, "Changing Concepts of Managerial Leadership," *IMC Bulletin* (publication of the National Council of Industrial Management Clubs of the YMCA), January 1967.

[24]Carl Rogers, *On Becoming a Person* (Boston: Houghton Mifflin Company, 1961).

[25]This concept is an elaboration of the work of Dale Zand at New York University.

[26]Ron Zembe, "What Are High-Achieving Managers Really Like?" *Training/HRD,* February 1979, p. 35.

[27]Frank Ephraim, *Trust Formation in Work Groups in a Government Agency* (unpublished paper: Washington, DC: The George Washington University, 1964).

[28]H. Igor Ansoff and R. G. Brandenburn, *The General Manager of the Future* (paper presented at the Conference of American Society for Training and Development, April 1968).

[29]*Executive Role Study* (Washington, D.C.: Civilian Personnel Office, Navy Department, 1978).

[30]SES Candidate Development Program, Office of Personnel Management, U.S. Government, 1979, Addendum A., p. 8.

[31]Ibid., Attachment No. 1.

[32]Richard H. Tawney, *Equality*, 4th ed. (London: George Allen & Unwin Ltd., 1952), p. 175.

[33]Abraham Zaleznik, "Power Politics in Organizational Life," *Harvard Business Review,* May–June 1970, p. 47.

[34]John R. P. French and Bertram H. Raven, "The Basis for Social Power," in Darwin Cartright, *Studies in Social Power* (Ann Arbor, Mich.: Institute for Social Research, University of Michigan, 1959), pp. 150–167.

[35]Peter Blau, *Exchange and Power in Social Life* (New York: John Wiley & Sons, Inc., 1964), p. 23.

[36]Douglas McGregor, in Carolyn McGregor and Warren Bennis (eds.) *The Professional Manager* (New York: McGraw-Hill Book Company, 1967), p. 138.

[37]William Shakespeare, *Henry IV.*

[38]Chester Barnard, *The Functions of the Executive* (Cambridge, Mass.: Harvard University Press, 1938), p. 161.

[39]David Mechanic, "Sources of Power of Lower Participants in Complex Organizations," in Harold J. Leavitt and Louise R. Pondy (eds.), *Readings in Managerial Psychology,* 2nd ed. (Chicago: University of Chicago Press, 1973).

[40]James Lee, "Leader Power for Managing Change," *Academy of Management Review,* January 1977, p. 76.

[41]Robert R. Carcuff, *Helping and Human Relations* (New York: Holt, Rinehart and Winston, 1969), p. 87.

[42]William G. Scoll, *Organization Concepts and Analysis* (Encino, Calif.: Dickenson Publishing Company, Inc., 1969), p. 44.

[43]Adapted from Edgar H. Schein and Gordon Lippitt, "Supervisory Attitudes toward the Legitimacy of Influencing Subordinates," *The Journal of Applied Behavioral Science,* Vol. 2, No. 2, 1966, 194–209. Hereafter cited as Schein and Lippitt.

[44]William E. Hallal and Ghiyath F. Naskshbendi, *Dynamics of the Legitimacy of Influence* (unpublished paper; Washington, D.C.: The George Washington University, November 1979).

[45]Edgar H. Schein and J. Steven Ott, "The Legitimacy of Organizational Influence," *American Journal of Sociology,* Vol. 62, May 1962, 682.

[46]Ibid., p. 685.

[47]Schein and Lippitt, p. 201.

[48]Keith Davis, "Attitudes toward the Legitimacy of Management Efforts to Influence Employees," *Academy of Management Journal,* Vol. 11, June 1968, 153–162.

[49]Jay H. Heizer and Donald H. Litton, "Some Negro and White Views of Organizational Legitimacy," *Southern Journal of Business,* Vol 7, August 1972, 1–7.

[50]Wayne B. Kemp, "Organizational Influence and Its Relation to Perceived Leader Behavior," in Thad B. Green and Dennis F. Ray (eds.), *Management in an Age of Rapid Technological and Social Change* (Blacksburg, Va.: Southern Management Association, 1973), pp. 52–59.

[51]Arthur G. Bedian, "A Comparison and Analysis of German and United States Managerial Attitudes toward the Legitimacy of Organizational Influence," *Academy of Management Journal,* Vol. 18, No. 4, 1975, 897–904.

[52]Ibid.; adapted by Arthur G. Bedian and William E. Hallal in 1980 as an unpublished paper.

[53]Bronston T. Mayes and Robert W. Allen, "Toward a Definition of Organizational Politics," *Academy of Management Review,* October 1977, p. 626.

[54]Leslie E. This, *Method/Tactics to Secure Organization Support for Change Analysis Form* (instrument; Washington, D.C.: Development Publications, 1974).

[55]Marvin D. Dunnette, in Frederick R. Wickert and Dalton E. Mcfarland (eds.), *Measuring Executive Effectiveness* (New York: Appleton-Century-Crofts, 1967), p. 40.

[56]Gordon Lippitt and Warren H. Schmidt, "Crisis in a Developing Organization," *Harvard Business Review,* November-December 1967, p. 110.

[57]Gordon Lippitt, "Elements of Leadership Growth," *Leadership in Action* (NTL Reading Series; Washington, D.C.: National Education Association, 1961), p. 23.

[58]Marvin R. Weisbord, "Six-Box Method," *Organization Diagnosis: A Workbook of Theory and Practice* (Reading, Mass.: Addison-Wesley Publishing Company, Inc., 1978), p. 4.

[59]Corporate Managerial Development Program (New York: General Electric Corporation, 1978), p. 12.

[60]Bernard M. Bass, *Technical Report 60: Norms*

on Exercise Objectives of Managers from Thirteen Countries as of September 1972 (Rochester, N.Y.: Management Research Center, University of Rochester, 1972).

[61]Henry Mintzberg, *The Nature of Managerial Work* (New York: Harper & Row, Publishers, Inc., 1973), Chap. 5.

[62]Harry Levinson, "Criteria for Choosing Chief Executives," *Harvard Business Review,* July–August 1980, pp. 113–120.

6

managing stress, conflict, and agreement

Successful activity, no matter how intense, leaves you with comparatively few "scars"; it causes stress *but little, if any,* distress.

Hans Selye, M.D., 1907[1]

The stability of a society . . . depends on whether its proclivity for generating conflict is or is not balanced by its ability to resolve or contain the conflict that it generates.

Sir Geoffrey Vickers, 1906[2]

Any change—even a planned or pleasant change—produces stress in the human systems affected by the change. In Figure 6-1, stress is seen as the generating force that develops within human systems a need for coping, which, in turn, is a key element in the ability of human systems to renew themselves. For an individual, group, or organization to examine and channel stress into coping behavior requires personal and situational data collection. Data collection, however, is not enough. There is also a need to clarify the issues causing stress, and to confront these issues with appropriate modes of behavior that are either in conflict or agreement.

LOOKING AT STRESS

In a number of the literature sources, we are presented the evidence of increasing stress on human systems. Some of this evidence is at the global level and is reflected in Alvin Toffler's pertinent observations about the rapid and complex changes—technological, social, and economic—that make it exceedingly difficult to cope.[3] Sol Levine and Norman A. Scotch picture increased stress in interrelated societies confronted with such problems as energy shortage, inflation, and population explosion.[4] Some researchers see a direct relationship between the stress occurring in individuals, groups, and organizations—and our industrialized society.[5] This theme is also found in the writings of Jay Anthony and William H. Whyte, Jr., as they portray the effects on line managers from the problems of modern bureaucracies in our large organizations.[6,7] Eugene Jennings and Michael Maccoby also discuss how the effective line manager not only achieves a mark of success by coping with stress, but actually thrives on it.[8,9]

Hans Selye indicates that there is *good* and *bad* stress.[10] In a sense, to live a life completely devoid of stress may be unexciting, nonchallenging, and unproductive (see Figure 6-2). Stress is a natural part of

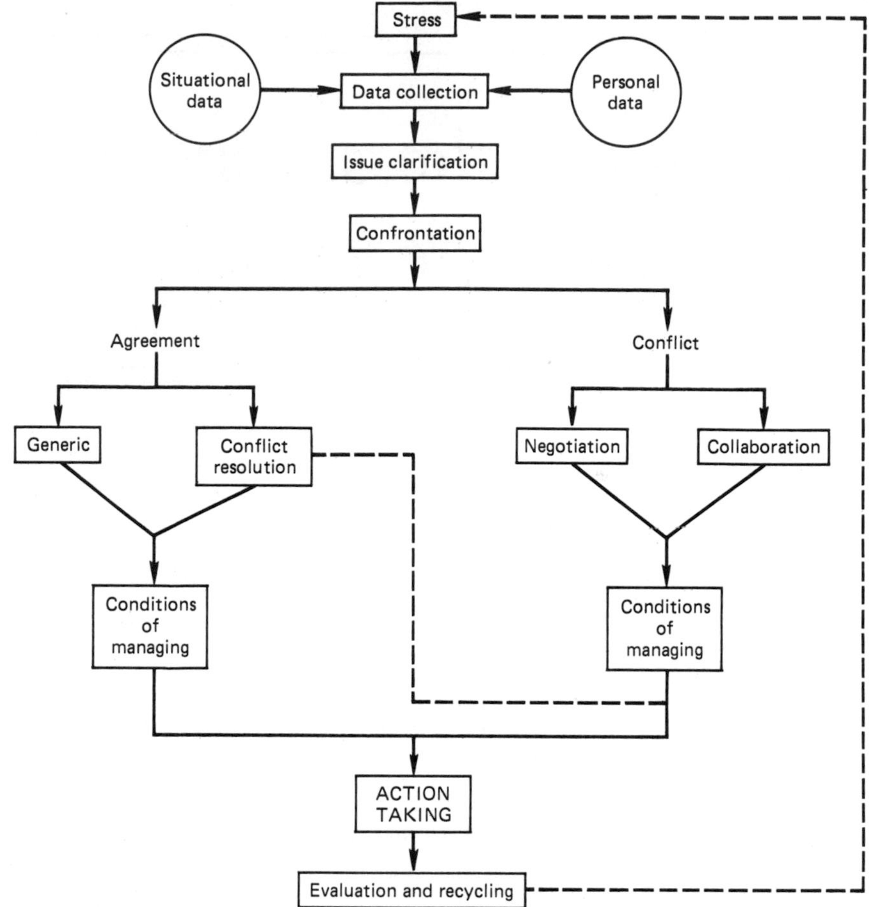

Figure 6-1 Model for coping with conflict and agreement

human functioning; the productivity of individuals, groups, and organizations is best under circumstances of moderate or optimal amounts of stress, but there is a need to differentiate between a reasonable amount of stress—and too much.

In this context, Selye postulates that there are a variety of environmental events or *stresses* that produce a specific pattern of physical reaction. If this reaction is too long continued, it can result in what Selye calls a "disease of adaptation," a condition that soon spills over into a dysfunction, such as cardiovascular disease. In attempting to link these behavioral and physiological views of stress, Michael Matteson and John Ivanevich define stress as a personal or internal experience creating within an individual a physiological or psychological imbalance.[11]

In enlarging upon this thesis and applying it to all human systems, it is appropriate to say that stress is an external or internal event that causes a disequilibrium in a system, thus creating a condition of homeostasis that can be overtly aided by the process of coping. But

(a) a great variety of environmental conditions are capable of producing

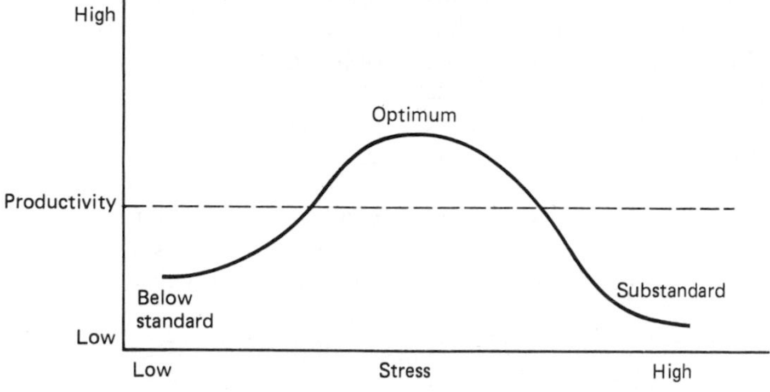

Figure 6-2 Stress and productivity

stress, (b) different individuals respond to the same conditions in different ways, (c) the intensity and the extent of the stress state within the person are difficult to predict, (d) the outcomes of prolonged stress may be physiological and behavioral, and (e) the consequences of prolonged stress may include chronic diseases.[12]*

There are differences in the amount of stress that causes dysfunctioning of the individual; they are based on such factors as heredity, personality, habits, and past accidents and illnesses:

> It has become increasingly apparent that stress is important as a factor in illness in general and chronic illness in particular. Many present day illnesses cannot be explained in terms of a single "cause." Research suggests that a significant portion of the population seeking medical care is suffering from stress-based illness.[13]

Aside from the physical defects it may cause, stress should also be explored for its effects on decision making, productivity, creativity, interpersonal relations, and the management of organizations.

*Although these conditions are cited for individuals, it seems possible that the same may be true of groups and organizations.

STRESS IN THE INDIVIDUAL

Events in one's life—such as a divorce, new work assignment, personal injury, or trouble with the boss—can produce stress and strain. Similarly, circumstances in the larger arena of society—such as inflation, lines at gasoline stations, or pollution—can induce stress and its physiological consequences. Studies of the effects of stress on health and an individual's competence caused the researchers to conclude:

> We found that the events of ordinary life—marriage, a vacation, a new job—can help trigger illness, because the effort required to cope with these events weakens resistance. The findings challenge our ideas about disease, and about the roles that psychology and sociology play in health. Perhaps illness is not just an interruption, a condition to be tended by a medical specialist before one picks up where normal life left off. Perhaps, instead, illness is a predictable result of life conditions. It may be that effective treatment of disease requires analysis of choices and actions, along with medical therapies.[14]

In another experiment, 394 persons were asked to rate the amount of social adjustment required to cope with forty-three different life events. In Table 6-1, the scale value of each event reflects the amount of stress and disruption it might cause in the life of an average human being. It is believed that an accumulation of more than 200 units during a year might cause some individuals to exceed their level of stress tolerance. Since individuals do vary in the tolerance of stress, these figures should be taken only as a rough guide:

In follow-up research on the original group of 394, expanded by additional persons, it was found that the odds of incurring a severe chronic illness within two years of accumulating a certain number of stress points was about four out of five. See chart below.

150 to 199 stress points	Mild	37%
200 to 299 stress points	Moderate	51%
300 or more points	Severe	79%

Table 6-1
Social-Readjustment Rating Scale[15]

Rank	Life Event	Mean Value	Rank	Life Event	Mean Value
1	Death of spouse	100	23	Son or daughter leaving home	29
2	Divorce	73	24	Trouble with in-laws	29
3	Marital separation	65	25	Outstanding personal achievement	28
4	Jail term	63	26	Wife begins or stops work	26
5	Death of close family member	63	27	Begin or end school	26
6	Personal injury or illness	53	28	Change in living conditions	25
7	Marriage	50	29	Revision of personal habits	24
8	Fired at work	47	30	Trouble with boss	23
9	Marital reconciliation	45	31	Change in work hours or conditions	20
10	Retirement	45	32	Change in residence	20
11	Change in health of family member	44	33	Change in schools	20
12	Pregnancy	40	34	Change in recreation	19
13	Sex difficulties	39	35	Change in church activities	19
14	Gain of new family member	39	36	Change in social activities	18
15	Business readjustment	39	37	Mortgage or loan less than $10,000	17
16	Change in financial state	38	38	Change in sleeping habits	16
17	Death of close friend	37	39	Change in number of family get-togethers	15
18	Change to different line of work	36	40	Change in eating habits	15
19	Change in number of arguments with spouse	35	41	Vacation	13
20	Mortgage over $10,000	31	42	Christmas	12
21	Foreclosure of mortgage or loan	30	43	Minor violations of the law	11
22	Changes in responsibilities at work	29			

A person's response to the accumulation of a relatively large number of stress points in a twelve-month period will vary according to self-knowledge, past experience with stress, breadth of interests, and coping skills.

Another view of stress in the individual results from examining the fundamental stages of transitions in a human life span. A classical theory of personality points out eight crucial conflicts during the stages of childhood, adolescence, and adulthood; and for the adult these conflicts are:[16]

Intimacy. Starting in the early twenties, this involves the establishment of genuine intimacy with a mate while attempting to establish a career.

Generativity. This is the turning outward of awareness that occurs in the forties and fifties—including parental interests, aiding in the development of skills in the younger generation, and extending one's creativity through others.

Ego integration. The age of the sixties, in which one philosophizes, reminisces, and realizes that the years gone by are a part of history.

During the past decade there has been a surge of interest in studying more closely the stages of adult development, and one researcher has identified six passages:[17]

16–22	Pulling up roots
22–29	Provisional adulthood
29–32	The "age 30" transition
32–39	Rooting
39–43	Midlife transition
43–50	Reestablishization and flowering

Daniel Levinson's study of this concept of transitions (or passages) was limited to adult *males,* with results that again emphasize the relationship between potential stress and passing from one life stage to another.[18] Harry Levinson thinks the age of 35 is a crucial midpoint in an executive's life, because it is the beginning of life's *second half,* the point at which mortality becomes a reality, and the facing of personal limitations is unavoidable. Fear of defeat and pains of rivalry lurk, and available positions upward begin to narrow.[19] It has been noted by Eugene Jennings that a change in executive responsibilities occur at this time, so that the work role gradually passes from technical to operational/managerial.[20] In the late thirties and early forties an executive may be expected to go through a crisis of values, failure of meaning, or feelings of incompetence. He or she may be "burned out" by the success-oriented life. By the age of 50, an executive will need to have coped with such an outer crisis period, and to have reached a plateau of individuality, developing a distinct style of behavior that establishes a unique individual. John D. Adams has developed a model showing a helpful way to look at this extraordinary challenge (see Figure 6-3).

The context of the "givens" inherent in any situation may serve to diffuse or to intensify stress. These givens include: (a) the personal characteristics and background of the individual; (b) situational factors; and (c) quality of support. We inherit strengths and weaknesses or develop them through good or bad personal habits, accidents, or abuses.

With an awareness of one's orientations and idiosyncracies, one has more choices available relative to avoiding overly stressful situations. Moreover, the nature of the organization one works in can either heighten or reduce stress levels. Factors such as the number of deadlines, manner of facing crises or the frequency and nature of client demands all need to be considered as to their role in increasing or decreasing stress.

Finally, people working in an environment lacking in social support tend to have more health and emotional problems than people working in more

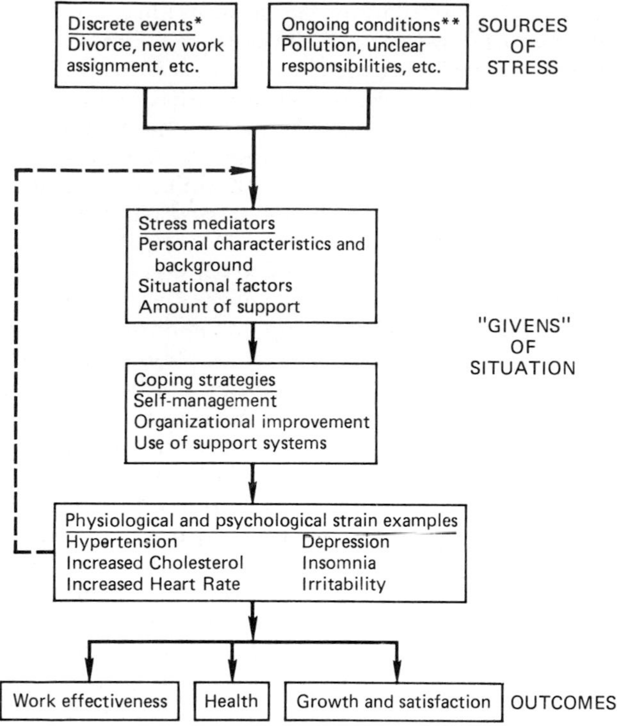

Figure 6-3 Experience of stress[21]

> supportive settings. We usually cannot easily change these factors (personality, nature of organization, quality of support) but the manager needs to develop an understanding of how they affect stress levels in order to promote effective [coping with stress].[22]

An experienced manager usually expects stress, to a certain degree enjoys it, and is used to handling a modicum of it in everyday managerial life. At the level of the individual, Adams feels that there are three ways to manage stress (see Table 6-2).

He refers to self-management, the creation and use of support systems, and the alteration of organizational practices. Self-management comprises individual practices that can aid the person in avoiding unnecessary stress and makes him or her better able to withstand the unavoidable stresses of life. Good nutrition is one of the key long-term prevention practices. Under stress, many people eat either carelessly or compulsively, causing their diets to become unbalanced. Those who had well-balanced diets (balance of dairy, protein, vegetable, and grain groups) enjoyed better health than both those with only somewhat balanced diets and those with poorly balanced diets. Because of the tendency of some people to eat carelessly (and to other dietary idiosyncracies), protein, vitamin, and

*Derived principally from the work of Drs. Thomas Holmes, Richard Rahe, and colleagues (1967).

**Derived principally from the work of Dr. J. R. P. French and colleagues (1972).

Table 6–2
Effective Stress Management[23]

Suggestions for effective stress management
1. Self-management
   A. Vigorous regular exercise
   B. Nutrition
      Good eating habits
      Vitamin and mineral supplements
   C. Letting-go techniques
      Centering and focusing
      Relaxation/meditation/prayer
      Finishing unfinished business
   D. Self-awareness
      Needs, desires, idiosyncracies
      Congruence/assertiveness
   E. Personal planning
      Time management
      Positive life choices
2. Creation and use of support systems
3. Altering stressful organizational norms, policies, and procedures

Characteristics of effective stress managers
1. Self-knowledge—strengths/skills/liabilities
2. Varied interests—many sources of satisfaction
3. Variety of reactions to stress—repertoire of responses
4. Acknowledgments and acceptance of individual differences
5. Being active and productive

mineral deficiencies are not as uncommon as we sometimes are led to believe. When this happens, one's diet itself becomes a stressor, increasing the likelihood of illness. Vigorous regular exercise is necessary to relieve tensions and to protect health. Some of the frequently recommended exercises include running, swimming, tennis, and bicycling.

It is also important to be self-aware as to the type of situations that are most likely to cause stress. For example, if one fears conflict, it is probably best to avoid a turbulent, technical working environment where new knowledge frequently is being created and where there is little stability in policies and procedures. Or by becoming aware of one's driving and competitive style (which is linked to higher coronary risks), one can undertake to develop a more relaxed approach to activities and develop noncompetitive diversionary habits. Such awareness can be facilitated by an individual through career and life planning.

Adams also emphasizes the fact that we all need other people to turn to for support. Most people have too few relationships they can count on as sources of support. In our complicated world a broad base of support is important. In addition to friends and family, individuals also need people to respect them, challenge them, provide access for them, and to be mentors, evaluators, experts, or energizers.

Before discussing the reduction of organizational stress, it is worth noting that the cultures of most highly developed industrial societies place a great deal of emphasis on achievement. This kind of drive is essential to the success and self-respect of some people, but current studies of stress seem to suggest that achieving persons need help in order to live and mature under the stress of achievement:

> The business executive does not enjoy the plateaus between achievements. He is never satisfied with himself, his success and opportunities; for each new success he posts higher goals for himself. The achievement drive increases geometrically to eventually become insatiable. For this reason he can never relax and enjoy internal rest.[24]

Such a person clearly has strength, while risking chronic health or mental problems when the stress becomes too great. Studying executive stress, defining its dimensions as explicitly as possible, developing appropriate individual, group, and system coping mechanisms, and applying them preventively rather than after the fact, are challenges that few organizations have yet confronted.

The Menninger Foundation suggests

that business managers, and others as well, take the time now and then to ask themselves:

What are my goals in life, and how realistic are they?
Is my use of time and energy helping me to reach these goals?
Do I have a proper sense of responsibility or do I try to do too much and fail to acknowledge my limitations?
How do I react to disappointments, losses?
How am I coping with stress and anxiety?
What is the consistency and quality of my personal relationships? Are my contacts with others superficial, meager, and unrewarding?
From whom do I receive and to whom do I give emotional support? Do I avoid getting support from others for fear of appearing weak?
What is the role of love in my life? How much time do I give to listen to and care for others?

At the end of this self-examination, a person should have a good idea of whether there are serious problems in his or her career or personal relationships. Being honest with oneself, the experts emphasize, is the first step toward problem solving.

From another source we learn other ways to reduce stress:[25]

Plan some idleness every day.
Listen to others without interruption.
Read books that demand concentration.
Learn to savor food.
Have a place for retreat at home.
Avoid irritating, overly competitive people.
Plan leisurely, less-structured vacations.
Concentrate on enriching yourself.
Live by the calendar, not the stopwatch.
Concentrate on one task at a time.

STRESS IN GROUPS

The individual will also need to cope in many ways with stress as a member of a group, organization, or larger human system. Every group that meets sufficiently often to have an ongoing life evidences certain similar phases of development that cause stress among the members.

Herbert A. Shephard and Warren G. Bennis have developed a useful theory of the phases of group development based on an analysis of many different groups in action.[26]

A group moves from one to another phase because of the standards, pressures, opposing forces, individual needs, members functions, and other such dynamics that are always present in any group. No matter how mature the members of the group may be, the group itself must start at birth and it may, therefore, experience growing pains as it develops maturity; and these growing pains create stress.

Recognition of the fact that every group goes through certain phases in its development—that it is at a given moment immature, maturing, or mature; and thus not a "bad" group nor a "good" group—can help us understand the realities of group life. A group lives in an atmosphere of uncertainty, and moves from a greater distance to a lesser degree of uncertainty as it overcomes obstacles to communication. The major areas of uncertainty in a group's internal relations must be reduced before it can cope with uncertainties in its external relations. These two major areas of internal uncertainties revolve about the group's:

Authority relations: members with the designated leader
Personal relations: members with one another

A group moves from preoccupation with the issues of power (authority relations) to preoccupation with the issue of intimacy (personal relations). It should be noted, however, that a group does not usually move steadily from one subphase to the next. It is a dynamic relationship.

In the *first phase,* which is called the *dependent phase* and in which the main issue is that of authority relations centering in the distribution of power, a group moves through three subphases of preoccupation, each of which can be a cause of stress:

1. Submission to authority
2. Rebellion against authority
3. Resolution of the dependence problem

In the *second phase*, which is called the *interdependent phase* and in which the main issue is that of personal relations centering in the degree of intimacy, a group also moves through three subphases of preoccupation, each of which can be a cause of stress unless lessened by the genuineness of the intimacy:

1. Enchantment over intermember identification
2. Disenchantment over individual identity
3. Consensus on interdependence problem

In both phases, the dependents and counterdependents, the overpersonals and counterpersonals, represent the extremes of member behavior at a given moment in the life of the group, thus reflecting the conflict going on in the group over the issue at stake. It is the action of members who are unconflicted over the distribution of power or the degree of intimacy that moves the group from one phase to the next. They emerge in the role of:

Independents: who function as the catalyst for group movement

It is important to remember, however, that a particular member cannot be identified with a particular role. In a given group that member may tend to be dependent or counterdependent, overpersonal or counterpersonal, or at some point may become independent and unconflicted over the issue of the moment. Each member needs to be comfortable with his or her own behavior in the performance of needed group roles.

Certain characteristics of a group can be identified in each subphase and traced as the group develops from one phase to the next:

Emotional tone of the group
Content theme of the group's agenda
Dominant *roles* emerging in each phase
Group *structure* determined by the roles
General *activity* in which the group is engaged
Group *movement* into another phase

These characteristics can be used to illustrate stress-producing elements in the functioning of a group. And it is becoming more apparent that there is a correlation between stress and membership (i.e., "Am I a member of this group?" "Who else is here?" "How will I fit in?"). The rush to meet membership needs—that is, to be included and accepted in a group—is directly related to the stress that a person is under or the stress the group is operating around.

Peggy Rutherford feels that stress can facilitate membership and that the amount of stress is directly related to the speed with which members seek acceptance and inclusion in a group.[27] She defines stress as a force tending to produce strain or tension. There are various levels of this force in a group:

Stress of *survival* by the group: the force to meet basic and essential needs, either physical (food, water, and shelter) or emotional (taking care of yourself, being taken care of, and keeping yourself emotionally together)
Stress of *belonging* to the group: the need to be a part of what is going on, to be recognized as having self-worth, to be connected to the others who are there
Stress of *productivity* by the group: to be working toward an end product, to work with others on a task, to use your own power to produce
Stress of *creativity* in the group: to bring into

being from one's own thoughts and imagination, to stretch oneself to the limit

Different groups experience these forces, some more strongly than others. A task group that is bent on productivity may not feel any survival stress at all. A group of people in a bomb shelter may not worry much about which member of the group expresses himself or herself in the most creative way. Other groups might experience all these levels of stress at one time or another throughout their lives together.

When high stress is occurring in a group, people can choose to exclude themselves, by leaving the group or by simply withdrawing into themselves. And the group itself usually has some part in that decision; it might even be the sole factor that is promoting the decision of exclusion. In a normal family relationship, no one is usually excluded from the group nor does any member usually choose to withdraw; but that does not mean that cooperation is present. One of the times when members of a family tend to pull together is a situation of mutual stress—a fire destroys the home, the family pet is hit by an automobile, the death of a parent.

People are essentially strong and can take care of themselves better than we normally believe. There is no reason, therefore, not to provide stressful situations with which people or groups have to deal. If, for example, the current problem is to facilitate membership, try "upping" the stress level of the group; it can bring it all together.

In examining actions potentially capable of coping with group stress, we usually think of the *team building* process* by which an appropriate amount of stress can be maintained and controlled. Excessive stress—which can block group growth, negate problem solving, and eliminate creativity—can be prevented.

*This process frequently is used in organizational development and organization renewal and is dealt with in more detail in Chapter 8.

STRESS IN ORGANIZATIONS

Organizations in crisis experience certain identifiable stages of stress: *shock, defensive retreat, acknowledgment,* and *adaptation and change.* The shock stage involves a threat to organizational patterns—a compelled change in the way things are. Defensive retreat is a condition of hanging on, anger, anxiety, disillusionment, denial, refusal to give up the way things are. Eventually, a stage of acceptance, realization, and acknowledgment takes over, new patterns and structure are established, and adaptation takes place. The ability of an organization to adapt to the new under conditions of stress is related to the old—what it has developed in the past: organizational policies and norms, management effectiveness, organizational structure problem-solving practices, and intraorganizational relations in the workplace. Although there is no intention here to belittle the importance of policies and norms, it does seem that these two things ultimately are what "really happens" in the workplace, an end result of rules, functions, and climate. A recent study[28] of 2010 men in twenty-three occupations, ranging from assembly-line worker to university administrators, revealed some interesting queries and answers:[29]

1. Long hours, heavy work loads, unremitting responsibilities, conflict . . . do these sound like the attributes of an ideal job? A recent study shows that workers in occupations that entail these apparent hardships are more satisfied, less anxious, and perhaps healthier than those in less demanding jobs. In fact, boredom and lack of responsibility may be hazardous to a worker's health.

2. The researchers found that job satisfaction had less to do with generalized

working conditions, such as the average number of hours worked each week and the quantitative work load, than with more personalized factors, such as opportunities to utilize skills and participate in decision making. The degree of job satisfaction, in turn, is correlated with the amount of strain in the form of anxiety, depression, or irritation that a worker experiences on the job, which frequently result in psychosomatic illness.

3. For example, of the twenty-three occupations included in the survey, family physicians ranked the highest in number of hours worked per week (over 55). Persons in this profession also put in a large amount of unwanted overtime, had one of the largest quantitative work loads, and reported that their jobs demanded high levels of mental concentration. In spite of these apparent hardships, these men reported the greatest amount of satisfaction with their jobs, low levels of anxiety, depression, and irritation, and few somatic disorders, such as difficulty in sleeping, loss of appetite, or fast heart beat.

4. In contrast, assembly-line workers—who do not have excessively long hours, unwanted overtime, large work loads or particularly great demands for concentration—reported the most boredom and the greatest dissatisfaction with their work load, as well as the highest levels of anxiety, depression, irritation, and somatic disorders. This strong evidence of strain, the researchers found, is attributable to job insecurity, to a lack of social support from immediate superiors and other workers, and to a lack of opportunity to use individual skills and abilities or to participate in decision making.

5. But the researchers found that the greatest single determinant of job satisfaction is the degree of compatibility (fit) between the demands of the job and the desire of the worker. If an individual feels that he wants a job which differs from the one he has in terms of complexity, work load, supervisory responsibility, or overtime hours, then he will invariably be dissatisfied with his present job, no matter whether it is deficient or excessive in these factors.

6. The researchers also report significant occupational differences in numbers of individuals with Type A, coronary-prone personalities. Previous studies have shown that these people are hard-driving, involved in their work, competitive, and persistent, and that they tend to seek out high-stress environments even though they are particularly susceptible to health-related effects of stress. The possibility that certain personality types may be predisposed to certain diseases confuses the positive correlation between job satisfaction, low strain, and health. The study found that occupations with the greatest concentrations of men with Type A characteristics (family physicians and university administrators) also have the highest satisfaction ratings.

In other studies[30–32] it was found that three elements in job stress are role conflict, ambiguity, and real work overload. Adams discovered stress factors in the workplace, such as:

Major changes in policies and procedures
Requirement to work more hours than usual
Increase in pace of work
New supervisor
New subordinates
Major reorganization of department
Change in nature of job
New co-worker

He reports that the amount of stress induced by one or more of these or other organizational changes is variable, and depends partly on how much preparatory communication takes place regarding them. In departments where managers did a good job of preparing their subordinates for changes, lower levels of strain and ill health were found and higher levels of work effectiveness and felt satisfaction and

Table 6-3
Organizational Readjustment Rating Scale[33]

	Values		Values
1. Transfer against one's will to a new position or assignment	81	16. Giving a major briefing or formal presentation	46
2. Being "shelved" (moved to a less important job)	79	17. Significant decline in environmental conditions (worse lighting, temperature, dining facilities, personnel services, less space, more noise, etc.)	45
3. Decrease in status (either actual or in relation to peers)	68	18. New boss	45
4. Being disciplined or severely reprimanded by one's superior	67	19. Significant decrease in the activity level or pace of work	43
5. Unable to transfer to new, more satisfying job	65	20. Significant increase in the activity level or pace of work	31
6. New line of work (a significant change in the nature of one's work)	60	21. Major relocation of workplace (move to new office or building)	31
7. Cancellation of a project you are involved in and consider important	60	22. Increase in status (either actual or in relation to peers)	30
8. Major or frequent changes in instructions, policy, or procedures	59	23. Frequently working more hours a week than normal because of crisis, deadline, etc.	29
9. Permanent change of duty station to or from overseas post	58	24. Transfer, retirement, or resignation of a close friend or valuable coworker	24
10. Being promoted or advanced at a slower rate than you expected	58	25. Being promoted or advanced at faster rate than you expected	24
11. Permanent change of duty station within continental United States	52	26. New subordinates	23
12. Anticipation of imminent retirement	47	27. New work schedule (change in time of day or days in week—total hours constant)	23
13. Major reorganization	46	28. New coworkers	21
14. Less recognition of accomplishments than before	46	29. More recognition than before of accomplishments	20
15. Major changes in technology affecting your job (computers, analytic or research techniques, etc.)	46	30. Significant improvement in environmental conditions (better lighting, etc.)	17
		31. Minor relocation or workplace (move desk in same office)	5

growth were reported than in departments where managers paid little attention to informing their subordinates of impending changes.[34]

As a result of this preliminary work, there was developed, as shown in Table 6-3, a readjustment scale based on organizational occurrences as contrasted to personal events.*

Some specialists recommend the development by appropriate organizations of

*See Table 6-1 for the social readjustment scale for individuals derived by Holmes and Rahe.

a *stress management program,* although the necessary medical, training, and research costs may be relatively expensive and difficult to "cost out." Labor/management differences are likely to occur. The organization that can undertake to so *manage* stress successfully probably will have these prescribed characteristics:

It will be large and financially able to support such a program.
It may already have a health maintenance service.
It will be progressive and humanistic in management philosophy.
It will have an active organization development program, through which related programs are offered.
Its top management highly values human resources.
Its labor/management relations are satisfactory and well developed.
It will be prepared to evaluate the crisis and social effectiveness of the program.

Given such an organization, and a firm commitment to develop a stress management program (SMP), Sharon L. Connelly, President of Resource Development Systems, Arlington, Va., recommends:[35]

1. Establish an SMP "planning committee" comprised of at least one presidential-level executive, the organization's two top medical and psychiatric staff, two middle managers who are stationary, two staff people who travel regularly, two spouses, two labor representatives, one retired member of the board of directors, and one consultant specialist on stress—a total of thirteen people.
2. Elevate management, maintenance, and development of human resources to the policy level, with an executive appointed to oversee such programming.
3. Gather baseline data on stress in the organization using a scale adapted to specific organizational needs.
4. Plan and conduct research on the relationship between stress and organization productivity, utilizing specially designed tools or instruments.[36]
5. Redefine the organization's health programs, including policies, objectives, practices, and resources in light of recent stress research.
6. Consider individual, team, department, and system approaches to reducing stress.
7. Design and use management development modules on:
   a. Detecting early signs of stress.
   b. Strategies for stress management.
   c. Wellness workshop, focusing on health instead of illness.
8. Conduct "change preparation sessions" for raising awareness about anticipated major changes, discussion, problem solving, and planning for such changes (e.g., reorganization, relocation, promotion, outplacement, retirement).
9. Create a means whereby all programs are evaluated.
10. Publish study materials and research results.

Stress is an elusive but pervasive phenomenon that has identifiable and sometimes costly results when it accumulates. It can contribute to chronic and mental health problems and can reduce organization effectiveness. Consultants, researchers, and practitioners are suggesting ways in which their findings might be applied to correct unhealthy working conditions. They cite some of the numerous experimental attempts to "humanize" work environments and alleviate the normal stresses of low-status jobs. But many of these experiments in work life have neglected to take individual differences into account; some have assumed that all workers on the same job are affected in the same way by stress factors, and they make unilateral changes to eliminate a problem. Some researchers argue that this sort of solution is often inappropriate, because what may constitute a decrease in stress for some individuals may constitute an increase for others.

The major contribution, however, will come from actions by leaders and individuals to plan for coping with stress, using these specific guidelines:

All events are stressful.
Stress is life-giving.
Stress is challenging.
Complete freedom from stress is death.
Stress is not to be avoided.
Distress is harmful and unpleasant stress.
Coping strategies are needed to neutralize the effects of stress.

CONFLICT

Fighting, hostility, and controversy, all of which can be called conflict, are nearly everyday fare for individuals and groups, although they do not always openly evidence themselves. Too often, there is emotional effort and involvement by many people that go largely unrewarded because they move in restrictive rather than constructive channels. By the same token, conflict releases energy at every level of human affairs—energy that can produce positive, constructive results. Two things should be recognized here: that such conflict is an absolutely predictable social phenomenon, and that conflict should not be repressed but channeled to useful purposes. Both of these realities lie at the heart of organizational renewal.

The goal of organizational leadership is not to eliminate conflict, but to use it—to turn the released energy to good advantage. The role of the behavioral scientist is to study, analyze, and report why people behave as they do, and to suggest ways in which research can be applied practically in human systems.

Conflict is almost always caused by unlike points of view. Because we have not learned exactly alike, and because we therefore see and value things differently, we vary in our beliefs as to what things are or should be. Because conflict, large or small, is inevitable, the extreme result at either end is a situation that is undesirably abrasive or dialogue that is creatively productive.

The American Management Association sponsored a survey of managerial interests in the area of conflict and conflict management. The respondents in the survey were 116 chief executive officers, 76 vice presidents and 66 middle managers. The results of the survey strongly suggest that the respondents see conflict as a topic of growing importance:[37]

They spend about 24% of their time dealing with conflict.
Their conflict-management ability has become more important over the past ten years.
They rate conflict management as a topic of equal or slightly higher importance than planning, communication, motivation, and decision making.
Their interests in the sources of conflict emphasize psychological factors, such as misunderstanding, communication failure, personality clashes, and value differences.
They feel the conflict level in their organization is about right—not "too low" or "too high."

These executives and managers also revealed what they considered to be the principal causes of conflict within organizations:

Misunderstanding (communication failure)
Personality clashes
Value and goal differences
Substandard performance
Differences over method
Responsibility issues
Lack of cooperation
Authority issues
Frustration and irritability
Competition for limited resources
Noncompliance with rules and policies

Nevertheless, that corporate executives and managers devote 24% of their working time to conflict management is considered to be quite low—by school and hospital administrators, mayors, and city managers. In these and similar fields, conflict resolution commands nearly 49% of the attention of such officials. The causes of conflict usually are the same as those cited above, but in a different order of rank. Most leaders look upon conflict as a negative experience. This is the key to the problem. We should take pains to see that conflict is a creative and positive occurrence; otherwise, we must recognize the destructive nature of conflict carried too far, too long:

It diverts energy from the real task.
It destroys morale.
It polarizes individuals and groups.
It deepens differences.
It obstructs cooperative action.
It produces irresponsible behavior.
It creates suspicion and distrust.
It decreases productivity.

But the list of positive and creative values inherent in conflict is equally long:

Conflict opens up an issue in a confronting manner.
Conflict develops clarification of an issue.
Conflict improves problem-solving quality.
Conflict increases involvement.
Conflict provides more spontaneity in communication.
Conflict is needed for growth.
Conflict strengthens a relationship when it is creatively resolved.
Conflict can increase productivity.

Parties to conflict, for the most part, find themselves in one (or more) of four areas of disagreement: *facts* (the present situation or problem), *methods* (the best way to achieve our goals), *goals* (how we would like things to be), and *values* (long-term goals and qualities we support). Generally, it is easiest to resolve differences over facts and most difficult to settle differences over values.

Conflict is a state of real difference between two or more persons where overt behavior is characterized by differing perceptions toward goals that, in turn, create tension, disagreement, and emotionality that tends to polarize those involved. Conflict is a topic of increasing importance to management. There are multiple reasons for this increasing importance, including the growing scarcity of natural resources; the complexity and increasing interdependence of relationships between individuals, groups, organizations, and nations; the values and life-style pluralism that characterizes people of all ages, sexes, and races; and the rising expectations and psychology of entitlement that are reflected in the motivation of employees, managers, owners, customers, and all others who interact in and with the organization.[38]

METHODS OF CONFLICT RESOLUTION

In a study of the constructive use of conflict, in which 57 managers were interviewed, five principal methods of interpersonal conflict resolution were identified (see Table 6-4):

Withdrawal: retreating from an actual or potential conflict situation
Smoothing: emphasizing areas of agreement and deemphasizing areas of difference over conflictual areas
Compromising: searching for solutions that bring some degree of satisfaction to the conflicting parties
Forcing: exerting one's viewpoint at the potential expense of another—often open competition and a win/lose situation.
Confrontation: addresses a disagreement directly and in a problem-solving mode—the affected parties work through their disagreements

It is important to depersonalize conflict by ensuring that the disputants do not sit in judgment of each other, and to focus the conflict on the basic issues by concentrat-

Table 6–4
Methods Associated with Effective and Ineffective Conflict Resolution

	Effective Resolution (N = 53)		Ineffective Resolution (N = 53)	
	N	%	*N*	%
Withdrawal	0	0.0*	5	9.4*
Smoothing	0	0.0	1	1.9
Compromise	6	11.3	3	5.7
Forcing	13	24.5*	42	79.2*
Confrontation-Problem-solving	31	58.5*	0	0.0*
Other (still unresolved; unable to determine how resolved; irrelevant to assignment; etc.)	3	5.7	2	3.8

*Percentage difference between groups is significant at the 0.5 level of confidence.

ing disagreement on factual ground. Progress in this direction, however slight, is usually self-continuing, and tends to reduce wholesale indictment to retail packaging. This limits conflict to manageable areas that are more likely to be subject to negotiation, accommodation, or compromise. When people are introduced to what they recognize as fact, they tend to become more objective—sensible, if you prefer. Unsupported opinion and implication generally cause an opposite effect. The leader, as a rule, should look at the issues coldly and at the people involved warmly.

Leadership in resolving organizational conflict creatively also requires empathy and equality, but not neutrality. The neutral position is damaging because by its nature it recognizes nothing. Empathy, on the other hand, means that leadership recognizes both the plight and the ideas of both sides in conflict, without necessarily agreeing totally with either. Equality

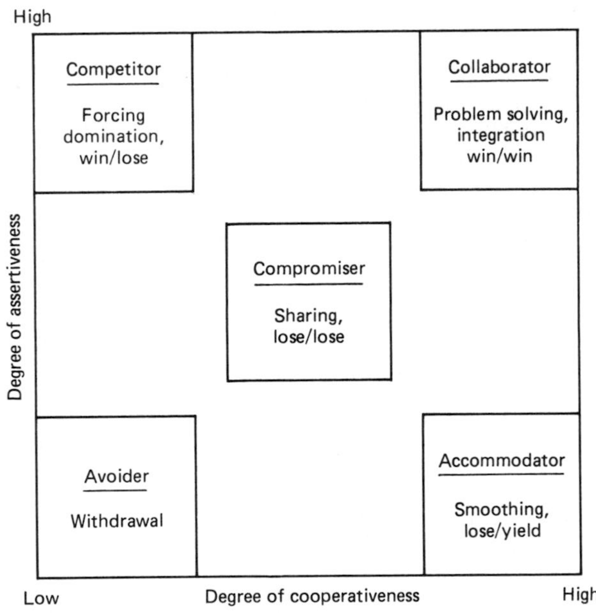

Figure 6-4 Conflict-management styles[39]

means that neither of the conflicting parties be made to feel inferior, for the alternative is greater jealousy and heightened competition.

Finally, adopting an attitude of one side winning and the other side losing is like pouring gasoline on the fire of conflict. On the other hand, the provisional try—honest fact-finding (all the facts), exhaustive exploration (both parties working together), and meaningful problem solving (with a lot of "what if we try this . . . ?" thrown in)—pries open the door to constructive creativity.

These are, of course, fundamental rules. The experienced leader knows that they do not always work as they should. It is necessary to contend with counterforces between those who passively refuse to engage in conflict and with those who deliberately develop conflict as a battleground for hatreds and greeds, as well as those to whom conflict is a healthy challenge for betterment. Nevertheless, management of human conflict is an objective of organizational renewal.

A helpful way to comprehend two particular styles of conflict management—that of *assertiveness* and *cooperativeness*—is illustrated in Figure 6-4. Each style has both positive and negative factors:[40]

Competitor. A competing style is high on assertiveness and low on cooperativeness. This style is power-oriented and approaches conflict in terms of a win/lose strategy. On the negative side, a competitor may suppress, intimidate, or coerce the other parties to a conflict.
On the positive side, a competing style may be necessary when a quick, decisive action is required, or when important but unpopular courses of action must be taken. In addition, competing may be required when "you know you're right" on an issue.
However, an avoiding style can make sense when a conflict situation has relatively minor implications for managerial effectiveness, when there appears to be little chance for a person to "win," and when the benefits of confronting a conflict situation are overshadowed by the potential damage of confrontation.

Accommodator. The accommodating style is low in assertiveness and high on cooperativeness. A person who uses an accommodating style as the primary approach to conflict management may be showing too little concern for personal goals. Such a lack of concern may lead to lack of influence and recognition. It means that conflicts are resolved without each party to the conflict presenting his or her view in a forceful and meaningful way.
However, like the other conflict management styles, the accommodating style has its uses. It is useful when a conflict issue is more important to the other person; when one of the other style's disadvantages outweigh those of the accommodating style; when maintaining harmony is important; when it is advantageous to allow the other person to experience winning; and when an accommodating style on one issue may make the other person more receptive on another, more important issue.

Compromiser. To some people the word "compromise" suggests weakness and lack of commitment to a position. A compromiser may be thought of as a person who puts expediency above principle or who seeks short-term solutions at the expense of long-run objectives. A compromising style results in each conflict participant sharing in some degree of winning and losing.
It is important, however, to recognize the potential value of compromise. Compromise is a common and practical approach to conflict management because it often fits the realities of life in organizations. This "fit" occurs when a conflict is not important enough to either party to warrant the time and psychological investment in one of the more assertive modes of conflict management. In addition, compromise may be the only practical way of handling a conflict situation in which two equally strong and persuasive parties are attempting to work out a solution.

Avoider. At first glance, an avoiding style may appear to have no value as a mode of managing conflict. An avoiding style may reflect a failure to address important issues and a tendency to remain neutral when there is a need to take a position. An avoider may also exhibit detachment from conflict, and a readiness to comply or conform, that is based on indifference.

Collaborator. Given the two dimensions of cooperativeness and assertiveness shown in Figure 6-4, the collaborating style is high on both dimensions. How is it possible to be both assertive about personal goals and cooperative about the goals of others? It is possible only if the parties to a conflict recast it as a problem-solving situation. What does this mean? A problem-solving approach requires the following conditions:

1. There is an attempt to depersonalize the conflict. That is, the parties to the conflict channel their energies to solving the problem rather than defeating each other.
2. The goals, opinions, attitudes, and feelings of all parties are seen as legitimate and acceptable concerns, and all parties are seen as playing a constructive role.
3. The parties realize that a conflict issue can make a constructive contribution to the quality of human relationships if the issue is worked through in a supportive and trusting climate in which opinions and differences are freely aired.

By developing an awareness of the elements of conflict and the conditions that foster it, you can maintain a low-conflict setting with the people with whom you associate. Some of the factors in the work setting that predispose individuals to engage in unnecessary conflict are:[41]

Poorly defined jobs, tasks, responsibilities, and ranges of authority

Prior history of conflict between two or more people or groups

Interdepartmental relationships that frequently place members at cross purposes; traditional adversary relationships such as sales versus engineering, production versus quality assurance, nursing versus administration, or district office versus regional headquarters

Unreasonable levels of pressure and pace in the organization

Severe economic downturn that jeopardizes the job security of organization members

Overly competitive climate fostered by top management and managers at various levels

Favoritism shown by managers to one or two employees

Punitive, accusative, or threatening style of treatment by a unit manager, leading to escapist behavior such as blaming others and shifting responsibility

Unclear or arbitrary standards for advancement and promotion in the organization; inconsistent patterns of rewarding accomplishment; overly secretive and competitive organizational politics

Great confusion or uncertainty about upcoming major changes or upheavals in the organization; inability of employees to define their future roles and interactions

By anticipating it, an effective manager tries to lessen the chance of *open conflict*; and it can be observed that the evolution of open conflict passes through five distinct stages:[42]

1. *Anticipation.* A change is to be made and problems are forecast.
2. *Conscious but unexpressed difference.* Rumors are out, but there is no confirmation. People do not like what they hear.
3. *Discussion.* Information is presented. Questions are asked. Sides of the questions become open.
4. *Open dispute.* The principals in the situation confront the sides of the argument. Differing opinions become clear.
5. *Open conflict.* The conflict sharpens up, with forces mobilizing behind each side of the question.

A good general approach to minimizing conflict and resolving the conflicts that do occur consists of the following three basic steps:[43]

Establish and maintain a low-conflict, low-stress climate, with cooperation being the general norm.

Isolate each significant conflict that does arise to a single, specific task issue or family of issues. Don't accept personality clashes but insist that the protagonists zero in on a concrete issue and its rational elements.

Help the protagonists to apply a rational problem-solving model or procedure to the issue; go for a workable compromise.

EXTREME CONFLICT

Some extreme acts of conflict do not lend themselves to rational modes of negotiation or conflict management. Conscientious leaders strive to take action and make decisions without losing touch with sound basic principles. Demonstrations, sit-ins, and other extreme conflict behavior should be duly heard and considered. But the inherent problems are these:

When does dissent become dissension?

How does one identify destructive disagreement?

When does freedom of speech become harassment?

The behavioral sciences can contribute some answers by helping to distinguish between legitimate, responsible, representative individuals and groups and those that might be characterized as "only troublemakers," and by pointing out some ways the irresponsible influence of the latter can be reduced.

The organizational leader should initially look for and evaluate the ultimate objectives of questionable or extreme behavior. If this is not found, or if what is found is immaterial or plainly subversive to a recognized good, it is reasonable to conclude that the members of the group are primarily interested in enhancing their own egos, "hurting" someone else, or exercising their ability to gain "power" through harassment. Typically, those who are only troublemakers cause discord and disruption for its own sake. They disdain the obligation to earn the right to wield influence. Rather than being interested in coping with a problem, they purposefully block any form of mutual accommodation that might lead to problem solving.

This is not to say that all dissenters are suspect, or that all outspoken small groups in an organization belong to the lunatic fringe. History shows us that some individuals and minority groups have stood against the majority, and the established way, in prophetic and sublime correctness. To confound the problem, we live in a world in which the most obvious truths have been gained only by the most extreme measures. Most of the trouble caused by extremists is generated by their unwillingness to proceed in accepted ways, or to exercise the patience needed to bring about change. By these reluctances they can be known.

There are modes of counterbalance against those who would destroy but not build. Although each situation of this type must be judged by its own demerits, these guides to intelligent action in response to incontinent criticism can be outlined briefly.

Evaluate the criticism. Is the source respectable and answerable? Can it fairly be demonstrated not to be so? Is the attack plausible? Or is it self-defeating by its own implausibility? Is it of substantial prominence in general acceptance? Or will denial create attention where none exists materially? Is there a risk of misunderstanding within the organization, even though the allegations are invalid? Does the criticism touch upon a legal or moral obligation? What effect does the criticism have upon the organization's appearance, where appearance counts?

Use facts as a suppressant. The best course is to promise a full response without delay. Then get facts quickly and accurately. Delay inflames the issue and strengthens the position of the critical. Destructive persons rely upon an inability to respond in time with indisputable, unslanted factual information. Avoid an immature, hotheaded response like the plague, but remember that wholesome indignation is generally looked upon as a healthy sign of mature concern.

Admit faults and accept valid criticism. Almost every attack by destructive persons depends upon a golden thread of truth, cleverly interwoven in a fabric of objective falsity. Find this thread and use it. No organization expects any person to be perfect, and its respect is enlarged by an unpanicked admission of oversight when it is accompanied by timely, appropriate action. Promptly acting upon the element of truth that it must have often so weakens the position of extremism that its adherents fade away, on that particular front at least. Essentially, however, the strongest rampart of defense is propriety in all past actions; the quickest road to disaster is fearful capitulation.

Avoid creating a martyr image. It is a part of the calculated plan of most disruptive individuals and groups to seek a semblance of martyrdom; an underdog posture gains sympathy for them that may later be hard to overcome. On the other hand, their very nature tends to make them talk themselves into a corner, to overplay their position so badly as to arouse disgust and rejection. No one is belittled by taking sincere and persistent steps to engage extremists in effective interfacing; on the other hand, stature is gained when they evade reasonable confrontation.

Keep the issues out in the open. A small minority attacking from an extreme angle must necessarily narrow the field of action in order to achieve concentration. From this concentration, which usually fails to consider broader issues the leader must keep in mind, it hopes to receive disproportional attention and, as a consequence, generate pressure upon its target. It will succeed in this tactic if an attempt is made to hush up the disagreement. Candor is disarming. Increase interest in the specific issue quickly, taking care to place it clearly in context. Do not widen the rift by borrowing from other issues, and do not generalize from individual or group to the whole organization. If the opposition is in the right, entirely or partially, the leader should act or explain satisfactorily why action cannot be taken on the issue on which they are right. If they are in the wrong, entirely or partially, that part in which they are wrong should be tried before the bar of open interfacing.

Harry and Bonaro Overstreet indicate that the principal countermove to extremist and lunatic groups and disruptive individuals is linked to the phrase: Don't be afraid![44]

> Don't be afraid of controversy.
> Don't be afraid to set standards of procedure and stick to them.
> Don't be afraid to say that some kinds of action are beyond the pale.

MANAGEMENT OF AGREEMENT

The essence of conflict management through confrontation, negotiation, and collaboration is to come to *agreement.* In many cases, however, a condition of general agreement may already exist—unrecognized, unspoken, unrealized. It has been rather well hypothesized that members of groups and organizations—as individuals—may be in agreement as to the nature of a situation or problem, but that no one individual has seen fit to lay his or her agreement on the table:

> Organizations frequently take actions in contradiction to what they really want to do and therefore defeat the very purposes they are trying to achieve. It also deals with a major corollary of the paradox, which is that *the inability to*

manage agreement is a major source of organization dysfunction.[45]

Frequently, people in organizations know how to cope with a problem, but do not share this knowledge with those who occupy the positions of authority or leadership—evidence of an unwillingness to communicate openly. As a result, all too often, invalid or inaccurate information leads to action that is contrary to the best interest of the organization. Members of the organization, finding themselves where they should not be, experience frustration, dismay, fear, anger, irritation, and dissatisfaction—whereupon the cycle repeats itself. Why does this occur? Jerry Harvey identifies six reasons:[46]

Action anxiety. People tend to be anxious about acting in accordance with their beliefs.
Negative fantasies. If we openly and positively correct a wrong, we may create new problems.
Real risk. The reality of life whenever we confront others; it might affect job, security, and one's role.
Fear of separation. If a person "opens up," it might threaten their acceptance in the group.
Fear of conflict (real or phony). Real conflict occurs when people have real differences. Phony conflict, on the other hand, occurs when people agree on the actions they want to take, and then do the opposite. The resulting anger, frustration, and blaming behavior, generally termed "conflict," are not based on real differences. Rather, they stem from the protective reactions that occur when a decision that no one believed in or was committed to in the first place goes sour. In fact, as a paradox within a paradox, such conflict is symptomatic of agreement.
Group think. A conforming pattern of group action that resists innovation, creativity, and deviation.

All this brings us once again to the conclusion that the management of agreement is a matter of confrontation, search, and coping. *Confrontation* has been called a process of interpersonal relating in which the behavior, the presence, or the mere existence of one person makes a difference in the behavior of another because they openly "face up" to the situation in which they are involved. To be productive, this process relies upon all the individuals involved communicating honestly and with integrity; but even so it generally tends to be inversely related to the intensity of domination which the involved individuals bring to bear. The highest levels of confrontation are usually found in human interacting in which conflict, threat, and domination—and hence the psychological necessity for defense—are negligible. Conflict, of course, is a kind of interfacing, and little interfacing takes place that is totally void of conflict, domination, or attempts to influence. "Direct confrontation of relevant situations in an organization is essential. If we do not confront one another we keep the trouble within ourselves and we stay in trouble."[47]

It may be well here to review some of the prominent factors of searching. Basically, what must be looked for by all concerned is an understanding of the position taken by the other person or group. Each person must do this in his or her own way, communicating clearly and avoiding all judgmental behavior so as to help establish a relationship of trust. If each person's autonomy and independence is to be preserved, there must be a minimal attempt by anyone to control anyone else. Thus a problem-solving, goal-oriented, continuously experimental approach must be adopted, and there must be considerable flexibility with respect to the acceptance or rejection of the ideas of others.

Contrasted to the questions of attitude and procedure, *coping* brings us down to the action in managing conflict and agreement. To cope requires an appropriate response to the situation, issue, problem, or relationship that has been confronted. Appropriateness may be in the "eye of the beholder," but in the context of organization renewal, appropriate management of conflict or agreement is related to solving the problem in such a way that the person involved learns from the process; the human subsystems are strengthened by the coping; the organization is aided in its growth; and in some minor or major way, the resolution or solution contributes to the environmental forces affecting the organization.

The importance of managing stress, conflict, and agreement have been discussed here not because they are negative forces, but rather because they are positive aspects of human system renewal:

> Diversity of orientation and differences in point of view ("fruitful friction") are essential if one seeks creative and effective organizations. Differences, of course, can result in irreconcilable, costly conflict unless the interaction—influence network and the problem-solving processes of organization channel the differences to productive and not destructive ends. There is need to develop more sophisticated social institutions and organizations that have the capacity to deal constructively with the conflicts caused by change or by diversity.[48]

If the conflict situation is in the healthy zone, skills and techniques for successful management can be learned and applied effectively. If the conflict situation is in the unhealthy zone, a different set of analytic skills and insights is needed. This is more complex and often is a longer process. It is important to know that unhealthy conflict can be managed as successfully as healthy conflict if there is a clear understanding of the nature of the conflict and the factors underlying it.

The management of conflict is assuming greater importance in the life of managers. In one study it was shown that in a sample of 293 managers, CEO's spent 18 percent of their time managing conflict, 21 percent of their time with presidents, and 26 percent of the time with middle managers.[49]

Thus, we have looked at importance and methods of handling change, communication, conflict, stress, and agreement—as key elements of managerial/leadership effectiveness. The leader's role in these things is that of facilitator of necessary confrontation, search, and coping for human system renewal.

QUESTIONS

1. What are examples of good stress? What are examples of bad stress?
2. What ways of coping with individual stress have you found valuable?
3. In organizational situations in which you have been involved or that you have observed, what kind of behavior or issues created the most stress?
4. What kinds of group stress have you observed most frequently?
5. In your experience, how have most conflicts originated?
6. What methods of conflict resolution have you found to be most effective? Why?

NOTES

[1]Hans Selye, *Stress without Distress* (New York: New American Library, 1974), p. 278. Hereafter cited as Selye.

[2]Geoffrey Vickers, *Making Institutions Work,* (New York: John Wiley & Sons, 1973), p. 161.

[3]Alvin Toffler, *The Third Wave* (New York: William Morrow & Company, Inc., 1980).

[4]Sol Levine and Norman A. Scotch, *Social Stress* (Chicago: Aldine Publishers, Inc., 1970).

[5]Walter Raab, "Civilization-induced Neurogenic Degenerative Heart Disease," *Cardiologia,* Vol. 41, 1962, 10.

[6]Jay Anthony, *Corporation Man* (New York: Random House, Inc., 1971).

[7]William H. Whyte, Jr., *The Organization Man* (New York: Simon and Shuster, 1956).

[8]Eugene E. Jennings, *The Executive in Crisis* (New York: McGraw-Hill Book Company, 1965). Hereafter cited as Jennings.

[9]Michael Maccoby, *The Gamesmen: The New Corporate Leaders* (New York: Simon and Shuster, 1976).

[10]Selye.

[11]Michael T. Matteson and John M. Ivanevich, "Organizational Stressors and Heart Disease: A Research Model," *Academy of Management Review,* Vol. 4, No. 2, 1979.

[12]Ibid., p. 348.

[13]Roger S. Lazarus, *Proceedings Of The National Heart and Lung Institute Working Conference on Health Behavior* (Washington, D.C.: National Institutes of Health, Department of Health, Education and Welfare, 1977), p. 5.

[14]Thomas H. Holmes and Minoru Masuda, "Psychosomatic Syndrome," *Psychology Today,* April 1972, p. 71.

[15]Thomas H. Holmes and Richard H. Rahe, "The Social Readjustment Rating Scale," *Journal of Psychosomatic Research,* Vol. 11, 1967, 213-218.

[16]Erik H. Erikson, *Childhood and Society* (New York: W. W. Norton & Company, Inc., 1950), p. 86.

[17]Gail Sheehy, *Passages: Predictable Crises of Adult Life* (New York: E. P. Dutton & Company, Inc., 1976), p. 14.

[18]Daniel J. Levinson, *The Seasons of a Man's Life* (New York: Alfred A. Knopf, Inc., 1978).

[19]Harry Levinson, "On Being a Middle-aged Manager," in *The Great Jackass Fallacy* (Cambridge, Mass.: Harvard University Press, 1973), p. 59.

[20]Jennings, p. 79.

[21]John D. Adams, "Improving Stress Management," *Social Change: Ideas and Applications* (NTL Institute), Vol. 8, No. 4, 1978, 3. Hereafter cited as Adams. Copyright © 1978 by NTL Institute for Applied Behavioral Science.

[22]Ibid., p. 4.

[23]Ibid., p. 5.

[24]Jennings, p. 207.

[25]Meyer Friedman and Ray Rosenman, *Type A Behavior and Your Heart* (New York: Alfred A. Knopf, Inc., 1974).

[26]Herbert A. Shephard and Warren G. Bennis, *Institute Take Home Packet* (Washington, D.C.: National Training Laboratories, 1972), pp. 14-18.

[27]Peggy Rutherford, *The Relationship Between Stress and Membership* (paper written for Association of Creative Change—(Group Development No. 1, 1979).

[28]Robert D. Caplan, Sidney Cobb, John R. P. French, R. Van Harrison, and Richard Pinneau, Jr., *Job Demands and Worker Health: Main Effects and Occupational Differences* (Ann Arbor, Mich.: Institute of Social Research, 1975).

[29]Adapted from *ISR Newsletter* (Institute for Social Research, The University of Michigan, Ann Arbor, Mich.), Spring 1975, pp. 3-4.

[30]Robert L. Kahn, "Conflict, Ambiguity, and Overload: Three Elements in Job Stress," *Occupational Mental Health,* Vol. 3, No. 1, 1973.

[31]Sidney Cobb, "Role Responsibility: The Differentation of a Group," *Occupational Mental Health,* Vol. 3, No. 1, 1973.

[32]John R. P. French, Jr., "Person Role Fit," *Occupational Mental Health,* Vol. 3, No. 1, 1973.

[33]Douglas Naismith, *Stress among Managers as a Function of Organization Change* (unpublished dissertation; Washington, D.C.: The George Washington University Library, 1975).

[34]Adams, p. 9.

[35]Sharon L. Connelly, *Executive Stress: Causes, Consequences, and Organizational Implications* (unpublished dissertation; Washington, D.C.: The George Washington University Library, 1978).

[36]*Michigan Organization Assessment Package: Progress Report II* (Ann Arbor, Mich.: Survey Research Center, University of Michigan, August 1975).

[37]Kenneth W. Thomas and Warren H. Schmidt, "A Survey of Managerial Interests with Respect to Conflict," *Academy of Management Journal,* Vol. 19, No. 2, 1976, 315-318.

[38]Robert Albanese, *Managing: Toward Accountability for Performance,* rev., (Homewood, Ill.: Richard D. Irwin, Inc., 1978), pp. 421–422. Copyright © 1978 by Richard D. Irwin, Inc. Hereafter cited as Albanese.

[39]Adapted from Kenneth W. Thomas, "Conflict

and Conflict Management," in Marvin D. Durnette (ed.), *The Handbook of Industrial and Organizational Psychology* (Chicago: Rand McNally College Publishing Company, 1976), p. 900. Copyright © 1976 by Rand McNally College Publishing Company.

[40]Albanese, pp. 429–431.

[41]Karl Albrecht, *Stress and the Manager* (Englewood Cliffs, N.J.: Prentice-Hall, Inc., 1979), pp. 273–274. Hereafter cited as Albrecht.

[42]Warren H. Schmidt and Robert Tanenbaum, "Management of Difference," *Harvard Business Review,* November–December 1960, p. 109.

[43]Albrecht, p. 274.

[44]Harry and Bonaro Overstreet, *Strange Tactics of Extremism* (New York: W. W. Norton & Company, Inc., 1964), p. 51.

[45]Jerry B. Harvey, "The Abilene Paradox: The Management of Agreement," *Organizational Dynamics* (American Management Associations), Vol. 3, No. 1, 1974, 66.

[46]Ibid., p. 75.

[47]Sheldon A. Davis, "An Organic Problem-solving Method of Organizational Change," *Journal of Applied Behavioral Science,* Vol. 3, No. 1, 1967, 13.

[48]Rensis Likert and Jane Gibson Likert, *New Ways of Managing Conflict* (New York: McGraw-Hill Book Company, 1976), p. 23.

[49]Thomas and Schmidt, p. 315.

III

Approaches To Organization Renewal

Organization renewal is brought about through individual, group, and organization development processes. Each level of the human system is relevant and important. In achieving such development objectives, both human and nonhuman resources need to be considered.

Chapter 7 examines the dynamics of individual behavior and ten processes that can be used to develop the full potential of the individual. The characteristics of group behavior are explored in Chapter 8; methods of optimizing the group are discussed, with a focus on ways to improve teamwork in the work unit. Chapter 9 presents a rich diversity of sixteen processes that have been used in organization development; and it is explained how these processes are derived from both management and behavioral science orientations. The importance of the quality of work life is stressed.

The shaded area in Figure P-3 indicates the portion of the systems renewal model that is covered in Part 3.

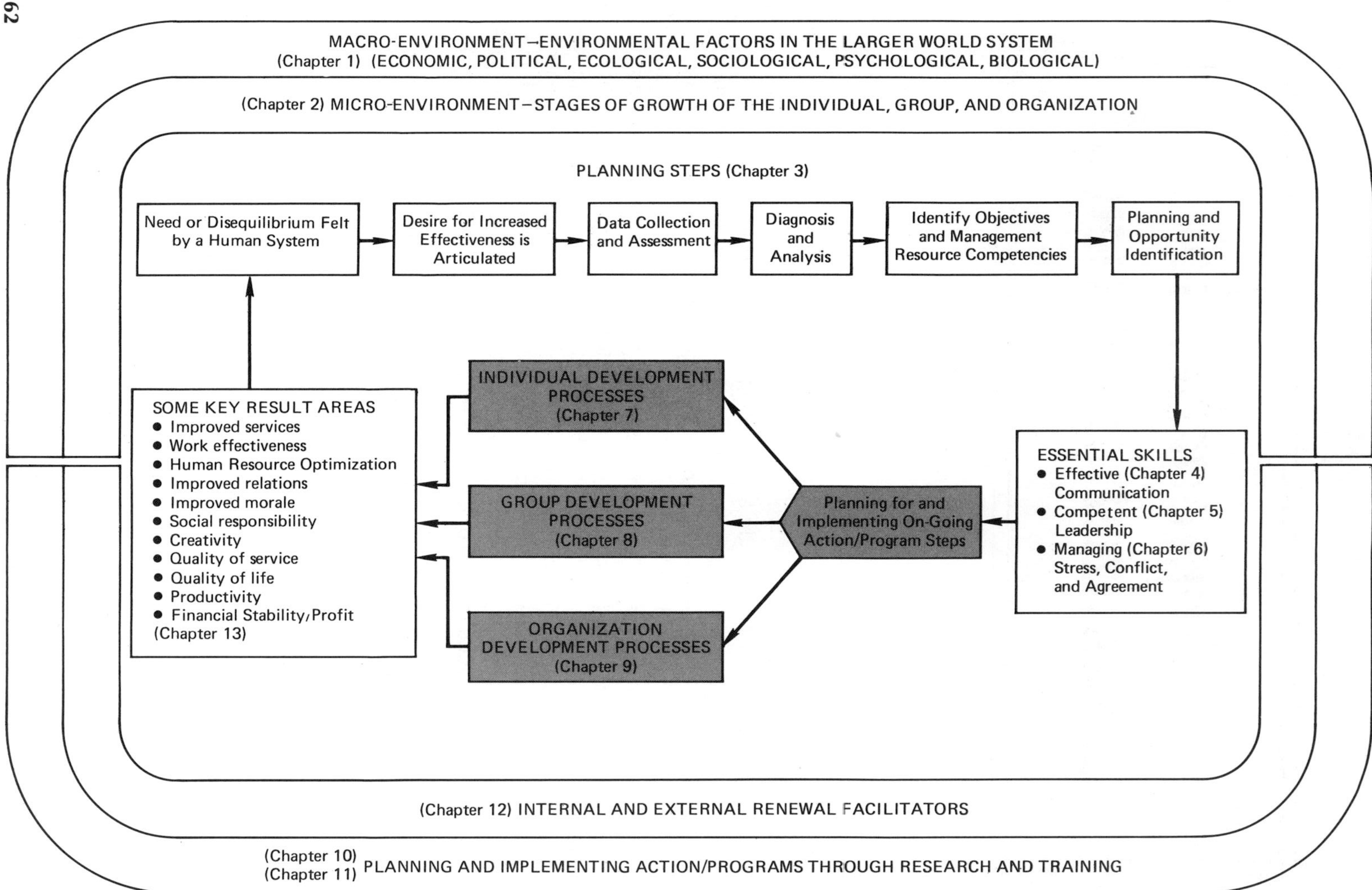

Figure P-3 Systems renewal model

7

individual development processes

Every science begins with individuals. From sensation, which gives only singular things, arises memory experience, and through experience, we obtain the universal which is the basis of art and science.
William of Ockham, died ca. 1349

In addition to those economic factors that are considered to be time-honored and traditional, management is affected by a host of changing, noneconomic factors. For example, the complexity of human resource development and utilization is seen as the key to achieving the objectives of organizations. The twentieth century has given society, through recognition of the importance of people, new insights about human behavior. Research is opening up insights about the changing needs, expectations, and goals of persons in the work situation.

Florence R. Skelly reports that new work values are emerging, particularly among employees under 35:[1]

- A concern for "meaningful" work—only 13% of the labor force think their work is "meaningful"
- A shift of energy and attention to leisure-time activities
- Renewed focus on money
- A strange combination of fear and superconfidence—a realization by young people that they have been judged against lower, less rigorous standards
- Apparent indifference to traditional penalties for poor performance
- Intense need for feedback on performance
- Stepped-up sense of time—"live for today"
- Receptivity to excitement at work
- A wider range of self-expression and life-styles

Such a list surely is not exhaustive, but it is indicative of the importance of a personalized and varied approach to the individual development that will be needed in the 1980s. This brings us to consideration of the ways in which individual development of adults is blocked, manipulated, or released by the behavior of the managers, the programs, the resources, and the climate of the organization. As in any field, there are many schools of thought brought to bear on individual growth and development in the workplace. A presentation of some of the basic beliefs about and approaches to individual motivation will be made here since those responsible for initiating human systems renewal cannot afford to approach their responsibility with outmoded or partially examined assumptions. As examples, once-honored concepts of motivation that held that human beings inherit most of their capability to perform well, and that they can be influenced only by reward and punishment, are no longer valid. We know now that employees and voluntary workers, and managers themselves, harbor expectations and needs that yearn for satisfaction. We know that employees are often motivated by social needs, and obtain many basic satisfactions through relationships with others. In these relationships, people want ego satisfactions as well as a feeling of accomplishment; self-identification and self-realization become increasingly important at various levels of the hierarchy of needs.

THE INDIVIDUAL AS A SOCIAL SYSTEM

Organization renewal is based upon the release of the human resources of an organization. It requires, therefore, renewal facilitators to become knowledgeable about the ways in which the personality and motivation of individuals will relate to the renewal process as part of the human system. In first looking at personality growth of the human being, we are brought face to face with the reality that organizational leaders must cope with adult human resources that have been molded primarily by past experiences. Any renewal process will need to be cognizant of this fact. The goal is not to change personality (this will be most improbable), but to understand the personality growth patterns that influence the functioning adult in the organization and to develop ways for people to continue their personal growth in the social system in which they work. Allport defines personality as "the dynamic organization within the individual of those psychophysical systems that determined his unique adjustments to his environment."[2] A later modification of this definition by White states that "personality is the organization of an individual's personal pattern of tendencies."[3]

Many scholars have worked at describing personality and the factors contributing to its existence. The false dichotomy between those who choose either heredity or environment as the major influence on personality has flooded lecture halls and filled books with evidence on each side. The early attempts to identify traits were succeeded by the pioneer work of Freud, who stressed the importance of early childhood experiences in the development of the adult personality. He also assumed a basic and dynamic personality structure involving outside reality (mainly other people) and three aspects of the individual: the ego, the superego, and the id. He defined the *ego* as the aspect of personality that strives to be logical and reasonable and to cope with the world of reality; the *id* as the composite of pleasure-seeking instincts, illogical and infantile in its seeking of immediate satisfactions, and completely out of touch with reality; and the *superego* as an infantile combination of conscience and ego ideal (the person one wishes to become). Since the work of Freud a number of personality theorists, among them Karen Horney, Erich Fromm, and Harry Stack Sullivan, have built on the contributions of Freud and placed a greater emphasis on social motives.

Erik Erikson took the basic stages of physical growth, related them to the environmental forces at work at each stage of life, and developed a very dynamic theory of personality development.[4] In developing his theory he maintained that the *ego qualities* emerge from critical periods (the eight ages) of development in which the ego attempts to integrate the timetable of the organism with the structure of social institutions in the environment. Upon entering each period, the organism and environment interrelate to present a "crucial conflict" in the growth of the person. The aspects of conflict in the eight ages (such as trust vs. mistrust) are, at the same time, (1) ways of experiencing for the individual, (2) ways of behaving, and (3) unconscious inner stages. This approach has been properly referred to as the "crucial conflict" concept of personality growth. The reason for elaborating on this approach to personality is twofold: first, it integrates the Freudian and environmental schools of thinking; and second, it highlights the considerable experience the individual has had in confronting life situations. His theory refers to interacting systems.

The major thesis underlying this approach to organization renewal is the need for the people in an organization to confront realistically the situations with which they must cope. Many individuals, managers, and leaders tend to avoid conflict, to "play games," or to cover up problems with pseudo-human relations. This is neither necessary nor desirable. Most normal adults have learned to confront life situations. They may not always have made the best reconciliation, but they have experienced confrontation.

In light of the compatibility between Erik Erikson's approach to personality and this view of human systems renewal, it is appropriate to examine our common ground in some detail. Table 7-1 is derived from the Fact Finding Committee for the Mid-Century White House Conference on Children and Youth. In the first column will be found the stages of physical growth. In the third column are those environmental forces that are key influences on that particular growth stage of the individual. The fourth row shows how this crucial confrontation is expressed. In the final column there is a projection of the alternative consequence in one's adult life, depending on whether the crucial conflict is resolved in a healthy manner. The mature personality accepts the life cycle as inevitable. It produces a sense of an alliance with time and history, permitting dignity to life itself and reflecting an appreciation for human striving in which life is a single coincidence among many lives.

It is important to realize that these social conflicts are being "worked" on by the individual prior to and after the crucial stages of his or her optimum confrontations. It is important for those of us involved in the renewal process to realize that adults can still change, but that some strong forces have forged the personality of those with whom we work and solve problems. The interrelationship between our social goals and concepts of healthy personality development is well defined by this comment:

> We are now working toward, and fighting for, a world in which the harvest of democracy may be reaped. In order to make the world safe for democracy we must make democracy safe for the healthy child. In order to ban autocracy, exploitation, and inequality in the world we must first realize that the first inequality in life is that of child and adult. Human childhood is long, so that parents and schools may have time to accept the child's personality in trust and to help it to be human in the best sense known to us.[5]

Since this creative work of Erik Erikson, some other writers and researchers have extended the examination of adult life stages. They have tried his seminal theories in the arena of pragmatic empiricism and found nothing that is contradictory and much that is supportive. While Erikson's theory provides an excellent descriptive framework for viewing the central issues of human development, it really is difficult to test empirically.

The most recent work on overall adult-life-span theory has been identified with several investigators: Bernice Neugarten, a social psychologist at the University of Chicago; Daniel Levinson, a social psychologist at Yale University; Roger L. Gould, a psychiatrist at UCLA; and Gail Sheehy, the author of the best-selling book *Passages.* All of them used interviews or

Table 7–1
Stages of Growth in Personality Development[6]

Stages (with approximate ages)	Psychological crises	Radius of significant relations	Psychosocial modalities	Favorable outcome
Birth through first year	Trust vs. mistrust	Maternal person	To get To give in return	Drive and hope
Through second year	Autonomy vs. shame, doubt	Parental persons	To hold (on) To let (go)	Self-control and willpower
Third year through fifth year	Initiative vs. guilt	Basic family	To make (going after) To make like (playing)	Direction and purpose
Sixth to onset of puberty	Industry vs. inferiority	"Neighborhood"; school	To make things (competing) To make things together	Method and competence
Adolescence	Identity and repudiation vs. identity diffusion	Peer groups and outgroups; models of leadership	To be oneself (or not to be) To share being oneself	Devotion and fidelity
Early adult	Intimacy and solidarity vs. isolation	Partners in friendship, sex, competition, cooperation	To lose and find oneself in another	Affiliation and love
Young and middle adult	Generativity vs. self-absorption	Divided labor and shared household	To make be To take care of	Production and care
Later adult	Integrity vs. despair	"Mankind" "My Kind"	To be, through having been To face not being	Renunciation and wisdom

questionnaires in trying to find patterns common to many lives.

Bernice Neugarten and her associates conducted over eighty separate studies probing for personality changes at various stages of life.[7] This work has been the most extensive examination of adult life to date. They found middle age to be a major turning point with both painful and gratifying aspects. The middle-aged were not only poignantly aware of their loss of youth, but also felt more in charge of their lives and incentive for further accomplishment. Neugarten also observed the effect that social class had on determining when the stages of life began and how long they lasted.[8]

Daniel Levinson and his colleagues began studying forty men aged 35 to 45. Although only males were studied, it was a special and diverse group, evenly divided among industrial workers (both blue-collar and white-collar), business executives, academic biologists, and novelists. After many hours of probing with psychological personality tests and interviews, Levinson discovered that he would not be able to understand middle life unless he knew what had gone before, and his interest widened to encompass the whole life span. Levinson took a broad approach which he calls the "individual life structure," which incorporates sociological, psychological, and development of personality approaches equally. He looked at all aspects of an individual's life, including the groups or institutions belonged to, the roles and careers, the personal meanings derived from these, and the aspects that are self-expressed or excluded. Occupation and family occupy the most time and energy in one's life and therefore were viewed as central components in a life structure with ethnicity, religion, peer relations, and leisure important secondary components.

The evolution of the life structure in Levinson's view is a dynamic sequence of alternating stable periods and transitional periods, with the stable periods lasting around six to eight years and the transitional periods lasting four to five years. The developmental task of each stable period is to establish the life structure securely and pursue goals and values within it. The task of the transitional period is to terminate existing structure and to change it into new structure. Each individual period reflects its place in the overall life cycle.

Added to this conceptual model, Levinson sees five major eras of 20 years each which include stable development periods and transitional periods linking and overlapping the adjacent eras. In each era the character of life changes not in a progression from low to high or from less advanced to more advanced, but being just different—like the seasons of the year. Levinson accounts for and describes each period based on his biographical research method. Preadulthood is terminated by the Early Adult Transition, which initiates the Getting into the Adult World (GIAW) period, in which the individual must pursue two conflicting tasks: to explore options and to create a stable life structure. This period is terminated by the Age Thirty Transition, in which the individual examines the progress so far made and determines whether or not to change the life course. For some this is a smooth transition, but for others it can be a bewildering developmental crisis. This initiates the second adult life structure, which begins with the Settling Down Period. Here a person has two major tasks: to establish a niche in society and to work at "making it," meaning to plan, strive, and progress along a timetable. Toward the end of the Settling Down Period, Levinson recognizes a distinctive phase which he calls Becoming One's Own Man (BOOM). A man or woman pushes to accomplish the goals of settling down, of having more authority, speaking his or her own mind, and becoming a senior member in the world.

BOOM is terminated by the Mid-Life Transition, which provides a bridge between early and late adulthood (see Figure 7-1). Levinson found that most of his subjects experienced moderate to severe crises because of struggles within themselves and with the external world. At this transition, the person must outgrow the illusions and immaturities of youth and confront, integrate, and balance life. It is the problem of steering "a course between worrying about growing old and trying futilely to stay young."[9] Middle Adulthood follows with Late Adulthood, and finally Late Late Adulthood.

Roger Gould studied 524 middle-class men and women who ranged in age from 16 to 66.[10] Although his methodology and conceptualization were different from Levinson's, Gould independently arrived at a similar sequence of adult developmental periods and a similar view of the life course. One of the patterns Gould recognized was the 16- to 18-year age group's

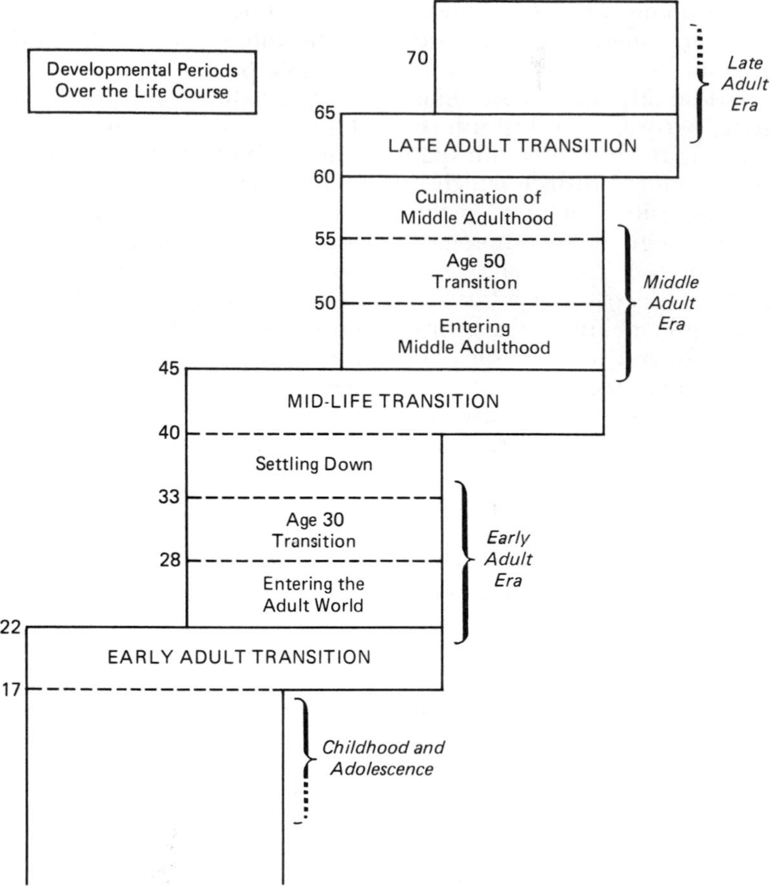

Figure 7-1 Developmental periods over the life course[11]

concern with escape from parental dominance. He saw that between 18 and 22 the emphasis was substituting friends for family. Gould found the twenties marked with confidence and optimism. In this period, adults "felt that they were the new generation," that "now was the time to live, and now was the time to build for the future, both professionally and personally." The thirties were more self-reflective; people questioned what they were doing and why.

Gould discovered that the forties brought awareness that time is finite as well as "reconciliation of *what is* with *what might have been*." In the fifties self-acceptance was even greater. There was a mellowing of feelings and relationships. Death becomes a new presence for this age group.

Gail Sheehy, an investigative reporter and nonacademician, did extensive research and over one hundred in-depth interviews. She also found that most of the research was being done by men studying other men. She eclectically draws from the theorists to identify the personality changes common to each stage of life. She then contributed to the theory by comparing the developmental rhythms of women and men. The asynchronization between the two sexes leads to her elaboration of predictable crises for couples (see Table 7-2). She performs a useful synthesis and, most important, has done more than anyone in popularizing the entire subject of adult life cycles.

Table 7-2
Predictable Crises of Adulthood[12]

Age Range	Descriptor
18-22	"Pulling Up Roots"
22-30	"The Trying Twenties"
28-32	"Catch-30"
35-45	"The Deadline Decade—Rooting and Extending"
45 plus	"Renewal"

The foregoing is a brief review of past and recent research on the individual human system. Roger Gould states the current situation fairly succinctly:

> We are many years away from having the experience and the studies necessary for an in-depth understanding of the adult period comparable to our current understanding of childhood and adolescence, and my formulations at this point are at best tentative. A number of other researchers are looking at various aspects of adult growth, and all of these studies are adding to our previously impoverished fund of knowledge about the subject.[13]

What are the implications of the research and concepts for the everyday managing of people? Certainly, it is not intended to help the management of an organization to deal with the more extreme psychological aberrations frequently found among employees, those termed by Harry Levinson, former director of Menninger's Industrial Mental Health Division, as "people problems."[14] He includes those who are suffering from undetected mental illness; those who exhibit various symptoms of hostility, such as the authoritarian who pushes people around; the irritable individual who "loses his cool" too often; the aggressive egocentric, and the psychological casualty; those whose job has grown too big; and those who are too impulsive or too unflexible. It also includes people who become despondent when pressed too hard for performance or who have a morbid fear of change. These are real concerns for management.

Argyris has pointed out some significant incompatabilities between individual personality growth and the organizational system:

> If the principles of formal organization are used as ideally defined, then the employees will tend to work in an environment where (1) they are provided minimal control over their work-a-day world, (2) they are expected to be passive, dependent, subordinate, (3) they are expected to have a short-time perspective, (4) they are induced to perfect and value the frequent use of a few superficial abilities, and (5) they are expected to produce under conditions leading to psychological failure.[15]

In describing maturation of personality, Argyris refers to the fact that an individual growing from childhood to adulthood moves from passivity to a more active social role, from dependence on the environment to independence, from specialized functioning to flexibility, and from a subordinate to a supraordinate position in life.

The concept and practices in many organizations are such as to delimit the opportunities for individual growth. Even organizations with lofty ideas and purposes—such as church, health, welfare, and educational institutions—while giving "lip service" to the practice of something they refer to as "democratic administration," actually execute only the rather obvious, good-intentioned kind of concern for others that may develop dependency and warmth but limits the individual's growth to achieve his or her highest needs.

Individual needs differ, collectively or singly, at any particular time. Nevertheless, certain levels of needs have been determined as common to human life experience. Abraham Maslow organizes these into a hierarchy of needs, as shown in Figure 7-2. At the fundamental level of a person's existence one finds the *physical needs.* Food, water, and air form the basic elements of life itself. One does not search for much else in life when these elements are not provided. Historically, even the earliest examples of coercive, industrialized civilization helped people meet some of these basic life needs.

With the basic physiological needs met, a person becomes interested in *safety and security.* The desire to be safe at work and to have a guaranteed wage with retirement benefits is important to most employees.

At the next level, however, we have the basic *social needs* for affection, belonging, achievement, and recognition. These are part of the motivational system of each individual. The historical shift in influence patterns from autocratic to benevolent systems (through organizations) was brought to the fore by an increasing standard of living in which human physical needs were being met, and by the aura in which we commenced wanting and expecting much more than mere subsistence. In the 1940s we began to see the management of organizations provide bowling leagues, retirement benefits, awards, annual picnics, and similar activities initiated by organizations to meet these "social needs." Such endeavors were motivated by multiple causes—desire by management to increase production, to combat increased unionization, to help the workers enjoy life more adequately, to meet the requirements of government regulations, and to help offset the increasing impersonalization of large organizations.

Figure 7-2 Hierarchy of Needs[16]

These endeavors to meet some of the social needs of individuals through benevolent patterns of activity and leadership have been partially successful. Certain improved working conditions, closer relationships with the worker, less stringent controls, and less frustration have resulted from the benevolent system. On the other hand, the paternalism implicit in this approach to relations with others creates dependence, does not account for human change and growth, and creates tension between the highest level of human needs and the organization at work.

As we view the higher level of needs we find human *ego needs* seeking satisfaction. The human need for identity and ego satisfaction surely is well annotated, and frequently reacted to by organizational management through office size, parking spaces, and other responses to the level of human needs actualization.

Maslow, in his interviews of selected subjects, found self-actualizing persons to be characterized by the following:

Efficient perception of and comfort with reality
Acceptance of self, others, and nature
Spontaneity
Problem-centered
Quality of detachment
Autonomy, independence from culture and environment
Continual freshness of appreciation
Effective in interpersonal relations

"Gemeinschaftsgefühl" (empathy for humankind)

As Maslow states, such persons are idiosyncratic in the expression of themselves, "for self-actualization is actualization of a self, and no two selves are altogether alike."[17] Other writers have referred to the concept of self-fulfillment as one of the highest human goals. These two concepts would seem to be closely linked.

A second aspect of the highest human needs is the expansion of the creative ability of human beings. In today's organization we need persons who will create new methods, new products, new ideas, and new solutions. Studies of originality undertaken in the past few years show that originality results from divergent thinking; it means getting out of a mental rut and looking at things in a new and different way. This kind of creative thinking occurs at these three distinct stages: the discovery phase, the insight phase, the inventive phase.[18] Such creativity is essential for organization renewal with effective problem solving. Most organizations have more creative talent than they use effectively. The need and ability for creativity are stifled by the size of the organization, its control factors, and its patterns of leadership.

The third part of the highest human needs is a sense of values. Our need to find meaning in existence, to develop a philosophy of life, to see the world as something of and beyond ourselves, and to give an expression of faith in something meaningful is one of the great human potentials.

If an individual is primarily concerned with physical needs, it is difficult to reach out for this "higher" person. It would seem that in most organizations, however, the challenge of a changing society will require functioning in such a way as to encourage the individual to achieve the highest goals and, in so doing, to contribute to the goals of the organization.

This does not mean that individuals function in a completely "free" way, unfrustrated and nonconforming. All of life requires mutual adjustment among law, order, and freedom. The concept of an organizational climate to provide growth opportunities for the individual does not imply that all human needs will or can be met. It does imply, however, that organizational leaders and members need to search and work diligently for those kinds of human relationships that will provide the best possible opportunities for an individual to reach full potential:

> This dilemma between individual needs and organization demands is a basic, continual problem posing an eternal challenge to the leader. How is it possible to create an organization in which the individuals may obtain optimum expression and, simultaneously, in which the organization itself may obtain optimum satisfaction of its demands?[19]

In operational terms the hierarchy of needs functions as follows. Needs at one level tend not to become activated until those at the next lower level have become satisfied. Once a level of need has been satisfied and remains satisfied, it tends to cease to be a source of motivation. As lower-level needs become satisfied, needs at a higher level emerge: the individual is never completely satisfied. Renewal must take into account the complex motivations of people in the work environment. No easy formula is applicable.

THE INDIVIDUAL IN THE LARGER SOCIAL SYSTEM

Most theorists have accepted the existence of a *psychological contract* between individuals and their organization. Harry Levinson refers to this as "reciprocation." In other words, managers enforce their expectations through the use of authority and power, while individuals enforce their expectations by attempting to influence the organization or by withdrawing all or part of their participation and involvement. Both parties to this psychological contract are guided by their assumptions as to what is equitable and justified. In reporting on the human–organization relationship, the Menninger Foundation study pointed out that the process of fulfilling a contractual relationship focuses upon the following concerns:

> The problem of dependency, and the balance between the necessary reliance on the environment for psychological support and structure versus the need to achieve some degree of autonomy and independence as an adult
>
> The achievement of appropriate and psychologically rewarding relationships with other people, thus avoiding both inappropriate intimacy and chronic isolation
>
> Coping with stressful aspects of the inevitable changes which occur within oneself and in the environment with the passage of time[20]

If we are to understand fully the implication of this psychological contract in the process of individual development, we need to explore the relationship between the job role, expectations, and performance, on the one hand, and individual personality and needs, on the other, as shown in Figure 7-3. Life in an organization requires a constant transaction between two sets of demands—those emanating from the requirements of organized work, and those coming from persons as persons.

Any large system is inhabited both by individuals and by subsystems of organizations. Organizations contain positions which in themselves have particular demands for particular behavior (e.g., the controller has to be concerned with where the money is going). If people were automata, the resultant behavior would be totally predictable, and totally "rationalized" in the sense of the early management theorists. But individuals have personality structures, which imply certain needs. If there were no additional work and family environment making demands on an individual, we might be able to predict his or her behavior from his or her needs.

If we emphasize organizational demands, the emphasis along line A_1–A_2 will be uppermost, and "effectiveness" will be high. But this says nothing about needs. Productivity can be high and morale low. If we emphasize meeting needs, line B_1–B_2 will be most important; but this suggests a happy organization that is not doing very much. If we can create conditions such that position demands are congruent with personality needs (e.g., the controller is a person with strong needs to keep things neat), then satisfaction is likely to be high. This

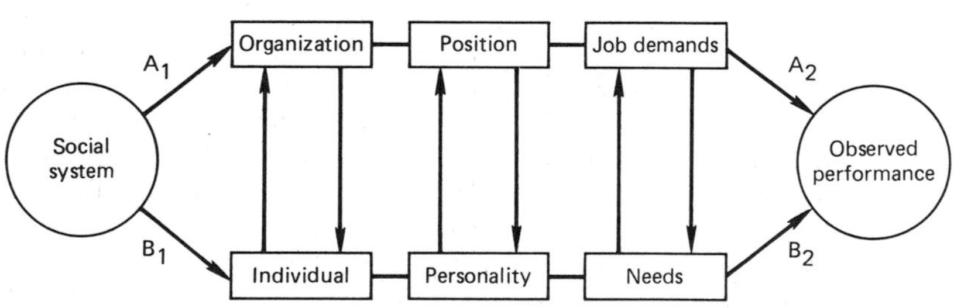

Figure 7-3 Individual Interacts With Work Situation

may or may not lead, however, to either organizational goal achievement or individual need meeting.

The antithesis suggested here is by no means this simple; nor must organizational and individual forces necessarily be opposed. When individuals really accept organizational goals, the suggested opposition decreases sharply. The significance of the interrelationships may be that it offers a concrete image of how organizational goal seeking can encompass or even enhance individual need meeting if such an integration begins to take place. But the fact remains that people get frustrated in organizations, and the working procedures inherent in "an organization" often prove unsuccessful in reaching the goals of people's careers and lives.

One of the consequences of the increased emphasis on large organizations in modern society is the sharpness of the distinction we make between *person* and *role*. This separation is reflected in many of our institutions (e.g., the company lawyer gives legal advice but is not a regular member of the management team). In organizational training and development generally, the aim is to help individuals to perform specialized roles in complex organizations. The training is oriented to the needs of the organization rather than to the needs of the individual. In many organizations the interest is in integrating various roles in the organization rather than organizing these roles to fit the persons in the organization. Even human relations training often aims only to teach a person to perform those interpersonal operations that are a part of an occupational role. In fact, many training activities are not supposed to be concerned with the development of the person. One of the unfortunate consequences of this distinction is the relative ineffectiveness of such an emphasis. We might say that "personality shows through" the role, meaning that the role has not been integrated into the personality; and so we find that a person may communicate one set of attitudes with words, and quite another set by his or her manner of speaking and acting.

Individual development processes leading to renewal need to integrate roles, goals, self, and methods. Ten processes, as examples, have been used in many organizations in attempts to integrate these multiple factors of an individual's behavior to the functioning of the organization:

1. Job enrichment
2. Restructuring work
3. Management responsibility guide
4. Management by objectives

5. Life planning
6. Career development
7. Interpersonal skills development
8. Developing technical skills

9. On-the-job coaching
10. Performance appraisal

The first four of these processes are related to work itself, the second four to personal skills, and the last two have to do with performance feedback and accountability. As indicated in Table 7-3, as part of the systems model, they are not intended to present all of the individual development processes, but rather they are some of the typical approaches to role integration, self-growth, and performance improvement.

JOB ENRICHMENT

If organizations are to meet the needs of people, it will be necessary to find not only what gives people satisfaction but what "turns them on." This fine delineation has come about in the studies of Frederick Herzberg, who differentiates between hygiene factors and motivation.[21] *Hygiene factors* are those that people expect at work, which if not provided will cause dissatisfaction. They are closely aligned with Mas-

Table 7–3
Relationship to Systems Model

Individual Development Process						Individual Development Processes			
Job	R	Management	Management	Life	Career	Interpersonal	Developing	On-the-job	Performance
E	e	R	by	P	P	skills	T	C	A
n	s	e	O	l	l	D	e	o	p
r	t	s	b	a	a	e	c	a	p
i	r	p	j	n	n	v	h	c	r
c	u	o	e	n	n	e	n	h	a
h	c	n	c	i	i	l	i	i	i
m	t	s	t	n	n	o	c	n	s
e	u	i	i	g	g	p	a	g	a
n	r	b	v			m	l		l
t	i	i	e			e	skills		
	n	l	s			n			
	g	i				t			
	work	t							
		y							
		guide							

low's first three levels of needs, and most of them are related to the job environment, such as work conditions, salary, company policy and administration, security, relationship with supervisors, and one's status. The *motivators* are growth factors that really "turn you on." These tend to be related to the job content and are such things as advancement, growth, responsibility, recognition, achievement, and the work itself. Herzberg feels that the challenge to organizations is to emphasize the motivation or growth factors while making sure that the hygiene factors are provided. The method he refers to as *job enrichment:*

> Job enrichment will not be a one time proposition, but a continuous management function. The initial changes, however, should last for a very long period of time. There are a number of reasons for this:
>
> The changes should bring the job up to the level of challenge commensurate with the skill that was hired.
>
> Those who have still more ability eventually will be able to demonstrate it better and win promotion to higher-level jobs.
>
> The very nature of motivators, as opposed to hygiene factors, is that they have a much longer-term effect on employees' attitudes. Perhaps the job will have to be enriched again, but this will not occur as freqently as the need for hygiene.[22]

Job enrichment is a diffuse, open-ended kind of concept, which is more an attitude or a strategy than it is a definable entity.[23] According to job enrichment concepts, large numbers of employees have much more to offer in the way of ability, potential, and general competency than most organizations ask of them. This discrepancy between potential and actual contribution creates significant frustrations for employees and significant costs to the organization. It is possible to restructure the work in order to give employees more of a say about what they are doing, including more responsibility for deciding how to implement their work, for setting goals, and more of a share in creating the excellence of the completed product. The results of such an approach should be improved employee morale, as well as increased productivity. Job enrichment also represents an attempt to move from a mechanistic to a humanistic model of work. The employee is given challenging or complete tasks, as well as more autonomy and discretion to perform those tasks. Such work is motivating in that employees are given an opportunity to solve the problems that involve them directly.

Giving employees more responsibility requires willingness on the part of leaders to delegate authority and to accept decisions made by the employees. Diffusing authority, however, does not imply managerial abdication; it simply means that decisions can be made by the person most involved and thus probably best qualified. Supervisors are spared the need to relay routine questions up the hierarchy—and decisions back down. Managers then have more time to manage, rather than having their time consumed by detailed problem solving. Another concept fundamental to job enrichment is that of organizing employees into teams. Individuals involved in small working units become concerned with helping their teammates and achieving common goals just as members of sports teams do. Although employees respond well to being members of a team and feeling they "belong," they also think it is important to be able to move up and to improve their job status. Most companies, therefore, trying to increase worker satisfaction through job enrichment, put careful emphasis on promoting from within, and make sure that the employees know it. Some of the broad advantages to implementation of job enrichment are shown in Table 7-4.

Although diffusing authority may give managers more time to manage, they often resist handing authority downward. They generally do not believe job enrichment will work, and if it does, they fear that their relative positions will be weakened. It is important, therefore, for top management to allay such fears and to explain fully the benefits to be derived from such an approach. This must be done well before an attempt is made to introduce job enrichment. Another change that occurs as a result of job enrichment is one involving level of communications between employees and management. Employees who have been afforded the freedom that job enrichment implies will be more confident in expressing their true feelings and attitudes and in pressing management to deal more directly with their concerns and frustrations. The implicit and explicit barriers to open, honest communications associated with traditional management will be lowered under job enrichment. The result will be a more open dialogue between employees and their supervisors. However, evidence of the problems associated with such an approach already exists. One study has described a situation in which job enrichment has demonstrated sizable gains in job satisfaction, but in which the affected employees report a similar increase in the amount of difficulty encountered in relationships with management.[24] Job enrichment, therefore, calls for a change in traditional communications systems.

According to Herzberg, job enrichment should be used on those jobs in which: (1) the investment in industrial engineering does not make changes too costly; (2) attitudes are poor; (3) hygiene is becoming very costly; and (4) motivation will make a difference in performance. In this sense, he is viewing job enrichment as a method of obtaining increased motivation, not as a method or technique of human systems renewal in a total sense. His prescription is only part of a much larger context.

An organizational adaptation associated with job enrichment is that there is no reason to believe that responsibility and achievement are everlasting. Motivated employees in enriched jobs ultimately will seek further heights. To deny this would

Table 7-4
Advantages to Job Enrichment

Principle	Motivator
Removing some controls while retaining accountability	Responsibility and personal involvement
Increasing the accountability of individuals for own work	Responsibility and recognition
Giving a person a complete natural unit of work (module, division, area, etc.)	Responsibility, achievement, recognition
Granting additional authority to employees in their activities; job freedom	Responsibility, achievement, recognition
Making periodic reports directly available to the worker rather than to the supervisor	Internal recognition
Introducing new and more difficult tasks not previously handled	Growth and learning
Assigning individual specific or specialized tasks, enabling them to become experts	Responsibility, growth, and achievement

be to deny the concept of self-actualization upon which job enrichment rests. To accept it, however, is to acknowledge a major change in the way employees will define, perceive, and relate to their work roles in a new environment. Once given the opportunity to assume a more responsible position, employees will become more interested and involved in the operation of the organization as they affect and define their potential. These motivated employees will not only be more involved in their jobs, but will also want to know the rationale for written and unwritten company policies, practices, and procedures that directly limit the degree to which they can play a responsible role. As time passes, however, one cannot but wonder how much of the added challenge remains, whether the broadened responsibility persists in its motivational propensity, or the employee merely paraphrases the well-known question, "What have you enriched for me lately?" Companies about to embark upon job enrichment must also answer or at least be aware of these questions: Enriching jobs are attempts to fit the job to the person—but which person? Do we have different sets and sequences of the same operations for people of varying competence, interest, and drive? Does turnover imply continual rearrangement? These are extremely important questions in light of the fact that individual development is an ongoing, continuous part of the renewal process.

RESTRUCTURING WORK

It seems appropriate here to explore, through case studies, the application of job enrichment and *job restructuring*.

U.S. Air Force[25]

The need for some type of organization change within the Air Force began to emerge in the early 1970s. At that time, the military services were returning to a peacetime environment, which, paradoxically, presents very difficult manpower management problems for a large standing military force. Following the end of the Vietnam conflict, military budgets were drastically cut and military strength levels sharply reduced. As the reductions continued and the dollar was shrunk by inflation, ongoing military missions began to be affected. "Doing more with less" and "enhanced productivity" became the clichés of the mid-1970s, and manpower became a real constraint within the Air Force.

During this period, the draft was ended and an all-volunteer military force became a reality. Although the Air Force had always been an all-volunteer force, it now became very concerned about attracting and retaining adequate numbers of high-quality recruits. About this time, changing attitudes toward work were becoming evident in American society, and these attitudes were reflected in the young men and women entering the Air Force. Generally, these young people had high expectations. A survey of Air Force personnel during the early 1970s indicated that 97% wanted a challenging job.

In retrospect, all these factors—the pressure for increased productivity, the all-volunteer force, greater demands for meaningful tasks, and improved quality of work life—were acting in concert to create a felt need for organizational change. Although the entire Air Force felt this need, certain subsystems felt the need more urgently than others. The Air Force Logistics Command (AFLC), for example, operates the Air Force's supply system and is responsible for depot-level maintenance of all aircraft and missiles. Because of the nature of its mission, AFLC was affected early by the call for improved productivity.

One step was to focus on the job of Security Specialist, which had long been extremely troublesome from a motivational point of view; these airmen guard nuclear weapons aboard bomber aircraft and missiles. They are frequently exposed to extremes of weather and spend extended periods of time repeating the same routine checks. In short, the tasks are, for the most part, dull, boring, monotonous, and frequently quite unpleasant. The Security Specialists who perform this duty had the classic symptoms of a problem career area—high disciplinary incident rates, rapid turnover, and low morale. In early 1975, a job-enrichment test program was set up at Ellsworth Air Force Base, South Dakota, within the Security Police Group.*

It was a slow, tedious effort at first to get the test started. Most people—particularly middle-level managers—were skeptical that job enrichment could make a contribution; a lengthy education program was necessary. Top-level management support was essential; without the support and encouragement of the commanders at several levels, neither project would have gotten off the ground. This high-level support continued to be critical as specific job changes were being staffed. Those whose jobs were being enriched were very enthusiastic about the process and the opportunity offered them to participate in the redesigning of their jobs; nevertheless, measurement of the effect of job enrichment was complex. In the case of the Security Specialist job, it was difficult to find an objective means to measure performance. Additionally, in both instances, follow-up measurement required that a lengthy period of time elapse after the job changes were identified and staffed.

Job enrichment produced positive results. The principal data came from productivity-type measures as a result of the initial emphasis. These data indicated significant dollar savings resulting from improved procedures and time-saving actions. The second kind of data includes a measure of job satisfaction and motivation. Both the productivity measures (e.g., absenteeism) and motivation scores showed significant improvements among those whose jobs were enriched. As a consequence of these positive results, AFLC decided early in 1977 to expand job enrichment to all of the other AFLC bases. Additionally, several other Air Force commands have requested assistance in determining if job enrichment may be applicable to their organizational situation. The growing numbers of requests have prompted the development of a comprehensive plan to make job-enrichment consultant services available throughout the Air Force.

This plan recognizes that job enrichment cannot be successfully mandated from above; it must be voluntary. The first-line manager must have the latitude to use or reject the technique in order to develop the real commitment that is so essential for success. Additionally, it appears that not all jobs can be enriched; the expansion plan requires a careful diagnosis of the potential for enrichment before a project is initiated. At the cornerstone of the plan, therefore, there is a small group of professionally trained consultants who are available to assist Air Force units with job enrichment when requested.

*Another experimental program of job enrichment was initiated at Hill Air Force Base, Utah.

American Telephone and Telegraph Company[26]

Mounting employee turnover in the parent company and its subsidiaries during the 1960s had caused top management grave concern. Aside from the fact that high turnover is a costly business in and of itself, other ramifications of it—such as poor productivity, low efficiency, and poor employee morale—were also powerful factors in the drive to get at the root cause.

Robert Ford, former director of the

Manpower Utilization Department, embarked in 1964 on a series of job-enrichment trials in the treasury department, where turnover was so high as to displease everyone. From these studies, a new concept of work motivation through the *Work Itself* idea was developed, and later introduced throughout the Bell System. Ford felt that job satisfaction and dissatisfaction arise from different sources, as had been expounded by Frederick Herzberg. Ford, along with Herzberg, felt that feelings of strong job satisfaction come principally from the task itself offering the employee a chance to achieve, to be recognized for his achievement, to obtain increased responsibility because of performance, to grow in knowledge and capability at the task, and to advance in the business. Conversely, that feelings of dissatisfaction come from job surroundings or from maintenance factors such as company policies and practices, supervision, working conditions, salaries, wages, and benefits. These are hygiene factors and must be present to prevent trouble.

This leads to the key notion that jobs may lack essential ingredients to give long-range satisfaction. Thus, to give a person a real chance of gaining true job satisfaction, the job must contain "work motivators" such as:[27]

Achievement
Recognition associated with an achievement
More responsibility
Advancement to a higher-order task
Growth in professional competence

There is a need to build in the long-range motivators. First, how does anyone sell the field managers the idea that a job such as that of the telephone operator needs to be restructured; second, how do the field managers actually restructure the telephone operator's job so that the motivators mentioned above are in fact incorporated into it; and third, once implemented, how do the field managers monitor the whole program and gauge its success?

There is a vast difference between staff and field operations, and this is where the headquarters people needed to bridge the gap. The staff had to get the field managers to see that they really do need to restructure jobs, and that they are the ones to translate job enrichment into action. The staff can only guide and lend support.

The approach used at AT&T was to assemble in a two-day workshop—at the level of a single system—a whole family of management personnel, from a vice president to first-line supervisor. In these *Work Itself* workshops, the field management team "brainstormed" or "greenlighted" ideas. This is how Ford was able to translate such mind-numbing generalizations as responsibility, achievement, recognition, and personal growth into specifics that relate to the work people actually perform. In the "greenlight" sessions, emphasis is placed on input of ways to innovate methods to improve service effectiveness.

Responsibility: How can we load increased responsibility into, for example, the telephone operator's job and achievement; that is, how can we provide the operator the chance to achieve or excel? *Recognition and personal growth:* What could be done that would result in more complete jobs for the telephone operator? With these two areas of concern before them, the field managers then "greenlighted" from 25 to 150 ideas. These ideas were grouped into categories:[28]

Change of module or slice of work
New responsibility
New form of recognition or feedback
A growth or advancement item
A roadblock that needs to be changed
A maintenance item that needs attention, such as working conditions

Ideas were then ranked according to excellent, good, and not-so-great. Those maintenance items marked excellent were implemented first. Then the motivator items were ranked and listed in order of importance. By the end of the second day, the group was ready to decide whether a job-improvement trial was to be started, and if so, when. Then those "greenlight" motivator items that were considered the best candidates for implementation to reshape a job were selected. The managers listed the obstacles they foresaw in implementing the desired job changes, and the steps they would have to take to overcome resistance. Now the managers were ready to restructure jobs in their districts and come up with a timetable for implementing the program. Thus, phase one of the program was to sell the field managers on the idea of restructuring jobs.

Let us review an actual case to see *how* a field manager actually restructured a telephone operator's job. A telephone operator's job at the switchboard historically is one that requires rigid discipline, close supervision, close adherence to a work schedule with limited breaks, conformity to dress codes, and conformity to telephone operating methods and practices. In other words, the operator is confined physically and is treated as a machine rather than as a person. How can we recreate or restructure this job to build in key input motivators such as responsibility and achievement?

The concept of the "Pro Operator" was developed at one of the workshops. Specifically, it is an attempt to restructure the operator's job, to build into it motivators such as responsibility and achievement, and to give recognition for past outstanding work while providing an opportunity for professional growth and advancement. A central office employs about 100 telephone operators. There are now at least one, perhaps as many as three Pro Operators in each office in a particular system area. They were selected by the entire management team to be Pro Operators based on their past performance. They are so designated by a distinctive headset. These Pro Operators are free of supervision. They are responsible for their own conduct and obligations. They have greater mobility and independence in that they can leave the switchboard when they choose, without obtaining permission from a superior. They are committed to good results for themselves and the customer, and they see that the customer is satisfied. Finally, and perhaps most important, they keep their own attendance records, their own productivity records, and their own quality of work checks; in short, they evaluate themselves. These persons are the best; they have to be, for they are the Pros. They are recognized by their co-workers and supervisors as Pros, and if they possess supervisory capabilities, they are at the top of the list for advancement. Thus, the telephone operator's job was restructured so as to load it with motivator items, to make it a more appealing and satisfying position, to accord it more dignity, and to upgrade its status. Not every operator has the ability or maturity to be a Pro Operator, but perhaps 25 to 30% of the work force does. What is more, everyone is trying harder to make the Pro ranks. This, in turn, is breaking the boredom of the job, getting operators to be more interested in their work, and getting them to produce more. Moreover, the operators are remaining longer with AT&T. It is making operators happier, more satisfied individuals since they now have a goal.

This concept of the Pro Operator was conceived as a calculated risk, but it has demonstrated monetary payoffs in terms of reduced operator turnover, higher productivity, better operating efficiency through reduced supervisory expense, and a psychic payoff in that happier telephone operators lead to improved morale.*

*Not all the Bell systems have implemented this concept.

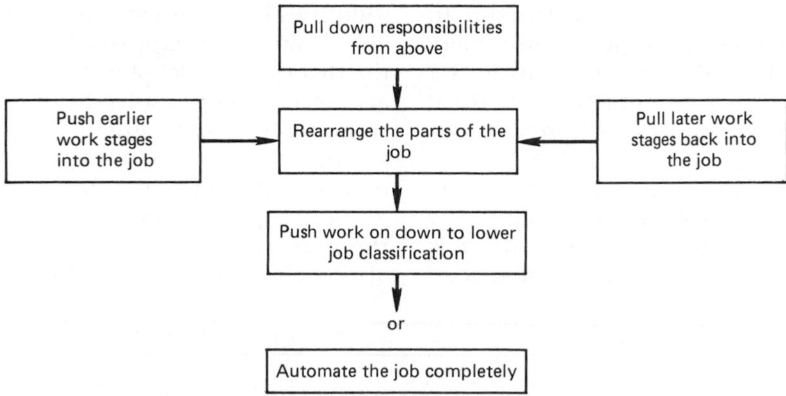

Figure 7-4 A scheme for thinking about improving work itself

Robert Ford feels that good job performance will lead to an improved attitude on the part of the operator towards the work and that "unless the work itself is improved, attitudes will not improve. Attitude change is generally a result, not a cause."[29]

A way of thinking about improving work itself is illustrated in Figure 7-4.

MANAGEMENT RESPONSIBILITY GUIDE

One of the major aspects of improved individual performance has been to bear down on the person's accountability. But how can we manage accountability, reduce interpersonal and intergroup conflict, and improve communications within our organizations? One approach is to use a *management responsibility guide** that fuses systems engineering and behavioral science concepts into an effective problem-solving process, capable of identifying and resolving problems that are otherwise ill-defined and ambiguous. Such a process, of course, must be viable enough to enable members of groups systematically to apply personal accountability to interface differences—within the context of the task to be done. There are five sequential phases in the process.[30]

Defining what needs to be done. Interviews are conducted to define what should be done to meet the organization's mission, not necessarily what is presently being done. The focus is on identifying operational practices and organizational concepts that are at variance with the basic purposes of the organization, as well as surfacing role and relationship issues that prevent the effective accomplishment of the job to be done. Task descriptors are then written which highlight the issues that have been identified. The task descriptors and relevant positions are then entered on a grid.

Determining how individuals perceive relationships. Little role and relationship resolution—meaningful and lasting—can take place without a means by which individuals communicate and develop a mutual understanding. The process of the management responsibility guide meets this requirement by providing a common

*This process was developed by Robert D. Melcher, president of the Management Responsibility Guidance Corporation, and it has successfully been utilized by public and private organizations.

language that enables each participant to state precisely how personnel should relate to each task descriptor entered on the set of matrices. Figure 7-5 illustrates a form used to apply this process to a school system.

Identifying key issues and differences. The participants' responses are returned to the consultant, who prepares a composite view of the perceptions on a set of matrices, identifies key issues and problems, and develops alternative approaches for resolving the divergent perceptions. Some problems are often best resolved on a superior/subordinate basis, others within a group setting. More often than not, a combination of both methods is used.

Clarifying and resolving differences. In the most common group problem-solving approach, each participant is given a set of

Management Responsibility Guide		POSITION OR ORGANIZATION																							
NUMBER	TASK DESCRIPTION	Principal	Assistant Principals	Asst. Principal GL	Asst. Principal AN	Asst. Principal SS	Dir. Student Activity	Department Chairmen	Dept. Chairmen GL	Dept. Chairmen AN	Dept., Chairmen SS	Counselor	Activity Room Teacher	Teacher	Student	Parent		Board of Trustees	Superintendent	Asst. Supt. Area "A"	Asst. Supt. Area "B"	Asst. Supt. Business	Asst. Supt. Education	Dir. Cert. Personnel	Sr. Admin. Asst.
1.1	Develop annual operating budget of school.																								
1.2	Insure compliance to established budget.																								
1.3	Forecast finances necessary for new educational programs, equipment &/or facilities.																								
1.4	Insure that departmental instructional program objectives, plans & commitments are developed within established district policy.																								
1.5	Establish departmental instructional budget in light of program objectives, plans & commitments within district allotment.																								
1.6	Manage department within established plans & budget including transfer to capital funds.																								
1.7	Determine placement of certificated personnel required to meet teaching work loads in accord with master schedule.																								

RELATIONSHIP CODE	A	B	C	D	E	F	G
	OVERALL RESPONSIBILITY	OPERATING RESPONSIBILITY	SPECIFIC RESPONSIBILITY	MUST BE CONSULTED	MAY BE CONSULTED	MUST BE NOTIFIED	MUST APPROVE

	MANAGEMENT RESPONSIBILITY GUIDE APPROVAL C MRG CORPORATION 1971	DATE	PAGE 1

Figure 7-5 Example of Management Responsibility Guide grid[31]

composite matrices depicting almost all responses—with the exception of the superior, whose responses are omitted because they might unduly influence others. After each member reviews the composite matrices, the entire group is brought together to clarify relationships and to resolve differences. During these meetings, the participants share their perceptions and express their feelings regarding how they should be working together. When differences occur that cannot be resolved by peer participants, their superior decides what to do.

Once the members of a group have clarified their roles and relationships, they turn their attention to external groups. The initial group determines how external groups should relate to the defined tasks. Simultaneously, the external groups independently enter their perceptions regarding the same task descriptors. The responses from the internal and external groups are compared and differences resolved in a manner similar to the methodology used within the initial group.

Converting "what should be" to operating reality. During the previous four phases, decisions have been made that affect the concepts, policies, practices, staffing, and structure of the organization. A plan of action is developed and commitments are made regarding the best manner in which to implement the changes with the least amount of disruption to ongoing activities.

Perhaps the greatest disadvantage to using the management responsibility guide is the fact that the results depend mainly on how the consultant or superior handles the data. It is up to them to exhibit true leadership in deciding between what is true and what is not true. Should the facilitator, for example, award certain responsibilities to persons who have no particular aptitude in that job or area, the groundwork may have been laid for failure of the project for that organization. The individual or group that so lacks aptitude probably also lacks an attitude necessary for the desired output. If a work unit is barely enthusiastic about its duties—whether from lack of comprehension or ability to perform—lack of interest often occurs and results are minimal.

Its originator says that management responsibility guidance is successful because it:[32]

- Employs an approach that permits an objective and systematic delineation and definition of the job to be done, taking into account the task as well as the hierarchical structure
- Provides a common responsibility language that affords each manager the opportunity to indicate how he, his organization, and others should relate to the defined tasks or functions
- Involves managers and their superiors in jointly and actively clarifying and resolving their accountability interfaces, first within their own work group and then with other work groups

MANAGEMENT BY OBJECTIVES[33]

Management by objectives is concerned with collaborative objective setting and joint problem-solving exercises by subordinates and superiors engaged in any enterprise. It can be described as a concept, a process, or as an approach; it can be viewed as an individual development process because it focuses on mutually derived objectives as a guide in the organizational decision-making procedure and operation. As an antecedent, it requires collaborative diagnoses, thus providing a conceptual framework and philosophy—and the latter calls for the establishment of time-limited tasks or targets at every level in the organization.[34]

When applied totally, management by objectives is an organic process involving setting appropriate objectives throughout the organization, executing tasks to achieve these objectives, providing feedback on the performance of the tasks, and accordingly adjusting the objectives or the actions. Every step is based on the idea that every human subsystem has some influence on its own goal achievement as well as the goals of the organization. It is a process that meets the criterion of "ownership" of the organization by a large number of individuals in the organization.[35] In general, management by objectives can be summarized in this manner:

Top management sets the "corporate goals." These are direction-setting, long-term, higher-order ends that must be general enough to transcend the specific case and that must hold good over a long period of time for many organizational cases.[36]
Every unit within the organization independently sets its own objectives based on the corporate goals, but not restricted by them.
The unit objectives are presented to the executive level of management, which reviews the discrepancies between the corporate goal(s) and the sum of the unit objectives.
Where discrepancies exist, all affected units are asked to reconcile the differences.
A revised set of unit objectives are developed and set.
Units execute the prescribed actions with feedback to the executive level (for monitoring performance).
Reviews are conducted periodically to appraise performance and "fine-tune" the objectives as required.[37]

Management by objectives is ideally suited to organization renewal, conforming to the underlying assumption that a cornerstone of renewal lies in managing against goals at all organizational levels. Proper application, however, presupposes that a participative style of management is possible and appropriate.[38] Individual development demands:[39]

Genuine subordinate participation in objective-setting components
A team approach
Problem-solving dialogues continuously operative at all levels
Continuous helping relationships be established at all levels
Complementary attention to personal, career goals, and objectives
Trust be developed and encouraged
Skill in process matters be emphasized

The major thrust of management by objectives makes the organization and its subsystems *proactive* instead of reactive. In so doing, it generally eliminates "management by crises."

Management by objectives should not be perceived as a panacea for all organizational problems; it is one of many approaches. Furthermore, all of the significant weaknesses and pitfalls should be identified and thought through beforehand. Particular attention must be placed on the need to *train* supervisors to use the process itself, not just the forms that are instrumental.

CAREER AND LIFE PLANNING[40]

It is difficult to separate planning for career and planning for achievement of life goals. These two things are strongly interdependent. Finding a job and career that fulfills one's interest takes an understanding of oneself, opportunities in the 1980s, and what is meaningful. The dilemma of integrating and balancing one's personal and social life with one's professional and work life is an increasing paradox in modern society. Such a dilemma brings increased stress and strain to the lives of millions of people.

The most effective way to cope with these changing times is to develop a balance between one's work and social identity: *work identity + social identity = self-integration (quality of life).*

We are all acquainted with the term "workaholic." With a workaholic we have an example of a person whose life energy is so consumed by work that life is out of balance. Social and personal life are practically nonexistent and compulsive when it does manage to be evidenced. At the other end of the continuum of the unbalanced life is the self-indulgent. This person puts most of their life, time, and energy into their own social life—frequently accompanied by a feeling of unease, dissatisfaction, and emptiness. Such a person may be a part of the so-called "me generation" that received so much attention during the 1970s. The literature has been filled with the stories of those who, at age 50, became swingers in the free life-style. Many of these people seem to be trying desperately to be happy, but their search leaves them unsatisfied, restless, and unfocused.

The ability of a person to fulfill the potential for balancing social, personal, and professional work life is, of course, influenced by early events in one's life. One must give credence to the importance of the inherited health factors that will determine, to some extent, physical wellbeing. As we now know, we inherit our intelligence and certain aptitudes that influence our abilities, capabilities, and direction. One is also influenced in early life by parental love, authority, hate, and experiences. Whether one is a member of a large or small family has been found to be sociologically important. Whether one is the oldest or the youngest sibling has also been found to be a relevant factor in the maturation process. One cannot neglect the importance of socioeconomic status of the family as another part of one's "growing-up" process.

Research has also indicated the importance of the early work experience as a significant factor in attitudes toward work, and the balance between self and work. One's first part-time job in adolescence can make an important and long-term effect on one's attitudes. That first boss and his or her behavior in your first full-time job makes a contribution to one's attitudes toward authority and bureaucracy.

We are also aware of the fact that the culture in which we live creates norms and expectations relative to behavior of people. Such norms are reflected in dress, work habits, and expectations in an achieving society typified by the advanced industrial culture.

It has been pointed out that some of the factors that influence the ability of a person to be responsive to opportunities for growth are situational skills:

Mobility readiness: the ability and willingness to make a geographical move rather than always staying in the same place of either one's birth and family, or first job placement

Anticipate chance: an ability and desire on the part of a person to make out of a chance encounter an opportunity or event and significant improvement of one's balance of job and life

Life/career planning: the ability to project into the future your own life and career so that you have goals and targets toward which your life is directed

Visibility opportunities: providing opportunities for yourself to be visible by being active in citizens affairs, professional activities, a central position in volunteer or professional organizations, and other situations where visibility to others provides opportunities for growth of self, job, and promotion

Flexibility: the desire and ability to be able to adapt and adjust to changing situations and differing work patterns so that one is not tied to a particular skill, geographical location, or type of organization

A survivor: a person who has resiliency and is not "thrown" by crisis, defeats, or failures

Beliefs and values: a person who has a value system that extends beyond opportunism, self-centered focus, and living only for the moment

In Figure 7-6 there is presented a concept of achieving balance in the quality of personal social life and the quality of work life

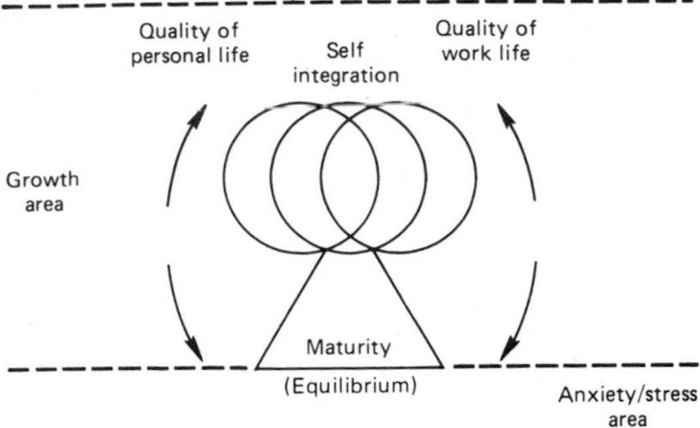

Figure 7-6 Optimal condition for achieving balance

by developing that self-integration which is the essence of maturity, including:

1. Security of one's psychological, physical, and economic self
2. Relatedness with other persons who provide support in one's life
3. Fun and adventure to make life a zestful experience
4. Multiple-role integration of one's function as a citizen, worker, companion, parent, and other roles
5. Peak experience opportunities that give one the thrill of lifelong memory
6. Flexibility and change so that one does not get bored with the tedium of life
7. Values clarification opportunities so that one can think and reflect about one's life in a more meaningful way, thus making a lasting contribution.

These two areas of life—work and personal—merge together to build self-integrity. In the context of self-integrity, therefore, we should include such items as:

Strength of one's ego
Clear life goals
Effective stress management
Acceptance of life cycle
Reality acceptance of one's own limitation
The contribution of others
Generativity to contribute to the next generation
Trust in one's self and others in the world
Spirituality; a belief in something that goes beyond self

Such integration and pulling together for effective balance in one's life is the challenge before all of us; and the achievement of a balance between one's personal and professional growth and life should actively contribute to six areas of human potential:[41]

1. *Achieving physical potential.* The physical potential is one's own awareness of one's own self as a physical being. Our body is the physical form that contains the human energy that makes it possible for us to be vigorous and to develop ourselves to the fullest.

2. *Achieving emotional potential.* The emotional potential of each person is achieved when we become aware that we have emotions that can be experienced and enjoyed. To be human is to experience a range of emotions from immobilizing anxiety to liberating ecstasy. Each person should be able to express his emotions fully, humanely, and spontaneously.

3. *Achieving socialization potential.* This potential involves one's overall awareness of oneself as a social being that is developed in interaction with others. In such a context, we develop the caring community in which we care about others.

4. *Optimizing one's intellectual potential.* In this potential a person becomes aware of his own mind. Through the use of our minds we can make of life a knowledgeable experience in which logic, imagination, information, and the sensors of the mind are utilized. Such intellectual potential means that the person is engaged in a life-long learning adventure.

5. *Optimizing the aesthetic potential.* In the aesthetic experience of one's life there is a recognition that we are part of the total universe and find beauty in the person, nature, a living thing, an inanimate object, a process, a product, or the expression by

these inanimate and living objects. Such appreciation for the sensuous value of beauty is a necessary part of both work and personal life. Integration is a performing art in which one utilizes all of one's senses to balance one's personal and work life.

6. *Achieving spiritual potential.* In this context we are rising above a level of the senses into an awareness of one's self as a holistic part of a larger meaning or pattern of life. Spirituality brings us into a feeling of awe about the realization of being interconnected with all that is in the process of becoming. It is a recognition of the ultimate questions of birth, life, and death. It is a reverence for life and a belief in the celebration of meaning that goes beyond what we now know.

These six areas of human potential can be achieved if individual life and work life are meaningfully integrated. Five steps can be taken by each of us to continue the process of achieving the self-integration necessary for the balance that is proposed:[42]

Step 1: Take charge of your own life. It is the responsibility of each of us to take any steps possible to increase our self-insight, to plan our own future, to assess our career and professional growth, and to focus on the targets and goals desired.

Step 2: Engage in mind, body, and spirit stretching. One should recognize the importance of having new experiences. Branch out into a multidisciplinary approach to learning and living. Develop new linkages with the people, organizations, and activities that develop new insights and experiences. This takes an experimental attitude that involves risk.

Step 3: Inventory your own life. Each of us needs periodically to inventory our capabilities, our desires, and our resources. In this process, we will want to review the constraints on our lives as well as the successes we have achieved.

Step 4: Develop an action plan. In any career or personal growth integration each of us needs to develop an action plan that will involve setting targets, reexamining our career fit, and examining our life-style to determine if it is meaningful and contributing to our potential. In this action plan we should review past learning experiences and reexamine lifelong learning plans for additional adult education, challenges, opportunities, and experiences.

Step 5: Plan for support, review, and evaluation. The process of growth and maturation is difficult. We will need, each of us, to identify and cherish the support of significant others in our life: those friends and colleagues who can give us feedback on our behavior, competencies, and limitations. We will need to build an evaluation of our new directions to assess their meaningfulness and satisfaction.

Despite the fact that life planning and career planning seem to be closely related, more organizations do pay more attention to the career aspect on the belief that it has a greater bearing on organizational responsibilities, benefits, and results. Nevertheless, career planning and development as an organization renewal process does focus on the individual rather than on an organization as a whole. Renewal efforts, of course, need to begin with the individual and proceed from there to ever-larger groups until it encompasses and benefits the whole organization. Human systems renewal is built on the premise that it begins with knowing one's self; and part of this necessary self-knowledge and self-confidence can be gained through career and life planning.

The average working American changes jobs every three years, and totally changes career fields three or four times during a lifetime. Organizations and job titles change, but the individual's skills and competencies provide the common thread.

In addition to the theme of change as identifying a need for career development is evolution to what we now call the quality of work life. In the past, employees were viewed as one of the factors of production, together with capital and equipment. With the evolution of modern management practices, the needs, motivation, and well-being of employees has become a major concern of most large organizations. This is not entirely altruistic; given the climate in which today's organizations operate, it has repeatedly been demonstrated that concern for the employee results in more productivity and reduces the loss of competent persons. The opportunity for career development is considered by most large organizations today to be an objective to be achieved.

Career development and planning refers to a process of clarifying work values, identifying skills and competencies, developing such skills and competencies, studying work settings in which these values, skills, and competencies are compatible, planning and implementing career decisions, and periodically repeating and reviewing the process. It is obvious in this context that one's career is primarily work, but it is also intricately involved with the values and style of one's life.

Some of the career planning steps being undertaken by organizations for employees are:

Job rotation: rotating persons into three or four challenging assignments during early years of employment

Job posting: announcing to all employees new positions that are available within the organization

Management development: providing opportunity for supervisors and managers to develop new competencies

Upward mobility programs: assisting employees with minimal education and skills to enhance both

Career counseling: using tests and interviews to examine career choices

Preretirement counseling: preparing persons for the retirement phase of life

Assessment centers: providing procedures for examining competencies in different behavior situations

Special programs for women managers: helping women to develop managerial skills and self-confidence

Surveys have indicated that the implementation of career planning research and career planning activities is increasing in organizations, and that the organizational interest in and need for career planning and development is well out in front of the response patterns of educational and human resource specialists.

INTERPERSONAL SKILLS DEVELOPMENT

In all the relationships the individual has in the organization, a key element is the sociopsychological atmosphere or climate that exists. Does the behavior of the leader suggest creativity? Is difference of opinion encouraged? Do we solve problems or subtly "attack" each other? These and other questions will answer the question as to whether a group or an organization has developed the kind of climate that encourages mature behavior.

In this sense, maturity connotes a permissive and informal atmosphere, for this determines whether the individual feels free to behave honestly and speak frankly. It not only encourages participation when a person is ready to do so, but actually makes it seem natural and easy to express ideas. By contrast, rigid and formal situations cause feelings and differences to remain unspoken, and this serves to disrupt and delay the problem-solving process. Rather than a climate which induces defensiveness, a climate of support must be developed.

One important aspect of such a supportive climate is an opportunity for two-way communication in which the individual may relate his or her achievements to group and organizational goals—a "feedback" communications system:

> Each individual needs to get accurate information about the difference between what he is trying to do and how well he is doing it. He needs to be able to use this information to correct or change his actions. Then, basically, he is steering himself.[43]

As individuals are involved both in making and carrying out decisions, thus providing them with a real feeling of influencing the direction and manner in which organizational objectives are achieved, more aspects of their abilities are uncovered and more opportunities for personal growth are made evident. This is vital, inasmuch as organization renewal always must be founded on individual growth; collaterally, in his face-to-face task group, the individual can be an important force in setting the norms of behavior and work output that affect goal achievement.

Self-insight is a vital element of interpersonal skills, and such necessary self-understanding can be obtained through group learning situations and by use of certain kinds of instruments. Among the latter are *Firo-B,* the *Managerial Grid,* or the *Keegan Type Indicator,* a recently developed tool that utilizes the concepts of Carl Jung.[44] It is suggested by Jung's work that there are four major personality styles that a normal individual can use in an approach to work and life. The emphasis given a particular style is based on the degree to which the individual chooses one approach over another:

STYLE	*FUNCTION*
Intuitor	Conceiving, projecting, inducing
Thinker	Analyzing, ordering in logical fashion
Feeler	Relating to and understanding experience through emotional reactions and response to feelings
Senser	Experiencing mainly on the basis of one's own sensory perceptions

Another helpful resource is the *Self Development Inventory for Multiple Role Effectiveness,* an instrument that helps a person examine his or her role as an individual or as a member of a group or organization. Inasmuch as the organization renewal process so frequently focuses on the need to stengthen interpersonal skills in operating groups, laboratory-type learning experiences and methods also are frequently utilized. Laboratory training usually includes the methods of group learning, individual feedback, skill practice, and information sessions. The theory behind such methods is based on a concept of learning which states that individuals can best learn interpersonal and group skills through actual experience when that experience is analyzed for the benefit of the learner. One of the underlying assumptions is that people best learn these kinds of insights by self-discovery.[45] It does little good to be "spoken to" about, or to read about, many of these kinds of learnings. The learning experience, then, must provide the kind of setting and methods that will best enable people to discover these insights and knowledges for themselves, and the methods used have been found most helpful to individual growth.

People develop their skill and awareness through various learning experiences. Any experience that can further interpersonal competence will need to provide the following conditions for learning:

- Recognition on the part of the individual of a need for improving his or her own skills
- An opportunity for the participant to interact in a learning situation so that actual behavior may be analyzed
- A supportive and helpful climate for learning created by the total experience
- An opportunity for trainees to give "feedback" on the effect of their behavior in

both structured and unstructured learning experiences

A basic knowledge of individual, group, and organizational behavior to give guidance to the learner

A chance to practice new skills of relating in person-to-person and person-to-group situations

An opportunity to relate learning to back-on-the-job situations

In evaluating the contribution to organization renewal made by interpersonal skills training, it is necessary to assume, first, that the training can affect organizational problems and, second, that individuals and groups are organizational problems. Some organizational problems are not the primary province of any kind of training. If the organizational product or service is not needed, wanted, or of an inferior quality—training is not the answer. Attempting to solve a problem such as that caused by a market that has fallen out from under a product because of technological or marketing factors is out of the range of training. There are some organizational matters that are the main province of other facets of organizational problem solving. Organizational effectiveness, in all its aspects, can never be equated with training or the lack of training, but too often organizations mistakenly see training as the answer to all their problems.

DEVELOPING TECHNICAL SKILLS

The competencies required to work effectively in an organization have been simplistically classified as *human, technical,* and *policy* development skills. We have seen that the first of these skills—the human, the interpersonal—can be learned in many ways; so, too, can technical skills. A few examples demonstrate the need for various types of workers to learn new ways to do things within their own vocational field:

A welder learning to weld titanium rather than steel

An accountant learning a new balancing procedure

A salesperson learning problem-solving methodologies

A manager learning word processing

A nurse learning a new shock-therapy technique

Organization renewal is not merely a matter of good intentions on the job. It involves the improved ability of persons in the organization to *learn* new skills. Some people feel that knowing how to work well is an inherited part of our nature. This may not be true, because research indicates that we generally must learn how to work. Facilitators of organization renewal face the fact that the learning of many persons is out-of-date. The knowledge explosion has antiquated many of our skills in human relationships, communication, management, and technical performance. To secure support for new skills, it will be necessary for most adults to "re-learn" so as to substitute new ideas, concepts, and realities for the outmoded knowledge, skills, and attitude they possess.

Learning as learning is rewarding. It satisfies curiosity, it provides greater personal power; it gives one a sense of achievement. On the other hand, learning may be uncomfortable. It says that the job of personal development is not finished. Cherished and comfortable assumptions and ways of doing things must be questioned. Employees are obliged to open themselves to anxiety and stress as they abandon earlier skills and fumble in ambiguity toward new attitudes, new insights, and new abilities.

ON-THE-JOB COACHING

In any human system, it is necessary to differentiate among performance improvement, performance appraisal, and a management inventory of promotable human resources. Performance improvement results from an individual's desire to improve in accordance with own goals—and, in some circumstances, as shared and discussed with a superior. The latter is a coaching and joint planning process. Performance appraisal is usually a function that is undertaken periodically so as to determine the movement toward and contribution by an individual or group in attainment of an organization's goals; collectively, these appraisals amount to a management inventory of promotable human resources, useful in making choices with respect to assignment and promotion. In many cases, a superior will use a completed appraisal form in the coaching relationship. Here understanding is aided by keeping in mind certain truisms about performance improvement:[46]

People perform better when they have a "say" about what they will do.
Subordinates are motivated by knowing that supervisors know and support their objectives for job achievement.
Organization objectives will be achieved only to the degree that individuals in the organization subscribe to and support them.
Individual objectives are the greatest support of organization objectives.
Individual objective setting is indispensable to personal growth.
Developing individual objectives increases organization productivity because it enables the individual to "stretch" and achieve on the basis of his or her own targets.
The individual needs to understand clearly his or her own role and job function.

Clarifying job functions and responsibilities should result in a concise, accurate statement of what the individual should *know* and *do* to accomplish successfully the task assigned. This statement should be in writing. In defining fuctions and responsibilities, the individual must come to know:

What he or she currently is doing, as well as what he or she *should be* doing
How he or she does it, as well as how he or she *should be* doing it
Why he or she is doing it, in terms of specific plans and objectives

The Institute of Industrial Relations at the University of Chicago suggests the coaching process shown in Table 7-5.

Table 7-5
Five-Step Coaching Process[47]

1. *Clarify functions, responsibilities, and authority (FR&A):*
   This is to involve in the process the person being coached, who will in turn crystallize the FR&A as he or she seems them.
2. *Reach agreement on FR&A:*
   This helps establish a firm base for coaching and development.
3. *Review job progress and problems:*
   This identifies specific areas for coaching and development.
4. *Analyze and work through problems:*
   This should involve seeking the causes of problems and developing alternative ways.
5. *Provide for continuing development:*
   Here there should be devised mutually agreed upon developmental activities, with means for interim evaluation.

A person engaged in on-the-job coaching should remember that an important element in achieving changed behavior is the environment in which performance is undertaken, and that the process of coaching, in and of itself, can be rewarding or punishing, depending upon whether or not it is two-way and collaborative.

PERFORMANCE APPRAISAL

One of the most persistent questions confronting professional managers today is the use—or misuse—of performance appraisals.[48] What, if any, is the real value of this management technique? Should a uniform "performance appraisal program" be applied through the various job levels and work environments in today's large-scale enterprise? What are the implications of management by objectives for conventional appraisal plans?

The conventional performance appraisal concept is expressed in terms of three goals: improving performance, setting individual management development goals, and helping to identify a person's future potential. These three objectives are both broad-gauged and complex, and the conventional appraisal approach very often ignores or underrates the complexities. In most cases, the appraisal forms produced are a rather naive "managerial grade card," designed to rate persons on personal traits or broad general characteristics. Very often a person's future prospects are decided by these crude judgments.

Typically, the appraisal interview, the heart of the process, is scheduled yearly. One basic assumption is that a judicious mixture of criticism and praise usually will motivate a person to change in ways indicated by a superior. Also implicit in the appraisal process are these lesser assumptions:

- That the current crop of managers are adequate to judge and stimulate the new crop of employee talents
- That the superior's management philosophy and behavior are worthy of emulation
- That the person being appraised has control over all the factors that make up the work situation and affect his or her performance
- That the appraiser really understands the current nature of the work and the skills and knowledge required to perform it
- That the person being appraised respects the judgment, ability, and values of the appraiser
- That a person can and will communicate in a tightly structured situation, and that sound communications can be established on "periodic" contact

Where appraisals are tied into organizational planning programs, there is also the assumption that appraisers share common performance criteria and use the broad yardsticks with the same general skill. There is, in fact, a wide gap between theory and practice. Appraisers frequently are biased and befuddled; the person being judged frequently is confused and resentful. Accordingly, a variety of new approaches have been tried. Some organizations have experimented with group appraisals; others have tried appraisals by peers. Bold innovators added to the process appraisals of superiors by subordinates. Others, finding that subordinates were not following through on recommendations, discarded the interview feedback and simply used appraisals as a form of managerial inventory taking.

The heart of the appraisal process is a goal-setting session in which manager and subordinate together discuss, clarify, and agree upon specific targets and timetables. Subordinates describe the direction in which they want to grow and how they plan to get there. The superior reviews organizational goals, makes certain they are consistent with the broader objectives of the unit, and helps translate these goals into a plan of action.

The conventional appraisal approach, on the other hand, is basically a control device. It is most appropriate when used with those individuals and groups, such as hourly personnel and many first-line supervisors, whose work merits or requires directive supervision. In modern organizations there is another complication. The higher and more complicated the manager's role, the more difficult it is to judge a person on the basis of acts for which that person is specifically accountable. This is especially true of higher-level staff functions. Top managers frequently make a crucial contribution not in the decisions they make themselves, but rather in the difficult-to-identify advice they give decision makers below them.

In the last analysis, the suitability of performance appraisal rests upon the organization's philosophy of personnel relations. There is little logic, for example, in an organization that wishes to encourage more individualism, innovation, and creativity among its professional personnel, moving toward the kind of directive counseling represented by conventional appraisal systems. There is nothing inherently bad about performance appraisal as a technique, but it must be remembered that its validity can be assessed only in terms of the mores, management policies, and general climate of a specific organization. Used at its appropriate level, for its appropriate role, the performance appraisal can be useful.

SUMMARY

The foregoing ten processes for individual development are certainly not all-inclusive. At best, they are suggestive of how the individual and the human system can be continuously renewed. This leads to the conclusion that the largest human system, and its renewal, starts with a system of one.

AN EXAMPLE OF AN INDIVIDUAL DEVELOPMENT APPROACH: *Whole-Person Executive Development in an International Corporation*

Recognizing the need for giving attention to the "whole person" in training and development activities, one international corporation is taking this approach:

1. *An executive development model was developed that gives equal emphasis to technical skills, organizational understanding, and human effectiveness (see Figure 7-7).*
2. *An executive profile is developed on each key manager identifying his or her strengths and weaknesses in each of these three areas.*
3. *An inventory is made of their career goals, interests, geographic preferences, and so forth.*
4. *A professional development plan is then developed for each person. This outline is a combination of planned experience, seminars, workshops, self-study, and so forth.*

The purposes of this plan are to:

1. *Integrate personal and organizational goals wherever it is practicable to do so.*
2. *To develop the skills needed in a position prior to moving into it, so as to avoid promoting someone on the basis of irrelevant experience.*
3. *To develop better-rounded management generalists at a variety of levels.*

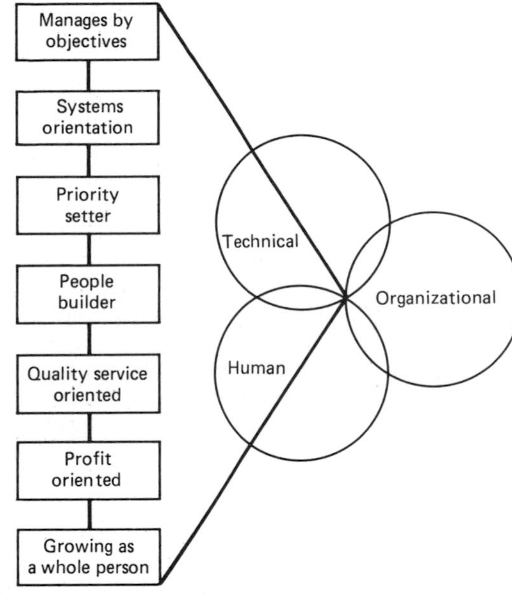

Figure 7-7 Executive development model

This company believes that a person's technical expertise will be more effectively applied if the person understands how this skill relates to the entire organization. The organization will be effective only to the degree that its management team can maturely interact.

Comment. *This organization has focused on important individual development processes related to a model they find helpful. Such an approach to organization renewal made "sense" to them. The company used both internal and external resources to implement the training and development process.*

QUESTIONS

1. In what additional ways do you believe that work styles are changing in today's society?
2. In what ways should leaders be aware of personality factors in themselves? In others?
3. What adult transition or crisis experience did you find to be a challenge? Why? How did you cope with it?
4. How do specialized rules in an organization affect a person's behavior? Cite some examples.
5. How do you feel that career and life goals might conflict? In what ways have you found that they can be integrated?
6. In what ways, in your work experience, were you or your superior able to enrich your job?
7. What types or methods of performance appraisal have you experienced? In what ways do you feel that performance appraisal is changing in today's organizations?
8. Of all the people who may have helped you in your life and career, which ones were most effective in coaching you? Why?

NOTES

[1]Excerpt from an unpublished study completed in 1979 by Yankelovich, Skelly and White, Inc., 575 Madison Avenue, New York, N.Y. 10022.

[2]Gordon W. Allport, *Personality: A Psychological Interpretation* (New York: Holt, Rinehart and Winston, 1973), p. 48.

[3]Ralph W. White, *The Abnormal Personality* (New York: The Ronald Press Company, 1948), p. 106.

[4]Erik H. Erikson, *Childhood and Society,* 2nd ed. (New York: W. W. Norton & Company, Inc., 1963), p. 166. Hereafter cited as Erikson.

[5]Erikson, pp. 11-12.

[6]Ernest R. Hilgard and Richard C. Atkinson, *Introduction to Psychology,* 4th ed. (New York: Harcourt, Brace & World, Inc., 1967), p.74

[7]Bernice L. Neugarten (ed.), *Middle Age and Dying* (Chicago: University of Chicago Press, 1968).

[8]Wilbur Bradbury, *The Adult Years* (New York: Time-Life Books, 1975).

[9]Daniel J. Levinson, *The Seasons of a Man's Life* (New York: Alfred A. Knopf, Inc., 1978), p. 57. Hereafter cited as Levinson.

[10]Roger Gould, "Adult Life Stage—Growth toward Self-tolerance," *Psychology Today,* February 1975, pp. 74-78. Hereafter cited as Gould.

[11]Levinson, p. 64.

[12]Gail Sheehy, *Passages* (New York: E. P. Dutton & Company, Inc., 1974).

[13]Gould, p. 74.

[14]Harry Levinson et al., *Men, Management, and Mental Health* (Cambridge, Mass.: Harvard University Press, 1962), pp. 23-37. Hereafter cited as Levinson et al.

[15]Chris Argyris, "The Individual and Organization: Some Problems of Mutual Adjustment," *Administrative Science Quarterly,* Vol. 2, No. 1, 1957, 10. Hereafter cited as Argyris.

[16]Abraham Maslow, *Motivation and Personality* (New York: Harper & Row, Publishers, Inc., 1954).

[17]Abraham Maslow, "Self-actualizing People: A Study of Psychological Health," *Personality Symposium,* No. 1, 1950.

[18]*Creativity and Conformity: A Problem for Organizations* (Ann Arbor, Mich.: The Foundation for Research on Human Behavior, 1958), p. 11.

[19]Argyris, p. 24.

[20]Levinson et al., p. 38.

[21]Frederick Herzberg, *Work and the Nature of Man* (Cleveland, Ohio: The World Publishing Company, 1966).

[22]Frederick Herzberg, "One More Time: How Do You Motivate Employees?" *Harvard Business Review,* January-February 1968, p. 62.

[23]Adapted from an unpublished paper by Howard C. Sakwa, *Job Enrichment as an Organization Development Method* (Washington, D.C.: The George Washington University, 1971).

[24]W. N. Penzer, "Managing Motivated Employees," *Personnel Journal,* May 1971, pp. 367-371.

[25]Adapted from an unpublished paper by Paul L. Roberson, *The Air Force's Use of Job Enrichment* (Washington, D.C.: The George Washington University, December 1977).

[26]Adapted from an unpublished paper by George J. Sears, *One Approach to Organization Development/Renewal: Restructuring Work* (Washington, D.C.: The George Washington University, November 1971).

[27]Robert N. Ford, *Motivation Through the Work Itself* (New York: American Management Association, Inc., 1966), p. 25.

[28]Ibid., p. 151.

[29]Ibid., p. 147.

[30]Robert D. Melcher, *Roles and Relationships: Clarifying the Manager's Job* (New York: American Management Association, Inc., 1967), p. 102.

[31]Robert D. Melcher, "A School District Learns Its 3Rs by Clarifying Its ABCs," *Thrust,* Vol 3, January 1974, p. 15.

[32]Ibid., p. 16.

[33]Adapted in part from an unpublished paper by Angelo J. DiMascio, *Management by Objectives: An O.D. Perspective* (Washington, D.C.: The George Washington University, November 1976).

[34]William R. Dill, Henry B. Eyring, and Harold J. Leavitt, *The Organizational World* (New York: Harcourt Brace Jovanovich, Inc., 1973), p. 20.

[35]Richard Beckhard, *Organizational Development: Strategies and Models* (Reading, Mass.: Addison-Wesley Publishing Company, Inc., 1969), p. 38. Hereafter cited as Beckhard.

[36]Robert L. Kahn and Daniel Katz, *The Social Psychology of Organizations* (New York: John Wiley & Sons, Inc., 1966), p. 265.

[37]Beckhard, p. 37.

[38]Carl Heyel (ed.), *The Encyclopedia of Management,* 2nd ed. (New York: Van Nostrand Reinhold Company, 1973), p. 505.

[39]Wendell L. French and Cecil H. Bell, Jr., *Organization Development* (Englewood Cliffs, N.J.: Prentice-Hall, Inc., 1973), p. 168.

[40]Adapted from Gordon Lippitt, "Integrating Personal and Professional Development," *ASTD Journal,* May 1980, pp. 12-18.

[41]Virginia Macagnoni, "Coming to Terms with Curriculum as a Human Agenda," *Life Long Learning* (yearbook; Alexandria, Va.: The Association for Supervision and Curriculum Development, 1979).

[42]B. J. Chakiris and Don Swartz, *Life/Work Goals Exploration Program* (Washington, D.C.: Development Publications, 1977).

[43]Leland P. Bradford, "A Fundamental of Education," *Adult Education,* April 1952, p. 85.

[44]Warren J. Keegan, *Keegan Type Indicator* (Washington, D.C.: Development Publications, 1979).

[45]Malcolm S. Knowles, *The Leader Looks at Self-development* (Looking into Leadership Monographs; Washington D.C.: Leadership Resources, Inc., 1961).

[46]Gordon Lippitt and Jaqueline Rumley, *Management by Objectives and Performance Appraisal: Leaders Guide* (Santa Monica, Calif.: Stephen Bosustow Productions, Inc., 1975), p. 10.

[47]*Coaching and Developing Individuals* (Chicago: Industrial Relations Center, University of Chicago, 1969), pp. 3-6.

[48]Adapted from Gordon Lippitt and Phillip R. Kelly, *Performance Appraisal: Useful for What?* (workshop paper; New York: New York Port Authority, 1971).

8

group development approaches

"There is nothing good or bad per se about a group."

"A group can be a roadblock to progress, enforcing 'group think' and conformity upon its members, paralyzing decision-making processes and smothering individual initiative."

"Under other conditions, a group can be a powerful synergism of talents, strengthening its members, speeding up the decision-making process and enhancing individual and personal growth."

Rensis Likert, 1903–[1]

In organizations, it is in the face-to-face work group where the individual potentially can satisfy personal needs, influence the organization, and attempt the integration of personal goals with those of the group and the organization of which the group is a part. As shown in Figure 8-1, a model of the "psychological contract" that takes place between the individual and the organization helps us to see the importance of the work group.

The concept of a psychological contract connotes the idea that the employee has certain expectations of the employing organization, and that the employing organization expects certain things from the employee. These expectations relate to work performance, quality of work, rights, rewards, roles, and the obligations of both parties. Only a portion of these expectations are ever expressed in a formal way, such as by job descriptions and performance targets. Often, they are in the unwritten manifestations of behavior. As organizations become larger, more impersonal, more structured, the individual finds that the face-to-face situation is usually the most likely way to resolve expectations, both of the individual and of the organization.

Another reason for the importance of the face-to-face group, according to research, is that these overlapping work groups enable group leaders to be a "link" between the various levels of organizational functioning. In the research work done at the Institute of Social Research at the University of Michigan, it was indicated that one of the general patterns of high-producing and high-morale types of organizations revealed a tightly knit and effectively functioning social system. The major feature of this system was that interlocking work groups had a high degree of group loyalty, a climate of trust between leader and members, and effective patterns of interaction. Or as Rensis Likert comments:

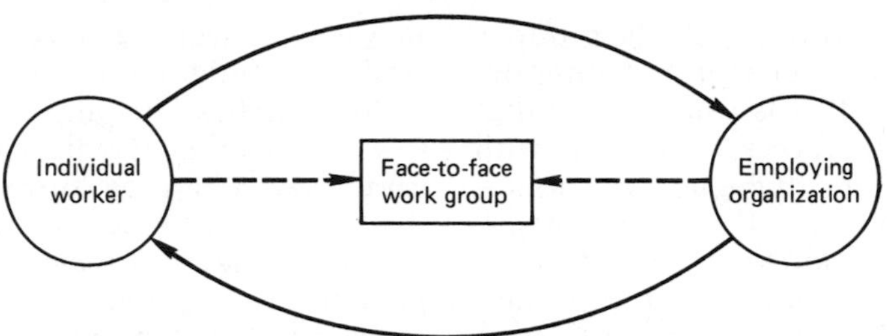

Figure 8-1 Psychological Contract[2]

Management will make full use of the potential capabilities of its human resources only when each person in an organization is a member of one or more effectively functioning work groups that have a high degree of group loyalty, effective skills of interaction, and high performance goals.[3]

The organization is a system of overlapping groups, as indicated in Figure 8-2. An organization leader is a member of one group in the organization with his or her superiors, and a leader of his or her work group, and serves thereby as a link between the two groups. A supervisor belongs to one group with superiors, to another group as the leader, and is usually a member of an informal group such as the carpool or coffeebreak group. This way of looking at an organization is more prevalent today, and more concurrently relevant to the real operations of a sociotechnical system. These groups link together the parts of the organization, and management personnel are the key linkers because of their multiple group responsibilities and involvements.

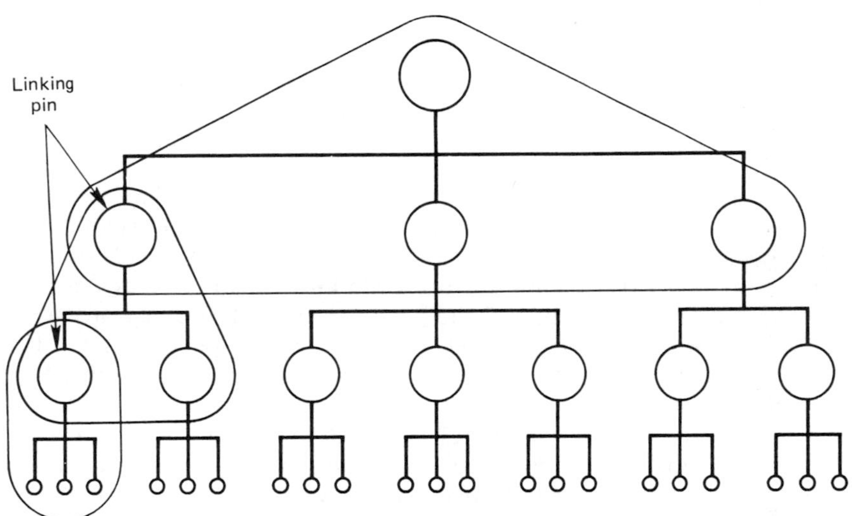

Figure 8-2 Overlapping Work Units in Organizations

In light of these two factors, the group is a principal point of focus in initiating organization renewal. It is usually here that interfacing—the process of coping with situations through dialogue, confrontation, and search—can take place most effectively. It is not enough for an individual to want change, but rather an important group or a number of groups must desire change if renewal and growth of the organization are to be achieved.

In such a context, we find a third factor supporting group development in an organization. The interrelationship between followship and leadership is rooted in group effectiveness. In the overlapping group concept, a person involved in the management of a human system will be a leader in a group of subordinates and a follower in a group of superiors.

> Perhaps the most significant learning to come from the many studies of leadership is . . . that it is determined by followership. There can no more be leadership without followership than there can be compass north without compass south, or for that matter east and west. The follower determines the leader. If we do not have followers, we do not have leaders. It is as simple as that.[4]

In other words, a person needs to develop concurrently the skills of membership *and* leadership in order to contribute to a group.

Generally speaking, the task assigned to or chosen by a group deals in some manner with a situation or a problem, and the resolution or solution usually involves effective teamwork. Herein lies one of the essential reasons why many leaders and managers decline to try to take advantage of group action when confronting organizational situations. The frustrations anticipated in securing teamwork—perhaps not without reason—are simply more than one cares to suffer. Insofar as organization renewal is concerned, however, these frustrations should and can be overcome.

Nevertheless, helping a group of people to work together is a difficult and complex undertaking, and a primary managerial decision is whether a working group should be asked to solve a problem or implement a program. To choose not to use work group action may block program or policy implementation, because the people involved in the program or affected by the policy had no hand in its development. Or it might reveal that the manager has no confidence in his or her own leadership and ability to work with people—or no confidence in the members of his or her own work unit. More important, it could suggest that the people working with the manager are not developed into the kind of team needed for the renewal process to be initiated. A manager, leader, consultant, or the organization development specialist, therefore, needs to be able to diagnose and release the human potential of persons in group situations.

THE GROUP AS A SOCIAL SYSTEM

Whether they have produced action or inaction, groups are as old as mankind. In recent years, our society has come to place increasing emphasis on them, partly because we have become more interdependent in the complex organizations we have created; we must necessarily rely on and collaborate with others. Paradoxically, as our lives and occupations as individuals become more specialized and fractionated, we experience a greater need to meet and work with others. Our expectations in this regard are not always fulfilled; but in spite of the complaint that "a camel is a horse put together by a committee," groups can be and frequently are effective.

During the years since World War II, behavioral scientists have devoted considerable valuable research effort to group phenomena—the "hows" and "whys" of group behavior. In trying to discover what it is that makes some groups effective and others ineffective, they have particularly examined the forces that normally determine the behavior of the group and its members. These forces are called the "dynamics" of the group:

> "Group dynamics" is not something that occurs or disappears according to the wish of the leader or its members. *Every* group has its dynamics—its unique *pattern of forces*. These forces describe the interaction in the group—the interpersonal relationships, the communications problems, the way the members make decisions. Although these forces may exist in varying degrees, an examination of any group shows that they are always present.[5]

Most groups fall into two categories. Our concern here is with the task-oriented group rather than the primarily social group. The task-oriented group performs two interrelated functions: first, the maintenance function—achieving viable continuity—and second, the task function—achieving an assigned or chosen goal. An effective task group must perform both of these functions well if it is to achieve effective teamwork.

Research conducted on the characteristics of groups, their dimensions, the functions of their leadership, their decision-making processes, and other factors now makes it possible to analyze the dynamics of a group and to prescribe ways it can better deal with its problems. It is from this research also that ideas regarding organization renewal have been developed. Generally speaking, these things are known about groups:

> Successful group productivity depends on the ability of the members to exchange ideas freely and clearly, and to feel involved in the decisions and the processes of the group.
>
> A collection of capable individuals does *not* always produce a capable group. Mature adults often form an immature working team. When people get together, they assume a character and existence all their own, growing into a mature working group or becoming infantile in their handling of problems. A number of investigators are now studying this area of group pathology, identifying reasons why some groups fail to be creative and productive.
>
> Groups may be helped to grow to maturity; they need not develop like Topsy. By using appropriate procedures, groups can become more productive, channel energies into effective work, and eliminate or replace internal conflicts that block group progress.
>
> The ability of a group to function properly is not necessarily dependent upon the leader. No group can become fully productive until its members are willing to assume responsibility for the way the group acts. Any group can benefit from a skilled leader, but to get creative group thinking, group decisions, and group actions, many different roles are required. The effective leader must realize (and help the members to realize) that each member must contribute to the total task of leadership.[6]

According to some studies, the average executive or manager spends as much as 70% of the workday in group relationships or conferences of one kind or another. The investment of so much time with other people indicates the nature of procedures and tasks in today's organizations, but many managers consider much of this involvement in face-to-face groups to be a waste of time. Therefore, since organizational growth relies so much on the effectiveness of work groups, we are challenged to learn more about how they can best be managed. Certainly the face-to-face work group is a key factor in the morale and productivity of any organization:

> Each of us seeks to satisfy our desire for sense of personal worth and importance primarily by the response we get from people we are close to, in whom we are interested, and whose approval and support we are eager to have. The face-to-face groups with whom we spend the bulk of our time are, consequently, the most important to us. Our work group is one of the most important of our face-to-face groups and one from which we are particularly eager to derive a sense of personal growth.[7]

The leader should not impose an intractable will on a group because the basic goal is to develop the potentiality of a group to work together. The advantages of either individual or group action should not be described in absolute terms, because both can be appropriate. As a matter of fact, meaningful group action more often than not reinforces the role of the individual:

> Social science, by discovering what happens in group situations and what causes different individual behavior, and by contributing to the recent growing movement of leadership and membership training, has aided materially in freeing and developing the individual rather than submerging him or her in the group.[8]

Similarly, an important element of organizational maturity, as well as individual growth, is the way in which work is accomplished with and through people. In this sense, groups should not be viewed as necessary evils, but rather as offering a viable opportunity for organizational growth when there is enough insight and knowledge to cause them to be productive.

The need for developing effective groups is a must for any temporary or ongoing work in the organization, but such group development will depend upon a dynamic balance being achieved in the group on four levels. Without implying an order of importance, these levels are:

Organizational expectation level. The organization has certain expectations of the work group. These may be in the form of production goals, quality work, company loyalty, creativity, or some other expectation of those who manage the organization or set up the objectives that govern a particular group in the organization.

Group task level. Most groups confront a task, and exist primarily to carry out that task. They are sometimes so conscious of the need to accomplish this particular task that they ignore or are unaware of the three other levels which are always operating simultaneously.

Group maintenance level. As people work on a task together in a group, they are also doing something *to* and *with* each other. Consequently, a group needs to have a growing awareness of itself as a group, of its constantly changing network of interactions and relationships, and of the need to maintain within itself relationships appropriate to the task. "Maintenance level" refers to what is happening to the members of the group as the task is being accomplished, and this has a direct bearing on the continuity of the group as a group.

Individual needs level. Each member of a group brings a particular set of needs that impinge upon both the group and its task. Individual needs may relate to all the different levels of men's and women's "hierarchy of needs." A group member may be getting psychological and safety needs met through external sources of a guaranteed annual wage, good physical working conditions, safe work environ-

> ment, and an adequate living standard. It is very likely, however, that the work group will be appropriate to meeting social, ego, and self-fulfillment needs.

As a group balances these four levels, it becomes a more effective and mature group. It acquires group teamness, and thereby contributes to organizational effectiveness. When one or more of these levels is neglected, the work of the group is impaired and its growth thwarted.

Although resenting anyone else saying so, a manager or supervisor may very well admit privately the ineffectiveness of many of the group problem-solving situations for which they are responsible. Usually, only a few members of the work group speak up in a frank manner, and one or two persons seem to dominate the decision-making process. Too much time is spent on details and minor differences and too little on the critical matters that are supposed to receive the group's attention. Under these circumstances, consideration of group and organizational effectiveness makes it appropriate to define factors affecting group leadership and group functioning. In other words, how can the functioning of a task group and the relationship of its members be improved? It is pertinent here to examine briefly some of the characteristics of a task group—any task group; these characteristics are neither "good" nor "bad" but as part of the reality of the group as a human system, they can be diagnosed by the leader and the members in terms of their affect on group action.

Group background. There is a history to each group situation before it even starts. Each member of the group brings to the group a "mental set." One might approach a group meeting saying to himself, "I wonder how long *this* meeting will take? or "I'm not going to let *anyone* jam anything down my throat!" Someone else will be thinking, "I hope I can get *my* idea pushed through this time," or "The boss isn't going to pull a fast one on me *again!*" And "This isn't the way we used to do it." These attitudes affect the behavior of all the participants.

Group participation patterns. Communication failures in group situations are usually the result of individual inability to express ideas clearly or significantly. The succinct statement is a rarity; rambling in search of a point is commonplace. The member who uses a technical or high-flown vocabulary to talk over the heads of others sometimes makes it nearly impossible for a group to function meaningfully. Nonverbal means of communications—those postures, facial expressions, and glances—can be disruptive and discouraging, or helpful and revealing.

Group cohesion. This is an immediate factor in working group productivity and morale—how effectively the group really functions as a team, how well it sticks together when the going gets rough or a crisis of decision arises. Groups are cohesive because of a variety of individual motivations that are strengthened in a cooperative situation in which each member has and is more or less aware of responsibility—without abdicating his or her right to independent thought. Cohesion depends more on goal commitment, wanting to belong to the group, and respect for others, than whether or not a member of the group agrees with or "likes" the others.

Subgroups. In any group situation, it is normal that subgroups of two or more members may be formed. Sometimes these subgroups are based on friendships, sometimes they gravitate around common agreement about a particular issue or common dislike of a situation. Individuals frequently change from one subgroup to another in the same group—agreeing with certain members on one issue, and then identifying with different members on another issue. When management is interested in organizational growth, it must be concerned with subgrouping that thwarts problem solving or healthy interpersonal relationships, particularly those subgroupings that tend to isolate or shut out other members of a group.

Group Atmosphere. This does not refer to the temperature or humidity in a room, although these comfort factors may be related to the group situation. Group atmosphere refers to the freedom or informality of the group situation, the permissiveness and friendliness that prevails in the work group. It bears on the frankness with which the members express their real feelings about issues, and the existence of an environment in which the members of a group feel free to speak when they have something to say.

Group standards. Here we refer to the mode of operation that the group adopts or is forced into, the sense of responsibility or nonresponsibility it possesses as it carries out its assignment or chooses its goals. It might be a standard of coming to work on time, of quality performance, or of being willing to "talk back" to the boss. Group standards are likely to be established fairly quickly, and to persevere. Various kinds of standards will emerge in any work group and affect the patterns of work, and they can be discerned by the leader and the group.

Group procedures. It is inevitable that a group will follow certain procedures, formal or informal, helpful or hindering. In most task group situations, except those involving large numbers of participants, there is little need for formality and, general speaking, informality encourages a permissive atmosphere. Even small and informal groups, however, require some ground rules.

Group goals. Goals can be of immediate, short, or long range; they can vary in their clarity and in the value the group places upon them; they can emerge from the group or be imposed on it; they can be realistic in relation to the resources of the group or completely unrealistic. Effective groups must continually check the clarity and validity of their goals.

Group leader and member behavior. Leader behavior in a group can range from almost complete control of the decision making by the leader to almost complete control by the group, with the leader contributing his or her resources just like any other group member. A leader can assume most of the functions required to provide leadership for the group; or these functions can become the responsibility of the members as well.

These characteristics affect all work groups as they strive to get their many objectives achieved, and try to meet the four levels of needs mentioned above.

There are several kinds of groups within the usual organization, each with its own pattern of behavior, communication, cohesion, goals, procedures, leadership, and membership which contribute to developing a complex of organizational processes and substance. These groups can be categorized under three principal styles of member activity:[9]

1. *Interacting groups.* Requiring the close coordination of the members in the performance of the primary group task (i.e., the ability of one member to perform a job may depend upon the fact that another member has first completed a share of the task). The leader's role is one of directing, channeling, guiding, refreshing, timing, and coordinating the activities of the members.
2. *Co-acting groups.* Although the members of this kind of a group have a common task, they each act independently of the others (i.e., each member is on his or her own and performance depends on that member's ability, skill, and motivation).
3. *Counteracting groups.* Individuals who are working together to negotiate and reconcile conflicting opinions and purposes (i.e., some members representing one point of view and others an opposing or

divergent point of view, and each individual working to achieve objectives at the expense of others).

Thus, there is a varying mixture of cooperation and competition among members of groups. This can be extended further to mixtures of cooperation and competition between groups. Such intergroup relationships can either promote or block organization renewal. The latter is particularly likely if the members of competing groups see one another as "the enemy." Distorted views of group values and loyalty can develop, together with stereotyped behavior in which the members of one group refuse to listen to the other.[10] Interaction, rotation of members from one group to another, avoidance of win/lose situations, and focusing on total group goals are useful ways to lessen intergroup conflict and to develop the collaborative relationships essential to organization renewal.

Theodore Mills has identified six models that are useful in studying and analyzing small groups, each offering a different perspective of small group processes:[11]

The *quasi-mechanical* model assumes that a group is like a machine; all behavioral acts in a group are seen as functions that can be categorized.

The *organismic* model assumes that groups are like biological organisms; that is, they have a period of formation (birth), a life cycle, and eventually a death. George Charrier has suggested that a group goes through a process of growth similar to the maturation process of individuals.[12]

1. The first step is called the *polite stage:* the members of the group are getting acquainted, sharing values, and establishing the basis for a group structure. The group members need to be liked.
2. The second step is *"Why are we here?"* During this phase the members define the objectives and goals of the group.
3. The third step consists of a *bid for power;* individuals attempt to influence other group members by changing each other's ideas, values, or opinions. This phase is characterized by competition for attention, recognition, and influence.
4. The fourth step is *cooperative;* the group members are constructive, open-minded, actively listening, and cognizant that others have a right to different value systems. It is the beginning of team action.
5. The fifth and final step is one of *unity, high spirits, mutual acceptance, and maximum cohesiveness.* It is a phase marked by *esprit de corps.*

This process, often referred to as "Cog's Ladder," is not absolute assurance of group growth; some groups stay at the first or second step and never mature. Some writers feel that while the group growth concept may be valid, one can classify groups into four types—with Cog's Ladder fitting the fourth model:

The *conflict* model assumes that a small group is a context for endless aggression and discord. All members of groups have to face the conflict of being truly independent versus conforming to some extent to the group's norms and expectations.

The *equilibrium* model assumes that groups and group members have a need to maintain some sort of balance. Conflicts between group members, for example, tend to be followed by attempts to smooth over hard feelings and to return to a state of interpersonal harmony.

The *structural/functional* model assumes that the group is a goal-seeking system that is constantly adapting to meet the new demands. It assumes that goal attainment is the primary source of satisfaction to its members.

The *cybernetic/growth* model shifts the emphasis from group survival to group growth. This model assumes the existence of group agents that help the group adapt to new information (or feedback). Thus, growth and development are attained by the group's responding to feedback from its earlier performance.

A seventh concept is offered by Stewart L. Tubbs, who looks upon groups from the orientation of general systems thinking.[13] Group interaction can most adequately be thought of as occurring in a system of interdependent forces, each of which can be analyzed and set in the perspective of other forces (see Figure 8-3).

Tubbs identifies three categories of variables.[15] *Relevant background factors* refers to attributes within the individual participants which exist prior to the group's formation and which will endure in some modified form after the group no longer exists. These background factors, such as personality, attitudes, and values, influence the group's functioning, and vice versa. *Internal influences* include (among others) the type of group, the style of leadership used, the language behavior, interaction roles, and decision style employed by the group. *Consequences* of small-group interaction will obviously vary with the background of the participants as well as with the nature of the internal influences. Consequences may include solutions to problems, interpersonal relations among group members, the amount and quality of information sharing, the level of risk taking, the amount of interpersonal growth of participants, and possibly the amount of change in any larger organization of which the group may be a part. The consequences are the outputs of the group's activities.

As complicated as group systems may be, they are a major key to organization renewal. Only by becoming convinced they can work with people effectively, through strengthening the skill of diagnosing particular operational situations, can managers find fruitful results through functioning work groups. Increasing insight into one's own ability, sensitivity to others, diagnostic ability about the problems the group faces, and the practice of membership and leadership skills make possible the development of people in groups so as to achieve organization renewal.

Table 8-1 displays seven distinct group development processes and relates them to the systems model. Although each of these

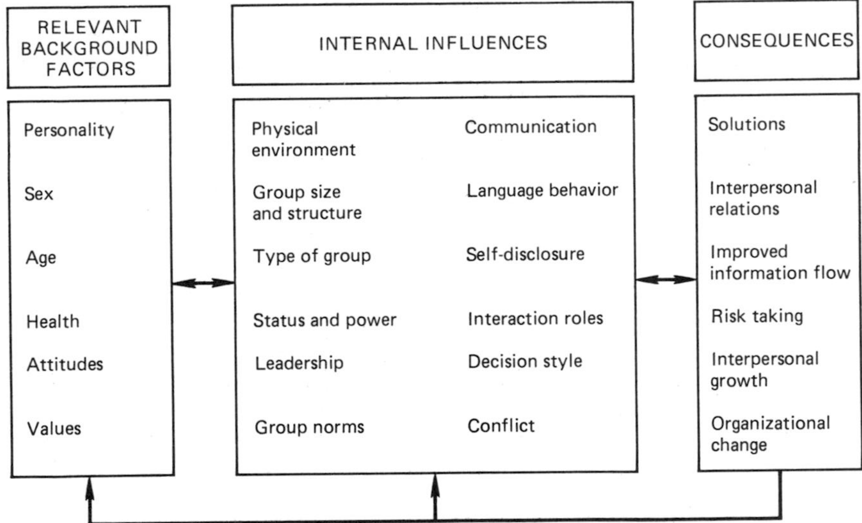

Figure 8-3 The Tubbs model of small-group interaction[14]

Table 8-1
Relationship to Systems Renewal Model

Group Development Processes							
Team building	Socio-technical systems	Role negotiations	Process consultation	Confrontation meeting	Inter-group problem solving	Matrix groups	Other processes

approaches is different, they all contribute to group teamwork and effective problem solving.

TEAMWORK

Teamwork, as used here, is manifested in the way a group is able to solve problems.[16] Let us examine some of the characteristics of teamwork and ways to achieve it.

Teamwork requires an understanding and commitment to the group goals. Whether a regular work group, a project team, or a special task force, the need for the group to determine and understand its goals is a prerequisite for effective team building. It is not just an understanding of the immediate task, but an understanding of the role of the group in the total organization, its responsibilities, and the morale objectives to which they are related. As indicated above, these goals operate at the level of the organization, task group, and individual. The goals will be both long- and short-range in nature. The members of the group, to achieve teamwork, will need not only to understand these goals but also to have a degree of commitment to them so as to work effectively toward their achievement.

Teamwork requires the maximum utilization of the different resources of individuals in the group. When a manager is confronted with a situation demanding change, it is necessary to ask whether the various aspects of the problem can be most effectively resolved through a memorandum, a report, or in an individual, person-to-person fashion. The group may be used effectively for problem solving when the type of problem to be solved is one in which there is a quantitative and qualitative need for various points of view and opinions. This might be especially true where there is a complex problem that has no easy solution within the resources of a single individual. Similarly, inasmuch as people tend to better carry out decisions in which they share, a decision might best be made in a group when the people comprising it will be the ones who will carry out what is decided. Thus, a leader or administrator will find it extremely worthwhile to involve in the process of making the decision those who will ultimately implement it. Different people in an organization will have had different experiences, background, and technical knowledge which frequently will be helpful in arriving at a decision:

> Frequently, in modern organizations, the complexity of a problem requires the specialized knowledge and experience of all the individuals in the group to find a realistic solution. A team knows the different resources of the individuals in their group. A supervisor and leader is the coordinator of these resources in getting group action. A good question (for the manager) to ask is: "Have I heard the ideas of everyone who can make a significant contribution to the solution of this problem?"[17]

It has frequently been said that many groups fail because the "wrong people meet the right problem." All too often the people who can best contribute to the solution of a problem are not asked to work on it. This does not mean that there are not many instances where, owing to the pressure of time, type of decision, or deferred area of responsibility, an individual may most appropriately make a decision. In other words, there is a place for individual as well as group decision making in most organizational situations. Teamwork, however, will maximize the utilization of individual resources to achieve group goals.

Teamwork is achieved when flexibility, sensitivity to the needs of others, and creativity are encouraged. A group of persons does not spring into mature group action just because its members happen to be assigned to the same section of the building or to a similar function. A group of persons may need to deal with some of the emotional problems of its members' interpersonal relationships before it can reach decisions effectively. Team action is a complex thing. Group decision making, at its best, depends on the kind of working relationships in which disagreement, creativity, and shared responsibility can flourish. When such an atmosphere is established, the group normally is ready to reach decisions effectively.

The old cliché that "two heads are better than one" is not always true. In some cases a manager can implement, develop, or think through various plans competently without getting the advice and suggestions of others. Conversely, when working on a new or complex problem, or a situation that affects a large segment of the organization, more effective resolution might be achieved if a number of people participate in a group problem-solving situation. A creative group should release the potential mental ability and resources of all its members.

Teamwork is most effective where shared leadership is practiced. A group of persons brought together in any problem-solving situation will not function at maximum efficiency if its members are "yes" women or "yes" men for a manager or leader. In such a situation, group leaders are merely communicating their own ideas. If a supervisor is interested both in assuming responsibility for leadership and in developing the membership of a group, so that the functions of leadership are shared, his or her attitude will go a long way toward achieving effective decision making. This criterion might be embarrassing to many who are reluctant to exert a team type of leadership. If a manager's motivation in calling together a group is selfish, he or she should not pretend to be seeking a group decision. Put another way, if you have already made up your mind, you should not imply consultation; you should *announce* your decision and communicate it to those who need to know. It is another matter if you are asking a group of people to think and act together as a means of helping to reach a decision. Leadership, however, will make or break the work of such a group. The supervisor, or anyone having the duty of guiding the group, must observe certain leadership fundamentals (see chapter 5) that are prerequisite to developing groups of persons into effective work units.

Teamwork requires a group to develop procedures to deal with a particular problem or situation. We are all familiar with the use of the voting procedure in group decision-making situations. There have been a number of research studies showing that in many cases it is not the most appropriate tool for group action. In fact, in many settings it is only a way by which the leader can keep control of the group—or, at its worst, an ideal procedure for "railroading" ideas. In most situations in which group action is taken, there is little need for a voting procedure.

There is a difference between unanimous decision making and a "consensus" decision. In a consensus-type decision, the members of the group agree on the next steps, with those who are not in agreement reserving the right to have the tentative decision tested and evaluated for later assessment. In other words, certain members of the group will agree that on a "provisional try" or a "first-time" basis the organization might try out a particular alternative; but they want to ensure certain evaluative means for testing whether or not the feelings of the majority indicate the most appropriate action. This is different from compromise, where the decision is taken from two opposing points of view and becomes something quite different from either of them. In the consensus decision, individuals in the group might be saying that they are "not sure" of the best decision, but realizing the need for action, they will accept agreement to one of the alternatives for action after thorough discussion and minority points of view are heard, and with the understanding that the temporary decision will be reviewed and evaluated at a later date.

Teamwork is characterized by the group's ability to examine its process so as to constantly improve itself as a team. When two or more people work together for a purpose, there tends to be interaction, interpersonal relationships, group goals, and communication, all with varying degrees of success. Someone has made the observation that a collection of normal individuals can make a neurotic group. In this sense, the word "neurotic" is used to describe a group that is unable to focus on the problem, is erratic in group discussion and unable to reach a decision, and which constantly bickers and fights. Such ineffective behavior is only one example of the pattern of forces and group dynamics that every task group inevitably exhibits. The leader and each group member might well ask some pertinent questions so as to learn from interaction:

What are the motivations of the various members of the group?
What are the real reasons for these people wanting to be members of the group?
What are the various relationships among them?
Are there underlying animosities that will reduce the group's productivity?
What effect will conditions of status have on the group?
Will any members of the group have difficulty in communicating with other members?
Can the group maintain a clear purpose?
How cohesive is the group?

By setting up a process of analyzing its own actions, a group can learn from its experiences how to improve its teamwork. A manager should always devote some time to developing group effectiveness—by helping the group confront its own process and initiating appropriate team-building opportunities.

For a group to function effectively as a team, the climate of the organization should encourage the manager to utilize the practices of participative leadership. Most managers behave in accordance with the example set by their superiors, and with the implicit and explicit reward systems existing throughout the organization. If the top management of an organization tends to feel that the only good decisions are individual decisions, a subordinate manager probably will feel uncomfortable in using groups very frequently to aid in the problem-solving process. On the other hand, if top management puts value on those leaders who utilize and develop others through team experiences, they will feel encouraged to use group action whenever it seems appropriate.

Teamwork utilizes the appropriate steps and guidelines for decision making in the solution of problems. As work groups, task forces, management teams, project groups, or other types of groups initiate and decide an action in the renewal process, they should use the appropriate steps and guides in decision making, which can be identified as follows:

A clear definition of the problem
A clear understanding as to who has the responsibility for the decision
Effective communication for idea production
Appropriate size of group for decision making
A means for effective testing of different alternatives relative to the problem
A need for building commitment into the decision
Honest commitment of the manager or leader to the group decision-making process
A need for agreement on procedures and methods for decision-making prior to deliberation of the issues

Teamwork requires trust and openness in communication and relationships. An important dimension of effective leadership is the ability to develop a trusting relationship among one's associates (see chapter 5). Such a trust relationship will encourage open and frank communications. It will manifest a high tolerance for difference of opinion and personalities. Teamwork is manifested best when such behavior is common to all members of the group, including the leader.

Teamwork is achieved when the group members have a strong sense of belonging to the group. A degree of cohesiveness is needed for teamwork to be manifested. Such cohesiveness will be built upon commitment to the goals, commitment to the group, and respect for the members of the group. This sense of belonging is not just a matter of blind loyalty, but a sense of wanting to work with other members of the group in accomplishing goals that are meaningful to the individual members. It is not predicated on everyone's liking each other, a highly unlikely occurrence, but is a more mature level of respect and openness which emerges out of common commitment to the task and to working together to accomplish the goal.

It should be apparent from all that has been discussed so far that teamwork depends as much upon the behavior and contribution of each member as it does on the skill of the leader, but this is not to say that the leader is unimportant. The group supervisor or leader is an essential factor in effective group functioning and growth. Different types of situations unquestionably demand different responses by the leader, but organizational growth requires the leader to exercise at least six basic functions:

1. Help the group to decide clearly its purposes and objectives.
2. Help the group to become conscious of its own procedures in order to improve its problem-solving capability.
3. Help the group to become aware of talents, skills, and other resources existing within its own membership.
4. Develop group methods of evaluation, so that the group will have ways of improving its process and become aware of how others think and feel.
5. Help the group to accept new ideas and new members without conflict, to learn to accept discipline in working toward long-range objectives, and to learn to profit from failure.
6. Help the group to create new task forces or subgroups as needed, and to learn to terminate them when it is wise to do so.

Such leadership skills will be needed effectively to develop the teamwork necessary for a group to cope with its responsibility in the process of organization renewal; and appropriate intergroup relationships are vital to organizational growth:

> Although the small group lies at the foundation of society and persists despite the rise and fall of institutions in the larger social structure, it is also true

> that the effectiveness of large scale organizations depends, in large measure, on the development of effective small groups. Not only must groups build their own cohesion and continually resolve their own internal problems, they must also maintain a positive identification with other groups and with a larger organization. The fact that small groups satisfy important human needs assures their survival as a form of organization. But this does not assure the development of effective groups and consequently effect organizations in the larger institutions of society.[18]

Now let us examine some useful methods of developing a group as a human system, and some ways to increase intergroup collaboration and cooperation.

TEAM BUILDING

Team building or team development is a process in which a group of people analyze and evaluate their interactions in an attempt to improve the process through which they do work.[19] For it to be true team development, the group members should have a common goal or purpose, and their work should be highly interdependent. The group can use team-building activities to focus and work on the type of task that they perform jointly (perhaps decision making or goal setting), or to focus on their interpersonal and intragroup reactions, role conflicts, group dynamics, and processes that underlie and influence all task accomplishment. No matter which focus is taken, the objective of the team-building activities is to remove barriers to effective functioning and to plan ways to improve unit achievement. An additional objective is to develop the group's skills in team maintenance, its ability to initiate and carry out team-building activities whenever the need arises.

Most definitions of organization [illegible]velopment or organization renewal incl[illegible] direct or indirect reference to the team or group as an essential focus at some point in the process. This is the medium through which work gets done.

A team is either a functional organizational element with a single managerial head in which the members participate in determining operation of the element, or "a number of people with different backgrounds, skills, and knowledge, and drawn from various areas of the organization who work together on a specific and defined task."[20] Teams are either permanent or temporary. Permanent teams are typical of the main functional segment of the organization where a systematic hierarchy exists. Temporary teams are typical of the project teams within a matrix organization. It is possible within a matrix organization to have both types of teams in existence at the same time and to have specific individuals in both team types simultaneously.

Each individual brings to the team a unique set of skills. These skills include technological, managerial, psychological, and communications skills. The team is a mixture of complementing and, in some cases, conflicting skills.

An essential ingredient to any decision to implement team building is a "felt need" on the part of the group to improve its product and/or its process. There must be an existing awareness that their current effectiveness is not optimal. Without this felt need, members will not be sufficiently motivated to participate actively in the team-building activities. The leader must also feel this need. Among many others, here is a partial list of symptoms indicating a need for team building:

- Loss or decrease in output of product or service
- Loss or decrease in quality of product or service
- Increase in grievances or complaints

- Increase in turnover
- Conflict or hostility in the group
- Decisions not implemented properly
- Apathy within the group
- Lack of creativity (routine answers to nonroutine problems)
- Ineffective meetings
- Lack of communication to people in need of information
- Continued unaccounted for increase in costs
- Resistance to directions from manager
- Poor self-image of team
- Upcoming big changes in the way the team is expected to produce
- New team startup: leader may have to market the felt need; group must accept the idea that the way they interact deserves some attention

Conversely, again among many others, there are these indicators that team building should *not* be used:

- When no felt need for improvement exists (i.e., just because "everybody ought to")
- When it is a management problem that team building cannot solve
- When the manager is using team building to achieve an ulterior motive
- When the manager is not well prepared to change or to heed feedback
- When the manager is not willing to share leadership and decision making
- If work is done primarily on an individual basis and members interact only on a limited basis
- If the manager and/or group does not fully understand the commitment of time and energy or the long-term nature of team development
- Lack of time and availability of personnel to work in the program
- Lack of willingness to look at one's own behavior, to analyze group processes, to give and get feedback
- People in power will not back up team solutions and team development activities

Team building is a process that can be used to make a good team better by clearing up some of the barriers to more effective functioning and by processing conflicts to provide for more energy for achievement. It can be used to start up a new team, efficiently and effectively, by setting "team process" out in the open as an important agenda to be considered. The multiplicity of uses and the multiple options for the structure of team building grow out of the very fact that the team is the pivotal factor in the success of any organizational improvement effort.

One of the factors contributing to the emergence and growing use of team building is the demand for greater organizational flexibility.*

The long-term objective of team building is to make the team self-sufficient, to incorporate the processes of team building into the team's normal way of functioning. Thus, in the future, lead by the manager, the team would interrupt its work on a task to work on its own process of functioning; there would be constant give and take between the two, but much attention would be paid to the process itself.

There are short-term objectives that vary with the assessed need and the type of team building selected. For task-oriented team-building activities, the goal is to improve the method of getting the task done. For example, goal setting often will help everyone work toward the same goal; practice in rational decision making will help the group better analyze its options; system analysis may uncover some blockage in the very system by which the team does its work.

For process-oriented team-building activities, the short-term objective is to address and improve the underlying dynamics of getting the job done. This means that members of the group must

*William Dyer provides us with a three-part checklist for assessing the need for team building, and how to structure it. One part focuses on the felt need (problem identification), the second on whether group climate will permit or assist team building, and the third on whether an outside consultant should be used.[21]

work on the way they interact, the way they define roles, power structures, and their own group dynamics. The objective is to clear up any dysfunctional dynamics so that they no longer provide barriers to effective team functioning.

There is a third kind of team building which can be called organizational team building because its focus is on the entire organization and all its teams. This kind of team building covers the entire organization and works its way down from the top, working with individual teams all the way down. The team building is primarily process-oriented, although undoubtedly it will address task improvement at times. It, too, has the short-term objective of clearing up barriers to effective functioning. Its long-term objective is related to the overall objective of altering/improving the management process (and ability to self-maintain) of the entire organization.*

The variations on team-building options are innumerable. It is truly a case where the activity/intervention must be tailor-made. It is, however, very possible to pin down the basic process, especially as it is fundamentally identical to all other organization renewal intervention processes. Team building must be based on accurate data; it must have the involvement of concerned personnel in more than a passive way; it must be carefully planned and implemented in order to acquire continuing support and involvement, particularly from those who will have to change; it must concern itself with many issues of power and security which are not readily visible. To accomplish this, as shown in Figure 8-4, the leader, group, and consultant must put great emphasis on action research, repeated data gathering, and involving group members as early and as much as possible. This model is useful in that it illustrates the continuing, cyclical nature of team building. It lacks one key

*These approaches are discussed in Chapter 9.

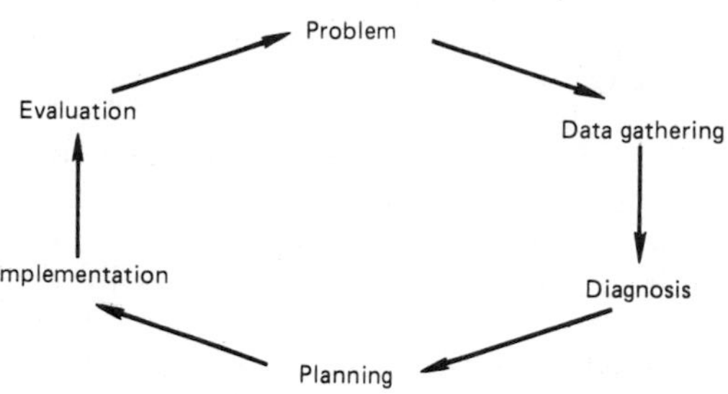

Figure 8-4 Team-building cycle[22]

point, however: that the steps are frequently pulled out of order or repeated. This is because, in various stages of the process, new data will emerge. Also, group dynamics or reactions may alter the way the planned activities can be implemented. It may be necessary, therefore, to adjust the process and go back to previous steps. It is a very dynamic and interactive process. Some of the factors that influence the possibility of success are:

Time allocated
Team's willingness to introspect
Length of time team has been together
Length of time team will be together
Frequency of turnover
Significance of felt need
Member commitment to resolution of felt need
Degree of sensitivity to felt need
Timing of team-building intervention
Degree of freedom the team has to implement solutions
Level of uncertainty and change inherent in the normal work environment (i.e., how accustomed to change they are)
Security/insecurity of team members and of manager
Support of management
Openness of manager
Clear roles and reporting relationships of members
Current patterns of communication
Advance planning—quantity of action plans
Follow-up and adjustments to action plans
Competency of professional resource people used (internal and external)

Prior experiences of members in other groups

The variations of team-building efforts are innumerable. The activities and interventions must be tailor-made to fit the needs of different people and situations in different groups. Therefore, not only the processes and combination of techniques used, but also the steps and short-term objectives, are likely to differ. No two team-building efforts are the same, but some of the more frequently used processes are:

Action research occurs in every successful team-building effort. At some point in the process, through some activity, all of the steps of action research must occur: problem recognition, data collection, feedback, and action plan—and finally, recycling of the process.

Short- and long-term planning, properly accomplished, can lead to successful team building.

Startups of new groups can take a different form depending upon the members' past experiences. Members should be asked to explain their expectations, their concept of the objectives of the group, and their understanding of their role in it. The purpose here is to try to develop teamwork before getting into action.

Interpersonal relationships are the foundation blocks of teamwork, and as such should be carefully developed along constructive lines. Typically, this kind of activity works best when it can be undertaken away from the group's primary activity.

Use of instruments is a way to help a group look at the factors of performance and level of team work. An instrument that has been used successfully enables members of a group periodically to repeat measurement of these two factors to learn something of their progress.

Team building, as such, is an important methodology of organization renewal and it will become even more so as we move into the 1980s. The potential benefits to a group are great. Whether team building occurs as a primary focus or as a part of diverse organization renewal activities, it is likely to be a difficult task. It is open to misdirection and misunderstanding; it requires great sensitivity and alertness on the part of the leader and all members of the group. It requires maturity, commitment, and most of all, trust in and among the team members. As a matter of fact, trust is a major factor in team effectiveness, and this trust is largely determined by the team leader:

> The truly trusting person is not the naive sucker, the innocent wide-eyed victim of the world's sharpies. . . . Rather, he is the tough executive who knows how to delegate responsibility; the leader who can build a task force of men and women in such a fashion as to release their creative and productive best. . . . Trust is an act, not a feeling.[23]

The value of trust is clearly presented by Gibb.[24] In his model, trust and emotional climate are related to communication flow, goal formation, and control. If trust is not present, the communications are distorted and restricted. The resulting goals are inaccurate and management may well be controlling the wrong goals. Within the team development, a clear and accurate goal is necessary for effectiveness; therefore, time spent on trust development is certainly worth the effort.

SOCIOTECHNICAL SYSTEMS APPROACH

Sociotechnical intervention is the group development approach that uses changes in task organization to much improve the functioning of an organization. Warner Burke and Harvey Hornstein refer to this method as technostructural intervention and consider Herzberg's "job enrichment" and Beckhard's "confrontation meeting" as examples of this approach.[25] Both these examples fit the description of sociotechnical intervention. The work of the Tavistock group is generally considered the foundation for changes in organizational structure; the classic description of this type of intervention is by Eric Trist, reporting on his work with the British coal mines.[26]

The emphasis by Trist and the Tavistock Institute is on the work group functioning, important to the nature of sociotechnical intervention. This approach looks at the work process. The group organization must have a logical fit with the task organization. This leads to questioning the definition of the tasks or task. The task should be defined as a process that a work group can accomplish. Although this seems fairly simple, there are basic production goals that can easily and logically lead to dysfunctional organization.

Sociotechnical interventions are based on the assumption that organizations are greatly influenced by technological and environmental restraints. This approach conceptualizes an organization as an open system with constraints placed on it by its environment but with the ability to change internally to achieve a steady state while still accomplishing its work. This analysis would include the technological requirements (environment) and the social structure of the organization—and the relationships between the two.

This approach is primarily utilized in complex, multishift production systems. It is a systems approach relying on the basic concepts of systems theory. The sociotechnical systems analysis considers the organization to be an open system with the technological constraints from the environment playing a major role in determining the self-regulating properties of an organization. In this approach, an effort is made to relate the technical system and the social system to each other.

Trist, in his work with the British coal mines, changed the organizational structure and the organization of work from a "conventional" system developed according to accepted industrial-engineering practice (work specialization, routine, repetitive, and individualistic) to a "composite" system in which individuals (1) worked on a variety of tasks, instead of a simple task, and (2) were themselves responsible for the quality of work, instead of having outside inspectors responsible.[27] In addition, Trist established a pay system based on a team's performance rather than an individual's. As a result of these changes, absenteeism, accidents, and costs were reduced. The assumption underlying these interventions and the interventions themselves have been discussed by Harvey Hornstein[28] and Louis Davis.[29]

Sociotechnical intervention recognizes the need to bring various task groups together into a corporate cycle group. The problem is concerned with bringing together and relating individuals performing different tasks in the interdependent phases. The objective is to provide a truly composite organization for an effective, continuous operation.

Trist describes four interdependent aspects of the composite organization:

1. *Composite work method.* This provides the task continuity that was present in single-place working. This requires the preparedness to carry out the next task, whatever it may be. This work method allows continuous cycle operation.
2. *Composite personnel.* Continuity depends on having persons in the cycle group who are competent, if not formally qualified, to undertake, under supervision, the necessary tasks as they arise.
3. *Composite work groups.* The team manning a composite longwall* is self-selected so that the range of personal abilities is ac-

*A method of coal extraction used in the British Isles.

cepted from the start. The team, as a whole, must be able to deploy sufficient resources on each shift to staff the roles likely to arise.

4. *Composite payment.* As in single-place systems, there is a common paynote in which all members share equally, since all are regarded as making an equivalent contribution. This system of payment places on the team as a whole the responsibility for all operations at the coal face, while relating total earnings to productivity.

The most important aspect in the composite organization is to assure task continuity. Task continuity provides the basis for cycle orientation. It also allows self-regulation by the cycle group to meet the cycle goals:

> Since men and officials on composite longwalls share the common goal of cycle completion, they can cooperate in a way not possible when task and cycle responsibilities are split from each other in terms of what belongs to management and what to worker. Identity of operational aim removes the "officials'" grievance. With the support of a self-regulating cycle group, the deputy has more scope for using his knowledge and experience of mining than when he is entrammelled in the wages system.[30]

This sociotechnical example did not proceed without problems. There was random selection of teams and poor understanding of the goal. The situation was treated in a "business as usual" manner, which it was not. After reorganization of the teams through self-selection and clarification of goals, the composite organization demonstrated the improvement expected. The advantage of this method is that it enables the organization renewal effort to encompass the tasks that need to be accomplished within the given technology, the kinds of skills required to carry out the tasks, the interdependence of the tasks required to accomplish the whole job, and the relationship of the social structure to the tasks. By this kind of diagnosis, the optimal social structure can be identified for the purpose of intergroup action. A disadvantage is that the organization renewal effort must use both a humanistic specialist and an industrial engineer. This limitation tends to limit the method to production-type organizations. It is not applicable to the management level, nor does it attempt to change the atmosphere of the organization to provide for better problem solving in the larger setting.

The ideal situation for sociotechnical intervention seems to be a group process task. It should be a task that requires some range of skills by a group over a period of time. The organizational and technological situations should be examined closely to provide evidence that there is a need for task continuity. Resources must be available for application to assure task continuity. There must be a sufficient pool of human skills to be applied over the period of time required for task accomplishment. The resources of mechanization must be used to complement the human resources.

Team building seems to be an important part of sociotechnical intervention. Aside from having the required technical skills, the group must have a strong maintenance ability. Self-selection seems ideal, but it may not be practical in all situations. In these cases there must be a development of mutual trust by other means. Sociotechnical intervention seems to be a powerful technique; however, it requires hard work and patience.

ROLE NEGOTIATION

Role negotiation is a planned change effort designed to affect the work relationships among members of a group.[31] It is a structured approach for identifying what task functions are in a group, who in the group is involved and their specific influences, the expectations of members for different task-related behaviors; then contracting, in writing, on a person-to-person "quid pro quo" basis for new behaviors. In other words, when a change facilitator arranges a series of exercises that result in each member of the work team having a list of specific behaviors that other members of the team should do more of, do less of, or continue unchanged (so as to enhance work effectiveness), the logical and effective closure is for each person of the existing dyads to agree to change some behavior which the other considers important. Each person making a request or demand for changed behavior on the part of another must be willing to accept a binding request or demand of equivalent value. The process, developed by Roger Harrison, while getting very specific about work-related behavior, is not designed to explore the likes and dislikes of members for one another and other personal feelings:

> This program which is called Role Negotiation makes one basic assumption: that most people in organizations prefer a fair negotiated settlement to a state of unresolved conflict. If the participants take the risk asked of them and do specify quite concretely the changes desired on the part of others, then significant changes in work group effectiveness usually can be obtained.[32]

Desired outcomes for role negotiation may be listed in this manner:

- Clarification of power, authority, and influence of members' roles in a group
- Agreements to change behavior, established by person-to-person written contracts on a "something for something" basis
- Changed behavior of group members
- Increased readiness to exchange task-related expectations in the future with less formality and structure (i.e., role negotiation becoming an organizational way of life)
- Increased productivity of work teams

Because of its various focuses on the individual and the group, role negotiation is considered helpful to group development, conflict resolution, and the enhancement of individual role and task performance.

The usual steps in role negotiation are:

1. *Climate setting.* An introduction to the process is begun whose length and breadth is at the discretion of the change facilitator. Certainly, the group must be willing to trust the change facilitator and acquire a belief in his or her competence. The group must feel free to discuss work problems among themselves and the change facilitator.
2. *Contracting* between the group and the change facilitator. This includes the following provisos:
   a. The consultant will not probe anyone's personal feelings or motives, since the intervention is designed to uncover job concerns; however, if feelings happen to be expressed naturally, they will not be labeled as being out-of-order. But role negotiation is not meant to be a gripe session.
   b. Openness and honesty about behavior is expected and is considered essential for the accomplishment of significant results.
   c. An individual's expectation or demand, to be considered fully communicated, must be written down and fully understood by both sender and receiver; no change process is to be started until the full communication transaction is completed.
   d. It is unreasonable for anyone to expect change to take place just because his or her demand or expectation has been expressed; mutual sharing of expectations and demands is required for contracts to change to be negotiated.

e. "Telling it like it is" and using various manipulative devices, such as threats and pressures, are not ruled out of the process. Neither are bargains to "not do this, if you won't do that." Wherever possible, bargaining chips should be positive.

f. The actual change process depends on bargaining, negotiation, and establishment of a written contract. It is not considered complete until an agreement for specific changes can be described with each party clear about what is expected.

3. *Diagnosis.* With ground rules laid out for open communication and closure, the group is led by the facilitator into the task analysis and development of task-related change proposals. Harrison suggests that an organization chart be discussed, bringing in the larger work environment and its influences: who and what else are players in the decisions of the group, and how this is beneficial or retarding to the quality of the decision. These discussions become the factual basis for group members to describe their individual satisfactions and dissatisfactions with the way decisions are made and events occur.

   Members are asked to complete three lists for each other person in the group, which state those things the other person should do more of, should do less of, and should continue to do. The lists are exchanged so that each person sees all the lists pertaining to his or her behavior.

   At this point, a discussion period, monitored by the change facilitator, takes place. The facilitator ensures that the discussion centers on clarification and improvement of specific work-related behavior. Argument, premature contracting, and discussion about the substance of work policy or methods are censored by the facilitator.

4. *Negotiation.* Actual contracting begins by prioritizing the personal lists, getting down to behaviors that are considered important and open to influence. On a one-to-one basis, members parley "I will do this if you do that" into formal agreements, written in specific terms, then signed. Subsequently, the agreements are published and made available to the whole group. The facilitator may consider it advisable to lead a discussion of the agreements, testing the good faith, reasonableness, and reality orientation of the members. Sanctions or penalties may be agreed upon by individuals for nonperformance of contracts.

5. *Follow-up.* After the first round of negotiation is complete, the members attempt to implement the agreements. Harrison suggests that an early date be set for the members to reconvene and review/renegotiate/reissue line items of or whole agreements that are no longer valid.

An alternative to role negotiation is the role analysis technique, which is also meant to clarify task-related behavior expectations of members, but it differs from Harrison's intervention in the manner of data collection and feedback, the absence of person-to-person contracting, and the creation of a role profile.[33] In role analysis, each role is sequentially examined; while it is being examined, it is termed the focal role. First, the role incumbent identifies such things as his or her duties and behaviors, and place in the organization; second, there are listed the expectations of the other roles in the group that affect behavior; and third, members of the group identify their expectations of the incumbent's role. In each of these steps, both the role incumbent and group members discuss and modify the listings until there is agreement. Finally, the role incumbent draws up a role profile:

> This consists of (a) a set of activities classified as to the prescribed and discretionary elements of the role, (b) the obligation of the role to each role in the set, and (c) the expectations of this role from others in its set. Viewed *in toto,* this provides a comprehensive understanding of each individual's role space.[34]

A related intervention with a similar name is called "planned renegotiation."[35] As shown in Figure 8-5, it is basically a conceptual model for viewing how roles are established and how change occurs, and it is complementary to role negotiation intervention.

> . . . relationships cycle through (1) the sharing of information and the negotiation of expectations, then (2) commitment to a set of expectations, which governs behavior during a period, (3) of stability and productivity, when, for the most part, you do what I expect of you and I do what you expect of me, until (4) disruption occurs and the possibility of change enters the system.[37]

Following the disruption of shared expectations, uncertainty and anxiety occur, resulting in termination, return to the way things used to be, or renegotiation. Knowledge of the model of planned renegotiation provides a way to introduce controlled change by anticipating disruption and renegotiation expectations in advance.

The best example of role negotiation is

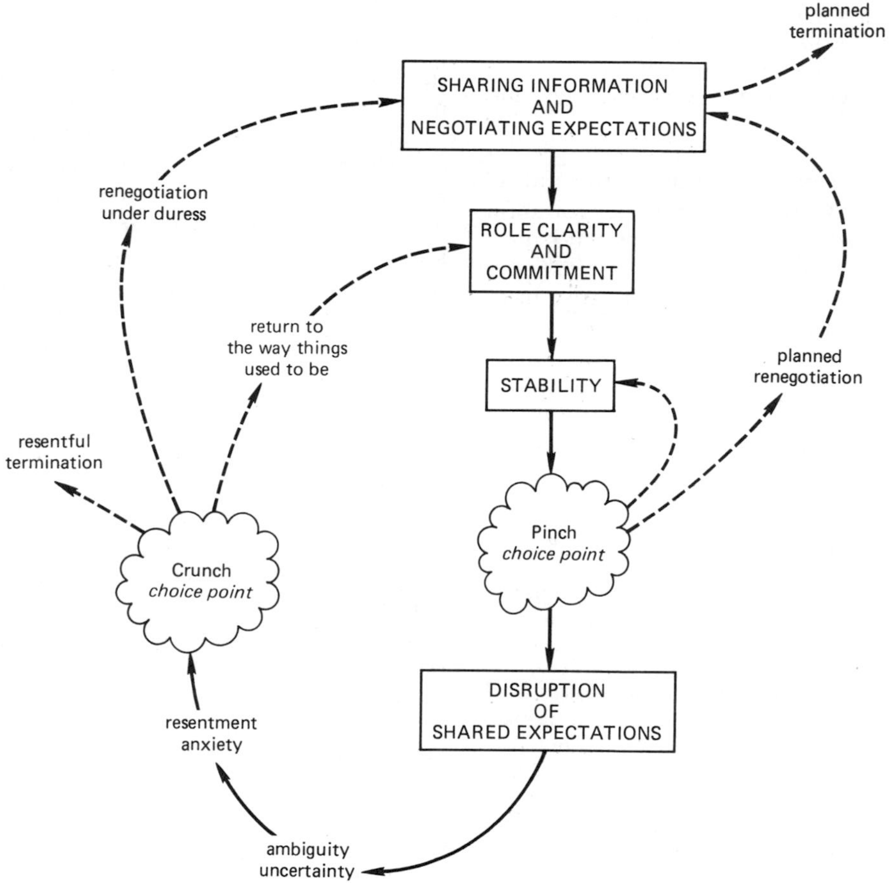

Figure 8-5 A Model for Planned Renegotiation[36]

the external consulting experience of Richard Hill and Irving Stubbs with the Diamond Shamrock Corporation.* They reported significant results:

> A more supportive climate throughout the corporation for participative management.
> Improved communication.
> Improved cross-functional collaboration. Many of the traditional interorganizational walls are dissolving.
> Numerous modifications of organizational structure.
> Many modifications of job and job assignments.
> Improved assimilation of relocated managers into new work situations.
> Individual skill improvement.
> Improvement in problem solving.
> Higher level of trust between managers and teams.

Diamond Shamrock intends to send all its managers to its role negotiation course.[39] Surveys of managers who have already attended reveal that over 90% believe that both teamwork and trust have increased as a direct result of the experience.

Hill and Stubbs found some resistance to change occurring in the application of their intervention, either because managers were unwilling to allow their teams to confront unresolved issues or to chance the loss of personal control over their teams. There is also instinctive resistance to being completely frank in remarks about bosses. There are occasions where disgruntled or sceptical team members get into over-heated confrontations with one another. These phenomena are recognized as part of the risks of making any intervention into the work situation. One distinctive advantage is that role negotiation "starts where the client is" (the client being the work team) and serves his or her needs. Although the climate-setting phase may introduce new concepts and some of the vocabulary of organization renewal, all steps in the intervention are designed with the client's specific organization and problems in mind. Insofar as the intervention itself is concerned, there is no normative concept for modifying power and influence within the client's team or for the kinds of contracts written. Challenging authority or changing management style is not designed into the intervention.

The process is simple, structured, and describable to the client in advance. The process of intervention centers around work behavior and is meant to raise problems and issues for which the client has both the interest, energy, and resources to change. Specific actions and results are identified throughout the intervention. In contrast to some other types of intervention, mere understanding of the need for role clarification is not an end in itself. Also, revelation of personal feelings is minimized. Client dependence on the facilitator is minimized. Learning skills and feedback are transferable to other parts of the organization. With minimal special training, an internal change facilitator can acquire the competence to conduct role negotiation sessions.[40]

As a disadvantage, role negotiation seems to presume, as a precondition, either the active awareness of a healthy psychological contract between team members or the shared perception that one is possible—in other words, recognition that mutual influence and mutual bargaining is an ongoing process in organizational life which can be dealt with openly

*They modified the Harrison approach and published both a manager's manual and a participant's workbook.[38] In their design, role negotiation takes place over a three-day period at a place other than the work setting, and involves a "family team," a manager from a certain level and his or her principal subordinates. Their procedure is more structured than Harrison's proposal and includes a climate-setting program of lectures and instruments.

(albeit under controlled circumstances) without loss of face or power by most line managers.

Related to the above is the open disclosure of how decisions are made and who influences the way they are made. This necessarily involves a review of past occurrences in detail, and this may be unpleasant or undesirable evidence of secrecy, deception, and manipulation, either by various members of the team or by higher-ups with team member(s)' collusion or silence.

It is possible that contracts may not be worked out because one or both contractors bargained at a superficial level or in bad faith, or because the rewards for modified behavior are not deemed to be worth the effort. Although the contracted-for behavior may not be sufficient to motivate, it is possible to add inducements in the form of penalties or sanctions.

Role negotiation has the potential to become widely used. As an organization renewal intervention, it can eliminate unresolved problems which are preventing attainment of organizational competence, replace unproductive thought patterns, and create a climate in which managers confront, in an open and candid way, the real issues underlying problems.

PROCESS CONSULTATION AND ANALYSIS

Another team development method is process observation of group functioning:

> Process consultation is a set of activities on the part of a consultant that helps the client [group] to perceive, understand, and act upon process events that occur in the client's [group's] environment.[41]

Process consultation assumes that, in many instances, the only way to arrive at a pertinent and feasible solution to any problem—a solution that the group will accept and implement—is to involve the group itself in the diagnosis of the problem and the generation of the solution. The process consultant may be a competent member of the group, a group process specialist from inside the organization, or an external organization renewal consultant.

Essentially, the process consultant endeavors to help groups function more effectively through diagnosing their own problems and shortcomings in one or more of the following areas:

Communications
Functional roles of group members
Problem solving and decision making
Group norms and growth
Leadership and authority
Intergroup cooperation and competition

This team-building method can be categorized under three typologies: (1) interventions designed to improve the effectiveness of dyads/triads in a group; (2) interventions designed to improve the effectiveness of teams and groups; and (3) interventions designed to improve the effectiveness of intergroup relations.[42] The setting for any of these typologies should have these characteristics:[43]

Selection of what to observe and a timetable for conducting observations should be collaboratively planned with the group and group leader.
It may and should be at any and all levels of the hierarchy of the human system involved.
Be amendable to observing all interpersonal and group interactions.
Not be contrived, but as nearly as possible approximating the real situation.

These procedures are relevant in implementing process consultation:[44]

Establish an open and trusting relationship with the group.

Clarify assumptions.
Define goals of the observation.
Decide what should be observed and how the observation should be conducted.
Implementation of data gathering.
Feedback to the group.
Action plan. The action plan can be more directive that the instrumentation used for the initial data gathering. Schein presents a broad categorization for possible interventions.[45] These include agenda setting, at which time the facilitator will grow increasingly deliberate about bringing attention to interpersonal issues; providing feedback during or immediately after meetings; coaching or counseling and structural suggestions regarding group membership; and communication and work arrangements (e.g., assignment of responsibility, distribution of authority).
Evaluation of results. Because of the lack of clarity of outcomes, and the lack of measurability that is inherent in a wide range of the outcomes, the successes or failures of the consultation effort often defy evaluation. Nonetheless, it is the responsibility of the process consultant to work collaboratively with the client to appraise the effort. The generic outcome of a process consultation is to increase the performance of an organization. This may involve increasing interpersonal skills and changing some of the values of the organization. Ideally, the specific skills and values should have been outlined at the initiation of the project. A variety of survey research tools can be used to generate information for the evaluation. Alternatively, more informal techniques, such as seeking feedback from participants without the use of a particular tool, can also be applied.

In summary, the primary concern of process consultation is the group's ability to carry on what the consultant role has introduced in terms of diagnostic techniques, and to solve its own problems. Although many types of consultants use their skills and knowledge only to solve group problems, the process consultant also passes on these skills and values to the group itself so that it eventually need not be dependent on an outside resource. The change process is accomplished within the context of process consultation by changing the values and learning skills of the group.

For a process consultation effort to work effectively, it should begin at the earliest stage in a group's development so that the possibility of defenses and distrust emerging might be reduced to a minimum. It is much easier to keep these negatives from developing in the first place than to try to undo them afterward.

CONFRONTATION MEETING

Whereas the foregoing methods of group development are relatively complex, the confrontation meeting is relatively direct and uncomplicated.[46] It represents a relatively simple technique for addressing a common organizational problem. During periods of major change it is not uncommon for management groups to become so engrossed in planning activities that they become detached from the day-to-day operating problems that concern middle and lower management personnel. This results in reduced levels of communication whereby middle managers and employees tend to feel left out. They also tend to feel uneasy about their own authority and they develop a lower level of ownership.

Often, decisions are postponed and fewer risks are taken until the "smoke clears." This results in increased levels of stress and anxiety, and the situation offers an opportunity for management to introduce a problem-solving technique such as the confrontation meeting.

The confrontation meeting is of greatest value for organizations undergoing a major change, such as leadership change, mergers, new technology, or rapid growth.[47] The basis for this conclusion lies in the primary objective of the confrontation meeting, which is "to assess accurately the state of the organization's health. How are people reacting to the change? How committed are subordinate managers to the new conditions? Where are the most pressing organization problems?"[48]

The confrontation meeting can be useful in many organization situations, but is most appropriate where:[49]

There is a need for the total management group to examine its own workings.
Very limited time is available for the activity.
Top management wishes to improve the conditions quickly.
There is enough cohesion in the top team to ensure follow-up.
There is real commitment to resolving the issues on the part of top management.
The organization is experiencing, or has recently experienced, a major change.

There are other useful objectives of the confrontation meeting in addition to assessment of the organization's health. In many respects, this method incorporates the major components of an organization renewal process, including diagnosis, process maintenance, and action. It will be obvious from the following description that these elements are combined into a relatively simple intervention method that involves the management group of an organization and requires five to six hours.* The initial session consists of three activities:

1. *Climate setting:* establishing a willingness to participate (one hour). This portion of the meeting, which includes the total management group, sets the tone for subsequent activities. It includes a statement from top management regarding the goals of the meeting, encouragement for participants to say what they think (without fear of punishment), and generally conveys support for the program. Also, it is useful to incorporate a brief information session by a facilitator (internal or external) that deals with such things as problems of communication, the need to be open, and the group problem-solving process. This portion of the meeting is extremely important because it sets the tone for subsequent sessions.
2. *Information collecting:* getting the attitudes out in the open (one hour). The total group is divided into small subgroups. Each subgroup should incorporate a heterogeneous, diagonal slice of the organization. That is, it should include a mixture of participants from different functional areas and it should not include superiors and subordinates within the same subgroup. Each subgroup is asked to discuss and define organization obstacles such as unclear goals, poor attitudes, or confusing policies. The subgroup should also discuss what changes should be made to make the organization more effective. The subgroup's conclusions are summarized and listed by a recorder/reporter.
3. *Information sharing:* making information available to all (one hour). The total group is reconvened and each subgroup's findings are shared with the total group. Each reporter writes the group's findings on one of a number of large posters that are displayed around the room. The meeting leader then suggests categories for the findings based upon subject area or type of problem (e.g., procedures, communication, top management).

During a break, the data sheets are duplicated for general distribution to the total group. The second session consists of steps 4 and 5:

4. *Priority setting and group action planning:* setting priorities and obtaining commitments (one hour plus). The data sheets are distributed and each participant is asked to categorize the data according to the subject areas earlier defined by the meeting leader. The participants are

*This usually consists of two sessions, one in the evening and another on the following morning and afternoon.

subdivided into their normal functional work groups for a one-hour session. Each functional group is "headed up" by its normal leader (e.g., unit manager), and is assigned three specific tasks:
   a. Discuss the problems and issues that affect its area. Decide on the priorities and actions to which the group is prepared to commit itself.
   b. Identify the issues or problems to which top management should give priority attention.
   c. Decide how to communicate the results of the session to subordinates.[50]
5. *Organization action planning:* getting top management support (one to two hours). The total management group is reconvened and:
   a. Each functional unit reports its commitment and plans to the total group.
   b. Each unit reports the items that top management should deal with first.
   c. The top manager reacts to this list and makes commitments (through setting targets, assigning task forces or timetables for action where required.
   d. Each unit shares briefly its plans for communicating the results of the confrontation meeting to all subordinates.

This completes the total group portion of the confrontation meeting; however, two additional meetings are required to complete the process:

1. *Immediate follow-up by top management* (one to three hours). The objective of this meeting, which comprises top management, is to formulate specific action plans together with a timetable for implementation. Information convering the various action plans are disseminated throughout the management organization within a few days.
2. *Progress Review* (two hours). A follow-up meeting is held with the total management group four to six weeks after the confrontation meeting. The purpose of this meeting is to report progress and to review action plans.

There is evidence that the confrontation meeting is helpful in terms of resolving group conflict and stress situations.

Beckhard reports two primary strengths of the confrontation meeting.[51] First, this method can provide for operational improvements such as the clarification of existing policies and procedures, initiation of new policies and procedures, as well as the development of task forces or temporary groups to solve specific operational problems. The second strength pertains to improvement of organization effectiveness through more open communication and problem solving.[52]

There are, of course, several weaknesses and potential problems inherent in the confrontation meeting. The four potential problem areas are:[53]

1. Management may not follow up on the action plans. Needless to say, this can have very negative effects.
2. If top management is using the confrontation meeting as a "snow job" to give the appearance of employee participation, the results can also be negative. The participants will soon realize top management's intentions and the reaction will be severe.
3. Implementation of action plans may not be possible, owing to the establishment of unrealistic or unachievable goals.
4. The most urgent problems brought out may not necessarily be the most important. The confrontation meeting may tend to focus attention on short-range problems.

In summary, the confrontation meeting is a useful tool by which to highlight critical problem areas and provide a mechanism to deal with them. It combines the key components of the renewal process into a one-day session. However, the most critical activities include "climate setting" and "follow-up" to ensure success through group action.

INTERGROUP PROBLEM SOLVING

The total organization is really a composite of its various working units or groups. The important thing for organizational accomplishment, whether the groups are formal or informal, is that these groups perceive their goals as being the same as the goals of the organization. On occasion, groups or parts of the organization come into conflict. The competitive atmosphere between groups can affect the total productivity of an organization. Basically, the problem exists when each group becomes more committed to its own goals and norms; they are likely to become competitive with one another and to undermine their rival's activities, creating ineffectiveness throughout the system.

Many unique dynamics take place within and between groups. During competition, each group becomes more cohesive; internal differences are forgotten for the moment as increased loyalty takes over. The group climate becomes more task-oriented as one's own group accomplishment becomes paramount. The leadership shifts more toward an autocratic style as the groups become more tolerant of each other and their own leadership. The group becomes more structured, with demands for conformity of members to present a solid front against the other groups.

At the same time, the dynamics between the groups are fierce. Each group sees the other one as the enemy and distorts perceptions of reality. Hostility mounts while communication decreases. If the groups are forced to interact, neither listens to the other or each biases remarks in its own favor.

In the win/lose intergroup situation, the outcome heightens tension between groups. If the win is clear cut, the winner often becomes complacent and is less interested in goal accomplishment. The loser develops internal conflict among its members by trying to fix the blame. In lose/lose outcomes, values and goals of each group become partitioned to the extent that neither group has much energy to contribute toward achieving the system's goals.

The negative consequences of intergroup conflict causes organizational management to seek resolution. The basic strategy of intervention is to find goals upon which groups can agree and reestablish valid communication between groups. This strategy can be implemented by any combination of the following: locating a common enemy, inventing a negotiation strategy that brings subgroups of the competing groups into interaction with each other, and locating a superordinate goal.

Sherif is helpful in identifying the main concepts for understanding intergroup conflict.[54] He defines the members of a group as (1) individuals who at a given time have role and status relationships with one another stabilized in some degree and (2) who possess a set of values or norms regulating the attitudes and behavior of individual members, at least in matters of consequence to them. He further identifies the appropriate frame of reference for studying intergroup behavior as the *functional* relations between two or more groups, which may be positive or negative. He is careful to point out that intergroup behavior (positive or negative) is *not* primarily a problem of deviant behavior. But attitude is of critical importance. Intergroup attitudes, including stereotypes, are defined as a set of categories within which a person belonging to one group locates other people as similar or dissimilar to himself or herself; and evaluates these similarities or differences as being in some degree acceptable or unacceptable. Of course, attitudes (and stereotypes) are affected by norms and shared images. Furthermore, it appears that cooperativeness and democratic interaction within a given group does *not* carry over to a group's treatment of the other group, or affect the image one group sustains of the other. Quite the reverse! Sherif's experiment showed that during the course of rising intergroup hostility, solidarity and cooperativeness within each group did increase.

There is obviously the need to "look at the past," to see the origins of group images and of group conflict. Basically, we are talking about the importance of awareness: about oneself, one's group, and "the other group."

Drawing from the work done by Sherif and Sherif, Blake and Mouton took a further look at small-group behavior in contrived research settings, exploring various phenomena emerging from intergroup competition situations. The first of their two studies began with the hypothesis that "even after full opportunity to evaluate and compare group products from both of the contending sides . . . group members will have greater factual knowledge of their own than of the other group's product." The hypothesis was supported and various conclusions emerged:[55]

Under competitive conditions members perceive that they understand other group's proposals when they really do not.

Losing groups, rather than accepting the winning product, react with hostility toward judges and antagonism toward the other group.

Resolving conflict is difficult in this sort of situation, for groups are not aware of how distorted the factual knowledge has become.

The second study looks at the role of the representative of a group elected to negotiate with other group representatives for the "winning" proposal (each group having submitted a proposal).[56] The authors describe the representative as having limited latitude for negotiation, for to compromise his or her group's proposal would be interpreted as defeat by them. The hypothesis of this study is that under win/lose competition, if the resolution of differences through representatives must result in the acceptance of one position as "better" and another as "poor" (no compromise possible), then it will more frequently end in deadlock (i.e., loyalty to a party line) than in capitulation. The results of the study confirmed that loyalty to an in-group position replaces the exercise of logic when two group positions are evaluated under win/lose conditions. This inability of representatives to adjudicate differences in points of view has resulted in a number of "neutral" groups whose function is to make impartial judgments. If negotiations between representatives could take place before group positions are made public, perhaps the possibility of reaching an acceptable solution may be increased; and by establishing superordinate goals for the competing groups, a win/lose situation may be avoided and a quality proposal designed.

The management of intergroup activities is crucial to the life and productivity of any organization. Schein suggests that management must understand the consequences of competition, collaboration, and autonomy in intergroup behavior.[57] There are a variety of techniques available through which one may learn about intergroup process:

Interview members of each group about their feelings toward other groups and how these feelings are translated into overt behavior.

Observe meetings in which both groups are present to assess the openness of such things as communication and cooperation.

Theorize what should happen between groups, then observe specific situations (e.g., observe group A's response to an error made by group B; were they supportive, sympathetic, helpful?).

Some intervention techniques and activities are available for groups that are experiencing strain or overt hostility among each other:[58]

Groups (or group leaders) meet with a change facilitator to confirm conflicts between respective units, and then are asked to commit themselves to the activity suggested. If they agree:

Each group meets separately to compose two lists: The first list reflects the thoughts, attitudes, feelings, and perceptions of the other group; the second list is a prediction of how the other group sees its own group.

The two groups come together and share lists. No discussion is to take place during this step and only questions of clarification are posed and responded to.

Once again the groups meet separately to discuss the lists and hopefully to discover the misperceptions and miscommunication revealed by the lists. The sharing of information often serves to reduce the problems perceived initially. After the discussion, each group separately prepares a list of the priority issues that remain unresolved between the two groups.

The two groups meet together to share and discuss the lists and to make a single integrated list of priority issues. Together they generate action steps for issue resolution and assign responsibilities for the actions.

A follow-up meeting is usually desirable to ensure that positive action is being taken.

In a similar exercise, groups are asked to make three lists:

1. A "positive feedback" list containing the things the group values and likes about the other group
2. A "bug" list of things the group dislikes about the other group
3. An "empathy" list containing a prediction of what the other group's list will include

After lists are shared, the group as a whole may prepare the master issue list, and then form subgroups to examine each issue. After another whole-group sharing session, a list of action steps are prepared.

One other method is the "organization mirror," in which a host group gets feedback from representatives of several other organizational groups about how it is perceived and regarded.[59]

If intergroup conflict is unavoidable, the resolution of conflict depends upon two factors: redirection of the intensity of the conflict and development of overriding organizational goals that include both parties to the conflict. Each resolution offers several options, and some creative management challenges. Differences between people and groups can represent fertile and legitimate grist for problem solving that results in high-quality decisions. This is the challenge of intergroup problem solving through collaboration born of differences.

MATRIX ORGANIZATION

The establishment of temporary and interdisciplinary groups within a human system is an important aspect of group development. This includes short-term task forces and long-term project groups that have specific tasks to accomplish outside the normal configuration of the organization. There is a need to develop new structures and processes to meet the rapidly changing demands placed upon these temporary groups. These new structures and processes will increase the need for the creative and flexible use of the human resources of the organization. More and more we will see the emergence of matrix organization concepts wherein people will be seen as resources to be utilized any time their capabilities are needed to solve organizational problems. The old concepts of "going through channels," autonomous departments, and line-staff delineation are no longer completely valid in modern organizational management. The use of project teams, task forces, and other types of "temporary systems" will be the appropriate way for organizations to optimize the different capabilities of its human resources:

> Organizations of the future . . . will have some unique characteristics. They will be adaptive, rapidly changing *temporary systems,* organized around problems to be solved by groups of relative strangers with diverse professional skills. These groups will be arranged on organic rather than mechanical models, they will evolve in response to problems to be solved . . . organizational charts will consist of project groups rather than stratified functional groups . . . . This is the form of organization that will gradually replace bureaucracy.[60]

It is frequently found that organizational problems are no longer the province of just one group, but that they cut across the multiple human, structural, and technological resources of an organization. The need for a matrix organization concept in practice is a trend in making modern organizational systems viable.

The development and utilization of special groups and subsystems in organizations to solve problems is an example of temporary societies. The characteristics of temporary systems are:

Time boundary (either chronologically or in terms of a task completion)
Insulation between the system and "outside" influences
Intensive involvement (in most cases)

These characteristics are reflected in the differences between mechanical and organic systems. The multidisciplinary task group within the matrix organization has some quite distinctive functions and unique composition:*

It is a special kind of problem-solving concept, in both form and function.
Its purpose is to solve problems that cannot be solved by conventional organizations, minds, or methods.
It (1) draws from a formal organization the men and women, machines, procedures, and techniques of diverse social and physical sciences, and (2) integrates them into a temporary group (force) having as a purpose, (3) the solving of a complex problem that the formal organization and routine method cannot solve; and (4) on completion of its task it is dissolved and its constituent members and parts returned to their functional homes.†
It has certain advantages not otherwise readily available to an organization:

1. *Results:* most effective means to accomplish some tasks; tends to cut bureaucratic red tape.
2. *Synergistic:* helps promote multidisciplinary contributions and develops halo effect.
3. *People:* enhances management testing, morale, and job enrichment.
4. *Management:* elicits management involvement in significant organizational problems.
5. *Communication:* provides, through group action, an improved interdepartmental communication and line-staff interaction.

*A newer approach to the solution of macroproblems—*The Multocular Process*—as developed by Gordon Lippitt and Reuben Stivers from the now more or less standardized view of the matrix organization, is a step beyond the project and task group concepts.[61]

†The U.S. Navy's concept of a *task force* is similar—that of a functional fighting unit comprised of a mix of various types of ships organized for a specific tactical or strategic purpose, and redeployed into groups of like-type ships when no longer needed for that purpose.

6. *Status:* participants often receive considerable visibility and heightened status.

But unless carefully conceived and handled, the use of project groups and task forces also introduce some problems and disadvantages:

1. The heuristic task group often duplicates an already existing functional group within the organization.
2. There is a tendency for functional groups to neglect their own work and to let the heuristic task group do it all.
3. There may be too much shifting of personnel from project group to project group as priorities shift.
4. There may be inadequate representation of useful disciplines.
5. The task group is not given adequate authority or resources or completion time.
6. The task group does not go out of existence when its mission is accomplished, and so becomes a part of the regular system.
7. Vested interests are allowed to block effective problem solving.

When people are presenting ideas in a heuristic task group within a matrix organization and, as is usually the case, working against time, some way must be established to sort out that which is useful and that which is not. Some way also should be found to determine periodically what progress the group has made toward the acomplishment of the task before it; group effectiveness is enhanced when this is done easily and smoothly. A concise statement of goals provides a criterion by which the appropriateness of each member's input can be evaluated, and a simple planning chart, always kept current, will serve to show the team how much remains to be done.

A common picture of the temporary group leader within a matrix organization is that of a frustrated diplomat struggling to cajole multifunctional representatives into performing the work on schedule and within allotted funding.[62]

The clarity of the task group's goals, communicative openness, and decision-making methods are important here as they are in any group development. The group leader and the group members will be continually working on four problems inherent in their psychological contracts:

1. *Problem of identity.* Questions each person in a group seeks to answer include: "Who am I in this group?" What kinds of resources do I have that will be useful?" "What roles will I play or be called upon to play?"
2. *Problem of power and influence.* Members are concerned about who will have power and influence; how much others will exert influence; how much others can be influenced. This leads to the matter of group power and influence, which, like goals, need to be understood by every member of the group.
3. *Problem of goals and needs.* "What are the needs of others in the group?" and "Will any of my needs be met?" are questions constantly asked by both the leader and members. In many groups little information is available to answer these questions because members are unaware of their needs or are unwilling to share their concerns and feelings. Whether needs are being met will be related to group cohesiveness, that is, keeping the members of the group together so that they function as a group. Whether or not a group remains intact and, to a large extent, its effectiveness depend upon the tolerance within the group of these differences and the means used to compromise them.
4. *Problem of acceptance and intimacy.* A group often confronts persons with the issue of their own needs, difficulties, hopes, and feelings of adequacy and inadequacy in forming close, trusting, and intimate relationships with other persons. For some persons, to be alone is threatening; to others, to be close is difficult. The problem of achieving appropriate levels of intimacy

is often worked out covertly as the group works on its task. Permanent projects groups and temporary task forces can benefit from a group development process so that those from different disciplines may work effectively to solve problems.

GROUP DEVELOPMENT INCREASES INDIVIDUALITY

The human resource development field has been attempting—through laboratory training, team-building efforts, and human relations workshops—to help develop more effective group action. In the past thirty years, the behavioral scientist has devoted a good deal of attention to group behavior and the problems of human behavior. Some people have expressed concern lest this research and emphasis detract from the importance of the individual.[63]

No more serious question could be raised in this age when individual freedom and growth throughout the world is threatened by various forms of totalitarianism. The submergence of the individual into blind and abject subservience faces us unless the democratic ideal of individual freedom, and the opportunity to develop according to individual potentialities, can be maintained and strengthened. As a matter of fact, our *basic* question today is how to help in the development of strong and wise individuals who can, alone and with others, reach good decisions about their problems. But we should remember these things:[64]

> There is nothing good or bad, per se, about a group.
>
> A group can be a roadblock to progress, enforcing "group think" and conformity upon its members, paralyzing decision-making processes, and smothering individual initiative.
>
> Under other conditions, a group can be a powerful, helpful synergism of talents, strengthening its members, speeding up the decision-making process and enhancing individual and personal growth.

The seven symptoms of "group think" are very much in the minds of leaders and managers:*

1. Illusions of invulnerability by the group
2. Collective rationalization in the group
3. Unquestioned belief in group morality
4. Stereotyping the enemy as evil
5. Direct pressure on deviant members in the group
6. Self-censorship of deviant behavior by individual group members.
7. An illusion of unanimity by the group

Recent activities in group behavior and team building, rather than submerging individuals, have had at the very core of their purpose the maximizing of the contribution of the individual, increasing the individual's personal worth in relation to others, and the development of a person's ability to make further contributions. The dangers of "group think" can be lessened through leadership education, management development programs, organization development efforts, and team-building processes. If done effectively and professionally, such efforts will reinforce and not submerge individuality.

To substantiate this point of view, let me elaborate upon some principles:

> Leaders, supervisors, and administrators trained in effective human relations are

*Irving Janis, in his provocative book entitled *Victims of Group Think,* states that (as a result of his analysis of major political events in the United States; that is, the Vietnam war, Cambodian bombing, Bay of Pigs, and Watergate) "group think" becomes a real factor in inadequate problem solving when the leader is surrounded by "yes" men who do not challenge assumptions and act creatively.[65]

more sensitive to the needs of individuals than are those who are not so trained.

In effective group relations, the group becomes sensitive to the needs of its individual members.

In effective team building, the individual shares in the setting of group goals that affect his or her own situation, and in determining the methods used in reaching such goals.

Expressions of individual differences of opinion and frankness of feelings are more likely in a supportive situation than in an autocratic, manipulated one.

The utilization of the consensus method of decision making, rather than majority voting, makes the individual important.

In effective group relations, the individual is encouraged to feel independent, is delegated responsibility and authority as the group members develop trust in one another, and is encouraged to grow and improve.

Group-relations research indicates that a wide range of individual contributions are needed.

Individual action and reponsibility are more likely to result from shared rather than autocratic decision making.

Leadership is a skill that is acquired, not inherited.

Professionals in the field of human resource and organizational development know the importance of the basic social drives of an individual. Among these basic drives are a (1) sense of belongingness, (2) a sense of achievement, and (3) a sense of recognition. In the complexity of today's world, in our industrialized society, the individual frequently does not develop the security that comes from the satisfaction of these three basic needs.

Groups can serve these basic drives. When a group has learned how to become sensitive to individual needs, each of its members is helped to feel that he or she belongs to the group and that the group wants him or her as a member. Such a group affords a person success and recognition.

Behavioral scientists can be proud of their work during the last thirty years in recognizing the importance of the individual. Individuals and their relationships with others are, and will continue to be, the prime concerns of those human resource developers who add to the knowledge and skills of how people work, learn, and play.

SUMMARY

In any process of organization renewal, the development of effective groups will be an essential process. The competent group leader and member are vital. Processes that can develop teamwork are needed in all organizational systems. Teamwork can be increased by use of team-building activity, sociotechnical methods, process consultation, confrontation meetings, intergroup problem solving, optimizing matrix group functioning, and other means. Developing such teamwork makes possible individuality and creativity rather than conformity. Group development in systems renewal is one of the most frequently used interventions in organization development and organization renewal.

CASE STUDY: AN EXAMPLE OF A GROUP DEVELOPMENT APPROACH

This case study involves organization renewal through team development. Traditionally, hospitals have encouraged the professional and vocational growth of their employees as a means of improving the quality of patient care and the efficiency of the institution. This sort of thing is usually implemented in the traditional ways—by organizing in-service programs, conducting seminars, supplying employees with periodicals and films, sending employees to national and regional meetings and conferences, paying tui-

tion fees for job-related technical and college courses, and so forth. Until recently, a large suburban hospital accepted this approach without question.

As a part of an ongoing quality evaluation program undertaken by its board of trustees, however, the hospital began critically to examine its approach. Employee motivation, communication, supervisory skills, interpersonal and interdepartmental relationships, and employee attitudes about their jobs, their fellow workers, their supervisors, and the institution itself were examined. It was soon apparent that increasing professional competence does not necessarily have an impact on complex intrahospital relationships and teamwork, both of which directly affect the quality of care rendered and the efficiency of the organization.

The hospital remained committed to the more traditional goals and methods of professional and vocational growth, but also sought a means of evaluating more complex organizational needs. The hospital lacked the expertise to properly evaluate its organizational needs.

Moving the organization from a formalistic direct-line management posture toward a participative mode was one of the major goals. The transition was achieved through team-building sessions for every unit, from the eight-member executive council to rank-and-file employee groups. As the program progressed through its various stages, supervisors and other employees were given special training by outside consultants and, in turn, became team training leaders.

The hospital's ultimate goal is the development of a cadre of trainers to assure team-building continuation without the assistance of outside consultants.

Comment. *In this situation we see an example of the use of outside consultants to help analyze organization-wide needs for moving into participative management. The team-building process was implemented with the development of inside resource trainers, and this will go a long way toward ensuring continued commitment.*

QUESTIONS

1. In what ways does the work unit provide means for the individual to influence the larger organization?
2. What do you believe are the major elements lacking in the teamwork of the groups with which you have been associated?
3. In what group have you experienced the greatest teamwork? Why?
4. Why do groups find it difficult to confront their own problems? How can this be overcome?
5. How do you react to pressures leading to group conformity? In what ways can a group lessen such pressures?
6. In your experience in organizations, have intergroup conflict and vested interest been a barrier to group productivity? How were they important?
7. When have you found project and task groups appropriate? Not appropriate?

NOTES

[1]Rensis Likert, *The Human Organization: Its Management and Values* (New York: McGraw-Hill Book Co., Inc., 1967), p. 67.

[2]Harry Levinson et al., *Men, Management, and Mental Health* (Cambridge, Mass.: Harvard University Press, 1962), p. 26.

[3]Rensis Likert, *New Patterns of Management* (New York: McGraw-Hill Book Company, 1961), p. 99.

[4]David S. Brown, "Leadership and Followership: The Twin Ingredients," *Management Quarterly* (a publication of the National Rural Electric Cooperative), Vol. 20, No. 3, 1979, 27.

[5]Gordon Lippitt and Edith W. Seashore, *The Leader Looks at Group Effectiveness* (Looking into Leadership Monographs; Washington, D.C.: Leadership Resources, Inc., 1961), p. 1.

[6]Ibid., p. 6.

[7]Rensis Likert, *Developing Patterns of Management* (New York: American Management Association, Inc., 1956), p. 7.

[8]Leland P. Bradford and Gordon Lippitt, "The

Individual Counts in Effective Group Relations," *NEA Journal,* November 1954, p. 487.

[9]Fred E. Fiedler, *A Theory of Leadership Effectiveness* (New York: McGraw-Hill Book Company, 1967, pp. 18–22.

[10]Robert E. Blake and Jane B. Mouton, "Reactions to Intergroup Competition under Win-Lose Conditions," *Management Science,* Vol. 7, 1961.

[11]Theodore Mills, *The Sociology of Small Groups* (Englewood Cliffs, N.J.: Prentice-Hall, Inc., 1967).

[12]George C. Charrier, *Cog's Ladder: A Model of Group Growth* (unpublished paper at Proctor and Gamble Company, 1965).

[13]Stewart L. Tubbs, *A Systems Approach to Small Group Interaction* (Reading, Mass.: Addison-Wesley Publishing Company, Inc. 1978).

[14]Ibid., p. 11. Copyright © 1978 by Addison-Wesley Publishing Company, Inc. Reprinted with permission of Addison-Wesley Publishing Company, Inc.

[15]Ibid., pp. 11–12.

[16]Adapted from Gordon Lippitt, "Guidelines for Managing Groups," *Credit Union Executive,* Winter 1965.

[17]Warren H. Schmidt, *The Leader Looks at the Leadership Dilemma* (Looking into Leadership Monograph; Washington, D.C.: Leadership Resources, Inc., 1961), p. 9.

[18]Abraham Zaleznick and David Moment, *The Dynamics of Interpersonal Behavior* (New York: John Wiley & Sons, Inc., 1964), p. 61.

[19]Adapted from an unpublished paper by Steve Harper and Gail Hughes, *Team Building* (Washington, D.C.: The George Washington University, November 1978).

[20]Peter Drucker, *Management* (New York: Harper & Row, Publishers, Inc., 1973), p. 146.

[21]William Dyer, *Team Building: Issues and Alternatives* (Reading, Mass.: Addison-Wesley Publishing Company, Inc., 1977), pp. 36–39.

[22]Ibid., p. 46. Copyright © 1977 by Addison-Wesley Publishing Company, Inc. Reprinted with permission of Addison-Wesley Publishing Company, Inc.

[23]Taylor McDonnell, *Group Leadership for Self-realization* (New York: Petrocelli Books, 1974), p. 68.

[24]Jack Gibb, *Trust: A New View of Personal and Organizational Development* (Los Angeles, Calif.: The Guild of Tutors Press, 1978).

[25]W. Warner Burke and Harvey A. Hornstein, *The Social Technology of Organization Development* (Fairfax, Va.: NTL Learning Resources Corporation, 1972).

[26]Eric L. Trist et al., *Organization Choice* (London: Tavistock Publications, Ltd., 1963), p. 112. Hereafter cited as Trist.

[27]Ibid., p. 106.

[28]Harvey A. Hornstein et al., *Social Intervention: A Behavioral Science Approach* (New York: The Free Press, 1971).

[29]Louis E. Davis, "The Design of Jobs," in Newton Margules and Anthony P. Raia (eds.), *Organizational Development Values, Process, and Technology* (New York: McGraw-Hill Book Company, 1972).

[30]Trist, p. 141.

[31]Adapted from an unpublished paper by William B. Johnson, *Role Negotiation: An Organization Renewal Technology* (Washington, D.C.: The George Washington University, 1977).

[32]Roger Harrison, "Role Negotiation: A Tough-minded Approach to Team Development," in W. Warner Burke and Harvey A. Hornstein (eds.), *The Social Technology of Organization Development* (Fairfax, Va.: NTL Learning Resources Corporation, 1972), p. 118.

[33]Wendell L. French and Cecil H. Bell, Jr., *Organization Development: Behavioral Science Interventions for Organization Improvement* (Englewood Cliffs, N.J.: Prentice-Hall, Inc., 1973), p. 81. Hereafter cited as French and Bell (1973).

[34]Ibid., p. 101.

[35]John J. Sherwood and John C. Glidewell, "Planned Renegotiation: A Norm-setting Organization Development Intervention," in W. Warner Burke (ed.), *Contemporary Organization Development: Conceptual Orientation and Intervention* (Arlington, Va.: NTL Institute For Applied Behavioral Science, 1972).

[36]Ibid., p. 87.

[37]Ibid., pp. 88–89.

[38]Richard L. Hill and Irving R. Stubbs, *Role Negotiation for Team Productivity: Managers Manual and Participants Workbook* (Washington, D.C.: Organization Renewal, Inc., 1976).

[39]Arthur M. Louis, "They're Striking Some Strange Bargains at Diamond Rock," *Fortune,* January 1976, p. 142.

[40]Roger Harrison, "Some Criteria for Choosing the Depth of Organization Intervention Strategy," in Richard Hacon (ed.), *Personal and Organizational Effectiveness* (New York: McGraw-Hill Book Company, 1972).

[41]Edgar H. Schein, *Process Consultation: Its Role in Organization Development* (Reading, Mass.: Addison-Wesley Publishing Company, Inc., 1969), p. 135. Hereafter cited as Schein.

[42]Wendell L. French and Cecil H. Bell, Jr., *Organization Development: Behavioral Science Interventions for Organization Improvement* 2nd ed. (Englewood Cliffs, N.J.: Prentice-Hall, Inc., 1978), p. 110.

[43]Schein, p. 91.

[44]Ibid., p. 102.

[45]Ibid., p. 104.

[46]Adaped from an unpublished paper by W. E. Bye, *Confrontation Meeting: An Update* (Washington, D.C.: The George Washington University, November 1975).

[47]Richard Beckhard, "The Confrontation Meeting," *Harvard Business Review,* March–April 1967, pp. 151–155.

[48]Ibid., p. 151.

[49]Ibid., p. 150.

[50]Ibid., p. 154

[51]Ibid., p. 152

[52]Ibid., p. 153.

[53]Ibid., p. 154.

[54]Muzafer Sherif, *In Common Predicament: Social Psychology Of Intergroup Conflict and Cooperation* (Boston: Houghton Mifflin Company, 1966).

[55]Robert R. Blake and Jane S. Mouton, "Comprehension of Own and Out-group Competition," in Bernard Hinton and H. Joseph Reitz (eds.), *Groups and Organization* (Belmont, Calif.: Wadsworth Publishing Company, Inc., 1971), pp. 373–376.

[56]Robert R. Blake and Jane S. Mouton, "Loyalty of Representatives to Ingroup Positions during Outgroup Competition," in Bernard Hinton and H. Joseph Reitz (eds.), *Groups and Organization* (Belmont, Calif.: Wadsworth Publishing Company, Inc., 1971), pp. 377–381.

[57]Schein, p. 101.

[58]Robert R. Blake, Herbert A. Shepard, and Jane S. Mouton, *Managing Intergroup Conflict in Industry* (Houston, Tex.: Gulf Publishing Company, 1964), p. 51.

[59]French and Bell (1973), p. 131.

[60]Warren G. Bennis and Philip E. Slater, *The Temporary Society* (New York: Harper & Row, Publishers, Inc., 1968), p. 127.

[61]Gordon Lippitt and Reuben Stivers, *The Multocular Process: A Working Paper* (Washington, D.C.: Development Publications, 1975).

[62]Robert Youker, *Organizational Alternatives for Project Management* (paper presented at the 8th Annual Symposium of the Project Management Institute, Montreal, Canada, October 6–8, 1976), p. 17.

[63]Adapted from Gordon Lippitt, "Effective Team Building Develops Individuality," *International Journal for Human Resources Development,* Vol. 1, No. 1, 1980.

[64]Rensis Likert, *The Human Organization: Its Management and Value* (New York: McGraw-Hill Book Company, 1967), p. 102.

[65]Irving L. Janis, *Victims of Group Think* (Boston: Houghton Mifflin Company, 1972).

9

organization development processes

Like people and plants, organizations have a life cycle. They have a green and supple youth, a time of flourishing strength, and a gnarled old age. . . . An organization may go from youth to old age in two or three decades, or it may last for centuries.

John Gardner, 1912–[1]

This level of change and renewal essentially differs from individual development and group development in that it is concerned with the total human system. Organization development has become a popular expression during the past twenty-five years, with many miniscule distinctions and fine differences applied to its goals and methods. Started in the 1950s, it is an outgrowth of techniques developed by social psychologists, such as T-groups and human relations laboratories. Over the years it has grown into a diffuse but recognizable body of work now occurring in hundreds of organizations throughout the world, with facilitation by outside consultants and in-house organization development teams or departments. In an early stage, it was defined as follows:

> Using knowledge and techniques from the behavioral sciences, organization development attempts to integrate individual needs for growth and development with organizational goals and objectives in order to make a more effective organization.[2]

In the pioneering efforts, it was indicated that these objectives are characteristic:[3]

- To create an open, problem-solving climate throughout an organization
- To supplement the authority associated with role or status with the authority of knowledge and competence
- To locate decision-making and problem-solving responsibilities as close to the information sources as possible
- To build trust among individuals and groups throughout the organization
- To make competition more relevant to work goals and to maximize collaborative efforts
- To develop a reward system that recognizes both the achievement of the organization's mission (profits or service) and organization development (the growth of people)
- To increase the sense of "ownership" of organization objectives throughout all the work force
- To help managers to manage according to relevant objectives rather than according to "past practices" or according to objectives that do not make sense for one's area of responsibility

To increase self-control and self-direction for people within the organization

In the systems renewal model, organization development is conceived as a series of processes that may be used to review the total organization or social system.

ORGANIZATIONS AS A SYSTEM

The total organization is a human system with birth, growth, and decline stages, and upon casual examination, several familiar variations in viewing the organization come to mind.

A system of authority. The organization is viewed in terms of conventional management theory—organization as a device to do a job too large for one person, as a division of labor with emphasis on processes of production and work flow.

A system of likes and dislikes. Here the criterion is personal preferences (whom we like and whom we do not like); the emphasis is on the "informal organization" as a friend or foe of the formal.

A system of communication. Here the criterion is who talks to whom, for what purpose, and with what effect.

A system of power and control. The emphasis here is on relative distribution of the total amount of power the organization can mobilize, and on the bases of power (rewards, coercion, legitimate, expertise, or personal) among members and leaders.

Other categories of systems could be listed that affect the total sociotechnical organization and provide the basis for the design, analysis, and renewal of organizations by giving joint consideration to the technological, structural, social, financial, personal, and ecological variables affecting them.

As illustrated in Table 9-1, the entire continuum of an organization's life falls within three developmental stages: birth, youth, and maturity. Some organizations succeed in reaching higher stages of development than others do, but organizations usually go into decline only because of internal mismanagement or drastic changes in external environment. The objective of organization renewal is to handle the key issues of development in such a way as to achieve higher stages progressively and to preclude a decline toward a lower stage. The birth stage is by no means limited to the level of a "cottage industry," nor is the maturity stage confined to the level of organizational giants. A comparatively small business organization may reach developmental maturity, and a comparatively large one may remain youthful. Thus, the criteria for determining the stage of development of an organization probably are found more in the manner of coping with predictable key issues than in the number of employees, market share, or managerial sophistication.

From this point of view, an organization is an assemblage of people, procedures, and facilities that is a *sociotechnical system* and which, during the developmental stages, experiences at least six critical concerns or confrontations. The fundamental issues posed by these concerns may occur at almost any time, and the problems they create tend to reoccur. The answers are partially supplied every day, directly or indirectly, by precedents set by the acts and words of managers and workers as they conduct the organization's affairs or produce its products or services. Nevertheless, at certain times it is inevitable that one of these issues will acquire exceptional importance, and that the organization must then recognize, confront, and cope with a paramount critical concern. This is similar to the problems an individual must resolve at certain times of life—the problems of puberty and aging, for example—if he or she is to have a healthy personality.

Table 9-1
Stages of Organizational Growth[4]

Developmental Stage	Critical Concern	Key Issue	Consequences If Concern Is Not Met
Birth	To create a new organization	What to risk	Frustration and inaction
	To survive as a viable system	What to sacrifice	Death of organization
			Further subsidy by "faith" capital
Youth	To gain stability	How to organize	Reactive, crisis-dominated organization
			Opportunistic rather than self-directing attitudes and policies
	To gain reputation and develop pride	How to review and evaluate	Difficulty in attracting good personnel and clients
			Inappropriate, overly aggressive, and distorted image building
Maturity	To achieve uniqueness and adaptability	Whether and how to change	Unnecessarily defensive or competitive attitudes; diffusion of energy
			Loss of most creative personnel
	To contribute to society	Whether and how to share	Possible lack of public respect and appreciation
			Bankruptcy or profit loss

Renewal—whether individual, group, or organizational—may occur at any time in the growth cycle.

The confrontations of an organization, within itself and within its environment, and the questions they raise, are as much a test of organizational growth as individual crises are a test of human fitness. Similarly, the answers that are provided reflect the will and wisdom of its leaders, and organizational maturity, just as an individual's responses to crises are a measure of aims, perspicacity, and success. Let us, therefore, examine in some detail the six critical concerns and response patterns in the order in which they are most likely to occur from birth through maturity of an organization.

Launching the venture. Here the entrepreneurs confront the crucial question: What and how much are we willing to risk? A number of years ago, two professors of psychology at a well-known southern university experimented with a new theory of programmed learning in which two learners worked together, each reinforcing the other. The professors created a unique methodology for this. Fascinated by the commercial possibilities of the theory and its potential contribution to society, the men decided to take the risk of abandoning their professorial seniority at the university and investing their savings to develop and promote their idea. Next, they persuaded others to join the venture. Friends put up "faith capital," and their employees took a chance on receiving a salary. An organization was born, but its chance of survival depended on many unknowns. It exists today as a successful enterprise only because all concerned gambled heavily.

The principle revealed in this simple illustration is repeated over and over again in our country. Every new restaurant, dry cleaner, or small electronics engineering firm, of which literally hundreds are born annually, rests on risk. Some of them, if they have taken the right risks, may succeed as did the Xerox Corporation. Joseph C. Wilson, then president of a small paper company, learned of a new process for electrostatic copying developed by an obscure inventor. He persuaded his friends and associates to undertake enormous risks to make xerography a success. Wilson expressed his philosophy in these words: "Great opportunities are given to those who are willing to take advantage of the new . . . [if they are] willing to accept great risk in doing so."

Management must decide how much risk to take in the light of two criteria: the goals by which achievement is to be measured, and the odds against success in reaching them. As we shall see, not only is risk involved in initial investment, it is also involved in each step along the path to full organizational development. But the concern is usually greatest at the beginning.

A person gets an idea for a new product or service. The idea alone is not enough. It must be linked to plans and resources and manpower to become a reality. A sociotechnical system must come into being. Many questions must be asked and answered—about markets, competition, location, costs, manpower, and procedures. All of these questions remain hypothetical, however, until this critical question is answered: Who is willing to risk the dollars, time, energy, and reputation to give this idea a chance to prove its worth? Once this commitment is made with sufficient strength to give the idea impetus, an organization is born and a new product or service is offered in the marketplace.

Survival and sacrifice. Now that it is underway, the organization quickly experiences its next crisis—the ability to survive as a viable system—and the question raised for management is: How much are we willing to sacrifice? Finding the answer may require agonizing soul-searching. A number of years ago, an organization was created by three leaders in the field of behavioral science, each of whom brought with him several pet ideas for marketable products, in addition to expertise in providing consultation and training for prospective clients. Altogether, the three entrepreneurs attempted to develop 28 new products, including, for example, an audience-reaction measurement device, prepackaged conference setups for hotels, a means of videotaping human behavioral actions in group situations, and a series of self-learning publications for managers. A rapid accumulation of debt and the spending of countless hours after the normal workday trying to cope with unfamiliar problems in production and financing soon forced the leaders to make a hard decision. They came to realize that most of the ideas they had favored were inappropriate to the organization they had created. It was painful to surrender the dreams, and difficult to go back to doing only what they did best. But survival dictated reliance on hard core consultation and training activity, with the sacrifice of all their beloved plans except the publications. The organization is eminently successful today only because it was willing and able to sacrifice.

It is axiomatic in risk enterprise that each gain, except a windfall, must be accompanied by the deferment of something else. Each gain in the struggle toward organizational development more often than not requires, usually in some combination, a corresponding individual loss of savings, leisure, energy, health, time with family or friends, comfort, or peace of mind. Or the loss may be represented by a deferment of something desired by the individual—for instance, adequate income, a new car, a vacation, or the opportunity to seize a tempting alternative outside the new enterprise. A critical concern develops out of the necessity to make a choice between values. The decision-controlling factors are the length of time the sacrifice must or can be tolerated, and the validity of the sacrifice in terms of survival. Here, as its leaders face difficult decisions while still in the birth stage, there can be exhibited an initial investment in organizational growth. In other words, the way in which these decisions are made contributes to the process of "growing up."

Some organizations remain a long time on a survival plateau, where dedicated effort results only in marginal returns and where continued survival depends on the confidence and commitment of the leadership.

Achievement of stability. If the organization survives, it is then confronted by a third concern, which raises the question: How willing are we to be organized and to accept and enforce discipline? A well-established firm, engaged in filling dispenser cans with liquids under pressure, had a highly effective vice president for marketing. He was young and personable, and most clients enjoyed dealing with him. He was, in fact, a driving force, a one-man show, and both employees and clients related to him naturally and by preference.

Then the market expanded under the demand for aerosol dispensers for household use, the founder moved up to become chairman of the board and the young vice president took over as president. There, instead of being a well-liked salesman, he had to be a professional manager. Although he was fully *capable* of filling his new position, delegation and efficiency eluded him because he also attempted to maintain all his former personal relationships. The abrupt withdrawal of so dynamic a leader from day-to-day contacts at the working level would have threatened the organization with chaos, but at the same time, the way things were going, he was threatened with personal failure as chief executive officer. Management consultants pointed out that he simply had to relinquish many of the tasks that he had once performed.

A director of personnel was employed who gradually established a rapport with the employees. A new director of marketing was introduced to all but three of the leading clients. A competent administrative assistant acted as a buffer between the new president and the many people who thought that he and he alone could make decisions. The storm was weathered, and the organization went on to exceptional success because it was willing to discipline itself.

Similarly, two young men conceived the idea of an organization that would offer its customers not only more flavors of ice cream, but also "far-out" flavors. The organization was immediately profitable, but as it grew by leaps and bounds, it became more and more enmeshed in nepotism. Regional franchises and leased outlets went to uncles, nephews, and even to second cousins; wives filled some important executive positions. A few of these relatives were efficient producers; most of them were only so-so.

Troubles loomed large as the organization expanded. It became obvious to the founders that the staff members would have to learn to work with strangers. The moment of truth occurred when a vacant regional managership was filled by an "outsider." Performance criteria were finally established, and all members of the management team participated in specific training. The key phrase became "shape up or ship out." Organizational discipline is hard enough to enforce among veteran employees; it is even more difficult to institute among members of a large family. Nevertheless, it was done, equitably and humanely, and the necessary organizational stability was achieved.

As an organization develops, the original leaders undergo varying degrees of trauma in surrendering personal leadership; the expanding hierarchy breeds factions and results in complicated politics; the maintenance of records becomes ever more burdensome; and there is a certain loss of freedom. It becomes hard to decide between further development, with concomitant stability and resilience, and the retention of close relationships and control.

In the birth stage, there is excitement in creation and challenge in survival. The youthful stage is far less dramatic; the organization is accommodating itself to its environment and adjusting its internal operations. Here is where the sociotechnical system becomes functional.

As the outside pressures (e.g., market uncertainties, creditors' demands) on such a system diminish, the internal defects become more evident. Interpersonal or intergroup tensions that could be overlooked in the early stage now clamor for attention. Differing expectations of the founders, managers, and workers are freely expressed. Compensation for sacrifices made earlier is demanded in the struggle to distribute recognition, rewards, and profits. Motivation is complicated by the conflicts between short-term personal gain and long-term organizational gain. Management faces problems of training and retraining personnel, developing a team spirit, stabilizing a core clientele, and developing a long-range plan.

Willingness to accept and enforce discipline means recognizing that expansion is not synonymous with organizational growth. The wisdom required to avoid overcommitment of resources is also involved, for this is a time to solidify gains before launching into larger arenas of action.

Pride and reputation. Next, the organization is concerned with its relationships with its "public." Executives are confronted with the question: How much are we willing to engage in self-examination? An established youth-serving, nonprofit organization established its reputation on various club and group programs for boys and girls from the ages of 8 through 24. As it expanded into most cities in the United States, it began to develop buildings with gymnasiums, swimming pools, and dormitories. The maintenance of such physical and program expansion required increased financial support from the community, particularly in suburban areas. As a consequence, in the late 1960s this organization confronted the reality that it was not serving the youth in the ghetto and inner city. The organization had built its reputation and pride on serving "all youth" regardless of race, creed, or color. In light of its desire to measure up to its own goals, the national policy-making group and staff set up a process of reexamination of programs and services, developed new means of reaching the underprivileged youth group, and directed a major share of its resources in that direction.

A large national airline, well organized

and managed, had consistently attempted to establish a reputation of outstanding service to the public. Management recognized that flight attendants were an important feature of this service, and had developed an extensive training program for individuals entering this occupation. When the company undertook an expansion of its flight attendant training facilities, management asked an outside consulting firm to evaluate the entire training program. This was undertaken cooperatively with the company's training faculty. The resulting study revealed a number of inadequacies, as well as strengths, in the content of the program. Disproportionate time and attention were being devoted to superficial aspects of the job while more basic functions were slighted. Teaching methods were often unimaginative, training facilities sometimes makeshift. The training faculty frequently felt harassed and unrewarded. On reviewing the findings, management and members of the training faculty moved to design imaginative training facilities and to streamline their entire approach to the program. This effort was costly in time and money, but the airline's pride and reputation depended on it.

Stability can become stagnation unless an organization's leaders are prepared to look critically at its products or services and at its internal and external operations. The organization's "ego" is now a sensitive reality. Basking in the youthful stage, and no longer quite as much threatened, it demands recognition. There is a tendency for leaders to be defensive when their creation is criticized by outsiders. Executives and employees want to speak with pride of their organization and what it does; they want to be respected by customers, competitors, and the public. Public relations assumes great importance and requires a larger proportion of time and thought. The budget for promotion is expanded; but promotional efforts are ultimately dependent on the stability of the organization, the quality of its output, and the performance of those who make up the managerial team.

Thus, the issue now at hand is whether management can face up to the constant need to monitor, review, evaluate, and improve. These actions may be considered by some of the managers to be an unfair reflection of their abilities—after all, the organization is successful, is it not? Any attempt to evaluate is interpreted by them as a threat; any attempt to improve their performance is seen as criticism. Quite often, a manager has capabilities that were sufficient only in the birth stage. Forced to choose between "stepping down" or "getting out," the latter may be chosen—and thereby almost invariably cause a shock to the sociotechnical system. With executive turnover, new managers must be trained in a climate that is new to the trainers themselves. It is because of this that many organizations go into decline. They are victims of two problems:

1. The turnover of personnel constantly alters the "image" received by clients or customers.
2. The new members of the management team cannot share other than vicariously the original feeling of sacrifice and commitment experienced by the founders.

Developing uniqueness. Having made decisions that resolved the crises of youth, the organization enters the stage of maturity and encounters new crises. The first of these has to do with its adaptability. The question before top management is: Are we willing to direct the changes necessary to make our organization unique? A public school that had achieved a fine reputation in the school district decided to develop a unique "human relations" approach to its educational program from the kindergarten through grade twelve. The superintendent, board of education, teaching staff, PTA, and students developed the concept and practice of educational experience as a human transaction in which student, parent, teacher, community, and the present social environment are involved. Through the use of sensitivity training for students, parents, teachers, and administrators, the group discussion process in all subjects and learning areas was implemented. Students learned from fellow students. Parents assisted the teacher. Administration became a resource to facilitate learning—not as a bureaucratic or monolithic system. Older students helped younger students. Teachers helped make learning a quest, not a ritual. As a result this school system became a unique demonstration of what a school organization could become and received the attention of educators, community leaders, and parents across the United States.

A Canadian engineering company, fifteen years old and with nearly 1000 employees, enjoyed an excellent reputation in the techniques of electrical power transmission. The expansion of hydroelectric systems in Canada confronted this organization with a basic decision. Should it attempt to compete with the gargantuan landline companies that were rapidly taking over with the help of enormous outlays of capital, or should it change to take advantage of the unique knowledge possessed by its engineers in the application of microwave technology?

The latter course was equivalent to starting over, rebuilding the engineering, marketing, and financial structures, and once more taking the risk of failure. On the other hand, chances were that most of the company's talented personnel would eventually relocate, and in time intense competition would force capitulation to its powerful antagonists.

After much painful self-examination, the officers and directors decided that the values of uniqueness were worth the gamble. Within a few years, this company was serving the governments of twenty-three developing countries throughout the world—designing, installing, and operating noncable, nonwire microwave communications systems.

At this stage, perhaps for the first time, management becomes aware of the basic truth in Peter Drucker's statement: "To manage a business is to balance a variety of needs and goals."[5] Thus far in its development, the organization's goals have been changing but are relatively clear cut. Now the need is for a kind of corporate "self-actualization" (to use Maslow's phrase[6] for one level in the hierarchy of human needs). The goal is a more subtle one—achievements dictated not by such criteria as survival, stability, and reputation, but by the desire to make full use of the organization's unique abilities. One might assume that no crisis could possibly arise at this mature stage of development, and that the solidarity created in the latter portion of the youthful stage would be immune to innovation or change. This is not always so. The drive for organizational self-actualization leads to decisions that once more involve risk. Certain reactionary forces within management feel that there is more to be lost than was the case in the initial stage of creating the new organism. They point out that the investment in technical experience, acquisitions, market identification, and goodwill should not be endangered without serious consideration. But such conservatism and a desire to avoid uncertainty lead to various harmful inhibitions.

Hopefully, the leaders will be sufficiently farsighted to realize that fear of change is the greater risk. To outdistance competition in a fluid market requires a constant search for special capabilities and for ways in which they can be applied advantageously. Thus, research and development—sometimes diversification—are introduced in the hope of establishing relative security in an always uncertain future.

Contributing to society. Only a relatively small number of organizations ever acquire "blue chip" security and stature. Most companies remain, often by preference, local firms, with simple organization structures, uncomplicated product programs, and ordinary ambitions. But some social systems do advance one step further. Their managements are confronted, as a result, with a new critical issue, one involving the organization's responsibility to society. The question that top executives must wrestle with is: What are we willing to give to society without expecting a direct return?

The president and a few of the top executives of a major automobile manufacturing company determined that their firm should introduce new safety devices on every car. This forward-looking program met with opposition from many of the company's directors and not a few of its sales executives. Those opposed to the idea pointed out that the objective of the organization was to outdo its competitors in price as well as in quality; that bankruptcy would make the company unable to serve society at all; or that the provision of extraordinary safety was essentially a calculated public relations program and therefore reprehensible. The president prevailed in this contest, but the attempt to "market" safety was a flat failure. The public simply was not interested. This company, a year or two later, bitterly opposed the federal government's automotive safety campaign. It had acted independently in its pioneering program, but the experience had been both expensive and disillusioning.

Once orderly internal control and a comfortable financial position are achieved, a company often feels a powerful desire to gain society's respect and appreciation. This desire differs in nature from the external attitudes sought by promotional and public relations activities, which are manifestations of bargaining between the organization and its markets. By contrast, the search for respect and appreciation for their own sake is prompted largely by defensiveness or morality. The search may also be self-serving, but that is not the primary motive.

It is not the manner in which these image-building actions are executed that creates an organizational crisis, but rather the degree of organizational growth and the capacity of that growth to handle properly the soul-searching decision of whether to undertake them at all. The achievement of a particular kind of attitude requires the expenditure of funds and entails some risk that many stockholders and not a few controllers and directors can neither understand nor accept.

Institutional advertising in its pure form, and various kinds of community relations programs, such as publicized antipollution efforts, are typical of the defensive methods used by business to forestall the castigation once dealt out to "heedless robber barons" and "heartless trusts." These efforts may also produce indirect benefits in the marketplace, and in a few cases they may help to protect the company against legal threats (e.g., more stringent antipollution laws).

Because the force behind these maturation/actions is often obscure, they are not always conducive to tranquil relationships in managerial hierarchy. There is always another demand for the money, always an investment opportunity somewhere that cannot be exploited if the larger contribution program is carried out. Lately, however, some organizations have accepted the idea that contributions to the social, political, and environmental welfare of the community, state, and/or nation are valuable in themselves.

Less defensively oriented but not less self-serving are actions to improve organizational employees as people. Management, in its search for organizational growth, looks inward and asks: How can we help our executives and workers to develop themselves? It also occasionally looks outward and asks: "How can we help our community, our nation?" or "How can we use our resources to improve the quality of human life?"

Positive answers to these questions take many forms. Scholarship programs are originated, educational television is sponsored, executives are loaned to government, key personnel are encouraged to perform civic services, foundations are established. Yet almost all activities of this nature involve some potential risk created by the complications of politics, taste, discretion, opinion, or equity. The severity of crises generated by efforts to be respected and appreciated as an organization depends on the extent of the conceived organizational need, the organization's financial status, and its own self-image. It also depends on how much the anticipated benefit happens to irritate certain people. There is no intention here to imply that attempts to make worthwhile contributions —for any reason—should not be made by organizations. The truth is that our society is becoming more or less dependent on such contributions, and that a corporate system probably reaches its zenith in development when it finds itself able and willing to so contribute.

The attention of most organizations fluctuates between the six critical needs and issues described above, and perhaps other issues as well, with executives dealing primarily with one now, and then primarily with another. Failures do not happen so much because managers do not manage what they know should be managed, but because they do not recognize the significant crises that occur in the organizational life cycle. Or in John Gardner's words, "Most ailing organizations have developed a functional blindness to their own defects. They are not suffering because they cannot *solve* their problems, but because they cannot *see* their problems."[7]

Recognition of the problem, however, is only the beginning. Problem solving involves developing a common understanding of the problem and all its implications. If all the members of a management team recognize the developmental stage of their organization, they are better able to understand why certain ambitions must be curtailed while others are advanced, and why and when another need is paramount in importance. This is the essence of organization development.

Table 9-2 shows a broad model of some typical results arising from correct and incorrect responses to critical issues. Bear in mind that the crises mentioned above do not always occur in consecutive order, and an organization may find itself facing an old crisis all over again. For example, new competition, declining markets, or other developments may repeatedly thrust a mature organization or one of its subsystems into a survival confrontation.

Confusion and intolerance occur in an organization when the true nature of a crisis is misunderstood, and its priority is therefore depreciated. If one group at the management level is striving for organizational stability while another group believes the essential need is to build a reputation, each group may become highly critical of the way the other spends money or time. The two groups tend to become competitive rather than supportive, simply because they do not understand the basic assumptions being made by their colleagues. It is the function of leadership to clarify such differences and to direct the consolidated efforts of the organization toward the resolution of the basic issue that is paramount at the moment.

Once the organizational leadership has well established common understanding among subunit managers, it must remember that the way an organization deals with each crisis inevitably affects its capability and flexibility in dealing with succeeding or recurring issues.

Table 9–2
Results of Handling Organizational Crises[8]

Critical Issue	Result If the Issue Is Resolved: Correctly	Incorrectly
Creation	New organizational system comes into being and begins operating	Idea remains abstract. The organization is undercapitalized and cannot adequately develop and expose product or service
Survival	Organization accepts realities, learns from experience, becomes viable	Organization fails to adjust to realities of its environment and either dies or remains marginal—demanding continuing sacrifice
Stability	Organization develops efficiency and strength, but retains flexibility to change	Organization overextends itself and returns to survival stage, or establishes stabilizing patterns that block future flexibility
Pride and reputation	Organization's reputation reinforces efforts to improve quality of goods and service	Organization places more effort on image creation than on a high-quality product, or it builds an image that misrepresents its true capability
Uniqueness and adaptability	Organization changes to take fuller advantage of its unique capability and provides growth opportunities for its personnel	Organization develops too narrow a specialty to ensure secure future, fails to discover its uniqueness and spreads its efforts into inappropriate areas, or develops a paternalistic stance that inhibits growth
Contribution	Organization gains public respect and appreciation for itself as an institution contributing to society	Organization may be accused of "public be damned" and similar attitudes; or accused of using stockholder funds irresponsibly

The way risk is shared by the founders at the birth of a company will influence expectations, and therefore decisions, during the developmental stages. If one person takes too high a risk at the outset, or if the distribution of risk among several founders is very uneven, the effect may be to hasten and intensify the critical concern of survival during the birth stage, prevent adequate self-examination during the youthful stage, and eliminate any chance of progression to a more advanced stage.

Extraordinary sacrifices made by individuals during the birth stage can become a permanent and discouraging characteristic of their role in the organization, leading key managers to become fearful of further development on the grounds that such sacrifices may have to be repeated.

Efforts during the youthful stage to stabilize the organization and make it more efficient can lead to excessive restrictions and controls, and to the establishment of autonomous groups. The result may be to dampen creativity in decision making and encourage intergroup conflict.

Certain easily recognizable, nonfinancial crises occur in the life cycle of an organization. Management cannot control the emergence of these issues; it can only control *how* they are resolved. Effective resolution will involve many different areas of knowledge, skill, and attitude on the part of management as it copes with each critical need. With respect to leadership, a manager who is effective in one developmental stage may prove to be quite ineffective in another stage. The growth cycle is only one of a number of factors that influence managerial style, but it should be mentioned that leadership requirements differ at different stages of organizational maturation.

The manager who is good at setting short-range objectives and taking great risks at the birth of an organization may be much less useful in shaping long-range plans and laying the groundwork for growth when the organization is seeking stability during its youthful stage. The manager who can act directly and decisively in a crisis of survival may prove to be less than adroit in guiding the search for uniqueness within the complexities of a larger organization. The managerial capabilities required at various times in an organization's life cycle come into sharper focus when we examine specific issues together with the problems and needs for action that are precipitated.

Of course, management's behavior is only one element of the sociotechnical system. Management objectives and actions must be clear to all the members of an organization if they are to be prepared to confront and cope with situations successfully. For this, they need a common viewpoint and frame of reference. It is therefore more important than ever that managers of human systems keep asking the kinds of questions discussed earlier—in particular:

What is the critical concern we face now?
How clearly do all our key personnel recognize this concern?
How can we resolve this growth-stage confrontation in a way that creates a sound base for dealing with future crises?
What promotes organizational maturation?

By asking such questions candidly and resisting the temptation to indulge in sophistic detours in arriving at answers, managers can broaden their capacity to provide effective leadership in an organization. In the practical application of organization development processes, this will require those in leadership positions to provide opportunities for members of the organization to assess "where" they may be in the growth process and the implications of the particular stage of growth they are experiencing. Methods for implementing such a process will be illustrated below. The organization renewal process is built upon the need for managers and groups in the organization to confront such issues and initiate an appropriate response that will contribute to problem solving while strengthening the human resources, relationships, and growth of the organization.

What does all this imply for organization renewal? It implies that we must envision the renewal process within a total frame of reference: the human and nonhuman resources and the relationships between people, the situation, growth stage of the organization, and the external forces affecting the organization.

As mentioned above, *organization renewal* also involves the capabilities of the organization and its subsystems to achieve whatever may be its next stage of maturity. Some of the key decisions and actions required at various stages of maturity are indicated in Table 9-3. Development efforts should be organically related to the decisions and problems faced by the organization at the present time, and to what effect the solutions to these problems will have on the future of the organization. It becomes of prime importance, therefore, that any organization, or subunit of an organization, first diagnose its present stage before engaging in a development or renewal processes.

This concept of growth stages is not

Table 9-3
Key Management Decisions and Actions[9]

Organization Needs	Key Decisions and Problems	Actions Required
To create a new sociotechnical system	Marketability of product or service Fiscal procedures and funding Technical procedures Political or legislative needs Organizational leadership	Assess risk alternative Make firm decisions Move with speed and flexibility Employ fluid strategy and tactics, using internal and external opinions Provide for timely entrance of product or service into market
To survive	Focus of operation Accounting and recording procedures Modes of competition Recruiting and training procedures	Meet competition Hire high-quality personnel as cadre Obtain financial backing at appropriate times Introduce delegation Implement basic policies with one eye on the future
To stabilize	Long-range planning Proper responses to new competition Technological matters Internal reward systems for personnel Basic public relations policies	Take more aggressive action in market place Use systematic plans and objective setting Try to beat the competition Begin R&D as appropriate Train personnel for future needs Begin image building within and outside the organization
To earn a good reputation	Increasing the quality of goods and/or services Top-notch leadership training Escalation of public relations policies into the community service area	Meet special customer and supplier requests Update policies and philosophy Concentrate on posture and image—internal and external Assure sound financial foundation Contribute to community needs
To achieve uniqueness	Internal audit of resources and limitations Policies to develop balance in operations	Select and promote one special service or product, or range of services or products Increase delegation Provide for more effective communications, including upward flow of ideas Increase advertising and build corporate image Consider optimal size

(continued)

Table 9-3 (*Continued*)

Organization Needs	Key Decisions and Problems	Actions Required
To earn respect and appreciation	Long-range R&D Determination of self-actualization program for corporate personnel Scope of community and national service	Make heavier commitment in community (e.g., scholarships) Commit executives to national programs and assignments Utilize ideas of total work force Increase contribution to basic R&D, as appropriate Concentrate on long-range direction Flatten internal organization, allowing more freedom for individual responsibility Assess internal direction in relationship to total environment

only well supported by John Gardner's classic observation about organizational life cycles, but also by the conceptualization of Ichak Adizes, who sees an *infant organization,* a *go-go stage,* an *adolescent phase,* the *prime organization,* the *mature organization,* and finally an *autocratic position.*[10] But the idea of looking at an organization as a living system is not widely accepted as a valid way to deal with organization development processes. This may be because many cherished organization development activities are still no more than elaborated efforts directed at individual or group development. The need is for total organizational effectiveness that is capable of achieving total organizational maturity; the reality is that people do define and evaluate effectiveness in many different ways. As shown in Table 9-4, a recent study of perception of effectiveness resulted in identifying fourteen evaluative criteria.

In recent years there has been a trend toward recognition that organization development is not only a behavioral science process, but also includes management science and environmental forces that contribute to organizational effectiveness. Such an awareness recognizes that organization development efforts range across a spectrum of efforts: at one end is a "people" approach, with emphasis on human resources development, dealing primarily with individuals and groups; at the other end is a "getting the job done" approach, dealing with an orientation toward improved productivity and "bottom-line" results. In the latter category, a commercial organization comes to mind:

> Bechtel's [Bechtel Corporation, a construction company] tough-minded approach views OD not as a tool for increasing the value of human resources or for changing management style or organizational norms and values, but primarily as a tool that helps the line manager accomplish the tasks at hand and reach productivity targets.[11]

Another, the Heinz food company, has developed some specific areas as firm guidelines for developing annual organization development goals:[12]

Table 9–4
Frequency of Occurrence of Evaluation Criteria in Seventeen Models of Organizational Effectiveness[13]

Evaluation Criteria	Number of Times Mentioned (N = 17)	Percent of Total
Adaptability–flexibility	10	59
Productivity	6	35
Job satisfaction	5	29
Profitability	3	18
Acquisition of scarce and valued resources	3	18
Absence of organizational strain	2	12
Control over external environment	2	12
Employee development	2	12
Efficiency	2	12
Employee retention	2	12
Growth	2	12
Integration of individual goals with organizational goals	2	12
Open communication	2	12
Survival	2	12
All other criteria	1	6

Strategy and policy. Assure attainment of company objectives through the development and use of strategies and policies.

Accountability management. Assure that division, department, and individual position accountabilities are directed at fulfillment of company objectives, through personal goal setting.

Structure. Assure design of an organization structure that interrelates positions and departments for fulfillment of their accountabilities.

Working agreements. Promote intergroup accomplishment of results through working agreements about how groups will work together in specific situations.

Human resources planning. Assure human resources to fill structure through programs for forecasting and providing requirements.

Personnel administration. Assure that organization is staffed with people of high and improving performance through programs of selection, assessment, training and development, and compensation.

Managerial arts. Assure skills in the fundamentals of the process of management.

Norms. Enable people to fulfill own accountabilities and to help others attain theirs by encouraging favorable norms of behavior.

Operating mechanisms. Assure operating mechanisms that support accountability achievement, such as business planning, operating systems, control systems, office space planning, and employee communications.

A total systems approach looks at multiple aspects of organizational functioning and uses a multitude of organization development processes, as shown in Figure 9-1. It is interesting that in the light of the earlier association of organization development with behavioral or "soft" approaches, organizations such as Exxon and

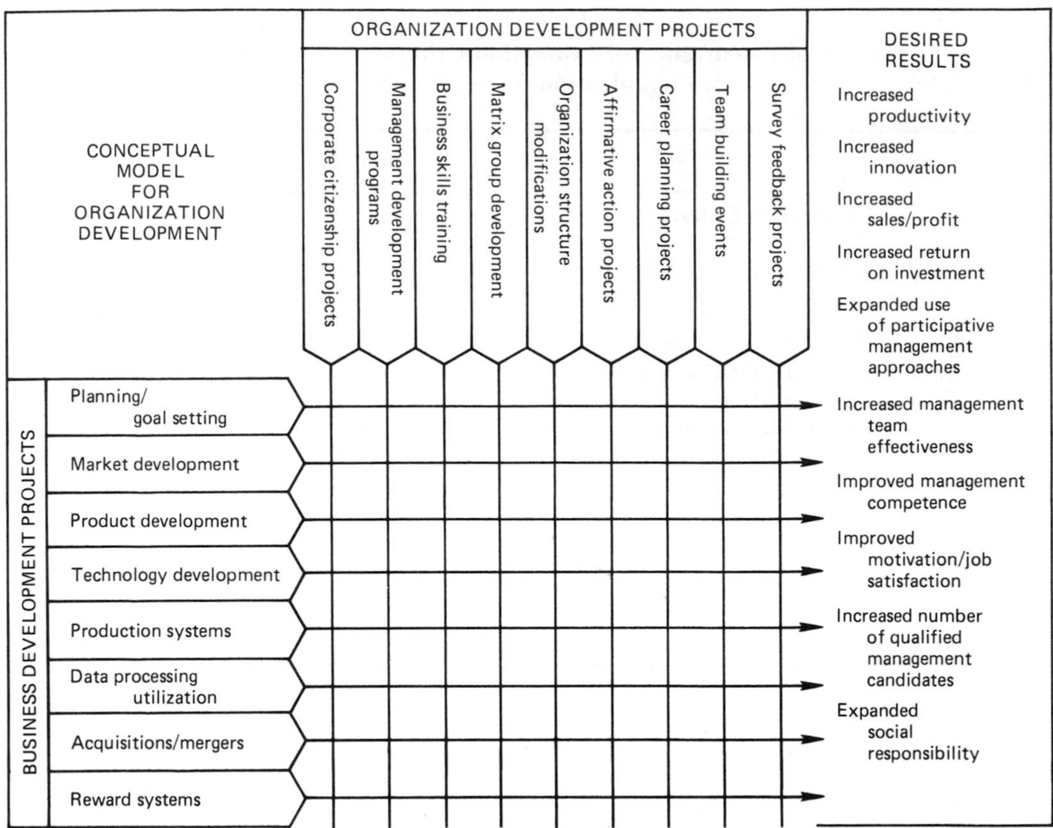

Figure 9-1 Conceptual model for organization development[14]

the U.S. Postal Service refer to their system-wide efforts as the Organizational Improvement Process (OIP), and that the U.S. Army refers to its efforts as the Organization Effectiveness Program (OEP). It seems appropriate, therefore, to define organizational effectiveness in terms of an ability to acquire and optimize available resources so as to achieve predetermined goals. This includes an organization's ability to compete and survive in a turbulent environment. Here is a frame of reference that seems to help our understanding:

> If we take a systems perspective, we can identify the four major categories of influences on effectiveness: (1) organizational characteristics, such as structure and technology; (2) environmental characteristics, such as economic and market conditions; (3) employee characteristics, such as level of job performance and job attachment; and (4) managerial policies and practices.[15]

And another:

> There is fairly general agreement on three major phases of OD: (1) same initial effort at diagnosis of the organization environment, and identification of the specific problems to which the OD effort will be addressed; (2) an intervention to ameliorate these problems, usu-

ally including the development of better communication and shared psychological investment in problem solving by the organization's various work group(s); and (3) a follow-up or maintenance stage to learn how the intervention is faring and to make continued consultation available, if desired, to help nurture whatever positive changes in the organization may have occurred. OD, then, is aimed at enhancing organizational effectiveness and job satisfaction.[16]

Sixteen organization development processes are discussed below under four categories or approaches. Table 9-5 provides a relationship to the overall systems renewal model:

Organization characteristics approaches
- Matrix structure
- Democratic principles
  - Scanlon Plan
  - Codetermination
- Reorganization
- Diversification
- Centralization and decentralization

Environmental approaches
- Existential crisis
- Internal pressures
- External pressures
- Federal legislation and regulations

Quality of work life and climate approaches
- Individual
- Nature of work
- Work output

Managerial policies and practices approaches
- Long-range planning
- Operations research
- Financial systems and budgeting
- Human resources accounting
- Flexitime
- Union negotiations and contracts

This list does not necessarily comprise a complete overview of organization development processes, but it does suggest the multiplicity of ways in which total systems can be changed.

ORGANIZATIONAL CHARACTERISTICS APPROACHES TO ORGANIZATION DEVELOPMENT

In any system-wide approach to increased effectiveness through organization development, it is essential to examine the role played by the existing structure or the probable effect of restructuring. There are in this regard at least five processes that are used to improve total organizational functioning.

Table 9-5
Portion of Systems Renewal Model

Organization Development Processes	
Matrix structure	Federal legislation
Democratic Principles	Quality of work life
Reorganization	Long range planning
Diversification	Operations research
Centralization and decentralization	Financial systems
Existential crises	Human resource accounting
Internal pressures	Flexitime
External pressures	Union relations

Matrix Structure

We are all familiar with the basic hierarchical structure found around the world. An organization of this kind is usually developed into *functional* elements such as manufacturing, finance, engineering, research, accounting, sales, and administration. The value here lies in making the most of specialization and in centralizing similar resources. The *product-oriented* organization, on the other hand, is built around activities according to the goals or services provided. The advantages of each of these types of matrix structure have been much debated. Numerous contemporary authors suggest that organizations, and the types of problems faced by organizations, are changing; they are becoming more complex. For example, for the increasing numbers of professionals and their adaptive requirements, the traditional bureaucratic structure may be ill-suited for many uses in today's organizations. Bureaucratic form does not meet (1) rapid and unexpected change, (2) problems of growth in size, (3) increasing diversity, and (4) changes in managerial behavior.[17]

Stafford Beer condemns the bureaucratic structure as being outmoded, stressing its inappropriate use in managing complexity.[18] Paralleling these concepts, others have stressed the need for renewal of organizations and the adaptation of temporary systems. Short-lived subsystems are created to fill the void between present organization ability and the necessary, almost vital, organization need to cope with change. Beer emphasizes that handling complexity is a major problem cutting across many current crises areas, and that some of our most powerful tools for meeting this challenge come from cybernetic science—the science of communication and control.

One central thesis of cybernetics is that there are natural laws governing the behavior of large, complex, probabilistic, interactive systems. Important examples are self-regulation and self-organization. System behavior is governed primarily by its own dynamic structure. Here the word "dynamic" refers to the speeds at which communication is effected within a system. "Structure" means the way in which the parts of a whole are interrelated and includes both the feedback loops by which systems regulate themselves and the conditional probability mechanisms by which systems learn and organize themselves.[19] Beer concludes that our increasingly complex society has outgrown the dynamic and organizing capacity of its current structure.

In filtering and refining the massive information overload—by means of data acquisition, storage, retrieval, and selection based on identification of system wants and recognition of system needs—we see the real utility of cybernetics. Cybernetics can help provide both the systems framework that will make information relevant and the systems methodology that will make information manageable.

From another viewpoint, Beer stresses that the "esoteric box" or "black box" (perhaps a firm, a profession, a social service, or a government agency) is the entity that will in practice develop these cybernetic information, knowledge systems. Right now the internal systems of the esoteric boxes are not responding adequately. Improved management of knowledge within the box is viewed as the rapid matching of sets of possible courses of action to sets of actual conditions and the rapid correction of mismatches by feedback processes. Improved management of information between boxes includes a metasystemic framework, an integral information network, a mutual trade-off of knowledge, and adequate temporary systems. In some cases, a project organization will be a permanent structure but utilizing resources from throughout the parent organization.

This concept of matrix organization is depicted as evolving relationships so aligned as to be responsive to problems of varying complexity and novelty, its chief characteristic being the extension toward "extraorganization."[20] Most of the personnel assigned to a project or task group would be drawn, as might be least disrupting to all concerned, from their regular positions within the structure of the parent organization (e.g., a federal government or department thereof, a corporation or a division thereof); it is reasonable to assume that upon self-destruction the members of the group return to their former positions to reflect upon the significance of their decisions and, more important, to have those decisions reflect upon them, for good or bad.

The matrix organization is a total system response by the organization as it endeavors to cope with its environment. Its relationship to other techniques of organization development is that that exists between tactics and strategy. The organization development practitioner must make a careful analysis of the situation to determine whether a matrix structure is applicable, and what supporting efforts may also be needed; in any event, thorough diagnosis of management goals and practices is necessary.

The Democratic Principle

Organization development processes that postulate the democratic principle within an organization for *all* employees are rare in the literature, and among those mentioned there are differences regarding both the mechanism of implementing the principle and the structural alternatives to the conventional form of managing.[21] In approaching the democratic principle it is helpful to give a frame of reference for the overall methods and purposes of organization development; this is a focus on the differences in perception of the democratic principle and the ways it gets concretized structurally. An attempt to put these differences in perspective will serve a dual purpose. First, it will help to conceptualize the elements of participation and democratization (implementation of democratic principle). Second, it will help focus the discussion on the political dimension and make it possible to evaluate the relationship between democratic interventions and organization development.

Paul Bernstein has developed a keen analysis of the maintenance of democratization:[22]

Participation in decision making, whether direct or by elected representation (some forms of profit sharing include no forms of participation at the decision-making level)
Frequent feedback of economic results to all employees (in the form of money, not just information)
Full sharing with employees of management-level information and, to an increased extent, management-level expertise
Guaranteed individual rights (corresponding to basic political liberties)
An independent board of appeal in case of disputes (composed of peers as far as practicable)
A particular set of attitudes and values (a participatory/democratic consciousness)

Although most of these elements are quite self-evident, the relevance of participation and democratic consciousness deserves explanation. Bernstein maintains there are these dimensions of participation:

The *degree* of control employees enjoy over any single decision
The *issues* over which that control is exercised
The organizational *level* at which it is exercised

Optimal participation includes a high degree of influence over a wide range of issues at many levels of the firm. This is not to say that every decision need be made by every worker at every level of the organization. Such a system would clearly lead to reduction of productivity, if not paralysis. Nevertheless, in an ideally democratized organization, provision is made for a workable mix of democratic control and managerial authority so that the enterprise may prosper. Whatever form this mix takes, power equalization is the outcome. In practice, there are two forms of democratic and participatory mechanism: one originated in the United States and is called the *Scanlon Plan;* the other originated in West Germany and is called *codetermination.*

The Scanlon Plan. The Scanlon Plan is an organization-wide incentive system developed by Joseph Scanlon in the 1930s. Scanlon had been working in Pittsburgh as an open-hearth production worker in a steel company that was close to bankruptcy. Costs were high and equipment was obsolete. Union demands for higher wages and improved working conditions compounded the problems for management; it seemed that if the demands were granted, the company would go broke.

Scanlon had taken a leading role in the organizing drive of the local union; in 1936 he was elected president. Recognizing the severity of the problems the union was facing, he convinced the president of the company to join a committee of union employees at the office of the International Union—to seek advice and help.

Under Scanlon's leadership, and with management's full cooperation, the company set out to implement, in a thorough and systematic manner, the suggestion to reduce costs and improve efficiency. Requests for higher wages were temporarily shelved. Before long, costs were substantially reduced, and the quality of the products improved. The company survived and was able to grant the wage increases while still making use of the obsolete equipment.

Both the management and the employees were proud of the role they played in keeping the company above ground while attaining wage levels comparable to those of their more prosperous competitors. This was the practical result of teamwork in a sustained cooperative effort involving workers and their superiors. What happened in this instance laid the foundation for what has since come to be known as the Scanlon Plan.

Other companies and other unions heard about the success of the steel mill and sought Scanlon's help. As a result, it was finally decided to establish the Production Engineering department of the United Steelworkers of America, with Scanlon as director.* In his position as director, Scanlon strove to find ways to improve operations and reduce costs, so as to provide more take-home pay for employees. The idea was for individuals in the company to have a voice in how they did their job. This was accomplished by workers being represented at meetings with company management; thus, worker representatives and company officials cooperated to improve productivity and to share the benefits.

One of the first major instances in which the Scanlon Plan gained national attention involved the LaPointe Machine Tool Company, which manufactured machine-cutting tools. Several articles concerning LaPointe appeared in national magazines. At LaPointe, during the first two years, 513 suggestions were received, of which 45% were put into effect; bonuses averaged 18% of base wages; and profits increased. In addition, delivery times shortened, grievance rates declined, and quality improved. It should be remembered, though, that something like the Scanlon Plan requires both new organization structure and new organization philosophy before its adoption is feasible.

There are three interdependent ingre-

*Later, Scanlon joined the staff of the Industrial Relations Section at the Massachusetts Institute of Technology, where he became active in both lecturing and field work.

dients of the Scanlon Plan: a theory regarding people, a system of participation, and a system of equity. Thus, the plan is a philosophy of organization. This philosophy recognizes that the workers like to fully express themselves in their workplace and given this opportunity, under the right circumstances, the philosophy holds that workers can and do make meaningful contributions to the ultimate goal of organizational efficiency. Given that employees have constructive ideas with respect to improving organizational effectiveness, they must be given the opportunity to express themselves:

> Scanlon deeply believed the typical company organization did not elicit the full potential from employees, either as individuals or as groups. He did not feel the commonly-held concept that "the boss is the boss and the worker works" was a proper basis for stimulating the interest of employees in company problems. Rather, he felt that such a concept reinforced employees' belief that there was an "enemy" somewhere above them in the hierarchy and that a cautious suspicion should be maintained at all times. He felt that employee interest and contributions best could be stimulated by providing the employee with a maximum amount of information and data concerning company problems and successes, and by soliciting his contribution as to how he felt the problems might best be solved and the job best done.[23]

Under the Scanlon Plan such participation is facilitated by a committee structure. A production committee is usually made up of a department supervisor and one or more elected employees of that department. This committee meets at least once a month to determine ways of reducing waste and improving organizational efficiency. Employee suggestions are considered and may be put into effect, provided that the suggestions do not affect other departments and are not too costly. Often, employees who have made suggestions are invited to speak before the production committee to discuss and clarify their concepts. A screening committee is made up of an equal number of representatives from the production committee and from top management. This committee screens and discusses all suggestions referred to it by the production committees. Reaction to suggestions are often discussed among representatives of the various departments to determine their overall feasibility. The final determination of whether to accept or reject a suggestion rests with management. One of the primary responsibilities of the screening committee is to discuss and analyze the amount and distribution of bonuses. Results of such discussions are then communicated to the rest of the organization, usually by written memorandum.

The third interdependent ingredient of the Scanlon Plan is equity. Given that employees are allowed to contribute to the effectiveness of the company, it follows that they should be equitably rewarded for their contribution. Typically, this is done through a bonus distribution.

During the time since the plan was implemented at LaPointe, the Scanlon Plan has been applied successfully in many companies. In 1977, more than 120 firms in the United States were actively operating under the plan. However, it has never really gained widespread acceptance or application. Nevertheless, it is still very much in existence today, with the same basic mechanisms developed by Scanlon years ago. As interest in quality of work life grows, and the need for organization development in union plants increases, the Scanlon Plan is receiving more attention from management:

> The Scanlon Plan has come a long way since the days of its reputation for limited applicability to small, family-

owned manufacturing plants. In fact, as recently as 1977, Edward Lawler felt the plan would most likely succeed only in small plants (fewer than 500 employees), where it was possible to produce a simple, stable measurement of performance. One year later that notion was discounted at the 1978 Scanlon Plan Conference, where diverse firms were represented—several successful plants of more than 1,500 employees, a number of companies with sales of more than $1 billion, others that had successfully developed complicated measures of performance to cope with changing product lines and the 1974-1975 inflation, and at least one installation in a service technology, namely, a distribution center.[24]

German Codetermination. The history and development of codetermination are strikingly different from the Scanlon Plan, although they share some elements in common. Basically, codetermination is a unique system of labor-management relations legislated in 1947 for use exclusively in the coal and steel industries of West Germany. Later, the principles were applied to other German industries, but to a lesser extent; and most of the research on codetermination has been on the coal and steel industries as the most fully developed form. Although similar arrangements are extant throughout Western and Eastern Europe (especially in Sweden, Great Britain, and Yugoslavia), codetermination is uniquely West German.

For over a hundred years, German labor sought the principle of "parity" in decision making in all spheres and at all levels of economic activity. The idea of parity is embodied in the concept of industrial democracy, which maintains that the liberal revolutions of the eighteenth and nineteenth centuries—which brought democracy to the political sphere through constitutional governments—must be extended to the economic sphere as well. Thus, the legislation of codetermination was an economic and political victory for German labor. The primary reason for its enactment after World War II was to limit the power of the German coal and steel industries.

To understand how codetermination actually works, some understanding of the distinctive features of German industry and labor is necessary. In Germany over 40% of the entire work force belong to trade unions; in the United States the percentage is only around 27%. German labor also represents both blue- and white-collar workers, so that the range of the national population represented by labor unions is much wider there than in the United States. Also, the structure of organized labor is different from that in the United States, and has three basic units. The first is the National Confederation of Unions. The second is the national trade unions, which have regional offices in towns or districts but are not "locals" as in the United States. The third, at the plant level, is the "works council—which has no affiliation with the unions and acts independently, although most of its members belong to various unions. Collective bargaining, as practiced in the United States, is not found in Germany.

The organization of West German industry is also unique. The first of these is the Board of Supervision, the highest authority. It is usually composed of eleven members and makes decisions about large expenditures and the hiring of key personnel (i.e., the members of the Board of Management). This management group usually is composed of three members and is the ultimate decision-making body. Members of this board are the actual directors and are responsible for all operational decisions. No one can serve simultaneously on both boards.

Under codetermination in the coal and steel industries labor is represented in both boards. Five of the eleven members of the Board of Supervisors are chosen by the owners, five are chosen by labor, and the last person is elected by the other ten members. Of the five labor representatives, one must be a wage earner, one must be salaried, two are selected by the national labor union, and one must be an "outsider" to the particular industry.

The Board of Management is composed of a Commercial Director, a Technical Director, and a Labor Director. The Labor Director is nominated by the workers through the works council to serve as a full-fledged member of management. This nomination is approved by the Board of Supervision, which also appoints the other two members.

It was assumed that there would be great divergence on matters between owners and labor, and that there would be many split votes. Labor agreed that in the case of a five-to-five deadlock on the Board of Supervision, they would acquiesce in management's choice. But the fear that there would be many such deadlocks has not been borne out in the experience of the steel industry. Because of several factors, unanimity rather than division has been the rule.

An important factor involved in the decision-making process in German codetermination is the use of certain techniques of accommodation and compromise. These have arisen out of a desire to reduce incidents of disagreement. The first technique is *tabling* or postponing issues on which there is no immediate agreement. This is also the reason decision making does take much longer under codetermination—but this is true as well under a consensus or a win–win decision-making process. The second technique is the use of *trade-offs,* or making concessions on issues of primary interest to one faction, with the tacit agreement that this attitude will be reciprocated where the interests of the other faction is at issue. Thus, in effect, labor has added influence in personnel and labor matters in return for giving ownership more freedom of action over other traditionally management-decided matters. This is, in fact, a practical *alteration* of the theoretical basis of codetermination which gives labor *equal* voice in all matters.

The third technique of accommodation is the use of a *special committee* within the Board of Supervision to decide on controversial issues—with the prior agreement that its decision will be binding. This is used where a formal vote might be embarrassing to members who are dependent on support from outside groups, such as the unions. In this case they are not required to make a formal commitment, but merely agree to go along with the smaller committee decision. There are three types of situations involving conflict of interest:

1. Where labor representatives vote contrary to the immediate objectives of the works council, their sponsoring organization
2. Where conflicts occur between local union and national union representatives
3. Where a vote involves a difference of loyalty between plant management and the trade union

A Labor Director is appointed by the Board of Supervisors after nomination by *ownership, works councils,* and the *unions.* There is considerable behind-the-scenes consultation and negotiation needed in this selection process. He or she is given primary control over wages and working conditions in return for a free hand in other matters. The composition of the work team is the primary factor in determining the influence the Labor Director has on nonlabor matters. In some cases, the Labor Directors have been so effective that they dominated the Board of Management, and have had influence in all matters; but they usually become isolated in the personnel function. The degree of involvement as members of the Board of Management has depended on their qualifications and the ability of all three to work together. At best, however, the Labor Director retains a limited veto power in issues outside his or her field.

The chairmanship of the Board of Management is usually rotated weekly, and the principle of equality is carefully observed. Some boards work together quite informally, generally depending on the degree of acceptance the Labor Director is able to garner.

Similar to the experience of the supervisors, there have not been many cases of unresolvable conflicts among the three managers. Issues with differences of opinion most often occur around labor matters involving the rank and file, wage decisions, labor policy, and financial policies where these affect the availability of funds for worker benefits.

Both the Scanlon Plan and codetermination can be considered processes of organization development. Certainly, the Scanlon Plan is a planned and systematic process in which the goal of organizational improvement is sought through hard work and the reduction of labor costs, with the participation and suggestions of the workers. The fact that the Scanlon Plan has a basic philosophy that values "the individual's head as well as his hands" is some indication that behavioral science knowledge is applied, and it should be mentioned that the Scanlon Plan is a philosophy of organization and not an intervention per se. Codetermination is more difficult to relate to organization development. Industrial democracy is not considered in the literature to be an intervention for organization development. In the usual organization development concept, the parameters of technical/professional approaches to change do not include such a political assessment. Second, some authors feel that organization development must apply behavioral solutions to labor-management conflicts, without any judgment regarding power equalization.[25] This posture limits an open-minded understanding of the many ways in which organizational efficiency is achieved.

Codetermination is an attempt through legislation to resolve the struggle for authority between labor and management. The behavioral solutions to organizational problems assume a free choice by all parties. This is not the case in codetermination; management leaders of the German coal and steel industry did not and would not have chosen such an arrangement. The solution, therefore, was political, although it had ramifications on the behavioral level.

Industrial democracy is not, in itself, an intervention for organization development; *but it can be.* This raises, however, a crucial issue for the field of organization development and takes us back to the discussion about the elements of democracy in an organization.

The professional/technical frame of reference for organization development, out of which most consultants operate, assumes political neutrality. The special focus on the interpersonal and behavioral dimensions of organizations—often to the neglect of structural considerations—reinforces the apolitical framework of organization development as generally practiced.

Empowerment is not incompatible; it is a part of organization development. But the question of *who is to be empowered* should be answered. Recognition of that reality not only reduces the ambiguity about democratic values, but also makes conscious the political choices that are always present in organization change.

Thus, both codetermination and the Scanlon Plan raise the issue of political choices and democratic values within the field of organization development. The application of human system interventions could be very productive in the codetermination context. The application of more creative methods of decision making would serve the interests of all involved. Yet the opposing interests represented by the owners and the different groups within labor would require an organization development facilitator to exercise skills both in dealing with conflict and in clarifying the political dimensions of power distribution. The Scanlon Plan would also require a choice regarding the issue of democracy and control. Such a choice might be incompatible with the professional/technical, behavioral science conception of organization development, but it would not be incompatible with a concept that recognizes the necessity of operating out of a set of values that include the political dimension.

Reorganization

A favorite form of structured intervention is the process of reorganization, an activity that is supposed to lead to reform and improved effectiveness.[26] Because of this belief, reorganization seems to be continuous in almost all bureaucracies. It may be defined as any change in the distribution of responsibilities, or decision-making power, or the relationship between functions. A reorganization usually entails organizational changes on a macro scale, and the problem associated with such changes are magnified by the scope of the functions, relationships, structures, and people affected. In effect, reorganization cannot be considered a single, identifiable technology of organization development, but rather it is simply an activity that disturbs the status quo of a system. There are many reasons to initiate reorganization; among them, frequently, are growth, declining economic performance, changes in managerial personnel, altered managerial trends, and the effects of external events.

Growth may take many forms, such as expansion of output or market, diversification of product line, merger, new technologies, or vertical integration. Certainly a major reason for reorganization is declining economic performance. This produces a powerful urge to reorganize, and often encourages top management to want to centralize its control and authority. This desire could well have been the very thing that contributed to the conditions that produced the poor economic conditions in the first place. But reorganization often generates a general cost-reduction program that makes the reduced administrative costs and immediate economies of centralization seem attractive.

A change in management personnel, especially a different president or chief executive officer, usually produces changes in the organization. Often the changes are merely superficial and reflect the fact that there is a "new broom" in charge. The personality of the individual is generally evident in such changes. There are also instances in which new management personnel are brought in for the express purpose of facilitating or implementing organizational revision. In this age of enlightened management, popular trends have been known to serve as the impetus for reorganization, merely because it is the "in" thing to be doing.

Many kinds of external events can initiate reorganization. Among these are advances in technology, governmental regulations, the actions of competitors, the expansion or contraction of markets, national and world economic conditions, social responsibilities, and in the case of public agencies, the effects of budget or manpower reductions.

The goals or objectives of reorganization are also multiple and varied. They may be explicit or implied, clear or unclear. There may be a single purpose for the effort, or the objectives may be several, complementary, or contradictory. Some of the common goals of reorganization are to reduce administrative expenses, to decentralize, to enhance coordination, to strengthen authority, to increase promotional possibilities, and to promote innovation and creativity. For each of these goals, the exact opposite also is valid as a goal; centralization, for example, is altogether as valid as decentralization.

Any reorganization will have some goal or objective that lends a greater or lesser measure of legitimacy to a person or group at the management level. The technology that will be brought to bear depends heavily upon the intentions of those initiating the reorganization. As one author put it:

> There may, however, be other more sinister reasons. Reorganizations frequently occur when new people take over. They may, as some feel, want to show their power and choose this way to do it. Or it may be a smoke screen to hide some other action they expect to take. In the confusion which surrounds reorganization, people who have held positions of influence suddenly find themselves out in the cold with little or no possibility of recovery.[27]

There may be a number of organization development technologies that are applicable to the process of reorganization; those that are suitable will be determined by the state of the organization in question, the objectives of the change, the perception of the problems, the commitment of the participants, and many other variables.

Perhaps the most useful and logical view in conducting a reorganization is seeing an organization as consisting of a number of significant interacting variables that cut across or are common to each part. These variables concern goals, tasks, technology, structure, the human-social subsystem, and the external interfaces that affect the organization. As is true of any effort to change a total system, acceptance of reorganization depends upon the way it is done. Some authorities on administrative practice find reorganization to be overrated in value as a management tool:

> That reorganizing means reform is, of course, a myth and a most dangerous one at that. It is a myth also that it will result in either changed behavior or improved results. Sometimes it is useful and there are times when it may even be necessary. But it is only one among many approaches open to the executive to what is usually a complex and often a chronic problem and in no way the cure-all that so many take it to be.[28]

There are, in fact, serious disadvantages to reorganization:[29]

- Disruption of ongoing operations
- Lower morale
- Loss of confidence in organizational leadership
- Possibility of internal power struggles
- Departure of key personnel
- Increased union activity
- Involvement in the organization of people from the outside
- Further reorganization
- A general reduction in both efficiency and effectiveness

Suffice it to say that reorganization, as a method of achieving system-wide change, has had very little evaluation. In terms of effectiveness and benefit, the millions of dollars expended through management man-hours, employee disruption, and organization disequilibrium might well be wasted. It is necessary here again to emphasize that any process used in organizaton development must be carefully considered before making the assumption that it is the way to improved performance.

Diversification

An organization that undertakes to diversify its service or product line is making a strategic decision—one that may change its basic nature and involve both reallocation of resources and redirection of talent. There is no generally accepted definition or measure of diversification. (Does a firm producing bicycles diversify when it begins to turn out tricycles, or when it acquires a corporation manufacturing motorcycles, or when it begins a new venture, say travel vacations via bike or motorcycle?) Variously used by researchers have been (1) a simple count of the number of products, (2) methods of growth—internal or external, and recently (3) statistical measurements of specialization, product or service relationship, and vertical integration. Nevertheless, diversification has been one of the most important changes in the conduct of business of the postindustrial era.

In terms of economic performance, product type of diversification has a potentiality for higher performance, and the key is the way a firm relates its new businesses to its old. In other words, building upon or extending a set of common skills, resources, markets, or purposes (not necessarily vertically integration) has been the most successful approach to successful organization development:

> The critical resource of the modern, diversified, divisionalized firm is general management skill, and the change from the old to the new industrial structure has multiplied several-fold the number of general management positions to be filled in industry. The training and effective employment of generalists must become the prime concern of any firm that has goals that include growth by diversification or participation in the new technologies that quickly produce a proliferation of new products.[30]

Thus, diversification, properly viewed in a systems context, leads to the requirement for organizations to adapt structure and talent for viability and strength. The process by which an organization diagnoses, plans, implements, and evaluates a diversification of its services or products can, in at least one way, serve as a valid and significant organization development intervention—because it does require a thorough reexamination of the goals of the organization.

Centralization and Decentralization

The issue of centralization versus decentralization is one of the major sources of difference of opinion within the management of many organizations. This is a false issue—because every organization must do some of *both*. The challenge is not to decide which to do, but rather to analyze the situation to determine which functions may need centralizing (i.e., a management information system, or purchasing) and which functions may need decentralizing (i.e., governance, or local office personnel practices). Such a determination can be helpful to the organization's philosophy, values, and practices.

As organizations have become more diversified, larger, and geographically spread out, the need to decentralize appears to be evident, but such action should be based on certain underlying principles:[31]

Decentralization should place authority to make decisions as close as possible to where the action takes place.

Decentralization is likely to get best overall results by getting the greatest and most directly applicable knowledge and most timely understanding into play on the greatest number of decisions.

Decentralization will work if real authority is delegated; and it will not work if details then have to be reported or, worse yet, if they have to be "checked" first.

Decentralization requires confidence that associates in decentralized positions will have the capacity to make sound decisions in the majority of cases; and such confidence starts at the executive level. Unless the chief executive officer and all the other officers of the organization have deep personal conviction and an active desire to decentralize full decision-making responsibility and authority, actual decentralization will never really take place.

Decentralization requires understanding that the main role of staff or services is the rendering of assistance and advice to line operators through a relatively few experienced people, so that those making decisions can themselves make them correctly.

Decentralization requires realization that the natural aggregate of many individually sound decisions will be better for the business and for the public than will centrally planned and controlled decisions.

Decentralization rests on having general objectives, organization structure, relationships, policies, and measurements known, understood, and followed; but also in realizing that definition of policies does not necessarily mean uniformity in methods of execution in decentralized operations.

Decentralization can be achieved only when higher executives realize that authority genuinely delegated to lower echelons cannot, in fact, also be retained by them.

Successful decentralization of management depends upon development of a system of controls that permits extension of the widest practicable grant of authority to local units in the system. Even so, in the process of decentralization, those in charge can review the characteristics of the organization, develop guiding principles, and institute a system of controls; but in the end, the act requires primarily a conscious change in attitude. Given this change in appropriate degree, some of the frequently articulated advantages of decentralization are:[32]

Decentralization distributes the management load. As an enterprise increases in size and complexity, it becomes more difficult, and finally impossible, to effectively handle it from some remote location. It becomes increasingly necessary to develop management initiative, responsibility, and authority at logical centers, closer to the scene of action, throughout the company.

Decentralization multiplies management effectiveness. Instead of a single center of management, decentralization stimulates and multiplies management initiative, resourcefulness, and the sense of profit-making responsibility throughout the organization.

Decentralization capitalizes on the natural decision-making advantages possessed by management on the spot.

Decentralization strengthens, simplifies, and speeds the management process. It minimizes the amount of detail that must be referred to headquarters; it eliminates unnecessary red tape, multiple handling, and overloading of central offices and staff costs.

Decentralization develops strong, self-reliant managers. It multiplies the opportunity for development of well-founded executives. It tends to produce leaders rather than leaners.

Finally, decentralization gives added challenge, stimulus, zest, importance, and value to "management-on-the-firing-line." There is nothing more challenging and interesting than being on your own, with full responsibility and accountability for results. Because of the heavier responsibilities entailed, decentralization substantially enhances the importance of management positions.

Neither management executives nor organization development facilitators will discover certainty in a finalized decision to centralize—or to decentralize; but the process of making the decision is so much an exploration of the total system that it can, and often does materially contribute to organization development.

ENVIRONMENTAL CHARACTERISTICS

Organizational effectiveness is affected by the environment in which the total system exists. It certainly is not feasible to attempt here to name all the environmental forces that influence both small and large organizations, but we can list a suggestive few: such things as inflation, high interest rates, war and the threat of war, pollution and the efforts made to correct it, drought, and depletion of sources of energy have their impact on all systems.

Much is to be said regarding the role of the organization in its environment and the manner and trend in which accelerated change affects the total organization. Evolutionary processes occur in the environment of organizations as well as in the organizations themselves. Ideal types of environmental conditions, spawning mere transactional interdependencies, are those in which (as in classical organization theory) the firm is able to maintain a relatively safe degree of self-control, isolating itself at will from its environment, if not choosing with accuracy and success what areas of the surroundings with which to become associated (i.e., only those areas that promise to be of most benefit to the organization).[33]

Adaptability in the face of change, although necessary, becomes increasingly difficult as each environmental stimulus becomes more reactive, more violent, and often more incongruous with the needs of the organization. This turbulence is becoming an increasingly complex field of forces and events; in terms of casual interconnections in the environment, it has itself reached crisis proportions.

As organizations have become interdependent with many external systems, the extent to which a system can change and react successfully to such induced changes in its adaptability is measured by its viability—and the viability of an organization is its insurance of survival. Thus, organizational adaptability, in gross terms, is a function of an ability to learn and perform according to changing environmental contingencies—an action fundamental to organization development.

A climate of constant and necessary reevaluation of goals, tools, and systems of operational and social design can be healthful for a system, especially when the time for reevaluation conveniently can be chosen by management and the organization development facilitator.

For the purpose of explaining the impact of environmental factors on organization development, five examples of the things with which management can expect to cope can be cited.

Existential Crisis[34]

An organizational system may be described as in a state of crisis when its methods of dealing with problems become ineffectual. Most crises are marked by a specific event that poses a threat to the continuance of organizational objectives.

Central in every organization is a strong need for survival, a force that provides an impetus to slake the covert symptoms of crisis, and the forces that maintain organizational homeostasis are equally strong. These forces tend to blanket each other unless homeostasis or growth are unbalanced. Crisis, therefore, does not well lend itself to organization development. Nevertheless, if management is so optimistic as to capitalize on crisis, there is advantage in the objective certainty that action must be taken. Crisis management creates a necessity for serious and questioning reevaluation of existing organizational structures soon after the shock phase has set in. Unfortunately, reluctance to change and the need for homeostasis occasionally can manufacture a crisis out of a routine organization development process. In any case, crises are never planned, and reorganization is doomed to be ineffectual if the situation acts to destroy the organization. Crisis, as an organization development method, is used only when an actual crisis has produced a stimulating shock—and at this point, by the nature of the situation, an organization is already faced with high risk and a dramatic fountainhead for reevaluation.

In its relationship to other methods of organization development, the crisis situation is closely allied in causes and effects to the intrusion of a change facilitator. A crisis situation puts an organization in a confrontation predicament, in which it is free to operate, to deal with, and to work around its severe problem. Frequently, however, there is an inability accurately to perceive the environmental factors that allowed the crisis to develop (e.g., strike, walkout, building damage, recession). Such factors are existential facts, forces to be dealt with by strong reaction, threats to survival of the system. Here lies an immediacy that can exist in no ordinary methodology of organization development, and existential crisis is marked by these characteristics:[35]

Demand for a sink-or-swim solution (i.e., liquidation or profit) for the firm.

Decisive action will be required (there exists no option to "do nothing," as in most other situational decisions).

The crisis itself is unexpected.

No problem exists with respect to resistance by management or staff. The change, or need of it, is imposed, either from the outside (e.g., market shift) or from a force on the outside emerging on the inside (e.g., strike).

The goals of the organization are challenged.

Compelled reaction is substituted for voluntary action.

Adhering to the concept of environmental relationships, the reactions of an organization in crisis are best understood as a scramble toward equilibrium.[36] With or without a change facilitator, management attempts to establish unification, to redefine its objectives, to restructure or rebuild as appears necessary. This affords a change facilitator, internal or external, an opportunity to effect elements of organization development that would not otherwise be as readily accepted:

Targets for change can be identified quickly—What can the organization do to eliminate its immediately pressing problem?

Normative goals can be established or reestablished.

Realistically clear social structures and administrative hierarchies, with congruent formal and informal groups and procedures, can be set up.

New systems can be created that promote interdepartmental, interpersonal, and extraorganizational dynamics.

Relationships with the environment can be redefined in terms of expected postcrisis behavior.

The functions of management can be strengthened and improved—in terms of providing subsystems for resolving conflicts; eliminating threatening, backbiting situations; clarifying incongruities between goals and activities; and directing the organization toward being a process-oriented, goal-seeking entity.

The organization can be stimulated to use the instruments, techniques, and programs of organization development in communicating, assimilating data, and developing and implementing priority actions.

Internal Pressure From Employee Groups

Most organizations have developed ways to keep in touch with the feelings, concerns, and gripes of employees—including such communication processes as an employee-edited newsletter, suggestion systems, and climate surveys; and involvement processes such as employee councils, recreation programs, and training supervisors with good listening capabilities. Organizational change, however, takes place more often these days as a result of a group of employees making known their desire for an alteration in the system through initiating pressures and even class-action law suits. Such actions have been taken by minority groups, women, office employees, and disgruntled field representatives. If handled effectively, strong, overt expression and movement by employees can contribute to organization development, as demonstrated by the following real-life example.

A group of low-paid employees at a prominent research hospital unit exerted internal pressure on the director to implement change in the management of their work environment, the hospital laundry. They were concerned with a change in the behavior of their immediate supervisors, as well as more management intervention in the structure of their work tasks. Once organized, the employees decided that the most effective means of presenting their grievances to management was through a recognized activist group at the hospital which had a reputation for seeking equal employment opportunities for all employees, especially minorities.

This activitst group, Action for Concerned Employees (ACE), decided first to determine the validity of the grievances. Second, they met with the laundry employees—whom they felt would neither be threatened nor intimidated when asked to speak out about the management of the laundry. Accomplishing these objectives, ACE forwarded a memorandum to the director of the hospital, requesting that fourteen changes be implemented at the facility, and that a task force be appointed to immediately investigate the reasonableness of the requested changes. The director ordered the personnel manager of the hospital to work with ACE in resolving the complaints. Representatives of the AFL-CIO, of Equal Employment Opportunity Advisors, of the personnel manager, and of the concerned employees thus became the agents for change.

There followed a number of positive, management-initiated approaches to problem solving, indicating that organized pressure groups can indeed demand and secure recognition from management. This also indicates that organization development was accomplished through the use of internal expertise. A memorandum, from the executive officer of the hospital to all laundry employees, responded to each of the 14 grievances.

The change that has occurred at the laundry is a direct result of the pressure exerted by an internal unit of employees. Management, recognizing that this dissonance was impeding its overall mission, responded immediately in seeking a solution. It was an organizational development effort that affected each employee in the laundry; it was effectively administered from top-level management, and it increased the organizational effectiveness of the laundry—resulting in increased job performance.

Many similar attempts to effect change through internal pressure have not gone as well as this particular example; in such instances, however, the basic principles and methods of organization development remained relevant.

External Pressure Groups

During and since the Vietnam conflict, we have seen an increase in the use of external pressure groups on government agencies, power companies, automobile producers, the Congress, and almost every type of human system—and they have a powerful impact on the entire organization.[37] Such influence can be handled legally, defensively, or with an organization development approach of confrontation, search, and coping in a problem-solving mode.

An external pressure group may be defined as a partisan, extraorganizational association of individuals who seek positive or negative legislation, special service, change of policy or practice, redress, or administrative aid in attempting to achieve certain interests and objectives. The propriety of special-interest groups was recognized in our constitutional system from the beginning. Pressure groups have become a vital part of our country's mechanism—pointing out problems and determining the direction of change. Although it is difficult to categorize pressure groups as they exist today, some general groupings can be drawn.

Of prime influence in our governmental structure are *political* pressure groups, whose prime purpose is securing legislation favorable to their particular interest. Most represent specific organizations, and the activities of most come under the classification of lobbying. A list of the ten most powerful lobbies would probably include such names as the American Automobile Association, the American Medical Association, the National Rifle Association, the AFL/CIO, the League of Women Voters, and the National Education Association. Interesting additions to political pressure have been the Common Cause and Nader organizations, so-called grass-roots groups that might be termed "the middle-class American's lobby." It is an attempt to combat the tremendous influence wielded by the large lobbies and to emphasize the interests of the so-called average American consumer. Their existence bespeaks the new aggressiveness of the individual citizen and of consumer groups.

How successful have the large lobbies been? They are probably the single greatest influence over any piece of legislation considered by Congress.[38] A prime example is the lack of any stringent legislation restricting the use of firearms in the United States today, and this can be attributed almost exclusively to the lobbying efforts of the National Rifle Association. "Despite widespread concern over crime and a decade that saw three widely publicized assassinations, this powerful lobby has been able to forestall or weaken drastically all gun legislation introduced in Congress."[39]

A second type of pressure group is the *nonpolitical interest group.* Such a group is primarily concerned with promoting a product or an organization, and does not engage in politically oriented activities. Some trade or professional associations fall in this classification.

A third type of pressure group is the *rights group.* Such organizations are concerned not only with political, but also with social and educational change. They are devoted to securing increased opportunities for their particular sector. Prime examples of rights groups are the National Organization for Women, the National Association for the Advancement of Colored People, the Jewish Defense League, and certain youth groups. These groups are almost exclusively the product of the twentieth century and their influence is of relatively recent origin; but today their impact on organizations, and on society in general, is pervasive.

A fourth type of pressure group is the *consumer* group devoted to representing the buyers or users of a particular product or service. Such groups derive most of their impetus from the movement begun by Ralph Nader and his book condemning the auto industry, *Unsafe at Any Speed.* Nader's efforts were, as most are aware, the foundation for the many pieces of auto safety legislation that have been enacted. Not only has the auto industry been forced to concentrate its funds on improving its cars instead of its profits, but it has become increasingly consumer-oriented since the Nader confrontation.

How do these groups work? How do they achieve their goals? Their secret lies in their ability to cultivate public opinion and use it as a driving force to secure governmental, legislative, and organizational change and cooperation. Most crucially, their success lies in an ability to reach others and win them over to their concerns, thereby increasing their constituency and attracting funds.[40]

The ultimate tool of the pressure group, however, is legislation. Only through legislation have blacks been granted increased opportunity, and have consumer groups succeeded in obtaining improved safety standards. Hence, pressure groups have directed their attention and techniques to where authority is lodged, or where interpretation of existing laws takes place. They have also concerned themselves with appointment of agency personnel, cabinet members, and members of the judicial branch.

Pressure groups have not only drastically affected what our society does and how it has changed, but also their success has influenced the way we think about accomplishing things within an organization. They have given us a new awareness of responsibility. Prior to the rise of pressure groups, employees had what has been called a "collective moral neutrality."[41] Therefore, even though employees might be directly involved in dumping tons of polluting waste into their town's river, they rationalize thus: "We weren't doing it, it was the Company."

What this foretells in organizations is the need for proactive and collaborative management. This means involving individuals and groups, in one form or another, in organization decisions, and in securing their support of organization policy. Collaborative management also entails giving people meaningful work that they can have a hand in shaping. The rise of pressure groups also has meant that the various communities and individuals affected by organization decisions expect to influence the actions taken, and this has given cause to a need for "external legitimization."

Many social scientists and psychologists have offered partial solutions to this challenge facing today's organizations. A team of Harvard Business School professors, for example, suggest that corporations engage in "social audits" which measure the worth and impact of their actions on the public. Rensis Likert suggests "anticipatory management" in which the company leader stimulates the organization to think about and devise strategies to cope with anticipated problems.[42] But one thing seems clear—organizations are going to have to become more humanistic to survive:

> The corporations must forget their nonsense about "private sectors." It is not just that government contracts and subsidies have long since blurred the line between public and private sectors, but that every American individual or corporation is public as well as private; public in that we are Americans and concerned about our national welfare. We have a double commitment and corporations had better recognize this for the sake of their own survival. Poverty, discrimination, disease, crime—everything is as much a concern of the corporation as is profits. The days when corporate public relations worked to keep the corporation out of controversy, days of playing it safe, of not offending Democratic or Republican customers, advertisers or associates—those days are gone. If the same predatory drives for profits can be partially transmuted for progress, then we will have opened a whole new ball game. I suggest here that this new policy will give its executives a reason for what

they are doing—a charge for a meaningful life.[43]

External pressure groups offer to organization development and the change facilitator a constant variation with which the organization and its leaders must cope. Given the amount and speed of expected change, the leader's chief role in the future will be to help the organization adapt to revolutionary and evolutionary forces. In particular, the organization development process will have to focus on three main issues:

1. Help the organization sensitize itself to the impact of pressure groups.
2. Help the organization develop criteria for evaluating the legitimacy of what a pressure group is suggesting.
3. Help the organization develop strategies for realigning its goals in the direction of valid change.

Precisely how this is done will differ according to the situation, but the importance of the response cannot be underestimated. In an era where rapid changes are expected in both our structures and our value systems, individuals who can facilitate such change properly will be providing solid leadership for their organization. And this kind of total system impact can benefit an organization development process if it is seen as a way to reexamine goals, processes, and values.

Federal Legislation and Regulations

If you ask the leaders of public and private organizations what factor has the greatest impact on their organizations, a high percentage indicate that it is the legislation and regulations produced by the federal government, and that these roadblocks and restrictions are constantly a bone of contention and source of irritation to most managers. Some governmental restrictions, however, become a challenge to the organization development process; coping with them can be a constructive, educational, and enhancing aspect of organization life. Consider, for example, some of those in the United States:

The Occupational Health and Safety Act of 1970 (OSHA)
The Federal Mine Safety and Health Act of 1977
Title VII of the Civil Rights Act of 1964, as amended by the Equal Employment Opportunity Act of 1972
Title IX of the Education Act of 1972, citing nondiscrimination by reason of sex

The enactments of law can be turned into a positive, system-wide response, rather than doing no more than absorbing time, creating hostility, and causing the fruitless expenditure of resources. Beyond the elimination of these wastes, the organization development process can help by confronting the laws and regulations as an opportunity to reevaluate practices, to educate managers and employees, to plan a positive organizational response, and to avoid fines, lawsuits, and decisions made in courts of justice.

Theoretically, regulations are the practical interpretations of the law—law with its sleeves rolled up. But all too often managers have discovered that the regulations which "interpret" laws create as many problems as they solve, and a kind of problem/solution chain reaction is then started. The result is that management requests the organization development facilitator to design a program that will do two things at once: satisfy requirements of the regulations that create potential compliance headaches for management, and design ways to avoid those situations for which the regulations were written in the first place.[44]

Many organizations responded with training because of interventions by the courts. An organization development effort can take the offensive and respond to the regulations and guidelines before the defensive team, the lawyers, has to be called in. This calls for a certain amount of organizational self-evaluation, which in itself is valuable:[45]

It affords the system an opportunity for the development or refinement of procedures and mechanisms that may be used for the continued monitoring of any program or process relating to the law or regulation.

It ensures that the organization and its employees are protected from unintentional acts that could result in violations of the law or regulation.

It provides an opportunity for informing all organization leaders and employees about the law or regulation while involving them in the assessment and modification process.

QUALITY OF WORK LIFE AND CLIMATE

Human resource programs designed to address improvement of working conditions should be unique, situation-specific attempts to embrace a concept encompassing growing social and economic concerns of the postindustrial society—one that defines a way of working, or an approach to work that incorporates the following precepts:[46]

The work environment is cooperative, not authoritarian.

The work process is evolutionary and change-oriented.

The work process is open rather than rigid.

Work cannot be rule-based; hence, it must be more informal.

Emphasis must be placed on interpersonal aspects of work relationships, not mechanistic.

Problem-solving skills are critical.

Relationships of managers, supervisors, and workers are based on mutual respect.

One cannot separate *quality of total life* from *quality of work life,* and it is the latter with which we are dealing here. In the late 1970s and early 1980s, however, a number of criteria of quality of life have been explored. Studies have shown that the pace of life in developed countries produces more unpleasant events than pleasant ones.

One way we effectively cope with events of life is the degree to which work is meaningful. Our search for quality of work life is an important part of coping with the environment.[47]

All animals perform a certain amount of work in order to protect and feed themselves, to provide for themselves the necessities for sheer survival. Human beings, in their uniqueness, also must work to obtain economic, sociological, and psychological satisfactions. For this reason, there is built into most of the great religions an ethic that prescribes work as morally and socially desirable. The various civilizations, therefore, have seen work as a good thing, have managed to establish a seemingly irrevocable relationship between work and a good life. Moreover, it has been taught (and it may be true) that work is its own reward.

Why, then, in the past few decades in our society that is based on Western civilization, has there occurred what seems to be a slow but steady deterioration in the common attitude toward work? Why is the quantity of work accomplished apparently disparaged, quality of work declining, worker productivity lessening?

Work, of course, is done by an individual; but human beings discovered a million years ago that more could be done if the work of two or more individuals is combined in series or in parallel. Thus, by successive refinements, men and women "working together" more or less systematically were able to do such things as hunt and kill other animals, protect their offspring, keep warm, use the energy of other animals, and build communities.

The refinements of working together were continued by the ancients, reaching a peak in military use, but in the civilian sector tending toward the artisan, craftsman, and cottage industry simply because most arduous work could be laid off on slaves. As craftsmen developed products and services that by their availability became needed, the perpetuation of each craft required the learning, subservient apprentice and the stagnated journeyman. Similarly, in the feudal period, heavy labor in construction and agriculture was the lot of the serf, while skilled artisans and scribes were influential citizens frequently organized into monopolistic and reactionary guilds, some of which were more powerful than the nation-states in which they existed. The guild system fell before better communications and the expansion of trade by export and import, and by the appearance of the capitalist and the entrepreneur.

Capitalism destroyed the guilds, but in their quest for ever-greater efficiency and productivity, human needs were often sacrificed by capitalists on the altar of the organization. As Western civilization moved from feudalism into an industralized society, a system evolved by which the work of many individuals could be regimented within an organization under the control of a few. These few—we call them corporate executives now—believed that to produce profit through productivity or effective services, it was first essential to achieve efficiency by limiting the variety in the work of each individual worker. All other things being equal, this concept usually made the organization profitable. But by eliminating such things as creativity and responsibility, it tended to reduce the contribution of the worker to prideless drudgery. Although the tendency was to create organizations as if they existed without people, it cannot be said that such a system was wholly without merit—for in its practice the Western world built great cities and massive industrial bases served by railroads, banks, schools, farms, and factories. Men and women accomplished the necessary work, however, in compliance with the expectations of their employers.

Generally speaking, classic theories of work and of organization for working evolved through several centuries along more or less parallel lines. In the postindustrial society, however, we see human values in a new light.

First, acceptance of deviation from organizational expectations as a manifestation of human instability was recognition that the workers themselves had to be taken into account. Second, this tacit admission was then bolstered by introduction of still another social invention that would, in a different way, hopefully relate the workers to the organization—scientific management took its place as the latest in a succession of work systems that included slavery, serfdom, bonded servitude, and bureaucracy. Third, although not without violent resistance and acrimonious struggle, the workers themselves restored a small conceptual remnant of the ancient guilds to form skill-related labor unions by which to force improvements in both working conditions and material compensation.

Management, scientific or not, countered unionization by shoving the pendulum toward paternalistic recognition of what seemed to be the workers' needs. The company dwelling, the company store, and the company cafeteria were outward indications of "taking care of" company employees as a means of making work more acceptable to them. For largely self-serving reasons, corporate organizations introduced pensions and government undertook to assure its citizens a measure of economic security within the social system. When behavioral scientists pointed out a collateral need for ego satisfaction, incentives were devised that served not so much to provide satisfaction as to delineate status. The mistaken idea that job status is interchangeable with job satisfaction has produced such amenities as the empty title, the rug on the floor, the in-office conference table, the water carafe, and—highest symbol of all—a parking space near the entrance. As a coup de grace to the problem of happily relating the worker to his assigned task, dollars have been expended on piped music and air conditioning. Yet people have not responded by enjoying work.

What kind of reality is developing with respect to work? Erich Fromm, in *The Revolution of Hope,* predicts a once more dehumanized society in A.D. 2000.[48] He agrees with Lewis Mumford that the age of the *megamachine* will be upon us. He foresees that work, as well as personal environment, will be dominated by impersonal social systems of decidedly negative impact on the individual. In a society that increasingly stresses quantity and consumption, and that measures progress by increases in things rather than in terms of quality of life, he senses that workers will become pathologically passive, without the capacity for individuality and creativity.

With survival and security needs more or less satisfied, with even-handed treatment fairly well secured for every worker, with greater job mobility possible, workers in every field of endeavor have become concerned with what has come to be called "quality of working life." The trend is away from being grateful for merely being employed, no matter how dull or meaningless that employment might be, toward being resentful for having to perform activities that make less than a full demand on one's capabilities.

"Quality of working life" is a broad concept. It refers to the degree to which work provides an opportunity for an individual to satisfy a wide variety of personal needs—from the need to survive with some security to the need to interact with others, to have a sense of personal usefulness, to be recognized for achievement, and to have an opportunity to improve one's skills and knowledge.

In a recent survey, interviewers gave people a chance to sum up their own opinions about work by simply asking them: Why do you really work? Three categories covered the main reasons:

1. Economic necessity and security or to raise money for a special purpose—59%
2. Personal interest and liking the job—29%
3. Convention and gregariousness—7%

If approximately 60% of the people work purely for economic reasons, while high job satisfaction develops from interest in the job and a sense of achievement, then there is reason for concern over quality of work life. Numerous studies show that the quality depends on meaningful work, the challenge in learning and problem solving, in control over one's job and a chance to collaborate with colleagues.

Criteria for Quality of Work

R. E. Walton offers the following conceptual categories or criteria for quality work:[49]

1. *Adequacy in compensation.* This concept also entails sufficient income to maintain a socially acceptable standard of living, limit on the gap between executive and hourly worker pay, and may mean pay proportionate to the number of jobs one is able to perform well rather than the number actually scheduled to be done.
2. *Safe and healthy working conditions.* This includes reasonable hours enforced by a standardized normal work week beyond which overtime premiums are required, those physical working conditions that minimize risk of illness and injury, and age limits on work that is potentially harmful to those below or above a certain age.
3. *Immediate opportunity to use and develop human capacities.* Included in this category

are autonomy, multiple skills requirement rather than repetitive application of narrow skills, feedback on results of one's own action as a basis of self-regulation, whole tasks rather than fragmented ones, planning as well as implementation activities.

4. *Opportunity for continued growth and security.* This concept encompasses work assignments and educational pursuits which expand one's capabilities, the prospect that one can use newly acquired knowledge and skills in future work assignments, advancement opportunities, and employment or income security associated with one's work.
5. *Social integration in the work organization.* Components are freedom from prejudice, egalitarianism, mobility, interpersonal openness, supportive face-to-face work groups, and a sense of community in the organization that extends beyond these primary groups.
6. *Constitutionalism in the work organization.* Included are privacy concerning nonwork matters, free speech without fear of reprisal, equity, and due process.
7. *Work and total life space.* This means a balanced role of work—work schedules, career demands, and travel requirements that do not take up leisure and family time on a regular basis and advancement opportunities that do not require frequent geographical moves.
8. *Social relevance of work life.* This includes social responsibility of the organization in marketing techniques, waste disposal, employment practices, and so forth.

It has been pointed out by Ted Mills* that one of the problems with the term is that "quality of work life" is not a single, specific notion. Rather, it subsumes a whole passel of terms and notions, all of which he feels really belong under the umbrella "*quality of work life*":[50]

Industrial effectiveness
Human resource development
Organizational effectiveness
Work restructure
Job enrichment
Organizational restructure
Sociotechnical systems
Work humanization
Group work concept
Labor-management cooperation
Working together; work involvement; and worker participation
Cooperative work structures

Each of these, in varying degrees of inadequacy, identifies a part of the larger whole that "quality of work life" seeks to identify. Quality of work life actually is the sum of all these various attempts to label a general new direction for work, working, and work organizations in the late twentieth century.

There is a new expression of individualism abroad in the land. People are insisting that in all their significant activities—including work as an important part—they want to be free not only from such negatives as hunger, insecurity, deprivation, and arbitrary reprisal but also free positively to express their unique skills and capabilities.

Figure 9-2 is a conceptual model of the processes in the search for quality of work life, based on four essential factors:

1. The *work itself,* which generates higher levels of accountability and responsibility because it is characterized by systems that encourage direct feedback on performance, clear work goals, fewer controls with more accountability, and appropriate involvement in decision making.
2. The *individual* who grows personally and professionally through his or her work roles and relationships, fostered and consistently improved through processes of role clarification; opportunities for individualization, self-identity, and learning; linking individual, work, and life goals; tangible support from superiors.
3. The *work output* of improved quality resulting from enlarged responsibilities, in-

*Director, American Center for Quality of Work Life.

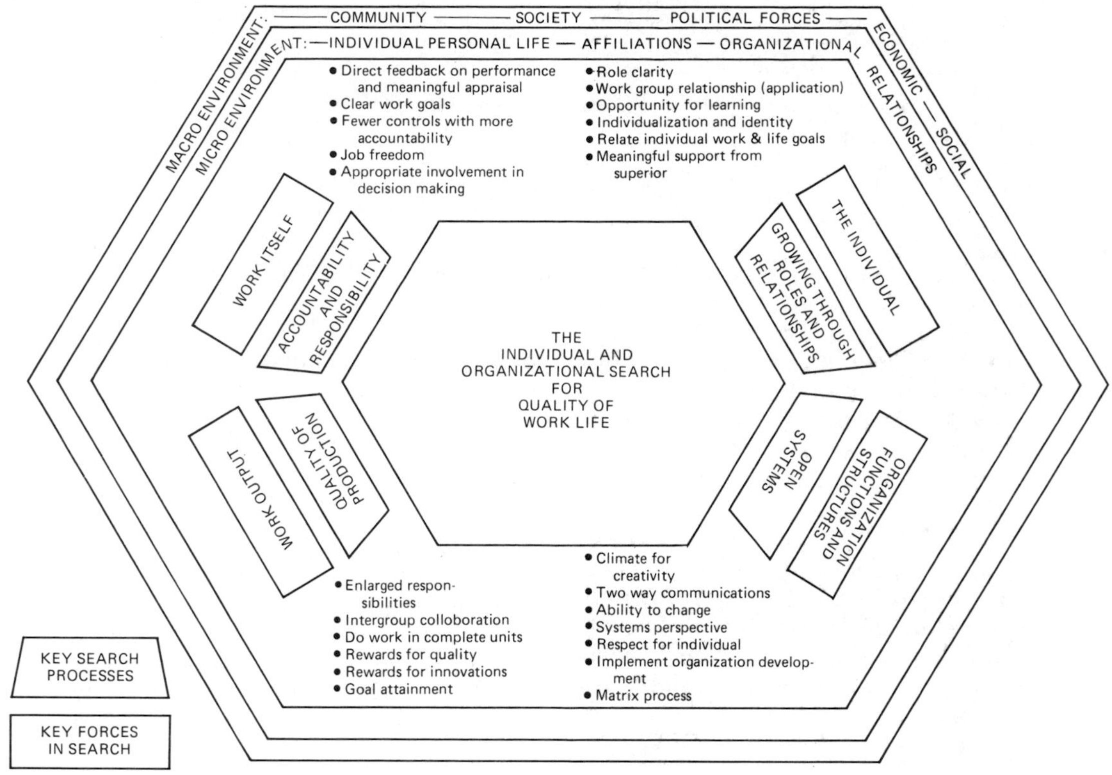

Figure 9-2 The search for quality of work life[51]

tergroup collaboration, work completed in units rather than in fragments, rewards for quality and innovation, and measurable goal attainment.

4. *Organizational functions* and *structures* built in an *open system* and providing a climate for creativity, two-way communication, a system perspective, respect for the individual, and ongoing organization development.

This model indicates that there may be a substantial overlap of individual and organizational needs—more than has so far been generally recognized. Conversely, an organization may unknowingly deny quality of working life by curtailing opportunities for its employees to satisfy their individual needs. These strong possibilities explain why managers, supervisors, and union leaders are looking for greater mutual understanding of ways to *humanize* work.

Success in the attainment of quality of work life lies in our belief in the desire of everyone, including ourselves, to live to the full measure of our capabilities and to be reaching beyond that.[52]

Emery and Phillips conclude their study with summing up the relationship between quality of work and quality of life[53] as illustrated in Figure 9-3.

If a person has a high-quality job—a challenging and interesting job—that job will also have other good work factors and altogether lead to high job satisfaction. This again, all other things being equal,

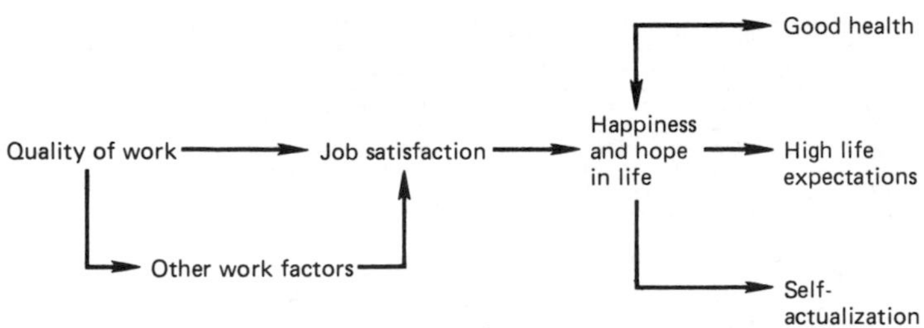

Figure 9-3 Relationship between quality of work and quality of life

leads to happiness and a sense of hope about the future. People in such jobs are also likely to have better health, high life expectations, and self-actualization.

Let us examine more closely the elements in Figure 9-3.

The Individual. The organization of the future will base its control and effectiveness on the growth and accomplishment of persons within the organization. The old "command" by authority or even benevolent paternalism will become less viable as a way of managing.

This new kind of relationship is built upon the confidence persons have in one another's integrity, goal orientation, and commitment to a problem-solving process. Such confidence does not need to depend upon authority or status for its success. It derives from some basic trust between the parties without which quality work will be illusory.

Many factors in the traditional organizational pattern caused persons in an organization to be seen as "doers of work." The task was the first concern of the supervisor. In the new approach, the supervisor's major responsibility will be development of others to adult patterns of self-control and achievement.

Work Itself—Accountability and Responsibility. When jobs have been redesigned in a number of different organizations we have seen that, in contrast to the learning and growth we were trying to imitate, the opposite happened. In the bureaucratic work organization, the following has tended to occur:[54]

Meaningless jobs with little variation lead to:

1. Little learning on the job
2. Little participation in decision making on the job

Such jobs mean:

1. Little pride and social support
2. Very little social significance outside work
3. Not much of a future except through promotion in the hierarchy of the organization

The consequence of this vicious circle is that people who have been in jobs for some time give up and withdraw from any challenge in terms of variation in the job—learning, participation—and so on. The bureaucratic principles are in this way effectively blocking any other form of organization.

Goals for a satisfactory organization of the workplace are as follows:

Diversity in job assignment for each worker
Opportunity to learn and continue learning
Decision-making power
Recognition
An opportunity to relate to what one does or produces

Management needs to strive to develop effective work functioning and to focus on the "person-centered" needs so as to "release" rather than control the potential of others. Fortunately, this fits the job to the person rather than fitting a person to a job description.

To improve performance, the manager will create opportunities for a person to set his or her own "targets" for achievement, work standards, and personal growth. Through "target-setting" type of experience, the individual meets task goals in terms of personal drives, standards, and needs linked to clear objectives of the organization. These objectives need to be achieved. The need is to lessen control but increase responsibility and accountability of the individual and the work group.

Work output. The work output should demonstrate competency and craftsmanship. It should be in keeping with goals set collaboratively by the worker, work group, and management. The worker should be accountable for output that is as close to error free as possible, with minimal rejects. Wherever possible the work should be done in complete units where job enrichment and variety is possible. Management should reward workers who are creative and innovative in accomplishing goals. Effective productivity should exist where subunits collaborate with a minimum of redundancy.

Organizational function and structures with open systems. Let us anticipate that our grandchildren will at least give us credit for starting to face some basic problems in work life. They will be able to judge our record when, around the end of the century, they know the answers to questions that are open today:

1. Are more open work roles, such as participant forms of work organization and flexitime, passing fads—or are they the beginnings or real alternatives to bureaucracy as the dominant form of organization?
2. Are careers and professions, as well as the institutions of learning, going to be more open and flexible, or are they to give continued support to bureaucratization?
3. Will the more open forms of work organization lead to a less fragmented society, a society where the young and the old, the sick and the disabled, are not sealed off from work and community life?

The need for instituting proper management and information systems in organizations is self-evident. New technology in closed-circuit television, intercommunication warning systems, computer terminals on managers desks, conference phones, and so forth, are all part of the arsenal of modern information storage and retrieval devices. It does not become communication, however, until it becomes a two-way process with those who want and need the information. Effective management must understand the need for open communication and be secure enough to share information, not hide it.

These four areas form the underpinnings of the thrust toward quality of work life. Certainly, one of the important contributions to organization development will be the nature of employee attitude, interest, commitment, and the climate of the work setting.

MANAGERIAL POLICIES AND PRACTICES

The policies established by its leaders and managers necessarily reflect the values, beliefs, mores, and codes that guide the destiny of an organization. It is a remarkably simple characteristic of a policy, however, that it is useless unless put into consistent practice—policy is not a document, it is what people *do.* We could discuss an extensive list of policy-oriented practices that are related to organization development, but it may be of greater value briefly to focus on six areas of policy and practice not ordinarily in organization development literature—even though they are system-wide elements that permeate the essence of organizational functioning. Each of these six practices represents a deliberately chosen policy on the part of management; the way they are implemented can be affected by the organization development approaches of diagnosis, data collection, goal setting, involvement, training, and evaluation.

Long-range Planning

Organizations are clearly affected by constantly changing social and economic conditions, making it imperative to plan well ahead.[55] Organizations must anticipate the turbulence of decades ahead and formulate mechanisms for attaining their objectives in advance, and implicit in these mechanisms are instruments of control in terms of resource allocation and consumption.

Long-range planning involves determining basic long-term goals and objectives of an organization, adopting courses of action, and allocating resources necessary for attaining these goals and objectives. Long-range planning also involves the desire on the part of top management to take steps into the unknown. If managers wish to take properly planned steps into the future, they must have an appropriate conceptual framework, or a concept of the mission, around which systematic information gathering and analysis is organized.

From the outset it is vital to state that the term *long-range planning* refers to a time dimension, usually ten to twenty-five years. Thus, long-range planning and strategic planning are not synonymous because strategic planning is not necessarily long-range. Some strategic plans, such as the acquisition, sale, or liquidation of a business, can be carried out in a few months. Still, since objectives tend to be enduring and basic strategy seldom changes overnight, strategic planning usually has a long-range focus.

Strategic planning is concerned primarily with how objectives and goals can be achieved rather than when, although the time it will take to carry out alternative strategies affects their relative attractiveness. It is true that strategic planning is forward-looking.

Long-range planning is a total system effort that can utilize organization development philosophies and methods, linking current decisions and behavior to future activities. This means that the plans and decisions we make today restrict our alternatives in the future. The quality and type of people we select today will largely determine the kind of organization we will have in the future. The product plans made now will determine the markets we can enter next year. Because the planning decisions have such long-range implications, it is important that they be made in context. Before we decide what action we will carry out tomorrow, we must determine whether that action will help or hinder progress toward a goal we want to reach at a later time.

It should be realized that, in effect, long-range planning is invariably planned change. In this regard, the greater the departure of planned changes from accepted ways, the greater the potential for resistance from the people affected or involved. It is necessary, therefore, to build into long-range plans provisions for overcoming the resistance of employees, and such provisions should include organization development efforts. Resistance may occur because of a lack of confidence in the planners. If past proposals have proved unsound, or have failed, the new propositions are dubiously received. Sometimes plans wear the obvious habit of the ivory tower—they are fully clothed in large generalities, they fall short in their assessment of the current situation, and they are out at the elbow in logic. These plans are often met with attitudes of distrust and resistance. Timing is important. Sudden changes should be avoided. People should be given enough time to understand and implement the plan. When participants clearly can see the plan's inner workings, and have an opportunity to visualize the end results, this familiarity will act as a potent self-persuader and will encourage them to accept the plan. Whenever possible, a plan should be made a continuation of something that is already being done. A good plan starts from where people are now, then carries them forward to the new aspects of the plan—constantly using proper diagnosis, goal setting, training, and involvement.

Operations Research

Most people define operations research as a collection of mathematical tools for solving operational problems, such as linear and nonlinear programming, game theory, Monte Carlo techniques, and probability.[56] But some operations research advocates, principally Stafford Beer, view it only as an approach to problem solving in which mathematical tools may be useful. Operations research, according to Beer, is a problem-solving method that incorporates objective and interdisciplinary analysis of complex problems in order to discover (1) the real nature of the problem, (2) the systemic relationships that cause the problem, (3) how the system can be changed to solve the problem, and (4) new systemic abberations that are likely to result from these changes. The operations research process often employs mathematical techniques as tools to assist in this process, but the tools do not define the process any more than a physician's instruments define a remedy.

Beer's formal definition of operations research is:

> Operations research is the attack of modern science on complex problems arising in the direction and management of large systems of men, machines, materials and money in industry, business, government and defense. Its distinctive approach is to develop a scientific model of the system, incorporating measurements of factors such as chance and risk, with which to predict and compare the outcomes of alternative decisions, strategies or controls. The purpose is to help management determine its policy and actions scientifically.[57]

Operations research has also been defined as a scientific approach to problem solving for executive management, and the assertion has been made that its application involves:

> Constructing mathematical, economic, and statistical descriptions or models of decision and control problems to treat situations of complexity and uncertainty . . . [and] analyzing the relationships that determine the probable future consequences of decision choices, and devising appropriate measures of effectiveness in order to evaluate the relative merit of alternative actions.[58]

Operations research is the use of both the basic research techniques of mathematics, statistics, and simulation theory—as well as the applied use of scientific method to decision making by government, business, and industry. It emphasizes fundamental measures that are relevant to the situation and, in doing so, links itself with the scientific basics of measurement, sorting, and classification. It can be applied to the monitoring of an organization's ongoing activities (e.g., its daily operations such as production scheduling, inventory control, facility maintenance, and repair or staffing of service facilities), and it can treat organizational problems that bear only indirectly on daily activities (e.g., that have a planning orientation, determine the breadth of a product line, or develop a long-term program for plant expansion).

Operations research, then, is a way of looking at the structure, form, and pattern of organizational life in an effort to determine causes (inputs), effects (outputs), and interactions (black boxes). It is characterized more by its spirit of inquiry than by its tools of inquiry. It examines the structural relevance of variables in a system and how they change over time.

The stages in a classic operations research solution are normally constant and equate closely to that of the scientific method: (1) diagnosis or identification of critical factors; (2) formulation of problem and objectives; (3) construction of the model; (4) analysis, sensitizing the model, and calculation of the mathematical or statistical solution or derivation of the simulation solution; and (5) implementation of findings and updating of the model. The various stages in applying operations research do not necessarily have to be separate; they can proceed in concert. The first—the *diagnostic phase*—has as its *task* the identification of what seems to be the critical factors in a decision situation: what principal decisions there are to be made, where the measures of effectiveness are among these choices, what trade-offs among these measures are likely to ensue in a comparison of the alternatives, and how the decision maker sees the problem. In the next phase—the *formulation of the problem*—the *task* is to establish the confines of the analysis, to state the problem elements from the preceding diagnosis—not only the controllable or decision variables, and the uncontrollable variables, but also the restrictions or constraints on the variables, and the objectives for defining a good or improved situation.

In the next phase—the *building of the model*—the operations researcher's *task* is to decide on the proper data inputs and to design the appropriate information outputs. The researcher identifies both the static and dynamic elements and devises mathematical formulas to represent the interrelationships among the identified elements. The operations research specialist can either hypothesize the constraints affecting the variables or, if the problem calls for it, forecast the probabilities of the system. A time horizon is then chosen by which to evaluate the selected measures of effectiveness for various decisions, and this, in turn, influences the nature of the constraints imposed. *Performances of the analysis* entails the *task* of calculating the mathematical solution, or the derivation of a simulation. This process begins with a given model and its parameters, as specified by historical judgment and technical data, and can require the redoing of any or all of the previous stages. A major part of the analysis is determining the sensitivity of the solution to model specifications, with particular reference to the accuracy of the input data and structural assumptions.

Implementation of the findings is the most critical stage of all. Here the operations researcher's *task* is to present a model and a proposed solution for action by the decision maker. Implementation is at best a problem of modification of behavior, and unless the decision maker has been brought in at the beginning—and his or her confidence and participation maintained—an operations research analyst is apt to collide with inadequate implementation of the decision.

Philburn Ratoosh comments on problems with implementation in operations research: "Although presentation of results is not enough to assure implementation, presentation together with persistent active support from within the group greatly increases the likelihood of acceptance."[59] He also points out a characteristic weakness in operations research—its lack of competence in dealing with human systems—either as problems or during an implementation stage. Operations researchers often shy away from implementation because of their own fears and conflicts about change; they have often stumbled at this point when they have to interface with human systems. They frequently and wrongly assume that managers are always rational.

Under these circumstances, therefore, it is helpful to relate operations research to organization development—particularly with respect to the behavioral science approach that Warren Bennis prefers to call "planned change." He sees these similarities and differences:[60]

Similarities

1. Both are recent developments.
2. Both are problem-centered.
3. Both are normative—they attempt to optimize certain goals.
4. Both rely on empirical science.
5. Both depend on a relationship of confidence and valid communication between the client and change facilitator.
6. Both work best with complex, rapidly changing, science-based organizations.
7. Both share common jargon, such as "equilibrium," "homeostasis," and "self-regulating".
8. Both place strong emphasis on the organic features of organizations (dynamic, self-adjusting, growth).
9. Both feel that in order to change a system one must first understand it.
10. Both eschew trial-and-error approaches to problem solving.
11. Both share an experimental attitude toward the planning of change.
12. Both are existential approaches.

Differences

1. Disagree on strategic variables—thus operations research selects economic or engineering variables—planned change practitioners pick less quantifiable human variables.
2. Disagree on the perceived importance of valid relationships with the client—operations research practitioners are less concerned with human interactions.
3. Operations research spends more time in research —planned change spends more time in implementation.
4. The idea of a system is less stringently upheld in the behavioral sciences.
5. The interdisciplinary team is more central to operations research.

Harold Leavitt cites three factors that represent potential strategies for organizational change: people, technology, and structure.[61] Each attracts specialists who favor one factor over the others as a lever for improving organizational effectiveness. Commenting on Leavitt's hypothesis, Louis Barnes notes that:

> The people specialists tend to focus on personnel placement, management development programs, job counseling, and human relations within organizations. Technology specialists approach change as production engineers, computer experts, systems designers. Structural specialists work on organization planning, work flow procedures and staff-line configurations, among other things.[62]

The foregoing discussion has tried to support the validity of considering operations research as an organization development technique by showing the extent of the similarities with the behavioral approaches to planned change, and by illustrating the usefulness of operations research methodology and some of its technical trappings to the understanding and solution of organizational problems.

It would seem, therefore, that any approach which aspires to create a more healthy organization is worthy of the term *organization development.* What operations research offers to the development of organizations is not a set of rules, values, or assumptions for the practitioner to follow, but rather a science-based form, a procedure, a way of building models through which the organization can be viewed.

The major implications of operations research for the organization development practitioner concern the nature of change interventions.

Financial Systems and Budgeting

When organization development consultants, internal or external, help analyze any organizational system, process, or network, they are confronted with procedures, means by which the organization communicates or operationalizes its various activities and functions; one of these techniques is the financial system and budgetary process.[63] The intent here is to consider several of the behavioral benefits that permit a change facilitator to intervene in the financial process, in contrast to the conventional mechanistic, quantitative approaches to money. It is the behavioral support which the financial process can lend to the organizational environment that makes budgeting a substantial tool in total system planning.

Budgets have long been viewed as accounting-oriented tools of management used in planning the future activities of the organization, both internally and in regard to the organization's interaction with the marketplace. Budgets are often viewed as management control mechanisms that are constructed at the hierarchical level of the organizational structure and then superimposed on the operational constructs of the enterprise.

These perceptions are noteworthy as negative aspects of finance and budgeting. The purpose here is to consider the possible implications and benefits of budgeting in terms of organization development. However, rather than to challenge the traditional control function of budgeting directly, a noncontrol role for budgeting is suggested. Although budgeting, as it is currently conceived, may well be accounting- and control-oriented, it can also be a very humane and beneficial function as it relates to the social and behavioral environment of the organization. A mature attitude, accentuated by organization development, can allow budgeting to become a mutually beneficial tool for all members and levels of the organization stratum.

Financial systems can be viewed as having two broad functions. The first of these is related to fiduciary responsibility; it is primarily concerned with keeping track of things and answering such questions as: "Did we get what we paid for?" and "Do we still have it?" Costing techniques that are designed primarily to provide cost and inventory data for financial statement purposes might also be included under the heading of fiduciary statements. The second major function of financial systems is to furnish information that is useful as a basis for decision making at all levels of the organization. This function provides managers with the data required for planning, coordinating, and controlling activities; but it also includes the operation of a system that assists in motivating individuals to make and implement those decisions that lead to the accomplishment of organizational goals. It is important to recognize that information for the decision-making function of financial systems places a heavy emphasis on influencing behavior.

Financial systems do indeed play an important role in influencing behavior at all of the various stages of the management process, including the setting of goals, informing individuals what they must do to contribute to the accomplishment of these goals, motivating desirable performance, evaluating performance, and suggesting when corrective actions must be taken. In short, management should be vitally concerned with the impact of organization development on financial systems because the information for decision-making function of financial systems is essentially a behavior function.

Although a financial system will demand the use of financial and accounting specialists, the way a budget is developed can involve various levels of management, as well as employees. We all know the "power of the purse" and the new golden rule: "Those that have the gold will rule."

The more that operating and field personnel can be involved in budgeting, the better will be the fundamental information and commitment. In the 1980s at least three methods are being used to make the budgetary process more rational and effective: Program Budget Management Systems (PBMS), Zero-Based Budgeting (ZBB), and Human Resource Accounting.* The PBMS process is intended to have program managers look at the costs of particular efforts to determine financial allocations. The purpose here is to make annual reviews of program goals, objectives, alternatives, cost–benefit, and thereby to determine increase or decrease from previous allocations.

Into this arena came zero-based budgeting. In theory, ZBB is allied with the comprehensive approach and, indeed, is a major component of program budgeting. Under program budgeting and the more formalized PPB system, there is no inherent "right" of any program for continued funding. Each program should be examined *in toto* (i.e., from a zero base) and would compete not only for a portion of the increases each year but also with every other program for its base. Theoretically, all dollars spent on one program would be in competition with all dollars spent on any other program.[64]

There are three basic steps in virtually any budget preparation, in both the private and the public sectors:[65]

1. Determining those programs/functions/activities for which significant budgetary decisions are to be made. This is called *identifying decision units.*
2. Preparing justification statements that include information necessary for managers to make judgments on these programs/functions/activities. For each decision unit, this is called *preparing decision packages.*
3. Identifying the relative priority of programs/functions/activities. This is called *ranking the decision packages.*

*Human resource accounting is discussed below, separately and in some detail.

The important things about *any* new financial system are the accounting procedures, the controls, and the involvement of people. Within this broad bracket, we can say that since most organizations must provide some product or service in the marketplace to afford economic maintenance, marketing estimations of demand is realistically the logical starting point in any budgetary process. Although this task falls primarily on the shoulders of the specialized marketing function, the process should provide for input opportunities from other functions, such as production, accounting, and engineering. After sales projects have been quantified, they should be evaluated at the various operational levels of the organization. The process calls for team and individual analysis, confrontation, and consensus.

Work unit members should make a conscious search of its membership to determine the various competencies and expertise available to the group in an attempt to maximize the rational process of budget construction. If data and advice are available from nongroup members, it should be pursued but never permitted to become a determination of objectives unless the group has reached a consensus that is supportive of the external proposal. As a group and as individuals, there must be a mature, conscientious attitude regarding the parameters within which decisions must be made. Information, data, and perceptions must flow readily from group to group, and from individual to individual, so that conclusions are not based on an isolated collection of specialized factors; reasonableness also requires acknowledgment that there are practical limitations to this process, but those practical limitations need not be overstated or used as artificial restrictions to data flow.

To avoid the construction of barriers between groups and functions, there should be a constant attempt to restrict secrecy regarding individual and group perceptions of organization objectives. Open communication is vital to an openly derived consensus. Conclusions and decisions based on secrecy and a closed evaluative process lend themselves to abstractions or misperceptions of real conditions, interrelationships, and interactions. The budget that results from abstract perceptions is dysfunctional and only adds to the harmful aspects of differentiation. Budgets derived in isolation as abstractions are often inconsistent with the predominant organizational goals and objectives, and escalate conflict between individuals and groups to the level of open hostility.

The financial system and budgetary process can and should incorporate not only plans for the continuous operation of the organization, but also planned change. Planned change is necessary for an organization to create negative entropy, and thus provide for the continuation and success of the organization. With every new budgetary process comes more planned change; participatory decision making and a participatory budgetary process are the most equitable means of meeting the resistance to change. Hostilities and dysfunctional confrontation that arise from fear of the unknown, and distrust of manipulative practices by management, are encountered in both the planned-change aspect of the budgetary process and the traditional control nature of the budgetary process. When management provides workable parameters for a participatory budgetary process, cooperation is optimized, dysfunctionalism is minimized, task group norms are consistent with organizational objectives, and the organization has a greater chance for success in dealing with those organizational economic/environmental problems that are not a function of management style.

Human Resource Accounting

A third system-wide process related to the "bottom line" of organizational finances is *human resource accounting* (HRA).[66] In a literal sense, this means accounting for people as organizational resources. It is the organizational measurement of the cost and value of people. It is the process of identifying, measuring, and communicating information about human resources to facilitate management effectiveness. Eric Flanholtz believes:

> Ultimately, perhaps the greatest impact of human accounting will be on the management of people, per se. The notion of human resource value will lead to a value-based paradigm for the management of people. Because of the attention directing effect of measurement, management will become more conscious of the need and opportunity to appreciate the value of human resources and, in turn, the value of the enterprise as a whole.[67]

The purpose of developing a method of human asset accounting is to provide for more accurate financial criteria: "(1) to estimate dollar investments made in building the human organization, and (2) to estimate the present discounted productive value of that human organization."[68] It also considers the development and implementation of human asset accounting essential to the success of organizational operating effectiveness.

In any organization, capital assets are a triangular configuration consisting of physical assets, financial assets, and human assets. HRA's purpose is to provide an organization with the information on where and how much it invests in these human capital assets. This information can then be utilized in two major areas, managerial decision making and financial reporting:

1. *Managerial decision making.* Every time managers hire, train, assign, develop, transfer, and replace personnel, they have to make value judgments about human resources. HRA helps managers make those judgments and supplies information to analyze those decisions in the same manner that they now evaluate other capital expenditure decisions.
2. *Financial reporting.* HRA's goal is also to assist an organization in its accounting procedures by providing data that would allow the capitalization of its human assets.

There are two major approaches to HRA:

1. *Cost approach.* This approach is designed to measure the amounts already invested in the human organization. The measurement is centered on objectively verifiable data which are classified into four areas: recruiting and acquisition, formal training and orientation, on-the-job training and familiarization, and formal development.*
2. *Value approach.* The measurement of the human resource costs does not reflect changes in the underlying value of human resources. The changing motivations of employees may be much more significant than the measurement of costs alone. This approach places substantial reliance upon the use of social psychological measurement techniques in measuring trends in the productive capability, hence the value, of the human organization.

*To date most of the application of HRA has centered on this approach and has been closely associated with William C. Pyle and Rensis Likert.

The quantifying of costs or value, and considering them as investments in human assets, should result in managers protecting these assets as they do the tangible physical assets. If managers knew how much it costs to replace existing human resources, they would realize the importance of maintaining their human resources. This should result in the raising in the collective managerial consciousness of the worth of the employee, the human resource, within the organization. In turn, managers would see the need for organizational renewal, for organizational change, in order to maintain and improve its human resources, and therefore maintain and improve its human assets. If the value of organizational improvements accomplished through interventions could be quantified, managers would be more willing to authorize and support such interventions. HRA can also be utilized to establish an information system that not only includes assessments of management practices, but also manifests how they are related to the long-run success or failure of an organization.

But human relationships, motivations, behaviors, and attitudes are difficult to measure in terms of dollars with a high degree of accuracy. An organization does not own its human resources in the same manner as it owns its physical and financial assets, and thus its investments may not be recovered in the same manner. Because of these two problems, accounting and auditing procedures presently question the concept of HRA for purposes of capitalization. This resistance, when coupled with the relatively high costs and the amount of time required to develop the requisite data, makes the implementation of HRA a slow process within an organization. Nevertheless, organizations such as R. G. Barry, American Telephone and Telegraph, and Touché Ross and Company have pioneered the development and implementation of accounting for investments in human resources. The usefulness of HRA is described in this manner:

> We use human resource accounting information in strategic decision-making. The information is employed in evaluating alternative investment opportunities. We have rejected the conventional return-on-assets approach because it does not recognize human investments. In evaluating a project, we take the physical assets into account as everyone else does, but we also add to that the investment to be made in the human resources required to support the opportunity. And when we develop relationships to profit, it is the relationship of all of those resources, tangible and human, to a particular profit opportunity.[69]

Extensive use of HRA, with respect to either cost or value, has been slow. This will continue to be true until sufficient criteria and more definition has been established—so that accounting procedures will accept capitalization of human assets and thus make it financially beneficial. One of the major areas of future study is assessment of the reliability and validity of models and methods developed by measuring the original and replacement costs of human assets.[70] Testing the reliability of present data is essential to the development of HRA, because management will not have confidence in the unknown.

One positive outgrowth from HRA, however, has been an increased awareness of the need to identify costs as they relate to human resources; with such assets ranging from 20 to 80% of an organization's costs, this kind of awareness will make financial planning much more inclusive and realistic.

Flexitime

Flexitime is a modern concept of work that allows individual employees to select their own hours—within some limits.[71] The most common form of flexitime incorporates morning and afternoon "core periods." During these times, usually two to three hours each, all employees are required to be at work. The flexibility portion of the workday is in starting, lunch, and quitting times. Flexitime does generally retain the eight-hour day and five-day week; however, there are numerous variations which do not.

Where flexible working hours have been implemented, the employee response has generally been enthusiastic. Flexitime allows a better integration of work and social life, which is so important with the current emphasis on leisure time. Employees have the option of sleeping in or playing a round of golf before dinner. Furthermore, many people perceive themselves as morning people or night people. The concept of flexitime lets the individual match working hours with these personal preferences. It allows one to better utilize evenings for family activities, social events, night school, or recreation, and thereby integrate work and leisure. It is also possible to transact personal business, including errands, shopping, and medical appointments during the day without losing vacation time or pay, leaving the weekends free for recreation and leisure-time activities.

The reality of one-parent families and working wives in our society is another argument for flexitime. Statistics indicate that there has been a striking increase in the proportion of working wives: from 23.8% in 1950 to 51% in 1979, a trend that is predicted to continue. Flexible working hours would permit one parent to go to work early, facilitating supervision of the children in the afternoon, while the other could go to work late, after the children are off to school. This system could also be used to reduce the cost and related problems associated with child supervision or day care centers.

From an employee viewpoint, some of

the conflict between work life and family life can be alleviated by flexitime. When flexitime was introduced at the First National Bank of Boston, "the system appeared to have a positive impact on employees being able to arrange their work and home responsibilities."[72] A General Accounting Office report on flexitime indicates that a major advantage is "introduction to the work force of skilled persons who cannot work standard hours—mothers with young children, students, or the handicapped, for instance."[73]

Studies indicate that flexible working hours appear to contribute significantly to humanizing the job and improving the quality of work life—major problems in transition to a postindustrial society. In the words of one employee, "choosing my own time for arrival makes me feel like a human being. It gives me tremendous control over my own life, that I'm not a wage slave."[74] This helps to fulfill the psychological and cultural demands to improve the quality of work life and becomes part of participative management. Flexitime is compatible with systems theory and treating the employee "as a whole person with needs outside of work as well as at work."[75]

As with any work systems concept there are, as far as the employee is concerned, negative aspects to flexible working hours. The requirement for more sophisticated timekeeping and the fact that "many white-collar workers consider the introduction of any formal time recording system a professional insult" are drawbacks. On the other hand, "Union eagerness for this new approach has been so marked that in one agency they have tentatively agreed to the installation of time clocks where none has ever been used."[76]

In the balance, however, the advantages to the employee seem to exceed the disadvantages. The evidence supports the conclusion that many workers now on flexitime would not want their employer to return to the old system of inflexible hours. From the employee perspective this is a valuable concept that probably costs the employer nothing.

Flexible working hours have many and varied advantages to the employer as well. In fact, management usually reports increased productivity with flexible working hours. There are several reasons for this positive result—including physical and psychological ones. First, the worker who arrives calm and relaxed is far better prepared to concentrate on the job. Second, the natural staggering of working hours, which occurs under flexitime, precludes some of the early morning and late afternoon "coffee clique" activity which is prevalent with fixed hours. Furthermore, early and late in the day, outside the core period, the office should be quieter and more conducive to concentration and high output.

From a management perspective, improved morale is an added benefit of implementing flexible working hours. Flexitime is consonant with many of the classical theories of motivation: the Hawthorne effect, participative management, job enrichment, delegation of responsibility, high job satisfaction, return to the work ethic, and the convergence of employer and employee goals.

There are costs to management for utilizing flexible working hours, which must be weighed against the benefits. Initially, there will be additional administrative costs incurred resulting from timekeeping. Some firms are experimenting with new timekeeping devices and equipment, whereas others are modifying their old systems or putting employees on the honor system. Regardless of the timekeeping procedure, management must assess the costs associated with the fact that some employees will find a way to "beat" the timekeeping system, just as they did under the inflexible work schedule. Care must also be taken to "ensure that more diligent workers are not saddled with the work left incomplete by those who might mistake the merits of flexibility for a release time of nonaccountability."[77]

Some manufacturing operations will not lend themselves to application of the flexitime concept without a significant restructuring of the job. Highly specialized sequential operations on an assembly line, shift work, and work teams are examples of this. Restructuring of such jobs would lose some efficiencies of operation, but would go a long way toward job enrichment, participative management, and improved job satisfaction. Flexible working hours may pose a problem where security, office cleaning, or maintenance are required. Careful planning and coordination can easily alleviate this problem.

The benefits of flexible working hours clearly outweigh the cost to management. For the few firms that had implemented flexitime and later returned to fixed working hours, poor planning and implementation could be identified as the cause of the failure.

Studies and research indicate a trend toward the establishment of flexible working hours: "Given the need to increase productivity, given the psychological and cultural demands to humanize the workplace, and given the sheer logistics of moving more and more people from home to work over crowded roads and in crowded trains, one may predict that soon working time in this country will become more flexible and better planned than in the past."[78]

With something more than 200 organizations using flexitime, it is predictable that by 1990 perhaps 50% of our nation's working population will be employed on some kind of flexible work hours scheduling. The determination, planning, and implementing of flexitime, of course, is considerably aided by adherence to relevant organization development procedures.

Union Negotiations and Contracts

These two things are considered to be a part of the organization development process because they are systemwide reflections of management policies and practices that contribute to organizational effectiveness. A union contract, sometimes called a collective bargaining agreement, is an agreement between the management of an organization and an organized group of its employees, called a union. The union contract is complex and usually spells out in great detail the conditions of pay, work, and fringe benefits under which the union representatives have agreed that union members will work during the period of the agreement. A union contract becomes a vehicle for organization development when it is written in such a way that it involves both the union and management in the planning, development, and problem-solving process of the organization.

The old-line, bread-and-butter attitudes of traditional unionism have changed. Instead, there is a strongly developing trend toward the more "cosmic" in union objectives and goals. Like the people they represent, many union leaders typify the younger generation. These youthful officers of labor are concerned with broader goals than the more elemental organizing and dollars-per-hour preoccupations of their predecessors. The fact is that today's younger union leaders chafe at what they regard as the conservatism of the old leaders. The new aim is to exert union strength to achieve "community goals"—that is, to cope with social problems, civil rights, and housing, as well as to improve education and training, and to forge stronger links with free-world trade unions.

Since the familiar "basics" have already been attained, modern labor officers argue that the unions' efforts should now be devoted to the attainment of broader benefits. Indeed, in 1966, steelworkers' president I. W. Abel predicted that areas of negotiation someday would include benefits traditionally restricted to white collar and executive personnel. Abel cited stock options, portal-to-portal pay from home to plant, employer-purchased homes for transferred workers, guaranteed annual wages, and profit sharing. This prediction is, of course, in tune with current union aims to organize the white-collar worker.

Organization development approaches provide a framework for a better approach to bargaining, already tried successfully by employers. This new approach recognizes union-management conflict and strikes as failures; and it directly treats these causes to restore mature relations. This is "integrative bargaining" or problem solving bargaining, because it takes a problem-solving approach to get joint gain for both parties through mutually integrated action.

Experience with integrative bargaining has shown that useful innovations can be made—innovations that will help the participants solve their own problems instead of depending on outside force. One easy first step is to begin bargaining with problem definition rather than demands and counterproposals. Conflict can be constructive, but it is questionable whether the whole bargaining process needs to have a conflict orientation, as it usually does in traditional win/lose bargaining.[79]

Management usually looks upon the union as that part of the total system with which they have to cope in order for the organization to continue to operate. It is no wonder that the union contract is usually not used for organization development. Actually, the union could make a positive contribution to the organization if management would enlarge its vision of the potential of the interrelationship. But for the union contract to be a vehicle for organization development, it has to be written in such a way that it will involve the union as well as management in the basic processes of organizational effectiveness rather than just working conditions, security, pay, and fringe benefits. Before this can happen, the attitudes of management and union leaders have to change. In most collective bargaining situations both management and labor approach it as a win/lose proposition; consequently, each girds itself to combat the other.

A better approach has been provided by behavioral science theory and has been tried successfully by employers.[80] This approach—called integrative bargaining or simply problem-solving bargaining—recognizes union-management conflict as failures in problem solving; it attempts to help the two groups find the causes of its failures, and it directly treats these causes to restore mature relations. It takes a problem-solving approach to get joint gain for both parties through integrated action. The effects of the union contract reach all parts of the organization, not just management. Conventional organization development methods, although they directly affect management, may leave rank-and-file members of the organization untouched and suspicious of management's new attitude. The integrative process requires that many blocks be eliminated: the average union worker believes what is good for management cannot be good for labor; the union contract is developed by "experts" whose livelihood depends on maintaining the adversary relationship; when labor leaders make concessions to management, or show a willingness to cooperate, the members may reject them; and organization development is rarely understood by management, unions, or workers.

To eliminate these fears, both management and union must build that mutual trust necessary for the maintenance of a high degree of cooperation. Each must acquire the ability to approach a problem from more than its own limited point of view. To do this there must be someone in top management who is a forthright leader—who can effectively meet any situation through confrontation, search, and coping—and union leadership that has the initiative and intelligence to understand the productivity side of the business. When these two requirements are met, the union can maintain its institutional integrity and sovereignty, and perform positively and constructively in organization development. Where such initiative and leadership qualities have been displayed, the union "becomes the instrumentality which has served to unlock the storehouse of work experience of the individual members and release the accumulated ideas, resources, and ingenuity that have seldom been encouraged to find expression or application."[81] When this occurs, true organization development happens and what amounts to a contribution to the quality of work life takes place.[82]*

CASE STUDY: AN EXAMPLE OF AN ORGANIZATION-WIDE APPROACH TO RENEWAL

This case involves an operation roadblock, and the use of action research, training, and action. A large midwestern paper company was involved in an interesting approach to organization renewal that was developed around the identification and solution of "roadblocks" facing the company.

The process began with recognition, by the president and other top officials of the company, of the need for improving personal, group, and company performance. It was decided to involve all members of management in all phases of the renewal process. Supervisory personnel began to identify the operating problems that stood in their way. The questions asked in each work group were: What are the roadblocks that prevent us from doing our most effective job? What can we do to remove these roadblocks?

More than 500 supervisors undertook to identify these roadblocks in departmental meetings. Some 4500 roadblocks were identified, and these steps were taken:

Problem-solving conferences
Work unit meetings to plan action steps
"Operation Follow-through"

The latter was a means for all key persons to work together in acting on suggestions, ideas, and information drawn from such sources as:

Opinion research survey
Five conference sessions
Employee complaints
Customer complaints
Safety meetings
Management planning reports
Employee suggestions

An overall follow-up task force was appointed at corporate headquarters. At each manufacturing division and in the general office, full-time teams were organized to help supervisors expedite the work of doing something about all the ideas, criticisms, and suggestions that were advanced.

Probably the greatest gain in this process was one that could be realized only in months and years to come—a method of working together to improve productivity and to make the company an even better place to work. Many departments began holding frequent meetings to pinpoint and solve problems as they arose.

The project continued for two years, but was

*This extensive examination of some of the system-wide influences that contribute to organizational effectiveness has not included the traditional, well-known, and modulized organization development methods. Some of the latter are discussed in Chapter 13, with examples of their application. What I have intended above is to indicate, primarily, that many organizational events and processes can be influenced by the appropriate application of organization development philosophy.

somewhat curtailed by the sudden death of the president and a major economic downturn that brought a merger into the situation. It proved, nevertheless, to be, a significant venture in organization renewal that had lasting effects.

Comment. *In this example we see the use of data collection, feedback, and action taking on an organization-wide basis. Top management was again a vital factor in setting the climate and plans.*

SUMMARY

An attempt has been made here to look at ways in which a complex social system, called an organization, can experience development. Organization development processes should be related to the stage of maturity in which the organization finds itself. Organization development processes usually include the phases of diagnosis (data collection), an action alternative to meet the problem need, and a follow-up to evaluate and maintain the organization-wide change effort.

There is merit in a multidisciplinary approach to organization development that involves the behavioral and management sciences, values, and technology. Each has validity under relevant conditions of disequilibrium, relevant needs assessment, and appropriate resources to meet the need.

QUESTIONS

1. What stages of organizational growth have you observed or experienced? Cite examples and give reasons for each stage.
2. In what ways can a matrix type of organization be helpful? Under what conditions?
3. Why does management tend to feel that reorganization efforts will solve their problems?
4. How can management use federal rules and regulations as an organization development process?
5. When is it appropriate for management to use financial planning and budgeting as an organization development process? How can this be done?
6. What is meant by the term *quality of work life?* How would you initiate a quality-of-work-life effort in an organization?
7. Is flexitime always helpful? Under what conditions do you think it will work? Under what conditions will it not work?
8. What do you predict will be the trend in union-management relations in the future? Why?

NOTES

[1]John W. Gardner, "How to Prevent Organizational Dry Rot," *Harper's Magazine,* October 1965, p. 32. Hereafter cited as Gardner.

[2]"What Is OD?" *NTL News and Notes,* Vol. 2, No. 3, 1968, p. 1.

[3]Ibid., p. 1.

[4]Gordon Lippitt and Warren H. Schmidt, "Crises in a Developing Organization," *Harvard Business Review,* November-December 1967. p. 103. Hereafter cited as Lippitt and Schmidt.

[5]Peter F. Drucker, *The Practice of Management* (New York: Harper & Row, Publishers, Inc., 1954), p. 62.

[6]Abraham H. Maslow, *Motivation and Personality* (New York: Harper & Row, Publishers, Inc. 1954), p. 102.

[7]Gardner, p. 20.

[8]Lippitt and Schmidt, p. 109.

[9]Ibid., p. 111.

[10]Ichak Adizes, "Organizational Passages: Diagramming and Treating Life Cycle Problems of Organization," *Organizational Dynamics,* Summer 1979, p. 26.

[11]Milan Moravec, "A Results-oriented Approach to OD," *Training and Development Journal,* September 1978, p. 26.

[12]*Organization Development Guide,* Vol. 1: *Principles* (Pittsburgh, Pa. Heinz, U.S.A., 1972), 8-9.

[13]Richard M. Steers, "Problems in the Measurement of Organizational Effectiveness," *Administrative Science Quarterly,* Vol. 20, 1975, 546-558.

[14]Irving Stubbs, *Conceptual Model for Organization Development* (Tryon, N.C.: Tryon Associates, Inc. 1977).

[15]Richard M. Steers, "When Is an Organization Effective?" *Organizational Dynamics,* Autumn 1976, p. 59.

[16]Wendell L. French and Cecil H. Bell, Jr., *Organization Development: Behavioral Science Interventions for Organization Improvement* (Englewood Cliffs, N.J.: Prentice-Hall, Inc., 1973), p. 18. Hereafter cited as French and Bell.

[17]Warren Bennis, *Organization Development: Its Nature, Origins, and Prospects* (Reading, Mass.: Addison-Wesley Publishing Company, Inc., 1969, p. 26.

[18]Stafford Beer, "The Management of Information and Knowledge," *Managing Modern Complexity* (Washington, D.C.: Committee on Science and Astronautics, U.S. House of Representatives, 1970).

[19]Adapted from an unpublished paper by Fred Wood and Robert Shouldice, *The Matrix Process: An Organization Revolution for Managing Modern Complexity* (Washington, D.C.: The George Washington University, January 1971).

[20]Gordon Lippitt and Reuben Stivers, *The Multocular Process: A Working Paper* (Washington, D.C.: Development Publications, 1975), p. 6.

[21]Adapted from an unpublished paper by Marge Schuler and Thomas Rimmer, *The Scanlon Plan and Codetermination* (Washington, D.C.: The George Washington University, November 1978).

[22]Paul Bernstein, *Workplace Democratization: Its Internal Dynamics* (Kent, Ohio: Kent State University Press, 1976), p. 18.

[23]Frederick G. Lesieur and Elbridge S. Puckett, "The Scanlon Plan Has Proven Itself," *Harvard Business Review,* September 1969, p. 110.

[24]James W. Driscoll, "Working Creatively with a Union: Lessons from the Scanlon Plan," *Organization Dynamics,* Summer 1979, p. 65.

[25]French and Bell, p. 36.

[26]Adapted from an unpublished paper by Arthur Rimback, *Reorganization* (Washington, D.C.: The George Washington University, December 1975).

[27]David S. Brown, "The Myth of Reorganizing," *Journal of Systems Management,* June 1979, p. 7.

[28]Ibid., p. 6.

[29]Ibid., p. 8.

[30]Richard P. Rumelt, *Strategy, Structure and Economic Performance* (Cambridge, Mass.: Harvard University Press, 1974), p. 106.

[31]Ralph Cordiner, "Decentralization at General Electric," in Max D. Richards and William A. Hielander (eds.), *Readings in Management* (New Rochelle, N.Y.: Southwest Printing Company, 1963), p. 219.

[32]Lounsbury S. Fish, "Decentralization Reappraised," in Franklin G. Moore (ed.), *A Management Sourcebook* (New York: Harper & Row, Publishers, Inc., 1964), pp. 253–254.

[33]Shirley Terreberry, "The Evolution of Organizational Environments," *Administrative Science Quarterly,* Vol. 12, No. 4, 1968, 590–613.

[34]Adapted from an unpublished paper by Leslie Ward, Jr., *Existential Crisis* (Washington, D.C.: The George Washington University, December 1971).

[35]Muzafer Sherif, *In Common Predicament: Social Psychology of Intergroup Conflict and Cooperation* (Boston: Houghton Mifflin Company, 1966).

[36]Douglas Carter, *Power in Washington* (New York: Random House, Inc., 1964).

[37]Adapted from an unpublished paper by Diana Chapin, *External Pressure Groups as Agents of Change* (Washington, D.C.: The George Washington University, November 1977).

[38]Grant McDonnell, *Private Power and American Democracy* (New York: Alfred A. Knopf, Inc., 1966), p. 142.

[39]Roger M. D'Aprix, *Struggle for Identity: The Silent Revolution against Corporate Conformity* (Homewood, Ill.: Dow Jones-Irwin, Inc., 1972), p. 19.

[40]Saul D. Alinsky, *Rules for Radicals* (New York: Random House, Inc., 1971), p. 83. Hereafter cited as Alinsky.

[41]Richard E. Walton, "Frontiers Beckoning the Organizational Psychologist," *Journal of Applied Behavioral Science,* Vol. 8, September–October 1972, 601–630.

[42]Rensis Likert, *New Patterns of Management* (New York: McGraw-Hill Book Company, 1961), p. 190.

[43]Alinsky, pp. 195–196.

[44]Kenton Pattie and Tina LaBoe, "Federal Regulations: A Boon to A/V Oriented Trainers,"

Training and Development Journal, December 1979, p. 11.

[45]Martha Matthews and Shirley McCune, *Complying with Title IX: Implementing Institutional Self-evaluation* (Washington, D.C.: Research Center on Sex Roles in Education, National Foundation for the Improvement of Education, 1976), pp. 133–134.

[46]Ted Mills, *Quality of Work Life, What's in a Name?* (Washington, D.C.: American Center for the Quality of Work Life, 1978), p. 20.

[47]Adapted from Gordon Lippitt and Jacqueline Rumley, "Living with Work: The Search for Quality in Work Life," *Optimum,* Vol. 8, No. 1, 1977, 37–43. Hereafter cited as Lippitt and Rumley.

[48]Erich Fromm, *The Revolution of Hope* (New York: Harper & Row, Publishers, Inc., 1968).

[49]Ibid., p. 141.

[50]Ted Mills, *Quality of Work Life: What's in a Name?* (Detroit, Mich.: General Motors Corporation, March 1979), p. 7.

[51]Lippitt and Rumley.

[52]Paraphrased from "The Growing Dissatisfaction with Workaholism," *Business Week,* February 27, 1978, p. 97.

[53]Fred Emery and C. Parks Phillips, *Living at Work* (Canberra, Australia: Australian Publication Service, 1976).

[54]Einar Thorsrud, *Quality of Work Life* (Chicago: National Conference on Higher Education and National Conference of Alternative Work Schedules, 1977).

[55]Adapted from Gordon Lippitt's portion of report, *The Planning Process for State Arts Agencies,* Deborah Dokken (ed.) (Washington, D.C.: National Assembly of State Arts Agencies, 1978), pp. 5–15.

[56]Adapted from an unpublished paper by Richard Christensen, *Operations Research, Organization Development, and Organization Renewal* (Washington, D.C.: The George Washington University, November 1975).

[57]Stafford Beer, *Decisions and Control* (London: John Wiley & Sons, Inc., 1966), p. 92.

[58]Harvey M. Wagner, *Principles of Operations Research, with Applications to Managerial Decisions* (Englewood Cliffs, N.J.: Prentice-Hall, Inc., 1969), p. 4.

[59]Philburn Ratoosh, "Experimental Studies of Implementation," in John R. Lawrence (ed.), *Operations Research and the Social Sciences* (London: Tavistock Publications Ltd., 1966), pp. 251–262.

[60]Warren G. Bennis, *Changing Organizations* (New York: McGraw-Hill Book Company, 1966), p. 85.

[61]Harold J. Leavitt, "Applied Organizational Change in Industry: Structural, Technological, and Humanistic Approaches," in James G. March (ed.), *Handbook of Organizations* (Skokie, Ill.: Rand McNally & Company, 1965), p. 1144.

[62]Louis B. Barnes, "Approaches to Organizational Change," in Warren G. Bennis, Kenneth D. Benne, and Robert Chin (eds.), *The Planning of Change* (New York: Holt, Rinehart and Winston, 1969), p. 80.

[63]Adapted from an unpublished paper by Peter Cirafici, *Budgetary Process: A Behavioral View* (Washington, D.C.: The George Washington University, Fall 1975).

[64]Frank D. Draper and Bernard T. Pitsvada, *Zero-based Budgeting for Public Programs* (Washington, D.C.: University Press of America, 1978), p. 52.

[65]Ibid., p. 59.

[66]Adapted from an unpublished paper by Kenneth Kalscheur, *Human Resource Accounting* (Washington, D.C.: The George Washington University, November 1975).

[67]Eric Flanholtz, *Human Resource Accounting* (Encino, Calif.: Dickenson Publishing Company, Inc., 1975), p. 337.

[68]Rensis Likert and David G. Bowers, "Organizational Theory and Human Resource Accounting," *American Psychologist,* June 1969, p. 588.

[69]William C. Pyle, "Monitoring Human Resources—On Line," *Michigan Business Review,* Winter ed., 1972, p. 27.

[70]"Report of the Committee on Human Resource Accounting," *The Accounting Review* (publication of the American Accounting Association), Vol. 48, Suppl., 1973, 169).

[71]Adapted from an unpublished paper, prepared as a group project and edited by Giovanni Coratolo, *The Rearranged Work Week* (Washington, D.C.: The George Washington University, November 1976).

[72]"Productivity Draws New Attention," *Banking,* Vol. 68, No. 5, 1976, 14.

[73]Wilson Norris, "Flexitime Bill Passed by House," *The Washington Post,* May 7, 1976, p. C2.

[74]Robert Meyers, "Workers Banish Time Clock," *The Washington Post,* August 3, 1976, p. A1.

[75]Alvar O. Elbing, Herman Gadon, and John R. M. Gordon, "Flexible Working Hours: The Missing Link," *California Management Review,* Vol. 17, No. 3, 1975, 54.

[76]Robert T. Donahue, "Flexible Time Systems: Flex Time Systems in New York," *Public Personnel Management,* Vol. 4, No. 4, 1975, 214.

[77]"A Note of Caution about Flexitime," *The Washington Post,* August 17, 1976, p. A16.

[78]Robert Lawrence, "Flexible Working Hours: A New Key to Productivity," *Best's Review,* Vol. 77, No. 1, 1976, 77.

[79]James L. Stern, "Collective Bargaining Trends and Patterns," in Benjamin Aaron (ed.), *A Review of Industrial Relations Research,* Vol. 2 (Madison, Wis.: Industrial Relations Research Association, 1971), 130.

[80]Jerome M. Rosow, "Now Is the Time for Productivity Bargaining," *Harvard Business Review,* January-February 1972, p. 83.

[81]Frederic G. Lesieur (ed.), *The Scanlon Plan* (New York: John Wiley & Sons, Inc., 1958), p. 123.

[82]Adapted from an unpublished paper by Lorna Polk, *Union Contracts as a Tool for Organization Development* (Washington, D.C.: The George Washington University, November 1975).

IV

Essential Competencies For Organization Renewal

Although organization renewal is the responsibility of line management, with or without the help of internal or external facilitators, certain competencies can be identified that are beneficial to all renewal leaders. Whoever initiates and takes responsibility for organization renewal, the need for data collection and research is evident—in order to properly target the renewal effort. Most development processes indicated by the research findings will require training for needed skills before effective action takes place. Renewal demands that leaders learn new knowledges, skills, and attitudes.

Chapter 10 presents an understanding of the research process as an essential first step in any planning for organization renewal. Chapter 11 deals with training and development as a prerequisite for organization renewal; and such training must be based on the learnings needed to meet the changes facing the system. Chapter 12 involves the skills, knowledge, and experiences required of a competent organization renewal leader. Chapter 13 examines the organization of the future and discusses the demands the future may place on effecting organization renewal efforts. Such an examination of the future and of criteria to be used in systems renewal is an important final note in this search for ways to improve organizational functioning.

The shaded area in Figure P-4 indicates the portion of the systems renewal model that is covered in Part 4.

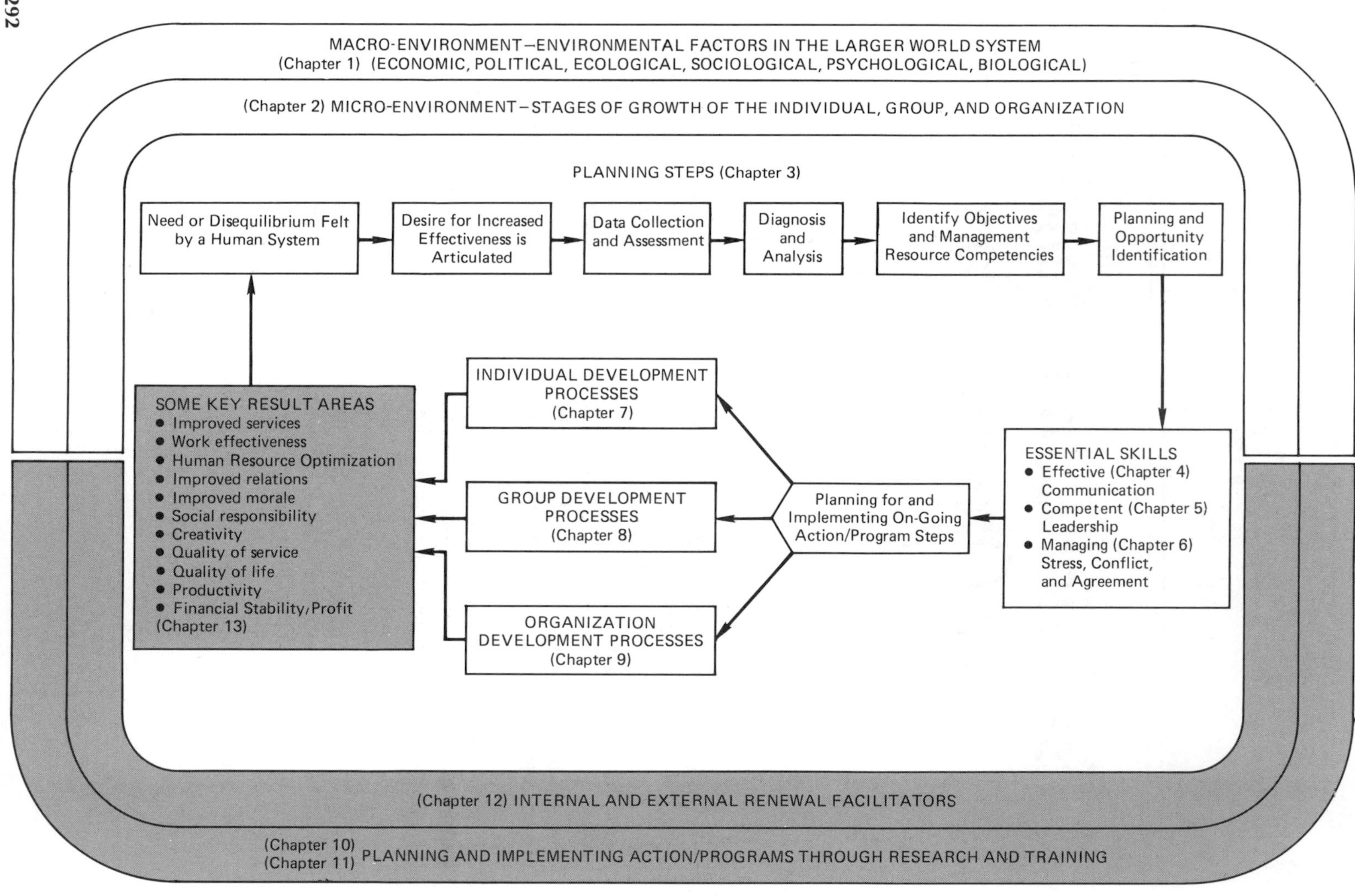

Figure P-4 Systems renewal model

10

using research in human systems renewal

The routine of custom tends to deaden even scientific inquiry; it stands in the way of discovery and of the active scientific worker. For discovery and inquiry are synonymous as an occupation. Science is a pursuit, not a coming into possession of the immutable; new theories as points of view are more prized than discoveries that quantitatively increase the store on hand. It is relevant to the theme of domination by custom that the lecturer said the great innovators in science "are the first to fear and doubt their discoveries."

John Dewey, 1859–1952

It may not always be possible to get real, hard criteria data, but this should always be the goal of every change facilitator. It is necessary to reiterate that data collection is integral to the process of organizational renewal, as well as vital to any evaluation of progress. Organization development is perceived as being increasingly involved in:

> studying the organization in depth to ascertain the what, where, and why of an organizational problem. Once a system of ineffective functioning is perceived, the first step toward treatment is diagnosis. . . . Diagnosis may be a complex procedure of surveying the organization to ascertain the "below surface" attitudes. . . . In addition to making an attitude survey—or perhaps instead of making one—organization development specialists interview individuals and groups to pinpoint the sources or locations of the problem and to identify its underlying causes.[1]

If one accepts the promise that organization development is a data-based approach to planned change in an organization, one must develop a conceptual framework by which to examine the use to be made of the information generated:[2]

There must be a belief in the validity, desirability, and usefulness of data about the system itself, specifically data about the system's culture and processes.

Specific kinds of data are preferred, for example data about the organization's human and social processes.

Data usually "belong to" and are used by the people who generated them. The data are public; the data are the property of all organization members; the data are a springboard to action.

Rather than viewing facts as good or bad, one looks at the consequences or functionality/dysfunctionality of the facts.

Data are described rather than evaluated—defensive postures are thereby less likely to be manifested.

Data are used as aids to problem solving rather than as "clubs" to enforce certain behaviors—they are used to supply answers to the central needs of the organization and its members.

Data collection serves several important and useful functions in an organization development effort. It reduces the degree of haphazard and unplanned change by creating a realistic information base for diagnosis. It eliminates pluralistic ignorance—the assumption by many that their perceptions are unique. It involves people at many levels of the organization in the assessment and diagnostic activities.

One of the interesting approaches to helping organizations evaluate themselves is a process initiated by the American Society of Association Executives (ASAE)—a procedure that helps in a logical and objective way to show association members:[3]

That their association is effective and responsive to needs
That finances are well managed
That the organization is working intelligently in the interest of its members
That staff is capable and productive
What opportunities exist for improvements and new activities
What activities are outmoded and should be discontinued

The guidebook for this procedure points out that association evaluation, properly done, can be a pleasant and rewarding experience; it can:

Create a better concept of basic association purposes and objectives
Build understanding and teamwork between elected officers and the staff
Provide useful information for future planning
Help members look at their association in a constructive way
Establish a way to compare an association's performance with the performance of similar organizations
Justify an increase in dues and other income
Improve current and future activities
Develop presentations showing the value of the association to members and others
Stimulate creative thinking by association leaders
Provide useful indoctrination material for new officers, board members, and committees

Evaluation is only as good as the evaluator. For this reason, it is important that the process be as objective as possible. One way to help assure objectivity is to see that there is at least one person in the evaluation group who has an impartial and objective view, and who is not a member of the association or its staff.[4]

The ASAE suggests that such studies are best undertaken by a committee having ample resources:[5]

1. President or chief elected officer, with broad concurrence and with consultation of chief staff executive, appoints an evaluation committee consisting of a chairman plus five other members, each to be chairman of a subcommittee.
2. Staff assembles exhibits and data for subcommittees.
3. President, with consultation of staff executive, appoints five subcommittees of five each, covering the following areas:
    a. Organization
    b. Program
    c. Staff
    d. Financing
    e. Headquarters and equipment
4. Set up meeting of evaluation committee for briefing session. At this meeting, establish time schedule for meetings of subcommittees and submission of reports.
5. Schedule meetings of five subcommittees. At these meetings each subcommittee will evaluate the area for which it is responsible.
6. Require written reports from each subcommittee.
7. Hold evaluation committee review of the subcommittee evaluations prior to preparation of the final report.
8. Submit final report to the board of directors.

9. After review, modification and approval by board, implement recommendations and incorporate in short- and long-range plans.

This ASAE approach is but one of many examples that indicate the need and procedures for organization self-evaluation by both inside and outside resource persons. But when a need for evaluation research presents itself, it must be formulated in researchable terms (not as a "should," "ought to," "value belief" question) and reduced to practical scope in time and cost. The data required must be defined, and the possibility of translating findings into action within the organization should be clearly ascertained.

Specialists are fond of asserting that the only truly effective development process is one that causes obvious and favorable changes. This is correct and valid. A major dimension of any projected research, therefore, must measure such changes; a before-and-after profile must be obtained in terms of specific criteria to fit a particular individual, group, or organization.

An organization must plan, organize, execute, and test. Testing is fact-finding. Research, usually starting with a stated hypothesis, is that phase of fact-finding which is not the by-product of regular operating procedure and reporting. Using the criteria indicated earlier, those initiating an organization renewal process should be able to develop a research design that can evaluate the organization's efforts and results.

A research design is the method of securing the data that have been defined as needed; such a design is aimed at reducing error and bias and economizing cost of collection; such a design will depend on whether the study is:

Formulative or exploratory: Establishing hypotheses or bases for study. Here design must be flexible, will depend much on insight, and can profitably use analysis of "deviate" cases.

Descriptive and diagnostic: describing a situation, and diagnosing reasons for it, and thereby suggesting action to be taken. Here selection or sample for data collection will be of great importance.

Experimental: testing the validity of a hypothesis. Here design can be laboratory or field in nature, and involves comparisons of an experimental group against some type of control observations.

To encourage research in and about organizational renewal, I suggest these action steps to cope with existing blocks to competent evaluation:

Change the attitudes of the client system toward the need for research.

Give research on change the status it deserves.

Encourage the client system to secure the financial backing required by data collection.

Generate within the client system the cooperation and coordination that is required for research.

Educate and train students and practitioners to appreciate the importance of research in problem solving.

Train students and client systems to use the tools and methods of research.

There is no single right way to evaluate the effects of organization renewal studies. Renewal systems should create research methods appropriate to their needs, based on proven principles of scientific inquiry. This is essential to the problem-solving process that constitutes organization renewal.

In keeping with the schema of organization renewal, the test will be whether the involved efforts solve a problem, improve the functioning of subsystems in the organization, deepen the process of interfacing, and contribute to the next stage of organizational growth.

The present-day approach to organizational change and development no longer considers individuals apart from the organization or the community in which they live. As a result of a historic trend away from the purely mechanistic, the directed development of managerial effectiveness in the individual and the group is now flexibly oriented to specific organizational tasks and values in a known climate. Self-understanding and productive relations with others are integrated with an ability to apply a variety of methods and solutions, as well as skills and knowledges, to problems that are themselves multifaceted.

In the future, those who assume responsibility for the development of individuals, groups, and organizations will be judged by their overall contribution to developing systems that create adaptable and viable conditions. Such judgments are best made in the light of parallel performance criteria, applicable on the one hand to the achievements of the organization in solving problems and, on the other hand, to taking steps toward its own increased maturity. This is why renewal facilitators need to concern themselves with the criteria and methods involved in the process of data collection.

In organization renewal, the task is even more difficult because there is no universal agreement as to how an organization should function, how it should be organized, and how it should be supervised and regulated—even what, really, it should be and do. Different systems, furthermore, are faced with different requirements depending on their structure, resources, size, products, and types of people serviced. On the one hand, an organization must be responsive to the values and perceptions of the people it serves; but to be effective, it also needs to exercise leadership and to follow sound human, technical, managerial, and financial practices.

It is important to restate that any individual, group, or organization development activity must involve data collection. Kurt Lewin was a strong advocate of the interrelationship of research, training, and action. He felt that all change should be based on data relevant to the situation, training designed to cope with the revelations of those data, and the ability thereafter to act with competence.[6]* In planning change, a person, manager, leader, specialist, or consultant should contemplate:[7]

Systematic data collection. Data may be collected through questionnaires, interviews, observation of behavior, or examination of organizational records. Frequently, these data are an integral part of the change, facilitator's diagnosis of the system, but data may also have other uses.

Data analysis. The change facilitator will work with the data, either alone or in collaboration with members of the organization, to aggregate, analyze, or interpret them.

Data feedback. The change facilitator will give the data back (perhaps with interpretations) to organization members in a form in which they can make use of it. Data feedback could either be immediate (as when a process consultant gives feedback to a group on its behavior) or delayed (such as computer analysis of questionnaire data or preparation of written reports).

The collection of data is basic to practically all change situations, and, in defining goals and diagnosing causes, both the client and the facilitator collect and analyze needed data:

> Collecting data on which to base a diagnosis can be as simple as brainstorming or as complex as a "grand design" research methodology involving hypotheses, instruments, and computer analysis. Complexity aside, there are four ways to collect data:

*See research in Chapter 10, training in Chapter 11, and action in Chapter 12.

1. *Observation.* Watch what people do in meetings, on the job, and on the phone.
2. *Reading.* Follow the written record—speeches, reports, charts, and graphs.
3. *Interviews.* Question everyone involved with a particular project.
4. *Survey.* Use standard questionnaires or design your own. Surveys are most useful when they ask for information not readily obtainable in any other way, such as attitudes, perceptions, opinions, preferences, and beliefs.

All four methods of data collection can be used to isolate the two major kinds of discrepancy—between what people say (formal) and what they do (informal), and between what is (organization as it exists) and what ought to be (appropriate environmental fit). The trick is not to use any particular methods, but to sort the evidence of one's senses into some categories that encourage sensible decisions.[8]*

Although these basic data collection methods are all useful, each of them also has certain disadvantages (see Table 10-1). Research is a phase of fact-finding that is not the by-product of regular operating procedure and reporting. Standard research usually starts with a hypothesis to be tested. Some research methods are more applicable than others to change situations. The choice of method depends on the nature of the inquiry and on how much control of variables is desired.

*Tests and the use of carefully designed instruments should be added to this list.

Table 10–1
A Comparison of Different Methods of Data Collection[9]

Method	Major Advantages	Major Potential Problems
Interviews	Adaptive—allows data collection on a range of possible subjects Source of "rich" data Empathic Process of interviewing can build rapport	Can be expensive Interviewer can bias responses Coding/interpretation problems Self-report bias
Questionnaires	Responses can be quantified and easily summarized Easy to use with large samples Relatively inexpensive Can obtain large volume of data	Nonempathic Predetermined questions may miss issues Data may be overinterpreted Response bias
Observations	Collects data on behavior rather than reports of behavior Real-time, not retrospective Adaptive	Interpretation and coding problems Sampling is a problem Observer bias/reliability Costly
Secondary data/ unobtrusive measures	Nonreactive—no-response bias High face validity Easily quantified	Access/retrieval possibly a problem Potential validity problems Coding/interpretation

THE USE OF INTERVIEWING

In Table 10-1, the first method cited is interviewing. No matter which research methods are chosen by the renewal planner, interviewing is a basic tool common to all except the research of written sources. All facilitators will use the interview as a data collection process sometime during the helping process. Such interview might be with an individual or a group. The group interview triggers more ideas, opens up communications, and starts appropriate action.

The results of an interview are always the joint product of the interviewer and the respondent in the interaction. Usually, respondents will communicate only when they feel that it is to their advantage to do so. The possibility of being able to check up on facts produces some extrinsic or negative motivation. There is intrinsic motivation in the satisfaction most respondents feel in having an opportunity to converse with an empathic listener. The interviewer thinks about what the other person is saying and why, rather than planning how to phrase the forthcoming questions. At the same time, the interviewer has to direct the conversation so that its content will meet the objectives of the interview. The wording of questions must bridge both the respondent's language framework and the interviewer's objectives. The respondent's frame of reference (personal experience) for using words can be revealed by the reasons he or she gives for a particular answer.

One version of this research method is called the *sensing interview*[10]—a depth interview between the change facilitator and a member of the system under study. This is usually done with individuals who represent a diagonal slice of the organization, and is conducted in some depth in order to obtain individual perceptions of the formal and informal organization. It is a diagnostic step used to "sense" the existing state of affairs. Obviously, though, one does not simply enter the premises of an organization and procede with a data collection effort; the people of the organization need to know what is going to happen and why; they need to recognize the interdependent nature of organizational problems, and to accept ownership of a search for solutions. One effective way to use the sensing interview is to erect a reality-based framework for organizational diagnosis that incorporates a means of data collection that is productive of change strategies. After securing the understanding and approval of top management, these steps are recommended to any person acting as a change facilitator:

1. Conduct initial meetings with various groups at various levels of the system—preferably groups that are aware of the existence of problems. Explain the organization renewal project in detail—its objectives, processes and interactions, stages of development, decision making, and roles and responsibilities. Confront issues directly. Structure the meeting(s) so that there is plenty of dialogue and interaction. Establish a climate for intervention and change. Explain what your role will be, your agreed-upon relationship to the organization, and the confidentiality of the responses made by individuals.
2. Identify the membership of any planning group that will receive your reports and work with you in developing appropriate strategies for organizational improvement. This planning group, or whatever it is called, should reflect a cross section of the organization, and should be drawn from among those willing to serve. This should be a mixed group, including the perennial gripers.
3. Obtain a roster of the total organization membership, from top to bottom. Select interviewees at random, every *n*th person. Describe the interview technique to them in detail, including protection of their anonymity.
4. Determine a location or locations to

conduct interviews. Off-site is preferable, and a site away from the respondent's immediate work area is necessary. Permit no interruptions.

5. Schedule and conduct the interviews in accordance with the information you are seeking. Certain questions are useful in exploring nine areas of concern in organization diagnosis:[11]*
   a. *Roles.* What areas of responsibility are you responsible for in the organization? What roles do you ordinarily play in this work group? How would you describe your job to another person?
   b. *Goals.* What are you trying to get done on your job right now? What short-term goals do you have for your job? What personal goals are you meeting at work? What are your long-range career goals? What do you want to be doing ten years from now? What kind of work would you not like to be doing inside this organization?
   c. *The job itself.* What do you see to be the predominant positive aspects of your job right now? What are its negative aspects? What parts of your job have the most personal meaning for you? What things do you do that seem not worth doing? What areas of responsibility might you have that you do not have now? What things do you do that might best be done by someone else?
   d. *Organization.* What is it about this organization that contributes to your effectiveness on the job? What factors around here hinder your performance? What makes it worthwhile to work for this organization? Why do people sometimes leave?
   e. *Interpersonal relations.* How would you characterize your relationship with your boss? What kind of relationship do you have with other persons at your level in the organization? How effective are your relationships with your subordinates?
   f. *Interpersonal perceptions.* What are the predominant characteristics of your boss? What would you see as his or her most noteworthy trait? How would you characterize the other people who are at the same level in this organization as you are? What kinds of subordinates do you have? What are their major personal characteristics? What shortcomings do you see in your subordinates? How do you measure yourself according to the characteristics by which you perceive the other people in your work situation? What are your own major strengths and shortcomings?
   g. *Work team.* What are the major problems facing your work team right now? How are decisions made in your team? What is the most serious concern you believe the team needs to face at this time?
   h. *Changes.* What changes do you believe that your boss needs to make right now? What do you believe ought to be changed by your work team right now? What changes would you like to see made on the part of the persons whom you supervise? What changes do you believe you should be making right now?
   i. *Here-and-now.* What feelings do you have about this interview? How are you feeling about the organization development project? What feelings are you experiencing in relation to the publication of the interview data? What is your attitude about the upcoming team-building session? How have

*These questions are intended to be instructive rather than directive or prescriptive. They are based, in part, on questions found advantageous by Chris Argyris.[12] It is important to explore these questions rather than simply asking them. The questions should be tested for clarity and understanding by the interviewee, and phrased in a nonthreatening manner.

you been feeling during this interview? What kinds of feelings do you have about me and what I am doing?

6. Gather and analyze the data. A factoring out process should indicate critical areas of concern, but it could also reveal that a change facilitator is not needed.
7. Feed the data (in rough form) back to the planning group. In such circumstances, the data should be presented to the entire client organization being studied, but not interpreted for the client. Change is best facilitated when the group analyzes the data and makes action plans.
8. The planning group can help you determine if you are on target, if the data seem to describe the problems, and if additional data are needed. It is vital to keep in contact with the planning group and to develop a rapport with them. The more they see of you, the better.
9. Compile your final report and submit it to the planning group. The report should be made available to any interested member of the organization who wants to see it. They own it. It is not made available to anyone outside the organization. Take the report to the planning group for their review. Discuss it with them. Negotiate any amendments to it that they recommend. Use the data base to resolve any conflict.
10. Design a model for meeting organizational needs and specific techniques for its implementation. This may include such experiences as goal analysis and clarification, role negotiation, problem solving and decision making, communication, process of change, leadership styles, transactional analysis, an management by objectives. Expectancies from the group will, in part, determine the methodology.

The sensing interview is a valuable diagnostic tool that deals with perception of people. It can be undertaken by an outside or internal consultant, or a trained person with the organization. But whether data collection is conducted by the consultant or the client with the consultant serving as technical adviser, the client has an important role to play in developing acceptance of the research, enlisting support of the respondents, and stimulating confidence in the results.

When deciding between the use of consultant-executed data collection or action research, one should consider which method does the following:

Establishes greater objectivity
Has a better focus on fundamental problems
Secures the required knowledge of the problem
Provides better cooperation and better utilization of findings
Is better at adapting the skills and resources that are available
Offers the better choice of financial byproducts—cash outlay, diverted cost of staff time, staff skill gained

Although interviewing is an important method and skill for any data collection process, it is valuable to examine various other research designs.

RESEARCH APPROACHES

Six kinds of research approach are most frequently discussed in the literature.[13]

Laboratory experiment. This method is especially suited for a situation in which precise control of the variable(s) is desired and possible:

> A laboratory experiment may be defined as one in which the investigator creates a situation with the exact conditions he wants to have and in which he controls some, and manipulates other, variables.[14]

Some advantages of the laboratory-experiment approach to research are that it offers:

More control of variable(s)
Better observation
Less expensive operation
Easier administration

Some disadvantages of the laboratory-experiment approach in data collection are:

The question of how typical the results are; do they represent reality?
The results are difficult to generalize.
Some criteria cannot be taken into the laboratory as variables.

Field experiments. The setting for a field experiment is an existing social situation. The experimenter manipulates real conditions in order to determine causal relations:

> Although it appears to be possible to study certain problems of society in experimentally created, smaller laboratory groups, we shall also have to develop research techniques that will permit us to do real experiments within existing "natural" social groups. In my opinion, the practical and theoretical importance of these types is of the first magnitude.[15]

Naturally, an advantage of field experiments is that they are more applicable to reality. Disadvantages of field experiments include:

The variables are more difficult to control.
They are more expensive.
It is necessary to get operations support.
Ethical questions.

Field studies. The field-study method provides a thorough account of the process under investigation. Field investigators study a single community or a single group in terms of its social structure. They attempt to measure and observe the ongoing processes, recording the social interactions that reflect the positions and attitudes of people. Some advantages of collecting data with the field-study method are:

It gives an overall picture.
"Living in"—getting a more accurate feeling for the natural environment or situation.

Disadvantages of field studies include:

The data are difficult to quantify.
There is a danger of subjectivity on the part of the investigator.
It is difficult to verify the data with other researchers.
Replicating the experiment is difficult.

Survey. The survey method of research depends on data collected directly from a particular representative sample of people. It is a tool for both basic and applied research and is frequently used in the consulting situation. Some advantages of the survey-research method are that it:

Measures directly the population that is being studied
Is relatively inexpensive
Is easy to quantify
Uses well-worked-out procedures

Some disadvantages of the survey-research method are that it:

Is applicable to only a point in time
Is essentially static and similar to a snapshot
Produces data difficult to interpret for action
Requires an appropriate sample that is difficult to select

Action research. The action-research method is usually used to solve a problem in operations. It involves the client in data collection, such as diagnosing a problem and evaluating the effects of action. Some advantages of action research are as follows:

People tend to utilize the findings.
People are likely to become involved in the process.
There is economy in the collecting of data.

Disadvantages of the action-research method include:

The necessity of training fact-finders.
The necessity of obtaining the support of people in the operation.
The subjectivity resulting from direct involvement.
The researcher must relinquish some decision-making power.

Research in existing written sources. A consultant and client often can find data from existing documents and letters, life histories, accounts of small-group process, annual reports, diagrams, and other sources. Doing research in existing written sources has the following advantages:

The sources are easily available.
The research is inexpensive.

Disadvantages of this research method include:

It is not always applicable.
The researcher may not be sure of some of the data.
The data are difficult to synthesize.
The data are selective.

Such an array of alternatives presents the system renewal facilitator with some obvious choices.

CHOOSING A DATA-COLLECTION APPROACH

Whether a certain method of collecting data would be relevant to a particular renewal situation depends upon how a number of factors are perceived by the client and the facilitator. The following questions offer some criteria for determining whether a particular renewal effort lends itself to evaluation and/or to research:

How complex is the problem? If the problem is really a number of problems or is very complex, it may not be possible to apply research methods to the process.
How much time will be required to get the information? If a change covers a span of years, it may not be possible to do research evaluation, although longitudinal studies are needed.
Is the question one of the values of operations? If the question is a matter of policy, rather than of measurable operations, it may arouse doubts of whether data collection is feasible.
What will be the cost of securing the facts? If the financial demand of such research is too great, it might make data collection impractical.
What will be the nonfinancial demands on the system? Any change plan should assess such matters as the need for support, time, public relations, and stress tolerance in determining the possibility of doing data collection/evaluation.
Is it feasible that the change process will be helped through the obtaining of evidence? If the data are difficult or impossible to obtain, it might be questionable whether evaluation will be possible.
Is starting some action the best way to collect the needed data?

Those who teach and practice system renewal and organization development have expressed some concern about the dearth of published research evaluating the change process.

In a survey of consultants and clients, it was found that there are some significant obstacles to research on the change process (see Table 10-2). According to the seventy-five persons surveyed, the principal obstacles are lack of time, inadequate frame of reference, and an inability to develop measurable objectives of the change

Table 10–2
Obstacles to Change Research[16]

Obstacles	Number of Responses[a] (n = 52)
Lack of time	20
Lack of a frame of reference	15
Failure of consultant and client to determine client expectations in measurable terms	14
Lack of money for research	12
Need to convince management	9
Lack of effective research methods and tools	6
Need for adequate facilities and resources	3
Lack of cooperation between client and consultant	2
Magnitude of the research	2

[a]Twenty-three respondents did not answer all the questions, and sixteen gave two or more responses.

process. Although it is understandable that lack of time and money is important, it is interesting to note the number of respondents who indicated their inability to establish a frame of reference for conducting such research. Another study of the use of evaluation by organization development specialists and consultants confirms the distinction of "soft" and "hard" data obtained as the result of an intervention*—examples of the latter being increased earnings, improved sales, fewer accidents, and greater productivity.[17]

The practices reported are significant on several accounts (see Table 10-3). First, there is indicated a definite interest in using hard criteria; this is to be expected because the respondents answered the questionnaire with reference to profit-oriented organizations. Without employing comparison groups, a practitioner cannot justifiably conclude that an organization development effort was responsible for the changes. Only about one-fourth of the respondents use a design employing a comparison group. Second, methods of collecting measures of soft criteria are: (1) observing and interviewing organization members, and (2) administering written instruments. It is significant that almost 60% of the respondents prefer to tailor instruments for each effort. This is an apparent expression that an evaluation should be keyed specifically to each organization development effort.

A third point of interest with respect to the practices is concerned with the experimental designs in use. The difficulties encountered in finding and using comparison groups explains why only one-fourth of the respondents use such designs. But the uncontrollable extraneous influences affecting the designs presently in use highlight the need for more scientific emphasis on evaluation.

The problems identified by the respondents were grouped into five subcategories (see Table 10-4). The problem most frequently mentioned was "selection and quantitative measurement of soft criteria." The source of this problem is probably found in the respondents' preference for tailoring instruments rather than using prefabricated ones. A second major problem was "difficulties of employing comparison groups." This is characteristic of practically all field research. The third most frequently mentioned problem is controlling for extraneous influences. Naturally, the experimental design selected determines which extraneous influences can and cannot be controlled. A design employing a comparison group is much more desirable, but much less prac-

*The questionnaire mailed had the dual objectives of determining practices followed and problems experienced in conducting evaluations of organization development efforts. The sample consisted of 269 practitioners in the field of organization development. Of the 127 replies, 101 were classified as usable responses from change facilitators.

Table 10–3
Summary Statistics of the Organizational Development Survey, Indicating Practices of Change Facilitators[18]

Practice	Number	Percentage
1. Frequency with which evaluations are performed		
a. Always	35	34.6
b. Frequently	41	40.6
c. Seldom	25	24.8
Total	101	100.0
2. Type of criteria		
a. Only soft	26	25.7
b. Only hard	1	1.0
c. Both hard and soft	74	73.3
Total	101	100.0
3. Methods of collecting measures of soft criteria		
a. Observation of and interviews with organization members	23	22.8
b. Administration of written instruments	2	2.0
c. Combination of *a* and *b*	71	70.2
d. No response	5	5.0
Total	101	100.0
4. Preference for:		
a. Existing written instruments	36	35.6
b. Tailored instruments for each organizational development effort	60	59.4
c. No response	5	5.0
Total	101	100.0

tical. A balance must be achieved between desirability and practicality.

Two other methodological problems are: (1) criterion deficiency which stems from evaluating efforts with work groups whose performance is difficult to measure (e.g., managerial workgroups), and (2) problems with time lags (i.e., the delay between organizational changes and accompanying changes in hard criteria).

These five problems constitute the methodological difficulties mentioned by the respondents. The only administrative problem was "difficulty in devoting time and financial resources. . . ." It was concluded that this administrative problem was largely responsible for the practices expressed in terms of (1) the frequency of evaluation, (2) type of criteria, (3) preferences for tailored instruments, (4) type of experimental design, and (5) the use of external and internal hard criteria. These practices are strongly influenced by the limitations of time and money imposed by organization decision makers; but these limitations are themselves a manifestation of reluctance that, perhaps, originates from two sources. One is the optimism that any organization development effort will result in an improvement in effectiveness. In other words, there appears to be a feeling of "since it has worked elsewhere, it will work here; why evaluate?" The second source is the pessimism arising from the

Table 10-4
Major Problems Encountered in Evaluating Operation Development Efforts as Identified by Change Facilitators[19]

Problem	Frequency
Methodological	
Selection and quantitative measurement of soft criteria	24
Difficulties of employing comparison groups	22
Controlling for extraneous influences	21
Criterion deficiency	4
Problems with time lags	3
Administrative	20
Difficulty in devoting time and financial resources to evaluation of organizational development efforts	
Miscellaneous	13
Communicating to managers what organizational development can and cannot do	
Conflict between adequate research design and helping a client	
Total	107

difficulties encountered in establishing internal validity. It seems some change facilitators share the feeling: Given all the methodological problems of conducting an evaluation, why waste the time and effort on evaluation?

EVALUATING THE CONSULTING SITUATION

In light of the extensive use of internal and external facilitators in renewal processes, it is valuable to examine a model and sources for evaluating the consulting situation. Figure 10-1 presents such a model, and the four interdependent elements are described in detail below.

Research and Evaluation Areas

Client/consultant relationship. This area related to the evaluation of the personal and professional relationships among client, client system, and the consultant. These relationships often have a major impact on the final outcome of the consulting process.

Evaluation of consulting/training events. This evaluation area covers significant con-

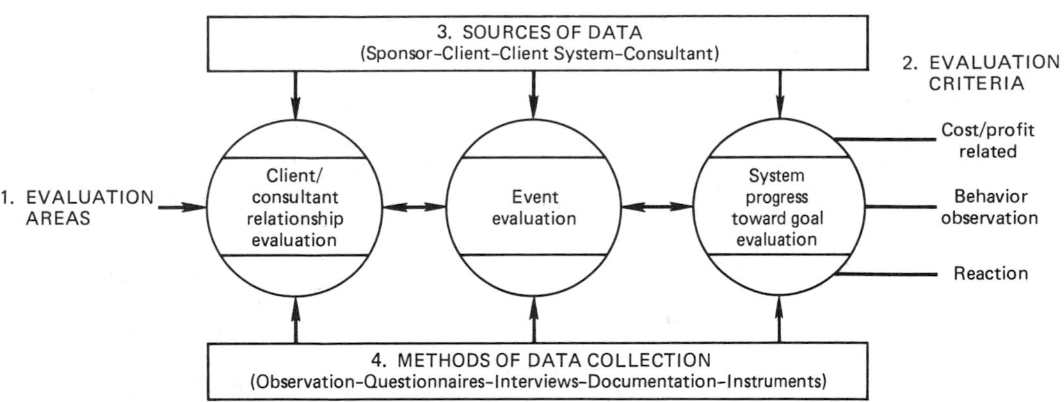

Figure 10-1 Evaluating the consulting process[20]

sulting interventions, such as survey-feedback meetings, skill training, conflict-resolution meetings, and other important milestone activities. Assessing the impact and contribution of each of these types of event on the overall project can provide important information, both for designing future projects with the client and for improving similar events that will take place in the current project.

Progress toward specific goals. This area relates to the client system's progress toward achievement of prestated goals and the contribution made by the consultation toward this progress. Evaluation of overall results helps to answer the client's question: "Was the money I invested in consultation returned, at least, by the results achieved?"

Research and Evaluation Criteria

Cost/profit-related. Some "hard-measure" criteria are developed to determine as directly as possible the effect of consultation on the achievement of specified results. Some examples of specified results related to cost/profit are:

Consulting time and expense (estimate versus actual)
Consulting-event outcomes that result in increased sales, decreased costs
Trend changes in safety record, grievances, turnover, absenteeism, theft

Within the cost-related evaluation criteria, three approaches to measurement can be considered:

1. Specific goal attainment by a specified time
2. Trend tracking versus a plan or estimated performance
3. Spot checks of performance versus hoped-for change (e.g., a downward trend has been reversed)

Behavior observation. These criteria call for documentation of significant changes observed in individual, group, or organizational behavior that resulted directly from the consulting process or from an event influenced by the consulting process. Some examples of observed behavior change are:

The client is much more relaxed and is functioning in a more assertive manner.
A change has occurred in the organization structure, simplifying lines of communication.
Event participants demonstrate that they can plan for and conduct problem-solving meetings.

Reaction. These criteria relate to the reactions of the client and the client system to the consulting process. They report feelings, attitudes, and points of view as these change over time. Some examples of reaction criteria measurements are:

The client's expressed feelings about the consulting relationship
The participants' evaluation of a training event
The reactions of the client system as expressed through a series of attitude surveys during the course of the consulting process

Sources of Data

Whatever type of evaluation is employed, there are four sources of data:

1. The *sponsor* is a person (or persons) who can significantly influence the consulting process and who has a strong interest in the initiation, progress, and final outcome of the consulting process. In some instances the sponsor is the client's supervisor. Many times (particularly when working at the top of the organization), the sponsor is the client (e.g., the president). The sponsor also could be a group of people, such as a city council, advisory board, executive committee, or board of directors.
2. The *client* is the person who makes the "go or no go" decision about events and

directions within the sphere of the project.

3. The *client system* is any person or group directly involved in, or affected by, the consulting project.
4. The *consultant* is the helper (or helpers) whose expertise has been contracted for by the client. The helper may be internal to the client system or external to it. There may also be a combination of internal and external helpers.

It is interesting to observe that questionnaires were most frequently cited as a *method* of data collection; but it should be reiterated that every consulting situation is a data collection process, and that action research was the most frequently mentioned purpose for data collection (see Table 10-5). However, there is some difficulty in attempting to look at action research as simply a research method or a technology of consultation, because the total change and renewal process is essentially a program of action research.

Action research was listed above as one of the approaches to data collection. In a sense, it is more the *way* the data are collected and used than it is a discrete method.

Table 10-5
Evaluation of Consultation

	Number of Responses[a] (n = 64)
Methods used	
Questionnaires	32
Interviews	16
Client reports	14
Efficiency reports	10
Discussions with client	9
Periodic testing	9
Inspections and visits	8
Consultant's ratings	8
Postevaluation immediately after consultation	7
Surveys of reactions to consultation	7
Surveys and operations audit	4
Follow-up testing (6 months to 1 year later)	1
	Number of Responses[b] (n = 75)
Purposes	
Action research on the problem	68
Evaluating the consulting process	55
Satisfaction of client	53
Improved skill or performance of consultant	38
Other[c]	23

[a] Eleven respondents did not list any methods, and thirteen listed four different methods.
[b] Fifty-four respondents indicated three or more purposes for evaluating consultation, and fourteen listed five purposes.
[c] The category "other" included such purposes as increased business income, change in organization relationships, value to organization, results in productivity and profits, program results, relationship to mission objectives, and supervisor's appraisal of value of consultation.

Action Research

If action research is considered a process—a continuous series of occurrences—it may be defined as:

> The process of systematically collecting research data about an ongoing system relative to some objective, goal, or need of that system; feeding these data back into the system; taking actions by altering selected variables within the system based both on the data and on hypotheses; and evaluating the results of actions by collecting more data.[21]

One of the important concepts involved in action research, therefore, is that the roles of researcher and subjects may change and reverse, the subjects becoming researchers and the researchers engaging in action steps. The model illustrated in Figure 10-2 shows a process that could involve an outside consultant or rely on individuals within the organization. The model also

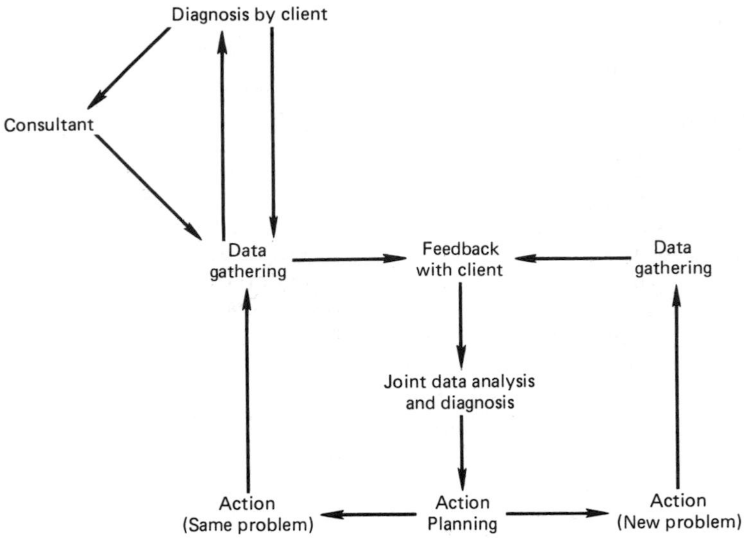

Figure 10-2 Action research in consultation

allows for the important point that action research is "sometimes treating the same problem through several cycles and sometimes moving to different problems in each cycle."[22]

When looking at action research as a process, we should include at least four major steps:

1. *Data collection may:* be preceded by a tentative diagnosis of a particular problem area (or may not be); utilize numerous instruments available for collecting data on task, environmental, or attitude climate; involve the training of clients in data collection skills and procedures.
2. *Feedback of data to client should be:* within a short period of time; worthwhile to the participants; specific enough to aid analysis and discussion; without value judgments; given in an open, supportive climate; relevant to desired goals of the client.
3. *Action planning should:* include in some aspect of the planning all the people who will be involved in the resulting actions; be relevant to the client's goals; be a close collaboration among the consultants, administrators, and participants involved; be feasible within the systems framework; be based on implications drawn from the data collected.
4. *Action should:* have built-in standards by which to measure progress and results; lead to further data collection and change, if evaluation shows it to be going in the wrong direction relative to the chosen goals; be continuously based on research, once the process has begun.

The use of action research began in the field of social science. Kurt Lewin is recognized as a major innovator and advocate of action research. He became aware that active practitioners were tackling problems without first having standards for measuring progress. He was concerned over efforts being expended without gaining the learning that results from knowing whether the action is heading in the right direction. Lewin felt that research (i.e., fact-finding and evaluation) could fill this gap and that action research was the link between the practitioners and the experimenters. Again the stress was on collaboration between the people of science and the people of action.

Action research lends itself to a diversity of goals, and the variations among practitioners are numerous. Lewin separated action research into the following two broad categories: (1) investigation of general laws, which contributes to theory and practice; and (2) diagnosis of a specific situation, which leads to the solution of pressing, practical problems. A consultant should be interested in both.

Action research can be broken down into four categories: (1) diagnostic (a researcher diagnoses and makes recommendations, which may or may not be put into effect); (2) participative; (3) empirical (requiring extensive records and posing several limitations); and (4) experimental. The experimental goal for action research is recognized as the most difficult but, like Lewin's investigation of general laws, it contributes to scientific knowledge and provides models of action research. The client's goal in action research is the one being emphasized in this discussion.

The basic four-step process may be altered or expanded to meet specific situations or projects. One weakness that may be ascribed to action research is that there is not a single and exclusive way to carry it out. On the other hand, this can also be considered a strength, especially in consultations. The variety of projects and areas in which action research has been utilized literally demands the flexibility that both the model and the process offer.

As with many other consulting technologies, action research may seem to be just common sense, to use parts of other technologies as its own, or to be but a part of another process. None of these can be considered weaknesses; if anything, they each add strength to the integrative functioning of the consulting process. Perhaps the difficulty in looking at action research as a separate consulting technology has been its similarity to the essence of consulting itself.

The essence of action research is the feedback to the parties so that it can be contemplated, planned, and implemented. Such feedback of the collected data might go to an individual, but it usually goes to a planning group, task force, operating units, or a total system. Most feedback processes include (1) establishing rapport, (2) establishing the context of the session, (3) establishing mutual expectations from the session, (4) encouraging the recipients to express his or her own perceptions, (5) describing and analyzing the data, (6) focusing on strategies for improving the performance, and (7) reaching a mutual agreement for follow-up activities.[23]

In establishing rapport, one should try to:

Create a socially relaxed atmosphere
Communicate an attitude of support and understanding
Draw out the receivers of the data by asking questions and encouraging him or her to talk freely

It helps to understand the context if the data provider is allowed to describe any particular situational factors that affected the data. A data-sharing session is the ideal time to identify all mutual expectations and to explore good and bad anticipations, to discuss performance strengths and weaknesses revealed by the data. The sharing session should provide both positive feedback to reinforce the participants and constructive feedback to help improve skills. It is important, too, to allow the participants time to think about what they want to describe and analyze, as they are encouraged to lay performance evaluations out on the table. Eventually, the discussion should come down to the analysis and its implications; and then there should follow real concentration on strategies for future improvement, generalizing about what specific skills or behaviors require improvement. In some cases, only minimal feedback is needed by receivers of the data in order for them to be aware of the need to change certain behaviors; in other cases, it may be necessary carefully to direct the group to conceptualize how the situation can be changed. The change facilitator should offer his or her own insights while helping the group to develop new strategies. Finally, the session should be ended with mutual agreement for follow-up activities.

It is generally better for the group to identify what its members feel can be changed, and therefrom to establish their own goals. If the members of the group make a commitment, they then assume the responsibility for improving performance; the change facilitator can only provide helpful support and guidance. During subsequent follow-up sessions, progress can be monitored and new targets for improvement highlighted.

Anyone who has experienced the role of providing feedback knows that the process has no simple formula. Feedback sessions are complex human interactions that require many different skills.

SEARCH FOR HARD CRITERIA[24]

All human system renewal efforts are marked by a constant need to "prove actual results." This pragmatic view leads to a requirement for continuing assessment of progress, and here a number of approaches can be involved. Most change interventions include training and group process events. It is often helpful to the client, the client system, and the change facilitator to evaluate these events in a procedure that allows learning reinforcement and permits needed corrective action to take place. Much has been written and said about event measurement, but only those methods that are used most frequently are discussed below.

In evaluation of the overall system's progress toward specific goals, it is usually difficult to isolate the effect of the change process.

The cost in time and money to isolate the change effort to show its contribution to the end result may be higher than the value returned to the client system. One way to evaluate progress is for the client and facilitator actually to develop a written contract with each other so that expectations as to goals, terms, and roles are spelled out for all concerned.

Experience indicates that it is a good practice to review the overall measurement possibilities with the client, and then to determine the level of sophistication necessary to achieve the measurements.

A cost–benefit criterion can be developed to determine as directly as possible the effect of change on the achievement of specific results. Some examples of cost/profit-related results are:

- Facilitator time and expense (estimated versus actual)
- Event outcomes resulting in such things as increased sales or decreased costs
- Trend changes in such things as safety record, grievances, turnover, absenteeism, and theft

Within the cost-related evaluation criteria, three approaches to measurement can be considered:

1. Specific goal attainment by a specified time
2. Trend tracking versus plan or estimated performance
3. Spot checks of performance versus hoped-for change

Here are two examples of evaluation criteria applied to client system progress toward goals (i.e., the attainment of a specific goal by a specified time):

Post-event measure

Use This Method When

1. There is no opportunity or little need for comparative pre- and post-measurement.
2. The trainer/consultant is really interested in the immediate reaction to the content and methodology of the event.
3. Consultant and client are satisfied with reaction data as the main basis for evaluation.
4. The event is not designed to result in a specific measurable behavior change. Rather, its purpose is to create awareness, internal motivation, inform, or educate.

Evaluation Criteria

1. *Behavior observation:* Consultant/trainer's observed behavior changes in participants during the event.
2. *Reaction data:* Post-event questionnaire is frequently used for these data.
3. *Post-event interviews:* These interviews are conducted with those individuals and groups involved by the consultant or client.

Pre-event and post-event measure

Use This Method When

1. The event is designed to help cause a specific observable behavior change in the participant.
2. The event is designed to increase the knowledge of the participants or understanding of a subject area, and it is worth measuring the degree of improvement.

Evaluation Criteria

1. *Behavior observation:* Documented observation of participant behavior by consultant and/or client before and after the consulting event.
2. *Reaction data:* Participant response to a pre-test and post-test, demonstrating an increase in knowledge and understanding, or expressing a change in attitude about an issue with which the event was concerned.
3. *Cost/profit-related:* Summaries of decisions made and problems solved as a result of the event, including cost–benefit estimate of each. This summary should be made by the participants and *they* should report it to the client or sponsor.

Pre-event and post-event measure with control group. This is a more sophisticated method of evaluating the payoff from consulting events in terms of performance on the job. The control group method can also be used for comparing post-event measurement between training group and control group. See the following list.

Use This Method When

1. It is possible to identify a control group that is experiencing similar variables as the training or consulted group (e.g., working conditions, supplies, tools, climatic conditions, terrain, etc.).
2. The control group and the training group each contain fifteen or more persons, so that the results are statistically reliable.
3. The consultant or client need good comparative performance data.
4. Identifying a control group will not create a "have" and "have-not" feeling in the client system.

Evaluation Criteria

1. *Behavior observation:* Documented observation of participant behavior by consultant and/or client before and after the consulting event.
2. *Reaction data:* Participant response to a pre-test and post-test, demonstrating an increase in knowledge and understanding, or expressing a change in attitude about an issue with which the event was concerned.
3. *Cost/profit-related:* Summaries of decisions made/problems solved as a result of the event, including cost/benefit estimate. This summary should be made by participants and *they* should report it to either the client or to the sponsor.

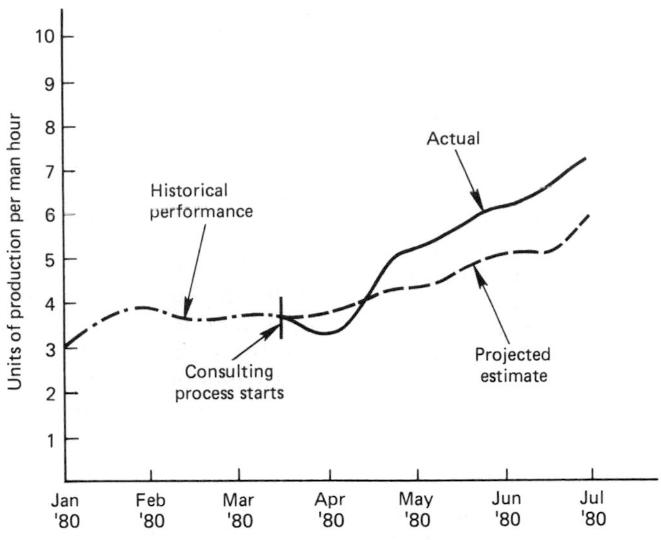

Figure 10-3 Trend Tracking versus Plan or Estimated Performance

1. To have a career development system in operation by January 1, 1981, at a cost not to exceed $50,000 for printing, training, and outside consultation
2. To attain an annualized production rate of fifteen tons per hour by reducing downtime required for maintenance through a concentrated, continuous training and problem-solving process for maintenance employees between January 1, 1981, and July 1, 1981

Figure 10-3 shows how historical performance and projected estimates may be used as a baseline performance standard against which to track client system performance over a period of time.

TREND TRACKING AND COMPARATIVE ANALYSIS WITH SIMILAR SYSTEMS

Let us examine a sophisticated comparative analysis of the safety performance of a large pulp paper mill as compared with the performance of other mills in the same area. The purpose of the analysis was to test the hypotheses that (1) the number of accidents in Mill A was significantly higher than that of the Mill B pulp and paper industry average prior to the intervention (see Table 10-6), and (2) that the number of accidents at Mill A decreased significantly after the intervention (see Table 10-7).*

In this example, the statistical analysis was accompanied by a documented account of significant planned and unplanned events which the consultant and client system considered as having an impact on the safety performance change.

*The null hypothesis was that the difference between the number of accidents in Mill A and the rest of the industry in general would remain relatively constant. A Mann-Whitney *U* test was used to test this hypothesis. This test combined the scores and ranked them in order of increasing size. The data were analyzed by comparing the preintervention data for Mill A and the Mill B industry average with the postintervention data for Mill A and the Mill B Industry average.

Table 10-6
Safety Before Intervention

	Mill A		Mill B	
1973 month	*Accident frequency*	*Rank*	*Accident frequency*	*Rank*
February	70.87	22	18.82	11
March	64.18	21	15.15	10
April	50.66	20	14.61	4
May	44.20	19	14.30	3
June	41.77	18	14.28	1
July	40.92	17	14.95	7
August	38.04	15	15.03	9
September	38.15	16	14.90	5
October	36.56	14	14.87	5
November	35.79	13	14.29	2
December	34.02	12	15.02	8
		$R_1 = 187$		$R_2 = 65$

Conclusions: The odds are 1:1000 that these results are due to chance. The accident rate was significantly higher for Mill A than for the Mill B industry average prior to the intervention.

Table 10-7
Safety After Intervention

	Mill A		Mill B	
1974 month	*Accident frequency*	*Rank*	*Accident frequency*	*Rank*
February	30.30	17	15.45	10
March	10.07	8	12.65	9
April	9.39	7	15.55	11
May	8.94	6	16.08	13
June	7.28	3	15.96	12
July	7.76	4	17.05	14
August	8.03	5	17.54	15
September	6.82	1	18.13	16
October	7.19	2	—	—
		$R_1 = 53$		$R_2 = 100$

Conclusions: The odds are 1:100 that these results are due to chance. The accident frequency is significantly lower for Mill A than for Mill B industry average after the intervention.

BEHAVIORAL OBSERVATIONS

Observable change in individual and organizational behavior constituted another set of criteria used to measure the effectiveness of the intervention. The observations reported here can be related directly to various intervention events, such as survey-feedback decision/action meetings, team development sessions, personal consultation, and productivity and effectiveness studies. In many instances, the intervention/events contributing directly to the observed change are themselves direct results of a specific intervention activity. An actual example of an observation measurement made after the process was completed is shown in Table 10-8; the observation data and conclusions were jointly developed by the internal consultant and the client.

It is always feasible to include reactions by the client and client system. Some examples of such reaction criteria are:

- Client's expressed feelings about the consulting relationship
- Participants' evaluation of a training event
- Client system's reaction as expressed through a series of attitude surveys during the course of the consulting process

As in the other evaluation criteria methods, there are multiple levels of sophistication:

- Sponsor/client reaction. The sponsor and/or client are invited to make spot-check observations of the project and record their reactions in writing.
- Client system reaction. This can be obtained through spot-check interviews by the client or an evaluation consultant. Client

Table 10-8
Example of Observed Behavioral Changes After Intervention

Observed Behavior Change	Intervention/Events Contributing to Change	Transferable Learnings
Before March 5, 1973, mill supervisors filed for certification to unionize After November 1, 1974, there was no threat of supervisors unionizing	Corrected inequities in salaries and compensation for overtime worked during construction and startup phases Conducted objective salary reviews Disclosed salary ranges Instituted performance bonus plan Team-building meetings to socialize front-line supervisors into management Heavy involvement of supervisors in labor relations strategy and procedures	Develop controllable SOPs and conduct performance reviews/reward reviews against these standards versus giving across-the-board "merit" increases Do not reward extra work with trips if dollars is the expectation; or at least give a choice Do not allow unrewarded overtime to pile up Overstaff with supervisors during startup to reduce fatigue and provide adequate training time Be absolutely open about salary administration plan and details so as not to create suspicion and distrust

> system reaction can also be determined through the multiple application of attitude questionnaires. They can range from homemade one-pagers to highly sophisticated and validated computerized attitude surveys.

The use of an employee survey can show indicators of change related to various work climate dimensions and issues. The data can be summarized on a graph and used as a diagnostic instrument during the consulting process. By collecting data from the client system at the beginning of the consulting process, at six months after the start, and again at eighteen months after the start, the consultant and client can view attitude trend changes that are consistent with behavior observation and cost/profit-related changes (see Figure 10-4).

In an age and time when people and

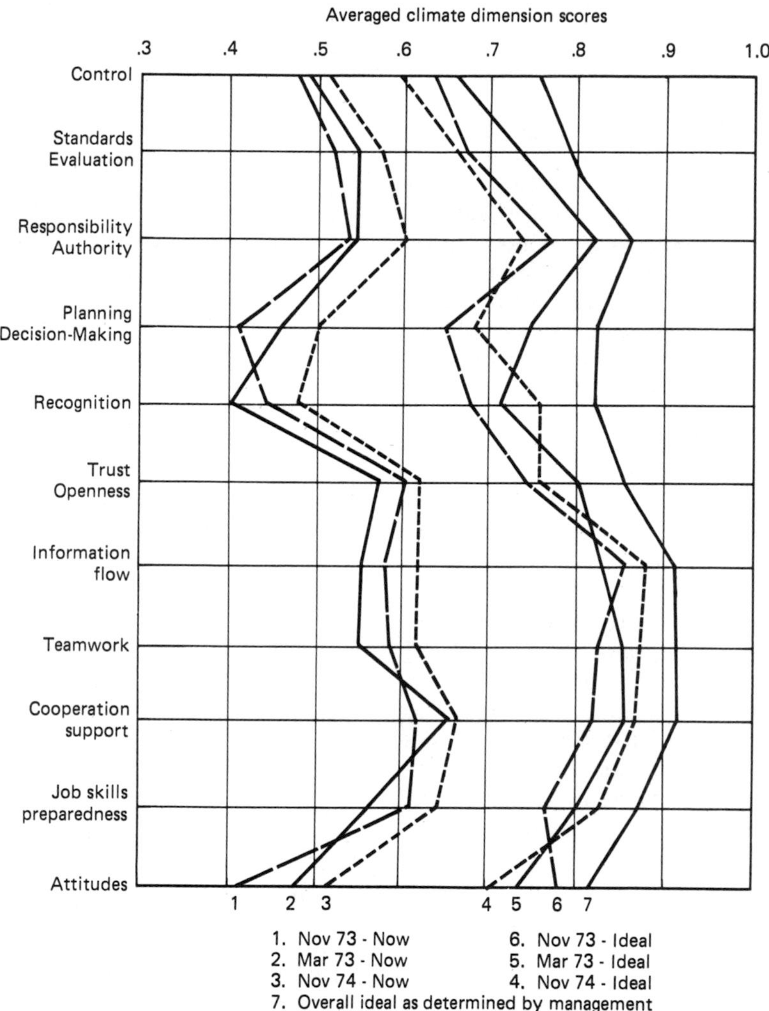

Figure 10-4 Averaged Climate Dimension Scores

management are results- and "bottom-line"-oriented, it is important to be able to measure the effects of change efforts. As proven with the practice of management by objectives, a stated and measurable objective is a force for probable achievement. Similarly, a human system that sees the results of renewal efforts will be reinforced to continue the process.

SUMMARY

The assessment of the results of learning or change experiences is a matter of concern to managers, educators, trainers, and professional groups interested in improving organizational productivity or in providing educational and developmental experiences for individuals, groups, and organizations. Two aspects must be considered in any meaningful data collection and evaluation. The first of these is the effect of learning or change experience on the individuals involved. This can be demonstrated to some degree by the use of before-and-after measurements that illustrate differences in responses and results. The second is the assessment of the effectiveness of the change experience when applied to the system's maturation, an evaluation that presents more complicated problems.

Ways to move from research to action-taking should involve those to be changed in the data collection, analysis, and plans for change. It is also valuable to be able to evaluate the effects of the renewal process in order that review and responsibility have a chance to be enacted. Another asset is the value of seeing progress by the individual, group, or organization involved in the renewal.

QUESTIONS

1. What data collection methods have you found most helpful? Why?
2. Why do people resist data collection?
3. How should interviews be conducted? Under what conditions?
4. When should action research be used as a data-based intervention? Why?
5. How can management be encouraged to support evaluation of development programs?
6. What is meant by "hard data?" Is the collection of such data always worth the cost and effort?
7. In your experience, what ways has management used to evaluate:
   a. the use of a new management technology?
   b. the value of a structural or product change?
   c. the value of their appraisal system?
   d. the value of their management development program?
   e. the organization's community relations?

   Why were different methods used? Why were they not used?

NOTES

[1]Harold M. Rush, *Organization Development: A Reconnaissance* (Report No. 605; New York: The Conference Board, Inc., 1973), pp. 6–7.

[2]Wendell L. French and Cecil H. Bell, Jr., *Organizational Development: Behavioral Science Interventions for Organization Improvement* (Englewood Cliffs, N.J.: Prentice-Hall, Inc., 1973), pp. 56–57. Hereafter cited as French and Bell.

[3]Charles Mortenson, *Association Evaluation: Guide for Measuring Organization Performance* (Washington, D.C.: American Society of Association Executives, 1975), p. 8.

[4]Ibid., p. 7.

[5]Ibid., p. 8.

[6]Alfred J. Marrow, *The Practical Theorist: The Life and Work of Kurt Lewin* (New York: Basic Books, Inc., 1969), p. 230.

[7]David A. Nadler, *Feedback and Organization Development: Using Data-based Methods* (Reading, Mass.: Addison-Wesley Publishing Company, Inc., 1977), p. 7. Hereafter cited as Nadler. Copyright © 1977 by Addison-Wesley Publishing Company, Inc.; reprinted with permission of Addison-Wesley Publishing Company, Inc.

[8]Marvin R. Weisbord, "Organizational Diagnosis: Six Places to Look for Trouble with or without a Theory," *Group Organization Studies: The International Journal For Group Facilitators,* Vol. 1, No. 4, 1976, 435.

[9]Nadler, p. 119. Copyright © 1977 by Addison-Wesley Publishing Company, Inc.; reprinted with permission of Addison-Wesley Publishing Company, Inc.

[10]Adapted from an unpublished paper by John Creighton, *The Sensing Interview as a Tool in Organizational Diagnosis for Organization Development* (Washington, D.C.: The George Washington University, December 1975).

[11]John E. Jones, "The Sensing Interview," *1973 Annual for Group Facilitators* (Iowa City, Iowa: University Associates, Inc., 1973), p. 28.

[12]Chris Argyris, *Intervention Theory and Method: A Behavioral Science View* (Reading, Mass.: Addison-Wesley Publishing Company, Inc., 1970), pp. 296–297.

[13]Adapted from Gordon Lippitt and Ronald Lippitt, *The Consulting Process in Action* (La Jolla, Calif.: University Associates, Inc., 1978), Chap. 6.

[14]Leon Festinger, *Research Methods in the Behavioral Sciences* (Hinsdale, Ill. The Dryden Press, Inc., 1953), p. 137.

[15]Kurt Lewin, "Research Center for Group Dynamics," *Sociometry,* Vol. 8, No. 2, 1945, 9.

[16]Robert Bidwell and Gordon Lippitt, *A Study of Application of Research to Training Activities* (research report; Washington, D.C.: The George Washington University, 1971), p. 6.

[17]Achilles A. Amrenakis, *Guidelines for Evaluating Organizational Development Efforts with Profit-oriented Organizations* (unpublished dissertation; State College, Miss.: Mississippi State University, 1973), p. 86.

[18]Ibid., p. 136.

[19]Ibid., p. 148.

[20]Adapted from Donald Swartz and Gordon Lippitt, "Evaluating the Consulting Process," *Journal of European Training,* Vol. 4, No. 5, 1975, 310.

[21]French and Bell, pp. 84–85.

[22]Ibid., p. 86.

[23]Adapted from an unpublished paper by Jeanne Freeman, *Evaluating Instructors: Systemizing the Training Management Process* (New York: Training World Conference, December 1979).

[24]Adapted from Gordon Lippitt, Betty J. Chakiris, and Donald Swartz (eds.), *Consulting Skills Notebook* (Washington, D.C.: Organization Renewal, Inc., 1979), pp. 4–11.

II

renewal as a training and development process

Intelligent behavior requires an apprenticeship; it is not the expression of ready-made inborn capacity, it is the outcome of learning. And it is not every kind of learning that avails; it must be learning that includes some perception of the relation of things.

Sir J. Arthur Thompson, 1861–1933

Human systems renewal is not merely a matter of good intentions or the identification of new objectives. It involves the improved ability of persons in the organization to *learn* how to solve problems. Some people feel that knowing how to confront problems effectively is an inherited part of human nature. Considerable research, to the contrary, indicates that we must learn skills of problem solving. Providing skills for persons before they act is the principal premise of Kurt Lewin's concept of research, training, and action. Before people take action they have to be prepared and competent.

Initiators of renewal face the fact that the learning of many persons is out of date. The knowledge explosion has antiquated many of our ideas about human behavior, communication, management, leadership, and organizational functioning. To secure support for new structures, processes, and action it will be necessary for most adults to relearn so as to substitute new ideas, concepts, and realities for the outmoded knowledge, skills, and attitudes they now possess.

Learning opportunities are usually confronted with mixed feelings of wanting to learn and, at the same time, resisting learning. People want to learn for a great variety of reasons. Learning satisfies curiosity, provides greater personal power, and gives one a sense of achievement. On the other hand, learning may be uncomfortable. It says that the job of personal development is not finished. Cherished and comfortable assumptions and ways of doing things must be questioned. We are obliged to open ourselves to some anxiety and stress as we abandon earlier pointers and fumble in ambiguity toward new attitudes, new insights, and new abilities.

Another complexity in the learning process is that many of us see learning as a passive process in the classic tradition. Because much of our academic and early life experience has led us to believe that we learn from listening to authorities, there is frequently a need to learn how to learn from real life experience.

In developing individuals and groups, we need to focus on the reality that learning is a continuous and life-long process, that it is complex, and that learning can take place in many ways through a variety of methods and circumstances. The term "life-long learning" is used to convey the idea that the search for human fulfillment is an unending search. A search for what? The six potentials for human fulfillment (physical, emotional, social, intellectual, aesthetic, and spiritual) were identified earlier.[1] Potential means moving to an improved state of competency—from being unconsciously incompetent, to consciously incompetent, to consciously competent, and, by maintaining skills, soon to be unconsciously competent.

It is suggested that each human system needs intentionally to strive to achieve these six potentials that give meaning to life. "Intentionally" means both the wish and the will to develop to full potential:

> Learning is not the accumulation of scraps of knowledge. It is a growth where every act of knowledge develops the learner, thus making him capable of even more complex objectives—and the object growth in complexity parallels the subjective growth in capacity.[2]

Life-long learning can be the way in which human systems gain control over the process of becoming mature, competent, and effective. As Leland Bradford has observed:

> The learning process should endeavor to help the learner learn how to learn more effectively so that more of his experiences can lead toward learning and change. . . . A basic purpose of education in all learning situations is first to help the individual learner open himself up for learning by being able to bring his problems and needs for learning to the surface and to listen and accept relevant reactions about his problems and behavior. A second purpose is to help the learner gain methods of experimenting, analyzing, and utilizing experiences and knowledge resulting from daily problemsolving.[3]

Attempts are often made to distinguish between training and education. Some educators feel that training directors and others similarly involved in adult learning activities are not engaged in education. Most such persons believe they are. Educators tend to make this distinction: training is narrow in scope and involves only learning that is directly related to job performance, whereas education is concerned with the total human being and insights into, and understanding of, the entire world. These attempts to distinguish between training and education seem petty inasmuch as both are concerned with the process of human learning.

Berelson and Steiner define learning as "changes in behavior that result from previous behavior in similar situations." Usually, but by no means always, behavior also becomes demonstrably more effective and more adaptive after the exercise than it was before. In the broadest terms, then, learning refers to the effects of experience on subsequent behavior.[4] From this we can deduce that for the renewal planner, learning would seem to imply:

- Knowing something intellectually or conceptually that one never knew before
- Being able to do something one could not do before—a behavior or skill
- Combining two knowns into a new understanding of a skill, piece of knowledge, concept, or behavior
- Being able to use or apply a new combination of skills, knowledge, concept, or behavior
- Being able to understand and apply that which one knows—either skill, knowledge, or behavior

Since those interested in human systems renewal are concerned with learning, it follows that they should be concerned with learning concepts. Many training and development people talk rather glibly about the learning theory that underlies their endeavors, but most of them do not have a good understanding of learning theories and their application to training and development efforts. Most such efforts in the renewal process are problem solving in nature:

Desired outcomes for the learning experience. They can range from complex comprehension of organizational dynamics to simple manual skills. Managers who underwrite educational programs normally stipulate entirely different sets of training outcomes. These usually are identified as reduction of costs, increased productivity, improved morale, and a corps of competent promotional replacements. Sometimes these things are confused by training directors as outcomes of training that are affected by learning practice.

Site for learning. Persons involved in planning learning experiences are concerned whether learning occurs best on the job, in a classroom, on or off organizational premises; or at a university or other formal site, cultural island, or at home.

Learning methods. These are seen as being on a continuum from casual reading to intense personal involvement in personal-relationship laboratories.

Grouping for learning. Grouping of learners can involve all combinations from individuals and dyads to audiences.

As learning planners deal with and manipulate the variables listed above, they tend to confuse them with learning theory. For example, a training director will say: "My theory of learning is that employees learn best when placed in small discussion groups at a training site removed from the plant." What is not clear to most training directors is that the variables identified above result in a myriad of devices and techniques derived from, and most effectively utilized by, a given learning theory. In and of themselves they are not learning theory.[5]

Learning theory has been confused with the variables of site or grouping, and use of the terms "learning theory" and "learning theory corollaries or principles" can be misleading. Usually, the learning theory can be stated very broadly; for example: "Learning occurs when a stimulus is associated with a response." From this generalization about how learning occurs, a number of specific laws of learning are derived: for example, "Repetition of a response strengthens its connection with a stimulus." Thus, the statement, "problems are difficult to solve when they require the use of the familiar in an unfamiliar way" is a corollary of the behaviorist learning theory school. It is corollaries such as this that most often serve as application guides.

Those concerned with renewal sometimes incorporate one or more corollaries or applications into a learning design. Sometimes the design applications have been borrowed from several learning theories and so would appear to be inconsistent. This may be quite valid, however, because the content and training objectives for a given training program may include both skill and conceptual training. Each of these kinds of training would tend to borrow techniques from different learning theories.

LEARNING THEORIES

Another discouraging aspect of examining learning theory is being able to discuss the subject in laymen's terms. Learning theories are to be found in courses in educational psychology and require a strong background in psychology, research, and statistics to be understood. Some of the differences seem to be exceedingly subtle. It is discouraging to attempt to understand either the individual theories or the difference between the schools embracing several theories. The first thing that strikes home is that most of the research on learning theory has been accomplished by using animals for subjects. Several authors comment that at least 95% of learning research has been accomplished on data received from experiments with rats, chickens, pigeons, monkeys, dogs, and cats. It is also interesting to note that research on animals inevitably occurs under one or both of two conditions: the animal is either very hungry or is sex-deprived. It may very well be that the designers of training programs have been overlooking some excellent motivational factors.

Animal research accepted, two other problems present themselves. First, it is not easy to differentiate the general schools of learning theory. Second, it is even harder to distinguish among individual learning theories within the general schools. This difficulty is compounded because of the technical language and equations used to express the theories. Usually, aspects of the theories are stated mathematically and then expressed in prose. Neither is done in a way that a practitioner can easily comprehend. He or she is then faced with the problem of trying to determine what the technical language expresses and to restate it in words understood. It may be helpful, therefore, to examine briefly the six general schools in which learning theories seem to fall.

The first school is known as the *behaviorist school.* Primarily, these theories hold that learning results from the reward or punishment that follows a response to a stimulus. These are the so-called S-R theories.

E. L. Thorndike was one of the early researchers into learning and, generally, he held that learning was a trial-and-error process. When faced with the need to respond appropriately to a stimulus, the learner tries any and all of his or her response patterns. If by chance one works, then that one tends to be repeated and the others neglected. From his research he developed certain laws to further explain the learning process—for example, the law of effect: if a connection between a stimulus and response is satisfying to the organism, its strength is increased; if unsatisfying, its strength is reduced.

Clark Hull introduced a new concept: stimulus and response were not the only things to be considered in learning—the organism itself could not be overlooked. The response to a stimulus must take into account the organism and what it is thinking, needing, and feeling at the moment. We now had the S-O-R concept.

B. F. Skinner is usually identified with the behaviorist school. Rather than construct a theory of learning, he seems to believe that by observation and objective reporting we can discover how organisms learn without the need of a construct to explain the process. He depends heavily upon what is called operant conditioning. He makes a distinction between "respondent" and "operant" behavior. Respondent behavior is that behavior caused by a known stimulus; operant behavior is that behavior for which we cannot see or identify a stimulus, although one may, and probably does, exist. If we can anticipate evidence of operant behavior, we can provide the occasion for the behavior by introducing the stimulus—but the stimulus does not necessarily evoke the behavior. Thus, the emphasis in learning is on correlating a response with reinforcement. This is at the heart of programmed instruction—a correct response is reinforced and reworded.

The second grouping is the *gestalt school.* These theorists believe that learning is not a simple matter of stimulus and response. They hold that learning is cognitive and involves the whole personality. To them, learning is infinitely more complex than the S-R theories would indicate. For example, they note that learning may occur simply by thinking about a problem. Kurt Lewin, Wolfgang Köhler, E. C. Tolman, and Max Wertheimer are typical adherents to this school. They reject the theory that learning occurs by building up, bit by bit, established S-R connections. They look at the phenomenon of insight, long-coming or instantaneous. To them, the whole is more than the sum of the parts:

> Central in Gestalt theory is the Law of Prägnanz which indicates the direction of events. According to this law, the psychological organization of the individual tends to move always in one direction, always toward the good Gestalt, an organization of the whole which is regular, simple, and stable.[6]

The Law of Prägnanz is another law of equilibrium.[7] Accordingly, the learning process might be presented as follows. The individual is in a state of equilibrium, of "good" Gestalt. He or she is confronted by a learning situation. Tensions develop and disequilibrium results. The individual thus moves away from equilibrium but at the same time strives to move back to equilibrium. To assist this move back to the regular, simple, stable state, the learning situation should be structured so as to possess good organization (e.g., simple parts should be presented first; these should lead in an orderly fashion to more difficult parts).

A third school is the *Freudian school.* This is a difficult school to encapsulate:

> It is no simple task to extract a theory of learning from Freud's writings, for while he was interested in individual development and the kind of reeducation that goes on in psychotherapy, the problems whose answers he tried to formulate were not those with which theorists in the field of learning have been chiefly concerned. Psychoanalytic theory is too complex and, at least at the present time, too little formalized for it to be presented as a set of propositions subject to experimental testing.[8]

A fourth school is that of the *functionalists.* These seem to take parts of all the theories and view learning as a very complex phenomenon that is not explained by either the gestalt or the behavioral theories. Some of the leaders in this school are John Dewey, J. R. Angell, and R. S. Woodworth. These men borrow from all the other schools and are sometimes referred to as "middle of the roaders."

A fifth so-called school is comprised of those who subscribe to *mathematical models.* To these researchers, learning theories must be stated in mathematical form. Some of these proponents come from different schools of learning theory but tend to focus on mathematical models, such as the feedback model, information theory model, gaming model, differential calculus model, stochastic model, and statistical association model. Rather than representing a cohesive theory of their own, they express the research findings of other theorists in mathematical terms.

LEARNING RHYTHMS

Before going on to examine the advantages and disadvantages of certain approaches to the design of training and development processes for renewal, I would like to discuss briefly a speculative theory about learning that makes particularly good sense to me—it has to do with something called *learning rhythms.*[9] Those of us who are consultants, trainers, teachers, professors, or managers know the occasional joys that come to us when students, employees, or clients successfully cope with a problem because of the application of a module presented during a training program. Or they did something unusually creative because of ideas innovated after an experience in a class, or improved their group productivity as a result of applying methods practiced in a team-building experience we had conducted.

Or a supervisor sees some on-the-job applications as a result of on-the-job coaching. Such occurrences may be the exception and not the norm. And although these rare and uplifting experiences do take place, they occur in a variety of ways, usually many weeks after the consultation, class, coaching, or training event that stimulated them.

What was different about that particular experience for that individual, group, or organization? Is it the participant, the leader, the phase of the moon, the context, or just an accident? It may be the culmination of several factors that have an effect upon learning. When basic aspects of a potential learning situation are in juxtaposition, a person will have an "aha!" experience, one that will provide the insight, creative impulse, or courage to change that surpasses a typical learning experience. This is a variation of Maslow's "peak experience." Such a learning experience involves the convergence of the right mix of factors to create the peak learning experience.[10]

In some ways, learning rhythms as derived from the concept of biorhythm theory, in which our physical, emotional and intellectual capabilities fluctuate in regular 23-, 28-, and 33-day cycles, respectively.[11] All three cycles start on your date of birth. "Critical" days are at the start, middle, and end of each cycle. At these times each faculty is the least reliable and may be dangerous to the individual. During the first half of each cycle one will supposedly find "positive days" when performance should be at its peak. The second half, however, is "negative" and performance will be below average. If all these cycles peak on the same day, one might expect outstanding performance. On the contrary, if one cycle is at a low point, it is a "critical day." Two lows mean a "double-critical day." If all three are critical on the same day—watch out!

This concept is not new. The idea was developed by German psychoanalyst Wilhelm Fliess in *Der Ablauf des Lebens* (The Course of Life), published in 1906. Since then it has been dormant until recent applications in the 1960s and 1970s in Japan, Britain, Canada, Russia, and the United States. Most of the studies have related to transportation workers,[12] pilots, and accident victims, and have examined the consequences of the "low" rather than "high" days of the cycle. However, a few studies on outstanding athletic performance did not confirm that such performance occurred at the time of three peak rhythm periods.

In the same manner that peak days are determined by the juxtaposition of these biorhythms, this theory of the convergence of learning rhythms (see Figure 11-1) states that under optimal conditions such interaction will create an infrequent peak learning experience (PLE). The chances for a PLE can be increased, but probably cannot be controlled or predicted. Those of us who teach, lecture, consult, train, and create development opportunities realize that learning is an "aha!" experience that may involve letting go, forgetting, remembering, analyzing, synthesizing, or just "making sense" out of many patterns of stimuli.

The Mind Has Rhythms

Jean Houston tells us that the mind has rhythms during conscious and unconscious periods.[13] Learning must take into account these rhythms to avoid being static, steady, nonrelevant, and unresponsive to the inner and outer spaces of the person.

Carol Tice supports this theory in her

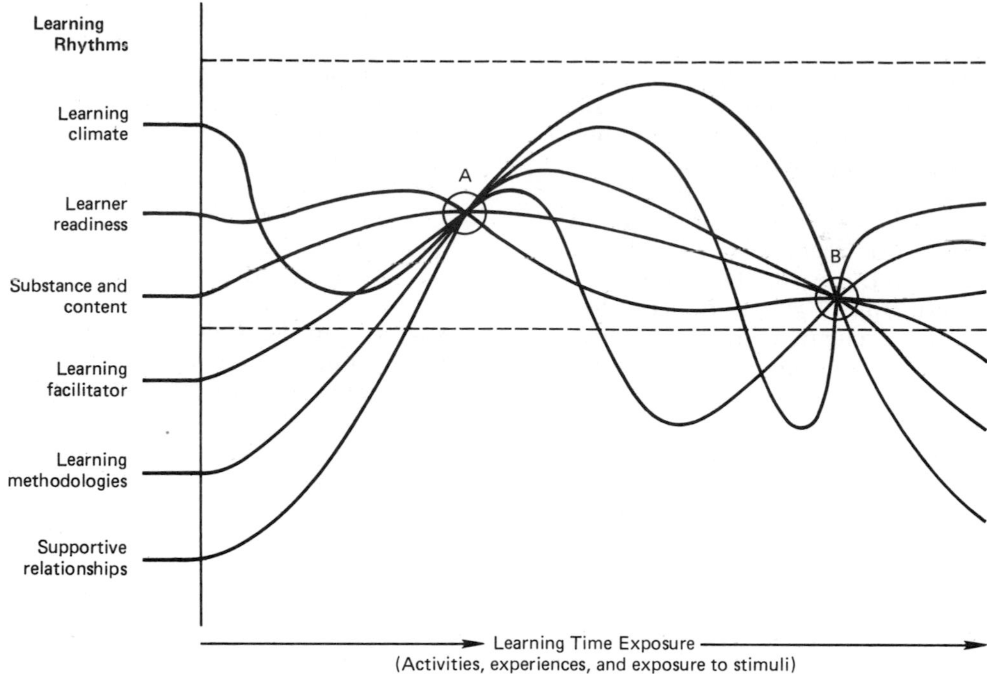

Figure 11-1 Learning rhythms in action

statement that "rhythms deeper than those of hand and mind and feet as the generations together, treasuring each other's knowledge and mystery, join the dance of new learning and new life."[14]

In Figure 11-1, two situations are illustrated—where the six learning rhythms intersect to provide a PLE. At intersection A, the supporting relationship rhythm, being strong and in concert with appropriate methodologies, relevant learner readiness, and other rhythms, create a PLE. At intersection B, an interaction again takes place with the learning facilitator and substance being relevant along with the other four rhythms to create a PLE.

One conception in this theory of convergence is that each rhythm needs to have optimal attention or intensity to enhance the chance of intersection. If too little attention is given to a particular learning rhythm, it will not facilitate PLE convergence. In a similar manner, if a learning rhythm is stressed too much or given attention out of proportion, it will lessen the chance of convergence (see Figure 11-2).

It would appear that if any one learning rhythm is neglected or overlooked, the resultant chances for intersecting other rhythms (A–B in Figure 11-3) will be low. On the other hand, if too much emphasis is put on one rhythm, it can also result in a low chance for intersection leading to PLE. This can be observed when so much attention is put on an audiovisual show that the medium gets in the way of the learning-rhythm intersection and a resultant PLE.

The creative challenge to educators, teachers, consultants, managers, trainers, and human resource developers is to attempt the orchestration of those learning rhythms they can influence so as to op-

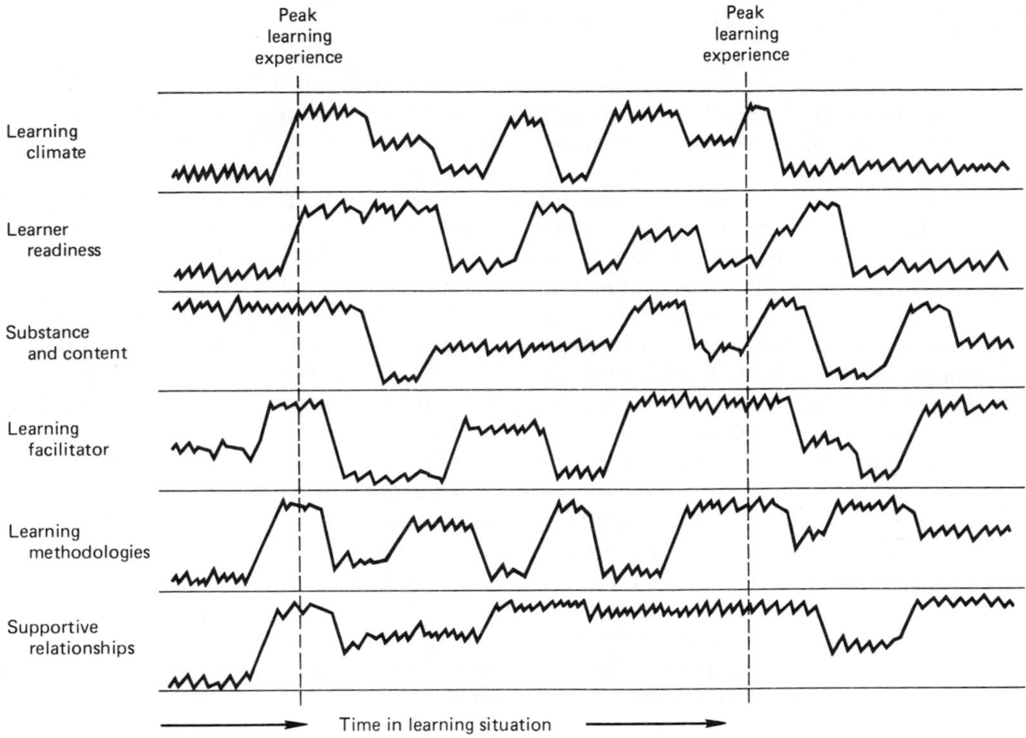

Figure 11-2 Learning rhythms intensity waves for congruence for PLE opportunities

timize the chances of convergence taking place for PLE. A description of each of the learning rhythms—and the effects of too little or too much emphasis—hopefully should clarify this aspect of the theory.

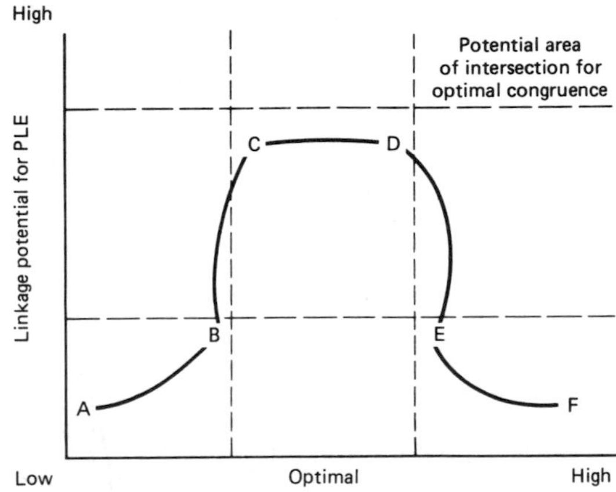

Figure 11-3* Intensity level of a learning rhythm and chance of intersection with other learning rhythms

*The author has repeated the same model as each of the six rhythms are discussed so as to reinforce the concept that the optimal level is desired for each rhythm to increase the intersection potential with the other rhythms so as to achieve a PLE.

Learning Climate Rhythm

This is an essential rhythm that is well known to those in the "helping" professions. The climate should be one in which the learner finds challenge, excitement, some stress, and respect for the potential for learning. A climate includes physical, psychological, and sociological elements of the learning space. We have all experienced the importance of the total surroundings in which a learning experience takes place.

It is interesting to note that the work of Dr. Georgi Lozanov[15] in Bulgaria in *suggestology* is now reaching the United States, and covers the twenty years of his work in both education and medicine. Suggestology, building on the right- and left-brain theories, uses relaxation, music, and temperature to allow the brain's left analytical and logical hemisphere to become a bit more passive, and to "turn on" the intuitive and emotional right half. Both halves are needed for learning. Lozanov points out that you must believe that you can learn. A supportive climate is essential (see Figure 11-4).

The optimal climate (C–D) is possible in a large lecture room or in a one-to-one dialogue. The key aspect of intersection potential is to give proper consideration to the learning climate. It can be influenced by those who try to help others discover themselves as well as by new insights.

Learner Readiness Rhythms

Each learner has goals. Whether an individual, group, or larger system, each will need to be dissatisfied with the status quo to optimize the readiness rhythms. Goal orientation is the basic need of the organism to make a PLE possible. The nature of the learner's readiness for entry into the learning experience is well annotated in research. The learner's "state of readiness" is a product of prior experience, life stage, expectancies, and existential state of the organism at the time of learning.

The PLE is basically an unique experience for that human system at that particular moment. It is a prerequisite for renewal that involves coping, living, loving, giving, and maturing.[16]

Figure 11-5 depicts the characteristics of an optimal learner readiness curve for encouraging intersection potential. All these factors relate to learner readiness, particularly the individual, group, or organization that is in a state of transition. We have been brought to an awareness that the lives of adults as well as children go through phases that create cornerstone life transitions. These periods of transition create anxiety, stress, challenge, coping needs, and the search process.

During such periods of role, life, or style transition, learner readiness rhythm is in an optimal state for many people. The transition provides a "force" for search for learning. Even in complex human systems,

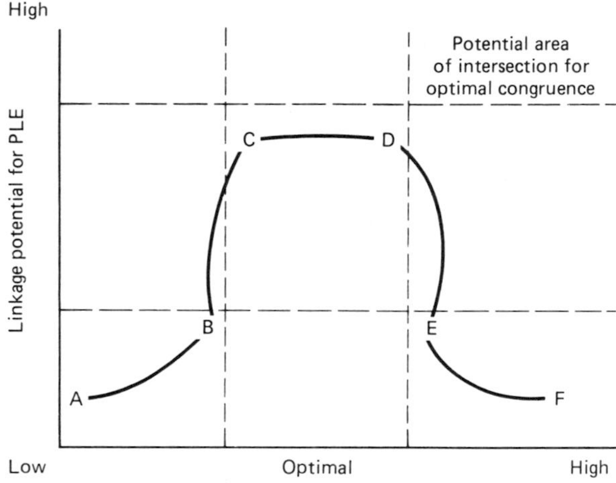

Figure 11-4 Intensity level of learning climate as it relates to intersection potential for PLE

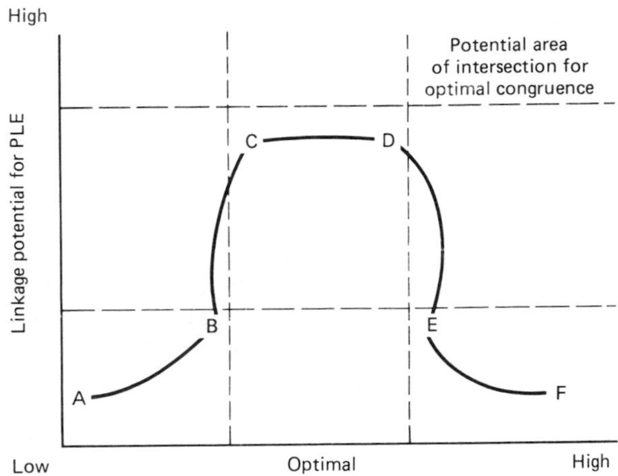

Figure 11-5 Intensity level of learner readiness as it relates to intersection potential for PLE

such as groups and organizations, learning and change will be affected by the stage of growth.

At the organizational level there are stages of potential growth through the birth, survival, stability, reputation, uniqueness, and maturity stages of organization life. At each stage the ability to mature to the next stage will be heightened if the system is aware of its potential for growth to the next stage and the need for renewal manifests itself. Organization renewal interventions are most valuable at these times of transition. In a similar manner, when an organization is experiencing a "transition," such as a merger, acquisition, strike, or decentralization, it will experience a need for learning "how" to get back into equilibrium.[17] Such conditions create a greater readiness for change and learning.

If learners (micro or macro) are forced into learning and do not really know "why" they are involved in the learning or change effort—chances of a PLE occurring are doomed to failure. Learning must be needed, whether voluntary or forced, so that it is perceived as relevant and helpful to the challenge and "pain" of transition. Such stress and anxiety will actually increase the probability of a PLE occurring.

Substance and Content Rhythm

This rhythm is related to the relevance and flow of the message received by the learner. A lecture given on a subject of great concern to the learner may be very timely. A presentation on the "meaning of death" may strike a responsive chord the day after a historical figure or loved one has died. An older employee facing the transition to retirement may be "ready" for information on hobbies, social security, and volunteer services. A youth or adult groping for the meaning of life may be profoundly influenced by the presentation of a messianic idea. The learner is usually goal- and problem-solving-oriented.

David Kolb presents a four-stage cycle of learning.[18] Here immediate experience becomes the basis for observation and reflection; these observations become assimilated into the form of abstract concepts and cognition that serve as guides to testing the implications of those concepts in new situations. The substance/content needs to have both practical meaning to the learner—as well as abstract—so as to provide guidelines for further experiences and reflective internalization.

The second dimension is the "flow" of substance to the learner's past experiences. Each learner comes to a new learning experience with a history of prior development and learning. The degree of prior success or failure will have an effect on the readiness to "hear" the new substance/content.

This concept of flow is related to Kurt Lewin's definition of behavior as a function of the person and environment.[19] This definition conceives of a dynamic unbroken field where behavior is a continuous process. It never stops but is always in flux. This is true in both the conscious and unconscious, as pointed out by Henri Bergson's concept of durée (duration), which he defines in terms of past-future relationship and a moving present.[20] The emphasis is on continuous process. The substance or content of the learning experience needs to be relevant to the moment and added to the flow of experience of the learner.

In Figure 11-6 are depicted some of the characteristics of low, optimal, and high intensity of this rhythm with related chance for convergence.

Learning Facilitator Rhythm

A fourth factor in the mix of learning rhythms is the learning facilitator. Whether this is a manager, counselor, trainer, or organization development professional, that person is a vital stimulus for learning. Although this role is essential, it is not the only force for PLE. The role of the learning facilitator is to support the organizing of the learner's experience and to help expand the learner's experience. The learning facilitator can contribute:[21]

- To help identify and relate to real problems and concerns of the learner
- To help set a climate related to the learner's readiness
- To create conditions for making experiences (past and present) explicit
- To clarify goals and their relevance from the facilitator's point of view and to attempt to relate to the learner's goals
- To put his or her own experience in perspective as it relates to the learner's experience

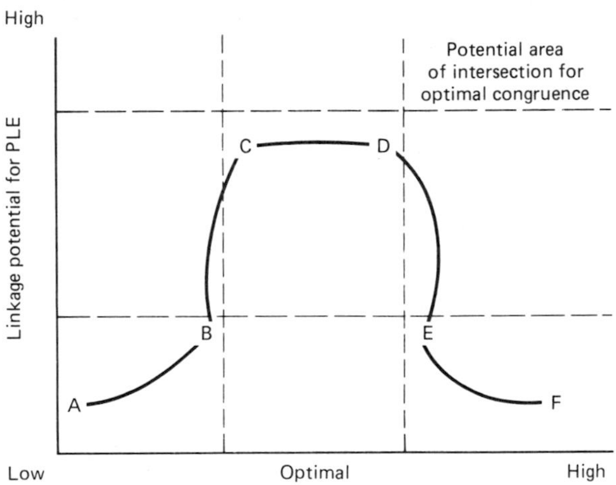

Figure 11-6 Intensity level of substance and content as it relates to intersection potential for PLE

To describe the intended process for learning
To provide new data and concepts for possible use by the learner
To help learners generate relevance and application from their past experiences
To allow people to learn in their way at their own pace
To be competent so as to "do your own thing" with interest, enthusiasm, and perspective

In a sense, what is meant is the value system of the learning facilitator. If you take yourself too seriously, overplan, overdirect, and assume that you have control of the learning, the chance for convergence for PLE will be lessened. This is indicated in Figure 11-7, where an attempt is made to describe the optimal conditions for creating a chance that linkage with the other rhythms will take place.

Learning Methodologies Rhythm

The fifth learning rhythm is the relevance of the learning methodology at that particular moment. At some point a challenging lecture may be relevant. In another, a visual stimulus is most valued. In some situations a chance to talk about issues and concerns with others provides appropriate learning. At other times a confrontation of one's lack of skill; in other situations the use of reflection time, a case study, an instrument, field trip, laboratory group, or problem-solving clinic might be the relevant method.

In other words, no one learning method will trigger a PLE. The learning facilitator, in conjunction with those wanting learning and change, must carefully and professionally design the experience to be relevant to the amount of time, number of participants, nature of the content, type of process, expectation of learning, and goals or need for learning and change.

The relevance or appropriateness issue, based on the design of the experience, is paramount. The need is for an organic blending of purpose, time, size, skill, expectation, and resources in the situation.

Although the concept of multiple stimuli for learning is well recognized, it is infrequently practiced. Those of us involved with learning and change tend to have our "pet" methods because of our reinforced comfort from frequent use of a particular method.

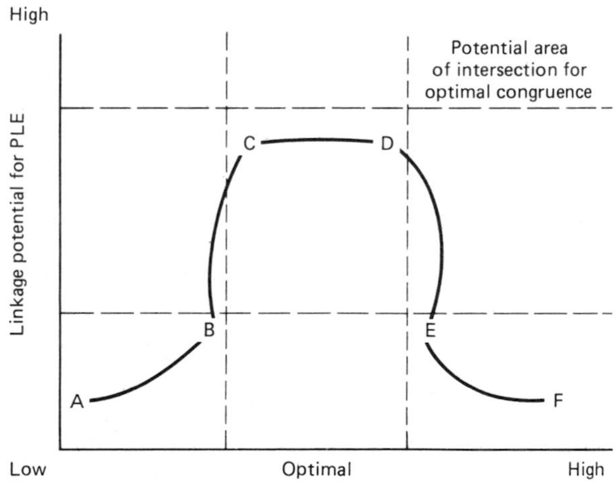

Figure 11-7 Intensity level of learning facilitator behavior as it relates to intersection potential for PLE

It might be helpful to refer to the classification of psychic factors proposed by Carl Jung (see Figure 11-8).[22] Although it might be ideal to fully utilize each of these functions and apply them to life coping, Jung feels that they are differentiated in the developed individual. For the sensation type of person, intuition may be the inferior function. In the thinking type, the inferior function is feeling. Although it is possible to determine a person's preferred way of perceiving reality by the Keegan Management Type Indication (KMTI),[23] in most learning situations all four functions should be present so as to strike a chord with that particular learner.

Research on the two hemispheres of the brain indicates multiple brain processes. We have long known that the left hemisphere controls many of the mind's most important functions, such as speech and language skills. However, the often-neglected right hemisphere also plays a vital role in the way people think. Recent research suggests that our right hemisphere responds to imagery and helps us to know things "intuitively" and to see things as a totality. As indicated by Dr. Joseph Bogen, a neurosurgeon in Los Angeles: "There is a clear inference that there are two quite different and parallel ways for the brain to process data and solve problems. When you're really doing well, you're using everything you've got."[24]

What we need is a balanced approach to Jung's four types and the hemispheres of the brain so that the learner's own preferences are given a chance. This is a strong argument for a varied approach to learning methodologies, depending on content to be learned, time, size of group, and other relevant factors in the learning situation. Whatever the methods, they should help further self-concept and a feeling of success and accomplishment in the learning situation. Both are essential for learning to take place.[25]

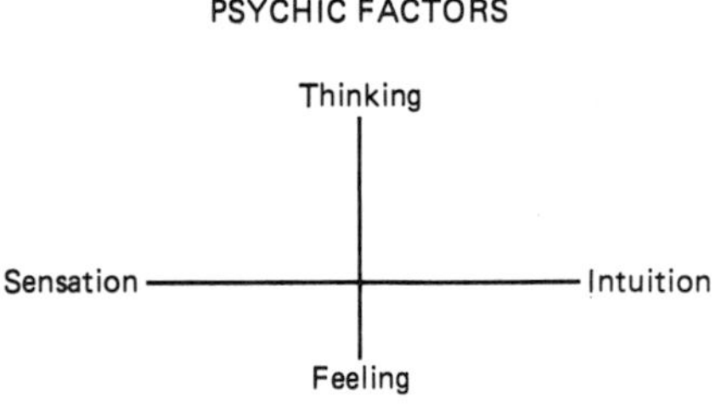

Figure 11-8 Psychic factors

In Figure 11-9 are indicated some of the considerations to take into account to create optimal conditions of learning methodologies for potential intersection with the other learning rhythms.

Supportive Relationships Rhythm

The final essential learning rhythm is the degree of support that is present in the learning/change situation. Some of the PLE support systems are:

Support of fellow learners (others in the situation). The importance of peer support is well known. To know that a colleague in the group, class, or situation is helping you—to learn and to analyze experience—is a valued element.

Support of spouse, family, and friends. To know that those who love you support your educational adventures is essential. One should not feel "guilty" about learning. If a manager attending an executive development program for two weeks feels neglectful of his or her family, it could negatively affect the learning potential.

Financial or technological support to help implement the PLE. Whether you volunteer or are told to participate in a learning experience and are financially supported in total or part, it makes you feel that someone else wants you to learn. This also is true if you are provided with such technological support as a tape recorder, books, or library resources.

Support of reinforcement materials and role modes. Learning is sustained more effectively with follow-up and reinforcement. Continuing to receive materials related

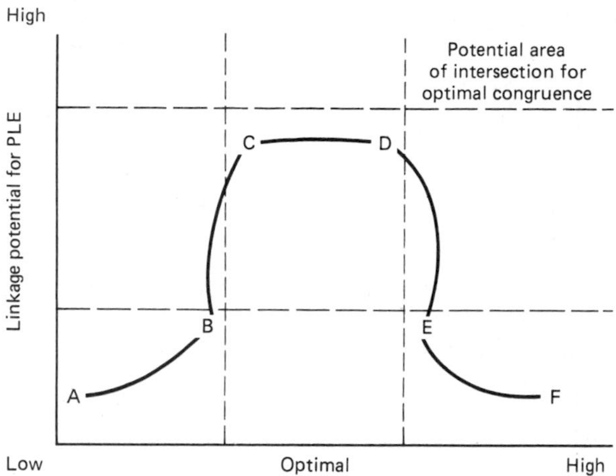

Figure 11-9 Intensity level of learning methodologies utilized as it relates to intersection potential for PLE

to the learning is helpful. It is also valuable to link with peers or others who have experienced related learnings and in their behavior reinforce the learned concepts, skills, and attitudes.

Support of opportunities to take risks and innovate. It is helpful when parents, teachers, bosses, and colleagues will permit the learner to try out new skills, enlarge one's responsibilities, and change one's old approach to job/career/life. Too frequently we are stereotyped by others in light of past behavior and not "allowed" to be different as a result of a learning experience. If this support is not present, we may remain in collusion with continued mediocrity or "going to Abilene."[26] In a classic article, Jerry Harvey points out that people in organizations frequently take action in contradiction to what they want to do because they cannot level, confront, or "face up" to their common desires or beliefs so as to manage their agreement.

Opportunities to be rewarded and to support the learner's PLE. In the latter context, it is valuable to "celebrate" those PLEs that help make meaningful transition possible for individuals, groups, and organizations. Celebrations can be a dinner with colleagues, wine and cheese with fellow learners, a new suit you always wanted to buy, a trip to see your favorite Broadway play, or other meaningful celebrations. These celebrations can support the PLE as well as the minor or major implementation successes that follow.

It is a well-known fact that a feeling of loneliness and alientation can create frustration, hostility, and resistance to change. Therefore, attention to the supportive relationships and the rhythm of learning is essential to encourage a PLE (see Figure 11-10).

Theory of Learning Rhythms Convergence

The underlying assumptions of this concept permit the proposing of a theory of learning rhythms convergence:

Learning rhythms are processes in a continuous "flow" that are experienced by the learner.

When learning rhythms intersect or converge for a person, group, or organization, a peak learning experience will occur.

Rhythms will converge in various patterns with different strengths, but will produce a synergistic effect.

Although it is not possible to tell which rhythm contributed most to the synergis-

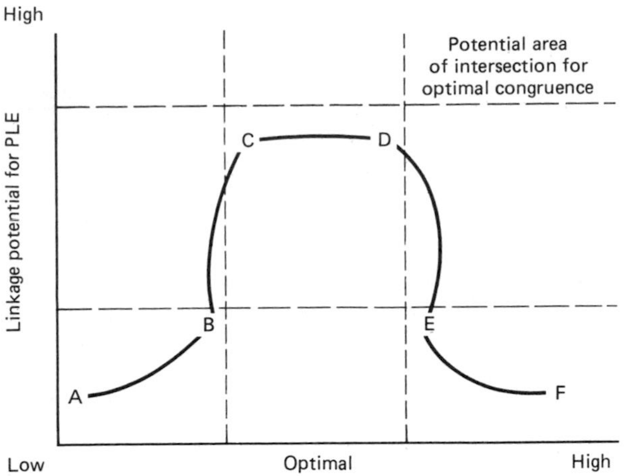

Figure 11-10 Intensity level of supportive relationships as it relates to intersection potential for PLE

tic convergence, it is possible to determine when the convergence occurs.

Although it is not possible to predict convergence of the rhythms, it is possible to increase the chances of convergence.

Transition periods in the lives of the learners will increase the likelihood of convergence.

If too little or too much attention is given to any one rhythm, the chance for convergence is lessened.

Although other elements in this theory will emerge as it is tried and revised by others, it provides sufficient basis for testing. This theory is not scientific, but rather speculatively descriptive of an intuitive concept.

Although we cannot control the occurrence of PLE, we can influence it as well as increase the change of a PLE occurring earlier and more frequently than leaving it up to chance. Stimulating the learner readiness to "surface," to come into consciousness, and to be confronted, can be encouraged by the learning facilitator:

To initiate need and readiness assessment without waiting for a "crisis" or to be asked to create a learning experience.

To enter into the learning situation with good preparation, professional competence, and enthusiasm for the joint learning experience

To develop clear and measurable objectives and goals for the learning experience, the learning situation, and learning facilitator

To select and develop a range of learning experience that meets the objective of the learning/change goals

To become innovative and professional in orchestrating a "design for learning" that creates optimum stimulus, excitement, and insight potential that will encourage the chance of PLE occurring

Such orchestration of learning rhythms requires commitment and competence. Although you cannot win every time, you can try. As professionals we need always to try to orchestrate learning rhythms—perhaps not as the conductor, but frequently as the first violinist.

As one plows into theory and concepts, the problem of motivation is confronted. Can a person be motivated to learn? Is the understanding of learning motivation a prime requisite for educational planning? It quickly becomes obvious that learning theorists do not agree on what motivation is or how it is stimulated. Generally speaking, these premises prevail: the learner must be self-motivated; the trainer must motivate the learner through an effective learning climate; not enough is now known about causes of motivation to discuss its role in the learning process.

Most managers and renewal advocates believe there is a factor called motivation. They seem to be evenly split as to whether the learner must be self-motivated, or whether the training situation or the trainer can develop motivation. Those who believe that learning must be self-motivated usually believe the trainer must provide the conditions under which self-motivation can occur. In practice, there is little to distinguish the designs of trainers who subscribe to differing philosophies. Designed conditions under which self-motivation can occur look much like the designs of those who attempt to motivate learners.

Such concerns about motivating individuals and groups to learn, and the recognition that there is such a thing as a learning process, have led to exploration of the conditions under which learning seems best to occur. Numerous lists of conditions for learning exist; they vary depending on the learning theory school to which the originator subscribes. As indicated above in our discussion of the concept of learning rhythms, however, there is no one "best" way to learn. In most organizations, the development and training specialists are generalists, and seldom do their activities and programs focus on a constant, single-objective outcome or method. It is perhaps inevitable, therefore, that guiding concepts and principles are a meld of many theories. But it is important that concepts and principles derived from theories of learning be used in a way that will accomplish the development objectives.

As the learning facilitator and planner explores learning theory, he or she finds several points of view. There are individual proponents of a given theory who insist that their theory alone accounts for the way people learn. There are those who insist that we do not know what learning theory is and that learning theorists do not contribute to the real problems of training and organization renewal. There are those who will be frank in saying to a training specialist, "You are on your own. Learning theory in its present state will not materially help you. Experiment. If it works and gets you the results you want—don't worry about what learning theory lies behind your success." It is important to keep our focus on the objectives and not become enchanted with the theories:

> Theories . . . attempt to organize existing knowledge, they attempt to provide guiding threads of hypotheses toward new knowledge, and they may also furnish principles by which what is known can be used. This practical outcome is seldom central in the thinking of the constructor of theory, and it is not surprising, therefore, that the person seeking advice from the learning theorist often comes away disappointed . . . . It turns out, however, that many of the quarrels of the theorists are internal ones, not very important in relation to immediate practical problems; there are, in fact, a great many practically important experimental relationships upon which the theorists are in substantial agreement. . . . If the theoretical differences are irreconcilable, and one position eventually wins out over the other, there will ultimately be an effect upon practice. But advice for practical people today need not wait for the resolution of these theoretical controversies.[27]

It is known that participants in training situations sometimes have better insights into the factors affecting their learning than do those who do the planning.

ACTION LEARNING AND THE LABORATORY METHOD

In light of the reality that adult learning tends to be most effective when the learner is active rather than passive, a good deal of emphasis is placed on *action learning,* a term that has become increasingly popular. It refers to various methods whereby people are encouraged to learn through set patterns of activity. This can involve a project or be an integral part of a person's ordinary job. The important point is that people are encouraged to learn from experience, a procedure very much in line with the philosophy expounded by John Dewey,[28] who argued that "there is an intimate and necessary relation between the processes of action experience and education." Such action learning methods include:[29]

- On-the-job training
- Job rotation
- Role modeling
- Work-oriented team building
- Skills practice
- Group problem solving
- Role playing
- Action taking with feedback
- Coaching

Each of these methods constitutes involvement combined with data collection, feedback, and additional experience.

One of the important contributions to action learning theory, practice, and application is the laboratory method. Some people narrowly refer to sensitivity training as being synonymous with laboratory method, whereas in fact it is but one example of application of the latter—the principle of laboratory education. The laboratory method is based on six premises:[30]

Perspective	*Premise*
A way of learning	People are helped to learn how to learn, with an experiential basis for learning
Process as content	One's experience can form the basis for new knowledge, learning, and skills
A way of planned change	Using skills and learning for personal, group, organization, and community change
A process of cooperative action research	Learning is an integral process of collecting experiential data for use in feedback for growth, improvement, and change
A process of knowledge utilization	Motivation of the learner is enhanced by applying research-tested knowledge
A way of resocialization and reenculturation	Learning involves one's ability to become an important part of the human organism's acceptance of responsibility with others in the same culture, so as to achieve relevant goals

Daniel Hogan has described the current situation in laboratory training very well:

> The potential value of human relations laboratory training for our society cannot be underscored enough. Technological change, alienation, social mobility, bureauratization, and the rigidity of traditional social institutions have brought about a situation where people in society have lost their sense of belongingness, their sense of stability, and

their sense of intimacy. The small laboratory group represents a place where these needs can not only be met, but where new methods can be learned to deal constructively with the problems in our society today.

Human relations training provides us with a tool to learn to adapt to change, and it has provided many techniques that have proven useful in psychotherapy. The research evidence indicates that human relations training can be useful for personal, group, and organizational development.

But, as is true with any powerful phenomenon, human relations training has the capacity for bringing about harm as well as benefit. It is this dual potentiality that makes the question of regulation so vital.[31]

His recommendations for regulation are for more effective professional standards and associations, not statutes. But consumers still need guidelines in deciding for themselves what kinds of laboratory training, if any, are appropriate for their organizations and communities.

DESIGNING TRAINING AND DEVELOPMENT

Proper design of a training experience is essential. It requires data, planning, resources, and experience; but the vital element is the learner. In Figure 11-11 we see the major components of life-long learning. First, the purpose, expectations, need, condition, readiness, and state of the learner are critical to the learning experience. Second, one must consider the experience, planned and unplanned, that contributes to learning; how it is perceived, evaluated, and used is an important factor. Third, resources are necessary—they can be such things as ideas, books, informed persons, libraries, films, inquiry centers, home, work space—and there is no reason why one cannot consider oneself as a resource, as well as seek the support and assistance of others. Fourth, in this context, authentication involves the importance and value of the learning, and these things need to be reorganized by the individual human system and, as well, for the sake of those things and persons that human system values in its life space.

The designing of training is a planned type of learning. Those doing such planning should be aware of the components of life-long learning and of some of the complications of maturation and change that will affect the training design. William Dyer presents these complications rather well, as shown in Table 11.1.

Keeping these two forms of reference in mind—*change conditions* and *training design issues*—the designer of training can effect an orderly progression in the design process. Figure 11-12 illustrates a step-by-step process.

Next, let us examine these steps in a bit more detail.[32]

1. *Analyze the needs of the organization.* The first step is to define the broad needs of the system, and then to focus on specific requirements for training. A need is something that must be accomplished in order for the system to achieve its purpose. Not all needs can be met through training.
2. *Specify job performance required to meet the organization's expectations.* The purpose here is to define what an individual should do on the job after training in order to accomplish the needs of the system. This definition should specify quantity and quality of performance; each statement should start with a verb, and describe behavior and actions.
3. *Define existing capabilities of proposed audience and define selection criteria.* Estimate needs that should be met by training. Defind course content for an average participant, but include material hopefully useful to those participants who are above

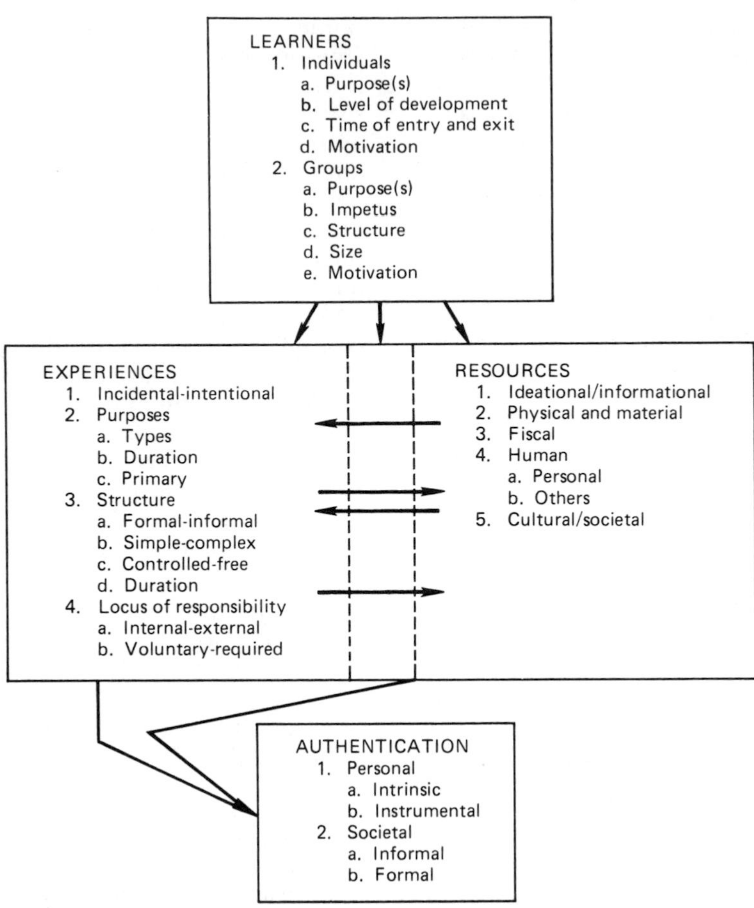

LEARNERS
1. Individuals
a. Purpose(s)
b. Level of development
c. Time of entry and exit
d. Motivation
2. Groups
a. Purpose(s)
b. Impetus
c. Structure
d. Size
e. Motivation
EXPERIENCES
1. Incidental-intentional
2. Purposes
a. Types
b. Duration
c. Primary
3. Structure
a. Formal-informal
b. Simple-complex
c. Controlled-free
d. Duration
4. Locus of responsibility
a. Internal-external
b. Voluntary-required
RESOURCES
1. Ideational/informational
2. Physical and material
3. Fiscal
4. Human
a. Personal
b. Others
5. Cultural/societal
AUTHENTICATION
1. Personal
a. Intrinsic
b. Instrumental
2. Societal
a. Informal
b. Formal

Figure 11-11 Major components of life-long learning[33]

and below the median. Then establish selection criteria that will keep the participants close to the norm—so that the material is relevant to each participant. This means that the capabilities of each participant entering training must be anticipated.

4. *Select program objectives and define specific learning objectives (knowledge, skills, attitudes).* The different types and levels of learning can be simplistically classified as (1) knowledge, which is simple access to information; (2) skill, which is the ability to use knowledge; and (3) attitudes, which is what is believed or the disposition toward knowledge and skills. These types and levels of learning should be kept in mind when selecting program objectives. The latter coincide with one or more of the major categories under job performance in step 2. Some program objectives will coincide with the major topics that comprise the training program itself; other objectives (e.g., developing an analytical questioning approach) might not be defined as a topic, but rather as something to be dealt with throughout the course. Specific learning objectives are the more detailed statements of what a participant should know, or be able to do, or believe at the end of the course. These statements define what the participant

Table 11-1
Checklist for Training Design[34]

Change Conditions	Training Design Issues
People change when there is a *felt need.*	Managers should go to programs in areas where they feel a need to improve—not because they are sent or it is "their turn."
People change when supported by a *respected other.*	Training should include a linkage with a respected other—hopefully one's superior. This person should understand and support the training goals.
People change when their change plan moves from general goals to *specific plans and actions.*	Training designers need to include a process where managers can spell out a specific plan or action for improving their managerial performance.
People change as they move from a condition of *lower to higher self-esteem.*	Too often training designs do not help managers see that the training will increase their feelings about themselves. In the past some good theory X managers felt threatened by the prospect of changing to theory Y.
People change as they shift from *old social ties to new or revised social ties.*	Too often training is not connected to the back-home setting. This results in a dramatic loss of learning when managers return from a training program. Training designs should link training into the back-home situation.
People change as they move from *external to internal commitment* to change.	Training designs should include opportunities for people to explore this commitment to change, to dialogue with others, and develop their own insight and understanding.

would be doing if subsequently observed on the job. Thus, in selecting program objectives, several factors must be considered, starting with the needs of the organization and of the learning situation itself.

One should take into account certain restraints in accomplishing program objectives (e.g., course length, lecturing staff, facilities and funds, type of course that can be taught, information transfer, technical skills, and social skills). Finally, there is a need for flexibility to accommodate change.

5. *Build curriculum (content and sequence).* Initially, a calendar should be developed, noting the topics of discussion for each session. When establishing the subjects and topics to be covered in the course, several factors are considered: time requirements, which are dependent upon the desired intensity of instruction, the resource person, and the level of sophistication of the participants. There are also several factors to weigh in development of a curriculum calendar. The first is "internalization." Participants should be given an opportunity for subconscious thought over a period of time, so as to relate the new material to their past experience. Thus, the instructor should allow some time between sessions on a certain topic, but not so much that the participants lose their train of thought. A second factor to consider is "boredom potential." Some instructors favor splitting up a subject—rather than give several consecutive learning sessions—in order to eliminate or relieve boredom, while providing time for internalization. Others argue that it is easier for the mind to grasp one subject fully before moving on

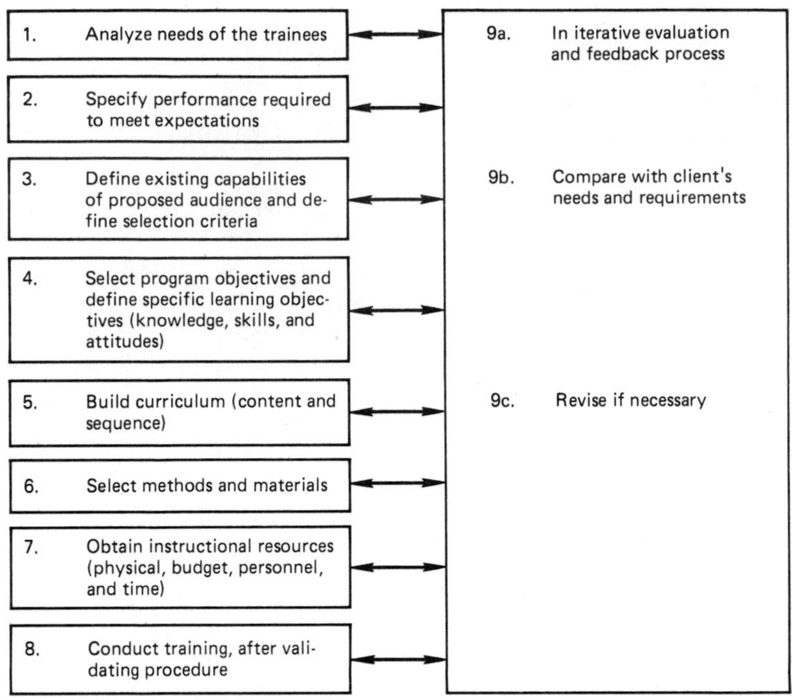
1. Analyze needs of the trainees
2. Specify performance required to meet expectations
3. Define existing capabilities of proposed audience and define selection criteria
4. Select program objectives and define specific learning objectives (knowledge, skills, and attitudes)
5. Build curriculum (content and sequence)
6. Select methods and materials
7. Obtain instructional resources (physical, budget, personnel, and time)
8. Conduct training, after validating procedure
9a. In iterative evaluation and feedback process
9b. Compare with client's needs and requirements
9c. Revise if necessary

Figure 11-12 Step-by-step process for defining, developing, and implementing a training program[35]

to another. If the instructor does split up a topic, he or she should intersperse lighter subjects.

6. *Select methods and materials.* Various methodologies are available to designers and resource persons: lectures, discussions, case studies, exercises, field trips, programmed teaching packages, role playing, workshops, games, and post-course workshops (see Figure 11-13). Methods and materials should be chosen so as to maximize learning, and here retention is a critical factor. Given one exposure to a topic—a lecture, for example—a participant may remember to look up a reading. The likelihood of this being done increases if the exposure actually involved the participant in an interesting discussion or an exercise. The greater number of such exposures, the greater the retention of learning. Vital topics should therefore have several exposures.
7. *Obtain instructional resources (physical, budget, personnel, time).* Before either the physical resources or personnel can be obtained, funding must be determined and secured. Then it is necessary to find adequate facilities and qualified staff.
8. *Conduct training.* This is the implementation phase. The first seven steps have been involved with defining and preparing the learning experience. If the methods have been selected wisely and teaching materials carefully prepared, then a group leader (who is thoroughly familiar with both the methods and the materials) can begin the training. New materials, however, should be tested before they are used.
9. *Evaluation and feedback process.* The purpose of a feedback process is to compare the accomplishments of each phase of the learning experience with its objective(s) (i.e., the needs and requirements of the organization). Revisions can be made, as

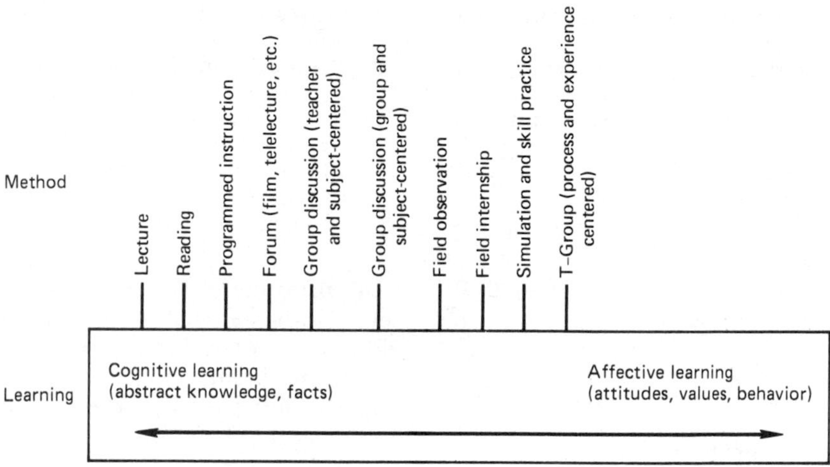

Figure 11-13 Training methodologies and types of learning results

necessary, in each of the preceding eight steps. Feedback can be formal or informal at various stages. During learning sessions, a group leader who has good rapport with the participants will encourage feedback. Informal feedback channels—during coffee breaks, at meals, parties, or social events—helps encourage those participants who might otherwise hesitate to voice their opinions, criticisms, suggestions, or approval. More formal evaluations—such as weekly questionnaires or relaxed debriefing sessions—are useful for planning future training.

These nine steps are rather typical of any effective design process.

TRANSFER OF LEARNING

Another problem that often confronts a manager, educator, or training director is the transfer of learning. In learning how to learn, we need to know how to transfer "learning from failure or incompetence" in one situation to achieve success in another situation.

Many a systems manager may question whether there is any real "payoff" to training (learning) activity. This concern is often well founded, particularly if the learning design, organizational climate, and supportive circumstance is not present and contributing to putting the knowledge, skills, and ideas into operation. In a research program on the effect of management training, Vandenput questioned sixty-two interview participants to ascertain the factors that aided or inhibited the transfer of learning to their work. He concluded that the organization has a specific influence upon the transfer of learning, and listed the major factors that seem to inhibit managers from transferring their learning from the training situation to the work situation:[36]

Ineffective relation between the trainee and other groups with which he or she relates (other age groups, other socioprofessional groups, other units in the organization)

Ineffective influence relations, making it difficult for him or her to influence other people

Other people's rigidity and conservativeness in the organization

Inappropriate organizational structures

Ineffective relations between the trainee and his or her superior
The organization's environment acting upon the trainee
The working conditions surrounding the trainee's job
The lack of (perceived) relevance of the training for his or her work

It is also clear from Vandenput's research that the factors encouraging people to apply their learning are:

A job giving an opportunity for team work
Support from innovation-minded staff groups
Top-level support for training
High wage rates
Openness between people
A job that is open to improvement
A situation where the trained person is seen as more valuable by his or her boss
A situation where the boss will delegate
Having position of decision
Support from external consultants
Contacts and comparisons with other companies

A similar study reinforces these points; the importance of organizational climate as a factor influencing the acceptance and use of new ideas derived from management education has been clearly shown by Baumgartel and Jeanpierre.[37] They studied a sample of 240 managers drawn from a sample of 2000 managers who had participated in one of seventeen management development programs. In all, the managers in the sample were drawn from more than 200 different industrial and commercial firms.

The researchers found that there was a positive correlation between six climate variables and adoptive effort scores. These were:

1. Freedom to set personal goals
2. Degree higher management is considerate of feelings of lower management
3. Degree organization stimulates and approves of innovation and experimentation
4. Degree organization is anxious for executives to make use of knowledge gained from management courses
5. Degree of free and open communication among the management group
6. Willingness of top management to spend money for training

In summary, Baumgartel and Jeanpierre indicate that if management development programs are to have a maximum likelihood of aiding participants to apply their learning, then the programs should:

Help participants deal with concrete problems facing them
Contribute to the personal growth and identity of participants
Have instructors and trainers who understand the participants' problems and have the capacity for beneficial personal relationships
Be well organized and at the appropriate level of difficulty

Furthermore, the managers who are most likely to transfer ideas and knowledge are those who are in positions of sufficient freedom and responsibility to influence events. It may be, however, that the sort of people who rise to these positions are innovators and the management program only provides the necessary ideas and stimulus for application. Indeed, the researchers suggest that personality variables such as motivations and attitudes can be major factors influencing adoption.[38] In light of these studies, the transfer of learning is identified as a critical element if training is to be effective, and some of the ways in which learning theories attempt to provide for this are:

Actually doing the "that" which is being learned. In this instance, the stress is placed on the belief that the transfer is best when learning occurs in live situations. This is so because little or no transfer is needed—what is learned is directly applied. Instances employing this technique are on-the-job training, coaching, apprenticeship, and job experience. This approach is the key to most organization renewal attempts.

Doing something that is similar to that which is to be learned. This transfer principle is applied when we use simulated experiences—the training experience and techniques are as similar to the job as possible. Sometimes we let the trainee discover the principles and apply them to his or her job. In other instances, particularly in skill training, work is done on mock-ups that closely resemble the actual equipment. Other techniques employed would include role playing, sensitivity training, and case studies.

Reading or hearing about that which is to be learned. The trainer or a book gives the trainee the principles and then discusses and illustrates them. The trainee must then figure out the ways in which what has been heard or read applies to the job at hand and how to use it. Illustrative training techniques would be lectures, reading, and most management and supervisory training programs featuring the "telling" method.

Doing or reading about anything on the assumption it will help anything to be learned. In this instance there is an assumption that a liberalized education makes the trainee more effective in whatever job is occupied or task is to be learned. This might be termed the liberal arts approach. It assumes that well-rounded, educated persons are more effective, and more easily trained in specifics, if they understand themselves, their society, their world, and other disciplines. Obviously, this would be a somewhat costly way of training for organization renewal inasmuch as it would involve perceptual living and generalized education.

Much research has gone into understanding the transfer of learning. Most of this occurs in the S-R theories.

Research into adult learning at the University of Nebraska indicated:

> The average older adult in an adult education program is at least as intellectually able, and performs as well, as the average younger participant.
>
> Adults who continue to participate in educative activity learn more effectively than similar adults who do not. This would simply seem to indicate that learning skills require practice to be maintained. Adults learn far more effectively when they are permitted to learn at their own pace.[39]

Some conclusions about the training required for adults to experience effective development can be derived from the foregoing analysis. The basic laws of learning are:

Readiness. People learn best when ready to learn.
Exercise. Things most often repeated are best remembered.
Effect. Learning is strengthened in a pleasant environment.
Primary. First impressions are strongest.
Intensity. Realism, dynamism, and firsthand experience are best.
Recency. Things learned last are remembered best.

Research and experience with the training and instruction of adults have also demonstrated the validity of these relevant guidelines:[40]

Adults learn what they feel a need to learn.
Adults learn best by doing (by being actively involved).
Adults learn best through problem solving.
Adults want to know how they are doing.
Adults prefer an informal learning environment.

What really counts is *what the learner learns,* not what the teacher teaches. To ensure that this emphasis is kept in mind, objectives should be stated in terms of what the learner should take away from the experience, not in terms of what the instructor does in the training session. The instructor should remember that in the final analysis all learning is really self-learning—with the instructor facilitating the process through stimulation, resources, and setting.

CRITERIA FOR EFFECTIVE HUMAN RESOURCE DEVELOPMENT[41]

From a review of learning theory, concepts, and methods it is possible to develop a set of criteria as guidelines for effective development processes at the individual, group, and organization level.

Relevant Needs

Does projected human resource development take into account, in its maturation process, the present state of needs and disequilibrium in the individual, group, organization, or community? Equilibrium can be restored. If an individual or group is under stress, the development process should relieve such stress. If the organization has low morale, the applied process should improve morale. In other words, the process should be applied where the system is "hurting." This is what is done in both Eastern and Western approaches to self-growth—in which such things as meditation, self-insight, and assertiveness training are responsive to the felt stresses in the lives of individuals. Organization development or renewal similarly aids the human system that faces upheaval, change, and survival. Neighborhood action groups, community ombudsmen, and urban planning commissions relieve stresses in today's modern community. Expressed another way, to be relevant the human resource development process must be targeted.

Clear Objectives

Is the projected human resource development based on clear and measurable objectives, so that progress can be gauged?

These objectives should be written down, and rewritten until they are succinct and thoroughly understood by all concerned. For an individual, the objectives might be specified accomplishments in a career plan. For an organization, they might be certain financial successes. Although not all objectives can be accurately measured, as many as possible should be stated in measurable terms—in terms of what the learner "takes away" from the growth experience, rather than what the helper, consultant, or trainer advocates or does. Effectiveness, then, would be calculated by determining what the participant learned, not by what the change agent taught—by specific behavioral or situational changes, not merely by intentions or hopes.

In addition to expressing, understanding and measuring the objectives, we know that human resource development is most effective when:

- The process is *internalized* by the system.
- The purposes are *known* and *accepted* by the system.
- The process is an *active process* that involves change in behavior.
- The process uses *feedback and a sense of progress.*[42]

Still, in the final analysis, it is all really self-learning facilitated by stimulation, resources, and setting.

Accomplishment

Is the projected human resource development based on successful growth, learning, and performance that is compatible with the environment in which the change takes place?

Each human subsystem operates within the context of a larger system—such as a group, organization, or community—in which there is or has been successful coping or performance that becomes a benchmark for accomplishment. In certain types of organization, achievement-based behavior is expected and rewarded. In some group situations, certain skills are a prerequisite for membership. Human resource development should be guided by these measures of accomplishment, even though these basic measurements will differ in different social systems.

Uniqueness

Does the projected human resource development meet the unique needs of the particular human system?

Standard methods, established theories, predesigned learning exercises or packaged programs may be used, but they must be pragmatically adapted to the situation—initially, and as other situations arise. There is no universal approach to human resource development; nor is there an unchanging method. It must be predicated on a need assessment and tailored to that need. Past experience is useful and valuable; we do not need to reinvent the wheel.

Flexibility

Does the projected human resource development meet the ongoing and changing need of the human system?

We are dealing with an active, involving, and evolving process. The professional must be flexible in terms of the needs that emerge during the process, as well as in helping the participants be flexible. The choice of resources may be redirected, or methods or situational surroundings altered. Experience brings realization of the requirement for flexibility as a particular event or growth rechannels an original plan or effort.

Skill Oriented

Does the projected human resource development stress skill development for competence in behavior or performance?

Skill development is readily discernible. It is the ability to perform and practice in real life the concepts one has learned, and this aspect should comprise at least three-fourths of the development process. The ability to *do* what one has learned is the essence of effective growth. Unfortunately, many human resource development activities do not sufficiently emphasize skill practice within the human learning system. The learner needs to practice, secure feedback, and repractice.

Professional Leadership

Is the projected human resource development led by a professional helper, trainer, or consultant?

Whoever is responsible for initiating and helping the human resource development process will need to manifest professional behavior and leadership.

Human resource development is not the province of any one group or discipline. It should, however, be planned, designed, and supervised by those who are prepared by education, practice, skill, and ethics—trainers, adult educators, counselors, therapists, consultants, teachers, or similar specialists. Working alone or with teams of other resource persons, the professional may come from inside or outside the system.

Future Perspective

Is the projected human resource development based on practical assessment of future needs?

A human system can usually "look ahead" to an image of its own potentiality, predicting where it wants to be in three to five years. Such a glance into the future can be predicated on individual growth parameters, group-growth dimensions, or stages of organization growth. It can also be based on pragmatic statements of "where I (we) want to be in five years."

It is only when an individual can target a desired career and life goal that meaningful human resource development takes place. The process can take place in individual or group situations. Organizations and communities, however, can also examine where they want to be in five to seven years in order to have future goals. Some professional helpers refer to this as developing an "image of potential." In this process, an organization or community is helped to develop a scenario illustrating achievement of its potential as those in the system perceive the future; but casting too far ahead tends to make planning unrealistic and nonrelevant.

Value System

Is the projected human resource development founded on an articulated value system in which its purposes are clear and philosophically consistent with norms, values, expectations, and goals held by that particular human system?

Values form the philosophy or standards toward which an individual, group, organization, or community is striving. Human resource development should enhance that effort by understanding and support. In an organization, goals might be bolstered by participative management; in a group it might be open communication; and with an individual it might be interpersonal competence:

> A person can develop into a socially adjusted and useful person and yet remain stillborn in a spiritual sense. If he is to develop into what he potentially is as a human being, he must continue to be born. That is, he must continue to dissolve the primary ties of soil and blood. He must give up certainty and defenses and take the jump into the act of commitment, concern, and love.[43]

Development is a growth process, and the goal of such growth rests on esteemed values. Human resource development should help people articulate the values in their system, because the identification of these values is an extremely relevant part of the growth process.

Evaluation

Does the projected human resource development include the technology, concepts, and methods that can produce meaningful evaluation?

After the process is under way, evaluation should mirror the reactions of the participants, and where possible it should have a controlled situation by means of which to compare results. If this is not possible, at least some before-and-after measurements should be used. In either case, appropriate advantage should be taken of confidential feedback from the participants. Such evaluation should be related to the objective, criterion, and skill development scales.

Evaluating effectiveness in meeting goals is an essential part of the human resource development process. In too many cases evaluation focuses on inputs rather than on accomplishment of intended purposes. Systematic evaluation will not always point the ways to better or less-expensive methodology, but it can be a guide for discussion. Lack of evaluation can be considered a flaw in implementation. On the other hand, there are a number of reasons why comprehensive evaluation is sometimes minimal:

Evaluation can be expensive and time-consuming.

- Many professionals believe "the value of my services cannot be measured."
- Explicit and systematic evaluation can be controversial.
- Professionals in the field of human resource development lack skill in quantitative techniques and analysis.
- Past evaluations have not been timely or helpful to sponsors, clients, or policymakers.[44]

As realistic as they may be, these difficulties do not negate a concentrated effort to evaluate with whatever resources, time, skills, and readiness exists within the system. Without evaluation we are unable effectively to measure progress, assess the worth of an activity, or improve programs.

Information System

Does the projected human resource development provide data that can be stored, retrieved, and updated to serve the human system, and make possible planning built on previous experience?

People involved in human resource development should know that analysis, diagnosis, and prognosis are taking place in a systematic and informative manner—whether or not computerized—for the sake of credibility, if nothing else. The key elements in such an information system make planning and feedback helpful:

- Human resource objectives consistent with and in support of the plans and objectives of that particular human system.
- A human resource audit (evaluation) of current assets to inventory those resources, and to determine how effectively they are currently being used.
- Forecasts of human resource needs for the individual, group, organization, or community; projection of requirements and statements of expectation as to how needs may evolve and how the present human resources will be available in the future to meet those needs.
- The identification of persons with potential.
- Training programs and other learning experiences to update people's technical and human resource knowledge and skills, and to develop a balance in human resource utilization.
- Programs for appraising the performance of people, with separate programs for appraising their potential to take on increased responsibility.
- The identification of career and life development paths.
- Feedback and adjustment of the plans as indicated by experience.

It is disappointing that so few organizations have a valuable human resource inventory that provides valid, up-to-date information about the competence of the people in the system. Such a system, small or large, makes it possible to draw the best from individuals and groups.

Organizational Support

Does the projected human resource development firmly commit the leaders in the system, and does it have their complete interest and involvement?

The process can make an impact only to the extent that it is encouraged by the policies, actions, and personal support of group, organization, and community leaders. They give legitimization to the process. In addition, such sponsors should be able to exert that amount of leverage required to influence the system.

At the individual level, a person is aided if he or she knows that family, friends, and peers are supportive of individual development activities. It is also valuable to know that one's organization supports career and life-enriching experiences. A group development process is also enhanced when an organization gives credence to and rewards team-building efforts.

It has long been known that organization renewal is most likely to succeed if it is seen as an integral part of the management ethos. A comment by a vice president of a nationwide organization at a time of recession and a necessary 10% cutback in the number of employees was: "We need human resource development more than ever in this organization. We want people to know that career development is still possible and we need to get the job done with fewer people than before. We will not cut our budget in this important field." Similarly, at the community level, it is important that a mayor, city manager, town council, or other officials support the values inherent in human resource development. Nevertheless, when the benefits are seen as a "luxury" or "reward" for faithful service, the process becomes a disincentive.

Participant Commitment

Does the projected human resource development strengthen desire to cope, solve problems, and mature?

It should increase the commitment of individuals to want to belong to the group, organization, or community, and to work to renew these human systems. If, conversely, it alienates the individual or group, it is a distinct disservice to the system. But participation in human resource development should be a voluntary act; there may be some exceptions, but these would be rare indeed. The process should be so conceived and executed as to increase the commitment of the individual to achieve goals; the group to achieve teamwork; the organization to increase effectiveness; and the community to cope with complexity.

Although the criteria cannot all be measured in absolute terms, most of the responses can be sufficiently quantified as to make it feasible to analyze trends, focus on differences, and identify needs. The purpose here has been to present the need for stated criteria for planning and evaluating the process of human systems renewal. When professionals and practitioners accept and apply some kind of explicit criteria—that process will become more responsible and relevant to the ability of people to cope with their lives and with the society in which they live.

THE CHANGING NATURE OF TRAINING AND DEVELOPMENT[45]

Whatever the future holds, training and development today is a field of constantly increasing maturity and professionalism. The following eleven trends highlight the change:

1. *There is greater emphasis on improving performance rather than merely increasing individual knowledge.* It is increasingly evident that the criteria used to evaluate the effectiveness of training development now anticipate change in performance rather than the lesser goal of having people "like" or "feel good" about a learning experience.

2. *More training is done to deal with situations as contrasted to improving the skills of individuals only.* Many educational experiences do not seem to bring about change within the trainee's organization. This has tended to increase the emphasis on training and development activities that focus on solving problems, with the result that situations are confronted and coped with more effectively. A word of caution, however: Although this is a trend toward supplementing the skills of the individual, it does not eliminate the need for skills training.

3. *There is more insistence on evaluation of training results instead of accepting them on faith.* If training and development is undertaken only because it seems to be "the thing to do," there is a tendency to overlook adequate evaluation and research values. In such cases, management also finds it difficult to justify the expense for educational activity even though they may feel it is necessary. At long last, we are seeing more sophisticated attempts to really evaluate the practical results of learning

and to be more selective about methods and emphasis.

4. *Trainers are increasingly designing activities that focus on learning how to learn.* Because organizational functioning is so complex and because so much diverse knowledge is required, it has become important that managers recognize learning as a continuing process. Learning must be gained from all of life's activities; it can no longer be confined to formal education or occasional training programs. Learning how to learn from situations is becoming a way of life for the successful manager.

5. *There is a move away from training that is unrelated to the learner's life experience or his or her organization's needs.* It seems that the trend is away from some esoteric types of training, which must be considered fads, to activities based on the real needs of people and organizations.

6. *Action learning is getting more attention than didactic, nonparticipative approaches to learning.* The gradual fading of the one-way-communication concept of training and development seems to originate in recognition that adults need to experience learning rather than be exposed only to cognitive learning.

7. *Reinforcement and follow-up experiences are being provided for trainees so that learning is enhanced by application.* A major criticism of educational programs has been that frequently there is no lasting effect of the learning. The observation that the new learning drops off quickly has been a matter of concern to many in our field. More and more career programs are being planned, with monthly follow-up sessions, planned reading programs, and a sequence of reinforcement activities.

8. *Training is being viewed as the way management gets its job done, not solely as a function of a training department.* Training and development, in the best sense, is a resource by which management uses organizational manpower to a maximum. This also happens to be a task and role of management. There is more and more awareness of the relationship between learning processes and organizational achievement.

9. *Training is being designed so that learning is self-motivated by the learners instead of being imposed upon them.* It has often been stated that people cannot be made to learn. A person will learn when a goal is realized, dissatisfaction with his or her own performance is felt, or the person wishes to achieve certain sociopsychological or economic rewards. In offering opportunities for individual or group growth, more and more training and development efforts are focused on the use of self-motivation principles.

10. *There is a greater emphasis on goal orientation instead of on the vague assurance that training will be "good for" the trainee.* Achievement and the solution of problems best motivate people and aid organizations. With this in mind, many organizations now direct more of their training and development activities toward certain goals. This is usually accomplished through programs of learning by objectives.

11. *Individuals are being trained as members of a group so that they will learn to function together in their organizational relationships.* Although there is some advantage to the individual being trained as an individual, there is greater advantage to an organization in the training of individuals as members of a real group. We are seeing more of this.

SUMMARY

The sophistication needed to understand and utilize the implications of learning theory have much to say about the kinds of qualifications and skills required for training and development activities.

Operational and organizational climate must support learning. In addition, managers need to be much more realistic and expect that very few entrenched responses can be changed in a week's training program or one appraisal interview.

It is suggested that renewal depends upon a process of continual learning. Norman Overly addresses this issue when asked: "Can we achieve the much needed learning society?" He responded:

> The answer is yes, but the task will require commitment to a lifetime of involvement and cooperative seeking as travelers rather than as tourists. We must individually reflect on and grapple with the parables of life, the opportunities and temptations, as well as the principles that point the way. We must read and inquire, observe, and think, and grow. The educator and the learner are both travelers on the learning road, seeking to engage each other in an understanding, appreciation, and attainment of their mutual and personal interests and goals. As travelers, we join together to become creators of a learning society.
>
> Those educational tourists seeking easy answers, instant, uniform learning, and unchallenged goals, may be on the same road as the traveler, but they see different things, and care little for the perspectives of others. They seek comfort and fuel at stations providing franchised familiarity, just like package tours. Whether teachers or students, they seek similar answers in the familiar educational institutions, regulations, and support systems that will provide information and degrees laid out in glossy catalogues and courses of study. The idea of a learning society extends beyond their immediate concerns and eludes them.
>
> On the other hand, lifelong learners see themselves as pilgrims, traveling into unknown byways, seeking truth where it is, no matter what the form or how it may be packaged. As we set the goals as a learning society, we must seek to move from an educational system patterned after a common, industrial model to a more open, non-competitive, self-selection model based on commitment rather than coercion. The best we can do is resolve to be travelers, pointing other travelers to some principles, utopian visions, and reformers' guidelines with the promise to join them on the journey.[46]

Effective learning methods assume that knowledge, skill, and attitudes have to be *discovered* by learners if they are to mean anything and make a difference in behavior. We learn not only from experience; we also learn, and perhaps we learn more, from *analyzed experience.* The renewal facilitator sets up conditions, including dilemmas and unsolved problems, where the learner can experiment, try things out, see what works, analyze, and generalize. The test of learning is not responses on a test, but whether the discovered learning makes any difference in the learner's life as he or she is constantly learning how to learn from every situation where the senses encounter opportunities for growth. This, then, is the challenge to those of us desiring to meet the critical problem of developing effective learning-how-to-learn experiences to meet the changing needs of today's society.

QUESTIONS

1. Recall a situation in which you feel that you learned a new skill, concept, or attitude. What factors contributed to that learning?
2. As you reflect on courses or classes you have experienced, what factors can you isolate as having helped your learning the most? What factors hindered your learning the most?

3. Can you remember a *directive* learning experience from which you learned something? Why?
4. Can you recall a *nondirective* learning experience from which you learned something? Why?
5. Under what conditions have you found a coaching or job-appraisal situation helpful? Under what conditions have you found such a situation unhelpful?
6. Do you feel that you have ever experienced a *peak learning experience*? If so, cite examples. Why did they occur?
7. How do you feel that training and development can contribute most to organization renewal?

[1]Norman V. Overly (ed.), *Lifetime Learning: A Human Agenda* (yearbook; Alexandria, Va.: Association for Supervision and Curriculum, 1979), p. 142. Hereafter cited as Overly.

[2]J. Quentin Lauer, S. J., *The Triumph Of Subjectivity* (translation of Husserl; New York: Fordham University Press, 1972), p. 105.

[3]Leland P. Bradford, "The Teaching-Learning Transaction," *Adult Education,* Vol. 8, No. 3, 1958, 18-24.

[4]Bernard Berelson and Gary Steiner, *Human Behavior: An Inventory of Scientific Findings* (New York: Harcourt, Brace & World, Inc., 1964, p. 83.

[5]Adapted from Leslie This and Gordon Lippitt, "Learning Theories and Training," *Training and Development Journal,* June 1979, pp. 5-17.

[6]Kurt Koffka, *Principles of Gestalt Psychology* (New York: Harcourt, Brace & World, Inc., 1935), p. 110.

[7]Pierre J. Marsh, *Selected Learning Theories: Their Implication for Job Training* (Master's thesis; Washington, D.C.: The George Washington University, 1965), pp. 56-57.

[8]Ernest R. Hilgard, *Theories of Learning* (New York: Appleton-Century-Crofts, 1956), p. 290. Hereafter cited as Hilgard.

[9]Gordon Lippitt, "Learning Rhythms," *Training And Development Journal,* October 1979, pp. 6-18.

[10]Abraham H. Maslow, *Religions, Values, and Peak-Experiences* (New York: Viking Press, 1970).

[11]Bernard Gittleson, *Biorhythm: A Personal Science* (New York: Warner Books, Inc., 1978), pp. 12-15.

[12]From studies made in Great Britain by the Railways Board in 1976; and by the Transport and Road Research Laboratory of highway accident victims (released in 1979).

[13]Jean Houston, "Holoverse: The Ecology of Inner Space," *Dromenon 1,* Vol. 4, June 1978.

[14]Carol H. Tice, "How Will We Score When Red, White, and Blue Turn to Gray? The Ultimate Accountability," *Educational Leadership,* January 1979, p. 286.

[15]Georgi Lozanov, *Suggestology and Outlines of Suggestopedy* (New York: Gordon and Breach, Science Publishers, Inc., 1979).

[16]Malcolm Knowles, *Self-directed Learning* (New York: Association Press, 1975), pp. 12-13.

[17]Richard Beckhard, *Transitions in Complex Organizations* (Reading, Mass.: Addison-Wesley Publishing Company, Inc., 1978).

[18]Adapted from an unpublished paper by David Kolb, *Individual Learning Styles and the Learning Process* (Washington, D.C.: The George Washington University, 1977).

[19]Alfred Morrow, *The Practical Theorist: The Life and Work of Kurt Lewin* (New York: Basic Books, Inc., 1969).

[20]Henri Louis Bergson, *Creative Evolution* (New York: Holt and Company, 1911), p. 6.

[21]Warren Schmidt, "Transforming Knowledge into Impact: The Teaching-Learning Process," *Optimizing Human Resources* (Reading, Mass.: Addison-Wesley Publishing Company, 1971), p. 79, pp. 80-84. Copyright © 1971. Reprinted with permission. Hereafter cited as Schmidt.

[22] Carl J. Jung, "Psychological Types," in *The Collected Works Of C. J. Jung,* Vol. 6, Bolligen Series XX [originally published in German as *Psychollische Typen,* Rascher Verlag, Zurich, 1921] (Princeton, N.J.: Princeton University Press, 1976).

[23]Warren J. Keegan, *Keegan Type Indicator* (Washington, D.C.: Warren J. Keegan & Associates, 1979).

[24]R. Jarnslovsky, "Brain Hemispheres Seen as Vital Factor in Way We Learn," *Wall Street Journal,* March 24, 1979.

[25]Benjamin S. Bloom, "Affective Outcomes of

School Learning," *Phi Delta Kappan,* November 1977.

[26]Jerry Harvey, "The Abilene Paradox: The Management of Agreement," *Organizational Dynamics.* Vol. 3. No. 1, 1974, 66.

[27]Hilgard, p. 485.

[28]John Dewey, *Experience and Education* (New York: Collier Books, 1975), p. 16.

[29]Eric Frank and Charles Margerson, *Training Methods and Organization Development* (London: MCB Human Resource, Ltd., 1978). Hereafter cited as Frank and Margerson.

[30]Kenneth Benne, Leland P. Bradford, Jack Gibb, and Ronald Lippitt (eds.), *The Laboratory Method of Changing and Learning: Theory and Application* (Palo Alto, Calif.: Science and Behavior Books, Inc., 1975), pp. 24–32.

[31]Daniel Hogan, *The Regulation of Human Relations Training: An Explanation of Some Assumptions and Some Recommendations* (unpublished thesis; Cambridge, Mass.: Harvard University Law School, April 1972), p. 112.

[32]Adapted from *Reading Book for Seminar on Teaching Project Analysis* (Washington, D.C.: Economic Development Institute, World Bank, 1977), p. 32. Hereafter cited as *Reading Book for Seminar on Teaching Project Analysis.*

[33]Overly, p. 181. Copyright © 1979 by The Association for Supervision and Curriculum Development; reprinted with permission of The Association for Supervision and Curriculum Development; all rights reserved.

[34]William Dyer, "What Makes Sense in Management Training," *Management Quarterly,* November 1979, p. 22.

[35]Adapted from *Reading Book for Seminar on Teaching Project Analysis,* pp. 31–38.

[36]Michael Vandenput, "The Transfer of Training," *Journal of European Training,* Vol. 3, No. 3, 1973.

[37]Howard Baumgartel and Francaise Jeanpierre, "Applying Knowledge in the Back Home Setting," *Journal of Applied Behavioral Science,* Vol. 8, No. 2, 1972.

[38]Frank and Margerson.

[39]Alan B. Knox and Douglas Sjogren, "Research on Adult Learning," *Adult Education,* Spring 1965, pp. 133–137.

[40]Schmidt, pp. 82–83.

[41]Adapted from Gordon Lippitt, "Criteria for Evaluating Human Resource Development," *Training and Development Journal,* June, 1976.

[42]A. Raia, *Management by Objectives* (Glenview, Ill.: Scott, Freeman and Company, 1974), pp. 127–128.

[43]Erich Fromm, *Escape from Freedom* (New York: Rinehart and Winston, 1961).

[44]H. Hatry, R. Winnie, and D. Fisk, *Practical Program Evaluation for State and Local Government Officials* (Washington, D.C.: The Urban Institute, 1973), p. 20.

[45]Adapted from Gordon Lippitt, "Training for a Changing World," *Training,* May 1975, pp. 45–49.

[46]Overly, p. 186.

12

qualifications and competencies for renewal facilitators

You know that medicines, when well used, restore health to the sick: they will be well used when the doctor, together with his understanding of their nature, shall understand also what man is, what life is, and what constitution and health are. Know these well and you will know their opposites: and when this is the case you will know well how to devise a remedy.

Leonardo Da Vinci, 1452–1519

The success of any human system renewal effort depends to a great extent on the qualifications and performance of the persons doing the initiating and the planning. Any individual or group that assumes such responsibility for renewal will be carrying out various roles and functions in the process. Whether the renewal facilitator is a manager, supervisor, staff specialist, a special organizational development task force, or a concerned group of board members, the courage and skill of initiating renewal will require a professional approach mixed with a sense of need and commitment. The needs of modern organizations are producing an enlarging role and increased responsibility for training directors and others skilled in manpower and organizational development. In an article written by Leonard Nadler and myself, we explored four major roles of modern human resource developers:[1]

1. As a planning leader
2. As an information and communications link
3. As a learning specialist
4. As a problem solver with management

It is my feeling that each of these functions requires somewhat different skills and abilities. In a small organization the renewal facilitator may perform all four functions, whereas in a large organization the "head of a division" might well be the facilitator for initiating change, but others will be involved in planning, data collection, and a potential planning process. Every renewal facilitator should be professionally prepared in all four roles and functions.

Planning Leader

As organizational complexity has increased, the administrative role of planning has begun to demand a major portion of the time, skill, and energy of the renewal facilitator. In this role, all the administrative skills must be applied. He or she will need to recruit, select, and involve others in the organization; plan meetings; set up the process of coordination and communications; carry out any financial plans related to the planning for change; and all the other functions of a leader:

> The [renewal facilitator] should know the principles and practices used in the administration of programs. They should also know the concepts of management principles, including areas such as problem-solving, the dynamics of organization, controls and reporting procedures.[2]

The planning function is increasing in importance within large human systems, and it is a critical area of skill for the sophisticated renewal facilitator.

Information and Communications Link

In this function the renewal facilitator serves as a seeker of information, clarifier of information, synthesizer of information, reality tester of information, provider of information, and as a communications "link" in the system.

As a *communication link* in the organization, a person should be the pivot for management, departmental and technical personnel, the organization specialists, and all others participating in the process. Obviously, such a person must be an effective communicator, and:

Be accessible to those who are working on the renewal process, or who will participate in it
Develop trust between themselves and all others concerned
Level with people on plans and problems
Keep the goals clearly in mind, and help others to do the same
Define the responsibilities of others
Develop his listening skills

Learning Specialist

An important aspect here is the ability to use learning theory and effective educational methods to meet the needs of a renewal process in which people will learn from their experiences. People contemplating renewal will not be inspired or motivated to change, "buy" an idea, or reexamine their own functioning unless they learn something from having done so.

The responsibility of an enlightened and effective renewal facilitator is to assure that one or more persons engaged in the renewal planning process is knowledgeable in the field of learning principles and practices. This will include the direction of certain activities, coaching the pivital leaders, selecting correct learning targets, and utilizing the best in human and technical resources. A great challenge to the renewal leadership function, therefore, is the increased sophistication required in making use of the rapidly growing body of knowledge about how people learn and change, and relating this to the best of renewal efforts and resources.

Problem Solving for Management

The most important function of the renewal facilitator is that of problem solver. The renewal function should serve as an example and a resource to management in the solution of problems.

The new challenge for the organization's renewal facilitator, then, is to develop skills and role in the organization as an internal organization helper on problem solving, change, and organization development.

The so-called "internal consultant" or facilitator role is important to the changing organizations of today's society; it will require increased professionalization and skills:

> In a sense everyone is a consultant. Everyone has impulses to give advice, information, or help. Teachers, parents, and friends are consultants. Specialists in management, human relations or finance are consultants. Also, everyone at times feels the need for help. In order that the consultantship between the helper and the recipient optimally meets the needs of both parties, appropriate relationships must be built. It is necessary that both parties have certain kinds of skills, knowledge, and awareness in order to establish these relationships.[3]

It is my feeling that more attention needs to be given by management to selecting and developing renewal specialists. As Richard Beckhard puts it:

> The consultant (or person in a helping role) always enters such a relationship as a person with authority achieved either through position or role in the organization or through the possession of specialized knowledge. To achieve an effective consultative relationship, it is essential that he understand the nature of this power and develop skills to use it in a way which will be viewed as helpful by the person receiving the help.
>
> A person entering a consulting or helping relationship must have the ability to diagnose the problem and goals of the person being helped, and be able to assess realistically his own resources to help in the particular situation.[4]

PROFESSIONAL IMPLICATIONS OF THE RENEWAL PROCESS

Carrying out any human system renewal effort requires competence that is professional in nature. As indicated above, the process of human systems renewal can be initiated almost anywhere by concerned leaders in a variety of situations—in divisions, departments, units—but it will not get very far if it does not quickly involve and link up with other individuals and groups in the system. Nevertheless, some individuals must serve as the initiator, stimulator, or spark to set the process in action. It may be a key executive, the personnel or training director, or the marketing or systems manager. What are the qualifications required in this person? Must the person be a behavioral scientist? Will one have to be so courageous as to personally strive to initiate change at risk to one's own job; does it require a person with unusual psychological maturity? These questions are logical and understandable.

Whoever is responsible for initiating renewal will need to manifest professional behavior and leadership. In a pamphlet issued by the Society for Personnel Administration, the difference between a profession and professional behavior is defined in this manner:

> *Professional.* A person who is in an occupation requiring a high level of training and proficiency. This person has high standards of achievement with respect to acquiring unique knowledge and skills. A person who is committed to continued study, growth, and improvement for the purpose of rendering the most effective public service. The level of training, proficiency, and ethical standards are controlled by a society or association of self-governing members. These people maintain and improve standards and criteria for en-

trance and performance in the field of work or occupation.

Professionalism. High level competence exhibited in action by people in a field of work. This behavior stems from an effective integration of a person's knowledge, skills, and attitudes which are derived from high standards of education and experience.[5]

It would be a prerequisite for effective renewal efforts that those giving it leadership manifest professional behavior. To understand this behavior, however, we need to see how certain professions such as medicine, law, and education have tried to achieve a professional status.[6] The literature in the field of management repeatedly gives evidence of the yearning of many management personnel for professional status. Statements, ranging from "Wouldn't it be nice to wear a gold pin indicating membership in the Association of Mystic Management Leadership?" to impassioned, learned pleas, can be found in the pages of professional journals, books on management, various study groups and committees, and convention speeches.

Part of this mutual exhortation, of course, comes from three usually unspoken motivations:

1. Desire for financial security that professional standing promises to enhance
2. Recognition and status
3. Lack of acceptance that certain jobs in management are seen as professional by "outsiders" and the necessity to find solace, compassion, understanding, and assurance of worth from fellow sufferers

Too often there unfortunately seems to exist some sort of naive faith among various management leaders that a cataclysmic change in public opinion, an enlightened act of legislation, or a Scrooge-like change in the vice president to whom those now engaged in training, renewal, or organization development report will miraculously create a professional status for them. This phenomenon, of course, is not peculiar to those engaged in human systems renewal; it is the problem of every new or emerging profession. Those of us engaged in the field of organization renewal and development are now beginning to realize that we will have professional status only to the extent that we achieve it with results that come from competent action.

One other resource to which we might turn to help us identify the criteria of a profession is to define the profession. One dictionary offers the following: "The occupation, if not commercial, mechanical, agricultural, or the like, to which one devotes oneself; a calling; as, the profession of arms, of teaching; the three professions, or the learned professions, of theology, law, and medicine."[7]

Other criteria may need to be added to meet the peculiarities of the human systems development type of endeavor. For example, criteria to demonstrate conclusively that the development process does have a very real dollars-and-cents and quality payoff. As noted earlier, this is an area in which the training and development field is trying many approaches. Another example might be tangible demonstration that a renewal process led by a person with professional qualifications is generally more successful than when change efforts are initiated by a person with no applicable background or skills. One of the difficulties we face is that human systems renewal deals in large part with human relationships and other intangibles, and everyone considers himself or herself to be an expert in these fields. Opposing concepts are difficult to prove or disprove because people in organizations have a way of learning dramatically even in unplanned or unorganized situations.

Current use of the term "professional" seems to be quite casual. Anyone who specializes in a job and does it better than anyone else today seems to be entitled to the term, but such use does not have the element mentioned above: "activities essentially intellectual."

The problem becomes even more frustrating when we find much evidence that employers follow this same pattern. When organizational development or training and development positions open, employers reach down into supervisory ranks and come up with an employee who seems to be able to do an ambiguous something better than any other supervisor—and becomes an organizational development director or training specialist. What it is this supervisor can do better than any other supervisor is not clarified.

COMPETENCY AREAS FOR HUMAN SYSTEMS RENEWAL FACILITATORS

Any list of the professional capabilities of a renewal facilitator is extensive—something like a combination of the Boy Scouts' laws, requirements for admission to heaven, and the essential elements for securing tenure at an Ivy League college. Nevertheless, these questions were asked of thirty-two practitioners:[8]

What are the skills, knowledge, and attitudes that are essential, in your mind, for a person to be able to carry out renewal services, processes, and activities?

What do you feel are the educational preparation and learning experiences that would equip a person to be able to function as a mature and effective renewal facilitator? (In other words, how could he or she become the person you discussed in the preceding question?)

What criteria can be used to evaluate your own effectiveness as it relates to the impact and contribution of consulting service?

The responses obtained from the questionnaire were varied, but certain trends were evident. It was obvious that aiding renewal requires a multifaceted group of competencies. As one respondent put it:

> In order to carry out consulting services, processes, and activities effectively, a consultant needs a host of multifaceted skills, knowledge, and attitudes. Some of these attributes are acquired, experienced, and known to the specialist, but I suggest that there are also internal resources, not consciously known to the specialist, that surface from time to time, and are dependent on situational circumstances.
>
> In my experience of trying to develop three different OD teams in recent years, I have not seen any two specialists develop with the same intensity or pattern. This might suggest that we do not have any concrete rules of order that can be draped as the "mold" for a consultant. Those successful specialists that have evolved under my observation (some unsuccessful ones, too) always seem to have a special quality that makes them credible to the client system. These qualities may be charismatic, professional competence, a flair for the dramatic, a warm personality, or a combination of all of these.

When the responses from the thirty-two practitioners are summarized, the competencies of a renewal facilitator seem to be:

1. *Knowledge areas*
   a. Thorough grounding in the behavioral sciences
   b. An equally thorough foundation in the administrative philosophies, policies, and practices of organizational systems and larger social systems
   c. Knowledge of educational and training methodologies; especially

laboratory methods, problem-solving exercises, and role playing

d. An understanding of the stages in the growth of individuals, groups, organizations, and communities; and how social systems function at different stages
e. Knowledge of how to design and help a change process
f. Knowledge and understanding of human personality, attitude formation, and change
g. Knowledge of one's self: motivations, strengths, weaknesses, and biases
h. An understanding of the leading philosophical systems as a framework for thought and a foundation for value system

2. *Skill areas*
   a. Communication skills: listening, observing, identifying, and reporting.
   b. Teaching and persuasive skills: ability to effectively impart new ideas and insights and to design learning experiences that contribute to growth and change
   c. Counseling skills to help others reach meaningful decisions on their own power
   d. Ability to form relationships based on trust and to work with a great variety of persons of different backgrounds and personalities; sensitivity to the feelings of others; ability to develop and share one's own charisma
   e. Ability to work with groups and teams in planning and implementing change; skill in using group-dynamics techniques and laboratory training methods
   f. Ability to utilize a variety of intervention methods and the ability to determine which intervention is most appropriate at a given time
   g. Skill in designing surveys, interviewing, and other data collection methods
   h. Ability to diagnose problems with a client, to locate sources of help, power, and influence, to understand a client's values and culture, and to determine readiness for change
   i. Ability to be flexible in dealing with all types of situations
   j. Skill in using problem-solving techniques and in assisting others in problem solving
3. *Attitude areas*
   a. Attitude of a professional: competence, integrity, feeling of responsibility for helping clients cope with their problems
   b. Maturity: self-confidence, courage to stand by one's views, willingness to take necessary risks, ability to cope with rejection, hostility, and suspicion
   c. Open-mindedness, honesty, intelligence
   d. Possession of a humanistic value system: belief in the importance of the individual; belief in technology and efficiency as means and not ends; trust in people and the democratic process in economic activities

Another way of looking at the required skills is shown in Figure 12-1. The taxonomy here is explained in this manner:

1. *Educating*
   a. Researcher: familiar with the theoretical bases for change
   b. Writer: able to write clearly and persuasively
   c. Designer: can design educational workshops and events
   d. Teacher: successful in helping others to learn
   e. Instructor: teaching related more to "training" tasks
   f. Trainer: beyond traditional "training"; able to "laboratory train," using heuristic methods
   g. Advocate: holding out for a point of view or plan of action
   h. Conference leader: able to lead, and teach others to lead, a participative meeting or conference
   i. Life/career planner: able to help clients plan careers

The Process of planned change:		UN-FREEZING		MOVEMENT			RE-FREEZING	
ROLES	CHANGE AGENT SKILL AREAS / PHASES OF PLANNED CHANGE	1. Awareness of Need for Change	2. Establish change relationship	3. Diagnosis of system problems	4. Examine options; set goals	5. Acceptance; take action	6. Generalization and stabilization	7. Termination
EDUCATING	Researcher		X	X	XX			
	Writer	X		X	X			
	Designer		X	XX			X	
	Teacher		X		X			X
	Instructor			X		X	X	
	Trainer			X	X	XX	X	
	Advocate	XR			XR	XR	X	XR
	Conference leader	X		X	XX	X	X	
	Life/career planner			X	X			
DIAGNOSING	Action researcher	X		XX	XX	X	X	
	Diagnoser	X		XX	X	X	X	X
	Instrument/survey designer			XX				
	Data analyst	X		XX	X	X	X	X
	Evaluator			X	X	XX	XX	X
CONSULTING	Role model	X	XX	X	X			XX
	Relater at all levels	X	XX	X	X	X	X	X
	Expert in consulting processes:							
	Survey feedback	X		XX	XX	X	X	
	Process observation	X		XX	X	X	X	
	Decision making		X	X	XX			X
	Problem solving	XX		XX	XX	X	X	
	Conflict resolution	X		XX	XX	X	X	
	Conference leadership	X	X	X	XX	X	X	
	Confronter	XR		XR		XR	XR	
	Intervenor				XX	XX	X	X
	Systems analyst	X		XX	XX		X	
	Designer/planner	X		X	XX		X	
	Adapter		X	X	XX	X	XX	
LINKING	Resourcer linker		X	X	XX	XX	X	XX
	Internal resources	X	XX	XX	XX	XX	XX	XX
	External resources							
	Special services			X	X	XX		
	In "thin" areas	(wherever help is indicated or needed)						
	Experts/theorists for action research		X	X	X	X		
	Referrer	X			XX			XX

Code: X-Relevant XX-Especially Relevant XR-Relevant but Risky

Figure 12-1 Taxonomy of Skills of Renewal Facilitator[9]

2. *Diagnosing*
   a. Action researcher: knows how to utilize research and survey data and systems theory to apply to present situation in the organization
   b. Diagnoser: ability to identify what needs to be analyzed, what data gathered, how to obtain and use them
   c. Survey designer: can get needed data in simplest way
   d. Data analyst: can draw correct con-

clusions from data and prepare them for presentation to client

3. *Consulting*
   a. Role model: can practice what one preaches; congruent
   b. Relater: uses interpersonal skills to maintain credibility with all levels of organization
   c. Expert in processes: possesses expertise in tools of the profession. Each of the examples listed in Table 12-1, although also an intervention, requires various skills that have to be learned
   d. Confronter: able to face issues and people head-on
   e. Systems analyst: can employ systems approach to change process
   f. Intervenor: can use an expanding repertoire of interventions appropriately and effectively
   g. Designer/planner: can plan and design and also execute interventions forcefully
   h. Adapter: applies his or her own experience and that of others in a creative and relevant way
4. *Linking*
   a. Resourcer linker: skill in linking the best resourcers with the correctly identified need
   b. Internal: identifies, enlists, trains, and employs resourcers within the organization to effect change
   c. External: identifies appropriate external resourcers, facilitates their entry and effective functioning; uses internal–external consultant relationship well
5. *Special tactics*
   a. Where internal renewal facilitator lacks skills or credibility: linking functions where skills are employed
   b. Theorist-experts for action research
   c. Referrer: able to assist client in employment of resourcers who do not require involvement of renewal facilitator

It seems that the qualities needed by a renewal facilitator fall into two broad categories: intellectual abilities and behavioral competencies. Intellectually, the renewal facilitator must have the ability to make a *dilemma analysis,* because the client that calls for help probably is faced with a situation that appears insoluble, or at least puzzling and difficult. The renewal facilitator must recognize that a dilemma, whether real or not, does exist in the minds of those requesting assistance. It is necessary to discover the nature of the dilemma and to help determine what really is causing it.

To cope with dilemmas (either real or not), the leader-facilitator must have a special type of diagnostic skill and the helping process itself creates additional dilemmas. It is only through skillful examination of the client situation that a consultant can see the relationships between various subsystems and the interdependent nature of individuals, groups, and the environmental setting. Insight, perception, and intuition are necessary to make multiple dilemma analyses. The renewal facilitator's toughest task is to penetrate the complexity and isolate the situational variables. Unless the important factors can be sifted from the maze of detail, and the causes are separated from the symptoms, accurate diagnosis is impossible.

In addition to diagnostic abilities, there is a need for implementation skills. Obviously, one must have some basic knowledge of the behavioral sciences and the theories and methods. But more than that, one needs imagination and experimental flexibility; dissolving a dilemma is essentially a creative process. No real situation is going to fit perfectly the mold suggested by typical techniques or textbook methods. Diversity and unique circumstances almost always exist; it is necessary to be imaginative enough to innovate adaptations and tailor their concepts to meet real demands. It is vital for helpers to be able to envision the impact or ultimate outcome of the actions proposed or implemented. But like most things, the work is as much a process of experimental trial and error as it is a matter of a priori solutions. The courage to experiment—and the flexibility to try as many approaches as are needed to solve the problem—are important ingredients in the practitioner's makeup.

Other major qualities of the renewal facilitator are what might be called interpersonal attributes, all couched in professional attitude and behavior. Success depends upon being as sincerely interested in helping the client as any good physician is interested in helping a patient. People in trouble are not necessarily fools; they can sense objectivity, honesty, and integrity.

A renewal facilitator entering a system needs a strong tolerance for ambiguity. One's first acquaintance with a client can be marked by a certain amount of bewilderment. It takes time to figure out the situation, and during this time one is going to experience a certain amount of confusion. The renewal facilitator must expect this to occur and not be worried by it.

Coupled with one's tolerance for ambiguity must be patience and a high frustration level. Helping a client system find goals and solve problems is likely to be a long and confronting experience. Quick results, full cooperation, and complete success are unlikely.

If people think they may be adversely affected, they will usually respond to attempts to change their relationships and behavior patterns with resistance or dependency, resentment or overenthusiasm, and obstructionism or rationalization. It is important for any person involved in renewal to be mature and realistic enough to recognize that many of their actions for change are going to be frustrated. Such maturity is necessary to avoid reacting with the defeatism and withdrawal that commonly accompanies the frustration of a person's sincere efforts to help others.

Anyone who objectively concludes that he or she cannot help a client system should, of course, withdraw, and, if possible, refer the client to some other source of professional help. This also requires maturity.

The best conceived and articulated plans for change can be destroyed if introduced at the wrong time. Timing is linked to a knowledge of the client, to the realities of the situation, and to the kind of patience that overrides one's enthusiams for wanting to try out a newly conceived alternative.

Beyond this, a facilitator's success will depend on persuasiveness in handling the contacts on which the change effort is based. Because such an array of skills and competencies is not easily achieved, each such helper should continue to evaluate his or her own skill and style:

> Most of the tactics or functions discussed (as interventions) cannot simply be picked up casually from a manual. They are skills which have to be learned. A good tactic badly executed may be worse than no tactic at all.[10]

Another study was conducted in 1979 to identify the principal skills needed by successful practitioners or organization development.[11] In Table 12-1, forty skills are categorized under four groupings, providing a way for a practitioner to engage in self-evaluation. In considering the knowledge areas relevant to an educational plan, we ought to take a look at some of the significant contributions the behavioral and management sciences can make:

Psychiatry: an understanding of individual dynamics, derivations, and the limits of training for the "average" and "normal"
General psychology: an understanding of personality growth and development

Table 12–1
Survey of Organization Development Skills[12]

Knowledge Skills	Consulting Skills	Conceptual Skills	Human Skills
☐ Organization development ☐ Organization behavior (individual, group, intergroup, and whole-organization behavior) ☐ Behavioral sciences management ☐ General business accounting, finance, marketing, management information system, budgeting, etc.) ☐ Training technology ☐ An awareness of current developments in OD	☐ Proposal writing ☐ Marketing programs and ideas ☐ Diagnosing organizations ☐ Synthesizing data ☐ Report writing ☐ Problem solving ☐ Team building ☐ Conflict resolution ☐ Process consultation ☐ Training and development skills ☐ An ability to identify and respond to an organization's real needs ☐ An ability to quickly adapt to changing situations ☐ An ability to quickly establish client trust and rapport ☐ An ability to obtain lasting results	☐ A sound philosophical base concerning human behavior, management, organization behavior, learning behavior, and organization development ☐ A systems view of organizations and the environments in which they operate ☐ An ability to visualize, design, and manage long-range programs, training, interventions, and follow-up programs ☐ An ability to understand and communicate theories, principles, models, and ideas ☐ An ability to innovate	☐ A genuine caring for people ☐ A positive attitude ☐ Self-awareness ☐ Self-discipline ☐ Good rational/emotional balance ☐ Integrity ☐ Helping skills (understanding, empathetic, good listener and coach, good at checking out perceptions, assertive, good at giving and receiving feedback) ☐ Sensitivity to organizational needs ☐ Leveling and confronting skills ☐ Persuasiveness and persistence ☐ A willingness to take risks ☐ An ability to successfully handle stress and frustration ☐ A good sense of humor ☐ An ability to model and practice healthy behavior

OD Skills Evaluation

Evaluate yourself on each of the OD skills by placing the appropriate answer in each box. Total your scores and divide by two and compare the result below.

1 = poor	2 = below average	3 = average	4 = good	5 = excellent
Excellent 90–100	Good 80–89	Average 70–79	Below average 60–69	Poor below 60

Social psychology: an understanding of interpersonal relationships, leadership, group behavior, and change

Educational psychology: an understanding of learning research, method, and theory

Business and public administration: an understanding of the dynamics of organizations, systems, concepts, and the importance of policy formation

Political science: an analysis of social systems, use of power, and conflict resolution

Sociology: an understanding of the forces in social systems and the role of organization in the larger community

Anthropology: an understanding of the function of a culture and the place of organizations as subcultures

General systems: an understanding of a holistic way of looking at input–output dynamics of organizations

Information technology: insight and appreciation for information processing

Quantitative methods: an ability to look at problems in mathematical terms

Economics: a sufficient understanding of micro- and macroeconomics as related to human systems

Being knowledgeable in such an array of areas may strike some renewal specialists as too unrealistic and broad an educational background. However, there is much evidence to indicate that most of management's disenchantment with past renewal efforts has been created by persons who turn knobs and pull controls without adequate understanding of the forces and factors they are trying to influence. The professional renewal facilitators of the future—no matter what they may be called—should be specialists of broad comprehension and ability, rather than merely book-bound manipulators of methods.

Such increased knowledge demand does not have to be satisfied solely, or even partly, by a formal degree program. It can certainly be part of a life-long learning process, anticipating the professional practitioner of the future. In this sense, it is rewarding to examine the roles in which the practitioner needs to be competent. An internal organization development facilitator has prepared a practical presentation of the personal attributes required to implement an effective, results-oriented approach to systems changes:[13]

Strong management background; knows what it means to be a manager and how decisions are made

Strong consulting background—knows how to do completed staff work, how to relate to clients, how to get things done without "authority"

Probably minimum of three years' work experience

Good, solid grounding in behavioral science, but not necessarily a major degree in the field

Masters degree or better in business, applied psychology, public administration, sociology, or *law* with business experience

Calculated risk taker

Willing to relocate as required

Pragmatic decision maker

Open to new ideas and creative in developing them

Able to be flexible in a dynamic environment and to keep focused on desired results

A "team player" in the sense of being able and willing to work within the quality constraints established for organization development activity

Very high tolerance threshhold for dealing with changing situations and frustrating behavior of individuals

Able and willing to talk and relate to the manual worker and the division manager, and maintain perspective

Politically astute, in a corporate sense; knows when to say things and how to say them, and when not to say them

Rapid learner

High energy level—demands of job are significant

Sensitive to where people are in mood, thinking, motivation

Good sense of humor

Although the foregoing lists of skills and attributes contain important information, it is well to keep in mind that activating and helping human system renewal is predicated on the practitioner's exceptional capabilities as *a person,* rather than familiarity with a prescribed order of skills and methods. Skill as a renewal facilitator may be related to academic background, knowledge of certain aspects of management, experience in the client organization, or interpersonal capabilities. It is also related to one's self-concept, style, and personal sincerity.

To act as a professional demands some specific standards. Although there is no clear-cut set of standards for persons who assure responsibility for system renewal, experience indicates that those who are likely to be successful will have some of the following characteristics.

Professional background. Often people with professional preparation in one of the following fields will have attained insights helpful in preparing for the role of renewal facilitator: sociology, psychology, business administration, educational psychology, public administration, personnel administration, and adult education. However, because of the wide variance of skills required in renewal, professional preparation does not guarantee competence, and conversely, people can be competent without such conventional academic training. Nonetheless, some knowledge in these fields is essential to a well-rounded renewal facilitator whether self-taught or academically learned.

Group experience. In addition to a professional background of some kind, the renewal facilitator should have met the practical problems of learning to work successfully as a group leader. Experience with groups, however, might simply have firmed up old habits of wielding authority and afforded practice in ineffective work habits. Experience, then, can be helpful or harmful, depending on its quality. Nevertheless, much of the renewal process will take place in task groups, project groups, functional units in organizations, and similar settings.

Self-understanding. This is an absolute essential in the role of the renewal facilitator. Facilitators must have sufficient understanding of their own motivations and sufficient control of their own defense mechanisms to prevent their needs from interfering with the renewal process, and to muster empathy with the interpersonal problems of others in the process of change. It is also a prerequisite to be an effective internal consultant to an organization.

Personal security. Together with organizational experience, a renewal facilitator must have sufficient personal security to permit taking a relatively nonpunitive role in initiating change, to be accepting in his or her relations with others, to have a genuine respect for them, to have a willingness to share leadership roles, and to relinquish authority as the renewal process proceeds. In short, sufficient personal security to participate adequately in a rather wide range of interpersonal situations where confrontation, search, and coping is involved is an indispensable requirement.

Multiple professional skills. With the proper background and maturity, one can probably learn enough planning, communication, learning, and consulting skills to carry out the complex functions involved in organization renewal. This assumes, of course, that the professional background of the person includes a working knowledge of the process of scientific problem solving and social change. These skills can be acquired. Obviously, the wider one's range of skills, the more effective the renewal facilitator can be applying them appropriately in the organization renewal process.

Democratic philosophy. A person who has a modest degree of each of the foregoing criteria will probably also exhibit a democratic philosophy of leadership and work. He or she will be able to encourage a renewal process in which persons learn for themselves. Such a philosophy will also imply a set of ethical norms that go with a democratic or collaborative planned change effort.

Ability to conceptualize. Tackling a process with such varied forces at work will require that the renewal facilitator be able to see the larger situation, to see the organization in its totality, and to see how the human, technical, structural, and economic forces interrelate. The broad perspective is a prime asset.

Although human systems renewal does require professional skills and behavior, it must have at the core of its leadership mature persons who possess a set of *personal values* that guide their life and work.

ETHICAL IMPLICATIONS OF RENEWAL

In contemplating, designing, and implementing human system renewal, we are confronted with the process of some individual or group initiating reflections, data collection, analysis, action, and out of all that, change. Who has the right to change a situation or persons? When is it unethical manipulation and when is change an appropriate initiation? First of all, who should be a renewal facilitator in an organization? It is anybody who deliberately sets out to help others to achieve change for the betterment of the organization. Certainly, every line manager is a renewal facilitator because he or she operates with other people to try to influence them to achieve effectively. Certainly, every human resource and organization development person falls into this category. The various specialists in the organization, the accountant, the corporation lawyer, the company physician, and almost everyone in a leadership position falls into this category at one time or another.

What is the central ethical problem of the renewal facilitator? On what grounds does he or she base a value judgment to influence others to change direction? This question is closely connected to the earlier, more technical question of how one effectively helps others to change. But they are different questions. Value judgments on which one bases an attempt to influence the thinking, behavior, and attitudes of others require one to reexamine the controlling values, as well as the grounds for their validation and justification.

Recognizing that many words have achieved evaluative weight, it might be well to divorce, for the moment, our value judgments from the processes these words describe. "Manipulate," for instance, means the arrangement of conditions so that change in a certain direction will take place. The schoolteacher who arranges the classroom setting, provides certain selected pieces of handwork, asks certain questions, demands certain homework, and creates certain motivational drives, is "manipulating," whether teaching physical fitness or higher mathematics.

In *The Ugly American,* the authors have Father Finian write in his diary: "What we discovered is that men are persuaded of things by the same process, whether the persuading is done by the Catholic Church, Lutherans, Communists, or democrats."[14] This would indicate that there are observable processes and forces at work in every system situation. By observation and analysis, these forces can be understood and, to some extent, their effect can be predicted from the nature of their influence. Further, skills can be developed to use, direct, or otherwise control present forces to meet desired, although not necessarily desirable, ends. People can and do influence, and sometimes control, such forces. This is a nonjudgmental statement; it is observable data.

This line of reasoning suggests, then, that the question is not merely one of the values of the forces themselves, but rather the value system that motivates a leader to use or not use them, and the ends he or she attempts to achieve. From this point of view, each person, acting or refusing to act as an influence for renewal places under critical judgment basic beliefs and out of those beliefs, an ethical system.

If we accept this line of reasoning, if we recognize that our commitment to a specific job in the organization often makes us a potential renewal facilitator, then I submit that the question usually asked, "What right have I to try to make persons and groups different from what they are?", must be reversed. The basic question that we cannot avoid is: "What right have I to withhold myself, my skills, and my convictions in a changing situation from helping that change to take place in a direction consistent with my convictions?"

Society has always been concerned about the ethics of those who wield power and influence. As control of the environment has increased, intense interest in the motives and values of leaders has also mounted. Today's gigantic organizations, mass advertising, and automated systems are controlled increasingly by professional managers who live in a world of continual tension and change. How do such persons self-guide their actions? What rules can be laid down to help the executive choose whether to put country above company, family above job, moral honesty above profit? Price-fixing scandals may arouse the public for a time, but the day-to-day struggles to find the right way to lead are fought on the lonely battleground of a leader's conscience.

In any area of helping, the renewal facilitator occupies a position of trust, and therefore the ethical aspects of his or her work and relationships occupy a significant place in the discussion of the renewal process. The work of all professional helpers requires the constant exercise of discretion and judgment. Their clients may not be qualified to appraise the quality of service being offered or the risks involved and therefore may have to rely for support and protection on the helper's standards of conduct, and, if one is involved, on a network of professional peers. The client is justified in expecting certain standards of conduct, and can derive confidence from knowing that a code of professional behavior and commitment will provide protection. Such professional behavior, however, encounters a number of complex values.

Once the awareness of the complexity of many ethical problems is granted, there arises the difficult task of defining what is and what is not ethical. A standard definition of "ethics" is that it is "the study of ideal human character, actions, and ends." The problem lies in the fact that differing ideas exist as to what is ideal human behavior.

Ethics is frequently interpreted as being "in the eye of the beholder." When a person wins something in competition with another individual or group, it is the superiority of his or her own ability; when the other person wins, it is easy to perceive "shenanigans" and to wish to expose him or her as unethical. Some people use the definitions of "legal" or "illegal" as an adequate definition of ethical behavior. Ethics is a set of standards, or code, or value system by which free, human actions are determined as ultimately right or wrong, good or evil. If an action agrees with these standards, it is an ethical action; if it does not agree, it is an unethical action.

Actions take on moral value in relation to the circumstances of a particular situation. Both theologians and practitioners have been focusing the modern concern for ethics on "situational ethics" rather than on absolutes that put all ethical confrontations in "black and white" terms. Can our complex ethical heritage be interrelated with the dynamic realitites of modern life? Is there a place for "ideals" that are consistent with the "practical necessities" of organization management? All too often organizational forces compromise the manager and, because of our heritage, one is left with a bad conscience. How did the present state of ethical dilemma develop? From what did most ethical norms emerge? Ethical behavior is based on moral tradition and beliefs. Our Western culture has given us a heritage of ethics that sometimes puts us in a position where any course of action we pursue will violate some ethical principle.

Samuel H. Miller, former Dean of Harvard Divinity School, delivered an introductory indictment of the oversimplified approach to ethical awareness adopted by many of the teachers, researchers, and leaders in the management field:

> We have reached a stage in our civilization where many different strands of ethical tradition have been woven together. Imbedded in the culture which conditions us and our relationships, and imbedded also in us as civilized, educated persons, are several distinctive ethical patterns. These sets of moral attitudes are contradictory enough to be competitive—both in their institutional forms and in their personal aspects. . . . [15]

Let us look at some of these "different strands of ethical tradition" that influence modern leaders and those they lead:

- Hebraic culture, based on the Ten Commandments—the "covenant" with the group was very important
- Christian system, based on the beatitudes of Jesus Christ, with emphasis on redemption of the individual born into the Kingdom
- Medieval way of life, based on penance, with emphasis on the future life
- Renaissance culture of the Reformation, based on the individual and his or her freedom
- Industrial Revolution, based on the technical application of science to production and distribution
- Scientific approach, based on the empirical method and the reign of law

There is an enormous gulf between the superficial and prestige attitude of the Agricultural Revolution and then the Industrial Revolution—and the fundamental ideas of the beatitudes of the Christian culture. The Industrial Revolution is in tradition and has been altered by the latest form of culture—the postindustrial society or "third wave."* This new phase, based as it is on empirical methods and laws, sometimes finds past cultures questionable as suitable foundations for building and renewing today's society.

Consistent with all these cultural influences has been the emergence of a social ethic and individualistic ethic. The individualistic ethic glorifies the freedom of the individual, competition between one person and another, and also self-determination as the value goals of life. The social ethic elevates the importance of the individual to the group, community, and larger society. It assumes that the group is the primary way of meeting human needs.

In some cases people perceive a clash between these two values. The social ethic advocates adaptation, equilibrium, and solidarity. Competition is no longer exalted. Although the individual is not neglected, his or her satisfactions are seen as derived from participation and membership in organized relationships (e.g., groups, clubs, organizations). Organization management has built upon both of these ethics for its values and practices. The individualistic ethic has focused attention on hard work, responsibility, individual goal achievement, self-development, and many other

*The term "the third wave" is used by Alvin Toffler to describe the next stage of world culture.

practices commonly or less commonly found in organizational life. One intensive survey made by the Church and Economic Life Commission of the National Council of Churches enunciated those individual values that are relevant to our economic system:[16]

Survival and physical well-being (productivity). Each individual should have access to the conditions necessary for health, safety, comfort, and reasonable longevity.

Fellowship. Each individual should have a variety of satisfying human relationships.

Dignity and humility. Each individual should have the opportunity to earn a position of dignity and respect in society.

Enlightenment. Each individual should have opportunity to learn about the world in which he or she lives. He or she should be able to satisfy intellectual curiosity and to acquire the skills and knowledge for intelligent citizenship, efficient work, and informed living.

Aesthetic enjoyment. Each individual should have the opportunity to appreciate aesthetic values in art, nature, and ritual, and in personal relations. Many aesthetic values are attainable through both production and composition.

Creativity. Each individual should be able to express personality through creative activities, to identify with the results of own activity, and to take pride in intellectual, aesthetic, political, and other achievements.

New experience. An important goal of life is suggested by such words as variability, spontaneity, whimsy, novelty, excitement, fun, sport, holiday, striving against odds, solving problems, innovations, and invention. Each individual should have opportunities for new experiences.

Security. Each individual should have assurance that the objective conditions necessary for attainment of the foregoing goals are and will continue to be reasonably accessible to him or her.

Freedom. Freedom is the opportunity to pursue one's goals without restraint.

Justice. The religious concept of love does not imply neglect of the self. The individual is to be as concerned about others as about self—neither more nor less.

The preceeding goals are stated in terms of the kinds of life experiences people wish to have. Goals can then be regarded as qualities of human personality; accordingly, a desirable personality would be defined as one that is favorably conditioned toward the various goals.

Fulfillment of such a list of individual values is a challenge to any manager, group, or organization, and it indicates some of the forces at work in initiating organization renewal. The individual values that have emerged in our culture sometimes conflict with a second trend, which focuses on social ethics.

The social ethic has emphasized the value of cohesive work units, use of specialists combined in team situations, associations in product and professional areas, responsibility to customers, and numerous other practical applications. In this context, management has differing responsibilities to various segments of society as it establishes goals, policies, and practices. These obligations try to secure and maintain a compatibility between management's relationship to society by legal and nonlegal means. The basic problem results as management pursues its operations, from the tension between organizational self-interest and social obligation. Some of the social responsibilities of organizational management are:

Ethical relations with customers. Whether an organization is providing services or widgets, it has an obligation to provide what is advertised, requested, or promised.

Ethical relations with employees. Management bears the obligation to provide a fair wage, proper working conditions, opportunity for promotion, appropriate fringe benefits, equal employment opportunity, and good personnel relations.

Ethical relations with suppliers. Managers have

a responsibility to treat suppliers with the same consideration as that given to customers.

Ethical relations with policymakers, shareholders, or sponsors. Almost every organization has a group of persons who have invested capital, trust, or energy into the life of the organization. The responsibility to inform, consult, reward, and be influenced by those groups is a prerequisite of ethical management.

Ethical relations with competitors. To work with one's competitors in such a way that fair practice results is another part of management's responsibility. This means avoiding price fixing, not stealing industrial secrets, cooperating in presenting one's field, and contributing to the development of the profession of management.

Ethical relations with the community. In the past twenty years, management has become more aware of its responsibility in community planning, community relations, and community problem solving.

It is necessary for today's leader to consider the importance of individual and social ethics. To apply these ethical standards to the organization, the group, and one's self is an essential undertaking. It is an even greater challenge to relate these ethical values to organization renewal and change. It is also important to understand clearly that there are some underlying assumptions supporting the need for organization renewal:

1. In today's organizations there are unavoidable human factors which involve varying degrees of interpersonal and intergroup tension and conflict that keep the organization from functioning most effectively.
2. It is better that such human problems be solved than that they remain unsolved.
3. Deliberate planning of solutions to these problems, which necessarily involve changes in the people, the groups, and institutions concerned, is necessary to a degree that it has not been in the past. Trial-and-error processes of historical accommodation are no longer adequate to the organizational needs of today.
4. The most promising source from which to derive principles of ethical control in the planning of change is in our system of democratic and scientific values. These values can be translated into norms or principles of method that can be used in the guidance and direction of organization renewal, of deciding what changes are needed, and in evaluating the changes produced. The alternatives are to identify "democracy" or "scientific" with one substantive solution or another. Some people who favor public housing will argue for it as "democratic"—others will identify private housing with the "democratic" way. Let us translate these values into norms of method acceptable to both sides. Through conflict they may work out a solution that may not be what either held in the first place, but which hopefully will be mutually satisfactory to both.

This thinking can be related to some guidelines for those who must plan changes that lead to human system renewal. The first guideline concerns motivation. A planner can be motivated, in part, by such individual needs as status, security, and prestige. One's own awareness of these motivations may clearly demonstrate a role. The approach to problem solving should be task-oriented rather than prestige-oriented. The essential concern should be that the new condition achieved be better than the first, not that the person initiating change should receive credit or have an enhanced standing in the eyes of others.

The processes by which renewal is planned should be collaborative; they should involve ideally all the people affected by the change. For example, as we set out to produce a change in the pattern of staff meetings in corporate headquarters, insofar as possible the changes planned and instituted should be arrived at collaboratively. All the people affected should have an opportunity to express themselves concerning the problem and to contribute to shaping the solution in terms of their particular relation to the decision. Often, resistance to collaboration operates within the people with whom we deal, as well as within ourselves. Attempts to complete self-effacement in the renewal facilitator may be a kind of dodge that covers up one's own self-interest in producing change. Widespread resistance to his or her attempts to influence should lead to reexamination of one's position, and reentry into the change arena with approaches that permit and sustain collaborative planning of change.

For the renewal facilitator to conform to democratic and scientific values, the methods of problem solving should be experimental. Although this norm may be most difficult to derive from basic democratic values, it is still very important. The opposite tends to be a kind of absolutist conviction that one's present views are right beyond question. Such an attitude often prevents genuine collaboration. If a human problem is a genuine problem, there is no single, pat solution. There may be many principles that apply, but no one knows in advance exactly which combinations best fit reality. An experimental attitude means giving any reasonable but novel plan a try; it also means building into the plan methods of evaluation that will reveal whether the altered practices approach the desired change goals. Almost always, solving a problem in human relations involves some interadjustment in all the people concerned, including the renewal facilitator.

The method used for renewal, if it is to be democratic and scientific, must be educational and/or therapeutic for the people involved, leaving them better able to face and control future situations. The objective is not to solve present problems in order to get away from future problems, but rather to know better how to deal with the latter as they arise. The idea is not to get away from problems, which is to move away from reality, but rather to know better how to confront, diagnose, and solve problems.

And finally, people initiating planned change must always be aware of accountability to themselves. The responsibility is to examine motivation, the results desired, and the methods employed to see how consistently they correspond with the value response required. Second, accountability extends to those who are affected by renewal efforts. In this it is a help, and further guide, to accept the fact that the renewal facilitator is always involved in and affected by the change produced. He or she does not stand over and above—a little god who calls the shots and determines the destiny of others. Such a person is involved and affected, whether as an outside consultant or a part of the system, never disassociated from a profoundly inextricable relationship with fellow men and women.

Let us take these guidelines for working in a democratic and scientific manner, as well as an operational definition of ethics, and apply them to the work of a renewal facilitator.

Leading or consulting with groups is required of all those who accept responsibility for changing the organizational systems of modern society. Today, fortunately, recent research results and new research techniques permit us to diagnose the behavioral phenomena associated with the achievement of constructive group action. With present knowledge it is indeed now possible to develop the diagnostic skills required for group leadership and consultation.

As leaders develop their capacities to improve group performance, it is well to examine the fundamental ideas and beliefs that undergird them, lending their efforts a value and central meaning. Group leadership skills have largely developed as they have because they were successfully related to a set of cultural and religious values. Only when a leader is guided by a value pattern is it possible to judge and evaluate his or her work with groups in meaningful terms. Here are some of the value orientations desirable in a renewal facilitator working with groups:[17]

1. *Worth of each individual in the group.* In Western society, a belief in the individual is an imperative in the development of group relation skills. We see the individual as an end, not as a means to an end—not as a pawn to be moved about as it may please an authoritarian to do.

It is essential, in leading groups, to be sensitive to the motivations and needs of the individual members as well as those of one's self. To understand individual needs is to be aware of the complexity of personality, its structure and capacity for growth toward self-hood.

The implications of the Western concept of individual worth are quite clear. To be successful, the group leader must consider each member indispensable to the group, and must help each member to be fulfilled within the context of the group. The psychological concept of Maslow's "hierarchy of needs" has all persons desiring self-fulfillment as their highest level of need. It is a modern form of the classical Judeo-Christian doctrine of the infinite value of the person, calling forth the affirmation of one's self as created in the image of God. An effective group leader will want each member of the group to be involved, to take part, and to contribute to the achievement of common goals.

2. *Group relationships should be authentic and satisfy the yearning for acceptance.* Of the many reasons why people participate in groups—for example, to secure representation, support, knowledge, experience, or to focus responsibility—perhaps the most basic reason is to obtain personal satisfaction. People search for social satisfactions through the development of close relationships that anchor the individual securely in some stabilized continuing group. When groups are ineffective, it is often because they are not satisfying the personal needs of members. Such failure, understandably, leads to apathy, loss of time, indecisiveness, and poor attendance at meetings. People yearn for acceptance in a fellowship. The history of the two ethics in Western culture—the individualistic and social—instructs us that both are of great significance in our lives.

The great challenge to working with groups is that of developing honest, nondefensive, and authentic fellowship in the life of the group. The group leader or facilitator should strive for unembarrassed communication among individual members of the group, with free exchange of ideas and feelings. In such an atmosphere, the sociological term "sense of community" takes on flesh and meaning. Frank expression and argument are viewed within this context by a mature leader as positive values that not only tolerate but encourage.

3. *Members must be able to influence group decisions.* Individuals should be allowed the right to influence the group, and group leaders should create a climate favorable to the exercise of that right if the decision is a group responsibility. In cases where the responsibility is in fact the leader's, or where a decision has already been reached, people ought not to be manipulated and led to believe otherwise at group meetings. Whenever the group is asked to reach a decision, its freedom to act and degree of responsibility should be made clear. The renewal facilitator should guide, not direct; and should seek opportunities for group, not personal achievement.

4. *The search for truth and use of mind.* The search for truth is another ethical principle that should guide group leadership and group actions. Group decisions must be based not upon friendship, nor upon likes and dislikes, hunches or intuition, but upon an objective search for the

right answer. Frequent references have been made to a supposed contradiction between the scientific method and religious values. It appears that this is essentially a semantic disturbance, a confusion of dogma and creed—which may indeed offend science—with the essence of Judeo-Christian thought. The scientist Wernher von Braun put it this way:

> I am certain that science, in its search for new insights into the nature of the creation, has produced new ethical values of its own. . . . Personally, I believe in the ultimate victory of truth. . . . The better we understand the intricacies of the atomic structure, the nature of life, or the master plan for the galaxies, the more reason we have found to marvel at the wonder of God's creation.[18]

Leaders and consultants who believe in the search for truth will encourage full play of members' minds in solving problems of the group. A good mind, encouraged to work, will penetrate half-truths and enlarge the incomplete view to encompass a broad perspective. Effective group action depends upon facing hard facts, interpreting them sensibly, and producing ideas—all a part of the problem-solving process. We must indeed use our minds if we are to survive.

While we seek new knowledge, we should also make the best use we are able of what we already know, always working toward the improvement of ourselves, other individuals or groups, the organization, and humankind itself. An effective renewal facilitator will employ problem-solving techniques to bring out the best in the minds of the members of the group.

5. *A group leader should stimulate creative free expression.* Most religious values emphasize the importance of "free will" and "free choice." All members of the group should be free to dissent, to be in the minority, or indeed to stand alone, and to differ with the leader without fear of reprisal. In short, each member of the group should be stimulated to release his or her creative best. Group activity is often criticized, and sometimes only too accurately, on grounds that it encourages conformity with the views of the leader or the hierarchy of the organization. However, an effective leader is usually one who provides a climate that releases the creative potential of individuals in the group and encourages spontaneity.

Expression of one's personality through group action is a rewarding experience that adds an immeasurable dimension to life. Such an experience is all too rare, but it lends life excitement and novelty as well as deep satisfaction. People want to take pride in achievements, be they intellectual, manual, aesthetic, political, or any other. This pride has a special value in group performance when a member's ideas or actions tend to be supported by the others during the problem-solving phase. Leaders and consultants should work to have the pardonable pride of individuals serve and advance the group objectives.

6. *Tolerate diverse behavior and do not sit in judgment of others.* A prime tenet of Western culture is the toleration of diversity, the recognition that many beliefs, attitudes, and personalities form the web of mankind. Most value systems caution that we judge not for we may also be judged. The concept of forgiveness, turning the other cheek, is prominent in our religious philosophy. Although effective group leaders will develop perceptions of other persons and feelings toward them, these perceptions and feelings should not affect their judgment of a member's contribution or of individual worth. As much as anyone else, the leader should exercise tolerance of people's behavior and recognize that hostility, aggression, and personal ill will are to be expected in group activity. The group leader must try to understand, in

order to communicate and progress. It is not unknown for a leader to use precedent as a substitute for democratic action when the group decision differs from his or her own. This, of course, is a poor way to "win," and organizations themselves should be flexible enough to prevent it.

We have been identified above some of the basic life values and methods that can provide guidelines for the responsible group leader and renewal facilitator. These have support in both psychological and religious knowledge; they put the leadership of group development in a frame of reference that indicates that growth of persons, freedom of will, use of the mind, meaningful fellowship, and the importance of the individual are the dynamic dimensions of qualitative group functioning in today's organiization. It may well become evident in the renewal process that there is a need to confront the overall values and operating ethics of the total system.

Persons who have had little experience in helping or planning change may wonder why it is not a simple matter to conduct all professional dealings in accordance with the highest ethical standards. The difference between the proper and improper should be clear enough. But it is not that simple. All too frequently, the consultant faces decisions that involve ethical questions not easily resolved. Some consultants may find themselves working in areas where ethical standards are vague and ambiguous. In many instances, the consultant must walk a decision-making tightrope, trying to balance fairly the sometimes conflicting interests of all those with whom he or she is professionally associated.

As a professional practitioner, the professional helper is a maker of value judgments.[19] Helping involves activities in which choices must be made between alternative courses of action. There are three alternative routes or approaches to follow in making ethical decisions: (1) legalistic, (2) lawless or unprincipled, and (3) situational.

In the legalistic approach, one enters into every decision-making situation with a whole code of preformulated rules and regulations. The lawless approach would have one entering into a decision-making situation armed with no principles or maxims whatsoever, except perhaps self-interest. The situational-ethical approach lies between these two. Since every situation is unique, one must rely on the situation itself, then and there, to provide its clues for the creation of an ethical decision. With this approach, one enters into every change situation equipped with the ethical maxims developed previously from experiencing somewhat similar situations.

Central to the use of ethical guidelines in most renewal situations is an awareness that circumstances alter cases. The person using situational ethics is willing to make full and respectful use of principles, treating them as maxims but not as laws. There is no real quarrel here between situational ethics and an ethics of principles, unless the principles become hardened into laws or regulations.

Three more specific ethical or value systems have been emerging that are relevant for consideration by consultants. These are the scientific ethic, the humanistic ethic, and scientific humanism. Each of these orientations has come increasingly to the fore in the last two decades in response to major social changes. Scientific values tend to emphasize rationality, moderation, flexibility, calculation, planning, and prudence as guidelines. Humanistic values stress freedom, spontaneity, creativity, participation, and self-acutalization. Scientific humanism is proposed as an integration of the other two frameworks.

Probably the most important evidences of the application of the scientific ethic are the new science-based analysis and decision-making techniques that are increasingly prevalent in business and government. These techniques, such as operations research and systems analysis, call for clarity in the specification of goals and therefore serve to make value preferences explicit. As evidence of the humanistic ethic, the humanistic trend in psychology developed by Maslow is probably most forceful and relevant to the interpersonal aspects of the consulting process. Maslow emphasized openness of communication, mutuality of decision making, personal growth, and fulfillment.

The growth of each person, however, seems to experience stages of moral understanding.[20] Lawrence Kohlberg proposes a sequence of moral reasoning that is derived from cross-cultural studies indicating six moral stages. At each stage there is an increased capacity to reason through moral conflicts in a rational, equitable, and constructive manner (see Table 12-2). The six stages are divided into three levels: the preconventional (stages 1 and 2), the conventional (stages 3 and 4), and the postconventional or principled (stages 5 and 6).

In *stage 1* there is an orientation toward punishment and obedience, toward superior power. The physical consequences of human action determine right and wrong regardless of their human meaning. At *stage 2,* right action becomes that which satisfies one's own needs. Human relationships are viewed in terms of the marketplace, reciprocity becomes, "You scratch my back and I'll scratch your's."

The conventional level becomes dominant in late preadolescence. Maintaining the expectations, rules, and standards of the group, organization, or nation become valuable in their own right. There is a concern not only with conforming to the individual social order but also in maintaining, justifying and supporting this order. At *stage 3* we have what is called the good boy/good girl orientation. Good behavior is what helps others and is approved by them. One gains approval by being "nice" or exhibiting behavior that will be approved by others. At *stage 4* there is a shift toward fixed definitions of social duty, concern with firm social rules, and a respect for formal authority; a recognition that laws and other social institutions have clear social utility and are justified in terms of their order-maintenance function.

The postconventional (or principled) level, first appearing in adolescence, is characterized by a major thrust toward autonomous moral principles. These principles have validity apart from the authority of the group or individuals. The principled thinker is able to evaluate the moral validity of concrete social rules and norms, through tests of more general principles of justice.

Stage 5 is a legalistic contract orientation, generally with utilitarian overtones. Law has a basis in consent and the welfare of citizens rather than simply in a respect for authority as at *stage 4.* Laws that are not constitutional, violate human rights, or are not in the general interest, are judged to be invalid at *stage 5.*

At *stage 6* there is a basis for rational agreement to moral principles. There is an orientation toward ethical principles appealing to logical consistency, comprehensiveness, and universality. The principles are abstract and ethical rather than appearing as concrete rules. They are universal principles of justice, ideal reciprocity, equality of human rights, and respect for the dignity of human beings as individual persons.

In this context, it is to be hoped that a renewal facilitator has arrived at stage 6 in moral judgement. A great deal of human behavior, however, is found at stages 3, 4, and 5. Some people are convinced that the 1970s were the "me" generation—with a stage 2 value system.

Both research theory and practical experience underscore the fact that the single most important factor in the practice of ethical behavior is the individual's personal code and standards. Each person

Table 12–2
Classification of Moral Judgment Into Levels and Stages of Development[21]

Level	Basis of Moral Judgment	Stages of Development
I	Moral value resides in external, quasi-physical happenings, in bad acts, or in quasi-physical needs rather than in persons and standards.	Stage 1: Obedience and punishment orientation. Egocentric deference to superior power or prestige, or a trouble-avoiding set. Objective responsibility.
		Stage 2: Naively egoistic orientation. Right action is that instrumentally satisfying the self's needs and occasionally those of others. Awareness of relativism of value to each actor's needs and perspective. Naive egalitarianism and orientation to exchange and reciprocity.
II	Moral value resides in performing good or right roles, in maintaining the conventional order and the expectations of others.	Stage 3: Good boy/good girl orientation. Orientation to approval and to pleasing and helping others. Conformity to stereotypical images of majority or natural role behavior, and judgment by intentions.
		Stage 4: Authority and social-order-maintaining orientation. Orientation to "doing duty" and to showing respect for authority and maintaining the given social order for its own sake. Regard for earned expectations of others.
III	Moral value resides in conformity by the self to shared or shareable standards, rights, or duties.	Stage 5: Contractual legalistic orientation. Recognition of an arbitrary element or starting point in rules or expectations for the sake of agreement. Duty defined in terms of contract, general avoidance of violation of the will or rights of others, and majority will and welfare.
		Stage 6: Conscience or principle orientation. Orientation not only to actually ordained social rules but to principles of choice involving appeal to logical universality and consistency. Orientation to conscience as a directing agent and to mutual respect and trust.

represents in his or her own life the influence of environment and experience, and this contributes to the criteria used to appraise the ethical implications of particular situations. Some people have used certain tests to evaluate the proper decision in a particular situation:

The test of common sense. Does the action make sense? In view of the situation, how will the proposed action look in practice and result in practical consequences? This common sense test may help to determine whether the proposed action is appropriate.

The test of hurting someone else. Will the action contribute "internal pain" to someone to the extent that it may endanger the integrity of a personality or cause excessive discomfort?

The test of one's best self. Each of us has a self-concept that may or may not fit our actions. As we consider a decision, we might ask if this action will fit the concept of ourselves at our best.

Persons operating as renewal facilitators can best guard against misuse of their own skills and knowledge if they are aware of their own major motivations. Often, we conceal our motives even from ourselves. We are more likely to violate our ethical norms when we use our knowledge and skill for purposes that we cannot or do not admit to ourselves. If we are concerned with ethical change, self-knowledge is essential. There is no royal road toward self-awareness, yet this is of primary importance for the person concerned with ethical or nonethical motivation toward changing other people's behavior. We are more likely able to fool others, the more skilled we are in fooling ourselves. Self-knowledge does not necessarily make one more ethical, but it does put the renewal facilitator in command of the forces operating on and through him or her so that dealing with them can be brought into line with ethical commitments.

The test of publicity. A simple test to apply to any contemplated action is to determine how the act would stand up to the light of public knowledge. What if people knew what you were doing? This is a searching and healthy test for any leader to ask introspectively when confused about the ethics of a situation.

The test of one's most admired personality. Most of us have one or two people who mean a great deal to us—such as parents, teachers, or bosses. What would such a model do in this situation?

The test of foresight. An important test of any decision or action is to explore the possible consequences of the behavior. What is likely to result from this action?

Managers and others who assume renewal responsibility have many other responsibilities to the organization and society of which they are a part. Legal and social obligations of management are to operate the organization in accordance with goals, objectives, and rights under which it operates. Equally important are its obligations to employees, customers, government, the community, and the public at large. These may at times be momentarily in conflict with the decisions and policy-making of management. However, the goal of management should be that its complex obligations and responsibilities should never jeopardize the application of high ethical standards.

The ethics of any decision-making situation are determined by looking at the effect of the decision on the decision maker and on those influenced by the decision, as both of these factors relate to the existing values of the culture. A leader must assess each situation in the light of relevant organization, group, and individual ethical standards. Over the past thirty years, organizations have continually attempted to demonstrate their eagerness to fulfill their social and individual responsibilities. They have initiated, and accepted from others, policies that have improved overall standards of conduct. Through these improvements, the requirements of effective leadership have steadily risen over the years. This, in turn, has had a profound influence on the performance of the scientific and industrial society in which we live.

In one sense, however, there is an additional factor that can help make sure that a renewal facilitator will manifest proper ethical practice. This is the extent to which we develop managing, leading, and consulting in the organization renewal context as a professional role and function. It is possible to develop adequate professional controls over attempts to produce change. Historically, one of the best methods of safeguarding the public from the misuse of expert knowledge and skill has been professional self-regulation. This is rather difficult to achieve in the organization renewal field because the renewal facilitator may operate in and through professional associations supporting many different disciplines. Here part of the problem is to get the several professional associations more concerned, more commonly aware that perhaps a common code of ethics should be developed.

An ethical code for a profession helps to assure fair treatment for clients and provides for the protection of their rights. More explicitly, these are ethical principles for helping behavior:

Provide professional guidelines, set by historical reference, regarding behavior that is attractive and justifiable to the client

Allow professionals to inspire faith in the client that the consultant will behave in a way beneficial to the client

Signify that the consultant is committed to do a good job in the client's interest in return for the client's trust and confidence

Codes that attempt to deal fully with the ethical dimensions of the professional's role in society serve a useful function. They are educational, providing members of a profession with guidelines for the kind of ethical behavior that, according to the historic experience of the group, is most likely to justify the confidence of the client. Codes narrow the area in which the consultant has to struggle with uncertainty.

The Association of Consulting Management Engineers has outlined the purposes of a code of professional ethics:[22]

It helps the practitioner determine the propriety of his conduct in his professional relationships.

It indicates the kind of professional posture the practitioner must develop and maintain if he or she is to succeed.

It gives clients and potential clients a basis for confidence that the professional person sincerely desires to serve them well, and places service ahead of financial reward.

It gives clients a basis for confidence that the professional person will do his work in conformity with professional standards of competence, objectivity, and integrity.

A number of professional organizations have developed codes of ethics for their members. It is worthwhile briefly to examine those of the American Society for Training and Development, the Academy of Management, International Consultants Foundation, the American Psychological Association, and the Association of Consulting Management Engineers.

The American Society for Training and Development has published a code of ethics from which the following items have been chosen as particularly relevant to the best interests of a consultant-client relationship. Consultants shall:

1. Not conduct activities that may cause any colleague or training participant unnecessary embarrassment or disparagement
2. Not violate confidences or break promises, unless disclosure of confidential information serves professional purposes or is required by law
3. Limit their activities as facilitators of change to functions for which they have been adequately trained, and shall abstain particularly from areas of psychological activity for which they have no professional qualification
4. Not knowingly distort or misrepresent facts concerning training and development activities to any individual, organization, or employer
5. Openly share information and data that will advance the state of the professional art
6. Maintain a professional attitude toward the introduction of new knowledge in the field of training and development
7. Recognize the desire of individuals and organizations to improve themselves and permit no exploitation of this desire by unethical use of the profession or its members
8. Recognize that society in general accords

status to consultants and that in return they have an obligation to serve the needs of society

The first three items relate to and uphold the aspect of the profession that encourages the validation of openness and trust between members of the client system and the consultant. Statements 4 through 6 concern ethical responsibility, and are designed to protect and support the growth of the profession. Rule 7 protects the rights of both clients and the profession. The eighth rule relates to the responsibility and obligation of the profession toward society in general. The profession should be able to recognize and justify the effect that its practices have on society at large.

The Academy of Management, Organization Development Division, has adopted a similar code of ethics.[23]

Reviewing a number of professional codes of ethics, the following list of principles for the professional facilitator or consultant is suggested:

1. *Responsibility.* The consultant:
   a. Places high value on objectivity and integrity and maintains the highest standards of service
   b. Plans work in a way that minimizes the possibility that findings will be misleading
2. *Competence.* The consultant:
   a. Maintains high standards of professional competence as a responsibility to the public and to the profession
   b. Recognizes the boundaries of his or her competence, and does not offer services that fail to meet professional standards
   c. Assists clients in obtaining professional help for aspects of the project that fall outside the boundaries of his or her own competence
   d. Refrains from undertaking any activity in which his or her personal problems are likely to result in inferior professional service or harm to the client
3. *Moral and legal standards.* The consultant shows sensible regard for the social codes and moral expectations of the community in which he or she works
4. *Misrepresentation.* The consultant avoids misrepresentation of his or her own professional qualifications, affiliations, and purposes and those of the organization with which he or she is associated
5. *Confidentiality.* The consultant:
   a. Reveals information received in confidence only to the appropriate authorities
   b. Maintains confidentiality of professional communications about individuals
   c. Informs clients of the limits of confidentiality
   d. Maintains confidentiality in preservation and disposition of records
6. *Client welfare.* The consultant:
   a. Defines the nature of his or her loyalties and responsibilities in possible conflicts of interest, such as between the client and the employer of the consultant, and keeps all concerned parties informed of these commitments
   b. Attempts to terminate a consulting relationship when it is reasonably clear that the client is not benefiting from it
   c. Continues being responsible for the welfare of the client, in cases involving referral, until the responsibility is assumed by the professional to whom the client is referred or until the relationship with the client has been terminated by mutual agreement
7. *Announcement of services.* The consultant adheres to professional standards rather than solely economic rewards in making known his or her availability for professional services
8. *Interprofessional relations.* The consultant acts with integrity toward colleagues in consultation and toward persons in other professions
9. *Remuneration.* The consultant ensures that the financial arrangements for his or her professional services are in accordance with professional standards

that safeguard the best interests of the client and the profession

10. *Responsibility toward organization.* The consultant respects the rights and reputation of the organization with which he or she is associated
11. *Promotional activities.* The consultant, when associated with the development or promotion of products offered for commercial sale, will ensure that the products are presented in a factual way

Nevertheless, the adoption of a code is not enough, no matter how complete and detailed. Members of the profession should study the code, know the reasons for its provisions, and understand its general importance as a part of professional competence. Regardless of how good a code of professional ethics may be, it will be ineffective unless there is some practical system of enforcement that is accepted by practicing professionals. A lack of penalties is the most basic reason why even well-constructed codes have not had significant impact on professional practice. Although a number of professional associations have developed well-defined procedures for handling alleged violations of their codes, some of the most clear-cut sanctions have been developed and publicized by the Association of Consulting Management Engineers and the American Psychological Association.

The most important aspect of formulating a code is the acceptance of a basic norm of morality that will properly sustain the code and indicate practical applications to consultants in situations too specific to be covered by the code. The effectiveness of this depends on the competence of the consultant.

Many of the older principles of professional ethics do not take into account the emerging new experience realities of mass communication, computers, invasion of privacy, and new drugs and chemicals which have complicated the working out of valid ethical controls.

Many persons responsible for organizational change do not belong to any profession. This creates an additional problem, to which there is no easy solution, since these people do not come under the discipline of any particular profession that might already have or may develop some appropriate group self-regulation.

It is important to highlight this area of concern in examining the whole effort of renewal. Planned change does have ethical implications that should be thoroughly considered by the whole body of practitioners. The moral and ethical standards that have become involved in this problem of individual and social responsibility should be the key to the future advancement in both the private and public sectors of our society. The responsibility for establishing and maintaining high ethical standards rests heavily upon managers and consultants in all kinds of systems. But every coin has two sides. This responsibility must, in part, be shared by everyone who has an influence upon the environment of our whole social order.

DEVELOPING PROFESSIONAL COMPETENCE AND SKILLS

The basis for competence usually lies in the mature adult whose early life was nurtured by parents who believed in the full development of the human species. And a formal education leading to a college degree, and specialized graduate work, although not absolutely essential, is certainly helpful. Something more is required, however, as stated by Alice Sargent:

> A curriculum for adult education needs to include many areas untouched by years of school or family socialization. It must encompass (1) the area of psychological education, developing a theory of personality development

which includes an adult learning model; (2) the development of attitudes and skills in interpersonal competence for a wide variety of situations including low, medium and high-intensity relationships in one-on-one as well as small group settings; (3) in communication skills, both oral and written, and (4) in the various stages of the problem-solving process, including planning, prioritizing and time management, goal-setting, decision-making, and implementation.[24]

In a broader context, it is helpful to look at a model of experiential-based learning relevant to developing adult skills and competence. David Kolb has designed a four-stage model of such learning in which he points out that adults learn from *watching, thinking, doing, and feeling.* (see Figure 12-2).

Unfortunately, the professional development of human systems renewal specialists has been a haphazard process. Only recently have workshops, experiences, and courses for developing such skills begun to emerge on a regular basis. To function effectively as a professional, one must have continuing learning experiences to reinforce his or her formal education.[26]

A human systems specialist can come from a wide range of disciplinary backgrounds. The key to the preparation of such a professional is a mixed background of interdisciplinary education and experience. What is important is that the practitioner have a working knowledge of many disciplines, including operations research, communications, general systems theory, information technology, finance, or cybernetics.[27] In other words, a rather broad educational background with as much mix as possible, balanced against enough in-depth training in certain fields to have a very solid academic foundation in at least a few fields. The whole purpose of the mixed interdiscipline approach is to give breadth and scope to the practitioner rather than narrow specialization. The problems involved in training tend to be interdisciplinary in character and not narrow. Thus, broad knowledge and multiple skills are needed.

However, keeping up to date and professionally competent in a continuous education mode is essential. The reader probably shares my experience that internalizing new concepts, and converting ideas and intentions into an available repertoire of skills requires time and testing and, most of all, the support of interaction with others while learning. Professionals should develop some strategy and design for their continued growth.

Eleven strategies that have proved useful, and that have been observed as successful supports for colleagues and practitioners, are:

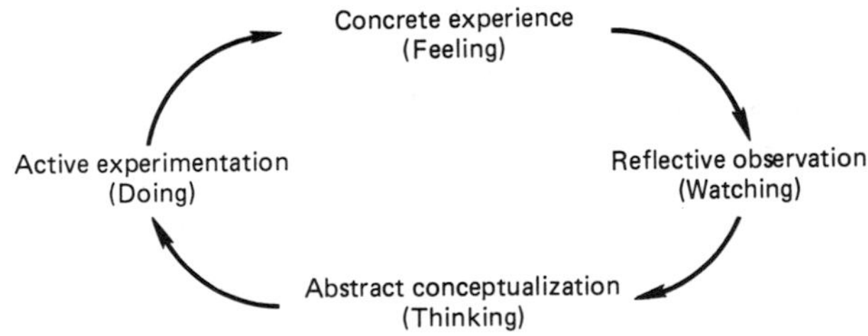

Figure 12-2 Kolb's model of adult learning development[25]

1. *Getting feedback.* A basic strategy of training and a great source of professional growth is the practice of collecting feedback data from those you are trying to serve. You should use some type of feedback tool as a part of every contact in renewal. There is no better way to build an effective working relationship, as well as to learn about your own performance during the process of change, than to review "how" things are going.

2. *Co-consulting.* Another great source of support and stimulus to a trainer's professional growth is to team with a colleague, either as a peer or as an apprentice. This requires planning together, which means sharing, testing, modifying, defending, and articulating values, concepts, rationale, designs, and techniques. Additionally, there is the opportunity to observe the performance of someone else, elicit feedback observations about one's own performance, debrief each other, and learn from the shared experience.

3. *Documentation, publication, and presentations.* Human systems renewal professionals should adopt as a goal the sharing of their discoveries and learnings with others. This is valuable because it is one of the most effective procedures for personal growth, a pathway to recognition by others, and a contribution to the practice of training.

Several activities assist in this area of growth. First, it is important to plan for the documentation of what you do as a trainer. Sometimes you can arrange for others to take notes, or you may want to write notes immediately after a session or record some verbal action on tape.

Another important step is to think and act as though the record of what you are doing will be useful and important information to share. It helps, therefore, to have committed yourself to the preparation of a report, publication, or a presentation concerning your learnings.

Again, as in co-training, there is value in a commitment to share the writing effort. This supports your motivation and makes the task more interesting, and the division of labor makes it easier to document and to write.

4. *Asking colleagues.* Most of us are inhibited in expressing curiosity about what our colleagues do and how they do it. However, this curiosity reflects a desire to learn, which can be very rewarding to others as well as to yourself. The exchange of concrete experiences of failure and success in renewal efforts is probably the most unused resource for a trainer's learning.

5. *Enrolling in learning opportunities.* In working with a team of internal consultants, it was found that they devote 10% of their work time to participating in opportunities for professional development and learning: courses, workshops, labs, seminars, conferences. This provides them with a rich menu of growth stimulation each year.

6. *Joining and being active in a professional association.* Some of the most interesting and supportive professional opportunities come from being an active member of a professional association. It helps a trainer's professional growth to be affiliated with one or more such groups, to participate in their meetings, to keep informed and connected through their literature. The feeling of being part of a larger professional colleagueship and part of a rapidly expanding diverse network of renewal professionals is helpful.

The American Society for Training and Development is one such group, but it might also be valuable to join such groups as the World Future Society, Adult Education Association, Association for Creative Change, NTL Institute OD Network, Organization Renewal, Inc., Academy of Management, or other such groups to broaden one's experiences.

7. *Joining an informal colleagueship.* In

many cities across the United States there are informal groups that get together without officers, dues, or formality to exchange experiences. A few years ago a group of oldtimers in ASTD formed the "Old Sages" group, which meets once a year for two days to share experiences.

8. *Personal self-development plans.* Personal setting of your career and life goals should be listed as a first step in professional development. It is essential that a professional person have clearly developed targets for his or her career and life. A number of inventories[28] and self-help[29] materials are available to aid in a process that can provide the direction and integration of the various activities in which one engages for professional development.

9. *Internships and sabbaticals.* It is becoming increasingly essential to have enough time off the job to focus on an educational experience and/or self-renewal. A number of organizations now make it possible for professionals to have a three- to six-month sabbatical, to have an internship, a program of study, or to develop professional growth.

10. *Consulting, moonlighting, and exchange of experience.* There is real value in going "outside" one's own organization to do consulting and training. Professionals will find that by volunteering to serve a community agency, by conducting a survey for another company, or by consulting on a human systems problem with an outside client, they will enhance their experience and learning. Many organizations are encouraging their professional people to spend one day a week in such activity. This would include the obvious value of teaching part-time at a community college or university. The required course preparation and reading in itself is a development process.

11. *Reading programs.* It is essential to develop a self-designed reading program. This would include not only an updating of selected texts, articles, and research papers, but also contemporary journals, papers, and magazines.

The challenge is in developing the self-discipline regularly to set aside a time period for reading and other study activities. The major supports for studying and self-development are a commitment to some time each week and a commitment to sharing one's learning with someone else. It is important, however, to read in a broad context.

Human systems renewal is requiring many new areas of skill development, such as management of stress, conflict resolution, limited resource management, and systems concepts, that are needed for effective organizational management. Professionalism in our field, however, is a performing art, not a science.

Professional standards, skills, and values are required. To help complex organizational systems, we need to broaden our ways of examining human systems beyond academic research and educational writings. Valuable sources of data about human behavior and management include *The New Yorker, Business Week, Wall Street Journal,* biographies, historical reports of TVA, World War II, Apollo II moon flights, and other sources that can broaden our concepts, practices, and values about individuals, groups, and organizations.

A poem from Chang-Tsu (fourth century B.C.) perhaps says it best:

How shall I talk of the sea to the
frog,
if he has never left his pond?

How shall I talk of the frost to the
bird of the summer land,
if it has never left the land of its
birth?

How shall I talk of life with the
sage,

if he is the prisoner of his
doctrine?

Truly qualified renewal helpers should consider their professional role as one that requires constant, life-long learning.

Some people have become pessimistic about being able to plan their own growth and development. Such pessimism arises when one leaves out personal assessment of needs, makes inadequate assessment of resources, has feelings of lack of support, has a limited view of alternatives, is not providing the time, and avoids taking action.

Professional development may take many different forms. It may be informal and completely within the work experience of the person, or it may be formal with plans that are fully written with specifications for carrying them out and with schedules and deadlines for their execution. The nature of the situation determines the formality, the detail, the responsibility, and the methods of planning your professional development. Whatever the nature of the development process, it is generally agreed that a plan is a most important part of the process. The only link between a professional desire to improve and its realization is the blueprint showing the parts needed, how they are put together, and the order in which to handle them.

SUMMARY

An effective renewal helper should have had experience as a line manager or leader with a group, organization, or community. Such experience gives depth, reality, and insight to one's role as a helper in coping with real problems, group decisions, organizational realities, and/or community conflict. It does require considerable knowledge and skill, as well as flexibility of responses, to be a professional leader today. As Warren Schmidt has said:[30]

> For there is a time of confront, but also a time to reduce tension;
> A time to use power, but also a time to use persuasion;
> A time to act, but also a time to diagnose;
> A time to accelerate change, but also a time to slow it down;
> A time to intervene, but also a time to refrain from intervening;
> But whether we confront or collaborate, intervene or analyze, let it flow from understanding and courage and love, and not from ignorance or cowardice or fear—for these cannot long survive on any frontier.

Schmidt is referring to the frontiers facing the postindustrial society. Such a frontier is going to require all the excellence that multiple-discipline consultants and leaders can bring to bear on complex and unknown problems.

If there are human systems renewal specialists with these kinds of values, attitudes, and beliefs, they may yet reinstitute a confidence in such facilitators as fellow human beings whose help can provide mutual growth for individuals, groups, organizations, and larger systems in our society.

QUESTIONS

1. In your experience, where has the initiative for organizational change been focused: Top executive? Line manager? Staff function? Why?
2. To be a renewal facilitator, is it really necessary to have a multitude of skills? Why?
3. As you reflect upon your experience and observations, can you cite examples of unethical behavior? Give examples.

4. Can you cite examples of socially responsible and ethical behavior? Give examples.
5. What do you feel has been the most valuable experiences that have helped improve your competency as a professional?
6. Are the skills of leadership and renewal facilitating the same? Are they different? Why?
7. What additional educational or learning experiences do you feel would be valuable to you in furthering your professional competence?

NOTES

[1]Adapted from Gordon Lippitt and Leonard Nadler, "Emerging Roles of the Training Director," *Training and Development Journal,* August 1967.

[2]Leslie This and Gordon Lippitt, "Learning Theories and Training," *Training and Development Journal,* April–May 1966, p. 14.

[3]Jack R. Gibb, "The Role of the Consultant," *Journal of Social Issues,* Vol. 15, No. 2, 1959, 1.

[4]Richard Beckhard, *The Leader Looks at The Consultative Process* (Looking into Leadership Monographs; Washington, D.C.: Leadership Resources, Inc., 1961), p. 7.

[5]Jack Epstein, *Personnel Professionalism Challenges the Status Quo* (Washington, D.C.: Society for Personnel Administration, 1965).

[6]Adapted from Gordon Lippitt and Leslie This, "Is Training a Profession?" *ASTD Journal,* April 1960, pp. 284–291.

[7]*Webster's New Collegiate Dictionary* (Springfield, Mass.: G. &. C. Merriam Company, 1961).

[8]Gordon Lippitt, *A Study of Consulting Competencies* (unpublished paper; Washington, D.C.: The George Washington University, 1976).

[9]Robert K. Menzel, "A Taxonomy of Change Agent Skills," *The Journal of European Training,* Vol. 4, No. 5, 1975, 289–291.

[10]Robert G. Havelock, *The Change Agent's Guide to Innovation in Education* (Englewood Cliffs, N.J.: Educational Technology Publications, 1973), p. 153.

[11]Don Warrick and Tom Donovan, "Surveying Organization Development Skills," *ASTD Training and Development Journal,* September 1979, pp. 22–25.

[12]Ibid., p. 23. © 1979 by the American Society for Training and Development, Inc. Reproduced by special permission.

[13]Walter Leach, *Characteristics of an OD Consultant* (interoffice memorandum, February 1976).

[14]Lederer, William J., and Burdick, Eugene, *The Ugly American,* (New York: W. W. Norton & Co., 1958), p. 186.

[15]Samuel H. Miller, "The Tangle of Ethics," *Harvard Business Review,* January–February 1969, p. 59.

[16]Howard R. Bowen, "Findings of the Study," in John C. Bennet (ed.), *Christian Values and Economic Life* (New York: Harper & Row, Publishers, Inc., 1954), pp. 47–60.

[17]Adapted from Gordon Lippitt, "Ethical Dimensions of Group Leadership," *Pastoral Psychology,* March 1967.

[18]Wernher von Braun, "Why I Believe," *This Week,* July 1965, p. 3.

[19]Adapted from Gordon Lippitt and Ronald Lippitt, *The Consulting Process in Action* (La Jolla, Calif.: University Associates, Inc., 1978), Chap. 5.

[20]Lawrence Kohlberg and Peter Scharf, "Bureaucratic Violence and Conventional Thinking," *America's Journal of Orthopsychiatry,* April 1972, p. 2.

[21]Lawrence Kohlberg, in Howard Munson, "Moral Thinking: Can It be Taught?" *Psychology Today,* February 1979, p. 48.

[22]*Professional Practices in Management Consulting* (New York: Association of Consulting Management Engineers, 1966), p. 6.

[23]Academy of Management, "Proposed Code of Ethics," *Organization Development Division Newsletter,* Winter 1976, p. 1–2.

[24]Alice G. Sargent, "Developing Basic Skills and Knowledge," *Training and Development Journal,* May 1979, p. 72.

[25]David Kolb, *Building a Learning Community* (Washington, D.C.: National Training and Development Service Press, December 1974), pp. 2–26.

[26]Adapted from Gordon Lippitt, "Developing Professional Skills and Expertise," *Training and Development Journal,* May 1979, pp. 65–70.

[27]"Personnel Widens Its Franchise," *Business Week,* February 26, 1979, pp. 116–121.

[28]George Ford and Gordon Lippitt, *Planning Your Future* (La Jolla, Calif.: University Associates, Inc., 1976).

[29]Don Swartz and Betty Chakiris, *The Life/Work Goals Exploration Workbook Kit* (Winnetka, Ill.: Organization Renewal, Inc., 1976).

[30]Warren Schmidt, *Organizational Frontiers and Human Values* (Belmont, Calif.: Wadsworth Publishing Company, Inc., 1970), p. 4.

13

organization renewal: a hope and challenge

If you can look into the seeds of time, And say which grain will grow and which will not, Speak then to me. . . .

Macbeth, Act I, Scene 3

We travel together, passengers on a little space ship, dependent on its vulnerable supplies of air and soil . . . preserved from annihilation only by the care, the work, and I will say the love, we give our fragile craft.

From the last speech of Adlai Stevenson, 1900–1965

One of the most difficult things to accomplish is the act of self-examination that can lead to renewal. It is a primary need, difficult to satisfy. Whether we take Socrates' admonition that "the unexamined life is not worth living," or a statement of a former assistant secretary of HEW who said, "Education is the only profession which has not had the guts to look at itself," we must recognize the universal need for renewal, including the renewal of most of our organized efforts.

It is desirable for us to examine the ways in which organizations can increase and maintain their relevancy to the needs of 1980 and beyond, ways in which organization renewal can be initiated, maintained, and evaluated. Such a process is not simple. The reason most organizations do not undertake such an effort is that there exist some false assumptions about organizational change.

It is generally believed, for example, that the promotion of "good human relations" among employees is synonymous with increased morale, productivity, and effectiveness. Research finds no grounds for this assumption. Even when our intentions are right and understood, others may not like them or may consider them opposed to their own interests. Nor should we assume that face-to-face meetings and personal association will necessarily engender loyalty and mutual accord. This idea somehow survives despite persistent reports of abrasive collisions between unions and management; and despite the obvious fact that some units of an organization that constantly deal with one another also fight with one another frequently.

Such broad assumptions are an inadequate base upon which to rest decisions; for example, to expand an organization's services or to spend limited resources on a new project, we must be more specifically concerned with the total organization, where it goes, what it does, and why it does it. Organizational renewal ought to produce concentrated and continuing efforts to relate the organization's technology, finances, structure, and people to the problems confronting the organization as it relates to the future.

No person or group of persons, however empowered, can prevent change from occurring. At best, they can only hasten or delay it. More important, they can cope with change at all only if they are aware of its nature and probable effect. In this sense, those responsible for the management of our organizations are faced with extraordinary difficulties in being always correctly informed and situationally knowledgeable. Organizational changes faithfully reflect the needs and interests of some of the people, but not necessarily all of them; therefore, they inevitably produce inequities. Since everything is the result of a change, competent managers cannot afford to overlook any change whatsoever, because every change is a seed from which some part of tomorrow's organization will grow.

In presenting a systems model for human systems renewal, the focus is on the matter of problem solving. Appropriate problem-solving response to complex situations will:

- Strengthen and further develop the human subsystems (individual, group, and organization)
- Further the use of the confrontation, search, and coping nature of the interfacing process
- Contribute to the next growth stage of the system, leading toward maturity
- Respond to the environmental forces interacting with the organization
- Utilize research, training, and action to achieve desirable ends
- Develop appropriate leadership, conflict resolution, model building, and planning skills so as to provide individual, group, and organizational development processes
- Develop and utilize internal and external renewal facilitators to stimulate, initiate, and maintain change

If such goals are universally desirable, why is it that they are so seldom achieved?

CRITERIA FOR SUCCESS OR FAILURE IN ORGANIZATION AND HUMAN SYSTEMS RENEWAL

In the past thirty years we have seen considerable research, action, publicity, and writing about organization development and renewal. Experience shows that during that time there have been many more failures than successes. It is possible to identify the conditions that affect either success or failure. It certainly is not a factor of intention or need. In these thirty years, however, numerous institutions of government, business, religion, education, industry, and civic organizations have initiated activities or processes of organization development or organization renewal. Some have hired consultants and others have put people on their full-time payroll with such titles as "Director of Organization Development" or "Director of Human Resources Development." Why can we not quote more success stories than those mentioned over and over again? Those cases that are initiated frequently end in failure, disappointment, or outright distrust of anyone involved in organization development or organization renewal.

The history of organization development reveals the evolution of the multiple interventions tried by practitioners.[1] This encompasses methods labeled "organization development" as well as those called human resources management, organization improvement program, renewal effort, and so forth. The common theme is that they are planned interventions, executed in an attempt to change, usually to improve, something; that they occur either in the workplace or with individuals or groups from the workplace; and that they are usually based on some behavioral science precepts. Many of these interventions have failed to achieve meaningful and long-term results. It appears necessary, therefore, to deal with concepts of success and failure.

Each intervention in organization development or renewal has inherent in it several sets of implicit and explicit goals. The interventionist may have one set, the "sponsor" another, the participant a third, and perhaps an academic theorist or facilitator, a fourth. In fact, there could be as many sets of goals as there are persons involved. Success or failure could be evaluated against each of these. Consequently, an intervention can be viewed as a success from one perspective, and as a limited success or failure from another. For instance, a personal growth type of intervention could be accepted as a success by the participants and the trainers, but viewed as a failure by a management who wanted immediate increases in production.

The time element also plays a role in the differentiation between successful and unsuccessful interventions. An intervention can accomplish all of its immediate goals and yet be a long-term failure. On the other hand, an intervention that appears to be a failure can from a long-term perspective be the critical element in reaching the goals of the organization and, therefore, be considered as a success.

Based on the literature and experience, many efforts in organization development do fail for identifiable reasons. The causes of failure can be divided into four main categories: collusion against accurate evaluation and reporting, discrepancies between assumptions in organization development and organizational realities, potential hazards surrounding the intervention, and the lack of integration of the organization development effort back into the total organizational system.

Published examples of failures in organization development are sparse; this phenomenon itself is interesting, and is quite possibly one cause of failure. If, as appears to be the case, such failures are not reported, studied, and made known to other practitioners, then mistakes, errors, and misapplications will be repeated. Instead of allowing the body of theory and experience to grow, turning a blind eye to negative feedback severely limits the amount of information available to organization development practitioners and decreases the potential for growth.

The reasons for not reporting failures in organization development are varied. It may be related to the emphasis placed in American society on success. Our culture is geared toward producing competitors who strive for success. Less than success has a negative connotation; it is a condition to be avoided and association with such a condition is to be denied.[2]

On a more practical level, both the intervenor and the organization in which the method took place have reasons not to report failures. The intervenor has a strong monetary and professional incentive for not reporting failures. Once a specialist becomes associated with failure, future job prospects are bleak. Why should an organization hire someone known to have failed when it can get someone else with an "untarnished" reputation? From the researchers' point of view, journals and magazines are not as interested in reporting experiments that did not work as they are successes.

From the organization's perspective, there are also forces that encourage or require that an intervention be termed a success and not a failure. If an internal renewal facilitator is involved, the forces surrounding protection of one's reputation come into play. The organization wants to be known for "attracting" a highly successful facilitator and having a successful change effort. In our present society, this has become somewhat of a status symbol. From another vantage point, to have had sufficient problems to warrant an intervention, and then to fail in that intervention, is like a double failure. The organization often makes it clear to the renewal facilitator that they do not want to hear negative feedback. When the intervention does not take place at the top of the organization, the subunit and the client often need a "successful" intervention to justify the service of the consultant.

In addition, the organization is frequently unwilling to approve the expenditure of funds necessary to evaluate whether or not the effort was a success. From their perspective they think they already know if it was a succcess, and if it was a failure, evaluation is "throwing good money after bad," as it may benefit academic research but not directly improve organizational functioning.

The result of these protective activities on the part of facilitators and clients is that efforts in organization development frequently are not evaluated and those efforts felt to be failures are reported even less frequently. This dearth of information retards the growth of the field and dooms practitioners of organization development to repeat failures.

A second major cause of failures in organization development is the variance between the assumptions practitioners make about organizational life and organizational reality. Three of these assumptions are basic enough to be categorized as philosophical differences. These concern the nature of humankind, the role of work, and the concept of motivation. The majority, although equally critical to outcomes, are more closely tied to norms and value systems. A few are not even differences in norms or value systems, but assumptions about what actually exists in most organizations. Whatever the source, the discrepancy between such assumptions and reality creates the potential for failure of efforts in organizational development.

In designing an activity in organization development, the renewal initiator and facilitator may make assumptions about the behaviors of individuals, groups, and organizations. Table 13-1 lists some of these assumptions together with the perceived organizational reality. If these assumptions are wrong and the perceived reality is true, then the basis of the effort in organizational development is flawed and the potential for failure is created.

As a consequence of the absence of congruity between the assumptions of the renewal facilitator and organizational reality, money managers began to look upon organization development as a soft, nonrelevant approach to the hard and tangible problems of the organization. The question is often asked: "What did the effort contribute to the bottom line?" Organization development frequently was viewed as a reward activity rather than as problem solving. Perhaps the stumbling block was the catch-all nature of the methods used: "Many people lifted the OD label and used it because of the popularity and reputation it had earned by the mid-sixties. Almost any activity concerned with development that took place within the organization automatically came to mean OD."[3]

Intervention into an organization is a complex process involving such things as the interplay of knowledge, skills, commitment, and value systems. The interaction of the variables adds to the potential for failure, and the primary potentials for failure in organization development are grouped below under five headings related to ingredients in the process rather than specific causes of failure.

1. *Organizational commitment and timing.* These two factors are the most frequent causes of failure in organizational development. Lack of commitment in terms of supportive behavior or resources dooms a project to failure. Artificial commitment is more insidious and in the long term more devastating because it raises peoples' expectations while the behavior of top

Table 13–1
Difference of Assumption and Reality in Some Organization Development Efforts[4]

	Assumptions	Reality
Behavior of individuals		
Nature of humankind	Good	Good and bad
Role of work	Central	Component
Task perception	Should enrich	Not always
Motivation	Intrinsic	Extrinsic
Goals	Compatible	Zero sum
Behavior of groups		
Power	Ignored	Real
Trust	Open	Not open
Leadership	Participative	Situational
Decision making	Participative	Centralized
Conflict resolution	Should resolve	Creates energy
Behavior of systems		
Work systems	Composite	Entity
Structure	Less bureaucratic	Bureaucratic
Reward structure	Planned with variations	Unplanned and structured
Culture	Cross-cultural	Western

management remains unchanged. The leading authors in the field would agree with the need for top-management support, or at least support from the individual at the top of the unit within which the activity is taking place. Some have gone so far as to write the need for top-management support into their definition of organization development. Timing can also be crucial to success. Reorganizations, labor negotiations, or governmental regulation may affect the effort if they happen concurrently or too close to the timing of the organization development intervention.

2. *Methodologies.* A discourse on the importance of accurate diagnosis and the appropriateness of individual methodologies is an important factor in the success or failure of organization development. It is not only the *kind* of intervention and its relevance to a diagnosed problem, but also the depth of such an intervention that constitutes a critical factor in the achievement of success. Intervention strategies can be categorized according to the depth of emotional involvement of the individual or group. There is a possibility of serious harm in choosing an intervention deeper than required. Robert Golumbiewski has developed some guidelines for anticipating the potential impact of organization development designs.[5] Roger Harrison has identified two criteria for selecting the appropriate depth of intervention: "first, to intervene at a level no deeper than required to produce enduring solutions to the problems at hand; and second, to intervene at a level no deeper than that at which the energy and resources of the client can be committed to problem-solving and change."[6]

There is another malaise, which lies somewhat deeper and is more crucial. When organization development facilitators in Great Britain, Canada, and the United States were asked to list their ideal goals for organization development, the goals mentioned were quite different from the list of organizational "hurts" usually identified by management; this, again, is a reflection of the gap between assumptions and reality. It can be postulated either that organization development interveners are not dealing with organizational ills, are tinkering at the edges, or that they are dealing with organizational problems *as presented,* being subject to discomfort because they perceive they are not fulfilling their mission.[7] Any of these situations creates the potential for failure of organization development efforts.

3. *Organization development facilitators.* The competency of the renewal facilitator, of course, is vital, and personal biases and interests affect his or her ability to diagnose.[8] Individual concerns predispose one to view the problem from a particular perspective. This can result in diagnosing every problem according to a particular perspective or bias (e.g., structure, centralization, interpersonal relationships). On the other side of the coin is the facilitator who has only "one bag of tricks" and recommends this intervention process as the solution to all problems. Both of these myopias substantially increase the potential for failure.

The role the renewal facilitator chooses to play must also be appropriate. Renewal facilitators, however, have tended to concentrate their efforts toward the nondirective end of the continuum, almost as a fad. This practice may not always have served the best interests of the client. There exists a continuum of roles and there will be interventions or occasions within an intervention when the directive end of the scale is the responsible choice.

Discussion of failures in organization development cannot be complete without mention of ethical considerations, including the potential for manipulation or misrepresentation of personal capabilities or of the available data. Ethical dilemmas are created by differing norms, values, and orientations. The renewal facilitator may be humanistic, whereas the tendency of management may be economic and political. Organization development failures can be traced to deterioration of client-facilitator relationships arising out of such conflict. Still, it is almost a cardinal rule that the renewal facilitator must not attempt to impose his or her own value system on a client; and this need not be done if the facilitator's role is limited to three primary tasks: to generate information, to prepare the organization to make free choices, and to develop internal commitment to the choices made.

4. *Congruency.* An organization development effort must be congruent with the remainder of the organization—or it is likely to fail because the effort will be out of phase with such organizational norms as trust, leadership, and decision making. It must also be consistent with the reward structure of the organization. At a deeper level, it must be congruent with the orientation of the firm. A training emphasis on interpersonal relationships, for example, may be too far removed from the task orientation of the firm for the training to have much impact. Lacking congruency, either the client will not try to implement desirable change or learning, or the attempts to do so will fail due to resistance or naiveté of the proposed solution.

5. *Lack of integration into the total organization.* Most organization development efforts deal with portions or subunits of a total system, and must be integrated back into the total system at the conclusion of the activity. Too frequently, organization development training for the individual or group simply finishes and the participants are left with the task of integrating his or her new self back into the organization. A lack of cognizance of the need for integration on the part of the renewal facilitator indicates a lack of competence on his or her part, and probably reflects inadequacies in the intervention activity.

Even when both renewal facilitator and client are aware of the need for integration, they can still encounter problems. The client may perceive lack of congruency, and not attempt integration. The remainder of the system may have no information about the change effort, and may react inappropriately because of this lack of information. The change effort may reverberate throughout the system and cause unforeseen consequences.

A frequent complaint from organizations is that the change effort worked for a while and then trailed off. This can be attributed to a number of factors: the major personality involved has left the job, the first blush of enthusiasm has worn off, provision for "celebration milestones" has not been built into the implementation, or the organization has changed rapidly in some other direction. Unfortunately, each of these is often identified as a failure in organization development.

The intervention here is not to imply that a majority of organization development efforts fail, or that organization development has little impact on organizational life. Rather, it is important to examine the underlying reasons why some efforts do not succeed. The profession is presently in the midst of a phase of self-doubt, partly as a result of a generalized pessimism in today's society and partly as a natural phase in the growth of the field. The potential for failure can be lessened through recognition of organizations as total systems and through a better understanding of organizational forms, values, and realities.

In looking at the organization as a total system and at approaches to help ensure success, some criteria can be suggested:[9]

Parameter approach. This relates to the importance for organization leaders to identify and commit the organization to a set of values, norms, and goals that will govern its activities, leadership, and problem-solving mode. This might be called the *parameter condition to organization renewal.* If an organization does not have a clear understanding of its values and management beliefs, efforts in organization development are doomed to failure. Such efforts become band-aids on a sick organism that does not know its purpose for existing.

Data-based condition of effective organization renewal. Successful organization renewal utilizes action research. The need to collect data and to feed that data back for planning and action is an essential element in successful organization development or organization renewal. This is where a system concept can be of real help—if it is collecting reliable and valid data.

Open communication systems. The organization must be willing to confront the research data. It must be willing to examine the implications of the data for organizational change. Organization development does not occur unless managers confront their own need to improve; confronting the data means facing up to reality; it means looking at things through clear glasses rather than either rose-tinted or dark-tinted glasses. But confrontation alone is not enough to bring about awareness, action steps, or organization change. It is only the beginning of the development of a two-way communications climate. Management of technological and complex organizations of the 1980s will require an openness of communication that is lacking in many organizations today.

Line management responsibility. The job of organization renewal is in the hands of line management. The staff specialist—even organization development or system specialists—will not change organizations. Those with authority and responsibility must commit themselves to the needed action steps. Staff specialists can consult, help, and advise, but the line manager is the key implementer.

Multiunit effort. For organization development or organization renewal to change goals, technology, and processes, it must be a multiunit responsibility. This does not take place with individuals charging around on "white horses." Different task forces, operating units, and project groups must be involved and committed.

General systems orientation. Organization development and renewal will revolve about the general systems approach that should and can effect the structure of the organization. The concept of sociotechnical systems is based on the reality that any production and service system requires both a technology and also a work-relationship structure that relates the human resources to the technological resources. To think about an organization as a social-technical system helps make viable the human-machine relationships as well as to integrate with the concept of human systems.

Commitment of human, financial, and time resources. Neither organization development nor organization renewal is a hobby or something easily done. It requires people who assume responsibility; it takes time and money. The effort can be worthwhile if such a commitment does take place; if not, it will be an exercise in futility.

As said above, the quality of work life and organization renewal are closely intertwined. The ideals of both are identical. The present practice of organization development, however, represents the limit to which a growing number of organizations are willing to go, while the quality of work life demands a broad scale, top-to-bottom approach that can be accommodated only in the exceptional organization. Thus, practitioners of organization development who undertake limited projects within small segments of organizations may be lighting candles while practitioners dealing with the quality of work life curse the darkness.

Several commonalities between the two approaches can be identified.[10] Both approaches:

Are planned

Have as their goal both increase of organizational effectiveness and development of individual members

Are a collaborative relationship between client and consultant built on mutual trust and an understanding of each other's values

View the consultant as a teacher of techniques and a resource in developing alternatives but not as a decisionmaker—all operating decisions are necessarily made by the client.

Strive to reduce client dependency on the consultant and build problem-solving skills within the organization

Are concerned with process and content

Look upon employees as adults capable of assuming responsibility

Encourage and set an example for open communication and confrontation

Take an action research approach which involves the client in problem definition and analysis, data collection, diagnosis, development and evaluation of solutions, setting up action procedures, and establishing a method for evaluation

Frequently use task forces made up of organization members

Probe for underlying causes

Focus on the roles people take in the work situation

Some people feel that neither *quality of work life* nor *organization development/organization renewal* is truly possible or practically feasible. Organizations are thought to be too bureaucratic, too large, and too old to be able to change. I do not agree. We can no longer shrug our shoulders and say, "You can't change people or our institutions."

Essentially, the development of people and organizations is dependent upon the values, norms, and beliefs of a given culture. If effective, it builds in problem-solving and coping skills for one situation that can be carried over and applied to another time or another place. It is, therefore, as prevalent at the level of the individual as at the level of the society. At whatever level, however, we must always recognize that the individual is at the center of any development or change process (see Figure 13-1). We must accept the

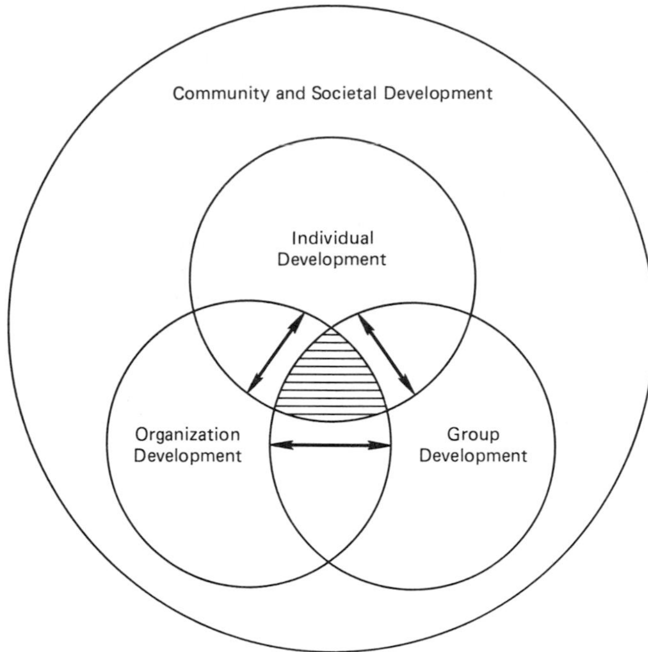

Figure 13-1 Areas of human resource development

concept of more than one level of human resource development in a holistic look at organization development.

Success in the development process results from creating disequilibrium in a system. Therefore, the need for regaining stability while changing and growing is the essence of human resource development in concept and practice. While renewal provides opportunity to change, it should also serve as a stabilizing force. Human systems, in the renewal process, need to diagnose those things that need to be changed and those that should remain the same.

In planning the human systems renewal effort to achieve this kind of change and stability for the total organization, and positive recycling, some principles about planned organizational change have been presented above. It is important to remember that renewal will most likely succeed if to top policymaking group is involved early in the process. If they do not want change or renewal, it will be difficult, if not actually foolish, to attempt very much real change. The sanction of those high in the present hierarchy lends necessary legitimization to the renewal effort. The leadership for renewal should come from this group even though some of the needed technical, fact-finding, and development skills for the process may be furnished by others in middle management. In periods of rapid change, a characteristic of our present era, organizational leaders must continually study the needs and interests of the people they serve as well as those who serve them in the organization, and assess the extent to which existing organizational efforts, programs, and responses are effective in relationship to these needs and interests. They must also revise, adapt, or create new efforts to meet foreseeable new requirements, and attempt to anticipate emergencies so as to plan ways to meet them.

Effective renewal leadership requires a certain degree of *futuring* in order to anticipate, plan, and partially control what is going to happen in both near and distant time.

PROCESS OF FUTURING

All of us want to understand and cope with the future. To the extent that we project images of the future, we find that such images can be utopian or realistic; descriptive or normative; and possible, probable, or preferable. Futurists do not agree as to which kind of images should be built. This disagreement is due in part to a difference in beliefs about the determinative nature of the images. Is our future already determined or can we control the future by planning for it on the basis of identified present and future needs? The answer to this question may indicate whether an image will be descriptive or prescriptive.

The value of futuring for organizational leaders lies in the fact that we can ill afford to wait until the future arrives. Futuring is essential to one's role as a planner, a link between what is happening now and what will happen in some definable future time. The relationship between planning and futuring is entirely practical. It is a basic shift in orientation to move from being an observer, an analyst, a reflector about what is going on in our world to becoming "part of the picture," an actor, goal-setter, doer. As we work at taking an intelligent "doing posture" about our future, as a person or organization, we discover there are several different sources of direction for defining our goals. Let us review these to remind ourselves of some springboards and restraints:[11]

Our past: "It worked before." Often, we depend for our future directions on what have been successful goal-achieving experiences in our past. "Having the governor speak got people out." "The annual dinner will raise money and get commitments."

Our past's future is still unrealized. It is sometimes instructive and embarrassing to ask, "Which of the goals we set a year ago are still unreached?" These goals may still be important to put in our future.

What seems to have been happening? Usually, we are sensitive to changes that have been going on in our environment or in ourselves. "Our members are becoming more insistent on having a part in goal setting," or "Resistance to our policy of closed membership has been increasing." We see these clues of change as trends to take into account as we plan for our future.

Pains of the here-and-now. Evidence from some analyses of goal setting is that future directions are often set by a desire to "get away from" some painful problem situation. Usually, this results in very limited, unrewarding steps into the future.

Adjusting to what "they" decided. Sometimes, a person or group "higher up" in the system has set goals that we are expected to fit into and help implement. Our future is oriented toward helping them actualize their image of the future for them and for us.

Interdependent neighbors. Most persons, groups, and organizations are interdependent with neighboring systems that want to be taken into account in our goal setting. They may have expectations (that we will share fund-raising efforts) or hopes (that we will not duplicate services).

Successful models. Sometimes someone we look up to, or compare ourselves with, demonstrates a very successful achievement of a goal. What we saw them achieve is something we'd like in our future, so we are motivated to set the goal that seemed to work for them. "They really got a payoff from automating."

Extrapolating from what seems to be going on. We are familiar with all the efforts to predict the future by extrapolating from the shape and rate of the curve of the past and what's happening now. "Looks like we will have 15% more membership in two years." "Teenage alcoholism will be rising and drug use decreasing."

Leaps of imagination into the future. The science fiction writers are perhaps the most innovative projectors of scenarios about the more distant future. They try to shed the bonds of past and present and imagine possibilities. They work on freeing themselves from "what is currently feasible" or "what they are ready for."

Preferred images of potential. Somewhere in between fantasized future and extrapolated possibilities there are projections ahead in time to observe future images of what has come to pass that are desirable and within the bounds of feasibility. This image-projecting may draw on all the other sources of ideas, but is a freed-up journey into the future.

Such practical steps can make futuring helpful in renewal planning:

> Perhaps the most important insight that futurists can offer is that the future cannot be predicted! The future is not a world that lies before us quietly awaiting our arrival but rather a world that we ourselves are creating. The future, then, is not fixed. Many different "futures" may develop out of the present moment in which we live. For that reason, we should explore a number of possible future worlds, not just a single "most likely" possibility.[12]

In keeping with this perceptive statement, Edward Cornish also offers three scenarios for the future. The first, practically enough, sees the 1980s as being a continuation of the not-easily-defined trends started in the 1970s, with uncertain reality and complexity. He also presents a pessimistic view of the last two decades of the twentieth century in which nations experience chaos through failure to cope with energy and food shortages, terrorism, unemployment, and ultimately World War III. A third prediction optimistically envisions technological advances, international interdependency, increased food and energy production, acceptance of birth control, and anticipatory democracy—all leading to worldwide peace and prosperity. In contemplating these three wide-ranging possibilities, however, it is well to realize: "It is not the task of futurists to predict exactly what people will do in the future, but rather to help people understand the possibilities of the future so that a better world can be created."[13] The concept of renewal suggests the chance of a positive future scenario becoming a reality.

Organizations are caught up in the massive forces that are changing the political, social, economic, and religious life of the world today. To ignore these forces would be folly. To respond to them by executing the same old programs and services would be to ignore a responsibility. To rush into ill-conceived programs is wasteful, and to be opportunistic is shallow. Any real attempt at organization renewal will need to fully comprehend the complexity of organizational life. As Harold Leavitt puts it:

> This is not to say that the complexity of the organization is so great that we can never tell what will happen when we do something. It is only to say that an organization is complex enough to make any simple *structural* or *technical* or *human* model inadequate. But we have made a lot of progress in understanding the complexities in the last few decades. We now know a good deal more about ways of acting on structure or people or technology; and we know somewhat more about how they are wired to one another. There is real progress in the organizational world.[14]

There is credence and reality to the interrelationship of technology, structure, financial, and human resources. The case example at the end of this chapter reports a massive system-wide renewal process undertaken by a large organization to assess goals and objectives for the future.

Organization renewal requires leaders and facilitators who can create the climate and process in which change in the tripartite nature of organizational functioning may take place. This thesis has been well stated by others, including Eli Ginzberg:

> Only men and women can develop the ideas that serve as the foundations for scientific and technologic process; only men and women—even in an age of giant computers—can manage organizations; only men and women can operate and repair the new machines which produce the goods which we desire; only men and women can provide services to the young and old, to the sick and well, to those seeking education, or recreation. Only men and women, not financial grants or ballistic missiles, determine the strength of a country.[15]

When people in organizations become agents of change, however, they find themselves caught up in many dynamic forces and new problems. These often occur while they are still in some phase of solving the problems created by earlier changes. This is the story of every person, and it is equally the story of every organization. Both human beings and our organizations can tolerate variations and modifications philosophically, even gladly; crises of greater or lesser importance develop when these things result in discontinuity, feelings of inadequacy, and inability to plan successfully.

The social environment of the nation is changing, as is its physical environment. Recent social forces centered around quality-of-life issues are placing new demands on organizations and causing a major break with age-old tenets of management through the forces and/or voluntary adoption of the "socioeconomic managerial philosophy." Managers today and tomorrow must be receptive, if not aggressive, toward the goals of society at large, in addition to their pursuit of traditional economic objectives. The great challenge ahead for organizations is to initiate policies and programs for the future that are mutually supportive to both economic and social goals.[16]

Some of the predictable trends, and their implications, can be stated for the managers of the future:[17]

The evolution of what might be called an "Argus person," as contrasted to a "Cyclops person." The demand of exceedingly complex, urgent, and total problems has come to require hundred-eyed, problem-solving groups, whose disciplinary membership is of a variety comparable to the problem's variety. This demand cannot be satisfied by cyclopean sensory systems and philosophical viewpoints of individual persons, or by conventional, monolithic, hierarchical organizations or quasi-matrix groups (committees, panels, project groups, task forces, elite "pickup" teams).

Administrators must understand and learn to apply the principle of matrix organizations. They will need to recognize that many early theories and assumptions about organizations are obsolete. Organization management must proceed from the assumption that people can and should be used anywhere in the organization that their talents are required. The focus will be on getting the job done. Systematic efforts will be made to prevent overemphasis on working through organizational channels which tend to choke and prevent organizational growth and effectiveness.

Managers must learn to make organization analysis and to interpret the results for the total system. They must place greater emphasis on being able to serve as problem-solving links within the organization. They must help people become comfortable in the presence of change and to work effectively within organizations characterized by continuous change and ad hoc group situations.

Development of all human resources will become a key responsibility of future organizations. The obsolescence rate of people in the organization of the future will make it necessary for individuals to cope with change in their own lives, careers, and organizations. People must have second and third careers in order to keep up with the rapid change required. The continued rapid growth of a service-oriented society will change the complexity and nature of many organizations and jobs.

In addition, adequate use of members of minority groups will be a constant challenge in an evolving and changing society. There will be pressure to evolve programs that use the total human resources of the country. Underutilized resources must be recognized at both individual and organizational levels. The middle-class puritan work ethic may be an inappropriate frame of reference for understanding the development problems of persons raised outside this ethic.

Many believe that the solutions will derive from management-sponsored education opportunities for all employees of the organization. The educational program of an organization must become an integral part of its organizational life.

There must be a better balance between focus on individual, group, and organization development so that the organization may adapt more effectively in meeting its objectives and in utilizing its human resources more creatively. New methods of training and development will emphasize the need for creativity and innovation.

Administrators must develop ways to recognize potential in all persons in the organization. The role of attitudes must be recognized and techniques developed for minimizing prejudice in the work situation. New ways to interpret and train people for the world of work will be required. This will require an ever-continuing involvement in creating new programs for effectively developing the capabilities of human resources. The administrator will need to be creative and supportive of an ongoing education and development process as part of the "management" of the organization. Implementing organization development and renewal process will become a key responsibility of management.

Mutual confidence, rather than obedience to authority, will provide the basis of work accomplishment. The organization of the future will base its control and effectiveness on the growth and accomplishment of persons within the organization. The old "command" by authority or even benevolent paternalism will become less viable as a way of managing. Forrester states it well:

> If the authoritarian hierarchy with its superior-subordinate pairing is to be removed, it must be replaced by another form of discipline and control. This substitute can be individual self-discipline arising from the self-interest created by a competitive market mechanism.
>
> To depart from the authoritarian hierarchy as the central organizational structure, one must replace the superior-subordinate pair as the fundamental building block of the organization. In the new organization, an individual would not be assigned to a superior. Instead he would negotiate, as a free individual, a continually changing structure of relationships with those with whom he exchanges goods and services. He would accept specific obligations as agreements of limited duration. As these are discharged, he would

establish a new pattern of relationships as he finds more satisfying and rewarding situations.[18]

This new kind of relationship is built upon the confidence persons have in one another's integrity, goal orientation, and commitment to a problem-solving process. Such confidence does not need to depend upon authority or status for its success. It derives from some basic trust between the parties without which quality work will be illusory.

Many factors in the traditional organizational pattern caused persons in an organization to be seen as "doers of work." The task was the first concern of the supervisor. In the new approach, the supervisor sees a major responsibility as the development of others to adult patterns of self-control. An effort is made to develop effective work functioning and to focus on the "person-centered" needs so as to "release" the potential of others. Fortunately, this kind of supervision fits the job to the person rather than fitting the person to a job description.

To improve performance, the manager will create opportunities for persons to set their own "targets" for achievement, work standards, and personal growth.

Modern concepts require freedom of access to information and two-way communication. The character and climate of an organization can be deduced from the way it extends and withholds information. Effective management should not monopolize information under the false assumption that to possess information is to possess power. Most people in organizations do not feel they have access to all the information they need to do their jobs well. Information is the outgrowth of communication, both of which can be stored and retrieved.

The major revolution in modern communication is that people want to "say it like it is," to have organizations tell them the truth, to be able to influence the situation, and to be "open" in the communication process. This requires managers in organizations to meet communications situations effectively, not with outmoded Madison Avenue techniques, but through managerial practices that give people access to the information processes and systems of the organization.

The need for instituting proper management and information systems in organizations is self-evident. New technology in closed-circuit television, intercommunications warning systems, computer programs, the paperless office, conference phones, and computer conferencing are all part of the arsenal of modern information storage and retrieval devices. It does not become communication, however, until it is shared with those who want and need the information. The effective manager must understand and be secure enough to share information, not hide it.

Effective administration needs good communications. It is hard to communicate between generations, among friends, between management and labor, and between departments in an organization; but without adequate communication, a person cannot be an effective manager.

The two-way process of communication is found in both the formal and informal aspect of organization life. Opportunities to see oneself and the effect of one's supervision are a prime necessity in effective organizational accomplishment. The need for a "feedback" communication system is essential.

An organization, through its policies, philosophy, and management practices, can develop a climate of acceptance that encourages this level of interpersonal and system feedback communication.

There is increased interface between government with other private and public institutions. Increased interface between the private and public segments of society will create opportunities and problems for organizations in the future. A better way will be needed to sense and identify the emerging problems before they become overwhelming. Opportunities for cross collaboration between organizations and government will be required. Interchanging personnel across these organizational systems will increase. More interdependence will emerge as a regular way of operating organizations.

Managers will move in and out of specific roles and assignments related to cross-agency coordination, planning, and problem solving. Managers will need to widen their perspective by working in various types of organizational systems and to develop collaborative skills with organizational systems other than their own. The administrator must learn where to turn to gain benefits from this kind of interchange.

There is a trend toward increased centralization and decentralization of decision-making areas throughout organizations. The process of involving persons in the decisions they will implement is an important new aspect of management. Obviously, all persons will not be involved in every decision, even though effective communication about decisions is one level of involvement. The degree of participation will depend on forces in the situation, forces in the leader, and forces in the subordinate groups. Those forces will provide guidelines for the degree to which an organization leader involves members in decision making that is relevant to their competency and experience, and meets the appropriate leader response to a particular situation. Some decisions will be decentralized to specialized units in the organization. Other decisions on overall policy in such areas as finance, legal guidelines, and growth rate will be centralized.

In general, however, people will expect to influence the position and role that they perform in the organization. In addition, organizations will be able to secure individual commitment and loyalty only if they prove that the work and organization objectives are relevant to both individual aspirations and social objectives.

Managers must:

- Help clarify which decisions will be centralized (system type) and which will be decentralized (human work type)
- Help people within the organization to establish targets and to achieve them—this will involve helping people "to do their own thing"
- Begin to see the organization as a system designed to release human energy rather than to control human energy
- Realize that organizations, like individuals, pass through levels of maturity, and that very often they get bogged down at the level of maintaining the status quo when they should be growing toward a mastery of change
- Help the overall organization set targets and objectives, particularly in relation to the development of human resources

Conflict, confrontation, and stress will increase as a norm of organizational life. Confrontation is not necessarily undesirable, but a way in which people "lay it on the line" and "tell it as it is." Millions of creative ideas have been lost in organizations whose climate does not allow for honest differences in judgments and opinions. Often, pertinent points of view are "filtered out" before they get to top mangement. It is desirable to avoid a win-lose concept in organizational and societal life and substitute, wherever possible, the concept of win-win. Openness, candor, and frank feedback should not be equated with hostility or obstructionism. Quite the contrary: those who shut off the ideas and contributions of their subordinates are really the obstructionists. There will be an increasing need to use confrontation and conflict in a constructive way. People are no longer ready to accept blindly the judgment or actions of bosses, superiors, or organizational leaders. Managers cannot change their organization or way of managing unless they confront the present needs of the organization.

Administrators must help themselves and others learn how to handle conflict and to recognize that confrontation is not simply a technique of "how to fight." As professionals, they must encourage the expressing of convictions and accept other points of view. The manager must help the organization determine when confrontation and conflict are appropriate and how they can be used constructively, and when they are not appropriate and could be destructive.

Effective face-to-face work groups will be the key unit of organizational accomplishment. Recent research has recognized the importance of the group as the key unit in the life of the organization. This recognition has been made particularly evident as a result of productivity and morale studies research.

It clearly indicates that if an organization is to make the maximum use of the human resources and meet the highest level of human needs, it will come to function best in situations where the individual relates effectively to those organizational groups of which he or she is a member and a leader. Such well-knit and effective face-to-face work units will develop out of conditions that provide the trusting relationship between supervisor and members. As organizations grow more complex and larger, the peer relationship of a work unit is even more crucial for accountability measures. A group can influence the larger system better than the lonely individual.

In the multiple roles, the administrator must recognize the necessity of taking into account factors of interdependence with the multiple groups in an organization. Supervisors must serve as helpers, trainers, consultants, coordinators, and stimulators of their own work units. Such group skill should be the focus of an enlightened supervisory-training program.

The most frequent advocated organization improvement practice has been the development and building of face-to-face "subsystems" of a permanent or temporary nature in the organization. In team-building sessions, the members of these groups are given an opportunity to analyze teamwork factors and to introduce the element of teamwork throughout the organization.

In addition to the top executive group in the organization, it is desirable to create the kind of teamwork that will make it possible for all functional groups to work together effectively, for project groups to relate effectively, and for professional specialists to build a work unit that will contribute to growth, accountability, and goals. In other words, an important need in the organization of the future will be to utilize groups effectively.

There will be greater utilization and application of general system concepts in organizations. Another series of activities or processes that will be more evident in organizations of the future will revolve about the systems approach to the organization that should and can affect the total organization.

An organization's total system provides the total set of human activities together with interrelationships to the technical–physical–financial resources and the process to make and deliver products or services. The future-oriented administrator will need to be aware, knowledgeable, and skillfull in the systems field. Managers will need to interrelate the various operating and human systems.

This list of characteristics of organizations of the future is incomplete and selective. However, a prediction model of the future potential of human organizations must be developed to elicit action that will be on the frontier of this transitional generation.

The proper approach to organization renewal no longer considers personnel or management technology apart from the human element within the organization or the larger environment. As a result of an historic trend away from the purely mechanistic, the directed development of organizations in the future is now flexibly oriented to specific tasks and values in a known organizational climate.

"Future shock" is neither a disease nor a disaster; it is a dilemma created by too many problems coming too fast from too many directions for traditional problem-solving tools and techniques to handle. It seems that groups of "Argus people," aided by both cybernetics (systems analysis) and electronic computation—as well as by behavioral scientists—are capable of integrating multiperson skills and disciplines into antidotal, discrete problem-solving organic entities of the future. There is an urgent need to develop and perfect this morphology, a new science of human/machine/organization dynamics:

> But whatever terms we use, something revolutionary is happening. We are participating not merely in the birth of new organizational forms but in the birth of a new civilization. A new code book is taking form—a set of Third Wave principles, new ground rules for social survival.[19]

Given these trends, an overall renewal approach would involve:

Conceptual models. Use as a means of integrating knowledge, providing understanding, and guiding developmental strategies.

Educational systems. Design to integrate knowledge and skill mainly through experience-based exercises.

Measurements. Develop and apply measurement tools to reflect people's perceptions of critical organizational variables and link these to operating performance to demonstrate relationships.

Data collection. Sponsor jointly with line management and union officials to diagnose problems, identify solutions, implement change, and reevaluate.

Demonstration projects. Carry out special projects, involving the joint sponsorship of the formal organizations, that may not be tied directly to an identified organizational need but may have long-term organizational implications.

Implementation of new concepts of organizational design. Apply sociotechnical principles to the design and operation of new facilities.

These principles, as implemented by appropriate concepts and resources, convert organization renewal into a total systems endeavor rather than merely a shopping list of methods and interventions.

CASE STUDY SEARCH FOR RELEVANCE: AN ORGANIZATION RENEWAL PROCESS

The purpose of this organization renewal process, as implemented by a nationwide volunteer agency, was to identify the crucial forces and directions of society for the 1980s, and to determine the organizational implications of these future developments.

A face-to-face consultation was held in which members of the organization's research council and important lay and staff leaders, together with social scientist consultants, reacted to projections of the future program direction.

The national board of the organization was vitally concerned that its total organizational resources be committed to producing programs that would be relevant to the fast-changing needs of its constituents. This meant it would be necessary to:

Identify changes in the social order that do or may affect the organization's basic values and traditional roles

Determine, by discovery or design, the most effective organizational responses, in terms of program and services, to these changed conditions

Recommend ways that local units of the organization could work most effectively with their own potential constituencies, using all available relevant resources in terms of programs and services

This renewal project included five elements: (1) analyzing current and future projections and exploring implications to the organization of crucial issues in American society; (2) examining roadblocks, resources, and capabilities in program services and organizational functioning that affect relevant organization response; (3) evaluating existing and potential program and organizational innovations; (4) setting targets for local-unit self-renewal and improvement; and (5) securing directions from local units as to possible goals for the total organization in meeting national issues and concerns. It all involves members and staff in subsystems, from metropolitan as well as from smaller communities (see Figure 13-2).

At a national convention, the task force reported the results of steps 1 and 2 above, with possible alternatives for programming. Thereafter, the targets set by local units were to be implemented and put into action. In this connection, the competencies and resources of all divisions and departments of the national board and its regional organizations will be made available. Experimental models, based on the 1980s, were to be developed, tested, and presented at all local units for adaptation to the local community as appropriate.

This organization renewal project was seen as extending over two and a half years, and presenting an excellent opportunity for the leadership of the organization, both lay and professional, to begin examining the course upon which the organization was then directed and to try, to some degree, to make a conscious choice for that direction in the future. In addition, it appeared possible to shape the nature of the future program development rather than have it shaped by conditions over which the organization exercised no control.

Comment. *This large-scale renewal effort is an example of an internal research and development office working in collaboration with a team of consultants. It was possible to facilitate fact-finding and fact-dissemination conferences. This case study also represents a massive in-*

Figure 13-2 Organizational Renewal Cycle

volvement process for redirection of a large agency while protecting the autonomy of its local units.

SUMMARY

What about the future of human systems applications to organization renewal? The ever-increasing complexity of organizations is a good argument for expanded use of the systems approach with its capacity for representing complex relations.

Expected trends in our postindustrial society will obviously require a systems approach. In discussing organizations of the future, Alvin Toffler says:

> These Third Wave organizations have flatter hierarchies. They are less top-heavy. They consist of small components linked in temporary configurations. Each of these components has its own relationships with the outside world, its own foreign policy, so to speak, which it maintains without having to go through the center. These organizations operate more and more around the clock.
>
> But they are different from bureaucracies in another fundamental respect. They are what might be called dual or poly organizations, in the sense that they are capable of assuming two or more distinct structural shapes, as conditions warrant—rather like some plastic of the future that will change shape when heat or cold is applied but spring back into a basic form when the temperature is in its normal range.[20]

As never before, the world needs creative organizational leadership that is looking for new paths, new methods, new approaches, and the search for innovations yet to come. To accept modern technology and to use it, rather than to be afraid of it, is essential. To see such technologies as tools to improve mankind, not to control people, is the proper attitude.

In conclusion, these words of William Faulkner are appropriate:

> What's wrong with the world is, it's not finished yet. It is not completed to the point where man can put his signature to the job and say, "It is finished. We made it, and it works."
>
> Because only man can complete it. Not God, but man. It is man's high destiny and proof of his immortality, too, that his is the choice between ending the world, effacing it from the wrong annals of time and space, and completing it. This is not only his right, but his privilege, too.
>
> Like the Phoenix, it arises from the ashes of its own failure with each generation, until it is our turn now in our flash and flicker of time and space which we call today . . . to perform this duty, accept this privilege, bear this right. . . . [21]

Here, then, is the hope and challenge of organization renewal both for ourselves, our organization, and all the people with whom we share the earth. We will, as individuals, find the ways of interfacing best suited to ourselves. When we do, we can bring—out of the experiences of today and tomorrow—effective coping, comprehension, and confrontation for the growth of both ourselves and our organizations.

QUESTIONS

1. In your opinion, why has organizational change and development been so difficult to achieve?
2. What examples can you give of failures in organization development? Why did the failures occur?
3. What examples can you give of successes in organization development? To what do you attribute these successes?

4. How can individuals, groups, and organizations plan for the future?
5. What are the differences between planning and renewal?
6. As you examined the case example at the end of this chapter, what elements of organization renewal were in evidence?
7. As you reflect back upon your reading of this book, what convictions of yours were reinforced? What new convictions did you develop?

NOTES

[1]Adapted from an unpublished paper by Gail Wicklund and Judith Meeks, *Why Does OD Fail?* (Washington, D.C.: The George Washington University, November 1979). Hereafter cited as Wicklund and Meeks.

[2]Philip Mirvis and David N. Berg, *Failures in Organizational Development and Change* (New York: John Wiley & Sons, Inc., 1977), pp. 9–11.

[3]Robert R. Blake and Jane S. Mouton, "Why the OD Movement Is Stuck and How to Break It Loose," *Training and Development Journal,* September 1979, p. 19.

[4]Wicklund and Meeks, p. 8.

[5]Robert T. Golumbiewski, "Some Guidelines for Tomorrow's OD," *Theory and Method in OD: An Evolutionary Process* (Washington, D.C.: National Training Laboratories, 1973), p. 93.

[6]Roger Harrison, "Choosing the Depth of Organizational Intervention," *Journal of Applied Behavioral Science,* Vol. 6, No. 2, 1970, 181–202.

[7]Noel Tichy and Harvey Hornstein, "Demise, Absorption, or Renewal for the Future of Organizational Development," in W. Warner Burke (ed.), *The Cutting Edge: Current Theory and Practice in Organization Development* (La Jolla, Calif.: University Associates, Inc., 1978), pp. 70–87.

[8]Noel Tichy and Harvey Hornstein, "Stand When Your Number Is Called: An Empirical Attempt to Classify Change Agent Types," *Human Relations,* Vol. 29, No. 10, 1976, 945–967.

[9]Adapted from Gordon Lippitt, *Quality of Work Life: Organizational Renewal in Action* (Distinguished lecturer series, Cornell University, May 14, 1977).

[10]Adapted from an unpublished paper by Virginia H. Martin, *Comparing Quality of Work Life and Organization Development* (Washington, D.C.: The George Washington University, April 1977).

[11]Edward L. Lindaman and Ronald Lippitt, *Choosing The Future You Prefer* (Ann Arbor, Mich.: Human Resource Development Associates of Ann Arbor, Inc., 1979), pp. 23–24.

[12]Edward Cornish, "An Agenda for the 1980s," *The Futurist,* Vol. 14, No. 1, 1980, 6.

[13]Ibid., p. 12.

[14]Harold Leavitt, *Managerial Psychology,* 2nd ed. (Chicago: University of Chicago Press, 1964), Chap. 21.

[15]Eli Ginzberg, *Human Resources* (New York: Simon and Shuster, 1958), pp. 169–170.

[16]*Tomorrow Begins Today* (Los Angeles, Calif.: Security Pacific National Bank, 1980), p. 14.

[17]Adapted from Gordon Lippitt, "Organizations of the Future: Implications for Management," *Optimum,* Vol. 5, No. 1, 1974, 36–51.

[18]Jay W. Forrester, "A New Corporate Design," *Industrial Management Review,* July 1965, p. 840.

[19]Alvin Toffler, "The Third Wave," *Playboy,* Vol. 27, No. 2, 1980, 274.

[20]Ibid.

[21]William Faulkner, as quoted in Gordon Lippitt, *My Quest for Dialogue* (Rufus Jones lecture; Washington, D.C.: Development Publications, 1966).

SUGGESTED READINGS ABOUT THE FUTURE

Robert Bundy, *Images Of The Future* (Buffalo, N.Y.: Promethus Books, 1976).

Arthur C. Clarke, *Profiles of the Future* (New York: Harper & Row, Publishers, Inc., 1964).

Business Week (Special Issue) *The Reindustrialization of America,* June 30, 1980. A McGraw-Hill Publication.

Edward Cornish, *The Study of the Future* (Washington, D.C.: World Future Society, 1977).

William J. Davis, *The Seventh Year: Industrial Civilization in Transition* (New York: W. W. Norton & Company, Inc., 1979).

Paul Dickson, *The Future File* (New York: Rawson Associates, 1977).

Victor C. Ferkiss, "Futurology: Promise, Performance, Prospects," in *The Washington Papers* (Beverly Hills, Calif.: Sage Publications, Inc., 1977).

Robert Fox, Eva Schindler-Rainman, and Ronald Lippitt, *The Humanizing Future* (Ann Arbor, Mich.: Human Resource Development Associates of Ann Arbor, Inc., 1976).

Draper L. Kaufmann, Jr., *Teaching the Future* (Palm Springs, Calif.: ETC Publications, 1976).

Edward B. Lindaman, *Thinking in the Future Sense* (Nashville, Tenn.: Broadman Press, 1978).

James Martin, *The Wired Society* (Englewood Cliffs, N.J.: Prentice-Hall, Inc., 1978).

John McHale, *World Facts and Trends* (New York: The Macmillan Company, 1972).

Gerald and Patricia Mische, *Toward a Human World Order* (New York: Paulist Press, 1977).

National Science Foundation, *The Study of the Future: An Agenda of Research* (Washington, D.C.: U.S. Government Printing Office, 1977).

Robert C. North, *The World That Could Be* (Stanford, Calif.: Stanford Alumni Association: The Portable Stanford Series, 1976).

OTA Priorities For 1979 (Congress of the United States, U.S. Office of Technology Assessment; Washington, D.C.: U.S. Government Printing Office, 1978).

Fred Polak, *The Image of the Future* (San Francisco, Calif.: Jossey-Bass, Inc., 1972).

Louis Rubin, *Educational Reform for a Changing Society* (Boston: Allyn and Bacon, Inc., 1978).

Taking Charge (New York: American Friends Service Committee, 1977).

Alvin Toffler, *The Third Wave* (New York: William Morrow and Company, Inc., 1980).

Max Ways, *The Future of Business: Global Issues of the 80s and 90s* (Elmsford, N.Y.: Pergamon Press, Inc., 1979).

name index

subject index